INVERCLYDE LIBRARIES

CENTRAL LIBRARY

1 3 JUN 2017	1 8 AUG 2017	Lou 7/17
- 5 OCT 2017	3 0 OCT 2017	2 1 DEC 2017
- 5 OCT 2018	Rerd 9/19	
- 8 NOV 2019	2 9 JAN 2020	

WITHDRAWN

This book is to be returned on or before the last date above. It may be borrowed for a further period if not in demand.

For enquiries and renewals Tel: (01475) 712323
www.inverclyde.gov.uk/libraries

'T. M. Devine's splendid new book . . . will remain the standard one in its field for some time . . . deservedly so . . . For those who want to know what it is like to be living in Scotland, its history and its society, it is a work of enduring distinction with the root of the matter in it' Neal Ascherson, *Times Literary Supplement*

'. . . Devine more than fulfils Devine's promise to provide a "broad, deeply researched survey" with an international perspective . . . an altogether exhilarating reading – innovative, dynamic, fresh . . . As anti-nationalists struggle to make the case the Union it has become increasingly clear that they could do worse than . . .'

'Dazzling . . . Of great importance . . . to a fuller and richer understanding of modern Scotland' Daniel Mulhall, *Irish Times*

'Both the sweep of the issues, and the depth of the analysis, particularly the impact of change on the lives of ordinary people, make it one of *the* books. It will certainly be one of my books of the year' The Rt Hon. Gordon Brown

'A treatise on the transformations of society . . . this book makes significant reading' . . .

'. . . all those with an interest in Scotland and those who want to know how we got to where we are . . . Devine's history – rich in detail, judicious in its conclusions, gripping and entertaining – will provide some, at least, of the answers' Allan Massie, *Scottish Review*

'Devine's commanding panorama . . . majestic analysis' Tom Nairn, *New Statesman*

D1346667

'Devine has synthesised the fruits of a revolution in Scottish historical studies and his book draws on its rich harvest of new research ... *The Scottish Nation* has synoptic power, lucidity of exposition and narrative force' Arnold Kemp, *Observer*

'A comprehensive, lucidly written history of Scotland ... a must read for anyone interested in Scotland's history' *Kirkus Reviews*

'Indispensable ... passionate, precise, unpatronizing ... this is the single volume history which will fill, with intelligence and breadth, the lamentable gaps in eduction left by a standard Scottish education' Catherine Lockerbie, *Scotsman*

'Indisputably the best single-volume history of Scotland we now have' Lindsay Paterson

'The chapters on the economy are outstanding – learned, lucid and unfailingly intelligent'
Nicholas Phillipson, *The Times Higher Education Supplement*

ABOUT THE AUTHOR

T. M. Devine is the Personal Senior Research Professor of History at the University of Edinburgh and Director of the Scottish Centre for Diaspora Studies. He is an honorary member of the Royal Irish Academy, a Fellow of the Royal Society of Edinburgh and a Fellow of the British Academy, the only historian elected to all major three national academies in the British Isles. In 2001, Professor Devine was awarded the Royal Gold Medal, Scotland's supreme academic accolade. Among Professor Devine's numerous publications is the bestselling *Scotland's Empire: The Origins of the Global Diaspora*, and *To the Ends of the Earth: Scotland's Global Diaspora*, both published by Penguin.

T. M. DEVINE

The Scottish Nation
A Modern History

INVERCLYDE LIBRARIES

PENGUIN BOOKS

PENGUIN BOOKS

Published by the Penguin Group
Penguin Books Ltd, 80 Strand, London wc2r orl, England
Penguin Group (USA) Inc., 375 Hudson Street, New York, New York 10014, USA
Penguin Group (Canada), 90 Eglinton Avenue East, Suite 700, Toronto, Ontario, Canada m4p 2y3
(a division of Pearson Penguin Canada Inc.)
Penguin Ireland, 25 St Stephen's Green, Dublin 2, Ireland
(a division of Penguin Books Ltd)
Penguin Group (Australia), 250 Camberwell Road,
Camberwell, Victoria 3124, Australia (a division of Pearson Australia Group Pty Ltd)
Penguin Books India Pvt Ltd, 11 Community Centre,
Panchsheel Park, New Delhi – 110 017, India
Penguin Group (NZ), 67 Apollo Drive, Rosedale, Auckland 0632, New Zealand
(a division of Pearson New Zealand Ltd)
Penguin Books (South Africa) (Pty) Ltd, Block D, Rosebank Office Park, 181 Jan Smuts Avenue,
Parktown North, Gauteng 2193, South Africa

Penguin Books Ltd, Registered Offices: 80 Strand, London wc2r orl, England

www.penguin.com

First published as *The Scottish Nation 1700–2000* by Allen Lane 1999
First published by Penguin Books 2000
Reissued with new material 2006
Reissued with further new material 2012

005

Copyright © T. M. Devine, 1999, 2006, 2012

All rights reserved

The moral right of the author has been asserted

Printed in England by Clays Ltd, St Ives plc

Except in the United States of America, this book is sold subject
to the condition that it shall not, by way of trade or otherwise, be lent,
re-sold, hired out, or otherwise circulated without the publisher's
prior consent in any form of binding or cover other than that in
which it is published and without a similar condition including this
condition being imposed on the subsequent purchaser

978-0-718-19320-1

www.greenpenguin.co.uk

MIX
Paper from
responsible sources
FSC   FSC® C018179

Penguin Books is committed to a sustainable
future for our business, our readers and our planet.
This book is made from Forest Stewardship
Council™ certified paper.

For my beloved son
John
1975–96
Aiġ foiś a niś

Contents

CONTENTS

Preface

For historians of Scotland the last three decades have been an exciting time. Research has boomed, established views are vigorously challenged and entirely new fields of investigation opened up which were uncharted in the older historiography. But at least so far as the universities are concerned, the great majority of Scottish historians are more concerned in their published works to address their own professional peers rather than a wider public audience. In part this is inevitable, given the demands of research assessments and the expectations of promotion boards. The consequence, however, is that the academic community might be accused of introspection at a time when Scotland is entering a phase of historic constitutional change when issues such as identity and culture are being reclaimed and contested both in the media and in public debate. The time is therefore now ripe for a new general history of modern Scotland which draws the threads of research together and presents them to a wider readership in an accessible form.

The purpose of this book is to present a coherent account of the last 300 years of Scotland's past with the hope of developing a better understanding of the Scottish present. It is a work which can be described as an interpretative synthesis. I have tried to absorb the path-breaking historical work of recent times into my analysis and narrative, while also giving it the stamp of personal interpretation. However, the basic foundations of the book lie in the monographs, articles and theses produced by the many scholars who have helped to transform the study of modern Scottish history. I hope that I have done some justice to their contributions, even if they do not always agree with the conclusions I draw from them.

The approach and structure of the book is based on several principles. First, I have adopted a broad and integrated definition of history and have incorporated detailed examination of society, politics, economy,

PREFACE

demography, religion, identity and popular culture into the text. Second,
I have tried whenever possible to look outwards in order to see Scotland
within an international context and sometimes against a comparative
framework of reference. We cannot know what was distinctive or
representative about the Scottish experience except by adopting this
approach. Third, due attention is given to the early decades of the
eighteenth century after the Union of 1707 and to the near-contemporary
history of Scotland since 1945. However, the core of the book lies in
the period between 1760 and 1914 because that was the era of massive
transformation in society and economy which above all else forged the
nation of Scotland as we know it in the twentieth century.

Tom Devine,
Research Institute of Irish and Scottish Studies,
King's College,
University of Aberdeen

Acknowledgements

This book was written during a sabbatical year granted by the University of Strathclyde after the end of my period of office as Deputy Principal in that institution. I am deeply grateful to the Principal and Vice Chancellor of Strathclyde, Sir John Arbuthnott, for his support, and to my former colleagues in the Research Centre of Scottish History and the Department of History for their stimulus and friendship over the years. My new colleagues at the University of Aberdeen have helped me to see the project to fruition with enthusiastic support and interest.

I am grateful to Richard Finlay not only for the loan of many books and articles but also for several informative conversations on politics and identity in modern Scotland and his perceptive scrutiny of the final text of this volume. Anne-Marie Kilday helped to research the material for the chapter on the Scottish City, while Ellen O'Donnell, Martin Mitchell and Henry Maitles allowed me to use their invaluable theses on the Lithuanian, Irish and Jewish immigrants respectively. Arnold Kemp, former editor of *The Herald*, provided expert comment on Chapter 24.

Earlier versions of Chapters 9 and 11 previously appeared in my *Clanship to Crofters' War: the Social Transformation of the Scottish Highlands* (Manchester University Press, 1994). The final version of the book was prepared by Margaret Hastie and Jean Fraser. In this project, as in so many areas, I am enormously grateful to them for their patient efficiency, especially when dealing with some intractable material.

Simon Winder and Ellah Allfrey at Penguin could not have been more helpful and understanding.

My principal debt as always is to Catherine and our children, Elizabeth, Noreen, Michael and Kathryna. They have shared with me the challenges of composition at a time of family tragedy for all of us. Quite simply the book could not have been completed without them. In that sense it is as much theirs as mine.

Maps

1. KINROSS
2. CLACKMANNAN
3. DUNBARTON
4. To KINROSS
5. WEST LOTHIAN
6. MIDLOTHIAN
7. EAST LOTHIAN
8. RENFREW

0   25   50 Miles

0   40   80 Km

CAITHNESS

SUTHERLAND

ROSS & CROMARTY

NAIRN   MORAY

BANFF   ABERDEEN

Aberdeen

INVERNESS

KINCARDINE

ANGUS

PERTH

R. Tay

Dundee

ARGYLL

FIFE

2   1

R. Forth

3   STIRLING

4   Edinburgh

5   6   7

8   Glasgow

R. Clyde

BERWICK

LANARK

PEEBLES

AYR

SELKIRK

ROXBURGH

DUMFRIES

KIRKCUDBRIGHT

WIGTOWN

IRELAND

ENGLAND

Belfast

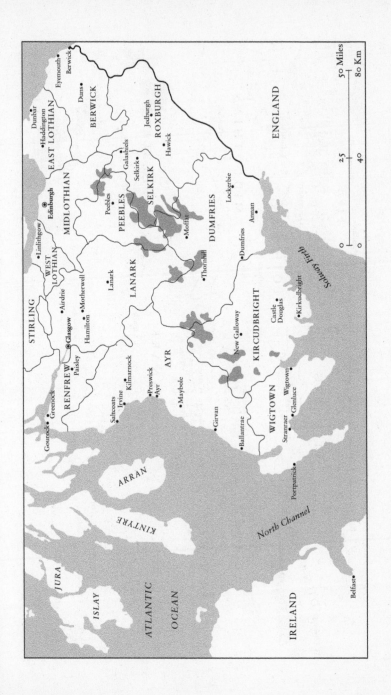

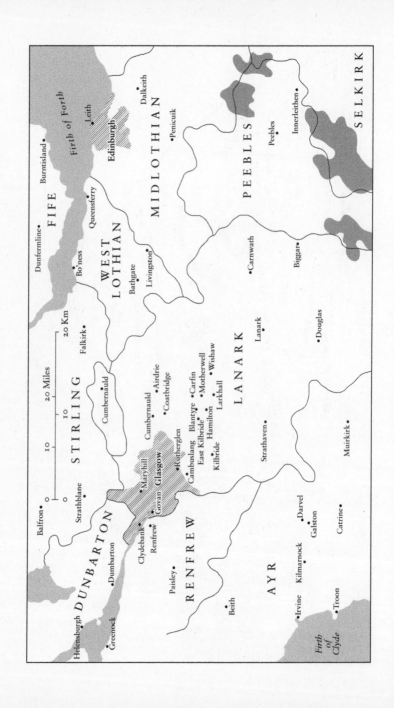

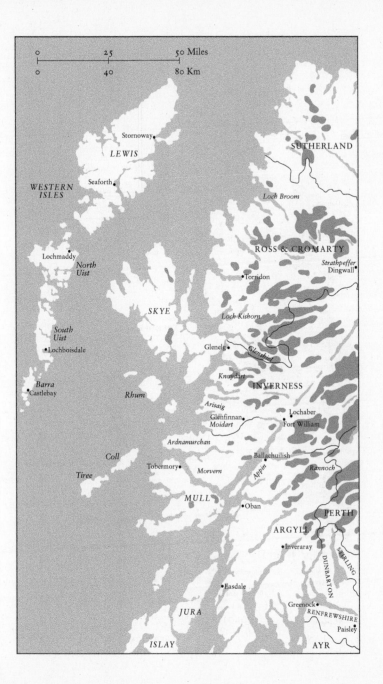

50 Miles
80 Km

Stornoway

LEWIS

WESTERN
ISLES

Seaforth

SUTHERLAND

Loch Broom

ROSS & CROMARTY

Lochmaddy
North
Uist

Strathpeffer
Dingwall

Torridon

SKYE

Loch Kishorn

South
Uist
Lochboisdale

Glenelg

Glenshiel

Knoydart

INVERNESS

Barra
Castlebay

Rhum

Arisaig
Glenfinnan
Moidart

Lochaber
Fort William

Ardnamurchan

Coll

Ballachuilish

Tiree

Tobermory

Morvern

Appin

Rannoch

MULL

Oban

PERTH

ARGYLL

Inveraray

DUNBARTON

STIRLING

Easdale

JURA

Greenock
RENFREWSHIRE

Paisley

ISLAY

AYR

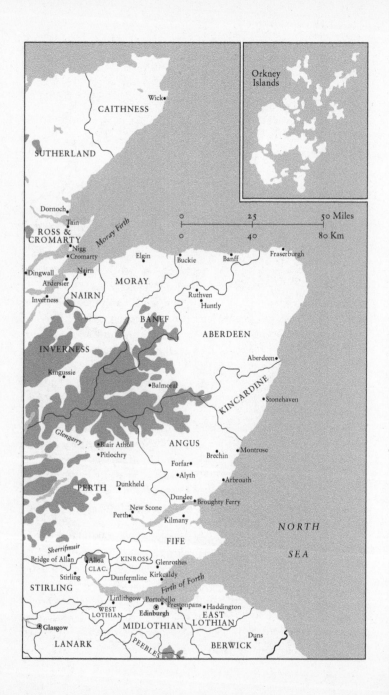

Foreword

Scotland in the later seventeenth century had an estimated population of a little more than a million inhabitants. This was about one-fifth the population of England and only one-eighth that of Spain. The country's population size was more akin to Switzerland's, and this made her vulnerable in an era when military power depended on a nation's numbers rather than technological prowess. Much of Scotland was dominated by mountain and moorland, and habitation therefore tended to concentrate on more favoured areas where intensive arable farming could take place. Even in the later twentieth century, after nearly 300 years of improvement and drainage, around two-thirds of the country is still suitable only for rough grazing. Not surprisingly, therefore, the main concentrations of settlement were in the more fertile areas: the lowlands of Aberdeen and Moray, the coastlands of the Forth and Tay, the Solway plain, the Merse and the lower Clyde valley. That said, however, population was more widely dispersed before 1700 than it was to become after industrialization in the eighteenth and nineteenth centuries, when mass migration was to alter the national demographic profile decisively in favour of the central Lowlands and the cities of Glasgow and Edinburgh and their booming satellite towns. Perhaps half of the inhabitants of Scotland lived north of the River Tay in the late seventeenth century, though parts of the Highlands were as sparsely populated then as now.

Overwhelmingly, Scotland was a rural-based society in this period. Landowners formed the political and social élite. The produce of the land – skins, grain, wool and coal – were vital trading commodities. On the return of the annual harvest depended the health, prosperity and food supply of the nation. If the harvest partially failed, emergency provisions would have to be acquired from Europe with scarce coin, and that could force a collapse in credit and a shrinkage of the cash base. The typical Scot was a country dweller. One estimate suggests that in 1700 only 5.3 per cent of the population lived in towns with over 10,000 inhabitants. This proportion was a long way behind more urbanized societies such as those in England, the Netherlands, Belgium, parts of Italy and even Spain and Portugal, and was on a par with the Scandinavian countries and some of the German estates. Even artisans, industrial workers and fishing communities had to have a stake in the land in order to cultivate their own food supplies.

But towns were becoming increasingly important, and changes were also under way in the pattern of Scottish urban development. Between 1500 and 1600 the proportion of the nation's population living in the larger towns nearly doubled, and it did so again by 1700. Edinburgh, the capital and biggest town, had a population of around 30,000 by the early eighteenth century. Aberdeen and Dundee had about 10,000 inhabitants each, while Glasgow had emerged as the second burgh in the land by the later seventeenth century, with a population reckoned at 15,000 and growing. Relative to Edinburgh and Glasgow, however, Aberdeen and Dundee were experiencing relative stagnation in the second half of the seventeenth century. Edinburgh's predominance in Scottish urban life was long-standing, but Glasgow's new pre-eminence reflected the growing importance of developing links to Ireland and the Atlantic economy, which were to prove so crucial to Scottish progress after 1700. The vast majority of other Scottish burghs were little more than villages in this period. Few, apart from Inverness, Stirling, Dumfries and Renfrew, had more than 1,000 inhabitants each. Nevertheless, in some areas, most notably the coastlands of the River Forth, the sheer number and growth of small burghs created a regional urban network to rival any in western Europe in density.

The growth in the number of town dwellers had major implications for rural society. Above all else, the new townsfolk had to be fed. In the later sixteenth century this would have proved difficult, since between 1550 and 1600 there were around 24 years of dearth on a national and local scale. But harvests improved after 1660. Between then and the devastating famines of the 1690s, food prices indicated serious scarcity only once, in 1674. Also in this period, several landed estates on the east coast were producing substantial quantities of grain for export. All this suggests that Scottish agriculture was not as inefficient as was sometimes suggested in this period. It may well be that the climate was also more favourable and the balance of food supply and demand was also helped by Scotland's demographic safety-valve, the huge levels of emigration to Europe and Ulster which prevailed in this period. From medieval times Scots had moved to continental Europe in large numbers as soldiers and traders, and there is some evidence that this exodus reached particularly high levels in the seventeenth century, especially when Ulster started to attract farmers and cottars from the south-west Lowlands. All in all, it is reckoned that Scottish emigration reached levels of between 78,000 and 127,000 in the second half of the seventeenth century.

But other influences help to account for the better times of the 1670s and 1680s. After the massive losses of blood and treasure in the Wars of the Covenant of the 1630s and 1640s, followed by the conquest and annexation of Scotland by Oliver Cromwell in the 1650s, there was now greater social and political stability. One illustration of the new order was the changing domestic architecture of the nobility as the tower house, designed mainly for defence, was being replaced by the country house. Some landowners were also showing greater interest in raising the revenue of their estates. Even in the Highlands full-scale clan warfare had become a thing of the past and most unrest was now confined to localized banditry and petty lawlessness. The reformed church also contributed powerfully to the new stability in the Lowlands. Its kirk session, consisting of the minister and elected elders, acted as a local moral tribunal supervising the conduct of the parishioners and punishing them when they were in breach of the Christian code. Already by 1620 most Lowland parishes and many Highland parishes had active kirk sessions which became effective agencies for the development of group discipline. In the 1680s there was also a kind of intellectual flowering which paralleled the greater economic stability of the time. This was the age of Stair in law, Bruce in architecture and Sibbald in medicine.

But the better times proved to be short-lived. Scotland's economy was small, her range of exports limited mainly to foods and raw materials, and the nation's political position weak in relation to the great European powers. This was an era of rampant economic national-ism when the leading states tried to gain advantage at the expense of their trade rivals through the aggressive use of prohibitive tariffs. The problem was that Scotland was ill-equipped to fight a trade war not only because she lacked any credible naval force but because her merchants traded in little that was regarded as either scarce or vital in overseas markets. Scotland would be hit badly by high customs barriers but equally she could not do much to retaliate. The policy of the Scottish parliament when confronted by rising tariff walls in several of the nation's traditional markets came to depend on a strategy of industrial diversification to produce the luxuries previously imported from abroad. Some manufacturers did prosper, especially those producing high-quality textiles, but by and large this laudable attempt at self-help did little to prevent a deterioration in Scotland's international economic position.

A second problem was with England. Anglo-Scottish relationships in this period were anomalous. The difficulties had their origin in the Regal Union of 1603 when James VI of Scotland succeeded Elizabeth I to the crowns of England and Ireland. James had been eager to go much further, and in 1604 commissioners from England and Scotland discussed a union of parliaments and a scheme of common citizenship. Despite James's keen support, the idea foundered. The Scottish nobility feared a loss of influence in a London parliament, while the English were concerned that the Scots would be favoured in the new arrangement by their royal master. Within a few years the projected union was off the political agenda and the difficulties of ruling Scotland from Westminster soon became apparent in the latter stages of James's reign – and even more so during that of his successor, Charles I, when they were instrumental in provoking the crisis that led to the outbreak of the Civil War. Union was enforced between 1652 and 1660 by Oliver Cromwell, but at the Restoration of 1660 and the return of Charles II it was dissolved, to the relief of the majority in both countries.

But Scotland was far from being an independent state. Scottish foreign policy had moved with James to London in 1603 and there was a great grievance that thereafter foreign policy for both kingdoms was exclusively designed to suit English needs. Thus the three Dutch Wars of the later seventeenth century were fought against a nation that was England's deadliest commercial rival but one of Scotland's main trading partners. Similarly, the fact that the Scots and English shared the same monarch did not prevent the London parliament levying punitive customs dues on such key Scottish exports as linen, cattle, salt and coal, at a time when England was becoming the single most important Scottish market. Increasingly Scottish interests argued that the Regal Union had to be amended and reformed because of the untold damage it was doing to Scotland. There can be little doubt that Westminster regarded most of these concerns as windy rhetoric or special pleading. In the 1690s, however, a series of crises transformed the debate on Anglo-Scottish union and made it a more pressing issue than it had been since Cromwell's armies marched north in the early 1650s.

PART ONE
1700–1760

I

Scotland in Great Britain

On 5 February 1705 the House of Commons in London passed legislation which would help to shape the entire future history of the United Kingdom. The Alien Act recommended to Queen Anne that commissioners be appointed to negotiate for Union between England and Scotland and, if the Scots did not comply and if discussions were not advanced by Christmas Day 1705, severe penalties would be imposed. All Scots, except those living in England, would be treated as aliens and the major Scottish exports to England of coal, linen and cattle would be suspended. This was a naked piece of economic blackmail, designed to bring the Scottish parliament swiftly to the negotiating table; north of the border the first response was one of outrage. In the event, the obnoxious clauses of the Alien Act were eventually repealed by the new Whig government at Westminster in November 1705 and this took some of the heat out of a growing crisis between the two nations. But the message of the Alien Act was clear. The historic English opposition to closer union with Scotland had been abandoned. Instead, many influential politicians and the monarch herself, Queen Anne, now regarded a parliamentary union with the Scots as essential for the future stability of the revolutionary settlement of 1688 and the security of the two kingdoms. Throughout the seventeenth century various schemes of union had been proposed but had foundered, mainly on the rock of English indifference or antagonism. James VI and I tried to bring the two countries closer after the Union of the Crowns in 1603, and further attempts were made in 1667, 1670 and 1690. As recently as 1702–3 joint discussions on union had come to nothing. A fundamental sticking point was always that London saw no reason to concede to the Scots freedom of trade with her colonies in America. As Sir Edward Seymour, the Tory Leader in the Commons, proclaimed in 1700,

Scotland was a beggar and '... whoever married a beggar could only expect a louse for her portion'.[1]

A first step therefore in trying to understand the making of the Union of 1707 is to explain why Westminster's political attitudes to the prospect of a closer political relationship with the Scots radically altered in the early eighteenth century. Equally, however, the Scottish position, and in particular that of the parliament in Edinburgh, deserves careful examination. There was nothing inevitable about a parliamentary union between the two nations. Difficulties were certainly emerging in the Union of the Crowns in the later seventeenth century, but there was scope for addressing these by amendment and adjustment rather than by more radical constitutional change. It is also striking how many Scottish politicians who favoured union in 1705-6 feared that it could not be delivered through the Edinburgh parliament. They were conscious of the deep animosity towards union passionately articulated by the national Presbyterian church, which was alarmed at the intolerable prospect of Anglican domination. John Clerk of Penicuik, one of the treaty negotiators who strongly favoured union, was later to write that he observed 'a great backwardness in the Parliament of Scotland for a union with England of any kind whatsoever' and felt that the efforts of himself and his fellow commissioners might come to nought.[2]

I

The Revolution of 1688 transformed the structure of Scottish parliamentary politics. William and Mary came to the throne of Scotland after the expulsion of the Stuart king, James VII and II, not through divine or hereditary right but by the decision and invitation of the Scottish Convention of Estates. At a stroke the balance of power between executive and legislature was altered. The Scottish parliament soon flexed its muscles in other directions. In 1690, in a crucial decision, the Lords of the Articles, the key parliamentary committee for drafting and initiating legislation, normally firmly under executive control, was abolished. In the same year the estate of bishops was removed. These two developments substantially increased parliamentary authority while at the same time reducing royal influence. The scenario for conflict now existed between the king's ministers, whom William still had the right to appoint, and a much stronger Scottish legislature. The Articles had been replaced by a number of *ad hoc* committees which were not as easily influenced by the executive and, as a result, for the next several years the government of Scotland became increasingly volatile. After 1695 the king's main strategy was to try to build a stable ministry around such powerful noblemen as Queensberry, Argyll, Atholl and Hamilton. The theory was that only these mighty aristocrats could deliver a pro-government majority in parliament through their personal followings and networks of clientage. This, together with an effective system of 'management', the promise of offices, pensions, fees and jobs in return for toeing the line, would ensure secure government. The hope proved illusory. The magnates were divided by bitter personal rivalries and by the craving for the spoils of office which were necessary not only for their own personal advantage but, equally crucially, to ensure the loyalty of their own supporters and dependants. Collaboration among these grandees for any length of time was impossible, and yet at the same time no single great man could dominate parliament single-handedly. To deliver power to one dynastic grouping was to risk alienating others, who would then promote a destructive opposition in parliament itself. Not surprisingly, business was often in a state of paralysis for long periods and it was increasingly difficult to extract agreement on financial supply to carry on the administration of the country.

This volatile situation was aggravated by increasing friction between England and Scotland. Between 1689 and 1697 William's wars with France were having serious effects on Scottish commerce while the Royal Navy was implementing the Navigation Laws with full rigour against illicit Scottish trade with England's American colonies. Conflict in the economic sphere was intensified by the collapse of the Company of Scotland's ill-fated expedition to Darien in central America. This enterprise was launched in a mood of great national optimism in 1695, but by March 1700 the attempt to found a Scottish colony on the Isthmus of Panama to trade with the Pacific and Atlantic simultaneously had ended in total disaster. The reasons for the catastrophe were many, ranging from poor planning to the lethal effects of tropical disease on the first settlers. But the blame was also laid squarely at England's door. English investment had been withdrawn from the original undertaking as a result of mercantile and political pressure from London, while the possibility of bringing relief to the Scottish settlement in 1699 had come to naught, in large part because the London government, conscious of the vital diplomatic need to maintain Spanish support against France, refused to send provisions or succour. The Darien failure had a serious economic impact because of the enormous national investment that had gone into it, but the political fall-out was just as significant. The disaster directly hit the pockets of the noblemen, lairds and merchants represented in the Scottish parliament precisely at the time when many landowners were already suffering from a collapse of rental income as a result of calamitous harvest failures in the 1690s. Simmering discontent gave way to strident criticism that Scotland's miseries were all rooted in the Regal Union of 1603. This alienation crystallized in the truculent opposition, shown during the parliamentary sessions of 1698 and 1700, which was so alarming that only the lavish use of patronage allowed the Scottish ministry to survive.

Long before the end of his reign, therefore, William had concluded that Scotland could not be governed within the existing context of the Union of the Crowns and that a union of the Edinburgh and Westminster parliaments was vital to national stability and security. The king was obsessed with winning the great war against the France of Louis XIV, and political volatility in Scotland threatened this strategy. This was not only because Scotland was an important source of recruits for his armies but also because support for the exiled House of Stuart was being encouraged by French money and promises of military aid. Nevertheless, while the union project had great appeal for the king personally, it still did not attract much support in Westminster. This attitude was to change radically after the session of the Scots parliament which met in 1703 in the reign of William's successor, Queen Anne.

This parliament now seemed virtually outside the control of the Duke of Queensberry, the Queen's Commissioner, and his ministers and supporters. The resentment which had been building up in earlier sessions boiled over with a vengeance. First, the parliament refused to vote the financial supply which was badly needed to maintain the civil government of the land. Second, an Act of Security, passed in open defiance of Queensberry and the Court or governing party, stated that the Scots parliament had the right to decide on Queen Anne's successor and that England and Scotland could not have the same sovereign in the future unless the London parliament granted the Scots 'free communication of trade ... and the liberty of the plantations'. In addition, the Union of the Crowns would be preserved only if in the current parliamentary session 'there be such conditions of government settled and enacted as may secure . . . the freedom, frequency, and the power of Parliament, and the religion, liberty and trade of the nation from English or any foreign influence'. This read like a manifesto for independence and was intended to be deliberately provocative. Not surprisingly, the queen initially refused to give her assent, although she conceded it, reluctantly, in the following year. The ministry was then forced to accept the equally contentious Act anent (concerning) Peace and War, which gave the Scots parliament the right to declare war and make peace if the two nations continued to share a sovereign after Anne's death. In the vain attempt to extract financial supply in return for these concessions, the ministry allowed this to pass, despite the fact that its whole emphasis suggested a separate and autonomous Scottish foreign policy. A third measure, the Wine Act, formally permitted trade with France during the war. The primary motive for this came from the governing party, which was keen to raise more revenue by boosting trade, but on the surface it also seemed driven by economic nationalism. Certainly the Wool Act, passed during the session the following year, was regarded as openly hostile by England by allowing the export and prohibiting the import of wool. As such it was viewed as an openly aggressive act against English trade.

The Scottish legislation of 1703 was the catalyst for Parliamentary Union because it convinced Westminster opinion that Scotland could no longer be governed effectively within the Regal Union at a time when the entire revolutionary settlement of 1688–9 had become uncertain because of Anne's failure to produce a living heir. The London parliament had attempted to deal with this vexed issue of succession swiftly by settling the crown on the German House of Hanover. But the Scots had failed to follow suit and so were in danger of placing the Protestant succession in grave jeopardy. Moreover, the belligerence of the Edinburgh parliament had come at the worst possible time. England and her allies were locked in armed combat with the might of the French state for dominance of western Europe. The War of the Spanish Succession was resumed in 1702. It was a critical stage and the outcome was far from certain. It was not until August 1704 that the Duke of Marlborough laid to rest the legend of French invincibility with his crushing victory at Blenheim. In the mean time, Louis XIV openly encouraged Scottish Jacobites, followers of the exiled House of Stuart, by recognizing the young son of the dying James VII and II as the true heir to the thrones of England and Scotland. By doing so he linked the issue of the English and Scottish successions directly to that of the European war. The Jacobites in Scotland had done well in the elections to the parliament of 1703 and had seen their strength in the country grow because of the unpopularity of the government. They were also being sustained by the interest shown by Louis and some of his ministers in an invasion of Scotland which would put even more pressure on the London regime. The continuing instability of the Scottish parliament therefore seemed only to be giving comfort to the mortal enemies of the state both at home and abroad. The source of the problem had to be tackled and quickly. It was certainly the threat of the French war which finally moved Godolphin, Queen Anne's Lord High Treasurer and Chief Minister, and Marlborough, her Captain-General, to opt for the union solution to the Scottish problem. Marlborough was concerned because so many of the crack troops for his armies were recruited from Scotland. Since the need to safeguard English national security was therefore paramount, only an 'incorporating union', which would both dissolve the Edinburgh parliament and create a new United Kingdom legislature, was ever acceptable to English negotiators. A federal solution, which might have perpetuated weak government, was never on offer.

Events now moved quickly. A joint Anglo-Scottish parliamentary commission met in the spring of 1706 and worked out a comprehensive draft Treaty of Union with 25 articles to be presented to the two parliaments. At the heart of the proposal was the cardinal principle of incorporation, which was absolutely indispensable from the English perspective. Most of the Scots commissioners were hand-picked followers of the Dukes of Queensberry and Argyll, both pre-eminent in the Scottish government and likely supporters of incorporated union. When this central component of the treaty leaked out, however, there was widespread anger and opposition. It would appear that some sort of improved accommodation with England and an improvement to the Regal Union may have appealed but not 'an entire union'. Initially, the proposed treaty alienated whole sections of Scottish opinion. The Kirk was very alarmed because it feared that, by closer association with England, bishops would once again be imposed on the church. The General Assembly and the presbyteries denounced the proposed union and the Kirk became the most formidable opponent of the project. The treaty was also anathema to the Jacobites, who rightly saw it as a grave threat to the restoration of the Stuarts. One enthusiastic advocate for union, the Earl of Roxburgh, argued that it was the most practical way to kill off Jacobitism once and for all, since after the union English armies would be able to move freely into Scotland and suppress any future Stuart insurrection. Anti-English feelings had reached a brutal climax in the spring of 1705, when Captain Green and two of his crew of the English ship *Worcester* were executed in Edinburgh after being found guilty on a trumped-up charge of piracy against a ship of the Darien Company. It was an act of judicial murder, aided and abetted by the Edinburgh mob. Rampant anglophobia continued into 1706 and, as the French spy, Nathaniel Hooke, reported to his masters, was likely to become even stronger as more details of the secret treaty negotiations leaked out in the months ahead.

Indeed, when the Scottish parliament met in October 1706 at the start of the historic session to debate the draft articles of union, it is plain that opposition had not subsided. Not all burghs and counties sent in petitions, but those that did were virtually all vehemently anti-union in content. Argyll dismissed these as mere paper kites, but it was significant that they were not balanced by any pro-union addresses. Presbyterian ministers remained loud in their denunciations, vigorously condemning the proposed union as a profane threat to the Scottish Protestant tradition. From the unionist perspective, Clerk of Penicuik lamented the yawning gap which he perceived between the parliament and the people on the issue. He estimated that 'not even one per cent approved of what the former was doing'.[3] The Kirk was by far the main influence on the opinion of ordinary people, and the continual preaching against union was believed in government circles to be a threat to public order. In Edinburgh, the Duke of Hamilton, the recognized leader of the parliamentary opposition against union, was cheered to the echo by the crowds who then attacked the house of Sir Patrick Johnstone, a strong union supporter. The Duke of Queensberry, the Queen's Commissioner, needed a military escort to Parliament House. From that point on, anti-union demonstrations were common in the capital. In November, rioting spread to the south-west, that stronghold of strict Calvinism and covenanting tradition. The Glasgow mob rose against unionist sympathizers in disturbances which lasted intermittently for over a month, while in the burgh of Dumfries the proposed Articles of Union were ritually burnt before an angry gathering of several thousand townspeople.

It was also rumoured that plans were being laid for an armed uprising.

This was to be led by the Cameronians, the militant Presbyterians from the western shires, in an unlikely alliance with the Jacobite highlanders of the Duke of Atholl in Perthshire. Some believed that a force of some 8,000 men could be mustered, which would be enough to break up the parliamentary session and defeat any government army that took the field against it. In the event, this great host never materialized. Nevertheless, the potential for armed opposition was clearly there, as is shown by recent research on the Jacobite conspiracy and threatened invasion in 1708 which was fuelled by strong anti-union feelings and was much better-supported than was once thought. The elaborate military precautions taken by government also shows its anxiety about the threat of insurrection. While the Edinburgh mob was taking to the streets, Queensberry ensured that the Scots standing army, 1,500 men in all, was camped near the capital, and troops were also quartered in the city itself. But the Privy Council feared that the Scottish forces at its disposal would not be enough if matters got out of hand. In late October, therefore, Godolphin assured the Scottish commander-in-chief, the Earl of Leven, that a powerful force would be ordered to the border to be in readiness in case the 'ferment' should continue to give 'any further disturbance' to the 'publick peace'. By December these infantry soldiers had been reinforced with 800 cavalry and were available for action on orders from the government in Edinburgh. More ominously, troops were also sent to the north of Ireland from where that major bastion of anti-union sentiment, the south-west counties of Scotland, could more easily be intimidated and, if necessary, attacked. In the event, an English invasion in support of the Edinburgh government proved unnecessary. But these very public preparations may also have fuelled popular fears that a vote against the union by parliament might well have caused Westminster to impose a military solution instead.

2

In 1706 the articles of the union treaty could not be easily guaranteed successful passage through the Scottish parliament. It was a single-chamber assembly, with a total of 147 members representing the nobility, the barons (or county members) and the burgesses of the towns, divided into a number of groupings, that were not organized and structured parties in the modern sense but looser alliances of political and personal interests. The largest was the Court Party, which, as its name suggested, was the party of government, helped to carry out the policies of London and controlled patronage which had been essential to the management of parliament since the abolition of the Lords of the Articles. It was the Court Party, under the Queen's Commissioner, the Duke of Queensberry, which had the responsibility for ensuring that the Treaty of Union was accepted by parliament. The mere fact of holding office and patronage gave the Court Party a cohesion and stability which the Country Party, the main opposition, manifestly lacked. Essentially this was an uneasy confederation of different and sometimes conflicting interests, many of which had little in common except opposition to the ministry of the day. So volatile was the party that the Jacobites would sometimes see themselves allied to it and at other times functioning quite separately as the 'Cavaliers'. The potential of the Country Party to be an effective opposition in the crucial session of 1706 was also significantly weakened by the ambiguous leadership of the Duke of Hamilton, whose contradictory behaviour in 1706–7 will be explored in more detail later. Finally, the 'New Party', soon to be known by the exotic name of 'Squadrone Volante', had emerged out of the Country Party in 1704. As events were to prove, this group of around two dozen members was to have a key role in the outcome of the union vote.

The union solution was a political response to a crisis of government, and there was no certainty that the queen's Scottish ministers could deliver in 1706–7 what they had signally failed to achieve in previous turbulent parliamentary sessions. The legislation of 1703 seemed to suggest that the Scots were bent on loosening the bonds of the Union of the Crowns rather than on closer association with England, and this appeared to be borne out by the anger which had built up around the country in the autumn and winter of 1706 as the parliament started its deliberations. There was indeed a lot at stake. The idea of incorporating union went much further than earlier ideas, and there were those who broadly approved of a closer relationship with England but firmly rejected incorporation because it meant the end of a Scottish parliament and the final transfer of legislative authority to Westminster. To some, the offer in the draft treaty of 45 Scots MPs and 16 elected peers in the proposed new parliament for the United Kingdom seemed meagre in the extreme, since it was based on the presumed taxable capacity of Scotland within the new constitutional context and not on her share of population. Yet, despite these potential obstacles and vociferous opposition both within and outside parliament, the Act of Union was finally carried. In a historic decision on 16 January 1707, parliament voted itself out of existence by ratifying the Act of Union by 110 votes to 67, a clear majority of 43. Apparently against all the odds, Queensberry and the Court Party had triumphed.

Basic to their successful strategy was the elimination of the threat posed by the Kirk, whose ministers had played such an important role in articulating anti-union feeling. By an Act of Security of the Church of Scotland of November 1706 the historic rights of the church and the Presbyterian system of government were guaranteed as a basic condition of union, and later accepted as an integral part of the treaty itself. Religious anxieties did not disappear, but the Court Party had effectively drawn the teeth of the opposition of the Kirk and in particular had placated the Commission of the General Assembly, the highest church court in the land. It was a master stroke which severely weakened one of the key elements in the anti-union campaign. One pro-union sympathizer noted:

in the churches, by and large, the trumpets of sedition began to fall silent. Ministers who had formerly meddled over-zealously in politics now learned to leave the direction of government to parliament. This greatly upset the Hamiltonians who saw themselves abandoned by those they most relied on to stir up anti-union sentiment.[4]

Several of the articles of the treaty itself also played to the Court Party's advantage. The English commissioners who helped to draft the treaty with Scottish representatives were mainly concerned with the vital issues of security and incorporating union. To help ensure that these essentials were agreed in the Edinburgh parliament, they were willing to concede ground elsewhere. In fact several of the clauses of the treaty were devoted to safeguarding the vested interests of those social groups who mattered in Scotland. Integration was confined to parliament, fiscal matters and public law. As well as the rights of the Kirk, the privileges of the royal burghs and their merchant élites were guaranteed. Scottish private law was protected and the heritable jurisdictions (or private courts) of the landed class maintained. The Scottish nobility were a particular target, since only 16 Scottish peers were to sit in the House of Lords. However, the majority who could not aspire to this eminence could draw comfort from being offered in the treaty the privileges enjoyed by their English counterparts. These included exemption from civil actions for debt – a not inconsiderable advantage, given the endemic financial embarrassment among the Scottish aristocracy at this time. Even more significantly, the Scots were granted free trade with England and her colonies, a concession for which they had craved for some years but which the English had always been stubbornly unwilling to concede.

How telling this inducement was in the final voting patterns is difficult to say and has been the subject of vigorous controversy among scholars. However, Article IV of the treaty, which allowed for 'Freedom and Intercourse of Trade and Navigation', attracted the largest single majority with only 19 votes against. This was not surprising, given the history of resentment against the English Navigation Laws and the fact that so many of the Scottish nobility were deeply involved in the cattle, linen and coal trade to England. On the other hand, most of the burghs, including Glasgow (later to become one of the great European transatlantic entrepôts), voted against, possibly because they feared the threat of English competition in the proposed common market. Perhaps even more crucial in carrying the treaty as a whole was Article XV, which dealt with the 'Equivalent'. This was an attractive inducement to the Squadrone Volante, the small party whose support the Court Party had to retain in order to achieve ultimate success, so finely balanced was the overall position in parliament. A sum of £398,000 (almost £26 million in today's values) was allowed to compensate the Scots for their estimated share after the union in repaying England's large national debt, which had been swollen by wartime expenditure. But some of this was also to be used to compensate the investors in the ill-fated Darien Company. Among the most significant of these were members of the Squadrone. When the first important vote in consideration of the Articles of Union was taken, it cast all its 25 votes in favour of the government. It was a spectacular volte-face because in 1704 and 1705 the Squadrone had not shown any commitment to union. Whether the lure of the Equivalent monies was a decisive factor in this swift and comprehensive change of mind cannot of course be determined absolutely!

If the Squadrone was important to the achievement of a pro-union majority, the Court Party itself was the fundamental basis of final victory. Computer-based analysis of the voting patterns in the last Scottish parliament has demonstrated its overall influence. The Court members, with the Squadrone, were the consistent supporters of the treaty through all of its 25 Articles, although this final outcome could not necessarily be foreseen at the start of the session. Moreover, the times were uncertain and the cohesion of the Court unpredictable. For this reason, political management, which had been employed with varying degrees of success since the later seventeenth century, was now deployed on an unprecedented scale. The promise of favours, sinecures, pension, offices and straightforward cash bribes became indispensable to ensure successive government majorities. Supporters had to be rewarded if disaffection was to be avoided, especially in such a miscellaneous group as the Court, which was made up of the disparate followings of several great noblemen each with his own personal agenda. Management which had abysmally failed in previous parliaments was now to achieve resounding success. The influential Duke of Argyll agreed to return from the armies in Flanders in order to support the Court in the decisive session. His personal rewards included promotion to the rank of major-general and an English peerage. £20,000 sterling (the equivalent of £240,000 Scots, and £1.3 million in today's values) was secretly dispatched north from the English treasury. Whether it was disbursed to pay office-holders whose salaries were overdue or as straight money bribes, as some have suspected, is in a sense immaterial. Payment of arrears to selected individuals was just as much part and parcel of effective management as handing over direct cash inducements. Once again, the Squadrone benefited handsomely from the distribution. Modern research has also identified as beneficiaries former members of the opposition, such as William Seton of Pitmedden, Sir Kenneth Mackenzie and the Earl of Glencairn, whose rewards seem to have encouraged a more favourable opinion of union. But not all parliamentarians were as susceptible. The voting record of at least 13 members shows that they supported the union without either cash inducement or promise of office. But the loyalty of the Court Party as a whole could not be taken for granted because there were allegations that some were unenthusiastic for incorporating union. Support had therefore to be shored up by lavish patronage. In this parliament there was to be no repeat of the débâcle of 1703.

The formidable political management machine presided over by Queensberry and his acolytes contrasted with the disarray of the parliamentary opposition which signally failed to capitalize on the national resentment to union which, if effectively led, could well have been a potent threat to the government. The anti-union forces suffered from three main weaknesses. First, the Country Party and the Cavaliers could always be relied upon to act together to make political mischief and embarrass the Court; but at a more fundamental level they were irreconcilable. The Cavaliers or Jacobites wanted the return of the Catholic Stuart Pretender, but this was anathema to the Presbyterian nobility who led the Country Party. Second, the leadership of the Duke of Hamilton was weak and indecisive at key moments which might have been exploited to advantage. So ambiguous was his position that some speculated as to which side he was actually on. The opposition tactic – of formally withdrawing from parliament in January 1707 and in effect boycotting proceedings so as to give a clear signal about the sheer extent of opposition to the treaty – came to nothing because of Hamilton. He failed to turn up in the first instance, complaining of being seized of the toothache, and, when he eventually appeared, he declined to lead the proposed mass withdrawal. The man who had been lionized by the Edinburgh crowds as the only hope for Scottish independence had again let his followers down. He had done it before, in September 1705, when parliament was deciding whether the Commissioners to treat for union should be appointed by the queen or parliament. Hamilton amazingly suggested that they ought to be the queen's nominees, thus ensuring a pro-unionist majority on the Commission. He was also later blamed for calling off the rising of Cameronians from the south-west and the Highlands in November 1706. Hamilton's behaviour demoralized the forces of opposition both in and outside parliament. Some have explained his hesitations as being the result of his personal position. Not only was he heavily in debt, he had in addition acquired through marriage large estates in Lancashire which he stood to lose if union did not succeed. His personal circumstances meant that he was also vulnerable to favours from government. James Johnstone, Lord Clerk Register and one of the Scottish officers of state, alleged that Hamilton was actively seeking assistance from London ministers with his debts in the winter of 1705.

The third reason for the weakness of the anti-union forces stemmed from the fact that their only real hope lay in an alliance between the parliamentary opposition and the disaffected population in the country, given the numerical strength of the Court and its ally, the Squadrone. But whether the leadership of the Country Party had any real stomach for a popular uprising must be doubted, especially since the Kirk was no longer actively or publicly opposed to the treaty. A civil war could have given comfort only to the Jacobites and would have threatened the restoration of the Stuarts through an invasion from France. The 1688–9 Revolution (which the Country leaders strongly supported to a man) and the Protestant succession could have been imperilled. Furthermore, there were grounds for believing that England might impose a military solution in order to safeguard her northern borders if the union project failed. Godolphin made veiled threats to this effect and, as has been seen, troops had been stationed in the north of England and reinforcements also sent to northern Ireland. There was no way of knowing whether these large-scale military preparations were simply sabre-rattling or had a more serious intent. They did, however, help to concentrate the minds of the opposition as they debated the Articles of Union in the last months of 1706. It was abundantly clear that they were playing for high stakes.

The Anglo-Scottish Union became law on May Day 1707. England wanted it for reasons of national security, at a time when she was fighting a major war in Europe. In Scotland there seems to have been overwhelming popular opposition to the loss of the parliament and angry hostility to the whole idea of an 'incorporating' union. Despite this, the treaty was passed by a clear majority. The powerful opposition of the Church of Scotland was weakened when the rights and privileges of the Kirk were solemnly guaranteed in the event of full union. A much improved system of management ensured the stability of the Court Party, and the treaty itself contained several clauses that were designed to appease key vested interests in Scotland. Freedom of trade was granted and the Equivalent helped to maintain the crucial support of the Squadrone. These were the carrots, but there were also some sticks. The danger of civil war if union failed was feared by some, and there were rumours that Westminster might use military means if the articles were rejected. In this situation the parliamentary opposition was fatally weakened by internal divisions and inept leadership and was in no position to exploit national disaffection.

3

The first article of the Treaty of Union proclaimed in sonorous language 'THAT the Two Kingdoms of England and Scotland shall . . . forever after be United into One Kingdom by the name of GREAT BRITAIN'.

The reality was, however, that a long and rocky road had to be traversed after 1707 before the new relationship between the two countries was finally formalized, and at some points along this difficult route the very survival of the new union was sometimes in grave doubt. The treaty had been born out of a marriage of convenience between the governing classes in Edinburgh and London, and its successful passage through the Scottish parliament was a close-run thing, delivered in the teeth of a good deal of popular hostility outside the House. This was hardly the context for the stable and harmonious development of 'Great Britain'.

Then again there was the continuing Jacobite threat, which was always more menacing in Scotland than in England, not least because the exiled House of Stuart could usually count on the military support of several of the strongest Highland clans. Jacobites were implacably opposed to the union since they viewed it – correctly – as a means of buttressing and perpetuating the Revolution of 1688–9 and so ensuring that the Stuarts would never again return to their rightful inheritance. Until Jacobitism was finally crushed (and this did not happen until after the '45), the union was always likely to be threatened to a greater or lesser extent. This was especially the case if France, with its enormous military and naval resources, chose to intervene on the Stuart side. Louis XIV and his ministers decided to play the Scottish card in 1708, in order to exploit the simmering discontent surrounding the union, and force some regiments from the Duke of Marlborough's victorious armies to be diverted from the campaign in Europe. In the event, the Jacobite expedition failed miserably through faulty navigation and bad weather; and the débâcle was completed when the French fleet missed its rendezvous with their Scottish allies on the Firth of Forth. The episode, however, tellingly illustrates the fragility of the post-union regime. John S. Gibson has convincingly shown the considerable numerical support for the rising in Scotland which, if the French had landed successfully, might have created a truly formidable force, much greater than the 1,500 troops available to the government at the time. Furthermore, James Stuart, the exiled 'Old Pretender' (or claimant to the throne), in his 'Declaration to the Scots Nation' had promised, *inter alia*, the restoration of the Scottish parliament in a deliberate attempt to attract the support of those disenchanted with the union settlement.

No one was more aware than Godolphin of the need to tread very carefully in this difficult situation. After 1707 he left untouched virtually everything in the Scottish administration, apart from establishing new Boards of Commissioners and Excise to try to secure improved revenues. The two existing Scottish secretaries, Loudon and Mar, were also retained. Godolphin's strategy seems to have been to do as little as possible and so keep the Scots quiet. On the whole he succeeded, apart from having to concede the abolition of the Scottish Privy Council, the chief executive organ of government in Scotland, in 1708. This had not been planned by Westminster but was the result of the machinations of the Squadrone, who were convinced that the Council was an instrument of the Court Party who used it to maximize their own electoral advantage. The end of the Privy Council was a key development because it gravely weakened the ability of government in Scotland to respond vigorously and decisively in crisis situations. The vacuum which it left at the centre of power could only give further comfort to the Jacobites. In response to the abortive Jacobite rising of 1708, the new United Kingdom parliament in 1709 extended the draconian English law of treason to Scotland against the concerted opposition of the Scottish members in the Commons. It was, however, imposed because the Scots had signally failed to punish the Jacobite plotters of 1708 in a suitably exemplary manner. Ironically, they had escaped retribution because the Privy Council was in the last days of its existence and was not interested in taking decisive action. But the issue of the treason legislation showed that Westminster would adopt an interventionist approach in Scotland when issues of national security were at stake, even if at other times it showed little interest in direct governance north of the border.

More provocative and serious were the inflammatory acts of the Tory government which replaced Godolphin and his Whig coalition at the elections of 1710. The High Church Tories seemed bent on a policy of cutting down the privileges of the Church of Scotland enshrined in the Treaty of Union. This was not so much hostility towards the Scots as such as a general campaign against Presbyterians in both England and Scotland by high Anglicans in the Tory Party. The initiative was enthusiastically supported by Scottish Tories, who were also noted for their Episcopalian loyalties. In 1711 James Greenshields, an Episcopalian minister, appealed to the House of Lords against his imprisonment by the magistrates of Edinburgh for defying the presbytery of the city and using the English liturgy. Recourse to the Lords was possible within the terms of the treaty of 1707, but the subsequent decision to allow the Anglican prayer book to be used for worship in an Episcopalian meeting house enraged the capital's Presbyterians. This was then followed in 1712 by two more provocative measures, the Toleration Act and the Patronage Act. The former granted freedom of worship to Scottish Episcopalians as long as they agreed to pray for the reigning monarch, while the latter re-established the primary right of patrons, who were usually local landowners, to appoint to vacant parishes and church offices. Patronage had been abolished as part of the Presbyterian revolution of 1690 because it conflicted with the rights of the community itself to decide on a candidate to fill a parish vacancy.

All this outraged the Kirk and seemed to undermine the Act of Security guaranteeing Presbyterian rights in the event of union, an enactment central to the acceptance of the treaty itself. But, in addition, the legislation of 1712 raised the issue of the nature of 1707 and the extent to which the treaty was an inviolate, fundamental law or subject to change at the whim of the sovereign legislature in Westminster. Perhaps of more direct impact, however, on the Scottish people was the new taxation regime within the union. A. L. Murray suggests that in the first few decades after 1707 there was a huge increase in customs and excise duties together with a significant extension in the range of commodities on which tax was paid. Partly, this was because the existing levels of taxation were simply not sufficient to cover the cost of Scottish civil government and administration, and London ministers were also soon appalled at the scale of smuggling and customs evasion. In addition, after the War of the Spanish Succession ended in 1713, the tax burden in Britain started to shift from the land tax to customs dues and excise payments on a whole range of commodities, including beer, salt, linen, soap and malt. These were all vital necessities of life for most people in Scotland. Salt, for instance, was the universal food preservative of the day and linen the most widely produced cloth. Equally, tax increases were likely to bite deeply because the Scottish economy was still in the doldrums in the first decade after union, and those pamphleteers who had optimistically predicted an economic miracle were now proven hopelessly wrong. Home salt, which had not been taxed before 1707, doubled in price when duties were imposed in 1713. That same year, the House of Commons voted to apply the malt tax to Scotland in direct defiance of the provisions of the treaty itself, a decision which would have significantly pushed up the price of ale, the most popular drink in Scotland at the time. The fury was such that the tax was never properly enforced.

To the Scots this was the climax of a whole stream of provocative actions which threatened to break the union. Scottish peers and members of the Commons came together in a series of meetings and agreed that the only solution was repeal of the treaty. What was remarkable was the unanimity of all parties on such a fundamental issue, a very rare occurrence indeed in the faction-ridden world of Scottish politics. The motion was put by the Earl of Findlater in the House of Lords in June 1713 and was only narrowly defeated by four proxy votes. The outcome demonstrated not only the disillusion of the Scottish nobility but also the fact that there was little enthusiasm in England for the union either. This alienation helped to feed the next great Jacobite rising, led by the Earl of Mar in 1715. Mar himself had been a crucial figure in helping the Court manage the votes for the treaty in 1706–7 and had then sat in the United Kingdom parliament. But he was out of favour with the new Hanoverian monarch, George I, and changed sides to the Stuarts, thus living up to his nickname, 'Bobbing John'. In 1715 Mar was able to assemble an army of 10,000 men, which was more than double the force that the government levies under the Duke of Argyll were able to muster. After the collapse of the '15, the Earl of Stair, an ultra-loyal Whig and British ambassador to France, noted that there was a real danger of another rebellion unless the ruinous consequences of the union were addressed. This was an admission by a high-ranking friend of the Court that the survival of the union was not yet assured.

However, Stair's hopes for an improvement in Anglo-Scottish relationships were premature since there was a fundamental cause of friction which would not easily or quickly disappear. The view from Westminster was that the Scots were not paying their way through taxation because of the enormous scale of smuggling and systematic revenue fraud said to be endemic in Scottish society. London merchants, for instance, were infuriated by the level of evasion in the Glasgow tobacco trade, and modern research has confirmed that between 1707 and 1722 the Scots paid duty on only half their imports from Virginia and Maryland. Fraudulent practices existed on a similar scale in other trades. On the other hand, Scotland had been accustomed to low taxes and relaxed methods of gathering revenue before the union, so that the new impositions after 1707 were bitterly resented both on economic grounds and because they were seen as an attempt by London to force Scotland to contribute to the English National Debt, which had swollen hugely to finance the Spanish Succession War. Popular retribution both against revenue increases and against more rigorous methods of collection was exacted through violence against the hated customs officers. The records of the Board of Customs are full of references to recurrent local disturbances which often resulted in mob assaults on servants of the Board and attempts to break into customs warehouses. At the customs precincts of Ayr, Dumfries and Greenock the position was so hazardous in some years that customs men dared not attempt to carry out their duties without armed protection, and a stream of reports came from all over the country of officers stoned, threatened or taken prisoner and goods seized from ships and warehouses.

These local incidents were nothing, however, compared to the national response to the decision in 1724 by Sir Robert Walpole's government to apply the malt tax to Scotland with effect from June 1725. The earlier attempt in 1713 had brought about a vote in the House of Lords which nearly dissolved the union, and this latest initiative unleashed a wave of popular anger in the summer of 1725, with riots breaking out in Stirling, Dundee, Ayr, Elgin, Paisley and Glasgow. The disturbances in Glasgow were by far the most serious. The local Member of Parliament, Daniel Campbell of Shawfield, was suspected of supporting the hated Malt Tax Act. The mob took its revenge by burning and looting his impressive town house, engaged in a pitched battle with the local garrison, which resulted in eight fatalities, and then drove the retreating troops out of the city towards Dumbarton. It took the intervention of General Wade with a force of 400 dragoons and accompanying foot to restore order finally and bring to an end a dangerous challenge to the union state. With other towns apparently ready to join in, Rosalind Mitchison has rightly described the enraged reaction to the Malt Tax as 'a movement of national resistance'.[5] Certainly the riots of 1725 concentrated the minds of Walpole's government on the Scottish problem. The insurrection itself was a serious matter, but of equal concern was the apparent impotence of the Scottish administration when confronted with such a major challenge to law and order. The Lord Advocate of Scotland, the country's senior law officer, Robert Dundas, had in fact opposed the Malt Tax and was dismissed as a result. The Secretary for Scotland, the Duke of Roxburgh, did little; and the vacuum in executive authority left by the abolition of the Privy Council was now very obvious for all to see. The Earl of Islay, younger brother of the Duke of Argyll, who was sent to investigate the situation, reported to Walpole that there had been 'a long series of no administration' in Scotland and the 'mere letter of the law had little or no effect with the people'.[6] This was tantamount to saying that Scotland was ungovernable within the union. It was not a situation which could be allowed to continue.

Walpole's solution was to sack the incompetent Roxburgh and appoint Islay to manage Scottish affairs. This was partly because the two men were friends and also because the parliamentary votes of the great Argyll political interest were valuable to his cause. The decision was a turning point in Anglo-Scottish relationships. Islay, later third Duke of Argyll from 1743, became the dominant political figure in Scotland between the 1720s and his death in 1761, excepting the brief few years, 1742-6. Such was his power that he became known as the 'King of Scotland'. His influence rested on a solemn contract with Walpole: Islay would deliver political stability in Scotland and the votes of most Scottish MPs in return for the lion's share of patronage and the authority to govern north of the border. The Walpole connection soon gave Islay immense sources of patronage which he deployed with great skill in alliance with his two principal agents, Andrew Fletcher, Lord Milton, and Duncan Forbes of Culloden, 'King Duncan' as he was dubbed in the Highlands. The civil administration, law courts, army, church and universities were all penetrated as Islay relentlessly built up a formidable empire of clients and dependants. It was reckoned that two-thirds of the judges promoted to the Court of Session owed their position to his influence, and the Campbell interest was also paramount in the appointment of sheriffs who, it was alleged, were 'little more than a list of the sons, sons-in-law, and alliances' of Islay's clients.[7] By the 1730s his power was such that King George II himself could describe him as 'Vice Roy in Scotland'.

Islay's effective management of Scotland gave a new stability to the union. He was a skilled politician who had done much in 1725 to defuse the dangerous crisis over the Malt Tax. But he then ensured that order was maintained and further civil disobedience avoided by trying to respond positively to Scottish concerns. Out of this came the foundation in 1727 of the Board of Trustees for Manufactures and Fisheries with a mandate to improve the Scottish economy. The sum of £6,000 per annum was to be devoted to the development of linen, wool and fisheries. In intent at least, this was the practical implementation of Article XV of the Treaty of Union, though not to the full extent actually agreed in 1707. But the law was also rigorously enforced against the Glasgow

Malt Tax rioters. The town was fined to compensate Campbell of Shawfield, and several of those involved in the disturbances were sentenced to transportation. This approach showed that Islay was able on the one hand to placate Scottish opinion but at the same time to satisfy London that Scotland was being effectively governed. As his system of patronage became more sophisticated in the next several years, so Islay's expertise in reconciling conflicting interest groups became ever more refined. In consequence Walpole trusted him to run Scotland with hardly any reference to Westminster. Indeed, not until 1737 did the government in London interfere in Scotland again in any direct fashion. This episode occurred in response to the Porteous Riot in Edinburgh in 1736, when the mob lynched the Captain of the Town Guard who had ordered his men to fire on the crowd at a smuggler's execution in April of that year. Porteous was under sentence in the city tolbooth because several people had been killed as a result of the Guard's actions. But the mob, inflamed that he had been given a brief reprieve, forcibly removed the unfortunate Porteous from gaol and hanged him. This brutal action incensed Westminster. Not only was the government appalled at the breakdown of law and order but it also suspected that the mob had been aided and abetted by the Edinburgh authorities. A bill was therefore prepared which proposed draconian punishments for the city of Edinburgh. The extreme measures were diluted only because of the determined opposition of the Duke of Argyll, Islay's brother, and resistance to the imposition of heavy penalties on the nation's capital by Scottish political opinion.

The Porteous incident damaged Islay's reputation as the man on whom Walpole and the London ministers could rely to run Scotland with minimal supervision from London. However, for over a decade his regime had done much to accommodate Scotland to the union. There was little additional pressure for assimilation of the kind that had seriously jeopardized the union in 1712. The cement of patronage had created loyalty to his rule in virtually all the key areas of Scottish civic life by the 1730s, and this in turn allowed Scotland to be governed almost as a separate polity within the union. Westminster was sovereign in theory, but in practice the real business of running Scotland was the responsibility of institutions inherited from the period before 1707. The treaty itself had protected the Church and the law from radical change, and now a basically Scottish form of national and local government was renewed. Edinburgh, despite the loss of the parliament, remained an important centre of law and administration. The major Scottish courts of Justiciary, Session and Exchequer, together with the Admiralty and Commissionary Courts, met there, as did the General Assembly of the Church of Scotland, the Convention of Royal Burghs, the Board of Excise, the Post Office and the Scottish Board of Customs. The system of justice at the local level, consisting of the sheriffs and justices of the peace, was inherited from before the union, while the two key social functions at parish level, those of education and poor relief, were the joint responsibility of the pre-1707 kirk sessions and local landowners. All of this represented a remarkable degree of legal, religious and administrative autonomy and continuity, which meant that most of the political decisions that really mattered continued to be made in Scotland itself. As long as Westminster kept a low profile, which in most years after 1725 it did, and skilled managers such as Islay were able to defuse possible causes of friction, Scotland's semi-independent status was assured. This in turn helped to mollify anti-union opinion and promote acceptance of the new relationship with England.

By the 1740s three other influences were also combining to strengthen the Anglo-Scottish connection. First, Jacobitism, one of the main threats to the union, disintegrated as a viable political and military force after the '45 ended in catastrophe at Culloden in April 1746. This was followed by the ferocious subjugation of disaffected areas of the Highlands. Second, the freedom of trade conceded in the treaty in 1707 finally seemed to be bringing the long-awaited benefits. The export figures for linen, cattle and tobacco, the leading sectors of the economy, all show significant increase at this time. The tobacco trade, for example, was already approaching the early years of its golden era. Eight million lb. were landed at Clyde ports in 1741. By 1745 the figure had climbed to 13 million lb. and, after a dramatic spurt, to 21 million lb. in 1752. Linen was also more buoyant, not least because of the provision of favourable bounties on exports from 1742. The key aspect to this economic advance was that all three commodities depended on freedom of trade to the colonies and the English home markets, plus the protection afforded by high tariff walls against foreign competitors put in place from 1707. The producers of linen, Scotland's major industry, sold nearly 70 per cent of their official output to England and the transatlantic colonies by the 1760s. It was now beginning to appear that the union was indeed of material benefit and that Scotland's future hopes of even greater prosperity depended on it.

Third, and perhaps most fundamentally, England and the English empire started to generate lucrative career opportunities for upper- and middle-class Scots. For centuries the Scots had been a mobile people in Europe, as merchants, small traders, intellectuals, churchmen and soldiers. Current estimates suggest that anywhere between 90,000 and 115,000 Scots migrated to Ireland, Poland, Scandinavia and other countries in the first half of the seventeenth century alone. The union soon gave fresh and even more attractive opportunities. Even before 1707 the foundation of Scottish colonies in New Jersey and South Carolina illustrated the slow change in the axis of Scottish emigration from Europe to the Atlantic. The ill-fated Darien enterprise, the grand design to establish a Scots commercial emporium on the Isthmus of Panama, though it was a costly failure, showed the new aspiration towards westwards migration. By the 1750s some Scots were doing rather well out of the union connection, with the nobility and lairds the first to exploit the richer pickings in the south. In 1733 Erskine of Grange complained that 'The country [Scotland] now, and for some years, has lookt on it self as deserted, not only by the courtiers but by the principall of its nobility and gentry.'[8] The attraction was London with its wealth of posts, sinecures, pensions and an abundance of career opportunities for those who were well connected. Several Scottish aristocrats were spectacularly successful. Some 46 per cent of Scots soldier peers managed promotion to the general staff of the British army between 1707 and 1745, compared with just over 17 per cent from 1660 to 1706. At a lower level, one in four regimental officers in the 1750s were Scots. It was, therefore, not surprising that several Scottish aristocrats opted to settle in England permanently, so continuing and accelerating a trend that had already been established before the union. For instance, the fifth Duke of Hamilton was educated at Winchester and Oxford, became a Lord of the Bedchamber to George II and died at Bath. Archibald Campbell, Earl of Islay, the uncrowned 'King of Scotland', was born in Surrey and attended Eton. The anglicization of the Scottish nobility had begun before 1707 but had further advanced by mid-century.

But it was far from easy for lesser mortals of Scottish birth to achieve success in the English capital in the fields of politics and civil administration before the 1760s, although an important exception to this generalization was the growing Scottish merchant community in London, many of whom had close family and business connections with the tobacco aristocracy in Glasgow. Partly because openings were fewer and prospects less attractive in the south for the majority of Scots, many were more attracted abroad to the empire, where their skills and educational background quickly enabled them to make their mark. In the 1690s the Company of Scotland Trading to Africa and the Indies, which launched the Darien venture, had signally failed to break the East India Company's (EIC) monopoly. After the union, however, the Scots began to infiltrate the Company's Directorate, and Scots banking families with continental associations, such as the Hopes and the Drummonds, were already prominent in its affairs by the 1730s. The first Scottish Director of the EIC, John Drummond of Quarrel, was appointed in 1722. Already by the 1750s, some time before Henry Dundas transformed the EIC into a veritable Scottish fiefdom, large numbers of Scots were serving as army and civilian officers in Bengal and Madras. Already by 1767, as Andrew McKillop has shown, there were 220 Scottish writers, the senior civil servants of the EIC in the Bengal and Madras Civil Establishment, or nearly 10 per cent of the total. This was a significantly higher figure than that of the Irish and the Welsh, who together accounted for less than 5 per cent of those who applied for writerships in the 1760s.

It was an even more developed pattern in North America, where an estimated 30,000 Scots settled in the first five decades after the union. In the Lowlands at least, this was a migration led by the educated professional and business classes. More than 150 Scottish doctors emigrated to America during the eighteenth century and became the main force in the colonial medical profession. Scots also dominated the Episcopal and Presbyterian Churches in the colonies, as well as supplying numerous teachers to the middle and southern states and other areas. They also managed to secure the majority of Crown appointments in East and West Florida after the Seven Years War, thanks to the influence of their countryman, Lord Bute, during his tenure as Secretary of State. Throughout the plantation economies of Virginia, Maryland and the Carolinas, Scottish merchants and planters had become key elements in the organization of the great transatlantic trades of tobacco, rice and indigo.

Scotland had the combination of an unusually effective and developed educational system including five universities and, in relative terms, only a limited range of openings at home for the sons of lairds, lawyers, ministers, merchants, doctors and teachers. It was a poorer society than in England and so, since time immemorial, it had been common to seek advancement abroad. The long tradition of international mobility in Europe and wide-ranging mercantile enterprise all over the continent stood the Scots in good stead after 1707. Emigration was a familiar experience in a society which was far from insular. The rise of the Scots to prominence in imperial trade, military service, administration and the professions was therefore a change of geographical direction rather than a new beginning. The Seven Years War of 1756 to 1763 gave further impetus to their aspirations, as victory over the French added huge new territorial gains in North America, the Caribbean, Africa and India which offered the prospect of even more glittering prizes while at the same time swelling the ranks of the army of empire and hence much greater openings for the Scottish officer.

The formerly disaffected Jacobite areas of the Highlands were now also enlisted in the imperial cause during the Seven Years War, and subsequently on an even greater scale during the American and Napoleonic Wars. The clansmen were transformed into the warriors of empire, and former chiefs were offered valuable additional sources of revenue by recruiting regiments for the British army from the people of their lands. The Highlanders were esteemed as a tough, loyal and mobile light infantry and, as Pitt the Elder admitted, "tis no mischief if they fall'. Six regiments of the line were recruited in the Highlands during the Seven Years War and another ten during the American War of Independence. Despite some incidents of mutiny if proper pay was denied or amalgamation threatened with Lowland regiments, the kilted soldiers soon became the feared spearhead of empire, with battle honours won by 1815 across western Europe, America, the Caribbean and India. In 1784 a grateful government restored the remaining Jacobite estates annexed after the '45 to their former owners. It was a decision partially influenced by the metamorphosis of the disaffected clans into an imperial army. In the Disannexing Act of that year the Highlanders were warmly congratulated by a grateful government for their heroic contribution during the American War: '. . . no subjects in any part of His Majesty's Dominions are more loyal or dutiful or better affected . . . many, of all ranks and descriptions, have performed signal services to their country in the late wars'.

London was not always so complimentary. Indeed, one confirmation of the growing Scottish success within the union was the Scottophobia that was generated in the capital in the 1750s and 1760s. This was especially so during the term of office of John, Earl of Bute, the first ever Scottish Prime Minister, when many of his fellow countrymen were rising to positions of public prominence in the government. Only eight Scottish MPs held state office in the years 1747–53, but 28 had achieved high rank between 1761 and 1767. The Scots were seen to be too much in the ascendancy, and English political cartoons of the time were savagely racist in tone, portraying Scots as treacherous mendicants who could not be trusted. Bute himself came in for some of the most scathing treatment, being portrayed in one ribald print after another as the well-endowed seducer of the mother of George III. As Linda Colley has pointed out, this representation was a direct sexual symbolism for the anxiety that the Scots were penetrating England itself in their craving for pensions and places. James Boswell certainly had his sense of national pride aroused at the famous incident in Covent Garden in 1762 when the arrival of two Highland officers at a play was greeted by the audience with roars of 'No Scots! No Scots! Out with them!', which was then followed by the throwing of apples at the unfortunate soldiers. Boswell was enraged and jumped up to cry, 'Damn you Rascals! I hated the English; I wished from my soul that the Union was broke and that we might give them another battle of Bannockburn.'[9] Even David Hume, the greatest philosopher of the age, encountered prejudice: 'Some hate me because I am not a Whig, some because I am not a Christian, and all because I am a Scotsman.'[10]

National pride was also offended by the Militia Act of 1757, which created a force in England and Wales for home defence, but not in Scotland. The suspicion was that the Westminster establishment even by the 1760s regarded most Scots as crypto-Jacobite who therefore were not to be trusted with the bearing of arms. This produced a storm of protest from many Scottish intellectuals, who began a campaign for the establishment of a national militia. But patriotic indignation and wounded pride were unlikely to disturb the union by this period. The Scottish nobility, merchant classes and intelligentsia were not prepared to sacrifice the material opportunities that were now flowing in great abundance from the political connection which had been forged in 1707.

Indeed, many were becoming more and more supportive of the idea of Great Britain. After all, it was a Scot, James Thomson, who wrote 'Rule Britannia'. Robert Fergusson and Robert Burns, major Scottish poets of the later eighteenth century, waxed eloquent on the theme of Britain. Fergusson referred to 'Thrice happy Britons ... the sons that hem Britannia round from sudden invasion', while Burns, in the 'Ode for General Washington's Birthday', spoke of 'the freeborn Briton's soul of fire'. Names such as Hanover Street, George Street, Queen Street and Frederick Street in both Edinburgh and Glasgow proclaimed the loyalty of the urban élites to Great Britain and the Hanoverian dynasty. Increasingly many of the Scottish landed classes were sending their children to school and university in England in order to enhance their career opportunities in later life, while the Scottish intellectuals of the Enlightenment, including figures of world renown such as David Hume, were becoming concerned about their 'provincial' accents and language. As the Select Society put it in 1761:

As the intercourse between this part of Great Britain and the capital increases, both on account of business and amusement and must still go on increasing, gentlemen educated in Scotland have long been sensible of the disadvantage under which they labour, from their imperfect knowledge of the ENGLISH TONGUE, and the impropriety with which they speak it.[11]

In order to deal with this problem, the Society proposed to import qualified English elocution teachers to provide instruction. Scottish historical scholars of the eighteenth century were increasingly seeing the history of the nation in negative terms. The leading historian of the eighteenth century, William Robertson, dismissed the Scottish past before the Revolution of 1688 as a dark story of anarchy, barbarism and religious fanaticism, and his scathing critique was repeated many times over in the volumes of other writers of less renown. A central theme in their work was an emphatic denial of the Gaelic-Irish heritage of Scotland and the complex racial origins of the Scottish people. Thus Sir John Clerk asserted, against all previous belief, that the Scots were indigenous to Scotland and that the *Scotti* had never come from Ireland. He further contended, in an extraordinary attempt to suppress the country's Gaelic-speaking past, that the early Scots spoke Saxon, which, despite political divisions, linked them with the Britons to the south and prepared the linguistic way for full and final union between England and Scotland in the eighteenth century.

Yet it would be entirely wrong to conclude that a distinctive Scottish identity was now being crushed beneath the unrelenting and irresistible forces of anglicization. Life in Scotland was still conditioned and fashioned by intrinsically Scottish institutions: the proudly independent Presbyterian church, civil law, the parish schools and the five universities. The Scots dialect was the language not only of the most humble but also of many of the greatest in the land. Scottish patriotism was alive and well among the mass of the people, as was demonstrated by the continuing and widespread popularity of the poems of John Barbour and Blind Harry, whose verse vividly recounted the heroic deeds of Bruce and Wallace, the great national heroes of the medieval wars of independence. Some of the intellectuals might revile the Covenanters of the seventeenth century as religious fanatics, but for the common people of much of the Lowlands they were the brave champions of Scottish Presbyterianism who had fought courageously for freedom of conscience against the oppression of the state. They too became national icons like Wallace and Bruce, and by the early nineteenth century it had become common for mass popular rallies to be held at Bannockburn, where Bruce had won his famous victory against the English, and also on the old battlefields where the Covenanters had fought and died. One of the crucial effects of the Covenanting tradition was to remind the Scots that Presbyterianism, their form of Protestantism, was distinct and separate from the Protestantism of England.

Popular texts such as *Scots Worthies* kept alive the Reformation and Covenanting legacies and even helped to inspire the later radical movements of the 1790s with their Calvinist vision in the equality of souls before God. Moreover, acceptance of the union at élite level was sometimes tempered by concern about some of its effects. In the early 1760s, as already seen, anti-Scots feeling in London reached a new intensity. John Wilkes whipped up English nationalism by depicting the Scots as an alien race who through the union were gradually infiltrating the highest levels of government and at the same time securing the most lucrative jobs in the empire. All this was exaggerated, but the 'Rage against the Scots', as Hume called it, did little to promote harmony within Great Britain and contradicted the cherished belief in Scotland that the union was a partnership between equals. It also made the Scots élite even more aware of their Scottishness. They were gradually developing a dual allegiance, a political loyalty to Britain which not even the most vitriolic abuse from the south could undermine, and at the same time they were maintaining a continuing sense of identity with their native land.

2

The Jacobite Challenge

I

Jacobitism is a subject littered with some of the most colourful personalities and familiar events in Scottish history. The story includes the exploits of Charles Edward Stuart, 'Bonnie Prince Charlie', the drama of the '45 rebellion and the epic last stand of the Highland clans at Culloden. These are all the stuff of myth, romance and legend, and it is not always easy to penetrate the historical reality behind the seductive smokescreen created by countless poets, novelists, dramatists, film-makers and songwriters, all of whom have found the rise and fall of Scottish Jacobitism a beguiling source for their own creative work.

At one level it is easy enough to define what Jacobitism was. The term derives from the Latin word *Jacobus* for James. Thus Jacobites were those who were committed to a return of the Stuart dynasty of James VII and II which had lost the thrones of England, Scotland and Ireland in the Revolution of 1688. James had begun a 'catholicizing' of appointments in Ireland after 1685, so that by 1688 a majority of the army officers in the country were Roman Catholic. Fears were instantly aroused among elements of the ruling classes in both England and Scotland, partly because Ireland might become a base from which to launch an armed counter-Reformation on the British mainland and partly because militant Catholicism was once again seen to be on the march in Europe, where the renewed persecution of the Protestant Huguenots in France culminated in their expulsion after the Revocation of the Edict of Nantes in 1685. James's policy of granting toleration and according civil and religious rights to dissenters and Catholics was regarded as the thin end of the wedge. Some suspected that his final intention was nothing less than the restoration of Catholicism itself.

When his queen bore him a son in June 1688, the continuation of a catholicizing policy looked to be assured into the next generation. This was too much for some of the English governing classes and they invited the unambiguously Protestant Dutch prince, William of Orange, to assume the throne.

At first, Scotland remained loyal to the Stuarts. Indeed, the Privy Council ordered Scottish troops under John Graham of Claverhouse, Viscount Dundee, to march south to London to give succour to the beleaguered monarch. But James was not made of the stuff to stand and fight and, as much of his political and military support in and around the capital started to melt away, he fled into exile in France in December 1688. However, his fate in Scotland was not yet sealed. All would depend on the reaction of the Convention of Estates, which met in Edinburgh in 1689 to consider the Scottish response to the revolution in England. Though proceedings were opened by a prayer led by the Bishop of Edinburgh that God should have compassion on James and restore him to the throne, the Stuart cause soon foundered when the assembly was presented with letters from the two rival claimants. William's was not only conciliatory above all but stressed his determination to ensure the security of the Protestant religion. James, on the other hand, was uncompromising and he even threatened those who might not be willing to submit to his rule. In effect, by this approach the last Stuart king committed political suicide. The Convention's decision to invite William and Mary to accept the crown of Scotland was therefore almost a foregone conclusion, especially since by this time the really committed supporters of the Stuarts were in a minority in the assembly. When it resolved that James had forfeited the crown, there were only four opposing votes. Nevertheless, the decision provoked the first Jacobite rebellion under Graham of Claverhouse, who raised the standard of King James on Dundee Law in April 1689. In the same month, William and Mary were proclaimed King and Queen.

This first attempt at Stuart counter-revolution seemed to demonstrate above all else the unpopularity of Jacobitism in the immediate aftermath of the Revolution. Claverhouse had left Edinburgh with 50 horsemen and he hoped to recruit widely before mounting an attack on government forces. In the event, he managed to attract fewer than 2,000 men. Most of these were drawn from a small number of West Highland clans, and hardly any mustered from the great aristocratic and landed houses of the Lowlands. Almost certainly there may have been more latent sympathy for the cause, but not many were yet prepared to risk life and property by rising in armed defence of Scotland's ancient royal dynasty. There was precious little sign during this first rebellion that it would develop a dynamic which would in time pose a potent threat to the new regime. In the chronicle of events of 1688–9, pride of place is often given to the exploits of Graham of Claverhouse, 'Bonnie Dundee', whose victory over government forces at the Pass of Killiecrankie in Perthshire was a notable feat of arms that conclusively proved the lethal effectiveness of the Highland charge and has been remembered ever since in popular song and story. Yet this was a false Jacobite dawn. Dundee himself was killed in the moment of victory; losses in his army were high, with nearly 40 per cent of his 2,500-strong army killed, injured or missing; and the attempt of his victorious army to break into the Lowlands was repulsed in vicious street-fighting in the town of Dunkeld. Finally, on May Day 1690, the Jacobite force was caught at the Haughs of Cromdale beside the River Spey and comprehensively routed by government cavalry. At that point the Stuart cause seemed to have little future in Scotland. The majority of Scotland's political élite had shown either hostility or indifference to it, and the spirited military challenge to the Revolution of 1688 was more or less dead by 1690. On 2 December 1691 James finally authorized his own supporters to submit to the new regime. Indeed, such was the lack of enthusiasm for the Stuarts that a more imaginative and intelligent government strategy over the next few years might well have eliminated Jacobite disaffection once and for all. However, it was state policy which soon gave a new and vigorous impetus to the cause.

A fundamental factor was the decision to impose a Presbyterian settlement on the Church of Scotland and abolish the estate of bishops. More than half the established clergy in Scotland refused to accept this resolution. These Episcopalians were also loath to take the oath of allegiance to William and Mary and their successors, because to have done so would have been in direct conflict with their adherence to the sacred hereditary principle of kingship and the absolute requirement of submission to royal authority. Those who refused to swear the oaths became known as the Nonjurors. In a typical response, for instance, Duncan MacRae, an Episcopalian minister from Wester Ross, utterly condemned the removal of James VII in 1689 as a heinous crime against the fifth commandment.

The Nonjuring factor in the development of Jacobitism became crucial. Ministers provided the moral and ideological backbone of the Stuart cause and helped to ensure its survival even in times of adversity. They refused to accept accommodation with the Presbyterian establishment in 1690, and even the toleration offered by the Hanoverian government in 1712. Areas of Episcopalian loyalty in Scotland became vital to popular support for the Jacobite rebellions of the eighteenth century. An estimated 15 of the 26 Highland clans active on the Jacobite side in the great rebellion of 1715 were Episcopalian in sympathy, and a further five were of mixed denomination. It was a similar pattern in the Lowlands. Overwhelmingly, Jacobite support in that region came from the north-eastern shires of Angus, Aberdeen, Banff, Forfar and Kincardine which, together with Perthshire, were all counties of Episcopalian tradition and loyalty. The tiny Catholic Church in Scotland, which had pockets of support in parts of the western Highlands, the north-east and the southern Hebrides, also developed a fierce loyalty to the Stuarts. During James VII's reign the Catholics had experienced a short period of formal toleration but this ended abruptly when the penal laws were reimposed in 1689. Catholics who were once again systematically excluded from public office could only look to the House of Stuart for succour. They were inspired not only by James's policies of toleration before 1688 but also by his uncompromising refusal afterwards to sacrifice his faith for reasons of political expediency in order to recover the crown he had lost. The Catholic commitment to Jacobitism was important but, because the church had few adherents (probably around 2 per cent of the Scottish population in c. 1750), it was much less decisive than the contribution of Episcopalianism. Indeed, the role of Catholicism in the Jacobite risings has probably been exaggerated as, in the 1715 rebellion, only six of the 26 clans actively involved were Catholic. Despite this, Catholic participation helped to shape the development of Jacobitism as an ideological crusade, founded on deep religious principles and not easily deflected by adversity, while at the same time it enabled the strengthening of contact with sympathetic Catholic powers in Europe such as France and Spain whose support was crucial to the movement's international credibility.

The Presbyterian settlement which had followed the political revolution of 1688–9 had significantly enhanced support for the Stuarts in the years after 1690 and it was soon followed by a number of other influences which added to the growing popularity of the Jacobite cause.

As already noted, the 1690s were a decade of economic crisis. War with France from 1688 to 1697 damaged Scottish overseas trade and could be blamed directly on the Williamite regime's more aggressive anti-French foreign policy. Poor harvests, in some areas resulting in actual famine, lasted for four years, with crisis peaks in 1696 and 1699. Of all the Lowland regions shortages, famine deaths and heavy emigration were especially acute in the north-eastern counties, all bastions of Episcopalian loyalty. The failure of the Darien scheme, which had attracted nobles, lairds and lawyers, as well as small merchants and craftsmen, was widely blamed on the new London government because of its failure to provide support for the ailing colony as it struggled to survive against the attacks of the Spaniards. The notorious Massacre of Glencoe of 1692 was a botched attempt to punish a small clan which had defied the government's policy of forcing the Jacobite clans to sue for peace terms after Dundee's rebellion. The MacDonalds of Glencoe failed to meet the deadline of New Year's Day 1692, when the clans had finally to submit to King William's authority. The Secretary of State, Sir John Dalrymple, Master of Stair, decided to make a brutal example of the Glencoe people: men, women and children were to be put to the sword. The plan failed and, although some perished, the majority of the clan survived despite being exposed to the harshness of a Highland winter. However, a huge propaganda gift had been handed to the Jacobites, who from that point on were able to exploit the bloody episode to the full as confirmation of the treachery, ruthlessness and vindictiveness of King William's regime.

By 1700 it seemed that the overthrow of the Stuarts had been followed by a decade of human and natural disasters. For a society that strongly believed in the influence of providence in human affairs it was easy to see these many miseries as a sign of God's awful and righteous anger which had been aroused when the Scottish people had committed the terrible sin of rejecting their lawful monarch in 1688. Jacobites could therefore describe the famine crisis as 'King William's Ill Years', while Catholic priests and Episcopalian ministers alike reminded their flocks of the dreadful consequences visited upon the Scots when King James was forced into exile and a foreign usurper crowned in his place. A few years after the humiliating end to the first rebellion the Jacobite star was therefore once again in the ascendant. A cause that apparently faced early extinction had been reborn and was now given further impetus by promise of European military support and the effect of the Treaty of Union of 1707 and its aftermath.

Jacobitism provided a means by which Britain's enemies could gain military advantage against her in an era of endemic warfare, economic rivalries and territorial ambition. The War of the Spanish Succession between 1695 and 1715 was one of the early stages in a titanic global struggle between France and England for mastery of Europe and the colonial territories in the Americas and the Indies. By assisting the Jacobites with army and navy support, the French monarchy could hope to deliver a crippling blow to its deadliest enemy. Louis XIV of France also personally believed that the removal of James VII was a great crime and act of blasphemy against the sacred rights of kingship. Not only did he provide the exiled Stuarts with a substantial pension of 600,000 *livres* and a palace at St Germain-en-Laye on the outskirts of Paris but, when James VII and II finally died in 1701, Louis immediately proclaimed his thirteen-year-old son, James, King of England, Scotland and Ireland. Even more significant from the Jacobite perspective, however, was that after several years of ambiguity in the French attitude there was now more public commitment of support from the greatest European military power of the day. This was to give much-enhanced political credibility to the followers of the exiled House of Stuart. The Jacobites with French treasure and French troops would now indeed be a force to be reckoned with. In March 1708 France organized an invasion force at Dunkirk to carry James Stuart and a body of soldiers to Scotland. Despite early misfortunes, including a delay when the luckless James caught measles, the fleet reached the Firth of Forth, where a group of Jacobite lairds awaited them. Since government forces were so thin on the ground in Scotland at the time, there was the real opportunity for a successful invasion. However, when a Royal Navy squadron appeared, the French commander decided to retreat. Despite this failure, the affair illustrated how, with the naval and military resources of France, Jacobitism might indeed become a serious threat to the British government.

The catalyst for the abortive invasion was the union of 1707, which had a transforming effect on the Stuart cause. As shown in Chapter One, the treaty had been carried against bitter opposition outside parliament and was eventually agreed only because of the threat of military sanctions, political management and the personal vested interest of some influential aristocrats. From the start, therefore, it was far from popular and, if anything, disaffection increased over time because economic expectations remained unfulfilled as much of Scottish commerce remained in the doldrums in the immediate aftermath of the union. The rising fiscal demands of the British state during wartime resulted in tax increases or entirely new impositions on necessities such as malt, salt and linen, many of which were in direct violation of the treaty itself. Discontent among members of the political élite was also fostered by the government's distribution of places, patronage and rewards among only a favoured few of its own supporters. Loyalty to the Stuarts had been originally founded on dynastic and religious principles, but now the Jacobites could pose as the champions of Scottish nationalism and the defenders of Scottish liberty. At the outset of both the major risings in 1715 and 1745 the exiled House of Stuart issued proclamations publicly committing the restored monarchy to repeal of the union and establishing once again an independent Scottish parliament. 'No union' became a common motto on Jacobite banners. Lockhart of Carnwath, an ardent champion of the Stuart cause, was committed to the view that repeal of the Act of Union should be at the very heart of Jacobite strategy because of the popular appeal the message would have.

Not surprisingly, therefore, the rising of 1715 led by John, Earl of Mar, reflected a much greater range and depth of support for the Jacobite cause than that of Dundee in 1688. Mar was able to muster around 10,000 foot and horse, the strongest-ever Jacobite host to take the field, against 4,000 in the government army commanded by the Duke of Argyll. Even more significantly, considerable support now came from some of the greater landed families of Lowland and especially north-east Scotland, who had been notable by their absence in 1689. The list of sympathizers included the Earls of Southesk, Panmure and Strathmore. At the same time, a Jacobite uprising in north-east England suggested the possibility of an effective military coalition between disaffected areas in each of the two kingdoms. From a Jacobite perspective, the prospect for the rising of 1715 was bright indeed. But when Mar, who as a general possessed a fatal combination of caution, timidity and ambiguity, failed to defeat the numerically inferior forces of the Crown in the inconclusive battle of Sherrifmuir in November 1715, the Jacobites completely lost the initiative. The failure of the rebellion was a crushing blow to their morale. Opportunities for real progress were there, but they had literally been thrown away by inept leadership.

Mar's indecisiveness cost the Stuarts dear and soon squandered the Jacobite military superiority. His delay in marching south from the movement's strongholds in the southern Highlands was crucial: 'Mar waited and waited: he waited for French help, he waited for the Duke of Berwick, he waited for the King, he waited for yet more recruits to make his position impregnable.'[1]

So confident had the Jacobites been of success that James himself had landed at Peterhead in December 1715, though he brought no help from France to augment his Scottish army. His triumphal entry into Dundee and then Perth was intended to be the prelude to a coronation at Scone. Instead, he soon had to beat a hasty retreat from Scotland via the port of Montrose. The fiasco of the '15 rising was then followed by the catastrophic failure of a Spanish invasion in 1719, designed to trigger a Jacobite revolt in both England and Scotland. The history of the main expedition was characteristically full of disasters. Severe storms in Spanish waters resulted in the scattering of the fleet and the cancellation of the main assault on the west of England. A smaller diversionary force pressed on to the Highlands, where it landed in Kintail off the Isle of Skye, only to be routed by government troops at the battle of Glen Shiel. It was indeed ominous that the Jacobites had been defeated in the very areas where they could claim most support.

Other calamities spread demoralization in their ranks. France was forced to abandon the cause of the Stuarts in the Treaty of Utrecht in 1713 which ended the Spanish Succession war, and the exiled court had to leave French soil. Even before this, however, French support was on the wane. From 1715 French policy was guided by the Regent Duc d'Orléans who, unlike Louis XIV, was unsympathetic since he was attempting to gain British recognition for his claim to be heir-apparent and was unwilling to compromise this by being seen to aid England's Jacobite enemies overtly. Not only did he fail to provide support for the rising of 1715, he also went so far as to dispatch some French troops to assist the British government in dealing with the attempted Spanish invasion of 1719. His successor, Cardinal Fleury, who was the major influence on French foreign policy from 1726 to 1743, maintained opposition to the Jacobite cause during the long peace with Britain which followed the end of the Spanish Succession war. With the settlement of the crowns of the United Kingdom on the House of Hanover and their descendants it was now easier and less costly for the French to threaten British interest in the new monarchy's German territories than by fitting

THE JACOBITE CHALLENGE

out an expensive and risky sea expedition in support of the Stuarts in
Scotland. Moreover, when the Jacobite court moved to Rome, British
agents seem to have become more effective in penetrating it through a
network of spies and informers who provided detailed reports on Stuart
planning. It looked as if the Jacobite menace had finally been crushed.
This was especially the case in England, where Jacobitism seemed to
enter irreversible decline after 1715. Paul Monod reckons that a quarter
of the English country gentry may have harboured Jacobite sympathies,
with the strongest commitment in northern counties such as Lancashire.
However, support and leadership for the cause were undermined by
the removal of Jacobite-inclined clergy in the Church of England and
by the passage of time since 1688, so that by the 1730s the 'Glorious
Revolution' had been given the veneer of permanence and solidity. In
Scotland, too, Jacobitism was in the doldrums. There were two major
crises of government in the 1720s and 1730s – the Malt Tax Riots of
1725 and the Porteous Riot in Edinburgh in 1736, which were both
significant challenges to the Hanoverian regime – but the Jacobites
signally failed to take advantage of either of them.

Yet while Scottish Jacobitism may have seemed moribund, it was
far from dead. Many supporters had strong ideological and religious
reasons for committing themselves to the exiled House of Stuart and
were not easily demoralized by immediate difficulties. This was especially the case among Catholic and Episcopalian laird families and the
dispossessed Nonjuring clergy. Moreover, there was a substantial
Jacobite diaspora in western Europe, which included intellectuals, merchants, financiers, bankers and clerics who often provided a network
of personal contacts and financial support for Jacobite families at
home. The cosmopolitanism of Jacobitism helped to sustain it when in
domestic terms it seemed to languish in terminal and impotent decline.
Moreover, after the '15 in Scotland there was little of the draconian
retribution from the state which eventually followed the '45. Although
19 Scottish and two English peers were attainted, only two were
executed, and in Scotland no wholesale dispossession of rebel estates
was enforced. Jacobitism was regarded as a real political alternative
north of the border: it fed off opposition to the union and other
grievances and there were simply too many well-placed Jacobites in
Scotland for drastic action to be applied. State terrorism might simply
have inspired more disaffection. As Duncan Forbes of Culloden noted,
there were 'not 200 Gentlemen in the whole Kingdom who are not very

nearly related to some one or other of the Rebels'.[2] The relative leniency of the government therefore did little to discourage sympathy for the Stuarts. Nevertheless, the disaffected intelligentsia did suffer. Those who had collaborated with the Jacobites in 1715 were systematically purged. In the north-eastern counties and in Perthshire numerous town councillors, clergy, teachers, solicitors, doctors and academics including the Principal of King's College, Aberdeen (a hotbed, with Marischal College in the same city, of Jacobite sympathy), were removed from office. They survived as a powerful source of bitter alienation from the Hanoverian regime.

Jacobitism also lived on as a potential revolutionary force because it still attracted continued loyalty from key Highland clans which gave the Stuarts the military muscle without which Jacobitism would have lost credibility in the years after the fiasco of the 1715 rising. The relationship between clanship and Jacobitism is complex. By no means all clans were Jacobite. The most powerful of all, Clan Campbell, was overwhelmingly anti-Stuart; several others, especially in areas where Presbyterianism was strong, were active supporters of the House of Hanover. These included Clans MacKay, Ross, Gunn and Munro. Again, even if there was latent sympathy for the Stuarts, actual military support for the Jacobites varied very significantly over time and space and within the clans. The evidence suggests, for instance, that even among the most loyal there was a weakening of support as the years went by. In 1689 an estimated 28 clans rose for the Stuarts, but by the time of the last rebellion, the '45, this had fallen to 18. Some families were split on issues of political and religious principle and few clans were committed wholly to Hanover or to the Stuarts in their entirety, if only because it was prudent to keep a foot in both camps in order to ensure the security of family lands. Thus, to take one example among many, the first Duke of Atholl was a staunch supporter of the Revolution of 1688, but three of his sons fought for the Jacobites under Mar in 1715. In addition, Jacobite loyalties were not confined to the Highlands. As earlier discussion has shown, the Stuarts attracted a good deal of support in most areas of Scotland north of the River Tay, particularly but not exclusively in the north-east, including the major towns of that region. Yet the centrality of the Highland factor still needs to be recognized. It is no coincidence that all the major risings began and ended in the Highlands and that Charles Edward Stuart launched the last and most remarkable rebellion of all from there. In 1689–91 the

Jacobite army was overwhelmingly drawn from the clans, and subsequently in 1715 and later in 1745–6 Jacobite Lowlanders were mobilized in much larger numbers. However, the clansmen remained crucial to the overall effort throughout. They were the front-line shock and assault troops who not only bore the brunt of the fighting but also suffered the heaviest casualties in battle. Thus, in all three major risings the clans formed the backbone of the Jacobite armies. Lightly armed, able to endure considerable hardship, more mobile than regular forces and responding to the social discipline of the clan structure, they were a formidable force and a major asset to the Stuart cause.

After the '15 there had been some erosion of clan allegiance to Jacobitism, but for the most part the old loyalties remained undisturbed. The fact that the state did not punish the disaffected areas after the 1715 rising sent out the wrong signals, and a power vacuum was created which helped to increase the chances of another rebellion. Even those estates that were forfeited by legal attainder were restored to the ownership of Highland chiefs after six years in return for sureties on their future conduct. The abortive Spanish expedition of 1719 led to the Disarming Act of 1725 which, if anything, had more impact on the government clans than on their Jacobite counterparts. Between 1725 and his departure from Scotland in 1740, General George Wade built 250 miles of roads and bridges to facilitate the movement of government troops throughout the Highland region. The routes were also designed to link the fortresses of Fort William, Fort Augustus, Bernera and Ruthven, which were to be the government's eyes and ears in Jacobite districts. By devoting so many resources to the Highlands, the state acknowledged the region's pivotal strategic importance for the Jacobite cause. But the grand strategy of containment was completely undermined from the later 1730s when government stripped the forts of adequate garrisons to supply troops for another European war, later known as the War of Jenkin's Ear. Wade's military roads were used eventually – but not for the purposes intended by the builders. The Young Pretender's Highland army force-marched across them in 1745 in order to speed their lightning descent into the Lowlands.

The '45 itself came after a quarter of a century, when Jacobitism was at a low ebb, and was triggered again by developments in international politics. In 1743, after the death of Cardinal Fleury, French foreign policy underwent a radical transformation. Once more, help for the Stuarts ranked high on the agenda because such a policy served French interest during the War of the Austrian Succession which had broken out in 1740. By 1743, a major Anglo-French conflict had developed which culminated in defeat for France at Dettingen in June of that year. Louis XV and his ministers once again decided to play the Stuart card and support a Jacobite invasion of England, which would force a withdrawal of British troops from Europe and perhaps ultimately bring about the destruction of the House of Hanover itself. As serious preparations began, the oldest son of the Stuart Pretender, 24-year-old Prince Charles Edward Stuart, journeyed to Paris from Rome in early 1744 to take up his position as nominal commander of the invasion force. The plan was ambitious: to land 10,000 troops on the south coast of England and bring the Hanoverian forces there to a decisive battle. Perhaps predictably, however, the strategy was leaked by a French spy in British pay and the Royal Navy was able to take pre-emptive action before the fleet was finally assembled.

The proposed invasion was postponed indefinitely, much to the chagrin of Charles, who had hoped to deliver the ultimate gift of the restoration of the Stuarts to his father. Out of the frustration born of the abortive invasion of 1744 came his fateful decision to force the hand of the French by leading a successful rebellion on British soil which would then force his allies into the provision of serious military support to complete the counter-revolution. This was the action of a bold and perhaps reckless gambler. The obvious place for a landing was in that Jacobite stronghold of the western Highlands of Scotland, far from the eyes and ears of the enemies of the Stuarts. Charles was not in the least deterred by the sober advice of the Scottish Jacobites that at least 6,000 French troops, arms for 10,000 more and a war chest of 30,000 *louis d'or* were the very minimum preconditions for a successful rising. Nor, apparently, was he concerned about his own military inexperience. When he landed in the Outer Hebrides in the summer of 1745, he came with a few companions, the 'Seven Men of Moidart', some arms and 4,000 gold coins. It was an extraordinary start to the most famous Jacobite rising of all.

Astonishingly, however, Charles's daring initiative was at first spectacularly successful. Relying mainly on the Jacobite loyalties of a few key clan chiefs, he managed to assemble an army of little more than 2,500 men, which moved rapidly into the Lowlands, took Edinburgh a month after he had landed, and then comprehensively routed the government forces under Sir John Cope at Prestonpans, south of the capital. Incredibly, only weeks after his arrival from France, Charles was master of Scotland. This triumph did not simply reflect the martial élan of the clans and the superb military skills of Lord George Murray, the most influential Jacobite commander of the '45. To a significant extent, Charles's success was also made possible because of the absence of an effective government response. The Scottish state was in a condition of virtual paralysis that summer. When the Stuart standard was raised at Glenfinnan on Loch Sheil in August 1745, Cope, the government commander, had a mere 3,000 troops at his disposal for defence of the entire country because of the heavy demands of the European war for veteran regiments of the line. The abolition of the Scottish Privy Council in 1708 immediately after the union had long since removed the main agency for expert intelligence-gathering and the Clan Campbell, the government's formidable strategic buffer in the western Highlands, had been weakened as a fighting force by the second Duke of Argyll's estate reforms after 1737 which had begun to undermine the traditional role and influence of the clan gentry. The unopposed march of the Jacobite army from Glenfinnan to Edinburgh graphically exposed the military weakness of the Scottish state and the ease with which it could be overthrown.

Because of this, many in Charles's Council of War argued that they should now halt, consolidate and strengthen their supremacy in Scotland as, with a firm base in the northern kingdom, the French might be more willing to send essential military support for the conquest of England. However, Charles's strong advocacy of invasion of England was finally carried by one vote. But in early November 1745, when the Jacobite forces of around 5,500 foot and horse crossed the border, the odds were increasingly stacked against them. The government had recovered from the shock of the defeat at Prestonpans and battle-hardened regiments were being swiftly withdrawn from the European theatre of war. The hoped-for French invasion did not materialize, although three French ships had brought some troops and munitions into the north-east ports of Stonehaven and Montrose in the autumn of 1745. But this was little more than a token gesture. Another major disappointment was the failure to attract significant support from Jacobite and Tory sympathizers in the north of England. Indeed the Manchester Regiment, consisting largely of Catholics, was the only English Jacobite unit raised during the invasion. It was a vicious circle: any remaining sympathizers in the north of England were reluctant to show their hand until the French landed, and that never happened.

Charles therefore received support from only two of his Council of War when he urged that the army should press on from Derby to London. Those who advised caution were doubtless confirmed in their view by information, whether true or false, from informers that three large Hanoverian armies were converging on the Jacobite forces. The return to Scotland in winter, through hostile territory and under relentless pursuit by vastly superior forces, was a remarkable exploit and a tribute to the tactical skills of Lord George Murray as well as the fighting qualities of the Jacobite army. However, after a further victory against government forces at Falkirk, in January 1746, the retreat continued inexorably into the Highlands, thus ensuring that the Jacobites were no longer able to finance the campaign through levies and taxation on the richer Lowland counties and towns. This collapse of Jacobite economic fortunes was but the prelude to eventual military defeat. While Scottish sources of revenue contracted or disappeared altogether, the failure of the French treasure ships to penetrate the coastal squadrons of the Royal Navy and provide much-needed succour had an equally disastrous effect. Charles decided to turn and fight at Culloden, outside Inverness, rather than engage in the guerrilla campaign favoured by some of his commanders because his cause was almost bankrupt. Inverness was the last town capable of being a Jacobite base and had to be defended at all costs.

The result was catastrophic. The battle of Culloden on 16 April 1746 was a total victory for the Hanoverian forces under the Duke of Cumberland and was effectively the end of the Jacobite rising and the prelude to a massive military, judicial and political assault on the clan society which had spawned Stuart subversion. Virtually every factor was against Charles's army on the fateful day. As commander-in-chief he had chosen a field of battle which gave a huge tactical advantage to his opponent. Culloden Moor is open, flat and exposed, almost designed by nature for the effective deployment of artillery firing case (or grapeshot) and the disciplined fire of well-trained infantry regiments. The Jacobites had also engaged in an abortive night attack on Cumberland's camp at Nairn, and this left many of the clansmen exhausted on the morning of battle. Because of this, as many as one-fifth of Charles's potential force may not even have taken part in the final engagement.

The Jacobites were also significantly outnumbered, by about two to one, by Cumberland's army of around 9,000 foot and horse. Charles compounded the Hanoverian advantage by exposing his crack front-line clansmen to a well-directed artillery cannonade for an hour before eventually giving the order to charge. Despite the subsequent rout, however, the Jacobite army did not disintegrate. Many of those who survived the battle, and others who arrived too late to take part, assembled again at Ruthven in Badenoch. It was only a message from Charles urging them to seek their own safety that finally led to their dispersal. After several months spent in hiding as a hunted fugitive in the Highlands, he himself escaped to France in early September 1746. For him the adventure was well and truly over, but the traumatic impact of the débâcle of the '45 was still felt by his loyal supporters throughout the Highlands long after he sailed away from Scotland for ever.

The Jacobite territories were now at the mercy of Cumberland's forces. A huge regular army, supported by units of the Royal Navy, had been drawn into the very heart of the Highlands. Effectively the Jacobite areas were under military occupation and the missed opportunity after the 1715 rebellion and the policy of leniency of that period were not to be repeated. The clans had to be broken once and for all because only their fighting skills and loyalty to the Stuarts had brought Charles close to ultimate success. An estimated 2,000 clansmen had been slaughtered during the carnage of the battle of Culloden itself and in the immediate aftermath. But even this military catastrophe had not apparently shattered the Jacobite spirit. The fact that so many of the defeated army had mustered again at Ruthven suggested to Cumberland that only extreme and radical action would finally root out their intolerable spirit of disaffection and recalcitrance.

At first Cumberland was attracted to a strategy of wholesale transportation of the clans to the colonies, but then he opted instead for a scorched-earth policy of burning, clearance and pillage. In May 1746 the Duke moved to Fort Augustus in the Great Glen, and a reign of terror was initiated in some of the most committed Jacobite areas of the surrounding region. Cumberland's explicit intention was to teach the people a lesson they would never forget. Numerous settlements throughout Glenelg, Kintail, Lochaber and Morvern were burnt, plundered and laid waste by four independent raiding parties, supported offshore by the Royal Navy. Even clans loyal to the Crown were not immune from the relentless depredations which lasted for nearly a year after Culloden. Cattle, the main source of wealth in this pastoral society and the means of buying in grain from more favoured areas, were confiscated on a massive scale. Fort Augustus, supplied from the booty plundered from the population of the surrounding districts, became for a time the largest cattle mart in Scotland. It was reckoned that in one year alone nearly 20,000 head of cattle were put up for sale, as well as numerous sheep, oxen, horses and goats. Long after the pillage had come to an end the state remained committed to a strategy of rigorous military control. The road system begun by Wade and others was extended, until by 1767 a network of over 1,000 miles had been built. Even more significant was the construction between 1748 and 1769 of Fort George at Ardersier, east of Inverness, the most formidable bastion artillery fortress in Europe and a permanent physical demonstration of the Hanoverian government's absolute determination that the clans would never again rise to threaten the Protestant succession.

When the military onslaught ended, the legislative attack on clanship began. Highland dress was proscribed as the sartorial symbol of rebel militarism. A Disarming Act stiffened previous legislation to prohibit the carrying of weapons of war. The abolition of heritable jurisdiction (the private courts of landowners) and military land tenures was supposed to destroy the power of the chiefs. In reality, clan loyalties were primarily influenced by the mind and the heart rather than by the law, and military tenures such as wardship were already becoming obsolete anyway because of commercial change in the Highlands. The Act to suppress Nonjuring Episcopalian meeting houses (one of the government army's main targets during the months after Culloden in the north-east counties as well as in the Highlands) was more significant since it was a recognition that Episcopal ministers were one of the key ideological supports of Jacobitism. Estates of rebel landowners were forfeited to the Crown and the majority were sold off to pay creditors, but 13 were inalienably annexed and managed from 1752 to 1784 by a Commission to promote 'the Protestant Religion, good Government, Industry and Manufactures and the Principles of Duty and Loyalty to his Majesty'. The thinking was that Protestantism should induce ideological conformity while prosperity would remove the poverty on which rebellion was supposed to feed.

Despite the ferocity of the onslaught, it would still be an exaggeration to say that it destroyed Jacobitism in the Highlands. In several areas the brutality of the Hanoverian forces produced a stubborn defiance in a people long inured to hard times. Indeed, Cumberland's successor as military commander, the Earl of Albemarle, became so frustrated that he once again contemplated a strategy of devastating whole areas and deporting the inhabitants. Moreover, far from inculcating law and order, the military occupation seems to have stimulated outbreaks of banditry not simply in traditionally truculent areas such as Rannoch and Lochaber but also in several other parts of the central and southern Highlands. Albermarle's reports show that, despite the best endeavours of the forces of the Crown, the people of the disaffected areas of Appin, Moidart, Arisaig and Knoydart still hoped for succour from the French as late as the winter of 1747. The reality was that Jacobitism did not simply or suddenly die on the field of Culloden or in the immediate aftermath of the battle. The forces making for its decline and final extinction went much deeper than that.

In 1715 there had been a real chance of Stuart counter-revolution, but this was much less likely by 1745. Jacobitism was unpopular throughout most of the Lowlands south of the River Tay; the central Lowlands in particular were mostly hostile and Glasgow and the western towns resolutely opposed. In 1715 opposition to the union of 1707 had been a major factor strengthening Jacobite support. By the 1740s, however, there was much greater acceptance of the relationship with England. Many Scottish merchants and landowners were now obtaining significant material rewards through the Clyde's expanding transatlantic trades and the impact of English and colonial markets on demand for linen, cattle, coal and grain, though it has to be acknowledged that some east coast ports, traditionally linked to Europe, were less fortunate. In addition, a fundamental obstacle for the Stuarts was their Catholicism. They were not prepared to sacrifice their faith for political ambition and so inevitably paid the price. Thus, by far the most effective propaganda agents for government were the Presbyterian clergy of the west, central and south-east Lowlands, effectively the economic heart of Scotland. They stoked up fears that the return of the House of Stuart would bring in its train an autocratic papist regime that would threaten both the 'liberty' and 'true religion' of Presbyterian Scots. Whig propaganda relentlessly identified Charles as a foreigner who had come from Italy (the home of popery) and every attempt was made to exploit the anti-Catholic passions of the people in order to encourage opposition to him. As one Whig diatribe had it:

47

From Rome a limb of Antichrist
Joined with a Hellish Band of Highland Thieves,
Came here in haste
God's Laws for to withstand.[3]

Culloden was therefore for many Scots a happy deliverance from the threatened dominion of the Antichrist. The *Glasgow Journal* brought out a special large-print edition to celebrate the defeat of 'Chevalier de St George's eldest son' and also to record 'the greatest rejoicings that have been known' in the city.[4] The heartlands of Presbyterian Scotland greeted the news from Culloden with relief and celebration, while throughout the entire rebellion only a tiny minority of the Scottish landed classes came out for the Stuarts. Even in traditionally Jacobite areas, the élites of some clans, such as the Macintoshes and Chisholms, were terminally split in their loyalties by the 1740s. Important Hebridean chiefs like Sir Alexander MacDonald of Sleat, Kenneth MacKenzie, Earl of Seaforth, and the MacLeod of MacLeod in Skye took no part at all. Scottish backing for the Stuarts during the rising was remarkably thin on the ground long before the crushing defeat of Culloden; it was this, together with the virtual disappearance of support in England, rather than force of arms in itself which ultimately ended their last hopes of restoration.

3

The Union and the Economy

I

In the years immediately before the union the Scottish economy was in crisis. The 'ill years' between 1695 and 1699 resulted in many famine-related deaths and a marked increase in emigration to Ulster, leading to an overall estimated fall in Scottish population of around 15 per cent. Merchants desperately tried to ship in from abroad emergency grain supplies which had to be paid for in cash, and this export of scarce specie disrupted credit while the spiralling cost of food cut back demand for manufactured goods. The impact of famine was aggravated by the French wars of 1689 and 1697 and the trend towards economic nationalism in western Europe which curtailed markets for Scottish exports. After 1689, absolute prohibitions were imposed on the valuable trade in fish and woollen cloth to France, and punitive duties were also levied on coal and some other goods. The failure of the Company of Darien with the loss of £153,000 sterling ended a decade of misery. It was reckoned that this disaster cost the country between one-quarter and one-sixth of its liquid capital, though no precise measurement of the financial impact can ever be known.

The serious effect of these catastrophes cannot be denied. However, it is less certain whether they reflected deep-seated structural weaknesses in the economy or were simply transient difficulties. The famines of the 1690s were certainly an aberration caused by a very severe but short-lived period of climatic deterioration which affected several countries in western Europe as well as Scotland. Indeed, one of the reasons why the crisis in food supply caused such widespread alarm among contemporaries was that in previous years they had become accustomed to better times. Since the 1650s there had been only one other period of significant harvest failure, in 1674–5. This more positive record can be compared with the horrors of the later sixteenth century, when food shortages affected at least some areas of Scotland in around a third of the years between 1560 and 1600. The most convincing sign that better times had become the norm was that the food supply policy of parliament and Privy Council radically altered in the later decades of the seventeenth century. Instead of protecting the consumers of grain by prohibiting exports, government now tried to encourage the sale of Scottish meal to foreign markets through the provision of subsidies. Indeed, an important Corn Bounty Act was passed in 1695, the first year that harvests began to fail in the 1690s. The long-term problem was quite clearly seen to be one of a recurrent surplus of grain which was adversely affecting the incomes of landowners and tenant farmers by driving down prices.

The reasons why in most years in the later seventeenth century before the 1690s the Scots were able to feed themselves and also to export more cargoes of meal and barley to Europe still remain obscure. What is clear, however, is that agriculture before the union was far from stagnant. Movement to enlarged single tenancies, longer written leases, expansion of rural market centres, and increases in yields through the use of lime and, in some areas, improved rotations have all been documented in recent research. In the eighteenth century all these innovations were adopted more systematically and effectively, but the origins of virtually all of them can be traced to the period before the union. It was an important line of economic continuity which helps to place the constitutional change of 1707 in perspective.

Continuity is confirmed in the approach of the Scottish landed classes. The single most important change affecting this élite had already taken place in the Lowlands before the union and it was developing also in several areas of the Highlands. Landowners had come to regard their estates more as assets from which revenue and profit could be extracted and less as sources of military power and authority. The indicators of this historic transition in the priorities of the Scottish governing classes were very numerous. It can be seen for instance in their domestic architecture. The last fortified house in Scotland, Leslie Castle, was built in 1660. The emphasis was now more on comfort and aesthetic appeal rather than on defence. The tower house was giving way to the country house. There also was a much greater involvement in the wider economy with the aim of extracting better returns from the landed estate. North-eastern landowners were heavily engaged in the seaborne grain trade to Edinburgh and the Scandinavian countries. Highland lairds were very active in the commercial exploitation of the native woodlands and in the droving trade to the south in black cattle. The great border landlords were energetically expanding the numbers of sheep and cattle on their properties. Between 1500 and the early eighteenth century, around 170 new burghs of barony were founded by landowners, with the majority established in the decades immediately before the union. Not all – or even the majority – were a success, but the commitment of the élite to small town and village development is undeniable. There were also instances of large-scale investment in harbour and port development, such as that of the Duke of Hamilton at Bo'ness, Sir Robert Cunninghame at Saltcoats and the Erskines of Mar at Alloa. Not surprisingly, the new economic priorities of the élite filtered through into the public policies of parliament and the Privy Council which they dominated. The records of these two bodies are full of references to attempts made to improve the national economy. These included Acts for the encouragement of colonial trade; domestic manufacturing; the foundation of the Bank of Scotland in 1695; the removal of the traditional monopoly rights of the royal burghs in 1672; and a series of statutes to facilitate agricultural improvement. Many of these initiatives were fine aspirations rather than real achievements. In a sense, however, this mattered little. What was more important was the confirmation that the Scottish governing classes were now on the side of material progress and lending their considerable political authority to the cause of economic reform. The fashion for 'improvement' was not unique to the eighteenth century; it had many of its roots in the seventeenth century.

In other ways, too, the pre-union period can be seen as an era of transition whose importance has been overshadowed by the crises of the 1690s. The ancient structure of external trade which had bound Scotland for centuries to European markets was in decay as life became more difficult for merchants trading to France and other countries because of the destructive effects of international war and aggressive protectionism. But elsewhere fresh opportunities were opening up which were being energetically exploited. By 1700 the trades in cattle, sheep, linen, coal and salt to England had become the single largest and most dynamic sector of Scottish commerce and were already reckoned to account for over 40 per cent of the nation's external commerce by value. Moreover, as the eastern links to some continental countries started to crumble, so now connections to the west were forged as the axis of Scottish trade started to shift towards the Atlantic world. Pre-eminent in this respect was the impact of Scottish emigration to Ulster. In the period 1650-1700, an estimated 60,000-100,000 Scots, mainly from Galloway, Ayrshire, Fife and Argyll, settled in Ireland. Effectively, Ulster had become a Scottish colony, and the colonists naturally looked to the home country for all sorts of necessities such as tools, shoes, saddles, coal and a host of other requirements.

Less significant at the time but more crucial for the future was North America. Scottish settlement in New Jersey began in 1683, and before the union the colony already had a Scottish governor. By 1700, East Jersey and Carolina together attracted well over 100 Scottish investors and nearly 1,000 settlers. Further south in Pennsylvania, the Scots were described as 'engrossing' the trade in tobacco, and the export of tobacco leaf and other colonial commodities, both directly to Scottish ports and also to English markets such as Whitehaven and London, was well established. This puts the Darien disaster in a different perspective because this spectacular failure has to be seen not as an isolated and over-ambitious adventure but as an integral part of a general drive to the west. These momentous changes were symbolized and influenced by the rise of Glasgow, Scotland's urban window to the Atlantic economy. The burghal tax assessments of the 1670s show that by that decade Glasgow had easily overtaken Aberdeen and Dundee to become the second most important town in the land and the nation's major centre of commerce and industry. The new direction of Scottish international migration was another telling illustration of changing times. In the early seventeenth century the Scots continued to go in large numbers to Scandinavia, Poland and Holland to seek their fortunes as mercenary soldiers, pedlars, small traders and merchants. Anywhere between 55,000 and 70,000 are reckoned to have emigrated in the half-century between 1600 and 1650. Scottish mercantile communities had also existed in such centres as Danzig, Copenhagen, Bruges, Quimper, Rotterdam, Dieppe, Rouen, La Rochelle and Bordeaux for many generations. But several of these traditional connections started to break down in the later seventeenth century. The formerly great migrations to Poland and Scandinavia fell away completely as the favoured destinations outside mainland Britain now became the New World and Ireland.

The period before the union was not therefore an era of economic darkness before the dawn. The crises of the 1690s have given a misleading impression of the Scottish economy in these years. What we rather see in embryonic form is the creation of the commercial structure centred on English and colonial trade which was to be at the very heart of post-union economic relationships. The landed classes had also already given abundant evidence of their interest in exploiting their estates on commercial principles as well as in promoting national development to further their own personal economic interest. The changes in patterns of overseas trade suggest a merchant class able to adapt, take risks and take advantage of new opportunities. In this, as in so many other respects, there were important continuities before and after 1707.

2

On the other hand, it is wise not to be too optimistic. There were many underlying constraints on development since, in the rural economy (which was overwhelmingly dominant at the time), subsistence farming was still the norm in most areas away from the Lothians. This was shown by the prevalence of payment of rentals in kind, which were only gradually being commuted in some parts of the Lowlands by c. 1700, and the large numbers of small tenancies, rarely producing much more than for family consumption and landlord rents, which fill the pages of estate records in this period. Above all, perhaps, the Scots looked vulnerable in international commerce. The old European trades were being relentlessly squeezed by the aggressive protectionist policies of the continental states and the Scots had neither the military nor the economic muscle to do much in response. The inexorable contraction of markets in Europe was to a large extent compensated for by new connections forged with England. But even the secure development of that commerce was uncertain because, like every other great European power, England was pursuing its own vital interests by raising punitive tariffs against the trade of competitor nations. In general, English customs duties were on the increase in the 1690s because more and more revenue was necessary to help cover the huge and escalating costs of the War of the Spanish Succession in which England had not only the financial burden of her own armed forces to meet but also the additional responsibility of providing subsidies to other states in order to cement the alliance against France. Ominously, tariffs were imposed on Scottish coal and salt, and in 1698 linen producers trading to England were faced with a substantial increase in duties. The threat in the Alien Act of 1705 in the prelude to union to prohibit entirely the entry of these key exports into England was an effective policy of economic blackmail simply because of the new Scottish dependency on this commerce to southern markets. It is not too difficult, therefore, to imagine a scenario in which, if the union negotiations had failed, the Scots would have been faced with the prospect of an English tariff wall at least as formidable as those which already confronted them in several parts of Europe.

3

Several clauses of the Act of Union were devoted to economic matters, but Articles IV and V were the two of most importance. Article IV provided for Scottish entry without payment of custom duty to the English domestic and colonial markets, while Article V stated that all Scottish-owned vessels would now rank as ships of Great Britain, so affording the Scots the privileges and protection of inclusion within the Navigation Acts. The union created the biggest free-trade zone in Europe at the time and gave Scottish merchants the liberty to trade legally in such profitable American commodities as tobacco, sugar, indigo and rum (a privilege not granted the Irish) and, at the same time, it afforded them the protection of the Royal Navy. It all seemed a very good bargain. On the other hand, there was considerable risk as well as much opportunity for Scotland in the new relationship. The bad times of the 1690s had seriously weakened the national economy. The 'Lean Years' had hit agriculture so hard that in some areas of the Lowlands farmers were still paying off rent arrears more than two decades later. In economic terms Scotland was not in good shape and was very exposed to more advanced and competitive English industry within the new common market. It was essentially because they recognized this danger that the last Scottish parliament bargained hard to ensure in the Treaty of Union that Scottish-made paper, malt and salt would continue to have a degree of protection after the union by being relieved of the need to pay the higher English duties for varying periods of time. The problem was that Scotland and England were at different stages of economic development. Scotland's manufacturing base was

both slender and vulnerable, while English industry, especially in textiles, was already the most advanced in Europe. The new political
integration might well have doomed Scotland to the status of an English
economic satellite: a supplier of foods, raw materials and cheap labour
for the more sophisticated southern economy but with little possibility
of achieving manufacturing growth and diversification in her own right.
This was roughly what happened to Ireland in the eighteenth and early
nineteenth centuries. Union could well have been the political prelude
to 'the development of underdevelopment' rather than the catalyst for
a new age of progress and prosperity. Why this was not the outcome
is one of the key questions of eighteenth-century Scottish history.

The first few years after 1707 showed that some of these concerns
were well founded. English competition soon crushed the finer end of
the woollen trade, which was already in difficulties before the union.
The levying of duties on linen in 1711 and 1715 imposed an additional
handicap on Scotland's most important manufacture. Other industries,
such as brewing and paper-making, were also badly hit, though it is
very difficult to know how far this was due to the harsh winds of free
trade after the union or to a more fundamental economic malaise
that was dragging on from earlier crisis years. Certainly there was a
widespread political consensus that the union itself was to blame and
some of the angry resentment that was generated spilled over into
support for the Jacobite rising of 1715. The Scots were also taxed more
highly, with some of the new impositions being in breach of the Treaty
of Union itself. In addition to linen, tax on salt rose in 1711 and, most
notoriously of all, on malt in 1725. These were basic articles of life,
and it is not surprising that the tax increases on them produced a furious
political response, including serious urban rioting in Glasgow in 1725.
Yet in the long run taxation hardly drained Scotland dry. Modern
estimates suggest only about 15–20 per cent of tax revenue actually left
the country in the five decades after 1707. Taxes went up, but apparently
most of the additional revenue was still spent on civil and military
expenditure in Scotland itself.

It is also difficult to gauge the real effect of what could have been
one particularly damaging post-union development. Increasingly, the
Scottish aristocracy and a few of the greater lairds sought political
opportunity, social position and family influence in London by setting
up residence in the capital during the winter months. This absenteeism
was not entirely new; it had already started before the union and became

greater after it. From one perspective the temporary migration of the Scots nobility could be regarded as a flight of capital, as aristocratic rentals were increasingly exported to the south to sustain opulent lifestyles in polite English society. Indeed, absenteeism almost certainly forced rents up because, as the Duke of Montrose complained in 1708, 'London journeys don't verie well agree with Scots estiates.'[1] On the other hand, there was also a positive side: the need for more revenue generated in the longer term a search for improved agricultural practices, since a prime determinant of agrarian improvement was the pressure on the Scottish landed class to extract more revenue from their estates in order to support a higher standard of life.

After these early difficult years some Scots merchants were beginning to exploit the new free-trade opportunities. Grain and meal exports more than doubled between the periods 1707–12 and 1717–22 and, as commercialization intensified, protests against meal exports became more violent in some parts of the Lowlands. In large part this may have been due to the extension of export bounties on grain after the union. The Levellers Revolt in Galloway in 1724 started when small tenants in the south-west protested bitterly against the large-scale cattle enclosures which were being built to secure more benefit from English demands for stock. These popular disturbances were one important sign that the post-union market was beginning to have an impact in some regions. Indeed, by the 1720s and 1730s the effect may have been more general. Recent research on the Lowland rural economy in these decades suggests that many of the estates studied were gearing their output of grain and cattle much more to the market. This is indicated by a widespread movement towards larger single tenancies and a general conversion of payment of rentals in kind to money values.

In the long run one of the key advantages of the union was that Scots merchants were able to trade legally with the English tobacco colonies of Virginia, Maryland and North Carolina. Even if the golden age of the Clyde tobacco trade lay some years in the future, there was already some evidence of dynamic enterprise by Glasgow merchants in the 1710s and 1720s. It was not so much that tobacco imports rose dramatically; that would have been difficult, because the general level of commercial activity in tobacco during these decades in the colonies and Europe was fairly stagnant. Where the Scots excelled was in undercutting their English rivals by developing smuggling on a grand scale. Indeed, smuggling was by no means confined to the American trades but became the great growth industry in Scotland during the decades after 1707. This reflected not only a desire to make quick profits but also widespread popular opposition to the new customs and tax regime which had followed in the wake of the union. In the tobacco trade most of the systematic fraud involved conspiracies between merchants and customs officers persistently to underweigh incoming cargoes. One estimate suggests that in the two decades after the union Scottish merchants were probably paying duty on only a half to two-thirds of their colonial imports. Needless to say, this gave them a significant competitive advantage over their rivals and, to the indignation of the merchants in Whitehaven, Liverpool and London involved in Atlantic commerce, the Scots went on to capture around 15 per cent of the legal trade in American tobacco to Britain by the early 1720s. This achievement was the foundation for even more spectacular success in the future.

Both the prophets of doom and the optimists were proven wrong as the union relationship entered its third decade. The nation's economy was not in ruins; indeed, there had been some modest recovery from the miseries of the 1690s in such sectors as agriculture and overseas trade. On the other hand, the economic miracle enthusiastically predicted by some pro-union propagandists had manifestly not taken place. Perhaps most crucially of all, however, Scotland had not been converted into a colonial appendage of the English economic system by the 1730s. With ultimate political authority now vested in London and the Scots exposed to open competition in manufactures from the most advanced economy in Europe, the scenario did exist for a dependent relationship. But two factors might explain why Scotland did not rapidly sink to the economic status of a satellite. First, England sought union for reasons of political and military security and had no economic ambitions north of the border. After 1707, Westminster seems to have been mainly interested in ensuring order and stability in Scotland, and when that existed – as it did for most of the time – the London government was broadly indifferent to the Scottish situation. Significantly, between 1727 and 1745 only nine Acts of Parliament were devoted exclusively to Scotland, and seven of these were concerned with minor matters. In general, Westminster was apathetic and, as shown in Chapter One, routine matters of government were normally delegated to the Scottish political 'manager' of the day, of whom the most powerful in the post-union decades was Archibald Campbell, Earl of Islay and later third Duke of Argyll. Indeed, the primary strategy of securing political stability could itself be of economic benefit to Scotland. The Malt Tax riots of 1725 undoubtedly made London sit up. Westminster was so concerned that in 1727 it established the Board of Trustees for Manufactures and Fisheries, which was to be funded from some of the accruals of the hated malt tax. This was a deliberate attempt to placate the truculent Scots by setting up a public body charged to improve the linen, woollen and fishing industries.

Second, the nature of the Scottish trade connection with England preserved a degree of protection. While commercial links were growing in the later seventeenth century, more than half of Scottish trade by value in 1700 was still conducted with non-English markets. This can be contrasted with the position of Ireland where, at the same date, between 75 and 80 per cent of the nation's external commerce was already carried on with England, the main market for Irish cattle, grain and wool and the principal source of supply of imported manufactured goods and essential raw materials. The Scots were not yet as integrated into the English trade network as the Irish. If they had been, the threat of southern economic dominance would perhaps have been more real.

Ultimately, however, the true test of the relationship between the union and Scottish development would come in the longer term, and a survey of the decades after c. 1740 does suggest a clear beneficial effect in that period. Linen was Scotland's most important eighteenth-century industry and one which experienced dynamic growth between 1740 and 1780, with output of cloth stamped by the Board of Trustees for sale rising fourfold over that period. In addition, it was to play a key role in the early stages of Scottish industrialization as the most important source of capital, labour and business skills for the cotton manufacture, the 'leading sector' of the Industrial Revolution. Linen's success seemed to rest to a large extent on the common market created by the union. In the 1760s, for instance, as much as two-thirds of stamped linen output was sold in the English home market or the American and Caribbean colonies. But for the union, this core manufacture would very likely have been confronted with an English tariff wall in competition with aggressive Dutch and German rivals. The Scots instead received protection within the union and were also aided from 1742 by a series of bounties to encourage exports. These, rather than initiatives to improve efficiency, seem to have been the decisive influences on growth. Linen, therefore, was one case where the record shows the impact of union to be clearly favourable in the long term.

To some extent it was a similar story with tobacco. The 'golden age' of the Glasgow tobacco trade dates from the 1740s and, astonishingly, by 1758 Scottish tobacco imports were greater than those of London and all the English outports combined. In 1771 the highest-ever volume of tobacco was landed, a staggering 47 million lb. Glasgow had become the tobacco metropolis of western Europe, and in the west of Scotland the profits of the trade fed into a very wide range of industries, founded banks and financed agricultural improvement through merchant investment. The transatlantic trades played a key role in the development of the Glasgow area, the region that was to become the engine of Scottish industrialization.

The legitimacy afforded by the union was crucial to this dazzling story of commercial success. As already noted, Scots traders had been active in the tobacco colonies before 1707, though on a relatively small scale, and much of it clandestine in nature. Certainly no London government would have allowed the enormous illegal growth in Scottish tobacco imports outside the union. Indeed, it was English protests against the boom in Scottish smuggling *within* the union that led to the wholesale reorganization of the customs service in 1723 and the formation of a more professional customs bureaucracy. This reflected the great political sensitivity of the issue since it was widely recognized that much of the Scottish success was at the expense of English merchants. Smuggling before 1707 clearly had its limitations; the union was therefore a necessary basis for the phenomenal Glaswegian performance in the American trades. Yet those successes were not inevitable. In the final analysis they were won by the Scottish merchant houses adopting more efficient business methods than many of their rivals. The big Glasgow firms were able to drive down their costs by a number of innovations in purchasing, marketing and shipping which made them formidable competitors in American and European markets. So the union did not *cause* growth in the Atlantic trades; it simply provided a context in which growth might or might not take place. Ultimately the decisive factor was the Scottish response.

This also conditioned the development of emigration within the union. Before the end of the seventeenth century there was already Scottish settlement in America at East Jersey and Carolina. However, the Darien fiasco demonstrated unambiguously that Scotland did not possess the necessary military and naval resources to establish her own American empire. The Earl of Stair put the point cogently in the union debates:

we followed the example of other nations and formed a company to trade with the Indies. We built ships and planned a colony on the isthmus of Darien. What we lacked were not men or arms, or courage, but the one thing most needful: the friendly co-operation of England. The pitiful outcome of that enterprise is too sad a story to be told again. Suffice it to say that the English did not treat us as partners or friends or fellow-subjects of a British king but as pirates and enemy aliens. The union of crowns gave us no security; we were exposed to the hostile rivalry of Spain; our colony was sacked; we suffered every cruelty an enemy can inflict.[2]

After the union, however, several parts of British North America became surrogate Scottish colonies. By the time of the American War of Independence, around 15,000 Gaelic-speaking Highlanders had already settled in Georgia and the Carolinas, while over 60,000 Lowland emigrants were concentrated mainly in the Chesapeake, the Carolinas, New Jersey and Boston. As Linda Colley suggests,

even the rawest frontiers of the empire attracted men of first-rate ability from the Celtic fringe because they were usually poorer than their English counterparts with fewer prospects on the British mainland. Having more to win and less to lose, Celtic adventurers were more willing to venture themselves in primitive conditions.[3]

Thus the Scots also became prominent in the East India Company (EIC) long before their position was further enhanced during the long reign of Henry Dundas as President of the EIC Board of Control after 1784. Unlike the pattern in the American colonies, where Scottish traders, clergymen and teachers were well established before 1707, the EIC had been able to prevent the involvement of Scots in India until after the union. However, in the eighteenth century they penetrated the EIC in much larger numbers than the Irish and the Welsh. Many were from landed backgrounds and, because the EIC strictly controlled the periods of service in India, Scottish writers, merchants and army officers often returned home with the accumulated profits of their Asian enterprise. They sometimes used these fortunes to invest in estate improvement, road building and village development.

This diaspora itself was not caused by the union, because the Scots had been mobile internationally long before 1707. What the Anglo-Scottish connection did, however, was to open up an unprecedented range of new opportunities where success was not guaranteed but depended on skill, enterprise, drive, education and luck. But the overall result of these increasingly global emigrations was to the massive benefit of Scotland itself. The Scottish international network later helped to forge trade connections in America and Asia which supported markets for industries at home. It was common for some colonial adventurers who had made their fortune to return home and buy a landed estate as physical proof to all and sundry of their material success. Contemporary observers like John Ramsay from Stirlingshire and Thomas Somerville from Roxburghshire identified men returning from the East Indies as the prime influences on the active land market in these counties and, in several other parts of Scotland, money from the colonies helped to sustain agricultural advances and the financing of rural industries.

4

What need to be considered finally are the reasons why the Scots gained from the union when in the long run they might well have lost. Union in 1707 could neither cause or prevent Scottish development; it simply offered an economic context with risks and opportunities. Three indigenous factors helped to ensure that the union was eventually turned to national advantage.

First, a crucial leadership was given by the landed élite and the business classes. The first signs of a concern for national economic improvement emerged in the decades before the union, but in the eighteenth century – and especially after c. 1760 – the greater landowners were in the van of agrarian modernization. The social élite played an energetic role in the founding of major banks, such as the Bank of Scotland, the Royal Bank of Scotland and the British Linen Bank, as well as in several provincial banking companies. To a much greater extent than their counterparts in Ireland, for instance, the Scottish governing classes developed a commitment to economic growth as a national goal. In addition, in the Lowlands they were much more directly involved in the process of driving forward agrarian improvement than even the majority of English landlords in the period after *c.* 1760. To this advantage was added the enterprising qualities of the Scottish merchant class. Already before 1700 the long-established merchant communities of the larger Scottish towns were considerably experienced in European, English, Irish and increasingly also in American trade. When commercial opportunities expanded dramatically throughout the transatlantic world in the second half of the eighteenth century, Scottish traders were well placed to exploit them.

Second, Scotland had the geological good fortune to possess abundant supplies of coal and iron ore close to water transport, large urban populations and centres of distribution and marketing. This advantage remained generally dormant for much of the eighteenth century, as water remained the main source of power for some time, but it became of critical importance early in the nineteenth century. Throughout Europe, regions blessed with such a favourable natural endowment became the leading centres of industrialization. Lowland Scotland was no exception.

Third, the Scottish cultural and educational inheritance deserves consideration. In the first decades of industrialization after 1750 there was significant technology transfer from England to Scotland, reflecting the quite different stages of economic development of the two societies. More advanced English methods were widely adopted in iron manufacturing, pottery, wool and glass-making. The new technology of Richard Arkwright in cotton-spinning became the basis of the Scottish cotton industry. It was also common to import English workers in order to introduce the Scots to new techniques and better practices. Carron Ironworks, in some ways the great symbol of the new industrial age, was dependent on skills and capital from the south. Yet Scottish innovators also made key contributions. James Watt was the father of steam engine technology, the basic source of power of the first Industrial Revolution. Bell's *Comet* of 1812 was the second successful commercial steamship in the world. J. B. Neilson revolutionized iron manufacture with his 'hot-blast' process. By the early nineteenth century the 'improved' agricultural system in Scotland had become world-renowned as a model of efficient organization. In banking and insurance the Scots also set the pace with a whole series of innovations such as the 'cash accompt' or overdraft. The list is not exhaustive, but it confirms that the Scots were not simply parasitical upon their more advanced English neighbours but made vitally important contributions of their own in technology and business organization. These achievements showed that Scottish society possessed the skills and the ideas to turn the union relationship to national advantage.

4

Roots of Enlightenment

I

In December 1696 an 18-year-old Edinburgh student, Thomas Aitkenhead, the son of a surgeon in the city, was tried for heresy. He was reported to have declared that theology was 'a rhapsody of feigned and ill-invented nonsense', that the Old Testament was 'Ezra's Fables' and the New Testament 'The History of the Impostor Christ'. Aitkenhead pleaded for mercy on the grounds of his youth, expressed contrition and solemnly promised to make amends.[1] Nevertheless, he was found guilty on Christmas Eve and condemned to be hanged, his 'body to be buried at the foot of the gallows and his moveable estate forfeited'. The Aitkenhead case epitomizes the rigid and intolerant Calvinism that seemed to clasp Scotland in a strong and unyielding grip during the last decade of the seventeenth century. The year after he was put to death, six other unfortunates were convicted of the crime of witchcraft in Paisley. Five were eventually executed and the sixth escaped public hanging and burning only because he committed suicide while in prison.

Again, in 1695 the Scottish parliament ratified an older statute making blasphemy a capital offence, thus confirming in law the unswerving official opposition of both Church and state to heterodox and deviant thought. In parallel a nationwide crusade was launched to enforce Presbyterian conformity after 1690. The victors of the Revolution of 1688–9 ruthlessly and energetically purged Episcopalians from both church offices and university posts. In parts of the Highlands and in the Lowlands north of the Tay the vengeful Presbyterians achieved only limited success. Elsewhere, their triumph was virtually complete as, between 1688 and 1716, no fewer than 664 ministers were deprived of their positions in the 926 parishes in Scotland, or nearly three-quarters of the total. Through its system of church courts, of assembly, synod, presbytery and kirk session, the Church had in effect more real authority than the state in many parts of the Lowlands and this was now deployed with full force to regulate, monitor and enforce orthodoxy of belief. It was believed that the years of Episcopalian domination before 1688 had resulted in a 'great decay of piety'. Now the nation had to atone for its numerous offences against God: 'profane and idle swearing, cursing, Sabbath breaking . . . fornication, adultery, drunkenness, blasphemy and other gross and abominable sins and vices'.[2] Aitkenhead's execution above all else demonstrated the commitment of the Kirk to root out sinners and free thinkers and cleanse the land of those who arrogantly offended against God's law.

To move from this Scotland of the 1690s to that of the middle decades of the eighteenth century is to enter a different world. Intolerance, conformity and resurgent puritanism seemed the hallmarks of the later seventeenth century. From the 1730s, however, Scotland was in the process of achieving an international reputation for wide-ranging intellectual inquiry in fields as varied as philosophy, history, science, law and medicine. In 1900 William Robert Scott introduced the term 'Scottish Enlightenment' to describe this extraordinary phenomenon and to capture the idea of a country which had successfully escaped from its benighted past and the shackles of Calvinist orthodoxy before blossoming into an intellectual powerhouse of Europe in the eighteenth century. Scotland became an integral part of the general eighteenth-century European Enlightenment, known as *Lumières* in France, *Illuminismo* in Italy and *Ilustracion* in Spain. As Alexander Broadie points out, the term was essentially one of self-congratulation used by those thinkers who saw themselves as 'enlightened' and who were literally living in the light of reason rather than in a world of darkness inhabited by those who relied only on faith and argument from the authority of ancient texts to advance human understanding.

The list of Scots who made world-class contributions to the new thinking was indeed remarkable. David Hume was the greatest philosopher in the English language. Adam Smith, through his masterpiece *The Wealth of Nations* (1776) and other works, is recognized as the major influence in the development of economics. Adam Ferguson, William Robertson and James Hutton were at the cutting edge of what became the disciplines respectively of sociology, history and geology. Thomas Reid developed 'common-sense' philosophy. The work of

William Adam and that of his sons, especially Robert, made Scottish architecture famed throughout the Continent. Joseph Black discovered both carbon dioxide and latent heat. William Cullen and the brothers William and John Hunter helped to make Scottish medical education the most progressive in Europe in the later eighteenth century. John Millar powerfully advanced understanding of the nature of social change over time and the interactions between law and philosophy. James Watt refined the separate condenser for the steam engine and so generated the essential source of power for the first Industrial Revolution.

But the Scottish Enlightenment was much more than a period of unparalleled creativity by a small number of 'great men' whose work collectively made vital contributions to the philosophical thought and scientific progress of the western world. Also central to it was the fundamental belief in the importance of reason, the rejection of that authority which could not be justified by reason and the ability through the use of reason to change both the human and the natural world for the better. In this new moral universe, intolerance, religious persecution and imposed orthodoxy of the type that were said to prevail in late-seventeenth-century Scotland were anathema. Nor was reason confined to the lecture theatre or the scholarly textbook. It affected all aspects of human behaviour. Thus the classic order and symmetry of the New Town of Edinburgh and the distinguished buildings designed by the Adam family are among the most compelling and enduring physical monuments to the Age of Reason in Scotland. So also was the ethic of rational 'improvement': of inspired planned intervention in the natural world which now came to be recognized as capable of amelioration by human effort. This helped to stimulate the late-eighteenth-century 'improving' movement in agriculture which contained all those elements of curiosity, optimism and a faith in reason that are to be found in the writings of the Enlightenment, though the Improvers were more interested in the practicalities of enclosures, drainage and new crops than in the detailed issues of philosophical debate.

The most gifted intelligence of all the *literati* (as the thinkers styled themselves), David Hume, in his *Treatise of Human Nature*, took the new confidence in the power of reason to its absolute conclusion by arguing for its ineffectiveness since it was impossible to prove the existence of things outside oneself. Elsewhere, he denounced the many evils that came from organized religion and condemned 'superstitions, piety and devotion'; and this a few decades after Aitkenhead had been hanged on a charge of blasphemy. Hume's scepticism may have cost him election to the chair of moral philosophy at Edinburgh University in 1745 but he was never stopped from publishing his views, was a welcome member of all the leading clubs in Edinburgh and also enjoyed a wide circle of friends and acquaintances among lawyers, ministers and university professors.

However, Enlightenment ideas were not confined to geniuses such as Hume and a small circle of well-known thinkers, but were also widely diffused throughout the ranks of the educated classes in Scotland. They were described, analysed, questioned and refuted in pamphlets and journals such as the *Scots Magazine*, in the contemporary press, in sermons and surveys like Sir John Sinclair's massive *Statistical Account of Scotland*, published in the 1790s, which provided an examination of the way of life of over 900 parishes compiled by the local ministers. It was this broad dissemination which ensured the social acceptance of basic ideas that might otherwise have remained arcane, remote and abstract. The Scottish Enlightenment was an intensely practical movement of ideas. Adam Smith's reasoning in the *Wealth of Nations* was often grounded on his own observations of the actual commercial and economic life of Scotland and Watt's technical virtuosity was as much part of the spirit of the age as William Robertson's renowned historical inquiries. Lord Kames was both a distinguished legal philosopher and also an influential publicist for improved farming through his classic text, *The Gentleman Farmer*. This interaction between theory and practice facilitated the transmission of enlightened ideas to the wider community. It is not possible, for instance, to understand the onset of rapid economic change in late-eighteenth-century Scotland without considering the acceptance of the idea that in this society man was now thought able to influence and control his environment to a much greater extent than had ever been thought possible before.

There is an obvious and striking contrast between these dazzling achievements of the eighteenth century and the intolerance and narrow puritanism of the 1690s. The age of Aitkenhead seems light years away from the era of Smith, Hume and Ferguson – the darkness of religious fanaticism, as it were, before the dawn of reason and enlightenment. But it is dangerous to draw too stark a contrast between seventeenth-century Scotland and the later decades of great intellectual achievement. Scotland before 1700 was far from being a cultural backwater. The country had five universities and a parish school system that was well established in most parts of the Lowlands and in some areas of the Highlands. The Act anent (concerning) the Settling of Schools of 1696 was the climax of a process of school foundation which had been going on apace in earlier decades. Gordon Donaldson showed that by the 1660s it was already a 'normal thing' for a Lowland parish to have a school under the supervision of the kirk session and partly supported by a tax on local landowners. It was a 'national system', not unique, but certainly still uncommon in western Europe. Moreover, the universities were already in the European vanguard in accepting the new thinking of John Locke and Sir Isaac Newton. By the 1690s Locke's *Essay Concerning Human Understanding* (1689), which challenged some of the basic contentions of Descartes in which the traditional curriculum was based, had already been adopted in teaching, although still condemned by the Kirk as theologically suspect. Locke's writings made little headway in either France or Sweden until later in the eighteenth century. Even more significant was the incorporation into university teaching of Newton's *Principia Mathematica* (1687). By about 1710 the natural philosophy courses at Edinburgh, Aberdeen, Glasgow and St Andrews were all basically Newtonian in emphasis, an innovation that took place here several years before it was incorporated into such distinguished centres of learning as Cambridge and Leyden. The Newtonian method later had powerful influence on social philosophy and was applied in such key texts as Smith's *Theory of Moral Sentiments* (1759) and Hume's *Treatise of Human Nature* (1739–40). Later, the Scottish universities would be at the heart of the Enlightenment, with many of the leading thinkers drawn from the professoriate. But this blossoming of talent did not occur in a vacuum. The reorganization of Scottish universities was already under way at Edinburgh under William Carstares, who was Principal in 1703–15, and by the 1720s was seen to have had considerable effect. Carstares and his brother-in-law, William Dunlop, who was Principal at Glasgow University, also managed to persuade government to increase endowment to the institutions.

The spread of Newtonian ideas before 1700 reflects one important link with the scientific achievements of the eighteenth century. But there were other crucial links in medicine and law. A fundamental feature of the Enlightenment was the discovery of knowledge which could then be used to improve the human condition. Perhaps the greatest advance in this respect was the progressive medical education associated with Glasgow and Edinburgh. The early pioneers were the *virtuosi*, the men of science, of the later seventeenth century of whom the most remarkable was Sir Robert Sibbald (1641–1722). In 1681 he was one of the founder members of the Royal College of Physicians of Edinburgh, and in 1685 became the first Professor of Medicine at Edinburgh University. As a physician he had a keen interest in botany and established a Physic Garden at Holyrood in 1670. This linked to Edinburgh's later reputation for medical studies, since the main function of the garden was to provide medicinal plants for teaching and research. The breadth of Sibbald's intellectual concerns is further demonstrated by his appointment as Geographer-Royal in 1682. The crucial point about Sibbald was that he was far from being unique. There was a real and lively Scottish intellectual community in the later seventeenth century which included such names as Archibald Pitcairn, Sir George Mackenzie of Rosehaugh, Andrew Balfour, James Sutherland and Robert Wodrow. From the 1680s, through their mutual exchange of ideas in clubs, societies and professional bodies they gave a new impetus to the scholarly life of the country and built a foundation from which the more celebrated achievements of the eighteenth century later developed.

It is important to stress that there was not necessarily any direct conflict between this flurry of scholarly activity and the stern Calvinism of the 1690s. On the contrary, religious belief could actually stimulate an interest in moral, philosophical and scientific questions, as systematic investigation of the natural world had a secure theological foundation in the desire of man to understand order and regularity in God's universe.

Nowhere was this connection more convincingly illustrated than in the work of James Dalrymple, Viscount Stair (1619–95), whose *Institutions of the Laws of Scotland* (1681) gave the country a codified, coherent and logical structure of laws for the first time based on philosophical principles. Stair's work was strongly influenced by the great European jurists such as Grotius and Pufendorf. But he was emphatically Scottish in his attempt, as a staunch Presbyterian, to harmonize his conclusions with scripture and theology, and so differed from some continental thinkers who argued that a rational system of law could exist independently of theology. For Stair, God was inherently rational and therefore law was primarily established according to His will. Stair's great work was followed by Sir George Mackenzie's *Laws and Customs of Scotland on Matters Criminal* (1684), the first textbook on the criminal law of Scotland. Mackenzie was also the formative influence behind the formation of the Advocates' Library in Edinburgh in 1682, which became a vital resource for scholars in a number of disciplines in the Age of Enlightenment. More generally, the new intellectual coherence of Scots law achieved by Stair and Mackenzie helps to explain why its separate identity could be formally accepted and incorporated in the Treaty of Union of 1707.

A lively Scottish tradition of scholarship therefore existed before 1700, and so the Enlightenment appears less of a completely new, eccentric and radical departure and more a continuation and a more powerful and brilliant expression of earlier trends. Recent research has painted an even more sophisticated picture by suggesting that the intellectual roots go much deeper in time than was once believed. Alex Broadie's explorations of the group of pre-Reformation philosophers around John Mair (or Major) has shown clear connections between eighteenth-century intellectual concerns and the logicians of the Renaissance period, while David Allan's work on the Scottish historians of the sixteenth and seventeenth centuries demonstrates that they built upon the humanists of the pre-Reformation period, such as Mair and Hector Boece, by stressing the status of learning and the value of history. There is also the idea of the 'latent enlightenment' in Calvinism. It was a theology which contained a strong intellectual element that appealed more to the head than to the heart. Apart from the fact that some of the *literati* were themselves committed believers, Calvinist moral and social principles can be found in some of the great works of the period and even in those of David Hume, a famous sceptic on religious matters.

The Calvinist concern with human morality in relation to the will of God which had obsessed sevententh-century Presbyterian divines was given a more secular orientation in the eighteenth century by those thinkers who saw the study of human nature as absolutely central to general understanding. The philosophers and historians strove to develop the 'science of man' – Hume regarded it as the essential basis of all the other sciences – while the great portrait-painters of the age, Allan Ramsay and Henry Raeburn, tried to capture the visual essence of human nature on their canvases. This interest in the study of humanity had theological roots in Scotland. In addition, several of the main figures of the Enlightenment were squarely within the Calvinist tradition. William Robertson was not only a cleric but the son of a minister, Moderator of the General Assembly of the Church of Scotland and leader of the Moderate Party in the Church of Scotland. Adam Ferguson and Thomas Reid were ordained ministers, the former for a time chaplain to the Black Watch regiment, and John Millar was a son of the manse. Calvinism was therefore a key element in a long-established Scottish philosophical tradition that created the context for the wide-ranging inquiries of the eighteenth century. However, it is doubtful if these could have flourished easily and generally in the climate of ortho-doxy and intolerance that existed in the later seventeenth century and which was so graphically illustrated by the execution of Aitkenhead and the repressive policies of the Kirk. Clearly some relaxation of this rigidity was a *sine qua non* for an Enlightenment which above all else advocated the values of civilized tolerance and the autonomy of reason. The discussion now turns to a consideration of these liberating influences which developed in Scottish society in the first decades of the eighteenth century. One vital factor was the European connection.

Scotland had always formed an integral part of the European com-munity of scholars since medieval times. Remarkably, between its foundation and the Reformation, 17 or 18 rectors of the University of Paris were Scots. In the late sixteenth and seventeenth centuries, Scottish students and scholars went to and from universities in the Low Coun-tries, France and Germany for training and teaching in divinity and law. Advanced legal education prior to the eighteenth century took place in Leyden, Bourges, Utrecht, Orléans and other universities, while for medical studies Scots attended the acknowledged European centre of excellence at Leyden in the Low Countries under the legendary tutelage of Hermann Boerhaave (1668–1738). Rome was the mecca for painters and architects, and a community of expatriate Scottish artists grew up there in the eighteenth century.

These connections were all conduits for the transmission of ideas and stimuli back to Scotland. Robert Adam spent four years studying in Rome, and the neo-classical style to which he was exposed there helped to make him the most celebrated and influential architect of his generation in Britain. The medical powerhouse of Leyden had a profound influence on the development of what was to become the world-famous medical school at Edinburgh. Alexander Monro (1697–1767), who had studied under Boerhaave, became the first Professor of Anatomy in Edinburgh in 1722 and founded a remarkable professorial dynasty consisting of son, Alexander *secundus*, and grandson, Alex-ander *tertius*, who effectively created the reputation of Edinburgh in the late eighteenth century as a centre for medical education without equal in Europe. One of the key reforms in Scottish universities at this time was the abolition of regenting (by which a single member of staff took the class through the entire curriculum) and the adoption of a system of professorships which eventually encouraged more specialist research and speculative thought. Here, too, the Dutch example was influential. William Carstares, later Principal of Edinburgh, had spent some time in exile in Holland before returning with William of Orange in 1688. His abolition of regenting at Edinburgh in 1708 was in part due to his admiration for the professorial system of the Dutch. The traditional cosmopolitanism of the Scots therefore made them aware of innovative ideas and practices in other European centres of learning and these blended with the Scottish intellectual tradition and the late-seventeenth-century academic developments already surveyed. However, a crucial stage in the context for Enlightenment was reached when a more liberal climate emerged for the exchange of ideas than had been possible in the 1690s. This in turn depended on changes in the Church of Scotland, progressive reform in the universities and a more appropriate political and economic background for intellectual discourse.

2

Though Scotland in the 1690s was in the grip of a repressive puritanism, the authority of the zealots was less in reality than might at first appear. In fact the force of the Presbyterian onslaught on heresy may in part have been due to an awareness of relative weakness, an anxious suspicion that the majority of the population were hostile to the Revolution of 1688-9 and so beyond the influence of the restored General Assembly. What happened in the 1690s to a large extent reflected the transitory over-reaction of religious counter-revolutionaries who had been out of power for some time and who were utterly determined to exact revenge on their old enemies and those who dissented from the true faith. But below the surface of public events, radical ideas were seeping in from Europe and England and were eating away at the more inflexible tenets of Calvinism. The works of Hobbes, Leibniz, Grotius, Pufendorf, Shaftesbury, Berkeley, Locke, Newton and many others were manifestly not those of the Westminster Confession of Faith which had been made the text of orthodoxy by the Church of Scotland in the Settlement of

1690. But the ideas of these men were already being aired in the university lecture halls and their effect on the new generation of the Scottish clergy can only be guessed at. Perhaps because of this, by the early eighteenth century the Church of Scotland was adopting a more pragmatic approach than before. It first opposed and then accepted (after guarantees for its own autonomy in the Act of Security) the Parliamentary Union between England and Scotland in 1707. This was a peaceful union between two states with profoundly different Protestant religious polities and could hardly have been contemplated a few decades before. It is possible, indeed, that eventually the union might have instilled an important new sense of Presbyterian security since it was the major obstacle to a successful Jacobite counter-revolution. As a result, the Kirk could have become less defensive over time. But any change that did occur was a gradual one. In 1715 John Simson, Professor of Divinity in the University of Glasgow, was tried by the General Assembly for heresy. He accepted the truths of Calvinism but considered there was further scope for debate and encouraged his students to think for themselves. But alternative opinion on theological matters was clearly not yet acceptable. The Simson controversy dragged on for several years until he was finally suspended from academic teaching in 1729.

In the final analysis, three factors helped to shape a more liberal climate. The first was the imposition by the Tory government at Westminster of the Patronage Act of 1712 reasserting the right of lay patrons to appoint ministers. This struck at the heart of one of the key principles of Presbyterianism, in which ministers were supposed to be selected by the local church community. When the new powers were generally deployed for the first time by landlords they immediately engendered serious tensions within the Kirk, culminating in a secession led by Ebenezer Erskine in 1740. A second and even greater schism took place in 1752 with the formation of the Relief Church. Some of those who left were of rigidly puritan inclination, especially in 1740, and their departure made it easier for more liberal opinion to become influential in the General Assembly, especially since it was likely that patrons would select ministers who shared their own values and avoid those branded as 'wild' and fanatical. At the same time, this fracturing of the Kirk was itself a telling sign that it was now becoming more difficult to impose monolithic conformity.

Secondly, Scottish ministers were trained within Scottish universities, and by the 1720s and 1730s significant developments in divinity education were taking place in some institutions. The most famous example was the impact made by Francis Hutcheson during his tenure as Professor of Moral Philosophy at Glasgow between 1729 and his death in 1746. Hutcheson was born of Scottish Presbyterian parents in Armagh, Northern Ireland, where his father was a minister. He had been influenced by John Simson's teaching when he was a student at Glasgow and had accepted his liberal views. Hutcheson in turn was to exert a powerful influence on a whole generation of Glasgow-educated divines. His most famous pupil was Adam Smith, who later referred to the 'abilities and virtues of the never to be forgotten Dr Hutcheson'.[3] Hutcheson's eloquent lectures were delivered in English rather than Latin; he held to the view that rational inquiry was the only effective method in theology, emphasized that benevolence was the basis of morality, and adopted a more optimistic approach to humanity than that suggested by the doctrine of the Fall and original sin. He summed up his aims to an Irish friend in 1740: since coming to Glasgow, he had tried 'to promote the more moderate and charitable sentiments in religious matters, in this country; where yet there remains too much warmth and animosity about matters of no great consequence to reall Religion'.[4]

Through the teaching of Hutcheson and his friend and successor, William Leechman, 'moderate and charitable sentiments' became an integral part of the moral philosophy curriculum at Glasgow and a key part of the education of future ministers. About one-quarter of the Scottish clergy in the mid-eighteenth century were reckoned to have studied at Glasgow. The Hutchesonian emphasis was moving towards tolerance, the justification of religious belief by reason as well as by faith and a stress on issues of morality rather than simply on matters of narrow theological significance. Alexander Carlyle wrote of the impact of Hutcheson and Leechman:

A new school was formed in the western provinces of Scotland where the clergy till that period were narrow and bigoted ... though neither of these professors taught any heresy, yet they opened and enlarged the minds of the students which soon gave them a turn for free enquiry, the result of which was candour and liberality of sentiment.[5]

These approaches at Glasgow and other universities contributed significantly to the third factor which helped to create a more liberal climate in the Church. This was the rise of the Moderate Party.

Puritanism within the Church had already been weakened by the departure of some of the more doctrinaire elements in the secessions in the 1740s and early 1750s. But tensions persisted due to the continuing effect of the Patronage Act and the unwillingness of many congregations to accept the minister nominated by the patron. There seemed also to be a threatened breakdown of authority, since even presbyteries were sometimes unwilling on grounds of conscience to obey rulings of the General Assembly on patronage issues. Such truculence raised fundamental questions about the relationship between the Church and the state which had enacted the patronage legislation in the first place. Concern about these disputes led to the formation of the 'Moderate Party' in the early 1750s. This was a group of young ministers that included William Robertson and Hugh Blair, who were determined to reassert the authority of the General Assembly on patronage disputes. Their reasoning was that patronage was the legal basis for the selection of ministers and only by enforcing the law of the land could the Church justify freedom from state interference. This was the price that had to be paid for ecclesiastical autonomy. Furthermore, Robertson himself believed that the system of patronage would deliver clergymen who were better educated and with more liberal values than those elected by the popular will.

There can be little doubt that if the Moderates gained influence there would be more scope for more critical discourse within the Church and a much closer relationship than ever before with secular values and secular authority. They advocated tolerance of doctrinal differences and accommodation with the political system of the day. Several had been robust supporters of the House of Hanover in the '45, and William Robertson himself, the leader of the party, had helped defend Edinburgh against the advancing Jacobite army in that fateful year. They also supported an enlightened clergy and religious freedom for those outside the established church so long as they kept the law. Little wonder that Thomas Halyburton, who had personally penned a vindication of the execution of Thomas Aitkenhead, complained 'that a rational sort of religion is coming in among us: I mean by it a religion that consists in bare attendance on outward duties and ordinances without the power of Godliness'.[6]

In a sense Halyburton need not have worried. Traditional Calvinism retained the greatest appeal for the vast majority of Scots, as is shown by the continuing influence of kirk session discipline described in the next chapter and by the enormous popularity of the new dissenting churches which emerged in the middle decades of the eighteenth century precisely at the time when the Moderate interest within the Church of Scotland first developed. The running sore of patronage, the refusal of many congregations to surrender their right of election to vacancies and the increasing incidence of bitter and violent opposition to unpopular ministers who were imposed on some parishes were all indicative of the continued power and passion of popular religiosity. In the early 1740s, for instance, a wave of evangelicalism swept through parts of Scotland, culminating in 1742 at Cambuslang in Lanarkshire when William McCulloch and George Whitefield preached to an estimated 30,000 people amid scenes of high emotion and mass conversion.

Nevertheless, the Moderates managed to achieve real authority by dominating the General Assembly in the decades after *c.* 1750 through their close connections with government and by their tenure of many university chairs. This influence in turn prevented a return to old-fashioned heresy hunts. Thus, in 1755 and 1756, when David Hume and Lord Kames came under the attack of the General Assembly, no action was taken, thanks to the intervention of William Robertson, leader of the Moderates from 1762 until 1780 and Principal of Edinburgh University from 1762 to 1793. Robertson went further and in his influential two-volume *History of Scotland* (1759) proceeded to revile Presbyterian tradition. He undermined the entire historic status of Scotland as a nation bound through the covenants of 1581, 1638 and 1643 to God by demonstrating that the idea of the religious covenant was not divine-inspired but came rather from the feudal practice of 'banding' together for mutual protection. He also emphatically condemned the bloody sacrifices of the seventeenth-century Covenanters (who were folk heroes to most ordinary Scottish Protestants) for their unacceptably violent and lawless actions. Here the man of the Enlightenment was distancing himself from what he saw as the terrible and irrational deeds, no matter how revered, of the nation's past.

But it would be quite wrong to suggest that the new liberalism meant that the *literati* were moving *en masse* towards secularism and that Calvinism was in decline. Religion remained very much at the heart of the Enlightenment and its influence remained all-pervasive. Echoes of Calvinist thinking are commonplace in the printed works of the period. For instance, both predestination and the 'invisible hand' of historical change feature in the writings of Adam Smith. The Moderates, far from ignoring religion, used it as part of their analysis of society, as when they justified the value of the hierarchical political structure in terms of God's divine plan for an orderly universe. Above all, the Church was still the dominant force in both the schools and the universities, the twin cradles of Enlightenment.

The universities merit serious consideration in any account of the Scottish Enlightenment. The majority of leading thinkers (with the notable exceptions of David Hume and James Hutton) held professorships and the teaching in the universities was the prime mechanism for disseminating the ideals of the Enlightenment to the new generation of ministers, schoolmasters, doctors and lawyers. The radical changes in curriculum that took place in the eighteenth century were based on Enlightenment values of improvement, virtue and practical benefit. The universities therefore enhanced the intellectual changes of the period and at the same were a vital manifestation of them.

Despite the ruthless Presbyterian purging of Episcopalian academics in the 1690s, several of the universities were already on the move before 1700 as Newtonian methods, Locke's principles and new ideas from Holland began to influence teaching practice and thinking. But this was but a prelude to the more wide-ranging advances of the eighteenth century. Only St Andrews remained virtually unaffected, being dismissed by Daniel Defoe in 1727 as 'looking into its Grave' and written off by Dr Johnson in 1773 as 'firmly in decay and struggling for life'.[7] The position was much better elsewhere. Student numbers rose rapidly: Edinburgh had 400 in the 1690s and 1,300 a century later; Glasgow's roll rose from 250 in 1696 to 1,240 by 1824; while at King's College, Aberdeen, the number of students stood at 50 in 1776 and 156 in 1812. At the same time, the traditional Scottish migration to continental universities fell away and instead the Scots institutions started to attract significant numbers of Presbyterian students from Ulster and dissenters from England who could not gain entry to Oxford, Cambridge or Trinity College, Dublin. Students entered university in their mid-teens and for this group the Scottish institutions had considerable appeal. Fees were significantly lower than the English universities and there was growing emphasis on subjects of direct vocational relevance, such as law and medicine. To a quite remarkable extent, for instance, universities such as Glasgow were able to draw on the merchant and tradesman classes interested in a practical education. The proportion drawn from this group rose from 26 per cent of the student population in the 1740s to around 50 per cent by the 1830s. Overall, Scotland had a higher ratio of university places to population size than other European nations, an achievement which was in large part due to the function of the parish and burgh schools as feeders for higher education.

Several features of the university system merit emphasis in this discussion of the context of Enlightenment. The abolition of regenting (first at Edinburgh in 1708), the adoption of English as the medium of instruction and the movement away from dictation from set texts in some subjects all in the long run allowed for more discursive and speculative teaching. Some of the great works of the Enlightenment, most famously Adam Smith's *Wealth of Nations* (1776) and John Millar's *Origins of the Distinction of Ranks* (1771) began life as lecture notes. Good teaching indeed seems to have been a hallmark of the Scottish universities at this time. In addition to formal lectures, some professors took part in 'catechizing' which involved discussion and questions on the lecture given previously, an approach very similar to the modern tutorial system. Some argued that excellence in teaching depended on the class fee system. Professors received a modest stipend but depended mainly on the fees paid by each student. There was therefore an incentive to be diligent and effective in order to attract a large class. Certainly there were many noted teachers whose inspiring lectures had a deep influence. Among them were Francis Hutcheson, William Cullen, Adam Smith, John Millar and Dugald Stewart, who all received lavish praise from grateful students. Of the last named it was memorably recalled by an admiring student that there was 'eloquence in his very spitting'. But since the professoriate was appointed on the basis of patronage and personal connection, by no means all came up to these high standards. In his last will and testament, John Anderson, Professor of Natural Philosophy at Glasgow, established a second institution of higher education in the city, named Anderson's University, which in the course of time eventually became the University of Strathclyde. Anderson made it clear to his trustees in no uncertain terms that the professors in his university were not to be 'permitted, as in some other Colleges, to be Drones or Triflers, Drunkards, or negligent in any manner of way'.[8] Despite its distinguished history in earlier years, Anderson accused his colleagues of abuses, faction-fighting and much else besides.

Allied to improvements in teaching was a remarkable dynamism in subject development. The universities had been seen by John Knox and his fellow reformers in the sixteenth century as divinity schools for the training of ministers. By the eighteenth century a much more secular emphasis was apparent. There was a transformation of the university into an institution with broad educational objectives but with a vital vocational function in the training not only of ministers but also of lawyers and medical doctors. The Moderate influence ensured that the universities were now committed to satisfying the new needs of society in a climate of economic change. Significantly, though there was little work of seminal significance in theology, many publications of high excellence were produced in philosophy, political economy, history and science. Similarly, a range of new chairs was founded in medicine, law, chemistry, botany and history, but with little increased academic endowment in divinity. By the end of the eighteenth century there were more chairs in medicine than in theology at Edinburgh, a telling illustration of the new interest in Man rather than God.

The urban location of four of the five universities (Glasgow, Edinburgh and both King's College and Marischal College at Aberdeen) was also significant. Edinburgh gained because of the pride of the council in the 'toun's college'. The rise of the city's medical school to a position of eminence in Europe was first given impetus by an effective partnership between Alexander Monro, *primus*, the Professor of Anatomy from 1720 until 1758, and Lord Provost George Drummond. The urban setting meant that academic and public cultures could interact, which also ensured dissemination of ideas. The Enlightenment was an age of conviviality, where issues were discussed and debated over port and claret (often in enormous quantities) in the many taverns to be found in the towns. There was a host of formally established clubs, such as the Select Society, the Poker Club and the Speculative Society, but an even greater number of more informal gatherings. It was entirely typical of the age that the Moderate Party first started to emerge as a significant entity after several meetings in an Edinburgh tavern.

At the same time, there is evidence of 'outreach' from the universities to the urban populations. In the 1750s, Robert Dick, the Glasgow Professor of Natural Philosophy, was offering popular courses in physics and astronomy to the townspeople. His successor, John Anderson, lectured on experimental physics to the same audience. Anderson put great emphasis on 'useful learning' which would be of direct benefit to commerce and industry. It was a demonstration of the way Enlightenment ideals of 'improvement' could be spread outside the confines of the university classroom and influence a wider urban public. Anderson was almost the opposite of the stereotypical moderate, tolerant and polite Enlightenment scholar. He was combative, firmly Evangelical in religion and uncompromising in opinion. When the repeal of the laws against Roman Catholics was being considered in the 1770s, Anderson challenged Thomas Reid to debate on the issue and compared 'the Papists to a Rattle-Snake, harmless when kept under proper restraints: but dangerous like it, when at full liberty; and ready to diffuse a baleful poison around'.[9] Nevertheless, in Glasgow and the west of Scotland, Enlightenment values, as Ned Landsman has shown, were to be found among those of *both* Moderate and Evangelical inclination. Anderson and men like him stood for a closer and more practical association between academe and society and an emphasis on the value of education. After his death, when the new institution he had planned in his will held its first lectures in the Trades Hall of Glasgow in 1797 under Professor Thomas Garnett, half those in attendance, uniquely for the period, were women. Furthermore, despite their apparent opposition to some of the classic principles of Enlightenment, Glasgow and west of Scotland Evangelical clergy were also strongly committed to those ideals of personal freedom and liberty traditionally associated with Moderatism. It was no coincidence that it was John Witherspoon, an Evangelical minister and resolute enemy of the Moderates, who, after emigrating to America, became President of Princeton University, a member of the first Congress and the only clergyman among the signatories to the Declaration of Independence of the United States. In Glasgow and the Presbyterian west of Scotland there was therefore no simple correlation between Moderate light and Evangelical darkness. The rational approach was widely diffused.

The political and economic developments of the middle decades of the eighteenth century were also conducive to intellectual inquiry. After 1707 tensions certainly existed within the Anglo-Scottish relationship in the early eighteenth century and Jacobitism's wide appeal still threatened counter-revolution. But by the 1740s these problems had disappeared. Scotland was now gaining from the union, although economic advance was still proceeding relatively slowly and was not yet causing the profound disruption in traditional social relationships characteristic of the era of industrialization after *c.* 1750. The disappearance of the Scottish parliament in 1707 had left a political vacuum in Scotland, and in many ways the debates in the General Assembly now more faithfully represented the real interests of the country than those of the MPs in distant Westminster. When the Moderates gained control in the 1750s, Church politics would be governed by the same standards of pragmatism that prevailed in the secular sphere. Scottish politics in mid-century were therefore intrinsically bland and devoid of conflict, but this provided an excellent context for the clash of ideas. William Ferguson makes the point that in an older Scotland the intellectuals would have been forced to take sides. Now civilized and objective debate and tolerant acceptance of different views were more possible.

Unlike the position in France, the Scottish philosophers faced no political constraints from the government of the *ancien régime*. The dominant figures in the Enlightenment were integral parts of the political establishment, virtually all Whig Hanoverians who regarded Jacobitism as a deadly threat to Protestant liberties and freedoms. The two universities in Aberdeen, King's and Marischal Colleges, located in the disaffected and Episcopalian north-east, did have to be purged after the '15. However, they remained loyal during the '45, and another Scottish university, St Andrews, went so far as to elect the Duke of Cumberland, the notorious 'Butcher' and victor of Culloden, as Chancellor. The highly effective patronage machine developed by the Earl of Islay, later the Duke of Argyll, and continued by Lord Bute ensured that political conformity would always prevail in appointments to university posts. It was reckoned, for instance, in 1764 that no fewer than seven of the 19 positions at Edinburgh and five of the 13 at Glasgow had been filled with Bute's support. As already noted, only David Hume's extreme scepticism and religious heterodoxy prevented him from election to chairs at both Edinburgh and Glasgow. Nevertheless, he was favoured with another establishment post, that of Keeper of the Advocates Library, in 1752. The Moderates were also committed to the maintenance of the existing social and political order. They were strongly supportive of law, order, discipline and hierarchy, which they regarded as necessary safeguards against the religious and political discords from which Scotland had suffered in earlier times. As William Robertson put it, 'there can be no society where there is no subordination'. To them, the Protestant Revolution of 1688–9 and the union of 1707 had produced the ideal combination of liberty and order. These men were essentially political conservatives who accepted the inequality of ranks as fundamental to the functioning of the social system and the unique right of a propertied élite to govern the country.

This conservatism was partly based on the new affluence of middle-class Scotland from the 1730s. At the beginning of the eighteenth century there seemed few material foundations for a vibrant cultural renaissance. The crises of the 1690s had impoverished the nation, while, in the short run, the union with England did little to improve the economy. Scotland remained one of the poorest countries in Europe, having also lost its court in 1603 and parliament in 1707. It seemed a most unlikely context for the remarkable cultural achievements of the middle decades of the eighteenth century. However, even in the times of most acute difficulty before 1700, there was some increase in agricultural productivity and a steady movement in external trade links away from Europe to the growing markets of England and the colonies. One contemporary observer, William Mackintosh of Borlum, noted as early as 1729 the beginnings of a revolution in the way of life of the landed classes. They lived 'more handsomely now in dress, table and house furniture'.[10] The wives of lairds were increasingly wearing French and Italian silk, and dinners were now often spiced with pickles, Indian mangoes and anchovy sauces. The career of the great architect, William Adam, illustrates their increasing prosperity. By the 1720s he was in great demand as a consultant and contractor for country house improvement, the most striking example of his work being the ambitious remodelling of Hopetoun House from 1721.

This greater affluence of the élites enriched the social context of the Enlightenment. More great men could now provide patronage for the *literati*; agricultural improvement meant a greater need for legal skills, which boosted the incomes and status of lawyers, a key group in the Enlightenment; and many more landowners were now willing and able to spend more money in elegant artwork, paintings and buildings. Economic expansion, therefore, did not cause the Enlightenment but it did facilitate its development. Moreover, much of the social analysis of the philosophers was grounded on economy. William Robertson regarded knowledge of how a society earned its living as the necessary first step to understanding it more broadly. As he put it, 'in every inquiry concerning the operations of men when united together in society, the first object of attention should be their mode of subsistence'.[11] Both Adam Smith and John Millar saw man's nature as the force driving him to better his material condition. They and other *literati* had a deep interest in how societies developed from primitive to civilized conditions, and again the economic factor was fundamental to the analysis. Smith was in fact the world's first and most celebrated economic historian. It can hardly be a coincidence that this interest in the material aspects of historical evolution matured to a high level of intellectual distinction in a society which was itself experiencing the beginnings of unprecedented economic and social change from agriculture to industry.

5

The Parish State

In the eighteenth century the Church of Scotland had important civil and judicial functions as well as religious responsibilities. People at the local level would be much more likely to experience the impact of the Presbyterian Church in all aspects of their lives than the influence of a distant state in London or Edinburgh. By the mid-seventeenth century the Kirk had already settled a minister of religion in almost all the 900 parishes in Scotland with the exception of some parts of the western Highlands. The minister was usually supported by a kirk session or permanent committee of lay-elders, who were elected and who entered into their office for life; and they were usually individuals of merit, piety or social standing in the local community. The kirk session's responsibilities were wide-ranging. It organized the collection and distribution of funds for the poor, with applicants being subjected to long and detailed examination about their circumstances before support was given. The parish school had to be supervised, and often the clerk of the kirk session was himself the local schoolmaster. Since the curriculum depended to a significant extent on the Bible and catechism, the religious ethos was central to elementary schooling. But the session also had a key judicial function: it exerted a close supervision on the moral behaviour of parishioners and was the lowest court from which more serious offences could be referred to the civil authorities. Indeed, the distinction between some ecclesiastical and civil crimes throughout the eighteenth century remained blurred. Kirk sessions heard cases of fornication, adultery, drunkenness and Sabbath profanation, but they also often dealt with assault, theft and wife-beating.

I

Few aspects of the history of Scottish Presbyterianism are more repugnant to the modern mind than kirk session discipline with its connotations of public humiliation, voyeurism and smug self-righteousness. But the supervision of the morality of the community had a basic rationale in Calvinist dogma and the function needs to be understood in the context of the time rather than be judged by the standards of a different and later society. Calvinism held that all humanity was corrupted by sin but that an omnipotent God had decreed that mankind should be divided into two groups: the elect, who would achieve salvation, and the reprobate, who would be damned for all eternity. The true church was that to which the elect belonged. The reformers in 1560 in the original Protestant Confession of Faith had stated that godly discipline was an important public function of the true church and this had been reasserted in 1690. Not only was discipline a moral obligation, it was also the most convincing public demonstration that the congregations of the church were members of the elect; and not to enforce discipline was the theological equivalent of accepting that the community was not part of that spiritual élite. In addition, there was the general Christian view, not confined only to Scottish Calvinists, that the awesome power of God could lead to punitive divine intervention in human affairs if the Creator was angered by the sinful behaviour of man. The force of this belief is shown in the custom, which lasted well into the nineteenth century, of imposing days of fasting and prayer after such disasters as famine and epidemics in order to appease the wrath of the Almighty. Godly discipline served an important purpose by demonstrating to God the wholehearted opposition of the Christian community to sin and its determination to root it out and exact punishment wherever it was to be found. The General Assembly proclaimed in 1694 that kirk sessions were to 'faithfully exercise church discipline against all . . . scandalous offenders' because:

God is dishonoured by the impiety and profaneness that aboundeth . . . in profane and idle swearing, cursing, Sabbath breaking, neglect and contempt of Gospel ordinances, mocking of piety and religious exercises, fornication, adultery, drunkenness, blasphemy and other gross and abominable sins and vices.

One crucial aspect of discipline was the 'testificat' system by which men and women could not move from parish to parish without a certificate of good behaviour, or testificat, signed by the minister. Kirk session registers of the early eighteenth century indicate that the use of testificats was very widespread and that ministers conscientiously checked details through their contacts in other parishes to ensure authenticity. There were of course ways of escaping the parish network by leaving the country altogether or by seeking refuge in the big cities or parts of the Highlands. But the testificat system and the overall cohesion of the Kirk before the 1740s made it more difficult for offenders to avoid discipline in lowland Scotland than in England where the proliferation of religious dissent made it more demanding for the Established Church to enforce its authority. But the nature and context of kirk session discipline was changing by the early eighteenth century. From 1690 the state was no longer willing to support church excommunication with civil penalties and, after 1712, lesser excommunication (the denial of communion) could not be referred to a sheriff for judicial action. Effectively from this date the Church was on its own and could not rely on the civil authority to support its disciplinary measures. Also from 1712, the Toleration Act allowed the Episcopalian Church to hold its own services and the Presbyterian Church of Scotland could not easily exercise discipline in parishes of Episcopalian loyalty without the agreement of Episcopalian clergy. Furthermore, the nature of the offences which kirk sessions prosecuted became narrower after the implementation of the Presbyterian Form of Process in 1707. This decreed that only sins which had showed outward evidence were to be dealt with, rather than those of the heart and the mind, such as pride and avarice, which could be identified less easily. Although seventeenth-century sessions had always shown a deep interest in sexual sin, the Form of Process gave even greater impetus to a concentration on fornication and associated offences such as adultery, 'scandalous carriage' (improper behaviour), illegitimacy and 'irregular marriage' (which took place outside the formal procedures of the Church). These were all visible actions which could be prosecuted through the careful and intrusive surveillance of local elders, followed by interrogation before the session. Thus, by the 1750s, sexual offences made up the majority of cases before most kirk sessions. Only profanation of the Sabbath and occasional drunkenness also featured significantly in the lists of complaints by then.

Certain social groups were also plainly outside the direct control of the Church. Foremost among these were the landed classes, not simply the aristocracy but also the petty gentry. There is abundant evidence that the social élite could offend with impunity and escape with a token payment to the poor fund of the parish. In 1719 and 1720, for instance, Alexander Robertson of Webster Straloch ignored demands to appear before the session despite fathering three bastard children by three different girls. Likewise, the Earl of Caithness, the Earl of Aboyne and the Earl of Wemyss all produced illegitimate children around the same period but were not subjected to any public discipline. Even the dependants, factors and servants of landed households seemed to have been exempt. A second group immune from discipline were army soldiers, who were not under the authority of the parish and could not be brought before the session. But if a soldier had fathered an illegitimate child with a local woman, she was still expected to do penance. Vagrants who were not attached to a specific parish were also less easily controlled. Some contemporaries suggested that there were large numbers of these rootless people outside the authority of Church and state alike. In 1698 Andrew Fletcher of Saltoun painted an intimidating picture of a vast army of vagrants living wild and preying on civilized society: 'In years of Plenty many thousands of these meet together in the Mountains, where they feast and riot for many days . . . at country weddings, Burials and other like public occasions they are to be seen both Men and Women perpetually drunk.'[1] He also accused them of ignoring the Christian religion and of practising incest and murder. Fletcher of Saltoun may have exaggerated the numbers considerably but at any one time, especially in years of poor harvest, many people would be on the road who were not permanently attached to a particular parish and hence not under the watchful eye of local sessions.

These, however, were the exceptions. In most parts of the Lowlands before the later eighteenth century the majority of the population appear to have accepted the discipline of the Church. This has recently been confirmed in a study of a large number of contemporary kirk session registers by Rosalind Mitchison and Leah Leneman which shows that the discipline of the Church and its punishments for breaching the sexual moral code were broadly accepted, despite the fact that the sanctions which could actually be used by kirk sessions in pursuit of offenders were relatively limited. Thus, although fathers of bastard children usually denied guilt or paternity at first, most in the end were willing to make public penance. Mitchison and Leneman estimate that in their national sample as many as two-thirds of those accused of paternity outside marriage eventually admitted to fatherhood within a month. This admission involved agreeing to contribute to the support of the child for a period of several years and enduring public rebuke and the humiliation of appearing before the congregation on a number of occasions before the session was finally satisfied that the sinner was truly contrite and could be absolved. Three appearances were formally required in church for 'simple fornication', six for a second offence or 'relapse', 26 for adultery and a year for incest. All these appearances were supposed to be made in sackcloth. A fine of £10 Scots was also levied which was waived in the case of the poor. Not everybody accepted these punishments. In the south-west region, the proportion of men admitting paternity was the lowest in Scotland and there was also a high number of cases in this region where women absconded rather than submit to session discipline. In addition, and co-existing with the puritanism of the sessions and their elders, a rich bawdy tradition flourished which was not only found among the upper social classes but was also an important part of the popular culture of tenants, cottars and servants, as is shown vividly in some of the songs of Robert Burns. Occasions such as New Year and Shrove Tuesday before Lent offered plentiful opportunities for heavy drinking and *hougmagandie* (fornication) which provoked a stream of angry but apparently ineffectual denunciations from the Kirk.

Moreover, by 1800 there were a number of signs that traditional discipline within the Established Church was beginning to crumble, though the formal structure of control did not finally collapse until the middle decades of the nineteenth century. It became much more common for kirk sessions to demand a monetary fine rather than the public appearance of the sinner before the congregation. Since these penalties were often channelled directly into support for the poor, the movement away from public rebuke may have been partly influenced by the need to increase payments to the poor in the later eighteenth century (as is described in the last section of this chapter). In earlier times, fines had principally been paid by members of the landed and professional classes who were anxious to avoid public humiliation and who had the ability to pay. But now the practice became more general. In the 1760s, for instance, the change was noted in Dundee, Alyth, several parishes in Aberdeenshire and a number in Ayrshire. But the public rebuke was still widespread and fines were still beyond the means of many who appeared before the session. Women in particular, because of their lower earnings, often had difficulty in making payment.

More fundamental in the changing nature of discipline was the undermining of the testificat system and the unity of the Church of Scotland. These two factors had ensured that the structure of discipline extended over most of the country and that there were few hiding places for the guilty. Now, after c. 1750, both came under pressure. The system of certificates of good conduct issued by the kirk session of the parish from which a person was leaving and without which the receiving parish would not formally accept the incoming migrant could function only when movement in general was limited and localized. As migration accelerated with rapid urban growth in the later eighteenth century it became much more difficult to enforce. Mobility in the countryside also became greater than ever before with the consolidation of tenancies, the removal of cottars and the foundation of rural villages, settlements and industrial centres. Emigration to North America became more common and by the 1770s Scotland was contributing proportionately more to the transatlantic exodus than any other part of the United Kingdom. One interesting sign of greater freedom of movement was a sharp increase in 'irregular' marriages which took place without the blessing of the Church among the rural population after c. 1750.

It was in this period too that the first serious impact of religious dissent began to be felt. The long-term effects of the Patronage Act of 1712, which asserted the rights of lay patrons to appoint ministers to vacant charges in the Church, now became much more apparent. From the 1730s, when patrons first started to enforce their powers, serious tensions emerged within the Kirk between those willing to accept lay influence and those who were resolutely opposed. In 1740 the General Assembly expelled a group of ministers, led by Ebenezer Erskine of Stirling, who were committed to the traditional rigours of Calvinism. They went on to form the Associate Presbytery (or Secession Church), which later split again into no fewer than four new dissenting Presbyterian congregations: the Old Licht Burghers and the New Licht Burghers, the Old Licht Anti-Burghers and the New Licht Anti-Burghers. The names of these bodies indicated profoundly different points of view concerning the loyalty of taking oaths to the civil authorities and whether or not earlier covenanting traditions of the seventeenth century were permanent and fixed or could be amended by changing circumstances. A second and much more important secession took place in 1752 and led to the formation of the Relief Church under Thomas Gillespie. This not only attracted much greater numbers than the Associate Presbytery but also offered a more liberal alternative to the Established Church. The Relief Church, for instance, imposed no doctrinal requirements on those who wished to attend communion.

Dissenting churches proved remarkably popular. One educated guess suggests that as many as 100,000 had already joined the Relief Church by the 1760s. Later figures are more reliable, and by the 1820s it was reckoned that as many as 38 per cent of the Scottish population were attached to dissenting or Roman Catholic churches, which recruited particularly well in towns and industrializing communities among the lower-middle classes, artisans and textile workers. This pattern demonstrates that discipline did not weaken because society in Scotland became less religious. On the contrary, the Christian message still had widespread popular appeal and the fracturing of the Established Church was one sign of the passionate commitment of large numbers of people to religious principles. But the development of dissent did have two effects. First, effective discipline depended on a network of communications between parishes in order to prevent those under examination by a kirk session absconding outside the jurisdiction of the Church. With larger and larger numbers attracted to the dissenting congregations, the system inevitably came under pressure. Second, while some dissenting churches were very committed to discipline of the traditional type, others, notably the Relief Church, were more influenced by other beliefs that stressed the conversion and commitment of individual Christians rather than the obligation to maintain the tradition of all the community and congregation as members of the elect. Thus movement away from preservation of the moral conformity of the group in favour of an individual route to salvation made public penance less significant. These currents of thought were also important in the Church of Scotland itself. Perhaps it was because of them that in the early 1800s the Kirk started to discourage the practice of public discipline which had been central to its mission since the era of the Reformation, though it did not finally disappear until the second half of the nineteenth century.

2

The Scottish system of schooling from the Reformation to the Industrial Revolution attracted lavish praise from contemporary commentators and later observers. Sir John Sinclair, writing in 1826, noted how 'in former times, the commons of Scotland were considered to be the most enlightened people of that rank in Europe'.[2] More recently, the distinguished English historian of the seventeenth century, Sir George Clark, broadened the geographical scope further and referred to the rural Scots of this period as 'the most enlightened peasantry in the world'.[3] In Victorian times, there developed the notion of the 'lads o' pairts', talented boys from humble background who had been able to rise above their station in life through the meritocratic system of schooling which offered a ladder of opportunity leading to the universities and on to the professions. The parish school was also seen as the cradle of the 'democratic intellect' where, it was said, the children of lairds rubbed shoulders with the offspring of ploughmen. This mixing of the classes produced, so it was argued, a more egalitarian society than England and was a way of asserting distinctive Scottish values in the one area where the Scots believed themselves not simply the equal but the superiors of the English. This section will consider the validity of some of these claims.

Scotland before the Reformation was not, as is often assumed, an educational wilderness. The Reformers after 1560 were building on foundations that had been put in place by the old Church. Three universities had been founded, at St Andrews, Aberdeen and Glasgow, most towns of any significance had a grammar school by 1500 and the schools attached to collegiate churches, abbeys and cathedrals were probably also open to the laity. However, the Protestant approach to education differed in three important respects from what had gone before. First, in the Calvinist manifesto, the *Book of Discipline*, the Kirk placed schooling and literacy at the very heart of its programme for religious revolution. It was the means by which the essential precepts of religious belief were to be instilled in the young. Schooling was not designed to liberate the mind but rather, in the words of the *Book of Discipline*, to foster 'the virtuous education and godly upbringing of the youth of this realm'. In addition, if all were now to be given direct access to the Word of God in the scriptures and if members of the laity were to play a central part in the governance of the church in their role as elders, then education took on a new significance. Second, the aspirations of the Reformers after 1560 were both systematic and coherent: they aimed for universal education with a schoolmaster in every parish in the land who would provide the foundations of literacy for all. They also had ambitious plans for linking the parish schools to town grammar schools and universities in order to develop an integrated system. Third, and most crucially, the Kirk was able eventually to gain the support of the state in support of its programme. In a series of Acts of the Scottish Privy Council and Parliament in 1616, 1633, 1646 and 1696, heritors (local landowners) were taxed in each parish to maintain a school and a suitably qualified master. The 1696 legislation used to be seen as the key development because it included measures for enforcing the mechanism of funding but it is now better viewed as the climax rather than the beginning of the process of state support. The system which had evolved by the end of the seventeenth century was unique in Britain. In England, for instance, elementary education was based on private fee-paying schools, charities and endowments until the later nineteenth century and, despite attempts in several countries to introduce a national system, the pattern throughout the continent remained very similar. In Scotland, however, the role of the state provided legal stability and permanence and, through the taxation of local landowners, helped keep school fees down. The influence of the Kirk was also central. Local ministers and presbyteries conscientiously monitored and inspected standards and ensured that the Bible and the catechism were the basic texts in the curriculum in which all should receive instruction.

It is not surprising that it took some time to realize this ambitious programme but evidence from the later seventeenth century suggests considerable progress had been made in several Lowland areas to achieve the ideal of a school in each parish. Advances were especially apparent in the Lothians and in the counties of the north-east. In the 1690s, at least 61 of the 65 Lothian parishes had schools and 42 of the 44 parishes in Angus. On the other hand, the picture in Stirlingshire, Ayrshire, Renfrewshire and Dumfriesshire was less rosy, with several parishes still without a schoolmaster. Clearly, despite legislation, some landowners continued to evade their responsibilities. Nevertheless, by the time of the *Statistical Account* a century later in the 1790s, the network of parish schools in the Lowlands seems to have become virtually complete. Donald Withrington has also recently shown that the Highlands and Northern Isles were not the educational deserts they were once thought to be. He estimates that nearly 84 per cent of parishes in Gaeldom and in Orkney and Shetland had schools in the later eighteenth century, though not necessarily all of those were 'parish schools' as strictly defined. Provision was especially well developed in the southern, central and eastern Highlands, but much less so in the western mainland and Outer Hebrides.

The development of the national system of parish schools established by law and under public control was a considerable achievement but it formed the most important part of a much broader and more diverse structure which was becoming more complex over time. The position in the urban areas was significantly different from that of the country. The burghs had a similar responsibility under law to provide schools as the rural parishes, but there were two key differences. First, before the Reformation the burgh councils had achieved control over schooling and this tradition was maintained afterwards. Second, the ideal of the single school in every parish required by law was not suited to the needs of densely populated urban areas. Smaller burghs compared well with neighbouring country districts in educational provision and councils in the larger towns often supported 'English' schools which taught reading and some arithmetic. But their main concern was the grammar school where Latin formed an important part of the curriculum and where instruction could lead to the universities. But as growth developed in the later eighteenth century, more and more migrants were moving to the larger towns where schooling for the majority of the population had traditionally been poorer than in the countryside. One estimate suggests as many as one-third of the inhabitants of Edinburgh were illiterate in the mid-eighteenth century.

In fact, the most dynamic feature of schooling in the large burghs was a response to the new needs of the expanding business and professional classes rather than the basic requirements for literacy of the urban masses. As early as 1695, Glasgow appointed a teacher of navigation and book-keeping, and Edinburgh in 1705 hired a former merchant as 'Professor of Book-keeping to the city'. These subjects were also introduced at Ayr, Dunbar, Stirling and Perth in the first few decades of the eighteenth century. An even more radical departure was the foundation of town academies, which were designed to provide an intensive education in modern subjects for those who intended to become merchants and manufacturers at a much lower rate than that currently charged by universities. These vocational schools would exclude classics and instead concentrate on mathematics, history, physics, chemistry, natural science and astronomy. The first academy was established at Perth in 1761 and a further eight followed between then and 1810 at Dundee, Inverness, Elgin, Montrose, Ayr, Annan, Dumfries and Tain. These were not private ventures but were supported by subscription funds and were either managed or strongly influenced by the local council.

In the countryside, too, any educational monopoly that the Kirk had had in the seventeenth century rapidly broke down in the eighteenth. Even in earlier decades there had been private fee-paying or 'adventure' schools outside the statutory system because parishes were often too large for one master to satisfy the demand. But the system came under acute pressure after 1750 with rising population and the significant increase in migration not only from country to town but also within the rural districts. The veritable explosion in the number of private schools at this time was, however, confirmation that there was a widespread popular demand for basic literacy. One typical local example must suffice to illustrate the point. In the 1750s there were no fewer than six schools in the Highland Perthshire parish of Blair Atholl. One was the parish school, which in 1755 enrolled 250 scholars; a second was a charity school; another was erected by the factor on the nearby forfeited estates of Strowan and Lochgarry; and the remaining three were all private schools. These foundations together taught 165 pupils. This pattern was a local microcosm of developments throughout rural Scotland. By 1818, a Select Committee of the House of Commons concluded that there were 40 per cent more pupils in the 'adventure' schools than in the parochial and burghal schools. In the west central region of extensive urbanization no less than two-thirds of the school population now attended private schools. Only in the Border counties were the majority of pupils still being served by the traditional system. There was also a good deal of informal education which is not revealed in precise terms in any record: women running 'dame' schools in their houses, parents in country districts distant from the parish school combining to employ itinerant teachers on a short-term basis, and instruction within the family, particularly of girls, for whom formal schooling was thought to be less of a priority.

The Highlands were the scene of the most ambitious organized attempt to supplement the parish school network with a charitable initiative. As already suggested, the Kirk had successfully established a number of schools in most Highland areas by the 1750s. Indeed, by the end of the eighteenth century it is reckoned that almost all parishes in the region had a public school, even if the immense size of some Highland parishes (Kilmalie in Inverness, for instance, was thirty miles wide and sixty miles long) together with the predominance of the Gaelic language limited their impact considerably. The foundation of the Scottish Society for the Propagation of Christian Knowledge (SSPCK) in 1709 came about because of Presbyterian anxieties about the apparent resurgence of militant popery in parts of the western Highlands and the north-east and the related potent threat of Jacobite disaffection. The SSPCK's mission was to establish schools to teach the true religion and instruction in English because Gaelic was viewed as one of the roots of the 'barbarity and ignorance' from which political disloyalty was generated. The number of the Society's schools rose from five in 1711 to 176 by 1758 with nearly 6,500 pupils in attendance. The SSPCK was only the first of several societies dedicated to the Christian instruction of the Gaels. It was followed in the early nineteenth century by the Gaelic Societies of Edinburgh, Glasgow and Inverness, which gave an important impetus to the evangelical revolution that swept across the western Highlands in those decades.

The pattern of Scottish schooling had therefore developed a rich texture between the seventeenth and early nineteenth centuries. The Kirk in combination with the state and local landowners provided an initial impetus, but the system had quickly achieved a remarkable diversity, particularly in the second half of the eighteenth century with the prolific growth of adventure and charity schools. A significant Scottish characteristic was, therefore, the widespread availability of education. In the parish system, fees were kept relatively low because the heritors contributed to the cost of the master's salary and the schoolhouse. In the 1790s in Midlothian, for instance, the rates were 1/6d (7.5p) a quarter for reading and writing and 2/- (10p) for Latin and arithmetic. These sums were typical of most areas. Kirk sessions were also supposed to assist the poor of their parish and throughout the eighteenth century were very reluctant to allow any increase in the fees for the core subjects of reading and writing in order to ensure that instruction in these basic skills was as widely available as possible. Almost certainly, therefore, education became cheaper in the later eighteenth century as average rural incomes in many parts of the

Lowlands rose in real terms from the 1770s. The other side of this coin was greater pressure on the living standards of schoolmasters. As early as 1749, their plight had led them to petition parliament, seeking redress and requesting an increase in stipend. Yet these very financial problems encouraged some rural schoolmasters to broaden their teaching to include 'new' subjects such as geography, French and book-keeping, since they were permitted to charge a higher fee on these. From at least the later seventeenth century, the parish schools had offered Latin to some pupils. For instance, in 1690 virtually all the 42 parish schoolmasters in Angus were able to teach Latin. Now the curriculum was broadening even further, to include subjects of direct vocational relevance which were also becoming more important in the burgh schools and central to the teaching of the new academies. This was a distinctive feature of Scottish education, not found to the same extent in England or in Europe, and a factor that was not without relevance to the precocious rate of Scottish economic development after *c.* 1760.

A major reason for the increasing scale of school provision in the eighteenth century was the demand for basic literacy. The *Statistical Account* of the 1790s is full of evidence that the rural population placed great value on education even though schooling was neither free nor compulsory. In the parish of Yetholm it was claimed 'parents will submit to considerable privations, rather than not send their children to school'.[4] Here, as elsewhere, it was a question of pride for many families. From Old Luce parish it was indicated that the poorer classes considered it a disgrace not to have their children taught to read and write. In the *General View of the Agriculture of Midlothian* (1793) the reporter noted that ordinary people 'would be ashamed if they could not at least read the English language'. The motivation for many was the ability to read the scriptures and the personal disgrace they might feel if they were unable to use the Bible in the kirk.

It is much more difficult, however, to determine the standards of literacy that were actually achieved through this wide availability of education. Full-time schooling, even in the parish system, was of short duration, with attendance usually starting at the age of seven, lasting no more than a year or two for poor scholars and less than four or five years for the majority. The *Book of Discipline* itself had stated that two years was sufficient 'to learn to read perfectly, to answer to the Catechism, and to have some entrance to the first rudiments of Grammar'. Attendance at school also fluctuated markedly, with numbers falling off dramatically in summer when children were needed for vital work at the harvest. The fee structure also had an effect on the skills that were acquired. Writing was more expensive than reading, was often charged separately from it and was taught later than reading. Not surprisingly, then, there is a good deal of evidence that many families were mainly interested in their children being able to read and that they regarded writing as a lower priority. In addition, there were profound regional variations in literacy. As already seen, significant efforts had been made to develop schooling in the Highlands but this had uneven results. Inquiries in the 1820s showed that in the central and eastern counties reading abilities were widespread, but in the far west and in many of the Hebrides the levels constrained by poverty and geography were much below those normally attained in parishes in the rural Lowlands.

It is against this background of changing influences that one scholar, Rab Houston, has tried to measure Scottish literacy in this period through the technique of analysing signatures in legal documents and other sources. He argues that by this criterion literacy among males was around 65 per cent in the 1750s but was much lower for women, with no more than 25–30 per cent able to sign their names on the sample of documents examined. These results suggest that Scottish literacy levels were no higher than those of northern England (though much superior to England and Wales taken as a whole), Prussia, Sweden and some Catholic areas of north-eastern France. Houston also contends that universal Scottish literacy was not only a myth but that literacy standards varied significantly across the social hierarchy and depended to a large extent on income and occupation. The ability to sign was widespread among the landed, professional and mercantile classes but much less developed among those of lower social rank.

Houston's work confirms that writing was not yet a generally developed skill in eighteenth-century Scotland for the reasons of cost and practical value already described. It does not follow, however, that reading was similarly constricted. On the contrary, in Denmark and Sweden, where excellent records exist, nearly universal reading ability has been documented, though sign-literacy was even less common than in Scotland and was not finally achieved widely until after state legislation in the nineteenth century. We cannot be as certain as this for Scotland because the available data are much poorer in quality but it is likely that at least in the rural Lowlands and the smaller towns by

c. 1760 reading literacy was very extensive. Indeed, despite the stresses imposed by industrialization, one survey of Scottish mill-workers carried out in 1833 suggested that the ability to read was virtually universal among them.

Whether the achievement in schooling promoted real equality of opportunity and allowed many 'lads o' pairts' to achieve upward mobility from the poorer classes is more debatable. Access to Scottish universities was certainly more open than in England and several other European countries. It was also cheaper to study in them. At Glasgow, for instance, the fee of £5 a year was one-tenth of the cost of attending Oxford or Cambridge. The Scottish universities also emphasized professional training in law, medicine and divinity and they were also increasingly expanding into areas of practical science. They certainly appealed to those seeking to make a career in the world on the basis of ability and training rather than of inherited position. There was no entrance qualification other than Latin (which made universities open to the products of the parish schools) and access was facilitated by the tradition of taking students at the young age of between 14 and 16. The number of places rose faster than the rate of national population growth in the eighteenth century, and virtually trebled from 1,450 in the 1720s to around 4,250 by the 1820s. The Scottish universities (and particularly Glasgow) certainly recruited from a much broader social range than Oxford and Cambridge which tended to attract students from mainly landed, church and professional backgrounds. In the period 1740–1839, for instance, almost half of those matriculating at Glasgow came from 'industry and commerce'. However, these were usually the sons of merchants, manufacturers, shopkeepers and skilled tradesmen rather than of labourers or the really poor. The universities aided the career progression of the lower-middle classes rather than the upward mobility of the vast majority of Scots. Robert Anderson's verdict for the 1860s that a minister's son was a hundred times more likely to go to university than a miner's son was almost certainly true also of earlier decades.

Not all the assumptions therefore made about the 'democratic intellect' and 'lads o' pairts' stand up to close scrutiny. Nevertheless, the achievement in schooling initiated by the Presbyterian Church in the sixteenth and seventeenth centuries was still impressive by any standards. Reading literacy was widespread and education available in most parts of the country at low cost. Close connections existed between the parish school system, the burgh schools and the universities. Profound differences of attainment did exist on the basis of gender, social class and region, but even these complexities cannot hide the fact that a national system had developed in the eighteenth century which was later enlarged by the dynamic expansion of private schooling in subsequent decades.

The general consequences for Scottish society were obviously profound. The fact that instruction in the parish and dissenting schools was based on scripture both reflected and enhanced the religious ethos that prevailed in so many communities. Some commentators go further and argue that education under the strong influence and control of the Kirk was a factor that did much to promote social conformity and disciplined acceptance of the existing social hierarchy and hence was one of the reasons lowland Scotland remained so peaceful during the great and disruptive changes associated with the Agricultural Revolution. But this view, that education was a channel for the inculcation of social passivity, can be questioned, not least because challenges to authority in the form of riots and disturbance were far more common in the eighteenth century than is implied. Indeed, one of the most enduring forms of agitation was robust protest in the Church of Scotland itself against unpopular ministers imposed on local congregations through the patronage system. Furthermore, the educational hegemony of the Kirk was breaking down in the eighteenth century with the dynamic growth of private schools and the expansion of the towns where the role of the Church had always been less significant and more secular subjects were entering the curriculum even at the level of the parish school. Some scholars suggest also that, since agricultural reform depended much on the initiative of the tenantry, 'the high level of literacy might have been an important bonus to Scotland: an educated peasantry more readily turns its back on immemorial tradition because it finds on the printed page an alternative form of authority, and much of the new farming technology was disseminated in books and articles'.[5] Just as crucial was the boom in middle-class education in the burgh schools, academies and universities which helped to equip Scottish merchants, entrepreneurs and professional groups to exploit the economic opportunities in the era of the Industrial Revolution. The rapid penetration of the Scottish middle classes into trade, administration and professional services in the empire after *c*. 1750 was in part due to the relatively limited opportunities at home but it was also facilitated by the training they had received in basic numeracy, literacy and often in an impressively wide range of vocational skills.

3

Like schooling, the foundations of Scottish society's provision for the poor were established before the Reformation. Statutes concerning the just treatment of the poor can be found as far back as the twelfth century and in the fifteenth and early sixteenth centuries legislation, not all of it effective, drew the important distinction between those able to earn their livelihood and others who had to rely on charity. Only this second group, the crippled, blind, sick or weak, were to be allowed to beg. The merely idle had to be found work, imprisoned or banished. In 1535 came the important act of parliament which confined licensed begging to the parish of the beggar's birth, thus stating the fundamental principle that each parish should have the responsibility for its own poor. What is usually seen as the basis of the Scottish Poor Law, the Act of 1574 entitled 'Anent [concerning] the Punishment of Strong and Idle Beggars and Provision for Sustenation of the Poor and Impotent', incorporated these previous enactments and, in addition, declared that the residents of a parish were to be taxed to support the poor. The 1574 legislation therefore did not simply continue past practice but stated the need for more generous provision for the poor, backed up by legal sanctions and a reliable source of revenue.

Unfortunately, however, the Act was virtually a dead letter until the middle decades of the seventeenth century. The Kirk was too much concerned to establish its own structure of parish organization through-out Scotland to have either the time, energy or resources to devote to the systematic provision of poor relief. Like education, provision for the poor was a longer-term priority. In 1574 the administration of poor relief became the responsibility of the provost and baillies in the towns, but from 1597 the authority in the country was the kirk session until another Act in 1672 entrusted the implementation of the Poor Law jointly to it and the local landowners who had the legal power to raise assessments in support of the poor. By this time, many Lowland parishes were active in providing for the poor, not least during the terrible harvest failures of the 1690s, and from the early eighteenth century the number of kirk sessions taking the responsibility more seriously also visibly increased. The vast majority of parishes developed some basic provision, except perhaps in the western Highlands where formal support was much more limited. Rosalind Mitchison has admirably summarized the general pattern:

Parishes regularly put the old and infirm on pension rolls, supported orphans and foundlings by boarding them out with pensioners, paid for the schooling of these children and of others whose parents could not afford school fees, arranged for the care of the insane, made contributions towards the cost of surgery or wet-nursing, joined with other parishes in supporting poor students at the University and buried paupers with a reasonable allocation of ale and tobacco for the mourners, while claiming whatever personal property these paupers left.[6]

This is an impressive list of contributions to the welfare of the poor and clearly reveals the impact of the Christian ethic in social action. Moreover, unlike the more rigorous approach which developed in Scotland in the early nineteenth century, the parish records even show assistance being provided to able-bodied individuals on an occasional basis because of temporary misfortune or disability. Kirk sessions seem to have taken the pragmatic view that, even though legislation of 1661 stated that no one was to receive relief if able to earn a living, helping those in temporary difficulty would prevent them becoming a long-term burden on the parish and that would eventually save money. The sessions could use the one-half of church collections not legally belonging to the poor for this purpose. This approach seems to have been widely adopted in years of crop failures such as 1772–3, 1782–3, 1795–6 and 1799–1800, when the cost of meal rose significantly. Indeed, it was as a result of support given during the last of these that the Court of Session itself (in the case of *Pollock v. Darling*) found that the able-bodied were entitled to relief under the Poor Laws. In this period also a number of parishes, especially in the Lothians, Borders and Stirlingshire, started to operate a system of subsidizing food because of sharp increases in meal prices in the 1790s. With the expansion in rural industrialization, more and more families depended on wages rather than growing their own food, and some parishes were willing to provide support in this changing world. The most famous example came from Prestonkirk in East Lothian, where oatmeal and barley were purchased by the parish and distributed to families at different levels of subsidies according to income.

This more liberal approach to poor relief did not come cheaply. Traditionally a significant proportion of the parish fund for the poor was based on charitable donations reflecting the Christian ethic of benevolent concern for the poor. Thus one-half of church door collections, mortifications (legacies) and other offerings went to support the poor, as well as income from fines, mortcloth dues, fees from the proclamation of marriages and the like. However, the more expansive Poor Law of the eighteenth century demanded more resources and this led to the spread of assessment involving the taxing of local landowners, who then passed on half the burden to the tenantry. Assessment did not become common everywhere; in general terms, it seems to have been mainly confined to the more prosperous regions of the Lowlands where landlords and tenants could support higher levels of expenditure. By the later eighteenth century some landowners at least were prepared to pay for a greater provision for need and more effective control of vagrancy. In addition to the expansion of assessment, individual landlords during years of harvest crisis such as 1740 made gifts of meal, money and coal for the poor not simply in their own parish but in adjacent areas. Throughout the century, landowners also came together in county schemes to suppress vagrancy and ensure that each parish supported its own poor. One large-scale project in the early 1770s covered 11 counties, from Argyll to Fife.

Some see all this as a result of the spreading influence among the governing classes of the intellectual fashion of 'civic humanism' which stressed the responsibilities of the élite for the creation of a better and more civilized society. But it might also be viewed as a more practical and realistic approach to support the poor and control vagrancy at a time of increasing economic change that could have threatened to undermine social hierarchy and traditional discipline. The fear of vagrancy, for instance, may reflect anxieties about an increase in the numbers of those outside the old structure of local conformity based on church, school and Poor Law as migration accelerated on a scale never experienced in the past. The rural Lowlands were remarkably free of social unrest during the classic period of agrarian transformation between c. 1760 and 1815. Arguably, the more flexible Poor Law and related schemes of support which developed at this time helped to provide a basic safety net for those dispossessed who were threatened with absolute destitution and so can be regarded as one of the factors that reduced the possibilities of serious social disturbance.

6

Scotland Transformed

I

By the middle decades of the eighteenth century the Scottish economy was on the move. Glasgow had become the leading tobacco entrepôt in the United Kingdom and one of the prominent port cities in western Europe. Some 47 million lb. of American tobacco were imported in 1771 and the Glaswegian merchants had carved out a greater and greater share of the British trade at the expense of rivals in London, Liverpool, Whitehaven and Bristol. As late as 1738, the Scots accounted for only 10 per cent of the total British importation; but by 1765 this had risen to an astonishing 40 per cent of a UK trade which had itself expanded remarkably in the intervening decades. One of the most important aspects of this dazzling success story was that the new tobacco commerce renewed the old connections with Europe that had been eroded by sea war and economic nationalism earlier in the eighteenth century. Over 90 per cent of the tobacco imported was eventually re-exported to French, Dutch and German markets. The dynamic growth of linen manufacture, Scotland's premier industry, paralleled the remarkable achievements in overseas trade as output rose fourfold in value between the years 1736–40 and 1768–72. At the last date, nearly 13 million yards were stamped for sale by the Board of Trustees, and linen then employed around 20,000 handloom weavers and a much greater army of female spinners drawn from rural and urban households throughout the length and breadth of Scotland.

There was also a series of landmark developments which seemed to signal a new age of prosperity and progress. The Royal Bank of Scotland was founded in 1727 and the British Linen Company in 1746. The establishment of the Royal soon led to the development of the 'cash accompt' in 1728, the world's first overdraft facility, while the Linen

Company was the only British chartered bank in the eighteenth century devoted specifically to the encouragement of industry. Banking also flourished elsewhere, notably in Glasgow with the Arms, Ship and Thistle banks, promoted vigorously by some of the city's wealthiest merchant princes. In 1759 came the foundation of Carron Iron Works, which was almost a symbol of economic modernity in Scotland. It was established to work and smelt iron on a large scale, using the latest techniques pioneered by the Coalbrookdale Company in England. The Prestonpans Vitriol Works had been set up 10 years earlier and also developed an enviable reputation at the leading edge of the chemistry of textile finishing.

In less spectacular but equally important fashion, significant developments can also be identified in rural society. Commercial forces were now undeniably having a much greater impact, both in the Highlands and in the Lowland countryside. The black cattle trade from the central and western Highlands was one of the clear-cut success stories in the decades immediately following the union. By the 1750s, however, exports of timber, slate and fish from Gaeldom were also becoming significant. Similarly, in many parts of the Lowland countryside, market forces were becoming more dominant. This is confirmed by the evidence of changes in the rental structure, where payments in kind were tending to become less common and were being steadily replaced by cash rents. On a number of estates a radical change in tenure was under way as proprietors converted more and more smaller holdings into larger individual tenancies which meant that the capitalist farming class of the Agricultural Revolution of later years was already emerging in embryonic form.

Manifestly, therefore, the Scottish economy of the 1750s was more stable, dynamic and prosperous than at the time of the union. Equally, however, the scale and significance of the changes should be kept in perspective. There had been real advances *within* the existing structure of economy and society, but precious little indication yet that the *overall* social fabric of Scotland was being altered. Overwhelmingly the country remained a rural society with only one Scot in eight living in a town (defined as communities of 4,000 or more) in 1750. In a European league table of 'urbanized societies' using a different measure (of the proportion of the population living in towns of 10,000 inhabitants and above) Scotland was 11th out of 16 in 1650, 10th in 1700 and 7th in 1750. The proportion of town dwellers was increasing but the overall Scottish distribution of population was still more akin to that of Ireland, the Scandinavian countries and Poland than to the more advanced European economies of England and Holland. In 1750, for instance, 17 per cent of the people of England lived in towns of 10,000 or more, compared to less than 9 per cent in Scotland at that date.

Moreover, the life of the countryside, where most Scots lived and worked, was still based within traditional structures that would have been recognizable and familiar to earlier generations. Contemporary estate maps show that in most areas, outside the progressive south-eastern counties, the landscape had hardly changed at all. Traditional rig cultivation and the scattered mosaic of irregular fields divided among different tenants were all very visible. Enclosure had made little progress outside the advanced enclaves and the 'improved' agricultural methods were rarely practised by most working farmers. As a result, average yields for oats and barley remained much the same as those of the later seventeenth century. The same pattern of continuity was also evident in social structure. Already by the early eighteenth century the three-tier social order of landlords, tenants and landless wage-labourers predominated in the midland and southern counties of England. In Scotland, however, the majority of the rural population maintained some connection with the land. Indeed, before the later eighteenth century, there were few entirely landless groups in the Scottish countryside. Cottar families with patches of land could still be found in large numbers in many parishes. Rural tradesmen, such as weavers, blacksmiths, tailors and masons, normally possessed a piece of land. All in all, therefore, Scotland's rural social structure had much more in common with that of most continental European societies than with its closest neighbour to the south.

This traditional pattern, of basic continuity marked by some changes at the margin, abruptly came to an end in the 1760s. That decade seems to have been a defining watershed because from then on Scotland began to experience a social and economic transformation unparalleled among European societies of the time in its speed, scale and intensity. The currently favoured view of English modernization, as a process charac-terized by cumulative, protracted and evolutionary development, does not fit the Scottish experience. North of the border there truly was an Industrial and Agricultural Revolution. In fact, recent research on comparative urban development in Europe suggests that the explosive Scottish rate of town and city growth was the fastest of any region in

Britain or the Continent between 1750 and 1850. In 1750, Scotland was seventh in the 'league' table of European 'urbanized societies', fourth in 1800 but second only to England and Wales in 1850. By then, over one-third of Scots lived in towns of more than 5,000 inhabitants, a figure that does not include those who were being drawn in from the countryside to the small factory towns and planned villages which multiplied in this period. At the same time, a general reconfiguration of the demographic map of Scotland was taking place. Migration was under way on an unprecedented scale since the towns could grow rapidly only by inward movement from the country. In 1851, for instance, over half the inhabitants of the 10 principal Scottish towns were migrants, not only from the Highlands and the rural Lowlands but increasingly also from the north of Ireland. The concentration of rapid urban growth in the Forth–Clyde valley, and particularly in the western towns, also had revolutionary effects. The Highlands and the Borders were losing people to the central Lowlands, which by the 1820s had absorbed more than half the Scottish population. The modern demographic structure of Scotland was now taking shape.

The engine of urbanization was industrialization and down to c. 1830 the main motors of growth were the textile industries of cotton, linen and wool. The omniscient Sir John Sinclair suggested that the making of fabrics together with silk production employed over 257,000 individuals in the early 1800s, representing nearly 90 per cent of all those working in manufacturing. The halcyon days of iron, engineering and shipbuilding were yet to come in the decades after 1830, and particularly from 1850. Despite the fame of Carron and the foundation of a further nine plants between 1779 and 1801, iron manufacture was much less successful than textiles before 1830. This sluggish performance was illustrated by the failure to build any additional works between 1798 and 1824 and the recurrent financial difficulties experienced by existing companies. It was therefore the textile sector above all which sustained the first phase of the Scottish Industrial Revolution and there were at least four aspects to its significance.

First, spinning was increasingly mechanized and production being concentrated in the mill complexes which, more than anything else, became the great physical symbols of the Industrial Revolution. Cotton achieved key technological advances with the adoption of the inventions from England of Hargreave's 'spinning jenny', Arkwright's waterframe and, above all, Crompton's 'mule'. When this last crucial innovation was linked to James Watt's steam engine, the cotton factories were liberated from the need to be close to sources of water power and could instead concentrate on a much bigger scale in towns and cities. By the 1820s, steam-powered flax spinning, after earlier difficulties, had transformed linen manufacture, while by the same decade all processes in the woollen industry, apart from weaving and knitting, could now be mechanized. Second, there were enormous increases in production. The average annual output of linen stamped for sale stood at 3,488,232 yards between 1728 and 1731 but had multiplied almost tenfold, to reach 30,700,100 yards, in 1818–22. The record of cotton was even more spectacular but is least amenable to long-term statistical description. Third, within the textile sector there was a recognizable trend towards regional specialization. The heart of cotton manufacture was concentrated in Glasgow, Paisley and the western Lowlands, while Dundee and the smaller towns of Angus and Fife became pre-eminent in linen and the Borders increasingly achieved a reputation as a centre of excellence for the spinning and weaving of woollens. By 1844, for instance, over half of all Scotland's worsted frames were located in one Border town, Hawick. Fourth, textile finishing experienced extensive growth and investment not only in the development of the numerous bleachfields which operated throughout the textile areas but also in the technical advances made in printing and dyeing. Perhaps the pinnacle of achievement in this respect was the establishment of the St Rollox works in Glasgow in 1799 for the manufacture of bleaching powder. It was primarily because of this initiative that Scotland began to emerge as a world leader in industrial chemicals.

Taken together, these diverse and mutually reinforcing activities of the textile industries generated a powerful dynamic for manufacturing growth at the heart of the Scottish economic system. Other activities, such as brewing, distilling and papermaking, also played a part, while recent research has demonstrated that coal mining in Scotland was more developed than used to be believed and that it managed to achieve output levels between 1760 and 1800 that were significantly higher than the British average. But textiles remained crucial before 1830. In yet another of his many estimates, this time published in 1826, Sir John Sinclair thought that over a quarter of a million people worked in cotton, linen and wool, of whom no less than 60 per cent were occupied in cotton alone. He reckoned also that only 13,000 were employed in the iron trade and 19,000 in other manufactures. It is also important to emphasize that there were significant continuities between the old and the new economic order. Even in cotton, the most advanced industry of the age, only spinning was fully mechanized before 1830, and the number of handloom weavers servicing all the textile trades continued to rise to a peak in 1840 of around 84,000. The machine was not yet triumphant and even for those labouring in industry the most common environment remained the home and the workshop rather than the mill or the large factory. It was also the case that most Scots, perhaps as many as two out of every three, still lived and died in rural communities rather than in the towns or cities.

Yet the combination of unprecedented industrial and urban expansion still had a transforming impact on Scottish society, with the effects embracing the islands of the Hebrides, and Orkney and Shetland in the north, through to the farms and the booming cities of the Lowlands. The voracious demands of the burgeoning urban and industrial areas for food, drink, raw materials and labour revolutionized agriculture and rural society throughout Scotland. The buoyant markets for kelp, fish, whisky, cattle and sheep commercialized Highland society, dissolved the traditional communal townships, encouraged the division of land into individual crofts and subordinated ancient landownership responsibilities to the new imperatives of profit. Similarly, customary relationships and connections between clan élites and followers swiftly disintegrated as the entire fabric of society was recast in response to the new rigour of landlord demands, ideological fashion and, above all, the overwhelming market pressures emanating from the south. In less than two generations Scottish Gaeldom was transformed from tribalism to capitalism.

The scale and speed of the revolution was no less remarkable in the rural Lowlands. There too the explosion in grain and meat prices after *c.* 1780 as a result of urbanization has been identified as the fundamental dynamic in rapid commercialization. It was in the two or three decades after *c.* 1760 that a recognizably modern landscape of enclosed fields, trim farms and separated holdings started to take shape in the Scottish countryside. The single farm under one master became the norm as holdings were consolidated between 1760 and 1815. By 1830, most of those who worked in Lowland agriculture were landless men and women servants whose lives were often as much subject to the pressures of labour discipline and enhanced productivity as were those who toiled in the workshops and factories of the larger towns. The market forces released by industrialism spanned the length and breadth of the land and brought a new social order into existence. Significantly, the population of all Lowland rural counties approached their peak levels by the census of 1831, and just less than a decade later in no county south of the Highland line was there a majority working in agriculture. Scotland was already set firmly on the path towards an industrial society and there had been a decisive break with the past.

2

The origins of such a transformation have long been the subject of debate among economic historians. One point is clear, as is confirmed by the example of Ireland: the process was not inevitable. In the eighteenth century, Ireland had shared with Scotland a common experience of commercial expansion. Indeed, in two key areas, linen manufacture and the trade in agricultural exports of beef, pork and butter, the Irish were significantly ahead of the Scots. But the promise of long-term growth then faded in the early nineteenth century with de-industrialization in textiles and the rapid contraction of intensive manufacturing to Belfast and the Lagan valley. To see the Scottish case as simply another regional variant of pan-European industrialization is equally unsatisfactory. This hardly explains the early timing of the Scottish transformation relative to all other nations apart from England, nor the particular and distinctive advantages which placed Scotland among a handful of European regions that successfully achieved the transition to an industrial society. The remainder of this chapter will consider these influences.

Markets

In 1755 Scotland's population numbered some 1.25 million. By 1801 this had grown to 1.6 million, and to 2.6 million by 1841. The rise in Scottish population was relatively slow and modest by comparison with other nations, with an annual rate in the second half of the eighteenth century of around 0.6, just over half that of England, and significantly behind the Irish increase of 2.1 per cent in 1791–1821. The home market in Scotland was therefore relatively small and not expanding in numbers very rapidly in the later eighteenth century. Nevertheless, the purchasing power for more goods and services was certainly rising. Urban development opened up more demand for foodstuffs, drinks, construction materials and coal. In addition, the middle-class element in the town populations was rising in both absolute and proportionate terms. Stana Nenadic reckons that the middle classes made up 15 per cent of urban inhabitants in the 1750s but around 25 per cent by the 1830s. These groups were demonstrating their collective identity in visible material terms by increasing expenditure on town houses, elegant furniture, fashionable clothing and numerous other items. At a different social level, agricultural wages, especially around the larger towns of the central Lowlands, were buoyant between 1770 and 1800. Farmers now had to compete more vigorously with manufacturers for labour precisely at a time when agricultural improvements were generating new demands for extra hands on an unprecedented scale. It is clear also that in many rural communities in the later eighteenth century family incomes were rising as many more women and children became involved in the labour market as spinners, bleachers, day labourers, factory workers and harvesters. The *Statistical Account* of the 1790s confirms that this new role for women in the labour market contributed significantly to increased working-class expenditure on coal, linen and cotton clothes, as well as on modest luxuries such as tea and sugar.

Despite its dynamism, however, the Scottish domestic market was overshadowed by the force of external influences, which became ever more powerful over time. Between 1785 and 1835, exports rose ninefold and Scotland became a key player in the Atlantic economy, the fastest-growing market place in the world in this period. Partly, the advantage came from the union of 1707, which provided duty-free protected access to the English domestic and colonial markets. Before the American War of Independence, for instance, these two areas together took over 60 per cent of the official output of Scotland's key linen manufacture. But the union connection became less crucial in the later eighteenth century. Scottish merchants were not content to rest behind the protective walls of mercantilist regulation. On the contrary, the disappearance of the major colonial market with the emergence of the independent United States in 1783 seems to have given them the impetus to expand on almost a global scale. During the first few decades of the nineteenth century, new Scottish trade links were established with South America, Asia and Australasia. At the end of the Napoleonic Wars in 1815, America and the Caribbean accounted for nearly 70 per cent of the tonnage leaving the Clyde. Much of the rest was destined for the European continent.

Natural Endowment

Success in the global market place was not inevitable but dependent ultimately on the Scottish commercial response. One favourable factor which conditioned this was geographical position and natural endowment. Not only did Scotland have a land frontier with England, the richest European economy of the eighteenth century, but it also had easy access by sea to Ireland in the west and Scandinavia and the Baltic in the east. This last connection had encouraged the migration of Scottish merchants, pedlars and soldiers in large numbers to Sweden, Norway and Poland in the sixteenth and seventeenth centuries. But when Ireland and the transatlantic economy became more influential in the later seventeenth and eighteenth centuries, Scottish traders found it relatively easy to transfer the focus of external commercial links from east to west. The rich hinterland of the central Lowlands through the ports of the Forth and the Clyde afforded the Scottish merchant classes a window *both* to Europe and to the Americas. Therefore, when Glasgow exploited the new transatlantic opportunities before and after the union, the city's merchants were able to draw on the capital, expertise and commercial traditions built up over centuries with northern Europe through the ports at the eastern end of this land corridor.

Indeed, the central Lowlands were almost fashioned by nature for industrialization. By 1800 they contained by far the largest proportion of urban dwellers of any region, with fully 60 per cent of the total town and city population of Scotland living in Glasgow and Edinburgh alone. Market demand was therefore concentrated and buoyant. Moreover, several areas (and in particular Ayrshire, Lanarkshire and Fife) were rich in coal and ironstone, the most important minerals for early industrialization, and had the additional bonus of close location to ports, sources of labour in the towns and water transport. The two great estuaries of the Forth and Clyde penetrated deep into the narrow waist of the Lowlands, a natural advantage which was then maximized by the building of three great canals, Monkland (1790), Forth and Clyde (1790) and Union (1822), all of them important for the carriage of coal and other goods low in value but heavy in bulk. With the construction of more roads and the continued expansion of the coastal trade, the central Lowlands acquired a first-class transportation network capable of large-scale exploitation of the very favourable geological advantages of the region. Some question the strategic importance of coal and iron in the first phase of industrialization since they really came into their own as crucial assets only after 1830. However, steam power, and hence the extensive use of coal as a fuel, was already widely employed in both cotton and linen spinning by the early nineteenth century. While water power did continue to be used extensively in all sectors of the economy, steam gave a new and decisive competitive advantage to the export-orientated textile industries not only by allowing unbroken production in all weathers but also through relocation of the mills from the countryside to the cities with their abundant supplies of labour. The Belfast cotton industry did not possess such easy access to rich sources of coal in the neighbourhood of the city, failed to compete with Glasgow and Paisley in the age of steam and fell behind from the 1820s.

Capital

In the seventeenth century, Scotland was one of the poorest countries in western Europe, as is shown by her persistently high levels of emigration and the experience of devastating famines in the 1620s and 1690s. Yet, a few decades after this last disaster, the country was on the threshold of a rapid economic transformation which demanded huge increases in investment in commerce, agriculture, industry and urban infrastructure. This presents a paradox and a problem for the historian: how did such a traditionally poor society finance industrialization? Four explanations might help to provide an answer.

First, the élite of the old society, the landed classes, mobilized resources on an impressive scale. Landowners were essential to the progress of agricultural improvement and invested large sums in enclosures, new farmhouses, roads and bridges. But many were also very active in financing industry, not least because so much of it was for a long period rural-based, and so manufacturing and mining could be regarded as an extension of and complementary to estate improvement. Coal, lead and ironstone mining proved particularly attractive investments to the flower of the Scottish aristocracy, such as the Dukes of Hamilton, Sutherland and Buccleuch and the Earls of Eglinton, Wemyss and Leven. Road-building, canal construction and banking were other favoured ventures of the landed classes. The nobility formed the most influential group of directors of the three chartered banks, the Bank of Scotland, the Royal Bank and the British Linen Company, and several other landowners were partners in the expanding network of provincial banks. Old wealth therefore helped to finance the new economic order. But it is important to recognize also that landownership was the main channel through which new money from the empire, the East Indies, government contracting and military service flowed back into Scotland and thereafter percolated through into industrial investment.

Second, the impact of the American trades was a direct consequence of the imperial connection and was especially significant in the west central region, the heartland of the Industrial Revolution. Colonial merchants funded 18 manufactories in Glasgow and its environs between 1730 and 1750, and a further 21 in the years 1780 to 1795. More than half the city's tobacco merchants had shares in industrial ventures in the eighteenth century into linen, cotton, coal, sugar-boiling, glass-making and many other activities. The tobacco lords also founded the city's first three banks, the Ship Bank (1752), the Arms Bank (1752) and the Thistle Bank (1761). Taken together, these activities represented a substantial influx of capital from commerce to industry. Third, Scottish society mobilized capital more efficiently through the banking system. The nation's banking assets per head rose from £0.27 in 1744 to £7.46 in 1802. Some argue that Scottish bankers were more adept in using these sums to facilitate industrialization than their more conservative counterparts in England. Certainly the banks were creative and innovative, notably in the development of the cash credit and also in increasing the small note issue. All of this helped. Nevertheless, all the detailed case studies of the accounts of industrial and merchant firms suggest that, while banking finance was commonly employed, its significance was much less than the reploughing of profits, personal and bonded loans, trading credit and often vital support from family and friends. Fourth, the new industries were built up by men of modest means who carefully reinvested as their businesses prospered. The most famous example of the breed was David Dale, who rose to become the greatest cotton magnate of his time in Scotland. He started as a weaver and then became a linen dealer and importer before founding the first of the great factory villages at New Lanark in 1786.

Technology and the English Connection

The early phase of Scottish industrialization was based overwhelmingly in borrowed technology and expertise. Ideas and skills were freely imported from Holland, France and Ireland, but England was far and away the major source. 'Technology transfer' on a remarkable scale took place from south to north, reflecting Scotland's relative backwardness and also the strategy of English businessmen who were on the lookout for cheaper labour and low-rented factory sites. The spinning revolution in cotton was entirely based on the seminal inventions of the Englishmen, Kay, Hargreaves, Arkwright and Crompton. Men with experience of English mill practice often became the managers of the early factories. The best-known of them was Archibald Buchanan who, after serving an apprenticeship at Cromford in Derbyshire, became the technical genius behind the rise of the great Scottish cotton empire of James Finlay and Co. Sulphuric acid manufacture was pioneered at Prestonpans in 1749 by Roebuck and Garbett after their earlier venture in Birmingham. The blast furnace and the coke process of smelting were both introduced from England, as was the coal-fired reverberating furnace, which was central to technical progress in the brewing, chemical, pottery and glass industries. Perhaps the most famous example of the penetration of English know-how came with the foundation in 1759 of Carron Company, Scotland's largest manufacturing plant of the day, based on the coke-smelting techniques pioneered at Coalbrookdale. The speed of Scotland's economic transformation also created technical bottlenecks and recurrent shortages of skilled labour which were often relieved by a steady trickle from England of experienced smelters, moulders, spinners and malleable ironworkers.

This is far from being a definitive list but it is enough to demonstrate that Scottish economic progress would surely have been impeded without English technical expertise and skills and, to a lesser extent, those of other countries. But these new processes were assimilated swiftly, confirming that Scotland had the appropriate social, cultural and economic environment to achieve fast industrialization. Like a latter-day Japan, having borrowed ideas from others on a grand scale, the country soon moved rapidly to the cutting edge of the new technology. A whole stream of key inventions started to emanate from Scotland including James Watt's refinement of the separate condenser for the steam engine (perhaps the fundamental technological breakthrough of the age), Neil Snodgrass's scutching machine, enabling wool to be processed effectively before being spun, Archibald Buchanan's construction of the first truly integrated cotton mill in Britain in 1807, where all the key processes were carried out by power within a single complex, Henry Bell's *Comet* of 1812, which pioneered steam propulsion for ships, and J. B. Neilson's invention in 1829 of the 'hot-blast process', which helped to transform iron manufacture by radically reducing the costs of production.

Labour

It is dangerous, however, to focus too much on technology when considering those distinctive advantages which gave the Scots a competitive edge during the Industrial Revolution. Most tasks, both in agriculture and industry, continued to be done by hand; even in cotton, the most advanced manufacturing sector of all, two of the three core processes, weaving and finishing, remained mainly labour-intensive until the 1820s. The cost of labour was therefore an absolutely crucial factor in Scottish industrialization, as was the way in which working people reacted to the strange new manufacturing processes and environments. Undeniably, wages in certain trades were rising in the later eighteenth century. For instance, agricultural workers experienced a substantial growth in real income, in the central Lowlands averaging between 40 and 50 per cent between 1750 and 1790. Nevertheless, most Scottish wages remained below those of England, and it was partly because of this attraction that English tycoons like Richard Arkwright were investing in Scottish factories in the 1780s. Arkwright boasted that the lower costs of production in Scotland would enable him to take a razor to the throat of Lancashire. Almost a century later, in the 1860s, when the first rigorous wage censuses became available, Scotland was still unequivocally a low-wage economy in most occupations compared to England. The key test of national differences in this respect was the balance of migration. When good figures were first produced in the 1840s, around 67,000 Scots and English migrated across the border. But over three-quarters of this number were Scots, who were plainly much keener to move to the greater opportunities in the south than the English were to move north.

A second advantage for Scottish entrepreneurs was the mobility of labour. Historically the Scots were a migratory people. But in the eighteenth century internal migration became more common precisely at the time when industry needed to attract more workers. Seasonal movement for harvest work from the southern and central Highlands for work in the Lowland harvests was significant after *c.* 1750. In the same region the first clearances for sheep, the transfer of people from the inland straths to the coastlands as the new crofting system was established, and the social strains coming from rampant commercializ-ation all led to more internal migration as well as promoting a large-scale exodus of people across the Atlantic after *c.* 1760. In the Lowlands agricultural improvement was radically altering the traditional social order and in the process drastically cutting back the large numbers who had always had a legal or customary right to land. The tenant class contracted further and cottar families with smallholdings possessing skills in spinning and weaving were steadily replaced by landless servants and labourers. Those who have little other than their labour power to sell are always more likely to be more mobile than a land-holding peasantry who, in the last resort, can rely on the land as a source of subsistence. Lowland Scotland certainly had larger numbers of people detached from land holding by *c.* 1800 than ever before and the resulting rates of short-distance migration were truly remarkable. One case study shows that two-thirds of the families listed for the village of Kippen in Stirlingshire in 1789 were no longer resident there in 1793. In the household of the Earl of Leven and Melville in Fife, 97 per cent of women servants and 90 per cent of men remained for only four years or less in the Earl's employment. Certainly by comparison with many rural parishes in parts of France and Germany, where most lived and died in the parish of their birth, Scottish internal mobility was a decided bonus for manufacturers keen to hire more labour.

Nevertheless, acute difficulties remained. Skill shortages abounded in coal and ironstone mining, pottery and glass-making, bleaching and nailmaking and, as already noted, could often only be made good by relying on English workers to hand on their expertise to the natives. More seriously, there was the major problem of recruiting labour to the new textile factories and large workshops. The mills crystallized the conflict between the culture of work in the old order and the new. E. P. Thomson showed that the traditional pattern was one of alternative bouts of intense labour and idleness. Full-time work, though not unknown, was unusual outside the towns and the majority of people had little interest in labouring for much longer than their basic needs required. But factory employment was radically different. Costly machinery had to be employed on a continuous basis and that meant long hours, a disciplined workforce and more rigorous supervision of labour. By the early nineteenth century, in the cotton mills even night working was not unknown when trade was brisk. Workers normally laboured for six days a week, with Sundays off and usually only a few further days annually. It was hardly an environment likely to attract large numbers of male workers at a time, in the 1780s and 1790s, when work in agriculture and handloom weaving was paying better than ever before.

But this potential recruitment crisis in the early years of industrialization was avoided. Scottish industry quickly developed a considerable dependence on women and children as sources of low-cost labour. Christopher Whatley has shown that by the 1820s they formed over 60 per cent of the total workforce in manufacturing industry and, in the cotton and flax mills, the proportion of women employed was significantly higher in Scotland than in the industrial areas of Lancashire. Women were also vital as bearers in the collieries, in the preparation of flax, the manufacture of woollen stockings and in the bleachfields. Again, unlike the pattern in Yorkshire and Lancashire, the immigrant Irish started to stream into the mills as early as the 1790s as both semi-skilled and unskilled labour. It was significant that when the powerful Glasgow Cotton Spinners Association emerged in the early nineteenth century the leadership was dominated by second-generation Irishmen whose families had earlier achieved a position in the industry in the late eighteenth century. In the early 1800s it was reckoned that around half the mill workforce in the city were either Irish-born or of Irish descent. By that time, national population growth in Scotland was starting to accelerate and in the cities the swelling number of migrants was relieving any scarcities that had previously existed in the industrial labour market. But for a period in the 1780s and 1790s, only the recruitment to the mills of Irish immigrants, Scottish women and pauper children prevented a slowing down in the momentum of industrialization.

Enterprise and Scottish Society

The proven advantages of favourable natural endowment and expanding markets would have been of little consequence if they had not been exploited effectively by enterprising merchants and manufacturers. In the Scottish case, overseas and especially imperial demand was particularly crucial to the key textile industries. It is best then to examine the quality of the business classes through their achievements in the international market place. The record is undeniably impressive.

The most striking feature is the radical geographical change in the axis of mercantile migration. By 1700 the long-established migration to Europe had dropped off and only the movement to Holland remained significant. Instead, by the later seventeenth century the Scots were starting to find new commercial opportunities across the Atlantic. In the British West Indies their role was at first less important than that of the Irish but they soon caught up and surpassed them in numbers, especially in commerce and plantation ownership. They became particularly influential in Jamaica, which produced more sugar than all the other British islands combined by the 1770s and where in 1771-5 Scots accounted for 40 per cent of the inventories after death of above £1,000. Over the same period, the share of the Irish and Jews was only 10 per cent. The impact was even more remarkable in North America. Clusters of Scottish merchants were to be found by the 1750s in the Chesapeake, where the Glasgow tobacco interest was dominant, New Jersey, Boston, Philadelphia, northern New England and the Carolinas. A few decades later, there is considerable evidence of Scottish commercial activity in India and Asia. Even before the end of the East India Company's monopoly, Scottish adventurers had set up agency houses which were permitted on licence from the Company to carry on local trade. By the 1790s, the dozen or so most powerful houses in Bengal and Bombay were dominated by Scots merchants, and jealous rivals vociferously criticized them for their clannish instincts which, they alleged, helped them to engross the business.

The jewel in the crown of this developing global network was the tobacco trade between the Clyde and the colonies of Virginia, Maryland and North Carolina. Here the Glasgow merchant firms were formidable and aggressive competitors. The first strategy in the commercial war with London, Bristol, Liverpool and Whitehaven in the 1710s and 1720s was to develop smuggling and fraud to unprecedented levels. The outcry of the English outports and government alarm led to new legislation in 1723 and 1751 and a reform of the customs service which meant that fraudulent practices soon went into rapid decline. Ironically, however, the 'golden age' of the tobacco trade started at this juncture, based on efficient business practices rather than clandestine smuggling. In 1758 Scottish tobacco imports were for the first time greater than those of all the English outports combined. Throughout these decades the Glasgow houses were carving out a greater and greater share of British imports at the expense of their southern rivals. As late as 1738, they accounted for only 10 per cent of the British total. By 1765 this had reached 40 per cent.

To some extent this achievement was based on the shorter sea crossing, and hence lower freight costs, between the Clyde and the Chesapeake compared to the voyage time from southern ports. But geography was not the decisive factor because the Scots had no such advantage over London in relation to the European markets of France and Holland where they sold most of their tobacco imports. Rather, the key influence was the effectiveness of the commercial methods of the Glasgow firms. The giant syndicates, such as John Glassford and Co., William Cunningham and Co. and Speirs, Bowman and Co., who together controlled almost half the trade, established chains of stores in the colonies run by Scots factors and clerks who bought up tobacco from the planters in advance of the arrival of the ships. This significantly reduced turnaround time in colonial ports and hence operating costs. This was an advantage which increased over time. The Glasgow houses moved from chartering ships to owning them. By 1775, 90 per cent of the Clyde tobacco fleet were 'company ships'. This allowed for better planning of shipping schedules and thus cut back the costly 'stay in the country' even more. It also helped to produce a pool of crack skippers who were absolutely familiar with the sea routes and whose skills further reduced passage time on the 7,000-mile return journey between Scotland and Chesapeake Bay. In 1762 the first dry dock in Scotland was opened in Port Glasgow with pumping machinery designed by James Watt to allow the speedier careening of the tobacco ships, especially vital because of their regular exposure to the teredo worm-infested waters of the Chesapeake. Ship design also improved. The move to provide the tobacco fleet with fore-and-aft sails, rather than square sails, enabled ships to sail closer to the wind, making it easier to navigate the shoal waters of the Chesapeake rivers where the stores were situated. Similarly, the carrying capacity of those vessels regularly engaged in the trade rose substantially over time. The average annual volume of tobacco carried per ship in the Clyde fleet increased from

219,800 lb. between 1747 and 1751 to 530,000 lb. in the years 1770 to 1775, indicating a notable gain in economies of scale.

These continuous improvements in efficiency were basic to the Glasgow success. In 1769 one observer, writing from America to a London merchant house, described that the Scots had 'a vast advantage' over the traders of the capital 'by sailing their ships so much cheaper' than they could achieve and, by doing so, were more able to retail their tobacco in Europe at lower costs.[1] The Glasgow firms relentlessly pushed down the average turnaround in Virginia from 53 days in 1750 to 40 in 1765 and then to 33 in 1775. In effect, the 'stay in the country' had been almost halved, a significantly better performance than the average reduction in overall port-times in the Chesapeake. This led to remarkable levels of efficiency. The Glasgow tobacco ships were sometimes able to achieve two round voyages across the Atlantic per year, a feat very rare in the British trade as a whole. For instance, the *Jeanie* of John Glassford and Co. completed 18 voyages in 11 years, while Alexander Speirs and Co.'s *Bowman* recorded the extraordinary total of 16 round voyages in the eight years 1757–65. After the prime cost of tobacco, the next major item was freight costs. The competitive edge of the Glasgow firms was based on their ability to drive these down to a much lower level than the merchants of other ports engaged in the transatlantic trades.

This short case study of the tobacco business reveals some of the qualities of enterprise and business drive that existed in the eighteenth-century Scottish merchant community. There is no reason to believe that the tobacco trade was untypical, other than in terms of its size, as it accounted for over half of the value of Scottish exports in the early 1750s. As has been seen, Scottish merchants were also pushing aggressively into the Caribbean islands and the British trading enclaves in India. Some have seen this thrusting commercial spirit as the result of Calvinist ideology which is said to have promoted the business ethic of hard work, thrift and the confident assurance which came from the awareness of membership of God's elect. But equally the Scottish capacity to exploit opportunities in the British Empire may also be explained by the long tradition of merchant adventuring in Europe in the fifteenth, sixteenth and seventeenth centuries which had broadened horizons, refined commercial techniques and reduced fear of foreign cultures. Whatever the influences, however, the internationally mobile

Scottish merchant, opening up markets from the Americas to India and beyond, was to prove one of the country's greatest assets in the age of industrialization.

7

The Rural Lowlands:
the Old World and the New

I

It is only in very recent years that historians have started to come to
grips with the reality of traditional society and economy in Lowland
Scotland before the wide-ranging changes known as 'Improvement'
which established the modern agrarian system. Indeed, the improving
writers of the later eighteenth century were themselves a major obstacle
to an understanding of how the old world worked. Their prolific
publications denounced the customary practices as archaic, hidebound,
wasteful and primitive in technique. Typical of the scorn and oppro-
brium heaped upon them were the views of Sir John Sinclair, editor of
the *Statistical Account* and doyen of the army of publicists for the new
farming. In a wide-ranging survey of the malpractices of the old order,
he condemned joint occupation of farms as 'work . . . where every one
claims an equal share in the direction can never be carried on with
success', ploughs, which 'were formerly of the worst description', and
the distribution of land into runrig which ensured 'all attempts at
improvement were in vain'.[1] In the writings of Sinclair and a host of
other commentators, a clear contrast was drawn between the golden
age of improved agriculture and the darkness before the dawn of
traditional farming. Such was the number, clarity and apparent authority of these commentaries that for a long time they also helped to
influence the thinking of later generations.

But the works of the improving writers require careful handling.
They were essentially propagandists who consciously sought to demonstrate the weaknesses of the old order. As the intellectual shock troops
of Improvement, their mission was not to understand traditional society
in its own terms but rather to provide the analytical justification for its
removal. Indeed, the wide dissemination of the improvers' publications

did give greater impetus to the spread of the most progressive ideas. They became an essential force, shaping the radical transformation which took place in the rural Lowlands in the second half of the eighteenth century. But in the process they were also overtly prejudiced against the old ways, which they dismissed as irrational, obscurantist and stubbornly conservative. It did not help that they also tended to see things from the perspective of the market-orientated society that developed after *c.* 1780. The rural society of an earlier era, when the market enclave was relatively weak and many on the land produced mainly for their own household and local needs, would inevitably suffer by comparison. In recovering the social history of the rural Lowlands before Improvement, modern scholars have tried to understand the old order in its own terms rather than by the standards of a later and quite different society. They have also started to research a much wider range of original sources, including landed estate papers, tax, church and legal records, in order to piece together the way of life of the Scottish people before the onset of agrarian capitalism finally changed rural society for ever.

It has to be recognized from the outset that agriculture was the very foundation of eighteenth-century society. In 1750, only one Scot in eight lived in a town (as defined as a community with a population of 4,000 or over) and there were only four towns with more than 10,000 inhabitants. The vast majority of the Scottish people made their living by cultivating the land and working in rural industries, especially spinning, weaving, fishing and mining. The grain harvests in August and September for oats, barley and wheat were absolutely critical to human existence. Eighteenth-century budgets indicate that at least two-thirds of the income of the labouring classes was devoted to food; before 1750, that meant the consumption of oatmeal, milk, some fish for communities near the coast and, occasionally, meat. Only later did the potato become significant. The novelist Tobias Smollett gives a useful description of the diet of ordinary Lowlanders: 'Their breakfast is a kind of hasty pudding of oatmeal, or peasemeal eaten with milk. They have commonly pottage to dinner composed of cale or cole, leeks, barley or big (a form of barley) and this is reinforced with bread and cheese made of skimmed milk. At night they sup on sowens flummery of oatmeal.'[2] Ale, made from malted barley, was the Scottish drink of the time and this explains the violent response provoked in 1725 by government attempts to impose a tax on malt. The land was also the source of a wide range of raw materials vital to the functioning of contemporary society: flax and wool for clothing; timber for building; charcoal for a number of industries; animal fats for use by soap- and candle-manufacturers; hides for tanners and then boot- and shoe-makers and saddlers; horn for cutlers; horses for town transport; straw for packing materials; sour milk as a bleaching agent (before dilute sulphuric acid became applicable in the later eighteenth century). And this is by no means an exhaustive list.

The working of land in the Lowlands depended on the tenants who rented their holdings from owners who took no direct part in the routine business of cultivation. There were indeed some owner-occupiers, or 'bonnet lairds', possessing small properties of a few hundred acres or less in a band of country from Fife in the east to Ayrshire in the west. But their numbers were in decline in the eighteenth century, and everywhere else in Scotland the tenant–landlord relationship was dominant. This structure, which was also to be found in most parts of England but which was uncommon in many areas of Europe, was important for three reasons. First, the relationship between tenant and landowner in the Lowlands by c. 1700 was emphatically economic in nature: access to land was given exclusively for rental in money and kind and a range of labour services due to the proprietor. There might, of course, be paternalistic overtones. On several estates at this time, landowners preferred to continue the family of the sitting tenant in possession. On the vast Buccleuch estates in the central Borders, for instance, the tenant's heir seems almost automatically to have been preferred as the successor. Proprietors might also allow arrears to accumulate in poor years rather than remove an insolvent tenant. But there is little hint of the cultural expectations which existed in the Highlands, where the clan ethic still demanded that the élites honour and fulfil the role of protectors of their people in the traditions known in Gaelic as *duathchas*. This crucial initial difference helps to explain the contrasting social response of the two societies to full-blooded commercialization after c. 1760.

Second, by the early eighteenth century tenants' rights to land were defined in law by a lease (in Scots, 'tack') for prescribed periods. These contracts commonly varied from nine to 19 years, with longer periods becoming more common as the century went on. Again, this was important because, from the landlord's perspective, it made the recon-figuration of land to increase efficiency relatively straightforward in theory. A number of tenancies could be gradually formed into a larger unit merely by refusing to renew leases for longer terms. Unlike many parts of Europe, there was little peasant proprietorship, buttressed with customary privileges, to resist the 'enlightened' progress of Improvement. Third, the tack gave the landowner enormous potential power because once the clauses of the contract were agreed they were defensible at law and tenants could be either fined or evicted for disobeying or ignoring them. The sheriff court records make it plain that several proprietors were willing to use the big stick if circumstances demanded it. Later, in the Age of Improvement, the 'improving lease' became a formidable weapon in the landlord's arsenal during the crusade to spread the new practices. Indeed, the Scottish tenant class had long been accustomed to the firm hand of landlord authority. One of the most remarkable aspects of the surviving tacks is the range of labour services that still survived and which later drove the improving writers incandescent with rage as they were said to be redolent of 'feudal servitude'. These services were really an additional rental paid in labour. Thus 'bonnage' (literally, bondage) service required tenants to supply labour for work on the proprietor's own home or mains farm, especially at the critically important harvest time when the tenants' own crops might be at risk from a sudden change in the weather. Other tasks included provision of carts and horses for carriage of the landowner's grain and the digging, drying and stacking of his peat supply for the cold winter months. 'Thirlage' meant that tenants had to have their corn ground at the landlord's mill, a custom that was still commonplace as late as the 1790s.

These services highlighted the dependent position of the tenants in relation to the landlords. But within their own communities, tenants were often men of status and significance. Their world was that of the *ferm-touns*, usually small settlements of little more than 20 households, dispersed across a countryside virtually bereft of the hedges, ditches, dikes, roads or any of the other man-made constructions that form the rural landscape today. The touns varied in size. In the more developed areas of the south-east in Lothians and Berwickshire, they were almost big enough to seem like villages. Elsewhere, there were as few as half a dozen families living in settlements apparently scattered randomly across the land. The names of these old places live on, either as settlements that have survived to the present day or in place names ending in '-ton', which are familiar references in modern Ordinance Survey maps. These clusters of people all had their own internal hierarchies, with tenants at the top and, ranked below them, cottars, farm servants and tradesmen.

Only a minority of the rural population held a lease and were responsible for paying rent which alone gave legal access to land in the early eighteenth century. In the 1690s, for instance, 30 per cent of those scheduled to pay the poll taxes in Renfrewshire and 12 per cent in Midlothian were tenants, though in parishes fringing the upland areas of the Borders in Ayrshire and Lanarkshire and on the marches of the Highlands small tenants made up a much higher proportion of the population. In Aberdeenshire, for instance, a clear distinction can be drawn between the richer arable coastlands, where tenants were fewer and more prosperous, and the hill country to the west, where almost half the poll tax payers in the 1690s were small tenants living much closer to the margins of subsistence. Tenants holding only a few acres of land were in the majority of leased farms in most districts. In Lowland Aberdeenshire and Renfrewshire, around half the possessions were under 30 acres, and even in the more 'advanced' county of Midlothian over a third fell into this category. The majority of farmers like this must have devoted their energies above all to subsistence husbandry in order to pay the rent and feed their families. Selling in the market was a decidedly secondary consideration. In the later seventeenth century this army of poor peasant husbandmen eking out an existence close to the margins of sufficiency demonstrates the limited impact of commercial forces before 1700 in whole areas of the countryside.

But the social pattern was far from static. The tenant class was steadily contracting in size, with thrusting individuals bettering themselves at the expense of others by absorbing more land in the townships. The most significant illustration of this trend was the expansion of holdings held by one tenant and a fall in the number of farms possessed by several husbandmen. The enlarged single tenancy was geared more to serving markets and less constrained by communal working practices. The farm under one master was to become the ideal of the Improvers later in the eighteenth century. A wide sample of holdings in five Lowland counties carried out by the present author suggests that more than half the farms were still in 'multiple tenancy' at the time of the union. However, in the next few decades this form of tenure was seen to be in rapid decline. Indeed, in most of the estates examined, by the 1740s single tenancy was overwhelmingly dominant, with only around one-fifth of all holdings now containing two or more possessors. Even within the old world, therefore, an embryonic rural middle class was emerging in some areas. Striking confirmation of this was the changing architecture of some tenant dwellings. The traditional long-house with living quarters, byre and barn under one roof remained common for most farmers. But, alongside these, the courtyard farmstead, common-place after *c.* 1780, was starting to develop. In this pattern the outbuild-ings were grouped in one or two wings, adjoining the dwelling house and enclosing a courtyard. This new layout symbolized changing times. Farmers with more land needed more buildings for storage, stock and tools and the spread of a more durable and elaborate layout also reflected increasing prosperity together with a greater confidence in the future coming from secure tenure. Typical of the kind of men who might live in these surroundings was William Nisbet of the parish of Crimond in Aberdeenshire. By the early years of the eighteenth century Nisbet had the whole tenancy of the Kirktoun of Crimond in his name and was master of a large community of six servants and herds, two subtenants, a cottar family and a few weavers, tailors and shoemakers.

The impact of the new tenantry was nowhere more apparent than in the Borders, where great sheep ranches with large areas of hill grazing and limited arable holdings in the valleys were well established in the eastern Borders by the late seventeenth century. One result of this territorial expansion was the unrelenting squeezing out of the rural population. Abandoned remains of touns which were inhabited into the early eighteenth century can be found throughout the Tweed valley and in Eskdale. Similarly, a number of the parish entries for this region in the *Statistical Account* of the 1790s describe once-populated settlements which were now visible only as mouldering remains. Over 100 years before the Highland Clearances, the advance of the commer-cialized sheep farms in the deep south of Scotland was causing wide-spread depopulation. In the western Borders, Sir David Dunbar at Baldoon near Wigtown built a great cattle park over two and a half miles long and one and a half in breadth to winter over 1,000 beasts. Dunbar was only one of several Borders proprietors who let their estates to commercially minded tenants for specialist stock-rearing. This process reached its climax in the 1720s, when several lairds acceler-ated the process by clearing out many small tenants and enlarging the stock-farms held by richer possessors. The arable lands were laid down to grass and the touns, now cleared of their inhabitants, were enclosed by dykes, with the aim of taking further advantage of favourable cattle prices in England after the union. This strategy provoked open rebellion from the people. A rising of several hundred armed men in the summer of 1724 broke down the dykes, killed and mutilated cattle and then confronted a military force of six troops of dragoons hurriedly sent in by a worried government. Nocturnal attacks went on for over six months until the turmoil subsided. This, the so-called Levellers Revolt, was the most serious rural disturbance in eighteenth-century Scotland. It was a telling reminder how, in the south-west in the 1720s, the conflict between traditional ways and market pressures, poor tenants and enterprising farmers with an eye for commercial opportunity, was already a reality before the more fundamental changes after *c.* 1760.

Much more numerous than the tenants in most of the farm settlements of the period were the cottar families. Indeed, it would be true to say that they formed the majority of the rural population in most regions. In the poll tax lists for Aberdeen, Renfrewshire, Midlothian and Berwick, for instance, between 40 per cent and 60 per cent of male heads of household and single men were cottars and tradesmen in the 1690s. Cottars held a few acres (usually less than five) from tenants in return for providing labour services for a number of days in the year and, occasionally, also making some rent payments. The tenant ploughed their smallholding and allowed them the keep of a cow. Tradesmen, such as weavers, carpenters, blacksmiths and other artisans, were also cottars, with tiny plots of land and a house within the ferm toun. The extraordinary numerical prevalence of the cottars throughout the length and breadth of Lowland Scotland reflected a number of factors. Cottar families formed the reserve army of labour in an agricultural system in which peaks of work were concentrated in only a few periods of the year, at the times of ploughing, harvesting and the gathering of peat. They were a guaranteed workforce at the busy times but could easily be laid off in slacker periods. This was also a world in which technology was limited and all tasks demanded a great input of labour. Enclosures were few, the land was open and much labour had to be employed in herding. Peat gathering demanded a huge effort from the local community through the summer months. Ploughing with the 'old Scots plough' could involve a few oxen, horses and several men. Again, it was useful for tenants, especially as their holdings increased in size, to have many hands ready to assist in the neighbourhood. Cottars could also help with the heavy burden of labour services exacted by landlords from their tenantry, and the fact that the reward to the cottar was in the form of land rather than cash was attractive when the money economy in some parts was still underdeveloped.

If we add the cottars and the tenants together within the social structure, it can be seen how the people of Lowland Scotland (like the Highlands) still depended overwhelmingly on the land. These two groups made up the vast majority of the rural population and few entirely landless groups assisted. Certainly there was a 'landless' servant class, consisting of both men and women. Married servants were to be found in the south-east and a few other areas. They were paid in kind, had a house and some land and were hired for a year. Single servants, the majority of the 'landless' workers before 1750, were mainly young men and women in their late teens and early twenties who were rewarded partly in money and partly in kind, lived with the farmer's family and were employed on contracts for periods of six months at a time. Many of them were born into cottar households before entering full-time service and at marriage some returned to the peasant way of life by obtaining a cottar holding. Cottars and the servants were therefore bound together by the common experience of possessing some land, no matter how small. This was a social pattern which sharply differentiated the rural Lowlands from England where, in most regions, the classical three-part social structure of landowners, farmers and landless servants/ labourers was already in place by c. 1700.

The way the people of this older society actually worked the land attracted scornful criticism from the improving writers. They reserved their most scathing condemnation for the 'infield–outfield' system and the 'rig and furrow' method of cultivation. Infield–outfield was the basic form of agricultural organization throughout Scotland before Improvement. The infield, normally located nearest the settlement and on the best soil, was cultivated most intensively and given an almost gardenly care. It had to produce crops year after year without being rested and if that regime was to be sustained the infield needed to be fertilized lavishly on a regular and systematic basis. Animal dung, rotted turf, shell sand, seaweed and urban refuse were all spread liberally. Outfields were given less generous treatment because they had a different function within the agricultural regime from the intensively cultivated blocks of arable infield. The quality of outfield land was poorer, but crops – notably oats – could be grown successfully on them by manuring plots by controlled grazing stock in folds. Also, this inferior land would be cropped for only a few years and then allowed to revert to pasture before being ploughed in due course. The outfields were also multi-purpose areas, supplying rotted turf for manuring the prized infields and providing grazing for stock and stone for building walls and dykes. Infield–outfield was the organizing principle of agriculture. The land was actually worked by ploughing it into a series of 'rigs' (or ridges) and furrows. On the rigs the crops were grown, while the furrows served as ditches to drain off surface water. Traces of this ancient system can still be seen to this day on the lower slopes of hills above the present level of cultivation. The width of the rigs depended on the needs of sowing grain by hand and then cutting it with the sickle. Estate maps also show that rigs were often substantial, with a breadth that could vary from 4 to 10 metres and stand as high as a metre or more. Generations of ploughing meant that the height of the rigs gradually increased as the earth cut by the plough was turned towards the centre.

The Improvers condemned all these practices as inefficient, wasteful of land and incapable of reform. It is true that crop yields, compared to the later eighteenth century, were comparatively low, for instance varying from 2:1 to 4:1 for oats in a survey of infield plots for the early years of the eighteenth century in Lanarkshire and Fife. Moreover, it is doubtful whether the traditional methods could have satisfied the huge increase in demand for foods and raw materials as a result of industrialization, urbanization and the rise in national population which took place from the 1760s. Yet in the pre-industrial age, the old system broadly met the needs of Scottish society. Judged over the period *c.* 1652– 1740, agriculture was remarkably effective in feeding the population and also in producing increasing surpluses for export, especially of cattle, sheep and grain. Between 1660 and 1700 there were significant harvest failures and shortages only in 1674 and 1693–7. The epic crisis of the 'Lean Years' in the 1690s was not confined to Scotland but also devastated several other countries in western Europe because of a period of unusually poor weather throughout the continent. After 1700 there were difficult times – but no subsistence crisis – in 1709, 1724–5 and 1740–41. Indeed, the central problem in the early decades of the eighteenth century was a stubborn stagnation in grain prices and the challenge of selling in depressed markets. This had also been a difficulty in the 1670s and 1680s, which explains why the Scottish parliament then transformed its traditional policy of protecting consumers to one of supporting farmers and landowners in order to export more grain in return for bounty payments from the state.

The cultivation methods and practices denounced by later commentators had a basic rationale when seen against the technical limitations of the old agriculture. The rig and furrow method was essential in order to provide some drainage in a wet country and for which there was no alternative before underground tile drainage became common in the nineteenth century. The splitting of land into strips and patches and the distribution of small plots to subtenants and cottars may have seemed illogical from a later perspective, but it was necessary in order to provide families with some ground for meeting their own vital needs for food. The communal working practices of the touns, which involved everything from house-building to peat-cutting, were an effective way of pooling the labour power of men, women and children when virtually every job had to be done by hand and 'technology' was mainly confined to tools like the spade, sickle and flail. A community approach was also favoured in the management of outfields. Each year, different parts rested as others were brought under the plough. The process could work effectively only if there was some planning and common controls so that different tenants followed an agreed sequence each year of breaking land in or deciding to return it to pasture. A similar strategy was adopted to prevent over-grazing by allocating each tenant a given number of animals through the practice known as 'stenting' or 'souming'. Regulation and co-operation had to be at the heart of the old system.

On the other hand, it was far from being static or inflexible. In some areas, a changing balance developed between each part of the system, with outfield expanding at the expense of infield as farmers and proprietors took advantage of the booming droving trade to England and the Scottish towns to lay down more land to pasture for stock fattening. In addition, in the main arable districts of the Lowlands, especially the Lothians and Berwickshire, infield systems had become very sophisticated, with four-course rotations of wheat, bere (a hardy form of barley), oats and legumes. Liming had steadily been adopted by more and more tenants during the seventeenth century; it helped to break down the acidity in the soil and was especially valuable in helping to open up areas of outfield to regular cultivation. The early systematic use of lime for this purpose can be traced back to the 1620s and, by the early eighteenth century, liming had become a common feature of Scottish Lowland agriculture. Through regular application, tenants in areas particularly well endowed for grain growing were able to expand their infields at the expense of outfields and specialize more in arable agriculture. In Roxburgh and Berwick by the early eighteenth century outfield cultivation had become much more intensive, with two-thirds under crop on some estates. In a sense, we are seeing here in outline a movement towards the unified pattern of cultivation which was to become characteristic of improved agriculture and the beginnings of an erosion of the traditional distinction between infield and outfield.

Behind the impression of ancient stability, therefore, significant changes were already under way in the rural Lowlands by 1750. The increasing dominance of the single tenant, the greater impact of the market, particularly for cattle and sheep, and the range of cropping refinements in arable agriculture were all important and indicative of the capacity of the old agriculture to change and evolve. Yet these developments were alterations *within* rather than *of* the existing structure. Most people still had some access to land, arable yields were relatively low in most regions, and the infield–outfield system prevailed throughout the Lowlands. The Scottish countryside of the 1740s, with its open fields, long sinuous rigs and huddled townships, had not changed very much in overall structure since medieval times. Yet within a matter of a few decades it would be transformed for ever.

2

Before the 1760s the process of social and economic change in most regions of the rural Lowlands was a story of slow and piecemeal adjustment at the margin in most regions. In that decade, however, there began a decisive break with the past. Between then and the 1820s, at a pace which varied among different areas and even different estates, the face of the Scottish countryside was radically altered and the way of life of the people fundamentally changed. By 1830 a recognizably modern landscape of trim fields and compact farms, separated by hedges and ditches, had emerged to take the place of the confused mixture of strips, rigs and open fields of the old order. New systems of crop rotation were widely adopted and produced yields two to three times greater than in the past. Before the 1750s, market pressures were becoming steadily more significant. But from the last quarter of the eighteenth century market forces established a complete dominance as the entire agrarian system in virtually every area of the Lowlands became geared to satisfying the needs of Scotland's burgeoning cities and towns for grain, butter, milk, cheese, eggs, meat and a host of other articles ranging from skins for leather goods to timber for building. Perhaps the most visible illustration of the comprehensive triumph of commercial relationships was the transport revolution which took place throughout the countryside in these decades. The construction on a truly massive scale of estate, parish and turnpike roads produced an intricate communications network that allowed market influences to affect all rural areas in a powerful way.

It was inevitable that this economic transformation would lead to basic changes in the rural social structure. As already seen, social change was under way before the 1750s, particularly with the movement towards larger, single-tenant farms. This trend now accelerated as the remaining multiple tenancies were eliminated and many individual holdings were brought together under one farmer. There was also an even more radical development running parallel with the consolidation of farms. The cottar system of allocating small patches of land in return for labour services came under widespread attack. The dispossession of the cottars was deeply significant, as in several districts in the Lowlands they had comprised between one-third and one-half of the total number of families. The continued contraction in size of the tenant farming class as a result of consolidation and the removal of the cottars (which was all but complete by the 1820s) created an entirely new social order in which only a tiny minority of the population had rights to land. The single exception in the Lowlands was the counties of the north-east region where the development of crofting from the 1790s maintained the land connection for many well into the later nineteenth century. Elsewhere, landlessness was predominant. The new social order of the agricultural communities was one in which a small number of rent-paying farmers, holding a lease for a given period, employed landless servants and labourers who were now dependent entirely on selling their labour power. The sheer scale and speed of social and economic change in the Scottish countryside in this period is remarkable and is probably unique in a European context at this time. By the 1830s, improved agriculture had triumphed throughout the Lowlands and Scottish farming, criticized for its backwardness in earlier years, had now become internationally renowned as a model of efficiency. It is worth outlining some key features before considering the origins of this transformation.

'Commonties' were uninhabited lands, varying in size from a few acres to several thousand. They were not 'commons' in the literal sense, because the rights to use them went with the lands adjacent to them. In essence they were part, though an individual part, of the private estates that surrounded them. Commonties were crucial sources of peat, stone, turf and rough grazing for small tenants and cottar families in the neighbourhood. The main legislation to allow final division of these lands among adjacent landlords had been passed by the seventeenth-century Scottish parliament, in an Act of 1695. But significantly it was only in the later eighteenth century that division of commonty really gathered pace. In a sample of four Lowland counties, 45 per cent of all recorded divisions from 1600 to 1914 occurred between 1760 and 1815. By the 1870s, virtually all Scottish commonties had been formally brought into private ownership – an extraordinary fact when it is considered that some estimates suggest around half the total land area of Scotland consisted of commonties in 1500. The drive to annex commonties to neighbouring estates is eloquent testimony to the rising profit levels of agriculture in the later eighteenth century and the absolute determination of landlords to secure these. It is interesting to note that, as commonties were being absorbed, leases to tenants were also becoming more rigorous, especially through the inclusion of clauses specifically reserving rights over coal, stone and minerals to the proprietor. All this symbolized the new view of land not simply as a family inheritance or as the basis of social position but as an asset to be prized and exploited in order to maximize returns.

Enclosure (or 'inclosure' in eighteenth-century documents) also changed the face of the countryside. The scattered patterns of inter-mingled strips of land were gathered into individual fields, separated by hedges, ditches or dikes. The same process hastened the dissolution of the infield–outfield system because it was designed to bring all the land into a regular sequence of productive cultivation using systematic fallowing and the new rotations to restore fertility. Inevitably, the pace of enclosure varied regionally and its costs were such that the level of investment in it dropped off during the crisis years like 1772–3 and 1782–4. Nevertheless, progress was still rapid. By the 1790s, an estimated 69 per cent of parishes in Angus, Fife, Ayrshire and Lanarkshire reported some enclosure activity, while more than a third indicated that 'most' or 'all' were already enclosed and divided.

At the heart of agricultural improvement was the ability of farmers to produce significantly more from a given area of land. Essentially, this meant increasing the yields from oats, bere, barley and wheat and expanding the numbers of cattle and sheep by extending the acreage under fodder crops such as turnips. There can be little doubt of the yield increases. The overall impression is that the average yields for oats in Angus and Lanark in the 1790s were 12 and 11 respectively, which was around three times the averages of the later seventeenth century. As William Fullarton reported in some astonishment in the course of his survey of Ayrshire in 1793, 'the third of the farms in crop supplied double or triple the yield which had been formerly taken from the whole'.[3] The achievement of significantly boosting grain yields was fundamental to the whole progress of urbanization and industrialization in late-eighteenth-century Scotland. The new productivity of the land allowed more and more people to move into jobs where they bought rather than grew their own food. If yields had not risen as population increased, food prices might have gone through the ceiling and the whole momentum of economic advance would have quickly faltered.

The key to the new agriculture was the more intensive application of traditional methods, such as fallowing and the application of lime and the rapid diffusion of sown grasses and turnip husbandry. In the old system, regular cultivation had been confined to the relatively small area of the infield because of the limited supply of manure. Sown grasses, such as clover, dramatically increased the amount of fodder, allowed more beasts to be kept and produced more dung to be spread as fertilizer. By 1800, according to the *Statistical Account*, the majority of farms in the central and eastern Lowlands were using rotations incorporating sown grasses. Turnips were less common in the later eighteenth century, but in the long run they were to become of even greater impact. They provided a heavy feeding crop which could be eaten on the fields. It therefore became possible even for farms that specialized in grain production to bring in animals from outside to be fattened and at the same time fertilize the arable land. It was a virtuous circle in which more beasts producing more dung added to the productivity of the soil on which still more fodder crops could be cultivated. The system particularly appealed in Scotland which, for reasons of climate and terrain, had tended to be more committed to pastoral husbandry. Now the areas of hill country and cattle and sheep farming were combined effectively with the lower-lying districts of arable agriculture. Particularly in areas north of the Tay and across the north-east counties of Banff, Kincardine and Aberdeen, turnip husbandry and cattle fattening became the basic foundations of the new system.

The way the land was worked also changed. Fundamental to this was the revolution in ploughing and in particular the movement from the heavy old Scots plough with its teams of horses or oxen to the lighter two-horse plough, designed and produced by James Small. It was not simply a sudden jump from traditional to modern. The old plough still had great value in the working of stiff land being reclaimed from the waste. It was also refined and adapted. With a shorter head, stilts and beam, it needed less animal power and human labour. The triumph of Small's plough could not be assured until larger stones were cleared, land drained and the unimproved landscape moulded into greater order and regularity. But when it did become popular (in most areas by the early nineteenth century), the two-horse plough became not only essential to the working of the soil but also the key determinant of the whole labour system of the new agriculture. The number of farm servants and the labourers who were hired depended on the ploughing capacity of the teams and the need to use the work horses in an effective fashion by ensuring their regular employment through the year.

Yet major technical advances in agriculture were rather unusual in the period down to 1830. Apart from the new plough, only the threshing machine was of primary importance as a labour-saving device. Invented in 1787, it quickly became popular, whether powered by wind, water or steam. But all the other farm tasks continued to depend on human effort: sowing, reaping, weeding, gathering, lifting and a host of other jobs. Labour became more effective not by being given technical support but by being better organized. One of the reasons farmers started to remove the cottars in large numbers was because they wanted a labour force that was much more subject to their own regular control and direct discipline. At the same time, in the improved farms now shorn of their cottar smallholdings the ploughmen became specialists, concerned only with their horse teams and they developed a sense of craft status and pride in their jobs. In short, they became the aristocrats of labour in the new agriculture.

The rural Lowlands had long been a complex mosaic of different farming systems. In the era of Improvement these distinctions became even sharper, as the stimulus of urban markets increasingly forced farmers to specialize in what they did best against a background of local climatic and geological circumstances. Thus the clay lands of Ayrshire, Renfrewshire and western Lanarkshire became more significant as centres of dairying with the growth of commercial cheese- and butter-making for the booming towns of the Industrial Revolution. Around all Scotland's major cities dairying developed as well as market gardening for potatoes, hay, grain and turnips to feed the teeming populations of the expanding urban areas. The south-east, including the counties of East Lothian, Fife, Berwick and Roxburgh, were traditionally the richest arable districts in Scotland. Their capacity was further enhanced by the rapid adoption of the new rotations, allowing intensive cropping of wheat and barley. The Borders, reaching northwards to the southern parishes of Lanarkshire and Ayrshire, specialized in sheep farming in the eastern and central parishes and cattle-rearing in the west. This was a long-established pattern. But, from the later eighteenth century, two developments may be noted. First, the region became more closely integrated with arable areas to the north and east, where their stocks were fattened for sale. Second, in the hill country of the central Lowlands, especially in Lanarkshire and eastern Ayrshire, the pastoral farms were becoming bigger and in the process forcing the removal of small tenants and cottars. There were complaints from parish ministers in the 1790s that social displacement and depopulation were widespread in some of these districts. In the north-east counties, the balance of agricultural activity was also altering as additional stretches of land were laid down to grass and more and more farmers became committed to cattle breeding and fattening. It was an early sign of this region's emergence as an international centre of excellence for stock-rearing later in the nineteenth century and the home of the celebrated Aberdeen-Angus breed.

Nevertheless, in all regions the improving theorists placed great emphasis on the size of farms and the relationship between this and the overall cost of working the land. Control of the holding under one man was taken for granted as the *sine qua non* for destroying the supposed constraints of co-operation and communalism which were believed to have obstructed progress in the old order. Now, more sophisticated calculations were made in order to ensure maximum efficiency. Thus, in the early 1770s, Robert Ainslie, estate factor to the Duke of Douglas on his large estates in Lanarkshire, Renfrewshire and Angus, was one of several commentators of the time to describe the optimum size of agricultural holdings. The key factor, as he saw it, was the relationship between farm acreage and the working capacity of a team using the new plough. He estimated that 50 acres 'in a good climate and middling soil' gave enough work for one plough. However, under an improved regime, half of all the land was in grass and the remainder under cultivation. Therefore, 100 acres was actually the minimum size for a viable agricultural holding. Even larger farms would, however, convey additional benefits in the efficient use of labour.

This kind of thinking, which quickly became the conventional wisdom of the time, was bound to have a decisive impact on the pace of tenant consolidation. Multiple tenancies, already being weeded out earlier in the eighteenth century, were now steadily eliminated. On the Morton estates in Fife, the proportion of multiple tenants fell from 20 per cent in 1735 to 8 per cent in 1811, while on the Duke of Hamilton's lands in Clydesdale the decline was of the order of 61 per cent between 1762 and 1809. In the hill country of southern Lanarkshire, for instance, there were scenes of depopulation which are usually regarded as more reminiscent of the Highland glens in this period. In the parish of Libberton in the 1790s 'the ruins of demolished cottages are to be seen in every corner'. The number of inhabitants had fallen by a half since the 1750s because, so the local minister alleged, of 'the letting out the land in large farms'.[4] In nearby Ayrshire there was a similar pattern. From the parish of West Kilbride came the report that the conversion of small tenancies to large grazing farms was producing a great haemorrhage of population '. . . in consequence whole baronies and large tracts of land formerly planted with families were thrown waste to make room for this new mode of management'.[5]

3

The transformation of the market for Scottish agriculture was the catalyst which accelerated improvement. Before the later eighteenth century, prices for oats and barley in particular were relatively stable. A broad balance existed between supply and demand and there was little incentive to invest in adventurous innovation. From the 1770s this equilibrium crumbled rapidly with the growth of national population and the expansion of towns and cities. Over the period 1755–1820, numbers rose from 1,265,000 in 1755 to just over 2 million, an increase of around two-thirds. From 1801 to 1831, the rate of Scottish town expansion was the fastest of any period in the nineteenth century, and as a result the proportion of the population living in urban areas of over 5,000 inhabitants rose from about one-fifth to nearly one-third of the Scottish total. It was not simply a question, therefore, of many more mouths to feed but that the numbers who no longer produced their own food directly were increasing even more rapidly. The new market context was graphically demonstrated in a steep upward swing in grain prices. Oat prices in one south-eastern county, Fife, which was not fully exposed to the demands emanating from the industrializing regions, illustrate the trend. Average prices for the years 1765–70 were 56 per cent higher than for the period 1725–50, and those for 1805–10 showed an increase of 300 per cent.

The market dynamic was intensified by two other developments. First, the rural transport revolution facilitated access to the burgeoning towns and cities. The best-known initiatives were planned by the turnpike trusts which, on one estimate, spent £2–3 million on roads and bridges between 1790 and 1815. But they were simply the most publicized aspect of a growing network of private and parish roads. The spread of more level surfaces and smoother gradients was essential to the expansion of wheeled traffic. As a result, savings were made on the costs of both human and animal labour as the cart became the normal means of carrying produce, stores and manures. In the central Lowlands, where, by the early nineteenth century, the majority of the population lived, the construction of the Forth and Clyde Canal was also crucial, enabling, for example, the booming commercial metropolis of Glasgow to be supplied with grain and meat from as far away as the farms of the Lothians and Fife. Second, the mushrooming of small towns and villages with an industrial emphasis in this period is an often neglected factor. Some 85 'planned villages' were founded in the Lowlands alone from 1700 to 1840, with the great majority being established in the years 1760 to 1815. But unplanned settlements were even more common as mining, iron-making and textile centres. Mining, spinning and weaving took place in the countryside, and the new industrial colonies brought the market for foods and raw materials much closer to farmers – a matter of importance in a business where costs were considerable for the carriage of produce that was often low in value but great in bulk. For instance, in the last decade of the eighteenth century, though the great market of Glasgow had a dominant influence, in rural Lanarkshire local farmers also supplied the new cotton mill villages at New Lanark and Blantyre, the lead-mining hamlet at Wanlockhead, the weaving communities in Hamilton and the thriving market towns of Biggar and Douglas.

The changing market context was decisive, but in the final analysis what mattered was the response of rural society to these opportunities. That is best considered with reference to both landowners and tenant farmers. In England the current historical opinion is that the great proprietors did not play a central role in the promotion of agricultural change. The main influences came from the lesser gentry, enlightened tenants and land agents. In Scotland the opposite seems to have been the case. In the Highlands, as in the Lowlands, the landed class was at the heart of the process, not necessarily through routine personal involvement but at a more strategic level through the support they gave to their professional factors and agents who actually enforced Improvement. Scottish agriculture was less advanced than English and so required a more interventionist approach. The basic advantage of the proprietors was that most land was worked through tenancies governed by leases. They therefore possessed full legal rights of eviction at the end of a lease. This not only allowed them to influence the size and composition of the tenantry on their estates but also to build into these contracts mandatory improving clauses enforceable at law. Sheriff Court records demonstrate that landowners had little compunction in using legal muscle to ensure compliance with cropping regulations set out in leases.

Legal developments had added to the power of Scottish landowners to promote improvement. As long ago as 1695, the 'Act anent lands lying run-rig' and a second statute in the same year relating to the division of commonties helped to facilitate the process. By the first, individual landlords could take the initiative to exchange and consolidate land held by different proprietors. The second Act allowed one landowner to promote a division of commonty rather than wait for a majority to be in agreement. The legislation put in place cheap and effective processes and was clearly designed to assist those lairds in the van of agrarian reform. The rights of Scottish landowners were buttressed further by the development of entail. Through the introduction of laws of entail in 1685 which safeguarded 'entailed' land from forced sales through debts, the succession to an entailed estate was confined to a definite series of heirs. Any proprietor who succeeded could not break this line and he was not permitted to contract debts that would put the property at risk. By 1825 an estimated half of the landed estates of the country were subject to strict entail. Entail's great attraction and obvious popularity was that it gave protection and security to the landed family over several generations. But the restrictions made it difficult to raise loans for investment which would then be passed on to succeeding proprietors. An Act of 1770 gave some flexibility by allowing an improving landlord of an entailed estate to invest in his property and become a creditor to his heirs up to the value of four years' rental.

But other influences were also significant. The costs of landownership were rising steeply in the eighteenth century. This was the era of competitive display when social standing was increasingly defined by material status. More elaborate country houses, interior decoration and the adornment of estate policies became not only fashionable but essential in order to maintain and demonstrate social position. It is noteworthy how many of the great houses of Scotland were either built or significantly renovated during this period. Inverary, Culzean, Hopetoun House and Mellerstain were only the most famous examples. This was the era when the remarkable Adam family of architects did their best work, much of which involved the comprehensive remodelling of castellated houses and fortified dwellings of an earlier and more turbulent age. In the later eighteenth century the number of aristocratic and laird houses built from scratch also multiplied. Nearly twice as many were constructed in the 1790s (more than 60) as between 1700 and 1720. Most of Robert Adam's commissions were for the laird class even though his best-known work was for the nobility. Also driving up costs was the revolution in interior design and furnishings. At the time of the union, the domestic furnishings of a typical laird's house were simple in the extreme. Less than 50 years later, the aristocracy was aspiring to standards of unprecedented splendour, with gilded ornamentation, framed paintings, lavish fabrics and elaborate ceiling mouldings. Mahogany furnishings, based on the designs of Chippendale, Sheraton and Hepplewhite, enjoyed remarkable popularity. Nor should it be forgotten that the assimilation of the Scottish nobility into the wealthier English aristocracy subjected them to special additional pressures of expenditure which increased the need to extract more income from their lands.

For all these reasons larger rent rolls became essential to service the new levels of conspicuous consumption and élite material competition of the landed classes. This 'Revolution of Manners' went hand in hand with the popularity of Improvement. But the influences at work were not only material in origin. They also came from the world of ideas. The Scottish philosophical revolution of the eighteenth century fed through into agrarian reform. The rationalism of the Enlightenment helped to change man's relationship to his environment. No longer was nature accepted as given and preordained; instead, it could be altered for the better or 'improved' by systematic and planned intervention. In a sense, therefore, Enlightenment thought gave a new intellectual legitimacy to the traditional interventionist role of the landed classes in Scotland by clarifying and systematizing the objectives of agrarian reform. Not surprisingly in a society where it dominated the economy, the theorists were fascinated by agriculture. Writers as varied as Lord Kames, James Anderson, Sir John Sinclair and the numerous contributors to the *Statistical Account* and *General Views of Agriculture* of the 1790s formulated ideas about the meaning of Improvement which offered a basic critique of the old order and a coherent approach to the development of the new. The crucial links between the intellectuals and the practice of agriculture were the factors and agents who managed the actual routine of farming on the great estates. These were often educated men who had attended a Scottish university and when they set out their schemes of improvement were in many instances simply putting into effect the new intellectual orthodoxy that was widely disseminated in the books, pamphlets and journals of the middle decades of the eighteenth century. There was remarkable unanimity about what was bad and had to be changed. Lands 'in a state of nature' were no longer acceptable and had to be enclosed and brought into regular cultivation. Farms held by more than one tenant had to be divided and recognized. The 'unimproved' regime was vigorously condemned as wasteful and ruinous. What was new was good; the old was bad. This gave the Improvers a robust moral and intellectual confidence as they vigorously went about the crusade of thoroughgoing agrarian reformation.

The new imperial context was a further influence on the momentum of agrarian change. By the later eighteenth century, as already noted many Scots were growing rich from the profits of colonial commerce to North America and the Caribbean, from service in the army and from trade and office-holding in India and the East Indies. It was common for some who succeeded to acquire a small landed estate and 'improve' their property from their personal fortunes. By the last quarter of the eighteenth century, for instance, the counties around Glasgow were ringed by the estates of the city's tobacco and sugar lords. At least 60 merchant families were involved in these land purchases between 1760 and 1815. It is striking also that many of the architect Robert Adam's clients were not members of the 'old' landed class but men who had made their money in law and commerce. The impact of empire on the land market and Improvement comes through in the literature of the time. John Galt's *The Last of the Lairds* concerns the appropriately named Mr Rupees, a 'Nawbob' who 'came hame from Indy and bought the Arunthrough property frae the Glaikies, who, like sae mony ithers o' the right stock o' legitimate gentry, hae been smothered out o' sight by the weed and nettle overgrowths o' merchandise ane cotton-weavry'.[6] Galt depicts Mr Rupees as a man committed to conspicuous consumption on a lavish scale and the generation of more and more profit from his lands.

Though profit-hungry proprietors might own the land they did not actually work it and the tenant farmers who did were censured vigorously by improving writers as conservative and hidebound. How then were the new ideas to be transformed into reality against this background of apparently unyielding orthodoxy and traditionalism? There were several explanations. For a start, not all tenants were as backward as the critics suggested. Even before 1750, the steady emergence of single tenancies and the decay of rentals paid mainly in kind meant more and more had direct experience of serving the market. These enterprising farmers, like their landlords, gained from rising prices after the 1770s. The 'latent' farming bourgeoisie described earlier in this chapter developed further in the new economic context. Nor should it be forgotten that many Scottish tenants were fully literate and that much of the new agricultural knowledge was spread by books, pamphlets and journals. Typical of the standards prevailing in many parts of the Lowlands was the pattern in St Ninian's parish, Stirlingshire, in the 1790s: 'Some of our farmers have been favoured with a liberal education. A few of them have been instructed in the rudiments of the Latin tongue. Almost all of them have been taught writing and arithmetic, as well as to read the English language with understanding and ease.'[7] Moreover, improving landlords used a range of incentives to encourage progressive practices. Some covered the costs of enclosure, liming and new farm houses set against obtaining returns through raising rents in the long run. The risk was worth taking because of the steep increases in rents after 1780. Contemporaries estimated that the general level was fairly stable to about 1750, started to move up from the 1760s, doubled between 1783 and 1793, and did so again from 1794 to 1815. Abatements of rent were also allowed in order to allow the result of the new practices to filter through and gain acceptance. As the Earl of Morton advised, rental should be kept at modest levels in the initial phase 'and not so high as to exceed the skill and industry of the tenants . . . as no General can expect good success with a bad disciplined Army'.[8] In order to attract able tenants, landowners also invested in new farmhouses. Some steadings, as in Fife in the early nineteenth century, for instance, remained in a 'barbarous' condition, but many others now had substantial, two-storey, slate-covered farmhouses, stables, cattle houses, barns, milksheds and strawyards.

Coercion was also used widely and systematically. The approach was based on the improving lease, which set out the detailed instructions for the new cropping prescriptions and to which the tenant had to adhere. Landowners could ensure compliance in a variety of ways: by fining, marginal increases in rent or eviction. Both estate and Sheriff Court records show that breaches of the lease were regarded as a serious offence and could be punished by the loss of the tenancy. These new leases were no longer conventional, generalized documents but contained several pages of written obligations and mandatory instructions concerning fallowing, liming and cropping routines. Nor were they simply paper contracts. On the great estates, bureaucracies of principal factor and sub-factors allowed for careful and regular monitoring. The Earl of Panmure was advised to appoint an inspectorate of three salaried officers to supervise the progress of the improvements on his Angus estate. If necessary, they should be supplied with assistants to 'take Inspection and make report annually as said is: That those who do well may meet with the Applause justly due them: That the Backward may be spurred on and that the Obstinately Negligent and Deceitful may be Undone and turned off as an Example *In Terrorem* of others'.[9] Here indeed was a telling illustration of the threatened use of seigneurial authority in the cause of Improvement.

4

Perhaps the most visible social effect of Improvement was the removal of the cottars. In Lanarkshire, over a quarter of parishes reported in the *Statistical Account* in the 1790s described their extensive dispossessions; for Angus, the figure was 22 per cent, and for Fife around one-third. The agricultural reporter for Lanarkshire commented in 1798 that in that county, 'It is vain to say anything of the ancient cottages . . . the former nurseries of field labourers for they may be said to be now no more.' He went on to add that 'the few scattered ones which still remain can scarcely be called an exception'. Witnesses were at pains to emphasize the radical and comprehensive nature of the removals, and this was shown in their colourful use of language. The minister of Kilmany in Fife referred to 'the annihilation of the little cottagers'. The reporter for Marrikie in Angus described how 'many of the cottagers are exterminated'.[10] Other observers noted the existence of numerous buildings in their parishes, formerly inhabited by cottar families, which were gradually falling into ruins. Elsewhere, cottar dwellings were being systematically demolished and the stone used to construct dikes and walls in the new farms.

All of this has a familiar ring, as these are the features usually associated with the notorious Highland Clearances, yet the social dislocation in the rural Lowlands in the later eighteenth century has virtually been overlooked and though the Highlands have stimulated a veritable scholarly industry the Lowland Clearances still await their historian. Ironically, however, while these great social changes have been almost all ignored by scholars, they did attract much contemporary concern. Some critics pointed out that the attack on the cottar system had effectively destroyed the traditional 'nursery of servants'. The sons and daughters of the cottars had usually provided the main source of labour supply for local farms, and recruitment was now difficult because in many areas cottar families had left the land. Other commentators, perhaps less convincingly, saw a relationship between the clearance of the cottars and the rising costs of the Poor Law in some of the larger towns. The links between migration, urbanization and the Poor Law were obviously more complex than this. Nevertheless, it is again indicative of the magnitude of cottar dispossession that some contemporaries regarded it as a vital influence on wider social developments in later eighteenth-century Scotland.

The cottars were under threat from a number of sources. They were being squeezed by division of commonties and the intaking of waste land. Commonties, moors and mosses were crucial to cottar life; they provided many of the family's basic needs at no cost other than labour. Building materials, such as stone, wood, heather and bracken, came from these marginal lands, which also afforded peat and turf for fuel. Commonties were also widely used by small tenants and cottars for grazing. In the second half of the eighteenth century, however, all these traditional sources of subsistence were being removed or drastically reduced as the commonties were divided and proprietors tried to prevent access to former 'common' land.

Farmers also now viewed the cottar system as uneconomic. Cottar families were traditionally provided with a few acres of land and additional grazing for both cattle and sheep. This was acceptable when several parts of a possession were underutilized within the old infield–outfield structure. It was less tolerable when all the land was cultivated systematically and intensively in a regular sequence of rotations. Rental inflation in the later eighteenth century meant that farmers looked much more critically at the real costs of land being used for cottar holdings. In Colmonell parish in Ayrshire, for instance, the cottars had possessed a house, yard, small piece of land and enough grass for one or more cows. The value of the holding was 'thought to be trifling while rents were low'. But much higher rentals meant that to the farmer the value of grazing the cattle of cottars increased. The balance of advantage had altered to encourage the use of cottar possessions for producing grain and stock for the market rather than for the maintenance of a reserve supply of labour.

Increasingly, also, other observers argued that cottars would place a burden on the Poor Law. This fear was not in itself new. Cothouses had long been seen as repositories of the poor, aged and infirm, and of migrants from other parishes. Thus the kirk session of Wiston in Lanarkshire proclaimed in 1752 that 'all persons who have coattages [sic] to set to beware that they bring no persons or families from other parishes who are not able to maintain themselves'.[11] Those who did so would be obliged to support them without assistance from the session. But this concern may have become stronger in later decades when there was much greater mobility of population. At the same time, the tendency to support the poor through rating or assessment, rather than primarily by means of voluntary giving, was on the increase. Also, as the number with rights to land declined, so the proportion of those seeking a parish settlement through obtaining a cothouse may have increased. Certainly, in some rural parishes, there was growing alarm about vagrancy in the last quarter of the eighteenth century. In the parish of Douglas, for example, reference was made in 1764 to 'the great number of vagrant persons and sturdy beggars' who were present in the area.[12] Again, in 1788, the lists of the poor in the parish were expanding as a result of the influx of strangers who were attempting to gain possession of vacant cothouses. By demolishing the buildings, farmers ensured some protection from this threat. It is significant that in several of the reports in the 1790s it was indicated that uninhabited cottar dwellings were not simply allowed to moulder away. They were often completely levelled.

Fundamentally, the cottar structure was in conflict with the new agrarian order. The system was well suited to a regime where demand for labour tended to concentrate in brief periods in the year around tasks such as grain harvesting and fuel gathering. It was useful in these circumstances for farmers to have a reliable pool of labour which could be called upon in the busy seasons and then laid off without any cash cost until required again. However, the needs of improved agriculture were radically different. The more intensive cultivation of the land, thorough ploughing, the adoption of new crops and of innovative rotations ensured that the working year started to lengthen. There was, on the whole, an evening-out rather than an accentuation of seasonal labour requirements within mixed farming. Inevitably, this development favoured the hiring of full-time workers. These were sometimes married servants hired by the year but, more commonly, in most districts, were single male and female servants employed for six months. Only these groups were suited to the regular toil increasingly carried out in improved Lowland farms. Ironically, the married-servant class was similar to the cottars in several respects. They obtained a house, garden, fuel, the keep of a cow and other privileges as part of the wage reward. The crucial difference, however, was that they were full-time workers, entirely under the masters' control during their term of employment, and could be dismissed at the end of it.

This position of subordination was crucial. While the independence of cottars can be exaggerated – they did possess land, but only in mere fragments and they had to obtain work in larger holdings in order to make ends meet – they were obviously less subject to the discipline of the masters than full-time servants. But the new agriculture demanded much higher levels of labour efficiency. Tenants were under pressure from two sources. Landowners were forcing up rentals in dramatic fashion and wages of agricultural workers were also rising from the 1770s, and especially from the 1790s, as industrial and urban expansion lured many from the country districts to the towns. One important response was the enforcement of policies designed to enhance the productivity of labour. The removal of the cottars can be seen in this context. In the most improved districts, where the old Scots plough was being replaced by James Small's plough, using a team of one man and two horses, the clearest effect can be seen. Gradually the whole work routine centred around boosting the efficiency of the horses. Hours of labour and number of workers were closely related to the number of horse teams and their work rate. Ploughmen took responsibility for a particular pair and their entire routine from early morning to evening was devoted to the preparation, working and final grooming of the animals. This system required that the ploughmen be permanent servants, boarded within the farm steading or in a cottage adjacent or close to their animals. The part-time labours of the cottars were now redundant as it became possible to tailor requirements to the numbers actually required for specific farm tasks.

Curiously, though, these Lowland Clearances were a silent revolution. Despite the magnitude of the social changes and the abrupt disruption to an old way of life there is hardly any evidence of angry protest or collective unrest. Even recent scrutiny of Sheriff Court records for the period of transformation has failed to come up with any hard evidence of direct action by the displaced cottars. One explanation might be that the loss of their land was not as serious a threat to their living standards as it was for Highland crofters. The cottars were being dispossessed when employment in agriculture and industry was booming in most years. Parish ministers in the 1790s were usually unanimous in their view that jobs were plentiful for all those who wanted them. The building of the towns and cities, the construction of roads, bridges and canals and the revolution in industry and agriculture created a hugely increased demand for labour in a society where technology had still to make a significant impact and where almost all tasks depended on human skill and muscle. In addition, Scottish population increase in the decades after *c.* 1750 at 0.6 per cent per annum was among the slowest in Europe, while the onset of war with France near the end of the eighteenth century drew many young men from civilian employment off into the army and navy. Many employers were therefore forced to concede higher wages in order to attract workers. This might well have been the context which helped to defuse any potential cottar unrest. Migration to the cities with their burgeoning demands for labour was one possible safety valve. But another was the easy availability of jobs in weaving, spinning, ditching, draining and casual labouring in most years throughout the many rural hamlets and villages that sprang up in the wake of the Agricultural Revolution.

8

Urbanization

Town growth in the period 1760–1830 forms a bridge between the old world of rural Scotland and the urbanized society of the later nineteenth century and modern times. In 1830 urban development had still some way to go before it began to ebb, but its acceleration from the middle decades of the eighteenth century had been dramatic. Recent work by Jan de Vries on European urbanization places the Scottish experience in an international context and his data are summarized in Table 8.1.

	1600	1650	1700	1750	1800	1850
Scotland	3.0	3.5	5.3	9.2	17.3	32.0
Scandinavia	1.4	2.4	4.0	4.6	4.6	5.8
England and Wales	5.8	8.8	13.3	16.7	20.3	40.8
Ireland	0	0.9	3.4	5.0	7.0	10.2
Netherlands	24.3	31.7	33.6	30.5	28.8	29.5
Belgium	18.8	20.8	23.9	19.6	18.9	20.5
Germany	4.1	4.4	4.8	5.6	5.5	10.8
France	5.9	7.2	9.2	9.1	8.8	14.5
Switzerland	2.5	2.2	3.3	4.6	3.7	7.7
Northern Italy	16.6	14.3	13.6	14.2	14.3	
Central Italy	12.5	14.2	14.3	14.5	13.6	20.3
Southern Italy	14.9	13.5	12.2	13.8	15.3	
Spain	11.4	9.5	9.0	8.6	11.1	17.3
Portugal	14.1	16.6	11.5	9.1	8.7	13.2
Austria-Bohemia	2.1	2.4	3.9	5.2	5.2	6.7
Poland	0.4	0.7	0.5	1.0	2.5	9.3

Table 8.1: Percentage of Total Population in Western European Territories Living in Towns with over 10,000 Inhabitants, 1600–1850.
Source: After J. de Vries, *European Urbanisation, 1500–1850* (London, 1984), pp. 39–48.

They confirm the conventional view that in the seventeenth century and in the early part of the eighteenth, Scotland was a predominantly rural society. In a league of 'urbanized societies' (as measured by the percentage of total population inhabiting towns of 20,000 or over), Scotland was 11th out of 16 in both 1600 and 1650 and was still only 10th in 1700. On the other hand, it has to be remembered that the threshold figure of 10,000 significantly underestimates the absolute size of the real urban enclave in Scotland before 1750. In the seventeenth century, for instance, there was considerable town development, not only through the expansion of the major burghs of Glasgow and Edinburgh, but in the rise of the salt and coal centres around the Forth estuary. The dynamism of the early modern town has been further clarified by recent research. Yet even recognition of the fact that there was more Scottish urban growth before 1750 than Table 8.1 implies does not entirely invalidate the proposition that the country was one of the least 'urbanized' in western Europe in the seventeenth century.

From that period, however, the data reveal a dramatically different pattern and indicate an explosive increase in the numbers in Scotland living in large towns. By the 1750s, Scotland was seventh in the league table of 'urbanized societies', fourth in 1800 and second only to England and Wales by 1850. Less than 10 per cent of Scots lived in towns with 10,000 inhabitants or above in 1750, but almost one-third did so in 1850. In the long-run perspective of historical development, a change of this magnitude represented a clear break with the past. Plainly, a new social order was in the process of formation. By 1800, according to Table 8.1, Scotland was already one of the five most urbanized societies in western Europe, alongside England and Wales, the Netherlands, Belgium and northern Italy. But it had achieved this position only in the previous few decades. The Netherlands, Belgium and northern Italy were already highly urbanized two centuries earlier and town development there did not intensify in the period after 1750. Similarly, there is no evidence of any other territory on the continent (apart from Poland, which started from a much lower base) experiencing such a rapid rate of urban expansion as Scotland between 1750 and 1850.

The Scottish pattern was exceptional also in relation to England and Wales. Throughout the 250 years after 1600, the tabulation suggests that a higher proportion of the population in the south lived in large towns than did those north of the border. But, equally, it is clear that the gap between the two countries, which had been enormous in the early eighteenth century, narrowed very rapidly after that. Table 8.2 confirms that, though England was still the more urbanized, the Scottish rate of growth in the later eighteenth century was significantly higher. Until 1800 the English pattern seems to have been one of a continuous and protracted process of steadily intensifying urban development. Town expansion in Scotland on this evidence was altogether more abrupt and swift and was therefore more likely to inflict much greater strain and pressure on urban relationships, amenity and sanitation. Furthermore, although by 1830 most Scots still lived in quasi-urban settlements, in country villages and in farm steadings, the growing urban areas had now become the strategic presence in the society and economy of Scotland. The towns were no longer adjuncts to an overwhelmingly rural social order but had become the dynamic centres of economic change. The lives of the country dwelling populace were themselves altered fundamentally by the needs of the teeming cities for food and raw materials and the impact these requirements had on the social structure and stability of countless rural communities in the Highlands and Lowlands.

	1600	1650	1700	1750	1800
Scotland	×	17	51	124	132
England and Wales	×	94	45	42	83

Table 8.2: Percentage Increase in Urban Population (as defined in Table 8.1) from Previous Data, Scotland, England and Wales.

Why Scotland should experience such a precocious rate of urban growth is a question that requires detailed consideration, since its consequences for the long-run development of Scottish society were so profound. The essential foundation, though not the principal direct cause, was the revolution in agriculture described in Chapter 7 which occurred in parallel with town and city expansion. Urbanization could not have taken place without a substantial increase in food production to sustain the needs of those who did not cultivate their own food supplies. However, for much of the period of this analysis, the urban masses mainly relied on grain, milk, potatoes and meat supplied from Scottish farms. They were fed through a rise in both the production and productivity of agriculture achieved by a reorganization in farm structure, a more effective deployment of labour, and higher yields derived from improved fallowing, the sowing of root crops and the adoption of new rotation systems. One knowledgeable contemporary, for example, took the view that from the 1750s to the 1820s the output of corn and vegetables had doubled in Scotland, while that of animal foods multiplied sixfold.

The process of agricultural reform also contributed directly to town growth at two other levels. First, the increasing orientation of agriculture towards the market further stimulated the function of urban areas as centres of exchange. There was a greater need than before for the commercial, legal and financial facilities which concentrated in towns. Perth, Ayr, Haddington, Dumfries, Stirling and several other towns owed much of their expansion in this period to the increasing requirements for their services from the commercialized agricultural systems of their hinterlands. Regional specialization in agrarian production also enhanced the need for growing centres of exchange. Inverness, for example, expanded on the basis of its crucial role as the sheep and wool mart of the Highlands as that area became a great specialist centre of pastoral husbandry in the first half of the nineteenth century. Second, the prosperity of Scottish agriculture during the Napoleonic Wars boosted the incomes of tenant farmers and inflated the rent rolls of many landowners. The increase in the purchasing power of these classes had major implications for urban growth because it resulted in rising demand for the products of town consumer and luxury industries, and for more and better urban services in education, in leisure and in the provision of fashionable accommodation.

Yet agrarian improvement was the necessary condition for Scottish urbanization rather than its principal determinant. Towns which acted mainly as exchange and service centres for rural hinterlands expanded only relatively modestly, at a rate which was only slightly higher than the national rate of natural increase. Moreover, the rise in population which occurred in all western European societies from the later eighteenth century encouraged food producers throughout the continent to increase their output in order to cope with enhanced demand. The nature of the Scottish Agricultural Revolution may have had distinctive

PART TWO: 1760-1830

features, but agrarian improvement was too common in Europe at this time to provide the basic explanation for Scotland's exceptional pace of urban development. It is more likely that Scottish town expansion was a direct consequence of Scotland's equally remarkable rate of general economic growth between 1760 and 1830. The Industrial Revolution before 1830 was mainly confined to mainland Britain, and it is hardly a coincidence that in this same period urbanization occurred more vigorously in England and Scotland than in any other European country. Scottish industrialization and Scottish urban growth were both results of the same economic forces because the town and city environment gave much easier access to dense concentration of producers and consumers.

This process had two interlinked aspects. The first was commercial in origin. In the eighteenth century, Scotland was in a superb geographical position to take advantage of the changing direction of international trade towards the Atlantic world. This momentous alteration in transcontinental commerce was a highly dynamic factor in port development along the whole western coast of Europe from Cork to Cadiz. Scotland was virtually at the crossroads of the new system, and the Clyde ports grew rapidly to become the great tobacco emporia of the United Kingdom until diversifying later into the importation of sugar and cotton. It was no coincidence that in the later eighteenth century four of the five fastest-growing towns in Scotland were in the Clyde basin. Commercial success was bound to foster urban expansion. The carriage and merchandising of goods in bulk were all highly labour-intensive in this period and demanded large concentrations of labour. Considerable investment was also needed to build up the complex infrastructure of trade: warehouses, ports, industries, merchants' mansions, banks, exchanges, inns and coffee houses. Greenock may be taken as the archetypal port town of the western Lowlands. It mushroomed in size from a population of 2,000 in 1700 to 17,500 in 1801 and to 27,500 by 1831. By that date Greenock had become one of the six largest towns in Scotland. Irish trade, coastal commerce and continuing economic connections with Europe also stimulated port development along both the east and west coasts.

But, in the long run, the expansion of manufacturing industry was even more critical for urbanization than the stimulus derived from international and inter-regional commerce. Of the 13 largest towns in early nineteenth-century Scotland, five at least trebled their population size between *c.* 1750 and 1821. In addition to Greenock these were Glasgow (from 31,700 to 147,000), Paisley (6,800 to 47,000), Kilmarnock (4,400 to 12,700) and Falkirk (3,900 to 11,500). Greenock apart, the inhabitants of all these towns mainly depended either directly or indirectly on manufacturing industry. It was the larger industrial towns and the constellation of smaller urban areas with which they were associated that set the pace of Scottish urbanization. It is important to emphasize, of course, that industry did not necessarily or inevitably generate large-scale urban expansion in the short run. As late as the 1830s, for instance, around two-thirds of Scotland's handloom weavers of cotton, linen and woollen cloth lived in country villages or small towns. The water-powered cotton-spinning factories of the last quarter of the eighteenth century were more often to be found in rural settlements such as Catrine, New Lanark or Deanston than in the cities. Throughout the period under consideration, both coal mining and pig-iron manufacture were also located in small towns and country villages. The continued presence of industry in a variety of forms in the countryside helps to explain why a majority of the Scottish people still lived outside large urban areas by 1830.

Yet, in the long run, there were obvious advantages in industrial concentration in towns. Manufacturers were able to gain from 'external economies': firms saved the costs of providing accommodation and other facilities for their workers from their own resources; they were guaranteed access to a huge pool of labour, and transport costs between sources of supply, finishing trades and repair shops could be markedly reduced or virtually eliminated by the close proximity of complementary economic activities. These advantages built up a dynamic for urban expansion even before 1800. Thereafter, the new technology of steam propulsion and conspicuous progress in transport developments through the construction of canals and roads steadily intensified the forces making for urban concentration. In cotton-spinning, and eventually in other textile industries, steam power encouraged industrial settlements on the coalfields and removed the one major obstacle that had previously constricted the expansion of manufacturing in the larger towns.

Glasgow provides the most dramatic case of the pattern of change. In 1795 the city had 11 cotton-spinning complexes, but rural Renfrewshire had 12. The fundamental need to have secure access to water power obviously diluted Glasgow's other attractions as a centre of textile industrial production. However, steam-based technology was rapidly adopted after 1800 and concentration accelerated on an enormous scale in the city and its immediate environs. By 1839 there were 192 cotton mills in Scotland employing 31,000 workers. All but 17 were located in Renfrew and Lanark, and 98 were in or near Glasgow. In Paisley, or its vicinity, there was a further great network of 40 factories employing almost 5,000 workers. A similar process of intensifying convergence evolved over a longer time-scale in the Border wool towns of Hawick and Galashiels and the linen centres of the eastern Lowlands: '. . . there emerged a strong urban concentration – Dundee specialised in heavy flax and tow fabrics, Arbroath was the seat of the canvas trade, Forfar and Brechin produced heavy linens such as osnaburghs and northern Fife specialised in finer linens and bleached goods'.[1] Before 1830, textile manufacturing was the principal motor of this process of agglomeration. Until then, for example, it was the cotton centres of Glasgow and its suburbs and Renfrewshire which grew most rapidly in the western Lowlands. Only thereafter, and especially from the 1840s, did intensive urban development spread from them to the coal and iron towns of Coatbridge, Airdrie and Wishaw in north Lanarkshire.

2

Despite fast urban growth, there remained considerable continuity between the old world and the new. The four major cities of the early nineteenth century – Edinburgh, Glasgow, Aberdeen and Dundee – were also the biggest Scottish burghs of the seventeenth century, although of course they had experienced substantial changes in size, occupational structure and economic specialization over that period. Again, the 13 largest Scottish towns of the early eighteenth century were the same, with only one or two exceptions, as those of 1830. The biggest urban areas, therefore, were all ancient places and the traditional county and regional capitals also continued to play a role whether as centres of administration or of local government or as markets for prosperous agricultural hinterlands. But by 1830 the Scottish urban system had also developed some characteristic features typical of the new era.

For a start, urbanization was mainly concentrated in the narrow belt of land in the western and eastern Lowlands. Between 1801 and 1841 never less than 83 per cent of the entire Scottish urban population (defined as those inhabiting towns of 5,000 or more) lived in this region. Within the area there was heavy concentration in Glasgow and Edinburgh, where, as early as 1800, 60 per cent of Scottish urban dwellers resided. Again, there was wide diversity within the urban structure. In very broad terms, most Scottish towns fitted into one of three categories: first, the four major cities; second, industrial towns; and third, local capitals in historic sites which performed marketing and service functions for their immediate neighbourhoods. In addition, there was a miscellany of other urban settlements, including the fishing ports of the Fife and Moray coast, the old coal and salt burghs of the Forth estuary and the new inland spas of Bridge of Allan, Peebles and Strathpeffer. Of these groups, the industrial staple towns and some of the cities were most likely to suffer the adverse consequences of expansion which are often associated with urbanization at this time. Such places as Paisley, Falkirk, Kilmarnock and Hawick grew swiftly, and their mainly working-class inhabitants were usually heavily concentrated in one or two industries which were often geared to overseas markets and hence were vulnerable to the changes in demand for international commodities. The ordinary people of these towns endured great suffering in the serious commercial depressions of 1816–17, 1825 and 1836–7.

In relative terms, at least, those who dwelt in the regional centres were better placed. Their typically moderate rate of population growth ensured that the existing organization of sewage and waste disposal was not so easily overwhelmed as elsewhere, though it must be stressed that at this time sanitary problems were a familiar feature of all Scottish towns, whatever their size. In addition, their occupational structure was more diverse than that of the staple towns and, because the economy of such centres depended primarily on their service function to surrounding rural areas, they were less vulnerable to the social crises provoked by cyclical unemployment. Again, however, distinctions should not be drawn too neatly because some towns of this type (such as Perth, for instance) had a considerable industrial presence and could not be entirely insulated from the ebb and flow of external demand for manufactured goods. The differences between centres like this and the staple towns were sometimes of degree rather than of kind.

The main contrasts in the occupational structure of Scotland's four cities are best studied from Tables 8.3(a) and 8.3(b). One similarity, however, is worth emphasizing initially. Except in the case of Edinburgh, the dominance of textile employment is very obvious and underscores the point made earlier in this chapter about the essential importance of cotton, linen and, to a lesser extent, woollen manufacture in Scotland's first phase of urbanization. The relative stability and balance of Edinburgh's economic base is also apparent. The majority of the employed population worked in small-scale consumer industries, many of which depended on demand from a middle- and upper-class clientele. Domestic service was far and away the largest employment of female labour. This occupational pattern reflected Edinburgh's metropolitan status, the significant numbers of salaried professionals in the city who represented a large pool of demand for services and luxury consumer goods, and the major functions of the capital in the areas of law, banking and education. Poverty and destitution were endemic in certain parts of the city, notably in the Old Town and elsewhere, but the ordinary people of the capital were less likely to experience the full horrors of cyclical unemployment on the same scale as their counterparts in Dundee and Glasgow.

Percentage of workforce in:	Glasgow	Edinburgh	Dundee	Aberdeen
Printing & Publishing	1.12	3.88	0.56	0.91
Engineering, Toolmaking & Metals	7.17	6.07	5.59	6.32
Shipbuilding	0.35	0.17	1.14	1.24
Coachbuilding	0.40	0.92	0.21	0.34
Building	5.84	5.73	6.05	5.99
Furniture & Woodmaking	1.06	2.73	0.77	0.87
Chemicals	1.22	0.24	0.19	0.37
Food, Drink & Tobacco	5.24	8.31	5.27	4.66
Textiles & Clothing	37.56	13.04	50.54	34.68
Other Manufacturing	2.90	3.02	1.29	3.18
General Labouring	8.40	3.69	3.84	6.87

*Table 8.3(a): Occupational Structure in the Scottish Cities, 1841 (*Percentage of Total Workforce).
Source: Census of 1841 (Parliamentary papers, 1844, XXVII) and R. Rodger, 'Employment, Wages and Poverty in the Scottish Cities, 1841-1914', appendix 1, in George Gordon (ed.), *Perspectives of the Scottish City* (Aberdeen, 1985).

Note that occupational classification in the 1841 census is questionable and imprecise. The precise figures presented here are unlikely to be wholly accurate; they provide an impression of overall structures rather than an exact measurement of them.

	Professional		Domestic		Commercial		Industrial		Agriculture & fishing	
	M	F	M	F	M	F	M	F	M	F
Glasgow (and suburbs)	4.53	0.57	2.03	31.60	15.09	2.87	73.92	64.59	4.43	0.37
Edinburgh (and suburbs)	13.34	1.93	6.53	70.36	14.10	2.71	62.26	23.61	2.77	1.39
Dundee	4.98	0.88	1.95	27.30	13.70	2.79	76.57	68.65	2.80	0.38
Aberdeen	6.46	2.24	4.05	40.37	14.57	2.44	68.71	53.98	6.21	0.97

Table 8.3(b): Occupational Structure in the Scottish Cities, 1841, By Sector (Percentage of Total Workforce).
Source: as for Table 8.3(a).

Aberdeen, though smaller, was closest to Edinburgh in occupational structure. It performed the same key legal, educational and financial services for the north-east region as Edinburgh did for the whole of Scotland. The proportion of professionals in the employed population was second only to Edinburgh, and there was also a significantly high number of domestic servants. On the other hand, there was extensive textile employment and, alone among the major cities, Aberdeen had a significant proportion of males occupied in fishing. By and large, the city possessed a relatively balanced occupational structure and, by the standards of other large towns, experienced a moderate rate of growth before 1830. Not surprisingly, therefore, it was spared some of the worst of the social problems that afflicted Glasgow and Dundee.

Glasgow and Dundee were alike in their heavy dependence on textile employment, the speed of their growth in the nineteenth century (though Dundee grew most rapidly from the 1820s and 1840s) and the relative weakness of the professional element in their occupational structures. It was these two cities which suffered acute problems of health, sanitation and poverty. In the short term, and especially before 1840, Glasgow's difficulties attracted most attention. In the long run, however, Dundee appeared even more vulnerable. Over half of its employed population were engaged in textiles alone and increasingly these were low-paid females occupied in the heavy linen and jute industries. Already by 1841, the urban economy of Dundee had become dangerously lop-sided.

3

Rapid urban growth depended on migration. Of the 10 principal Scottish towns in 1851, only 47 per cent of their inhabitants had actually been born in them. The majority of the migrants were young adults, more concentrated in the marriageable and child-bearing age groups than were the native inhabitants. High migration because of its age composition was therefore likely to fuel natural increase in the urban areas. Of those born in Dundee in 1851, only 37 per cent were aged 20 and over, but 70 per cent of the migrants to the city fell into that age group. The overwhelming majority of migrants had travelled only short distances. Most new Aberdonians, for instance, were from the north-eastern counties; the largest number of Greenock's Highland immigrants came from localities in the vicinity of the town in the neighbouring southern Highlands. During the 1820s, burial records show that one-third of those buried in Dundee who were not natives of the city had been born in the city's county of Angus, and most of the rest came from the surrounding east coast areas. The big towns all had population catchment areas which were usually in their immediate vicinity.

In the main, only the largest centres, such as Glasgow and Edinburgh, had apparently the capacity to attract many people over long distances. Despite Scottish myth, which sometimes portrays the Highlands as being emptied to furnish labour for the large towns, permanent migration to the south from the north-west before 1830 was relatively limited compared to the high levels of mobility in some Lowland country parishes. As late as 1851, however, only around 5 per cent of Glasgow's population were born in the Highlands and the majority of these came from the southern districts on the edge of the Lowlands rather than from the crofting region of the far west. Many of the people from the Hebrides clearly preferred transatlantic emigration to permanent movement to the cities in the early nineteenth century, though temporary migration to the Lowlands was also extensive and important.

Highland movement was dwarfed by Irish migration which accelerated from Ulster and eastern Connaught in the 1810s and 1820s due to the difficulties there of the native linen manufacture and the quicker and cheaper access to the Clyde ports afforded by the new steamships. The Irish immigrants of this period were both Catholic and Protestant, and it was the transfer of traditional sectarian animosities to Scotland as much as native Scottish prejudice which provoked religious and social bitterness in the wake of this movement. In 1851, after the even greater immigration of the Great Famine, 7 per cent of the total Scottish population were Irish-born, more than twice that of England. But this bald figure underestimates the Irish influence on Scottish urban life. J. E. Handley rightly stresses that those of Irish extraction should be included in the count as well as the Irish-born. Handley's revised estimates would suggest that in 1841 almost a quarter of the people of the western Lowlands were of Irish extraction. Moreover, Irish immigration tended to concentrate on specific urban areas, and global figures conceal the impact of the distribution. Thus 44,000 of Glasgow's population in 1841, or 16 per cent of the total of 274,000, were Irish-born. But if Handley is correct, it would mean that at that date around one in three of the city's inhabitants were of Irish descent.

No single factor was decisive in explaining the increasing scale of rural-to-urban migration within Scotland. There was undoubtedly a distinctive urban pull. As A. S. Wohl has suggested, 'urbanisation meant more jobs, a wider diversity of social contacts and infinitely greater colour and excitement in the lives of the masses'.[2] Higher wages than were usual in the rural economy and a greater range of employment opportunities helped to hasten migration to towns *in the later eighteenth century* to such an extent that Scottish farmers in the zones where urban growth concentrated were forced to raise wages in order to retain labour. Even after the Napoleonic Wars, when urban demand for labour slackened, and clear signs emerged of a labour surplus in some of the cities, the towns still retained their allure. The poor health record of the large towns did not deter migrants, and indeed there is evidence that urban crises of mortality were sometimes followed by 'replenishment migration'. The fact that the overwhelming majority of newcomers to the towns came from adjacent districts was itself confirmation of the importance of the 'pull' factor.

The close proximity between the source of migrants and the host towns facilitated migration. The urban areas were near and familiar. Migration did not mean that all contact with the native rural community was lost. There was much seasonal and temporary migration and a connection could be retained with kinfolk who normally lived short distances away. Many of the migrants to the cities already had some experience of town life. One of the biggest migrant streams was that which linked different urban areas: not all or even the majority of new arrivals were the rural innocents of legend. It should not be forgotten either that extensive migration was not unique to the era of urbanization. Mobility over short distances was common in pre-industrial Scotland long before the late eighteenth century. Again, the apparent obstacles to rural-to-urban migration were often more apparent than real. A crude contrast is occasionally drawn with the radical change in lifestyle forced upon peasant cultivators who moved to factory employment in the cities. But this stereotype did not necessarily apply to the majority of migrants. Most townspeople before 1830 worked outside the factory, in workshops, in homes and in the open air. There were, therefore, often important continuities between rural and urban employments, especially when it is remembered that before 1760 the spinning and weaving of textiles was so extensive in Lowland Scotland that most country families must have had some members with experience of industrial labour. The migrant could also ease the process of urban assimilation by lodging with kinfolk or with family friends from the same locality. Movement from country to town was in this way facilitated both by the previous experience of the migrants themselves and by the strategies they adopted to adjust to a new life.

The most controversial aspect of migration at this time is the question of how far people were 'forced' off the land into towns as the process of agrarian reorganization gathered pace from the later eighteenth century. As seen in Chapter 7, the numbers with either a legal or customary right to land in Lowland Scotland did decline rapidly after c. 1780 as main tenancies were consolidated and subtenancies eliminated when rationalization quickened. On the other hand, in the short run at least, the creation of the modern agrarian structure, through the construction of farmhouses, roads, fencing and dikes and the adoption of the new rotation crops of sown grasses and turnips, seemed to require more rather than less labour than the old system. The new ploughs were certainly labour-saving and labour productivity increased as work organization was improved, but most farm tasks remained unmechanized and there was an overall increase in demand for labour as production of foods and raw materials intensified. In addition, textile and other manufactures expanded in the country villages and small towns. There was therefore often less need for dispossessed cottars with craft skills to move to the big cities in order to make a living. Rather, surviving wage data for the later eighteenth century, when agrarian reorganization accelerated, suggest that rural employers were forced to offer increasing wages in order to compete with their urban counterparts. In that period, therefore, it would seem that many migrants from the country, far from being forced off the land, were being lured to the towns by the positive attractions of higher wages and a greater range of employment opportunities.

Yet there were indeed fundamental links between rural-to-urban migration in Scotland and the social changes initiated by the Agricultural Revolution, even if they were more subtle than is sometimes suggested. The creation of a landless labour force did not necessarily cause people to leave their rural environment, but it did facilitate it. Peasant farmers are notoriously reluctant to give up their holdings. Pierre Goubert's well-known aphorism is appropriate: 'No peasant willingly surrenders land, be it only half a furrow.' Landless wage labourers were, however, much more mobile. They survive through selling their labour power in the market and they could fall back on scraping a living from a smallholding, no matter how meagre. Again, outside the south-east Lowlands, Fife and some other districts, most regular farm workers in Lowland Scotland were unmarried male and female servants, hired on six-monthly contracts. At marriage, many were forced to move to alternative employments. They were a highly mobile group, and one option among several for them was movement to the towns. All the local studies demonstrate a great haemorrhage from farm service at age 23 to 25, the average age at marriage in Scotland at this time.

In the final analysis, however, the main momentum was probably generated by the acceleration in Scottish population growth, which occurred from the early nineteenth century, and the social effect that this had in country areas, as well as agrarian reorganization in itself. Scottish demographic expansion in the later eighteenth century was unusually modest by the standards prevailing in Ireland, England and several continental societies. Between 1755 and 1801, the annual rate of increase was only about 0.6 per cent. From 1801 to 1811, however, this doubled to 1.2 per cent and it increased again to 1.6 per cent per annum from 1811 to 1821. Such a rate of growth might well have swamped rural labour markets and the problem would have been aggravated by the great demobilization of soldiers and sailors after the Napoleonic Wars. Though farmers had a need for more hands, the demand for labour was not increasing at anything like the pace of population growth, especially as agricultural income and hence employment opportunities contracted with the slump in grain prices after the Napoleonic Wars. One might realistically have anticipated a huge expansion in unemployment in rural districts. This was the experience in the western Highlands – but not in the Lowlands, partly because of the expulsive force of the Scottish structure of engagement for farm service. In the later eighteenth century, it became a major principle of Scottish improving policy that only the population essential for proper cultivation should be retained permanently on the land. Accommodation in and around the farm was strictly limited thereafter to the specific labour needs of the farmer. Cottages surplus to these requirements were pulled down and the building of new accommodation strictly controlled. This inevitably became a mechanism for channelling excess labour off the land, especially when it is remembered that the able-bodied unemployed had no legal right to be relieved under the Scottish Poor Law, even if occasional assistance was sometimes provided at times of acute difficulty. The combination of this system, a natural and accelerating rise in population and only slowly growing or stagnant employment opportunities in agriculture after 1812–13 helped to drive an increasing movement of people from country to town. In the 1810s and 1820s Scotland had a growing problem of unemployment. But it did not concentrate in the Lowland rural areas and was instead mainly confined to the large towns, the western Highlands and the communities of industrial workers (and especially handloom weavers) in the countryside. Some of its effects will now be considered.

4

The speed of Scottish urban expansion did not have a significant impact on mortality rates until the second and third decades of the nineteenth century. The larger towns were mainly free of epidemic fevers from 1790 to 1815 but these diseases (mainly typhus) then reappeared at recurrent intervals in 1817–20, 1826–7 and 1836–7. Scotland also experienced in 1831–2 its first major attack of the dreaded cholera, which claimed 10,000 victims. Interpretation of mortality statistics for any period in the first half of the nineteenth century is hazardous. But the careful enumerations carried out by some pioneering city doctors leave little doubt that the cities were steadily becoming more lethal. In Edinburgh, where conditions were by no means the worst of the larger towns, the death rate which had fallen to 25 per 1,000 in 1810–19, climbed to 26.2 in the following decade and reached 29 per 1,000 between 1820 and 1839. So marked was the general rise in urban mortality rates that they help to explain why *national* death rates also began to escalate after sustained decline in earlier decades. There could be no more telling or ominous illustration of the new significance of the large towns in Scottish life. Indeed, by the 1830s and 1840s some were approaching a social crisis of unprecedented proportions. Meaningful efforts at reform rather than temporary palliatives were not even contemplated until the 1840s, and not before the second half of the nineteenth century were some of the worst aspects of the urban problem effectively tackled.

Urban growth brought major health problems throughout Britain, but both available statistical evidence and contemporary comment suggest that conditions were much worse in Scotland than in England. As Edwin Chadwick concluded in his *Sanitary Report* of 1842: 'there is evidence to prove that the mortality from fever is greater in Glasgow, Edinburgh and Dundee than in the most crowded towns in England'.[3] The influences that promoted environmental decline in cities in the first half of the nineteenth century have been chronicled in full detail by a number of historians and there is no need to explore them at great length here. They included, *inter alia*, the absence of effective sanitation; the Scottish tradition of accommodating people in high-built tenements, courts and wynds; little or no street cleansing in poor neighbourhoods; inadequate supplies of uncontaminated water; the inertia of unreformed municipal authorities; medical ignorance of the causes and nature of the major killer diseases; and ideologies which blamed poverty and squalor on weakness of character rather than environmental constraints. These and other factors ensured that rising urban death rates did not begin to come under effective control until the 1850s. But most were common to both England and Scotland and cannot in themselves explain the peculiarly bad conditions in several of the Scottish cities. To do that, distinctively Scottish influences must be considered.

Some are already obvious from the earlier discussion. Scottish urbanization was faster than probably anywhere else in western Europe between 1760 and 1830, and the rate of growth simply overwhelmed the contemporary structures of sanitation and amenity in a great rising tide of humanity. Much of Glasgow's notoriety as the unhealthiest city in Britain at this time stemmed from the simple fact that it was growing more swiftly than any other British city of its size, adding a staggering 5,000 every year to its population in the 1820s. It must also be remembered that the larger Scottish towns, especially those in the western Lowlands and Dundee, played host to migrants from Ireland and parts of the Highlands, two of the poorest regional societies in the British Isles. The Irish, in particular, often arrived in a semi-destitute condition, concentrated in the poorest quarters of towns, were more vulnerable to the diseases of the city and inevitably aggravated pressure on accommodation.

But the familiar plight of the Irish was but a part of a more general and deeper social crisis in early nineteenth-century Scotland. The rapid industrialization of the society was partially due to the fact that Scottish labour costs were lower than rates in England. This, in turn, was a reflection of the relative poverty of the country as many thousands in the booming towns of Scotland eked out an existence close to the margins of destitution, a condition aggravated by the rigour and meanness of the Scottish Poor Law. All the large towns had armies of casual labourers who worked in the varied urban tasks of fetching, carrying, loading and building. James Cleland estimated that almost a quarter of Glasgow's labour force in 1831 were casual workers who had to endure a life of very poor wages, broken time and employment which fluctuated markedly throughout the year. People like these had little economic power to create market demand for decent housing. Instead, they eked out a living in grossly overcrowded, subdivided tenements in the decaying heart of the booming cities, particularly the Old Town in Edinburgh and the notorious Wynds of Glasgow. Housing conditions in these areas were appalling simply because many had no alternative but to accept them.

The connection between poverty and urban mortality was vividly demonstrated during the three great industrial recessions, of 1816–18, 1825 and 1836. It was these rather than poor sanitation as such that precipitated the first sharp upswing in urban death rates in Scottish cities in the nineteenth century. Significantly, fever was much rarer in the early years of the century despite the fact that then, too, sanitary provision was very poor. Typhus only became a major killer in the crisis years of profound economic difficulty following the Napoleonic Wars. All three depressions were followed by savage epidemics in 1816–18, 1827–8 and 1837–9 which remorselessly drove up mortality rates in all the larger towns. Poverty and destitution were obviously as lethal as inadequate sewerage and poor housing. This was not the result of urbanism *per se* but rather the inevitable consequence of a general imbalance between population and employment opportunities in Scotland in the two decades before 1830. It was an imbalance that began to be contained only in the second phase of industrialization when iron, coal and engineering expanded from the middle decades of the nineteenth century, though even then appalling social conditions endured in the heart of the nation's largest cities. Industrial expansion and its offspring, urbanization, significantly increased the volume and range of jobs down to 1830, but not at the rate required to provide regular and decent employment for the constantly rising numbers of people entering the labour market.

9

The Disintegration of Clanship

It was once assumed that the old Highland society perished in the bloody carnage of Culloden Moor and was finally buried in the military repression and primitive legislation that followed the Jacobite defeat. Recent perspectives, based on wide-ranging archival research into both landed and government records, tell a different story. Culloden and the aftermath were the climax, not the beginning, of the imposition of state authority on Gaeldom. From the later part of the sixteenth century the monarchy of James VI was extending control, and the state became progressively more powerful during Cromwell's regime in the 1650s and after the first Jacobite rebellion in 1688–9. The Massacre of Glencoe showed the determination of the Williamite state in the 1690s to employ violence against recalcitrant clans. The construction in the 1720s and 1730s of Wade's military network of roads and bridges, though during the '45 ineffectual, also symbolized the penetration of government authority. The militarism of the clans was also in decline. Government and Whig propagandists portrayed clan society as addicted to rape, plunder and collective violence. The reality was that by the early eighteenth century cattle raiding and protection rackets were confined to particular areas such as the frontier lands of the Highlands and the more inaccessible parts of Lochaber. The notion that the clans were constantly at war or preparing for war is mistaken. The last major clan battle took place near Spean Bridge in 1688, more than 50 years before the last Jacobite rebellion of 1745. Despite the popular image, the vast majority of Gaels who fought in all the Jacobite uprisings had never seen military action before. It is significant, for instance, that before the battle of Killiecrankie in 1689 Viscount Dundee was concerned how his raw clansmen would react under fire. Daniel Defoe noted the decline of militarism in his *Tour Through the Whole Island of Great Britain*. The people of the central Highlands were 'a fierce, fighting and furious kind of men' but they were by 'the good conduct' of the clan élites 'much more civilised than they were in former times'.[1]

Commercial forces were already causing tensions in the social cohesion of the clans. Markets were developing to the south for Highland goods – above all for cattle which, alone of Scottish products, did very well in the years after the union – but also for timber, fish and slate. The returns from these trades helped to sustain absenteeism and consumerism among the clan élites. Household accounts show a growing appetite for elegant furniture, fashionable clothing, pictures, books and musical instruments. The clan bards were alarmed at the trends and lamented the habit of chiefs who spent longer periods in Edinburgh or even in London and neglected their traditional patriarchal duties. There were already signs that profit was starting to take precedence over the ancient social responsibilities of the élites. The commons of the clans expected the ruling families to act as their protectors and guarantee secure possession of land in return for allegiance, military service, tribute and rental. But the evidence suggests that this social contract was already under acute pressure in some parts of Gaeldom even before the '45. Rents were rising, especially in the great territorial empire of Clan Campbell, which included most of the county of Argyll. During the 1730s came the first significant emigrations from Sutherland, Argyll and the central Highlands to Georgia and the Carolinas. The most flagrant breach of the clan ethic involved the two most powerful chiefs in Skye, Norman MacLeod of MacLeod and Sir Alexander MacDonald of Sleat. They devised a scheme to deport some of their tenants, with their wives and children, to the American colonies to be sold as indentured labour for the plantations. In the resulting scandal both of them were threatened with prosecution at law.

It is also easy to exaggerate the impact of the '45 as a turning point in Highland history. The government's intentions were perfectly clear: first, to take a terrible revenge on the Jacobite clans and then finally to destroy the system of clanship which spawned rebellion and disaffection. As discussed in Chapter 2, the long-term results of these draconian policies are in some doubt. The reign of terror imposed by the avenging Hanoverian regiments, as secret government reports confirm, often bred defiance rather than quiescence. The proscription of military land tenures, such as wardship, and the abolition of heritable jurisdictions had little effect. Government made the mistake of thinking that the power of the clan chiefs lay in these legal controls. In fact the loyalties inherent in clanship were matters of the heart and mind rather than of the law. Wardship itself had already been made redundant as a result of the commercial developments of the later seventeenth and early eighteenth centuries. The state's ambitious military and legislative programme to eliminate clanship has to be seen against an ongoing process of decline in clan values which had already developed deep roots long before the 1740s. In addition, much more potent than government policy was the impact of market forces after c. 1760 and the transformation of clan chiefs into commercial landlords. As will be seen, these were the essential influences that finally killed clanship.

In the 1760s and 1770s as in the rest of Scotland there was a marked acceleration in the rate of social change and, in subsequent decades, material, cultural and demographic forces combined to produce a dramatic revolution in the Highland way of life. In simple terms, traditional society was destroyed in this period and a new order based on quite different values, principles and relationships emerged to take its place. Before this time, élite attitudes were changing, commercial influences increasing and government pressures on clanship in the aftermath of the '45 intensifying. However, the basic structure of Gaelic society in most areas remained broadly unaltered. What happened in the last quarter of the eighteenth century was a decisive change of pace which was brought about by an enormous expansion in the rest of Britain for such Highland produce as cattle, kelp, whisky, wool, mutton, timber, slate and a host of other commodities. The irresistible material and ideological forces which were unleashed transformed the Highlands for ever.

Commerce, and in particular the export of cattle and the import of meal, had long been vital to Gaelic society. But in this period southern markets began to exert such a dominant influence that the Highland region effectively became an economic satellite, with its population increasingly dependent for survival on demand for products from the industries and cities of the Lowlands and England. A full-scale process of commercialization was under way and one important indicator was the movement of rentals. Starting in the 1760s, but speeding up drastically during the Napoleonic Wars, rentals throughout the region soared to unprecedented levels to catch the surplus from rising prices.

It was the speed and scale of rent inflation that was new and different from the earlier eighteenth century and, in addition, most of it reflected surging external demand rather than a return on landlord improvement investment. Skye rents trebled in the third quarter of the eighteenth century, while those of Torridon in Wester Ross rose tenfold between 1777 and 1805. On the Lochiel estate in Inverness, the rental jumped from £560 in the 1760s to £863 in 1774, an increase of 54 per cent, with even more dramatic rises later. Glengarry rentals stood at £732 in 1768 but by 1802 had spiralled by 472 per cent to £4,184.

The raising of rents to this extent demonstrated that the Highland élites were now subordinating their lands to market production and new profit imperatives. The growing commercial economy of the decades before c. 1760 could be uneasily accommodated within the old social structure but the traditional order was no longer compatible with wholehearted agricultural production for the market at competitive prices. Important consequences ensued. The transition of clan chiefs and gentry to landed gentlemen, which had been under way for several generations, was finally achieved and the heritable trusteeship of clan élites, obliging them to secure and maintain the landed possessions of their kindred and associates within their territories, was abruptly abandoned in favour of other priorities. Land came to be allocated through competition to those bidders able and willing to offer the highest return. It was the resolute imposition of these new standards when tenancies were available for reletting which was one factor in stoking up the social tensions, stimulating wave after wave of emigration from the western Highlands in the later eighteenth century.

In addition, there was a sustained and widespread assault on the traditional township or *baile*. These group settlements of multiple tenant farmers, cottars and servants had formed the basic communities of Gaeldom from time immemorial, but over the space of two to three generations, starting in Argyll and Highland Perthshire in the 1760s and quickly spreading north and west in subsequent decades, the *baile* was broken up and virtually eliminated. By the 1830s and 1840s only a few remnants of a once universal pattern of settlement and cultivation remained. But the new structure that emerged to take its place was far from simple and reflected not only the strategies of individual landowners but varying physical resources, climatic advantage and market potential. Thus, in much of Argyll, Highland Perthshire and the eastern parishes of Inverness, lands were often consolidated into single tenant farms, some pastoral but many arable, with their dependent servants and labourers. In this region too were the crofts or smallholdings that were more typical of the north and west. The heartland of the new 'crofting' society, however, was the western seaboard to the north of Fort William and extending to all the Inner and Outer Hebrides. In this region the communal townships were steadily replaced by individual smallholdings or crofts with the arable land possessed by single small tenants and the grazing land still held in common. The core of the new structure, however, was division of the scattered strips or rigs of arable, which were the basis of the old system of joint farming, into separate holdings of only a few acres. In addition, throughout the whole Highland area, but especially before 1815 in the central and western mainland, commercial pastoral farms were advancing rapidly. The coming of the *Na Caoraidh Mora* or 'big sheep' posed a particular threat to the old society. Before the 1750s there were few commercial, specialist sheep ranches anywhere in the Highlands. Yet, as early as 1802, an official report of the Highland Society described how the hill country of Perth, Dumbarton and Argyll and the entire west coast from Oban to Lochbroom were already under sheep. Most of Mull had been invaded, and the sheep frontier was also starting to advance in Skye. The report concluded ominously that 'In Ross and northwards all parts capable of sheep are or soon will be occupied.'[2]

There were also important effects on social structure partly to do with the impact of the crofting revolution. The delicate and graduated social hierarchies of the *baile* were shattered and replaced by the virtually uniform small tenancies of the new crofting townships. Equally significantly, the traditional tacksman or gentry class was gradually reduced in number and social significance as the deliberate destruction of subtenure became a central theme of landlord policy from the 1770s. The action of the Duke of Argyll against the *daoine uaisle* of his estate had been unusual in the 1730s, but 50 years later it was commonplace as the landed classes sought to absorb the middlemen rentals. The demise of the tacksmen varied in speed and extent from estate to estate. Some who were wadsetters (that is, gentlemen who had received lands from their chief as security in return for providing loans) were bought out; others were placed in difficulty by having their rights to subletting reduced. Sharp increases in rental also put acute pressure on many, as in the 1750s much of the rent on many Highland estates would be directly paid by the tacksmen. A century later they were but a minor part of the social structure, and their decline was one of the clearest signs of the death knell of the old Gaelic society. The new middle class in many areas invariably comprised southern sheep farmers and cattle ranchers with little hereditary or ethnic connection with the people.

The new landlord priorities and incessant market pressures produced a massive and relentless displacement of population. Eviction and forced removal became an integral part of the destruction of the traditional settlements throughout the Highlands. This was the most direct violation of *duthchas*, the obligation on clan élites to provide protection and security of possession for their people within their lands. 'Clearance', as the process of dispossession became known to later generations, was far from simple. Too often it is equated only with the removals resulting from the creation of large sheep farms. But displacement took place by other means and for other reasons. The carving out of the monotonous lines of crofts from the scattered rigs of the *baile* sometimes led to the eviction of entire communities. It also became almost routine for estates in the north-west and the islands to move people from inland glens to the sea and to areas of moorland where new crofts were planted in the waste and the settlers encouraged to reclaim it by potato cultivation. Removal of the *bailtean* to create larger arable holdings was a marked feature of the southern Highlands. Today at Auchindrain in Argyllshire there still survive many of the buildings of an old farming township in a marvellous open-air museum. But in the 1760s in the half dozen miles between Auchindrain and Inveraray, the Campbell capital in Argyll, there were no fewer than a further six settlements. By the nineteenth century they had all disappeared.

This was a vivid illustration of the subordination of the human factor to the new needs of productive efficiency. Possession of individual areas of land had never been permanent in the old society, when clan territory had been lost by conquest, annexation and insolvency. It was common for subtenants and cottars, and even for principal tenants, to be moved from one farm to another. The later eighteenth century, however, brought dispossession on a truly unprecedented scale all over Gaeldom, with people on the move everywhere. Sometimes the pressures did not come by direct removal. The jacking-up of rentals in a peasant economy in which the balance between sufficiency and failure was a fine and precarious one also caused immense strain. The detailed research by Marianne McLean on western Inverness-shire shows that often rent increases were pushed above the rise in cattle prices and when the markets collapsed, as they did in 1772-3 and again in 1783-4, rent arrears spiralled and small tenants came under great pressure to surrender their holdings. Similarly, when farms were offered for letting at higher rents, reflecting the new commercial realities of the time, the poorer men had profound difficulty in competing. Loss of land was an inevitable result.

Undoubtedly, however, it was large-scale pastoral husbandry that led to the greatest social dislocation. Extensive cattle ranching was increasingly practised in parts of Argyll, Dumbarton and Perthshire and dislodged many peasant communities. One contemporary, John Walker, estimated that as a result of conversion of small farms into large cattle holdings, population had fallen in 17 parishes in these counties since 1750. Much more significant, however, was sheep farming. The new Blackface and Cheviot breeds were greedy for land and required different levels and types of land for the different ages and sexes of the flocks. The Cheviots in particular had special needs. Initially they enabled sheep farmers to pay twice the rent that was usually possible on land grazed by Blackfaces, but they could not easily survive the Highland climate without access to low ground for wintering, and this posed a potent threat to the arable lands of the traditional townships. At the same time, the sheep competed for grazing with the small tenants' black cattle. The sheiling grounds, where stock were taken into the hill country during the summer months while crops were growing on the arable land, were especially at risk. Sheep farming therefore weakened the basis of the old economy by means other than direct clearance. Thus in two sheep-grazing parishes in Sutherland (Creich and Assynt) between 1790 and 1808, the numbers of cattle fell from 5,140 to 2,906, while sheep increased from 7,840 to 21,000.

Much more cataclysmic, however, was the extensive and direct removal of peasant communities to make way for the big sheep farms. The new order and the old pastoral economy were fundamentally incompatible as not only was there intense competition for scarce land but the rental return from sheep was significantly higher than that from cattle. This was not only because of price differences in the market resulting from the new industrial demand for wool but also because sheep used land more intensively and extensively than cattle. They were able to graze in areas formerly underutilized in the old pastoral economy. Landlords also stood to gain from more secure returns. Sheep farms were normally run by big graziers who could guarantee the proprietor a regular and rising income in most years, whereas small tenants were much less dependable: their rent payments fluctuated with the weather and the state of the cattle markets. Nor could the indigenous tenantry hope to participate in the sheep economy in large numbers, as pastoralism was most efficient when practised on a large scale and this created an insurmountable financial barrier for most Highland tenants. There is evidence, for example on the estates of MacDonnell of Glengarry and Cameron of Lochiel in Inverness-shire of some townships building up small flocks of Blackface in the 1770s; but the landlords were too impatient for the massive profits to be obtained from grazing on a large scale, especially since there were now plenty of ambitious and enterprising farmers from the pastoral districts of Ayrshire, the Borders and Northumberland eager for Highland leases. The unexploited lands of the north had become too valuable to be let to the inexperienced native tenantry.

As the sheep frontier advanced, so also did clearance. The most notorious removals took place on the Sutherland estate where, between 1807 and 1821, the factors of the Countess of Sutherland and her husband Lord Stafford removed between 6,000 and 10,000 people from the inner parishes to new crofting settlements on the coast in the most remarkable example of social engineering undertaken in early nineteenth-century Britain. Old men looking back from the 1880s could still give the names to a Royal Commission of 48 cleared townships in the parish of Assynt alone. In its scale and level of organization no other clearance matched that of Sutherland. Indeed, the vast majority of removals probably involved only a few people at a time until the more draconian episodes of the 1840s and 1850s during the potato famine. Gradual and relentless displacement rather than mass eviction was the norm but, taken together, the numbers involved were very great and suggest a systematic process of enforced movement.

What is clear, nevertheless, is that most clearances before 1815 were not designed to expel the people. The conventional eighteenth-century assumption that a rising population was an economic benefit was only slowly being questioned, most landowners and improving theorists taking the view that the evicted represented an important resource that should not simply be discarded. A dual economy was envisaged, each part of which would in time be a source of increasing revenue. The people from the inner straths and glens should be moved to the coast, where they might find employment in kelp or fishing, and the interior districts would then become extensive sheep farms. This became the pattern along the whole west coast north of Fort William as the entire traditional settlement structure was transformed in the later eighteenth and early nineteenth centuries. On the Reay estate in north-west Sutherland the inland population was settled on the coast in the 1810s; further south, in Wester Ross and western Inverness, similar forced movements from the inland areas occurred in Glen-shiel, Glenelg, Morvern and other districts. The people no longer had traditional guarantees of land and the old social order was destroyed for ever.

2

The social experience of the Scottish Highlands in the decades after *c.* 1760 had its distinctive characteristics but it was far from being unique in Europe since, all over the continent and the British Isles, ancient social systems were increasingly under pressure. The eighteenth and nineteenth centuries were an epoch of persistent rise in population, urban growth and industrial expansion and in virtually every European country the rural economy had to produce more food and raw materials at acceptable prices to feed and support the growing urban masses. To a greater or lesser extent the new market orientation of agriculture imposed enormous strains on the older social patterns and in some regions caused considerable dislocation. The most potent threat came from the recognition that land was now principally to be seen as an asset and a productive resource to be managed according to its capacity for earning profit rather than as a basic source of support for the rural population. Enclosure and consolidation were the principal means by which this radical change was accomplished, and these brought to an end the old order (in which several members of a community had rights of use) and introduced a new condition (in which single occupants possessed complete control). There were echoes of this dramatic transition in the wave of clearances and land improvements that swept across the Scottish Highlands from the last quarter of the eighteenth century.

But there was also profound regional variation to these changes in markets and ideologies in western Europe. The peasant social order, where the majority of the people retained some rights of access to land, survived in most European countries, partly due to the varying impact and intensity of market demand but also, and more fundamentally, to the widespread nature of peasant proprietorship on the continent. To disturb land interests sanctified by both law and custom would have threatened to unleash massive social disorder and thus it was only in a few countries and areas that the full impact of the new agronomy and its revolutionary effect on traditional patterns of life and settlement was experienced. These included England, Scotland, Denmark, the Low Countries, Catalonia in Spain, some German states, such as Pomerania and Brandenburg and parts of Sweden; and even in these regions there was great diversity in the pace, nature and structure of agrarian change. This demonstrates that though the pressures making for reform of the rural economy were common across Europe, the responses to them depended ultimately on the particular political, legal, social, cultural and economic characteristics of each country. The case of Denmark, for instance, highlights the peculiar features of the revolution in land in northern Scotland. The Danes also mounted a sustained attack on communal agriculture and 'inefficient' patterns of landholding but the whole revolution was supported by the state and was managed in a way that markedly reduced the social costs which otherwise might be incurred as a result of the huge upheaval in peasant agriculture. State regulation was involved from the start when in 1757 a Danish Royal Commission produced a series of recommendations, later incorporated as state decrees, which provided for consolidation, rated the costs among individual villages and established a fund to help cover the costs of reform. But the striking feature of the Danish case was the degree of social benevolence employed to ensure social stability as the new structure was steadily built up and those who suffered loss from the reforms were to be compensated by a leasehold of four to six acres. Other legislation banned division of lands into areas too small to support a family.

The case of the Scottish Highlands could not have been more different. There, state action and control were minimal and landlords were virtually allowed complete freedom of action. Indeed, from the seventeenth century in Scotland the balance of law had swung ever more decisively towards the interests of private property. Acts of the Scottish parliament in 1661, 1669, 1685 and 1695 created the legal framework for land division and the consolidation of runrig, and an Act of the Court of Session of 1756 clarified the legal procedures for removal of tenants, which could be accomplished relatively easily through application to a local sheriff at least 40 days before Whitsun. The system of land tenure in Scotland was well suited to the exercise of landlord authority, since small peasant proprietors of the type who dominated the social structure of many European countries did not exist to any great extent. The overwhelming majority of the Highland population in the eighteenth century had no absolute legal right to land. They were either tenants whose rights were finite in time and were limited by lease or agreement or they belonged to the growing underclass of semi-landless cottars and servants who possessed no legal security of tenure whatsoever. It was the legal and customary defencelessness of the people which made the clearances possible in the Highlands and which simply would not have been feasible in many regions of the Continent where peasant ownership and legal rights and privileges built up over centuries were formidable obstacles to radical and rapid agrarian modernization.

There were, however, similarities with patterns of social change in the Scottish Lowlands. There too, as Chapter 7 shows, there was considerable population displacement. Just as the Highland *bailtean* were broken up, so also were the ferm touns of the traditional Lowland society. Over time, multiple tenancies and communal farming were steadily eliminated and by the early nineteenth century in most districts farms leased by individual husbandmen had become dominant. In several ways there were intriguing and close analogies with the Highland experience. From the middle decades of the seventeenth century, Border cattle and sheep ranching had expanded rapidly on the basis of the new demands from the urbanizing and industrializing areas of the north of England which led to extensive farm consolidation, annexation of peasant arable and grazing lands to feed and winter stock and inevitably the removal of many small communities in a manner similar to what happened later in the Highlands.

Clearance and dispossession were, therefore, not unique to the Highlands. The whole of Scotland in the last quarter of the eighteenth century was in turmoil as the new order took shape. Old tenurial rights, ancient patterns of settlement and traditional habits of working the land were being transformed everywhere in Scotland in these decades to a greater or lesser extent. But, nevertheless, there were distinctive aspects of the changes in the Highlands which mark the Gaelic experience out from the broader movement to agrarian improvement elsewhere in Scotland.

The movement from multiple to single tenancy occurred over many decades in the south, while in Gaeldom the break-up of the *bailtean* was concentrated in the later eighteenth century. The Highland experience, outside the southern and eastern fringes, was therefore more traumatic. The terrain of most of the north and west was best suited to large-scale pastoral husbandry which required much land but little labour, whereas over much of the Lowland areas farming was based on a mix of arable cultivation and stock rearing, which required more hands. Again, in the western Highlands and Islands, no successful alternative to agriculture developed. In the eighteenth century, kelp, fishing, distilling and quarrying all prospered, but after 1815 they went into rapid decline. In the Lowlands, on the other hand, the booming textile industries, many of them located in rural districts, and the creation of the elaborate new urban and agrarian infrastructures offered employment to those threatened with dispossession as a result of agrarian improvement.

One suspects also that the Gaels were more vulnerable to mass removal. The rural social system in the Lowlands, even before the Age of Improvement, depended on the tenant farmers who paid the rents to the landlord and employed the cottars and servants. This class had legal rights to their holdings over a given period, usually between eight and 15 years, which were defined clearly in written leases that were enforceable at law, and this made instant, comprehensive and widespread removal of entire tenant communities virtually impossible. Proprietors had to proceed with patience and weed out surplus tenants slowly as leases lapsed. In many Highland districts, however, the majority were much more vulnerable, as possession was invariably by custom or short annual leases which posed little obstacle to the enthusiastic Improver. Not surprisingly, therefore, in a society where legal security was minimal, clearances spread alarm and anxiety throughout areas still undisturbed and helped to push people into making preparation for emigration long before they faced the direct threat of removal.

The cultural distinction was also vital in understanding the impact of clearance on the psyche of the Gael. There was a quite different social relationship between élites and people in the two regions of Scotland by the middle decades of the eighteenth century. Due in large part to the much earlier pacification and hence more thoroughgoing commercialization of the Lowlands, landowners were no longer regarded as heads of kindred groups or of personal, feudal followings; they were simply proprietors. The rights and privileges of the tenants of their estates were defined in the written lease and, although labour duties were still required, the main factor in the relationship between lessor and lessee was the rental, paid either in cash or in kind, and increasingly in the former. Tenants had no right to land beyond the terms of the lease and could be removed from it as a result of a breach of the agreement or for persistent rent arrears. At the end of term, it was common for holdings to change hands and the connection between landlord and tenants was, therefore, a commercial and economic one. Land was property and there was a social acceptance of this fundamental fact by both parties.

This was not at all the pattern in Gaelic society. Even if the clan élites had developed new commercial assumptions and priorities, the people still clung to the principles of *duthchas*, in which the landlord had a basic duty as protector and the guarantor of land possession. Not only, therefore, was the scale of removal greater and faster in the Highlands, but the cultural trauma of dispossession by 'landlord-protectors' was likely to be much more devastating for the people. It is hardly surprising that the relentless violation of the values of clanship caused enormous collective disorientation throughout the Gaelic world and hence a basic difficulty in resisting landlord action in any effective fashion. As Allan Macinnes has put it:

That the occupiers of the soil adhered tenaciously to the traditionalist concept of *duthchas* long after clanship had been abrogated by the conduct of chiefs and leading gentry is testimony more to the cultural disorientation rather than outright cultural alimentation occasioned by the first phase of Clearance. Unlike contemporaneous Irish Gaels who were able to direct polemical attacks against the alien English forces of government, the landowning classes and the established church, Scottish Gaels seem prisoners of their own culture, thoroughly perplexed, demoralised and disorientated by the process of anglicisation effected by the assimilation of the clan élite into the British establishment. The criticisms of the poets – still the main outlets for public opinion within Scottish Gaeldom – were usually expressed deferentially through misplaced strictures against factors, legal agents, tacksmen, incoming tenant farmers and even sheep. On the rare occasions when landlords were indicted as instigators of Clearance, citations were depersonalised, the amorphous 'they' being held responsible.[3]

3

While the processes and outcomes of agrarian modernization may have differed between Highlands and Lowlands, the origins of social change were not dissimilar. Britain was the first industrial nation, and the demands on the rural economy for more food and raw materials were considerable; but in Scotland rapid economic change came later than in England and agrarian modernization took place within a shorter timescale. In simple terms, the depth and extent of the markets for all that the Highlands could export was transformed and the commercial forces were so powerful that social change in Gaeldom became irresistible.

Demand for traditional staples boomed. Cattle prices quadrupled in the course of the eighteenth century and total exports of cattle from the region probably quintupled. In Argyll, albeit to a lesser extent further north, commercial fishing of herring became even more significant with, for example, some 600–800 boats engaged annually in Loch Fyne alone. Due to changes in government revenue legislation and enhanced Lowland markets, demand increased persistently for illicit whisky, and the exploitation of Highland slate quarries at Easdale and Ballachuilish and elsewhere, and of woodland on many estates, continued apace. Textile production began to expand in Highland Perthshire, Argyll and eastern Inverness and in parts of Ross and Cromarty and Sutherland, and the production of linen cloth stamped for sale in the Highland counties rose steadily, from 21,972 yards in 1727–8 to 202,006 yards by 1778.

Southern industrialization had an insatiable and voracious appetite for Highland raw materials in the later eighteenth century and thereafter, with wool being in special demand. The Lowland cotton industry quickly achieved abundant supplies of raw fibre from the Caribbean and then from the southern USA, but it was more difficult for the woollen manufacturers. Overseas supply from Europe was limited and erratic during the Napoleonic Wars and it was only when Australia started to export in volume from the 1820s that overseas sources became really significant. In the interim, the gap was increasingly filled by Highland sheep farmers; in 1828 Scottish wool accounted for just under 10 per cent of UK output and for 25 per cent by the early 1840s. Behind these statistics lay the convulsion in Highland society unleashed by the inexorable advance of the sheep farms. Equally significant for a time, though in different ways, was the manufacture of kelp, an alkali extract from seaweed used in the manufacture of soap and glass. Industrial demand for it was on the increase, not least because cheaper and richer sources of foreign barilla were curtailed during the French Wars and kelp production seemed well suited to the western Highlands and Islands where the raw material was abundant. Cheap and plentiful supply of labour was vital since the process of production, though essentially a simple one, was very arduous with a ratio of one ton of kelp to 20 tons of collected seaweed. Kelp manufacture began in the west in the 1730s but not until after 1750 did it really begin to take hold: 2,000 tons per annum output were reached in the 1770s and 5,000 in 1790 and thereafter the industry boomed, achieving a peak production in 1810 of about 7,000 tons. By that date its main centres had become clearly established as the Uists, Barra, Harris, Lewis, Skye, Tiree and Mull, and on the mainland there was also considerable activity in Ardnamurchan and Morvern. To a considerable extent, however, kelp production was concentrated in the Hebrides, especially in the Long Island; and there, as will be seen in more detail below, it had profound social consequences.

British demand was not simply confined to the foodstuffs and raw materials of the Highlands. The market for human labour was also expanding as young adult Gaels, especially from Argyll, had taken up seasonal harvest work in Lowland farms earlier in the eighteenth century. After the 1770s opportunities increased as output rose in southern agriculture and the old cottar class, which had been the main source of harvest labour in the past, was steadily reduced in size. Highland migrants also took up seasonal employment in the herring fishery of the Clyde and in the bleachfields around the textile towns and villages. An even more spectacular growth industry was the recruitment of Gaels into the British army and navy in the later eighteenth century. Beginning on a small scale during the Seven Years War (1756-63) and increasing during the American War of Independence, recruitment multiplied to extraordinary levels during the Napoleonic Wars when, on one estimate, the Highlands supplied around 74,000 men for regiments of the line, the Militia, Fencibles and Volunteers out of a total regional population of about 300,000. This was a quite remarkable figure, even if probably much inflated by contemporaries, and represents a per capita rate of military recruitment probably unequalled in any other region of Europe. It was eloquent testimony to the impact of population pressures at the time and of the ability of the landlords to maximize recruitment to their family regiments by coercion and the promise of land in return for service.

On a much broader scale the role of the landed classes was fundamental in accelerating social change. As earlier discussion has shown, they were in a position of virtual omnipotence over their people, with full legal authority to transform their estates when they willed it. In theory, however, the hereditary duties attached to their position in the clan structure were a powerful impediment. The roles of chief and capitalist landlord were incompatible and there is evidence in the historical record of some landed families agonizing over the conflicts between these two functions. However, the forces making for the triumph of landlordism over tribalism were eventually triumphant.

Many Highland proprietors before the 1750s were increasingly acting in their own commercial interest rather than that of their clansmen. Moreover, if chiefs were becoming an integral part of the British landed élite, they could not remain immune from the material, intellectual and cultural goals of that class. Among the aristocracy and gentry the eighteenth century was an era of conspicuous consumption, of ornate and expensive building, foreign travel and a more opulent way of life. The atmosphere in élite circles was one of competitive display, where a family's place was defined by the grandeur of its physical surroundings. This was the world now inhabited by the Highland landowners, one which was a constant drain on the purse and in which they could not easily survive on the paltry returns of traditional agriculture. Again, clearance and dispossession could be and were given intellectual justification. The Highland élites, through education in southern schools and universities and travel elsewhere, had absorbed non-Gaelic values and objectives long before the '45. Alien forces were partly responsible for the destruction of traditional society through the post-Culloden pacification and the activities in certain districts of the Commissioners for the Annexed Forfeited Estates. Fundamentally, however, the revolution was achieved by the indigenous leaders of Gaeldom, who had absorbed and accepted the ideas current among their class elsewhere in Britain. These included a view of the existing social order as 'primitive' and urgently in need of reform, an uncritical belief in the values of individualism and a contempt for the traditional patterns of life and work as demonstrating the indolence, fecklessness and inefficiency of the people. These assumptions made it much easier to reorganize their estates along more rational and profitable lines. The landlords were not simply making more money, they could also justify the abrogation of their traditional responsibilities by claiming that it was a necessary evil in order to 'civilize' and 'improve' their estates.

The sheer force of market pressure was also fundamental. Demand for Highland commodities was advancing on all fronts at such a pace that few could resist the rewards. Indeed, it was the combination of the growing financial demands on the landlord class with the emergence in the later eighteenth century of huge new opportunities to satisfy them which was the basic catalyst for accelerated change. Most proprietors achieved what were essentially windfall gains because many significant sources of profit – kelp, cattle, wool, mutton and regimental recruitment – did not require significant investment but accrued to the landlord simply because of his rights of ownership. Little wonder that the period c. 1760 to 1815 seemed a bonanza for many Highland landowners, and it is scarcely surprising that the majority were tempted to remove the traditional society quickly and completely rather than embark on the more complex and difficult task of patiently developing a fusion between the old and the new.

In the long run, an even more potent threat to the traditional ways was the steady rise in regional population, which was becoming apparent in the eighteenth and which accelerated in the nineteenth century. This was part of a Europe-wide demographic revolution in which not only were traditional levels of population rise sustained, but the rate of increase became greater over time. Demographers are still divided about the origins of this historic change of direction, but it seems to have been based mainly on an increasing food supply, rising employment opportunities as a consequence of industrialization and some limited medical advances such as inoculation and vaccination against smallpox.

More important, however, than the causes were the social consequences for the Highlands, and closer scrutiny reveals that an explosive demographic problem was emerging. The southern and eastern rim of the Highlands experienced very modest growth because of high levels of migration to the Lowlands; whereas along the western seaboard from north Argyll and in most of the Hebrides, increase was more pronounced. Between 1801 and 1841 population in this region increased by 53 per cent. In 1755 the population of the island of Tiree was 1,509 but it had risen to 1,676 by 1768 and to 2,443 by 1792. The average population of each township on the island stood at 56 in 1768 but had reached 90 by 1800. Increases of this order could not have come about except through repeated divisions of tenancies and rampant subdivision, much of it abetted by landlords eager to swell the ranks of kelpers and fishermen and made possible only by the rapid spread of potato cultivation. A major demographic result in the short term was to limit emigration by anchoring population on the land on splintered and insecure holdings. There can be little doubt either that population growth outstripped traditional levels of agricultural productivity and the methods evolved over centuries for ensuring a basic living from a poor land and a hostile climate. All detailed studies show that the old agrarian economy was delicately and precariously balanced between a meagre sufficiency and occasional shortage. It could not easily have survived the population upsurge of the eighteenth century without substantial change.

4

By the end of the Napoleonic Wars two divergent types of tenure and settlement were visibly seen to be replacing the traditional Highland townships. The destruction of the *bailtean* was far advanced in the southern and eastern rim of the Highlands, including much of mainland Argyll, Highland Perthshire, central and eastern Inverness and the eastern parishes of Ross-shire. A distinctive social order was emerging here which, despite some differences within the region, had a number of common characteristics. The shape of the holdings and the layout of the land were not unlike those in many adjacent parts of the Lowlands where landlords had consolidated rather than divided tenancies. There were therefore fewer full tenants than in the older order, but there were significant numbers of servants, cottars, labourers and servants, who were employed by the new farming élite. Large sheep- and cattle-holdings existed throughout the region; but in other districts, especially in parts of Argyll and Highland Perthshire, family farms of 40–60 acres were engaged in mixed husbandry. There was a modest standard of comfort and little sign of the recurrent subsistence crises which occurred in the north-west. The potato was an important item in diet, but so also was grain and, in coastal parishes, fish. A feature of the region was the development of non-agricultural activities, such as the herring fishery of the Argyll sea lochs and the linen manufacture of Perthshire.

There can be little doubt that agrarian change in this region maintained and even improved standards of life, in part because it had more favourable natural endowment. Arable and mixed agriculture was possible in the great straths which run from west to east. The Highland massif is a great tableland that slopes towards the south and east, and this affords good drainage for the land surfaces of the area, provides some protection against the heavy and continuous rainfall that often devastates arable farming further west, and facilitates communication with the economic heart of Scotland. But material amelioration was at the expense of an enormous haemorrhaging of people from the region, partly because of widespread population displacement during the era of transformation as well as the job opportunities emerging in the Lowlands as a result of industrialization and urbanization. From 1755 to the 1790s, no less than 60 per cent of the region's parishes failed to increase population at all because of the huge scale of out-migration. Agrarian reform in the south and east channelled the people out of the area in large numbers, and to this day the poignant physical evidence of that great exodus can still be seen in the ruined steadings and crumbling sheilings scattered throughout the hill country.

Nevertheless, there were real benefits for those who remained. By the 1830s a relatively balanced, more secure and much more productive economic regime had begun to form in this region. The ratio of the population to available cultivable land was higher than elsewhere in the Highlands. In the early 1840s, for instance, arable acreage per head of population was reckoned at 2.18 in mainland Argyll but a mere 0.5 in Wester Ross and Skye. Land consolidation had broken up the old townships and produced a new farming class who employed a larger number of landless and semi-landless wage labourers who derived their subsistence partly from earnings at work and partly from their crofts. In both the south-west and north-east corners, dynamic fishing communities had developed. The economic backbone of the region was the small core of tenant farmers, for the most part natives of the area, renting medium-sized holdings of from £20 to £100. This class gave the southern and eastern Highlands a resilience notably lacking in the poorer parishes to the north and west. The region's stability was most obviously demonstrated during the potato famines of the 1840s as, while the west was being threatened with actual starvation, the districts adjacent to the Lowlands weathered the storm and experienced only temporary difficulty. As one famine relief organization concluded at the time:

The population of these parishes was in an entirely different position from that of the western districts. The different classes of society were in their proper place. There was a labouring class supporting themselves and their families by remunerative employment – a fishing population, carrying on that branch of industry as a permanent resource – and there were all the appliances of an advanced state of society, in which purchased food forms a principal feature of the subsistence of the people. The distress among them had been occasioned by a temporary disproportion between the ages of labour and the price of food, and the loss of the potato, which formed but a subordinate element in their means of subsistence.[4]

However, along the western seaboard, from Morvern to Cape Wrath and including most of the Inner and Outer Hebrides, a quite different social order was taking shape amid the ruins of the traditional society. Over great tracts of the region, especially on the mainland before 1815, but extending over the islands in subsequent decades, large grazing farms devoted to the raising of Blackface and Cheviot sheep had become dominant. But although the advance of pastoral husbandry had caused immense social disruption and the removal of traditional communities, it did not often result in this period in planned and overt expulsion of the inhabitants. Instead, relocation (and especially relocation in crofting townships) was the favoured policy so that profit could be extracted both from the labour-intensive activities of the crofters and from the more extensive operations of the big flockmasters.

Over less than two or three generations, as the *bailtean* were destroyed the crofting system was imposed throughout the region. By the 1840s, at least 86 per cent and in most parishes 95 per cent of holdings were rented at £20 or less. These small tenancies, only a few acres in size, were laid out in 'townships' or crofting settlements and had certain common features because they were the product of an 'improving' philosophy which was absorbed and implemented by virtually all landowners in these districts. At the core was the arable land, divided into a number of separate smallholdings, and these were surrounded by grazing or hill pasture which was held in common by the tenants of the township. The most striking feature, however, was that the croft was not designed to provide a full living for the family. Sir John Sinclair reckoned that the typical crofter had to be able to obtain at least 200 days of additional work outside his holding in order to avoid chronic destitution. Crofts were in fact reduced in size in order to force the crofter and his family into other employments. The holding itself should provide only partial subsistence and, to make ends meet and afford the rental, the crofter and his family had to have recourse to supplementary jobs.

These non-agricultural tasks were usually seasonal in nature. The crofting system provided a convenient source of subsistence for a reserve army of labour that was required only at certain times of the year. Crofting, therefore, became the *sine qua non* for the rapid expansion of kelp manufacture (in which between 25,000 and 40,000 people were seasonally employed during the peak summer months in the Hebrides), for fishing and for illicit whisky-making. Crofts were also used to attract recruits to the family regiments of the landowners, with tiny areas of land being promised in return for service. Throughout the process of transforming the joint tenancies into crofts there was one fundamental guiding principle: too much land would act as a distraction from other, more profitable tasks. The crofters were to be labourers first and agriculturists only second. In retrospect, this proved a disastrous policy for the people of the western Highlands and Islands.

Essentially, the whole social system of the region became bound up with the success of the by-employments which flourished down to the end of the Napoleonic Wars. But in the main these activities were ephemeral because, like kelp manufacture and military service, they often existed only on the basis of the transitory conditions of wartime. Moreover, in their heyday they had little positive effect on the crofting economy. Kelp, for instance, was noted for its volatile prices but, because of the great market expansion of the 1790s, became the principal economic activity in the Western Isles by 1815. But the working population gained little from this short-term bonanza as landlords in the kelp islands achieved monopoly control over the manufacture and marketing of the commodity and the 'earnings' of the labour force were mainly absorbed by increased rentals and annual payments to proprietors for meal.

Indeed, the economic expansion of the Napoleonic Wars, which had brought some material improvement to the southern and eastern Highlands, laid the foundations for later social catastrophe elsewhere in the region. Because of the labour needs of so many activities, most landlords were happy to see the unregulated division of lands among cottars and squatters, a fragmentation of holdings which tied the people to the land and inhibited permanent migration. The impact of these policies can be clearly seen in the demographic statistics. Between 1801 and 1841 along the western seaboard and the islands, population increased by 53 per cent while in the south and eastern Highlands the average was around 7 per cent. The reckless process of subdivision also depended on an equally rapid increase in potato cultivation. Potatoes had been grown in the early eighteenth century but by 1750 were still relatively uncommon. It was only where the croft became dominant that potatoes became a central part in the diet, and during the crofting revolution of the later eighteenth and early nineteenth centuries cultivation expanded on a remarkable scale. The transformation of land structures and the adoption of the potato went hand in hand. Because of its very high yield, the potato became the key source of support for the dense communities of crofters, cottars and squatters that were building up to service kelp and fishing. Sir John Sinclair reckoned that four times as many people could be supported by an acre of potatoes as by an acre of oats. The potato crop was also less vulnerable to climate, since even marginal and inhospitable land could be made to yield good returns through the process of lazybed cultivation, by which sandwiches of soil and seaweed were created and planted with potatoes, allowing a much larger population than ever before to make a living, at however basic a level, in the crofting region. But the potato also carried the enormous risk of over-dependency on a single crop and facilitated excessive subdivision of precious land resources in areas where the possibilities of a secure existence had always been delicately balanced.

5

The experience of the western Highlands is a salutary reminder that economic change is not necessarily for the better. Victorian observers were troubled by this, especially when the problems of the region eventually degenerated into acute destitution and famine. It then became common to blame the economic failures of the area on the conservatism and indolence of the people: they were seen as having a blind attachment to the old ways and to be lacking the enterprise which had brought prosperity and progress elsewhere. The Highlands became a 'problem' region where economic transformation had produced difficulties rather than benefits.

This outcome seemed all the more puzzling, given some of its advantages for development. The Highlands possessed an expanding and cheap labour force, were surrounded by seas that were rich in fish, and the potential of the region as a major source of raw materials had been amply demonstrated before 1815. The possibilities for capital accumulation were also very great because so much of the area's principal asset, land, was concentrated among a small group of proprietors. The Highlands were one of the few parts of Britain where, because of their strategic importance as a source of soldiers and sailors, the state invested on a considerable scale through the Commission for Annexed Forfeited Estates, the British Fisheries Society and an ambitious programme of road and bridge building in the early nineteenth century. But all to no avail; there was little long-term impact.

However, the argument that the basic cause of failure was the social conservatism of the Gael hardly convinces. Gaelic culture and values did not prevent the successful economic adaptation of the southern, central and eastern Highlands and there is also abundant evidence of Gaelic entrepreneurship, from the commercial activities of clan gentry in the cattle, fish, grain and slate trades before the 1760s to the successful organization of large-scale transatlantic emigration after that date. A population that responded to the cultural and economic shock of clearance by rapidly adopting a new subsistence crop (the potato) and adjusting to the new realities of crofting can hardly be described as conservative or rigid in outlook. Before 1750 the peasantry was constantly adjusting to the new demands of the landed classes. The records of the Commissioners for Annexed Forfeited Estates also show clear evidence of a willingness to adopt 'Lowland' crop rotations if they were deemed practical. So much of the approved system, however, such as enclosures and turnip husbandry, was not relevant to the Highland landscape.

Such pools of indigenous enterprises as did exist were inhibited in a variety of ways. The destruction of the old order, resettlement and rental inflation combined to produce a context of profound insecurity that was not conducive to small tenant investment. Crofters were allocated their holdings on an annual basis and were vulnerable to removal at the end of this term. Again, before 1760, while the expansion of the cattle trade brought capital into the Highlands, it failed to filter down to any great extent and produce more commercial values across the society, whereas in the Lowlands by the 1750s the ordinary tenants sold their grain and stock directly to the market. In the western Highlands, marketing was mainly monopolized by proprietors and clan gentry and, partly for this reason and partly because of the paucity of towns in the region, commercialization before the 1760s was confined mainly to the élites. The area lacked the large middle class of capitalist tenants, merchants, traders and manufacturers who were the shock troops of economic transformation in the Lowlands. The emigration of tacksmen and middle-rank farmers can be seen in part as a flight of capital from Gaeldom which diminished the entrepreneurial pool still further. The creation of crofting townships probably also decimated the ranks of that small group of tenants who had a significant surplus above sufficiency by shaving holdings down to a uniform and basic subsistence minimum.

Whether more effective management of the resources of the region by the landlord class would have resulted in a different outcome is an interesting question. Highland landlords were confronted with more formidable obstacles than their counterparts elsewhere in Britain: the climate was less sympathetic and the land much poorer, the élites did not possess the mineral and urban rentals of many more fortunate proprietors elsewhere and intensive arable farming which might have absorbed the population more easily was not possible in the north and west. By laying down more and more land to sheep, they were playing to the region's comparative advantage in pastoral husbandry and so their actions had an inherent economic rationality though with devastating social consequences.

But impersonal forces were not the whole story; several landlords directly contributed to the malaise of the region themselves. Some seem to have been more interested in extracting a quick profit than in sound investment and most of the windfall gains from kelp were recklessly squandered outside the Highlands. To change the entire social structure of their estates on the foundation of activities that were unlikely to last for much longer than the conflict with France was myopic to say the least. Yet some proprietors did try to fund fishing and industrial development on an ambitious scale, the most notable examples being the fifth Duke of Argyll in the later eighteenth century and the Sutherland family in the early nineteenth century. In both cases, however, the development strategy, after some initial success, came to little; this suggests that imaginative schemes, even if based on considerable sources of finance, faced major problems in the region.

In fact, the north-west had little scope for adjustment by the early nineteenth century. It was locked into an economic vice that was contracting inexorably. There were at least four major problems. First, by 1815 commercial forces had transformed the region into an economic enclave of British industry. In essence it had become a satellite, with its functions utterly subordinate to the production of foodstuffs, raw materials and labour for the southern cities. No longer were the people of the western Highlands dependent only on the climate, the price of cattle and the returns from the land; their fate was now also inextricably bound up with the fluctuation of distant markets for a range of commodities. Commercialization had ended their isolation and partial independence. Second, commercialization had fashioned an insecure and vulnerable economic structure, centred around crofting, the potato and by-employments; and at the same time much grazing land, vital in the old society, had been absorbed by the new sheep farms, which also tended to channel most of their economic gains out of the region. Commercialization, therefore, even in the short run had profoundly negative economic effects on the western Highlands as well as destroying the old cohesion of society. Third, the Highlands were now an integral part of the British market economy and one consequence was that the region was fully exposed to the direct impact of competition from advanced centres of industry such as the west of Scotland and the north of England. The Highlands lacked coal reserves of any significance, had few towns and, like other British peripheral regions such as the west of Ireland and the south-east of England, its small-scale textile industries were soon remorselessly squeezed by competition from the manufacturing heartlands. It was forced to specialize in sectors where it had a comparative advantage within the new economic system, and these were confined increasingly to sheep farming and the provision of casual labour.

Fourth, the collapse in prices after the end of the Napoleonic Wars made it impossible for even the most skilled form of landlord management to stabilize the crisis. Most areas of the British economy experienced some difficulty in the years after 1815, but in the north and west the outcome was disastrous. This was partly because in a recession peripheral areas tended to suffer worst but it was also because so much of the Highland boom was due to ephemeral wartime conditions, and much of the region's export economy fell apart with the coming of peace. Cattle prices halved between 1810 and 1830. Fishing stagnated, due to the erratic migrations of the herring in the western sea lochs, the withdrawal of bounties on herring in the 1820s and the decline of the Irish and Caribbean markets for cured herring. Kelp, the great staple of the Hebrides, suffered even more acutely when peace brought revived imports of foreign barilla, a cheaper and richer substitute. The reduction of the duty on foreign alkali combined with the discovery that cheaper alkali could be extracted from common salt also had a devastating effect. The price of kelp had already halved by 1820 and it fell further in later years. The coming of peace also led to the demobilization of the vast number of Highlanders who had joined the colours and before long even illicit whisky-making was also under severe pressure as a result of radical changes in revenue legislation in the 1820s. That decade was indeed a grim one for the people of the western Highlands as virtually the whole economic fabric which had been built up between 1760 and 1815 disintegrated. Even more ominously, though sheep prices stagnated they did not experience the collapse of other commodities, and it looked as if only commercial pastoralism, with all its implications for even further clearance and dispossession, had a real future.

10

The Old Regime and Radical Protest

I

In late-eighteenth-century Scotland a revolution in agriculture and industry was gathering pace and Scottish cultural and intellectual achievements were attracting widespread international acclaim. By contrast, the system of burghal and parliamentary government seemed archaic, moribund and corrupt and increasingly out of step with the dynamism of national development in other spheres. As in the rest of Britain, the ownership of property alone gave the right to vote because it was argued that only those with a firm stake in the land could be trusted to manage the nation's affairs prudently and responsibly. But in Scotland the dominance of property was carried to such a remarkable extreme that even the vast majority of landowners (especially middling and smaller lairds) and wealthy town merchants were themselves effectively excluded from the franchise. After the union there were 45 parliamentary seats in the Scottish counties and 15 in the burghs, each with 2,600 and 1,500 voters respectively. This amounted to approximately 0.2 per cent of Scotland's population in the later eighteenth century. This tiny electoral élite was unique even by the pre-democratic standards of eighteenth-century Britain, as both Ireland and England had a significantly larger franchise. For instance, the Dublin electorate of 3,000–4,000 was greater than the total number of those with the vote in all the counties of Scotland and nearly as much as the entire national electorate combined. But power was even more narrowly circumscribed than this. In the counties, for instance, it was generally feudal superiors rather than proprietors who had the right to vote. By splitting their superiorites among friends, kinsmen and clients, the greater landowners created a number of fictitious or 'faggot' votes which helped them to dominate local elections and at the same time extend their personal influence. As a result there emerged what Michael Fry has described as 'pocket counties', with the great noble houses of Argyll, Bute, Sutherland, Queensberry, Buccleuch and a number of others influencing a system of electoral manipulation that reinforced family hegemony throughout their estates and beyond.

A similar pattern of oligarchical control existed in the burghs where only a fraction of the merchant and tradesmen classes had the vote. The burghs numbered 66 in all and were divided into districts of four or five, to select the 15 representatives to sit in Westminster. The electorate was minute in size, with Scotland's proud capital of Edinburgh having a mere 33 people enfranchised. All commentators are agreed that brazen corruption and venality were rampant in burgh elections, with small, self-perpetuating cliques drawn from the merchant and craft guilds able to maintain their continued ascendancy with relative ease. It is hardly surprising that elections became a matter of indifference, to the extent that in some cases they were never even held. Remarkably, in 1790, at a time when the French Revolution was sending political shock waves around Europe, only nine county and burgh elections in Scotland were actually contested. This was in dramatic contrast to Ireland at the time where political activity at a local level was intense and the issues keenly fought.

The difference was partly due to the extraordinary success of Harry Dundas, the government's 'manager' or 'minister' for Scotland, in honing the techniques of political management so that he was able comfortably to control most of the Scottish electoral system in his interest by the early 1790s. In consequence, real opposition, in the formal, parliamentary sense, became both rare and pointless. Dundas in a sense was the heir of the Earl of Islay (later Duke of Argyll) who had controlled the electoral process so effectively in the first half of the eighteenth century. But the Argyll hegemony did not endure and, when Bute's ministry fell in 1763, there was no obvious replacement to fill the gap, maintain the link between London and Scotland, act as the source and distributor of patronage and effectively run the Scottish administration. The problem of government was compounded by the absenteeism in England of the greater magnates, the traditional leaders of Scottish society, and the Cabinet's indifference to Scotland as long as the country remained politically conformist and quiescent. Dundas seized the opportunity created by this vacuum to make his mark. Significantly, he was not of noble birth but a scion of the lairds of

Arniston in the Lothians, a family with strong legal connections and traditions. His rise was meteoric. He became Solicitor General in 1766 and Lord Advocate in 1775. Crucially, these posts were not simply confined to the law but extended to a whole range of other political and administrative duties. Essentially, it was the senior law officers who ran Scotland in the later eighteenth century.

However, control over patronage was the real key to power for Dundas. From 1779, as sole Keeper of the Signet, he became the decisive influence over appointment to government posts in Scotland and systematically used his position to build up a complex network of clients, voters and local interests who depended on him for favours, places, promotions and pensions. His ascendancy was further buttressed by his appointment first as a commissioner of the Board of Control of the East India Company in 1784 and later as its president from 1793 to 1801. Although Scots were finding Indian appointments in significant numbers long before Dundas came on the scene, access to the Company's vast patronage could only strengthen his position even further. Dundas was capable of serving many masters for his own ends and indeed in 1782–3 he had been a member of three governments, each of a different political hue. But thereafter his loyal and close relationship with the younger Pitt (which included sharing in many heroic drinking sessions) put the seal on his rise to pre-eminence. His position in the final analysis rested not on conviviality but rather on his ability to deliver what William Ferguson calls 'the well-drilled phalanx in the north' for Pitt's interest. In 1780 Dundas personally controlled 12 of the 41 Scottish constituencies contested; by 1784 this had risen to 22, and in 1790 to 34. 'King Harry the Ninth' was coming close to the zenith of his personal power in Scotland.

There is, however, a paradox here. The Dundas electoral machine was based on endemic corruption in the burghs and tightly managed elections in the country. It seemed at odds with the other Scotland of the Enlightenment which, in its universities, clubs and debating societies, was committed to the application of reason, the pursuit of knowledge and the clash of ideas. Much Enlightenment thought from Scotland had influenced radical politics in the American colonies and in Ulster. Francis Hutcheson, Professor of Moral Philosophy at Glasgow from 1729 to 1746, taught his students that a natural law existed which transcended the laws of the state. From this he concluded that man had an inalienable right to enjoy freedom of opinion and to resist the tyranny of oppressive

rulers. Ideas like these contributed powerfully to the political programme of the American colonists in the years before 1776 and of the
Irish radicals later in the eighteenth century. At a lower level, the
Scottish population was one of the most literate in Europe and political
ideas were increasingly disseminated widely through newspapers,
pamphlets and broadsheets. One character in John Galt's novel, *Annals
of the Parish*, noted that as a result of the outbreak of war with France
'. . . men read more, the spirit of reflection and reasoning was more
awake than at any time within my remembrance . . . cotton spinners
and muslin weavers, clubbed together and got a London newspaper'.

Furthermore, Scotland was by no means naturally submissive to
established authority. The eighteenth century saw a massive growth in
religious dissent and the fracturing of the Established Church of Scotland
with the emergence of the Associate Presbytery (or Secession Church)
in 1733 and of the Relief Presbytery in 1761, significantly as a result of
deep popular hostility to the use of patronage in Presbyterian parishes.
The same society which meekly accepted the Dundas regime before
1790 was also the one in which acrimonious and occasionally violent
disputes over ecclesiastical patronage were rife. Dissent flourished and
by the 1820s (only marginally reflecting Irish Catholic immigration)
nearly one-third of Scots no longer belonged to the Established Church.
This level of haemorrhage suggests a society with a robust independence
of mind and spirit based on the Calvinist inheritance of 'the equality
of souls' before God. It was an egalitarian tradition which fuelled the
fiery political radicalism of Scottish Presbyterian migrants to Ulster
(much more feared by their landowners than were Catholic tenants)
and the pivotal role played later by many of the 'Scotch Irish' during
the American Revolution and the rebellion of the United Irishmen in
1798. In Scottish religious tradition, the idea of the Covenant, a contract
between God and man and rulers and ruled, had been a powerful force
for political revolution in the seventeenth century. Out of this world of
the Scottish peasant also came Burns's great egalitarian poem, 'A man's
a man for aw that'. It would appear that where it mattered to them
most, as in the vital issues of religious belief, worship and church
government, the Scots were far from apathetic and dependent. Formal
'politics' for much of the eighteenth century, however, had far less
appeal.

This is hardly surprising because, even before 1707, the Scottish
'political nation' had been totally unrepresentative of the people as a

whole. The union ended the parliament and, in due course, the incipient 'parties' that had started to develop within it also withered on the vine. Scottish parliamentary politics as such disappeared. Westminster hardly ever spent time on Scottish business and, apart from a brief flurry of legislation after the '45, the London parliament showed only occasional interest. So it was not a question of sending MPs south to defend or promote Scottish concerns for these were rarely debated. Dundas's game was rather to maximize the number of loyal supporters in the House of Commons and by so doing to make himself indispensable to the government of the day and so consolidate and, if possible, expand his sources of patronage. It is generally agreed that in this last respect he was a past master. The number of places and sinecures in the navy, army, colonial, excise and government service taken by Scots increased substantially during his period of hegemony. By 1800, Scotland had obtained more than a quarter of all official pensions and one-third of state sinecures, a much higher proportion than was warranted by her size of population (one-sixth of England's) or national wealth. Success on this scale eventually provoked outrage in London and parliament determined that the volume of patronage to the greedy Scots should be drastically curbed. But the number of requests for posts was still far in excess of the supply. For the years 1784-90 alone, there survives in the National Library of Scotland a bundle of almost 600 petitions for everything from university professorships to peerages and these are not by any means the total received by Dundas during those years. As a result he was able to pick and choose, not simply ensuring rewards to political clients and associates, but also selecting on the basis of talent, ability and potential. This gravy train was vital to the careers and family prospects of many in the Scottish landed and professional classes and few were likely to risk preferment by rocking the boat too much.

The apparent political apathy in Scotland was also related to the actual business of running the country. Scotland was governed by the national institutions which not only survived the union but were guaranteed by it. The election of Members of Parliament had little to do with the actual process of administration itself. For the majority of the people, the Kirk was the most visible and significant arm of government at the local level. The parish state collected and distributed poor relief, punished minor civil as well as religious offences, educated most children in the rural areas and buried the dead. At the national level, the law was at the core of government. The senior law officers, the Lord Advocate, the Solicitor General and on occasion judges, such as the Lord Justice Clerk, formed the Scottish executive, though theoretically responsible to a minister in London, who from 1782 was the Home Secretary. More importantly, the judges of the Court of Session, to use Dundas's own words, 'were allowed a greater latitude and discretion' than elsewhere, and on the whole they seem to have used it with considerable impartiality and moderation. As Hamish Fraser has shown, their judgements, particularly on sensitive social issues, were genuinely independent and not necessarily dictated by class interest. The judiciary allowed workers to form combinations and established a reputation for dealing fairly in complex disputes over wages. Indeed, workers in a variety of trades were willing to seek arbitration from the Court of Session as a matter of course because they expected a fair deal. In this way some legitimacy was given to an established political order which in many other respects was notoriously corrupt and ripe for reform.

By the 1780s, however, the first public stirrings of criticism were becoming apparent. From 1782, freeholders interested in reforming the county franchise started to meet in the north of Scotland before holding a national gathering in Edinburgh in which most of the Scottish shires were represented. Their ambitions, however, were modest and confined to the abolition of fictitious or 'faggot' votes. Dundas himself recognized the need for something to be done about the scandal of 'made votes' and saw little to be concerned about in the proposals. By comparison with English reform bodies at the time, such as the Yorkshire Freeholders Association under Wyvil, the Scots were timid in the extreme, unwilling to extend the movement outside Scotland and interested only in the correction of some imperfections in the existing system rather than broadening representation in any serious way. Far from posing a threat to the regime, their activities only confirmed once again the general lack of interest in meaningful reform.

More significant was a movement which also began in the early 1780s to address the flagrant corruption and endemic nepotism of many of the Scottish burghs. It was triggered by a series of letters to the press by a rich Edinburgh merchant, Thomas McGrugar, who wrote under the *nom de plume*, ZENO. He denounced the closed corporations of the towns not because they were undemocratic – to him 'the dregs of the populace are disqualified by ignorance' – but because they gave no effective voice to the intelligent and propertied middle classes. McGrugar wished to see the franchise extended to the 'men in middle ranks of life who generally constitute the majority of every free country'.[1] This public intervention immediately struck a chord and in 1783 a committee devoted to burghal reform was established in Edinburgh, led by liberal advocates such as Henry Erskine, Archibald Fletcher and John Clerk of Eldin and a judge of the Court of Session, Lord Gardenstone. At the grass-roots level, however, the merchant class was the dominant force. This development was of interest for several reasons. First, to some extent it reflected a mood of profound disillusion with incompetent government as a result of the British defeat in 1783 and the humiliation and loss of the American colonies. Second, burghal reform was now firmly on the agenda because of deeper social and economic changes. The rapid growth of towns and cities, the mushrooming expansion of overseas trade and domestic industry and the brilliant achievements of the intelligentsia were all contributing to the development of a new Scotland. But the great majority of the merchants, manufacturers and professionals who were shaping this new world were still effectively excluded from any role in urban government. Now they were starting to demand a voice in public affairs, albeit at this stage only moderately and pragmatically. Third, the movement was designed to extend the franchise only within the propertied classes. The population as a whole was not included and the watchword was reform and not radical change.

In this spirit a parliamentary bill was drafted to correct burghal abuses, extend the franchise to all burgesses and establish annual elections. These were all worthy objectives, although Dundas himself privately remarked that 'It would be easier to reform Hell' than some Scottish municipalities.[2] There were also other obstacles. Not one Scottish MP was willing to introduce the bill in the House of Commons, and the case was eventually taken up by Richard Sheridan, the playwright and Irish MP, who thereafter brought it before parliament on an annual basis but to little effect. In the mid-1780s Dundas was still inexorably extending his grip on the majority of the constituencies in Scotland and was unswervingly opposed to a reform which he saw as a threat to the personal political ascendancy he had relentlessly worked to create. Year after year he scathingly and contemptuously repudiated Sheridan's arguments in the House. It seemed once again that a political movement feeding a latent middle-class discontent had effectively run out of steam. However, the outbreak of the French Revolution in 1789 changed everything and set the scene for an unprecedented challenge to the existing regime.

2

At first the stirring events in France were welcomed enthusiastically by reformers and conservatives alike. Cynical statesmen saw the revolution as a means of temporarily emasculating the French state which had challenged British power both in Europe and overseas for over a century. Whig politicians were pleased that the French had finally achieved the liberties the British propertied classes had possessed since 1688 and intellectuals such as Dugald Stewart and John Miller hailed the dawn of a new age of international co-operation and peace. When Edmund Burke published his *Reflections on the Revolution in France* in 1790 and robustly defended the existing order by harshly condemning what had happened in France, he was almost a lone voice crying in the wilderness. The Whig Club of Dundee was more representative of middle-class opinion in Scotland when, in its address to the National Assembly of France in the summer of 1790, it greeted the revolution as 'the triumph of liberty and reason over despotism, ignorance and superstition'.[3] At this stage, the revolution was not feared by the Scottish propertied classes but rather viewed as the mechanism by which the French had finally won freedom from arbitrary rule, a liberation which the Scots and English élites had achieved over a century before when the Stuarts were removed from the throne.

Nevertheless, even in 1790 the ideas of the revolution had a catalytic effect and gave a fresh impetus to political discussion and debate in Scotland. Not only did the number of newspapers increase, from eight in 1782 to 27 in 1790, but they generated much more intense argument on political issues than before. The discussion of reform ideas well beyond the political classes was given enormous stimulus by the publication in February 1791 of the first part of Tom Paine's *Rights of Man*, followed by Part Two a year later. Paine produced a comprehensive and penetrating critique of the corrupt political system, written in clear and accessible prose, which vigorously challenged some of the most sacred assumptions of the British constitution. He reviled the unrepresentative government of the day, eulogized all that had happened in

France and argued that, since the existing oligarchies were entirely incapable of reforming themselves, all the people should elect a General Convention of the Nation to carry through the necessary political improvement themselves. At the same time, he dismissed the nonsense that only those who owned landed property could be trusted to govern and he forcefully advocated universal suffrage instead. These ideas were not reformist but revolutionary and a direct challenge to the whole structure of contemporary authority. Paine went further by arguing for a much greater role for a reformed state which should divert funds used for the iniquitous practice of making war in the direction of free education, old age pensions and even allowances of £4 per annum for every child under 14.

The *Rights of Man* had a galvanizing effect on debate and at the same time awakened the interest of many previously not interested in political issues. By the end of 1793 it had sold over 200,000 copies throughout Britain and the market was also soon flooded with cheap editions and abridgements. Ironically, the government significantly added to the fame and popularity of the pamphlet by trying to ban it by royal proclamation in May 1792. Sales thereafter spiralled upwards, one Edinburgh journalist describing how in one north of Scotland town the local bookseller had only sold one copy of the *Rights of Man* before the proclamation and 750 a few weeks afterwards. Norman MacLeod, the reform-minded Member of Parliament for Inverness, observed that the proclamation had 'acted like an electric shock: it set people of all ranks a reading'.[4]

Meanwhile, during the spring of 1792 the burghal reform movement had received yet another rejection of their modest reform proposals when Richard Sheridan's annual motion was predictably talked out by the House of Commons. It was confirmation of the new political circumstances that this refusal was not greeted with the usual indifference but instead provoked a wave of anger in several parts of Scotland. Henry Dundas was burnt in effigy in Aberdeen, Dundee, Perth and Brechin, and the mob went on the rampage in Edinburgh for three days during the king's birthday celebration in June 1792, in the process breaking the windows of Dundas's house and those of his nephew, Robert, the Lord Advocate. It is true that these disturbances can to some extent be blamed on economic and social factors rather than on political discontent. In 1792, corn prices were the highest for a decade; the pace of rural improvement was also quickening and causing displacement of people and, with it, protest against large-scale sheep farming in Ross-shire. Nevertheless, the anti-Dundas riots of May and June 1792 do also suggest popular anger against 'Old Corruption' and its stubborn refusal to countenance even the most modest reform proposals. At the same time as some were taking to the streets, other Scots of relatively humble origin were starting to form 'Societies of the Friends for General Reform' which were still few in number but a portent for the future. Of course it would be a gross exaggeration to suggest that the Scottish people as a whole had become politically disaffected by 1792. The unrest was localized at first, with the western counties and industrializing towns hardly affected and the disturbances mainly confined to some areas on the east coast. Yet the agitation of that year was significant because it was the beginning of a new popular opposition to government on a scale not seen since in Scotland since the Union.

The establishment of the Scottish Association of the Friends of the People in July 1792 added a further momentum. Its foundation was a direct result of the frustration felt by the burgh reformers at the persistent and contemptuous rejection of their proposals by government. They had now come to the conclusion that the only way forward was reform of parliament itself. But the objective was emphatically not to start a Paineite revolution. At a meeting in Fortune's Tavern, Edinburgh, on 26 July a group of burgh reformers and some members of the parliamentary opposition allied to Charles James Fox, William Pitt's most formidable opponent, resolved on 'moderate, firm and constitutional proceedings' which would 'draw over the landed and borough interests to its view'.[5] Like the London Association on which it was modelled, the new body sought to direct popular feelings away from Paineite radicalism and towards reformism and constitutionalism which the propertied classes would be able to control.

However, before the inaugural meeting of the National Convention of the Scottish Friends of the People finally took place in December 1792, events in France took a dramatic turn. The bloodbath of the French nobility and clergy in the 'September Massacres' attracted widespread coverage in the Scottish press which did not spare its readers any of the gory details of the grislier executions by guillotine. From this point on, the revolution was represented as a grave threat to the entire social order, a political force careering out of control and sliding rapidly into murderous anarchy. From the conservative perspective, worse was to follow when the Duke of Brunswick's mighty army of coalition of the European powers, assembled to crush the revolution with all speed, was itself roundly defeated by the citizens' army of France. The revolutionaries then proceeded to terrify the ruling classes all over the continent in their Decree of 19 November 1792 by offering military aid to all other peoples seeking liberty from oppression.

All this transformed the political landscape in Scotland. The success of the French revolutionaries against all the odds convinced many who had never been part of the political nation that the *ancien régime* in Britain could also be destroyed by popular action and a new democratic order put in its place. The *Edinburgh Gazetteer* caught the mood when it proclaimed, 'Every patriotic heart must rejoice at the brilliant successes of the French in every quarter. Despotism has now been shook to the centre on the Continent and before the conclusion of next summer the Tree of Liberty will occupy the soil that has long been usurped by merciless tyranny.'[6] It was this wave of unrestrained optimism and sheer political excitement that fuelled an explosive growth of reform societies all over Lowland Scotland between October and December 1792. By the end of that year, local societies of the Friends of the People had been founded in all the towns south of Aberdeen and in a large number of country villages in the central belt. But this was only one aspect of the popular response. The authorities were alarmed not so much by the rise of an essentially moderate and worthy parliamentary reform movement as by a series of spontaneous riots that erupted in several towns along the east coast. These were emphatically political in nature, with the planting of 'trees of liberty' and the usual ritual incineration of countless effigies of the hated Henry Dundas, the very personification of Old Corruption. But little evidence has been traced of coherent links between the reform societies and the plebeian mobs. Indeed, most of the local associations, which were committed to constitutionalism, deplored the delinquent lawlessness of the crowds and even on occasion assisted the authorities to restore order. After one of the worst riots in Dundee, the mob went on the rampage for over two weeks, and only the intervention of two troops of dragoons finally brought a measure of calm. The Dundee Friends of the Constitution promptly denounced the disturbances as 'the most fatal enemies of Liberty'.[7]

Despite their protestations, however, conservative opinion in Scotland firmly condemned the Friends of the People, who were now deemed guilty of the heinous crime of stirring up sedition among the common people. The combination of the terrible events in France and the threat of plebeian revolt at home rapidly closed the ranks of the propertied classes. Even opposition Whig politicians who had previously dabbled in reform politics rallied to the cause of defending the constitution from 'the levelling spirit' which now menaced the whole social order and subverted the right of property to govern. Henry Dundas informed the House of Commons in December 1792 that he had just returned from several weeks in Scotland, during which 'he had been visited from every quarter, by the great manufacturers by magistrates and by gentlemen ... all expressing their alarm at the situation of the country; and requesting the interference of government to check a spirit which threatened the most dangerous consequences'.[8]

Therefore, even before the first Convention of the Friends of the People met, the reform movement was already vulnerable to draconian government reprisals. Eighty of the reform societies sent delegates to the Convention, but many of the leading figures in the movement stayed away (apart from several Edinburgh advocates, including the eloquent and fiery Thomas Muir and William Dalrymple of Fordell). It was now plain that only an isolated minority of the upper-middle-class reformers were prepared to take the risk of promoting the cause in the new circumstances. Indeed, much of the business of the Convention was devoted to a vain attempt to demonstrate loyalty to the established constitution rather than debating reform proposals. From this point, the Friends of the People were on the defensive and they never recovered the initiative. During the Convention, Thomas Muir read out a fraternal address from the Society of United Irishmen which was branded seditious and treasonable and gave the government the opportunity to move against the reformers. Muir himself was arrested in January 1793 and his trial in August 1793 has been made infamous by the notorious partiality of the presiding judge, Lord Braxfield. Muir, however, did not help matters. He opted to fight his own defence but showed little grasp of forensic skills in doing so. When Muir was found guilty, Braxfield handed down the sentence of 14 years' transportation to Botany Bay. Muir's trial has entered Scottish folk tradition but it was simply the most celebrated episode in what now became a campaign of systematic discrimination and retribution against the supporters of the Friends of the People.

The conservatives were given further encouragement when France declared war against Britain in February 1793. The Scottish supporters of the revolution could now be branded as the enemy within and the onslaught on them legitimized as necessary retribution against potential traitors. As John Brims puts it, 'Lawyers of allegedly "Jacobin" sympathies were deprived of briefs, radical journeymen and school-teachers were dismissed from their employments, and master tradesmen and shopkeepers of democratic political views were boycotted.'⁹ Ministers of the Church of Scotland and the dissenting congregations railed from their pulpits and roundly condemned parliamentary reform as a threat to the very existence of Christianity.

Against this background of hysteria, it was hardly surprising that the second Convention in April 1793 attracted only 117 delegates, compared with 170 at the inaugural meeting. The approach of members remained moderate rather than revolutionary, but morale was low and the movement would probably have collapsed altogether if an invitation had not come from the radical London Corresponding Society to unite all the parliamentary reform societies throughout Britain in pursuit of their joint objectives. William Skirving, the secretary of the Edinburgh Friends of the People, responded positively and a British Convention of the Friends of the People met in November 1793. The trials and subsequent punitive sentences on Muir and Thomas Fishe Palmer, an English Unitarian minister active in the reform movement in Dundee, had convinced the leadership that even existing liberties were now under grave threat from a government and judiciary that was becoming more tyrannical and despotic. The British Convention therefore moved decisively from a reformist to a radical approach. The Convention passed Paineite resolutions supporting universal adult male suffrage and annual parliaments, adopted French styles such as 'citizen' and 'section' and agreed to establish a permanent convention that would organize popular resistance if liberties were threatened. These provocative acts made it even easier for the authorities to crush the Convention. The use of French forms seemed to confirm the old conservative charge that the reformers were revolutionaries at heart, aided and abetted by a foreign power. Despite being ordered to disperse, the Convention continued to sit and the leadership was then arrested. Maurice Margarot, Joseph Gerrald and William Skirving received what had by now become the familiar sentence for convicted radicals of 14 years' transportation to Botany Bay. There was precious little popular opposition to these verdicts. For once, the 'mob' was silent and the middle and upper classes sided with the government. The Convention was deemed guilty of fomenting revolution on the French model during a time of war with the French enemy; for that it deserved enforced dissolution and the leaders severe punishment.

In this climate, the authorities were able to strike hard without provoking much reaction. Indeed, the formerly sympathetic *Caledonian Mercury* congratulated government on its decisive action 'before the guillotine was declared permanent'. The state's position was further strengthened by the so-called 'Pike Plot', a plan conceived by a former government spy, Robert Watt, to mount a revolutionary coup in Edinburgh. The pikes to be used in this attempt and which were found in Watt's house allegedly belonged to the British Convention. In the fevered atmosphere of the time, Watt and one David Downie were tried for high treason. Downie was reprieved but Watt was found guilty and executed at the tollbooth of Edinburgh, the only Scot put to death during the revolutionary era. His trial signalled the end of the era of open radical politics in the 1790s. From then on, such opposition as remained went underground. Now Dundas really took the gloves off. The Act against Wrongous Imprisonment, the Scottish equivalent of *habeus corpus*, was suspended and a general witch-hunt unleashed against any suspected radicals. The most famous victim was Henry Erskine, who was deprived of his office as Dean of the Faculty of Advocates. But there were countless other unknown figures who suffered, including many tradesmen whose businesses were boycotted and workmen who were dismissed. Dundas's popularity among the Scottish political classes rose to unprecedented heights and in the elections of 1796 he won the largest-ever number of seats. At least in the short term, the radical threat had been well and truly vanquished.

3

Unlike the revolution in France and the great rebellion of 1798 in Ireland, the pattern in Scotland seemed to be one of rock-solid political stability after the dramatic events of 1792–4. Even the years of dearth of 1795 and 1796 and rocketing food prices failed to disturb the surface calm. But the appetite for reform had been clearly demonstrated and was unlikely to die entirely, despite the powerful conformist pressures of loyalism during the French war and the hard line relentlessly pursued by the authorities. The clearest indication of survival was the emergence of the secret oath-bound society, the United Scotsmen, who were republicans committed to annual parliaments and universal suffrage and who advocated the lawful right of resistance against the tyranny of the state. The influence of the Society of United Irishmen on the organization and constitution of the United Scotsmen was considerable and it increased during the 1790s with the mass migration of weavers, pedlars and seasonal harvesters from Ulster to south-west Scotland. Repressive measures against members of the Irish Society from 1797 meant that a stream of political refugees crossed the North Channel to Wigtownshire and Ayrshire and the authorities suspected these men of boosting the numbers of subversive societies. The other connection was with the now-disbanded Friends of the People Associations. The chief ideologist of the United Scotsmen, George Mealmaker of Dundee, had written the Address of the Perth Reformers which had resulted in the trial and transportation of the Revd Fishe Palmer, and he then attended both the Second National Convention of the Friends and the British Convention. Government reports suggest that many of the old strongholds of the Friends in Stirlingshire, Forfar and Fife were also centres of activity by the United Scotsmen. Emissaries in the dissemination of ideas were often migrant Irishmen and tramping weavers, and the very patchy evidence of their activities reveals a growing network of around two dozen clandestine societies, stretching across the Lowlands from Ayrshire (where the Irish influence meant they were especially significant) to the east coast. The links with the United Irishmen gave them the support of the most formidable revolutionary organization in the British Isles and they also formed a link in the international chain of conspiracy which France hoped to exploit in any invasion across the Channel.

Nevertheless, it is hard to see the United Scotsmen posing any credible threat to the state. Elaine McFarland, the most recent student of their activities, concludes that the Societies 'at their height probably never attracted more than a few thousand members, active and nominal'.[10] An unknown proportion of this small number were transient Irish rather than indigenous Scots. In fact, when the Rebellion of 1798 broke out in Ireland, the Scots did not come out in support of revolutionary brothers but as loyal armed soldiers of the Crown, with a mandate from the state to crush the forces of papist insurrection. Scottish troops comprised no fewer than 13 of the 20 British regiments responsible for the defeat of the rising of United Irishmen. Several were known to have carried out their orders with uninhibited ferocity, as is indicated in this Scottish soldier's song of 1798:

Ye Croppies of Wexford, I'd have you be wise,
And not go to meddle with Mid-Lothian boys,
For the Mid-Lothian boys, they vow and declare,
They'll crop off your head as well as your hair.
Remember at Ross and at Vinegar Hill,
How your heads flew about like chaff in a mill,
For the Mid-Lothian boys when a croppy they see,
They blow out his daylights or tip him cut three.

The United Scotsmen might have expected a significant stimulus from the Militia Riots which erupted throughout the rural Lowlands in the autumn of 1797 and have been able to exploit them to advance their cause. In order to increase the supply of men for the national defence of the realm at a time when the war was going very badly for Britain, a Scottish militia was to be established. The terms of the Militia Act suggested that conscription was to be enforced and that the unfortunate recruits might well be sent out of Scotland for military service. The main targets seemed to be young men of the labouring classes; others of higher rank could hire substitutes if they were selected. The legislation generated a furious response. Riots spread from Berwickshire to Aberdeen, with the most serious outbreak in the mining village of Tranent in East Lothian. A bloody battle culminated in 12 people, including two women and a boy, being killed by a troop of dragoons who, driven beyond endurance by the mob, finally ran amok. Some members of the government thought all this was the nefarious work of 'Jacobin' conspirators. There is no evidence, however, that the United Scotsmen deliberately incited the riots, although some of the bolder spirits in the organization, such as Angus Cameron, did try to encourage armed resistance in the disturbed districts. But these efforts proved futile and, by mid-September, the Lord Advocate, Robert Dundas, could confidently report that any threatened insurrection had failed to materialize.

Two further serious blows to the morale of this small band of activists came in 1798. First, a key influence, George Mealmaker, was convicted of sedition and sentenced to transportation to Botany Bay. Second, and more seriously, the collapse of the 1798 rebellion of the United Irishmen had a crushing effect on political expectations; it demonstrated the failure of the French to provide anything other than minimal support and at the same time the sectarian bloodbath into which the rebellion degenerated appalled those idealists who had believed in the movement's aspirations to universal brotherhood. The year 1798 did not bring all Irish-Scottish liaisons to an end. On the contrary, the flight of refugees from the carnage of the rebellion added to the number of former United Irishmen in Scotland, and a skeleton network still survived *c.* 1800 in Glasgow, Fife, Perth and one or two other places. By 1803, however, the United Scotsmen had ceased to have political significance and disappeared altogether from government surveillance reports.

4

A revolution on the French model could not have occurred in Scotland in the 1790s because, a century before, the decisive shift in power between monarchy and aristocracy had already taken place. By 1700, the political status of kingship had been reduced and the position of the greater landowners and their kinsmen and associates among the laird and legal classes effectively consolidated. They had in effect become the governing authority in the land. The claim of the monarchy to rule over all by divine right was challenged in the civil wars of the middle decades of the seventeenth century and then destroyed at the Revolution of 1688–9. William and Mary reigned by the consent and invitation of the Scottish nobility not by inalienable right. This seventeenth-century revolution in Scotland, as in England, established the landed élite as the ruling class, in partnership with a constitutional monarchy whose powers had been drastically cut back. In one sense, then, the *ancien régime* which was overthrown in France in 1789 had already died in Scotland a century before. The resilience of the Scottish state therefore, in the 1790s, rested ultimately on the power of the Scottish landowners and their kindred and clients. It was *their* exclusive right to govern the country rather than that of the monarchy which was questioned by the Scottish radicals in the 1790s.

One reason why that challenge failed was that the landed class was probably at the zenith of its authority and power in the later eighteenth century. Their sense of confidence radiated most obviously from their great building programmes at this time. This was the era of the construction of the massively impressive aristocratic houses at Culzean, Hopetoun, Inveraray and elsewhere. They physically symbolized the dominance, wealth and territorial influence of the great men of Scottish society. The fact that rural Improvement accelerated in the last two decades of the century was further testimony to their complete assurance in their own right to rule. A class which feared for its own position would never have contemplated the revolutionary economic changes that became common in both Highland and Lowland Scotland at this time. The evidence that these fundamental alterations in both tenure and settlement provoked only limited, sporadic and isolated protest was itself a sign that the right to govern of the landed families who had ruled Scotland for centuries was still widely accepted.

The union of 1707 continued the traditional privileges of the landed classes and, at the same time, gave them, their kinsmen and their associates easier access to a richer network of patronage and career opportunities in London and the English empire. But the union did not threaten their right to govern Scotland. There was little impetus to assimilation. Instead, 'semi-independence' allowed for the exercise of traditional authority, while at the same time guaranteeing free access to English markets for such products of the landed estates as coal, salt, linen, cattle, wool and grain. Two developments a few decades later buttressed the position of the governing classes still further. First, the decisive defeat of Jacobitism in 1746 finally removed the possibilities of a counter-revolution and the danger of any return of absolute monarchy. Second, and at the same period, there was the emergence of the political dominance of the Moderates in the Church of Scotland. This did not necessarily mean that all churchmen became docile creatures of the lairds but the development did ensure that religion no longer posed a threat to aristocratic hegemony in the way it had done a century before in the era of the Covenanters.

The main material threat to the traditional order might have come from the impact on the population of the changing economic and social structure of Scotland in the eighteenth century. Ironically, however, the economic revolution, far from undermining the position of the old ruling class, helped in the short run to give it further resilience. In the eighteenth century, at least, economic growth consolidated the influence of the existing regime. One clear sign of the increasing material power of the magnates was the evidence that the territories of the larger estates were still growing in size at the expense of the smaller properties throughout this period. This had a variety of causes. Urban and industrial growth occurred rapidly in the 1780s and 1790s, but Scotland remained an overwhelmingly agricultural society into the nineteenth century. Economic diversification boosted demand for both foods and raw materials from the landed estate and led to sharply rising rentals. Industrialization and agrarian change were interrelated because much weaving, spinning and mining took place in the countryside rather than in the towns. The new economic order which was taking shape did not therefore threaten the hegemony of the landed classes. Many, indeed, were active agents in the transformation, through their energetic role as agricultural 'improvers', as founders of industrial villages, as partners in mining, iron manufacturing ventures and in banks, roads and canals. They may have been political conservatives but they were also economic revolutionaries who had a vested interest in and commitment to the new society that was emerging. This role did not develop suddenly in the later eighteenth century. As seen in previous chapters, the landed estate was increasingly viewed as a source of revenue rather than of military power by the later seventeenth century and commercial criteria were already dominant in many areas by 1700.

This had vital consequences for the survival of the old regime. The commitment of the existing ruling classes to economic change meant that for several decades the 'unreformed' political system was entirely capable of accommodating and implementing legislation crucial to the advance of merchant and industrial capitalism. By doing so it helped to perpetuate itself. The system of bounties on linen exports, which was crucial to the expansion of that strategic sector in the mid-eighteenth century, the establishment of the Board of Trustees for Manufactures and Fisheries in 1727, and the abolition of 'serfdom' in the collieries and saltworks in 1775 and 1799, which was designed to solve the problem of labour scarcity in these industries, were some examples of the measures designed to promote economic progress. Radical and innovative action in the economic sphere by the landed élite helped to defuse potential discontent among the leaders of urban society who might otherwise have felt a deep grievance at their continued exclusion from government. The 'unreformed' state was politically static but demonstrably very active in economic affairs. Ironically, many powerful merchants and manufacturers also helped to consolidate the power of the landed classes by themselves purchasing estates and seeking landed status in their own right. But this was no bourgeois conquest of the landed interest's traditional preserves. The numbers who managed to acquire land were very small, the average size of the properties that were bought was tiny, and even the wealthiest from the towns, such as

Glasgow's colonial merchants, found it difficult to move beyond the ranks of the lesser gentry because the sheer cost of acquiring large acreages was so great. The territorial hegemony of the aristocracy was not in the least impaired while at little cost a potential group of powerful critics was successfully absorbed within the existing system.

The endurance of the old order derived primarily from the series of influences that have already been examined. In the 1790s, however, the radical challenge was overcome because of a number of factors, specific to that decade, which also worked to the advantage of the ruling class. As already noted, the war with France and the bloody development of the French Revolution after 1793 made it possible for the state to brand all radicals as traitors and so legitimized the use of coercion against them. The excesses of the revolution, and in particular the Reign of Terror, seemed to confirm entirely the validity of the conservative position that popular democracy would lead inevitably to murderous anarchy. In Scotland, this prompted a rapid closing of the ranks of the propertied classes, especially since the British Convention of the Friends of the People, because of its more proletarian composition and overtly radical demands, held out the real threat of a serious challenge, not only to the old political system but also to the existing *social* hierarchy. The new spirit of political conformity was displayed in the widespread enthusiasm shown by both the professional and commercial classes to join the volunteer regiments in the later 1790s, in the public recantation of such celebrated supporters of the radical cause as Robert Burns, and in the sweeping success of the government party in the elections of 1796. The authorities encouraged 'gentlemen' to establish self-funded volunteer corps of infantry or cavalry for home defence against the French enemy. Because they attracted no state subsidy, they consisted primarily of the respectable classes, officered by landowners and merchants, with the rank and file recruited from shopkeepers, tradesmen, clerks, teachers and farmers. Scotland contributed disproportionately to the Volunteers. By the end of 1803 more than 52,000 Scots had enrolled in 51 regiments out of the 103 established for the whole of the United Kingdom.

The second factor was the growth and extension of the network of state patronage in the 1790s. The cement of the power structure was the patronage system, by which promise of posts and promotions within the army, navy, civil service and the legal system was dispensed by the influential and the governing party in return for loyalty and conformity. The favour of the great was essential for any gentleman who aspired to a position of significance. If sources of patronage had contracted in relation to demand, the regime may very possibly have been destabilized. There is some evidence, for example, in Ireland, that the scarcity of career opportunities for younger sons of the gentry and 'middleman' class in the 1790s helped to inspire the 'restless spirits' who played a significant leadership role in the extensive social disturbances of that decade and in the great rebellion of 1798. There was little danger, however, of this occurring in Scotland. As previous chapters have shown, economic growth at home and the physical expansion of the British colonies in North America, the Caribbean and India in the eighteenth century had generated new opportunities for the sons of the middle classes and the gentry. The huge expansion of the army and navy after 1793 created numerous new posts which could be used to strengthen government support; at the same time, India became, in Sir Walter Scott's words, the 'corn chest for Scotland', as a host of young Scots made their careers in the civil and military administrations of the sub-continent.

The third and final factor was the impact of economic change on the material standards of the majority of the people. In France, economic crisis, harvest failure and high grain prices were at the very heart of the revolution. In Scotland, too, there seemed abundant reasons for popular discontent. Meal prices rose sharply in the final two decades of the century, and they increased again from 1795. The way of life of countless communities in the countryside was changed radically as consolidation of land and dispersal of people intensified in the wake of the 'Agricultural Revolution'. Town workers were also exposed to new insecurities, demands and pressures as industrial development became increasingly linked to the rise and fall of international markets. But, given the scale of the upheaval, what is striking is the relative social stability of Scotland. There was little of the angry peasant rebellions or of the great surges of collective unrest that characterized Ireland or France at this time. Food riots did occur in years of particularly high grain prices, but they were much less common and frequently less violent than those in France, and far fewer even than the outbreaks which occurred in England. On the whole, there was little effective fusion in the 1790s between the meal mobs and the overtly political movements which sought constitutional change. Only after the Napoleonic Wars did a close association emerge between economic distress and political action, especially in the years before and during the Radical War of 1820.

Examination of the social history of the later eighteenth century reveals why popular protest was relatively unusual and in the event posed little threat to the existing regime. There was undoubtedly considerable social dislocation at the time; customary rights were challenged and the experience of economic transformation must have inflicted a great deal of pain and insecurity. But for much of the period the evidence suggests a modest rise in living standards for the majority of people between c. 1780 and c. 1800. Detailed surveys of occupational groups as varied as male farm servants, urban masons and rural handloom weavers indicate that, while grain prices were indeed rising, money wages were rising faster still. Only from the early nineteenth century was there a decisive break in this upward trend. This cushion of moderately improving living standards for the majority was of central significance. It helped to alleviate the effects of social change and reduced one possible cause of widespread popular agitation.

Improvement in living standards at this time was a distinctively Scottish experience. It was not, for example, paralleled in most areas of western Europe, or even in England, where, in the 1780s and 1790s, prices did apparently outstrip money income. Peculiarly Scottish factors help to explain the trend north of the border. Not only was there an unprecedented boom in urban, industrial and agrarian employment, but so much of the economic expansion depended on labour-intensive methods that it led to particularly significant increases in such major groups as handloom weavers and farm servants. At the same time, Scotland contributed disproportionately large numbers of soldiers and seamen to the war effort between 1793 and 1815. Added to that was the relatively slow pace of national population increase, significantly lower than that of Ireland, France and England in the later eighteenth century, which ensured that the labour markets were never in danger of being glutted with a flood of additional workers. The general result was that employers, whether in country or town, had to bid higher in most instances to ensure a regular supply of workers.

Potential unrest was also defused by the widespread opportunities for both emigration and migration. Population mobility in this rapidly changing society was unusually high by the standards of many west European countries. Transatlantic emigration was undoubtedly one alternative to physical protest against the onward progress of agrarian capitalism in the western and central Highlands. But the 'safety valve' of migration worked also very effectively in Lowland Scotland, where the close proximity of 'improving' areas of agriculture, the foundation and extension of planned villages and new towns, and the rapidly expanding cities of Glasgow and Edinburgh facilitated and encouraged temporary and permanent movement of people in large numbers. Dispossession did not pose so grave a threat when these alternatives not only existed but were close and accessible to many.

In the final analysis, however, the survival of the old regime depended ultimately on the role and responses of the landed class itself. In a hierarchical society, the legitimate right to govern was based not only on the inherited privileges of rank but also on the expectation of the performance of traditional duties to those lower in the social order. The tenant, for example, paid his rental in good years on the assumption that his landlord would be a source of support in bad times. Many Lowland landowners intervened in two key areas to alleviate social distress, and this also reduced the possibilities of social unrest. The first was by purchasing grain in years of scarcity and making it available at subsidized prices to local communities. The second and more recent development was the willingness of landowners to allow themselves to be rated for poor relief. It was at this time that local assessment became common in several districts of the Lowlands. In the later eighteenth century also no clear and firm distinction was yet made between the 'impotent poor', entitled to relief, and the able-bodied unemployed, who were not. Only in the nineteenth century did the system become more rigorous and discriminating. In earlier decades, however, poor relief was much more flexible and less parsimonious and it helped to provide a basic safety net for the worst off in years of economic crisis such as 1782–3, 1792–3 and 1799–1800. It was also common for tradesmen to petition Justices of the Peace and the Court of Session in wage disputes with their masters, and the judiciary was often prepared to use its powers to adjust wages to take account of rising prices. This kind of intervention was apparently becoming even more prevalent in the 1790s. Both JPs and judges played a key role as intermediaries, and this at once helped to check industrial confrontation and at the same time protected some groups from the impact of rising grain prices on their standard of life.

The free market in prices or in wages was therefore not yet a complete reality. Paternalistic regulation was jettisoned only in the early nineteenth century and, as will be seen, the removal of the old controls then did much to intensify the deeper social tensions which came to the

218

surface after 1815. But in the 1790s, paternalism, through the provision of food subsidies, a more responsive Poor Law and action on wage bargaining, still lingered on. The combination of these measures, a hard line by the state against radicalism and a fortuitous and ephemeral set of social and economic circumstances meant that the old regime came through the turbulent decade of the French Revolution remarkably unscathed.

5

For the next decade or so, radicalism was in the doldrums. Napoleon's meteoric rise to power in France seemed to confirm the old conservative prediction that the anarchy of revolution would inevitably be followed by the tyranny of military dictatorship. Further, the grave threat to British security posed by the French blockade and plans for invasion was likely to promote patriotism rather than disaffection. But beneath the political calm new conflicts were already emerging which would eventually provoke another eruption of popular radicalism on a much bigger scale than the disturbances of the early 1790s. At the heart of the problem was the impact of Scottish industrialization. The old relationships between masters and men in the traditional trades were now disintegrating rapidly. It was no longer possible for all these workers to aspire to move from apprentice to journeyman and, for a few, to the status of independent master. The vast majority of journeymen in a host of trades were destined to remain wage earners for their working lives. Increasingly, too, master manufacturers, facing the challenge of cut-throat competition in volatile overseas markets, set wages according to commercial demands rather than traditional standards. Over a whole range of crafts, a separation of interest between employers and employees developed from the later eighteenth century, and one result was the formation of permanent journeymen's societies among masons, tailors, shoemakers, wrights and many other occupations to defend workers' rights. The most famous symbol of the new age was the Glasgow weavers' strike of 1787, when a combination of escalating food prices and a slump in wages provoked a stoppage throughout the city and an unprecedented mass meeting of over 7,000 weavers and their families which stridently opposed the lower prices offered for work by the manufacturers. A violent confrontation with burghal authorities and regular troops followed, in which six of the crowd were killed. The impact of the market economy was now forcing many more to unionize, not simply for welfare and benefit purposes, as had been the main priority in the past, but to provide some form of protection against fluctuating wages, unscrupulous employers and the flood of semi-skilled and unskilled migrant labour that now threatened to undermine craft living standards. Thus, even if radical political activity virtually ceased in the early nineteenth century, the organization of workers through trade unions went on apace. In 1810 and 1811, calico printers were involved in a long period of industrial conflict that became known as the 'Reign of Oppression', and it was also between 1809 and 1810 that the first effective union of Glasgow cotton spinners, developed. At the same time, in many of the 'unionized' trades, masters' organizations were also growing up to strengthen the position of the employers against increasingly truculent workers and to ensure their right to hire at whatever level the market dictated.

Within this world of simmering industrial unrest a number of additional factors fuelled discontent. A fundamental influence was the acceleration in the rate of growth of towns and cities. In 1801, 21 per cent of the Scottish population lived in towns with 5,000 or more inhabitants. By 1831 this had risen to nearly one-third of a national population which was itself increasing more rapidly than in the later eighteenth century. This period of three decades of urban expansion was the fastest of any in the nineteenth century as a whole as migrants streamed into the towns and cities from the Lowland countryside, the Highlands and increasingly from Ireland. In general, it was the manufacturing centres of the western Lowlands that attracted most migrants and became the human melting-pots of the new industrial society. But despite the dynamic expansion of industry, these urban economies in the early nineteenth century did not have the capacity to absorb all or even the majority of new arrivals in regular and gainful employment. Especially during serious industrial recessions, such as that of 1816–18, there was terrible social suffering as employment collapsed in cotton spinning and weaving and destitution escalated. One index of mass poverty was that death rates in Scottish cities started to climb once again after falling for a time in the later eighteenth century. The central cause was typhus, the disease of poverty, which became a major killer in the recession years when jobs were harder to find and wages were often cut to the bone. One estimate suggests that about half of Scotland's handloom weavers, the country's largest single group of industrial workers at the time, fell below the 'primary' poverty line as defined by late-nineteenth-century social analysts. A pool of surplus labour was building up in Glasgow and some of the western industrial towns after *c.* 1810, and this was producing long-term unemployment and an army of casual workers living on a mere pittance on the margins of society. Scottish industry was now mainly geared to overseas markets which were notoriously fickle; when trading conditions were difficult, even the families of prosperous artisans were threatened with penury as orders slumped and workers were laid off.

For many, therefore, the new industrial world of the nineteenth century was characterized by uncertainty, anxiety and insecurity. Ironically, however, it was precisely at this time that the traditions of paternalism that had helped to defuse social conflict in the later eighteenth century were being abandoned. Taxation became more regressive as, with the abolition of income tax, revenue had now to be found from the mass of the population through levies on such basic necessities as salt, sugar, tea, shoes, soap and candles. Before 1800, the Scottish Poor Law had been remarkably successful in responding to such social crises as harvest failure through the development of rating to meet an increasing range of provisions for the old, orphans, the infirm and even for those in temporary distress. But the system was not geared to the needs of the expanding towns because it was founded on the parish network of the Presbyterian Church of Scotland and the administrative authority of the kirk session. But the establishment of new parishes and churches in the urban areas lagged a long way behind the steeply rising graph of town populations, while the influence of the Established Church was further eroded by the growing numbers of Protestant dissenters and Irish Roman Catholics in the cities.

But the Poor Law itself was becoming even more stringent and rigorous in the early nineteenth century. An intellectual revolution was under way initiated *inter alia* by T. R. Malthus, who in 1803 argued in the second edition of his *Essay on Population* that generous poor relief was counter-productive because by encouraging imprudent marriages it increased the labour force, so reducing wages and causing poverty to multiply further. The new thinking touched a nerve in Scotland, where the gross imbalance between the number of workers entering the labour market in the larger towns and the volume of jobs was already causing acute social problems by the second decade of the nineteenth century.

As late as 1804, a Court of Session judgement in the case *Pollock v. Darling* had stated that the function of the Poor Law was to relieve destitution no matter its origin. A few years later, however, resistance was building up to the imposition of rates to relieve distress and, even more crucially, to the idea that the able-bodied unemployed had a right to support. The changing climate was illustrated by the huge interest shown in the social experiment carried out in Glasgow by Dr Thomas Chalmers, the most prominent church figure of the day. In St John's parish, Chalmers carried out a practical demonstration of his belief that poor relief should be based on voluntary donation and not on compulsory taxation. His arguments made a significant impact on his middle-class audience because they suggested that rating would actually deflect funds from charity and hence destroy the Christian bond between giver and receiver which joined the different social classes together and which was now ever more necessary in times of potential social conflict. The widespread acclaim which greeted Chalmers's views confirmed that opinion was now in favour of more rigour in the Poor Law precisely at the time when severe post-war industrial recession was throwing out of work many thousands who had little means of alternative support. It was not a development conducive to social stability.

An even more powerful cause of friction came in the field of industrial relations. Until the early nineteenth century Scots Law had permitted tradesmen to organize to petition for increased wages to their craft incorporation, to the town magistrates and to the Justices of the Peace, who had powers dating from the seventeenth century to regulate hours of work and wages. They could even take the ruling of local magistrates to the Court of Session itself if they were dissatisfied. There is evidence, as has been shown earlier, that both Justices of the Peace and judges were willing in the 1790s to play the role of impartial arbiters and to adjust wages upwards in line with the steep increases in grain prices. This was obviously a vital safety valve and helped to channel energies away from militant confrontation. But within the space of a few years in the early nineteenth century, this legal alternative to strike action was effectively closed off. The catalyst was the great strike of 1812, when weavers' unions in the west of Scotland sought to establish minimum payments for their work so as to enable a weaver 'with fair hours and proper application, to feed, clothe and accommodate himself and his family'.[11] It was a final appeal to the 'social economy', now threatened by the relentless advance of the market economy.

The weavers proceeded in the traditional way, first by petitioning the Glasgow burgh magistrates and the Sheriff, and then taking their case to the Lanarkshire Justices of the Peace and the Court of Session. The courts were sympathetic but the manufacturers refused to implement the prices. The Court of Session for its part was then unwilling to enforce its decision; instead, despite the moderate and even orderly manner in which the strike was carried out, the Sheriffs of Lanarkshire and Renfrewshire moved against the leaders, partly because there was growing alarm at the sheer scale of the dispute, with upwards of 30,000 looms lying idle throughout Scotland. A number of the organizers received prison sentences, and soon afterwards the statute of 1661 which had given Justices of the Peace the right to regulate wages was repealed. The trial of the weavers' leaders also seemed for the first time to criminalize trade unions because they were charged with the offence of simple combination, a new departure in the law of Scotland and one with profound implications. The drive towards an unfettered market economy had principally come from the cotton merchants and manufacturers of the west of Scotland, where the speed of industrial transformation was most evident and where 'antiquated' regulation, it was argued, inhibited further economic progress. But the law itself was changed by judges and advocates, and the new generation of the legal élite, schooled in the universities of the Scottish Enlightenment, were converted to the virtues of the free market economy by the writings of Adam Smith and his acolytes. The concept of the social economy, which related wages to needs and to the cost of living, had been decisively rejected by the courts, and even trade unionism itself seemed to be outlawed. The only recourse now open to groups such as the handloom weavers was to move towards political radicalism in a desperate attempt to change the very nature of the unreformed state itself.

It was not surprising that the weavers were in the vanguard of this new radicalism. Their association with reform politics went back to the 1790s, when weaving villages had played an important part in the Association of Friends of the People, and specialist weaving towns like Paisley, with many families employed in the high-earning fancy trades, had sustained a lively culture of political debate and discussion. But the weavers had suffered a catastrophic decline from their old ascendancy as an aristocracy of labour. A great influx of labour had destroyed their traditional standard of living as numbers of weavers rose from around 25,000 in 1780 to approximately 78,000 in 1820. Between 1816 and 1831, Glasgow handloom weavers endured a fall of nearly one-third in real wages, with most of that decline concentrated during the hard times in the immediate aftermath of the Napoleonic Wars. Disaffection was born out of this crisis and the crushing of the weaving trade unions by legal decree in 1812. But alienation was not confined to the weavers. In Glasgow and some of the other western towns, the years 1816 and 1817 witnessed meal riots and bitter trade disputes involving shoemakers and colliers. The authorities also feared a rising tide of petty criminality which threatened to engulf urban society. In 1810, the Glasgow Commission of Police was referring to 'these dangerous times' and was alarmed at the untold numbers of 'Thieves, Rogues, Vagabonds and Defendators of every description' who, it asserted, were loose in the city, menacing both property and persons.[12] All of this had no overt political purpose, but the perceived incidence of rising crime demonstrated the depth of the social crisis which also fuelled radical discontent.

The radical revival was influenced by two English reformers, William Cobbett and Major John Cartwright. Cobbett provided a highly readable and penetrating critique of the new industrial society in his widely read weekly publication, the *Political Register*, which argued that only parliamentary reform in the final analysis could bring amelioration for those now enduring the misery of poverty. Cartwright was, if anything, even more influential. The veteran radical embarked on a Scottish tour, arguing his case for reform through annual parliaments, vote by ballot, equal electoral districts and payments of MPs. He insisted that the economic difficulties were the result of bad government and could be removed only if the entire system of government itself was changed. Cartwright's message triggered an enthusiastic popular response in 1816, a year of economic depression and high food prices, and large public meetings were held in Paisley and Glasgow to debate the issues. The Glasgow gathering in October 1816 at Thrushgrove on the outskirts of the city attracted an estimated 40,000 people, the greatest political assembly that had ever taken place in Scotland. At this stage, the movement was reformist and moderate, placing greatest emphasis on the petitioning of government and the holding of public meetings. Both middle-class representatives and urban tradesmen were active and a wide range of demands were articulated, from reductions in taxes to the abolition of pensions and sinecures in order to attract the broadest possible support. But the 'caps of liberty' worn by many of the protesters also proclaimed their loyalty to the radical principles of the 1790s.

Inevitably, petitioning failed and the 'moral force' approach seemed to be leading nowhere. By the end of 1816, therefore, and with no improvement in the economic situation on the horizon, a second phase in radical development began. Secret societies were first established in the weaving suburbs of Glasgow and then expanded through a clandestine network to Paisley, Perth, Dundee and other towns. A central committee was set up and efforts made to forge links with radicals in England. They drew on survivors from the 1790s' societies and some of the leadership were Ulster migrants who had had experience in the United Irishmen and with the tradition of using insurrectionary and violent methods to promote political change. To the alarm of the authorities it was reported that armed force was to be used to overthrow the government and the societies were suspected of being in possession of stands of arms, musketballs, gunpowder and cutlasses. The demobilization of soldiers meant that many in the radical ranks were also well experienced in the use of weapons. In early 1817, the magistrates in Glasgow arrested the leadership and 26 people were eventually gaoled for their part in the secret societies. This insurrectionary activity frightened off most middle-class support and brought to an end the alliance across classes that had promoted the moderate reform movement of 1815–16.

Not until economic depression returned again in 1819 did radical activity revive. Again the direct inspiration came from England. Joseph Brayshaw advanced the novel idea of 'union societies', in which all members would agree not to purchase goods on which excise was levied. The theory was that this would then cause a massive fall in the tax revenue and would bring down the government. Associated with this were also demands for universal suffrage and annual parliaments. Brayshaw's economic ideas may have been naïve, but the union societies had considerable popular appeal. They were designed to provide political education for the working classes and they also developed a new organizational structure for radical activity. This was soon necessary as the government unleashed a systematic campaign of repression against all public demonstrations in favour of reform. The turning point was the Peterloo Massacre in Manchester in August 1819, followed by the 'Six Acts' which, *inter alia*, outlawed meetings of more than 50 people. Thereafter most committed radicals began to meet in secret through the union societies, and in the counties of Ayrshire, Stirlingshire, Renfrewshire, Dumbartonshire and Lanarkshire they were transformed from discussion clubs into insurrectionary cells bent on achieving the overthrow of government by physical force. Given the nature of these clandestine associations, it is impossible to be entirely certain about their number, purpose and potential, but details pieced together from government informers, trial depositions and government reports do provide an outline of their activities. The underground societies had a central co-ordinating committee; arms (usually pikes) were available and military drilling was alleged to be under way in some districts. In addition, the associations had a network that stretched across the five counties of the west of Scotland, and substantial contacts had also been achieved with radical groups in the north of England. There can be little doubt that an armed revolt was being planned against an intransigent government which once again had met even moderate demands for reform with repression and judicial retribution.

This was the background to the so-called 'Radical War' which was signalled on April Fool's Day 1820, with the circulation throughout the union societies' heartland in south-west Scotland of the *Address to the Inhabitants of Great Britain and Ireland*, compiled by 'the Committee of Organisation for forming a Provisional Government'. It proclaimed the unity of all classes and called upon the army to stop supporting despotism and instead assist in the fight for freedom. It urged workers to 'desist from labour' until their rights as free men were recovered. But the principles advanced were not necessarily egalitarian: 'the protection of the Life and Property of the Rich Man is in the interest of the Poor Man' because the 'interest of all classes are the same'. The *Address* had an immediate and remarkable effect in Glasgow, Paisley and some other towns. From Glasgow, Lord Provost Monteith confirmed to the Home Office that 'almost the whole population of the working classes have obeyed the orders contained in the treasonable proclamation by striking work'.[13] Around 60,000 people, both in the city and elsewhere, across a whole range of trades, were said to be involved in the action. A full-scale armed uprising was to follow which would be triggered by the outbreak of a popular revolt in England. The signal to confirm that rebellion in the north of England had indeed broken out was that the mail coaches to Scotland would be halted.

Yet while some disturbances did take place in Yorkshire, there was no general rising. When the mail coaches arrived from Manchester, to the open relief of the authorities on 4 April, the plans for widespread insurrection in Scotland were aborted. Despite this, a small group of around 20 radicals, most of whom were weavers, after a meeting on Glasgow Green decided to march on the Carron Iron Works to seize some cannons. They were joined by others at the village of Condorrat but the foray ended at Bonnymuir when, after a bloody skirmish with a troop of cavalry, remembered ever since as the 'Battle of Bonnymuir', 18 radicals, including the two ringleaders, Andrew Hardie and John Baird, were taken prisoner. The last military act of the uprising involved a group of 100 Strathaven radicals who had taken possession of their village and, led by James Wilson, a veteran of the reform campaigns of the 1790s, marched towards Glasgow behind a banner that read on one side 'Strathaven Union Society, 1819' and on the other, 'Scotland Free or a Desart'. However, by the time they reached the town of Rutherglen it became obvious that the national insurrection had failed and the rebels swiftly disbanded. A few days later, most of the strikers had returned to work and the authorities engaged in a series of mopping-up operations in areas of disaffection. Ruthless suppression followed. Three men, James Wilson, Andrew Hardie and John Baird, were executed for the crime of armed insurrection, while many other rebels were sentenced to transportation. Employers exacted revenge on suspected radicals by excluding them from employment. The middle classes, terrified by fear of revolution and the danger to property, closed ranks behind the government and, as they had done in the 1790s, filled the ranks of the yeomanry and volunteer regiments established to police potentially seditious communities.

Over a long period the Radical War has become encrusted in myth and legend and not all popular beliefs about the events of 1820 can be sustained by modern historical scholarship. The familiar notion that the rebellion was provoked by mysterious *agents provocateurs* who were attempting to give government an excuse to move against the secret union societies has now been largely discounted. The key figures in the production of the *Address* which triggered the rising were three weavers from Parkhead in Glasgow rather than spies in the pay of the Crown. It is clear that the burghal and central government authorities were also initially caught off guard by the turn of events and, as the Home Office papers confirm, had then to work hard to regain the initiative after the general strike began on 1 April. Equally unconvincing is the more recent belief that 1820 was a pan-Scottish nationalist uprising that sought as one primary objective to achieve liberation from England. Certainly there was a distinct Scottish dimension to the radical movement, as can be seen by the many references to the heroic figures of Bruce and Wallace as symbols of both nationhood and freedom at political demonstrations. The banner of the Strathaven men in 1820 with its famous inscription, 'Scotland Free or a Desart', had similar overtones. However, one of the striking features of the history of radicalism since the 1790s had been the close association between Scots and the English proletarians in a shared struggle for rights and liberties. This started with the involvement of English radicals in the General Convention of the Friends of the People in 1792 and developed further with the influence on the Scottish movement of Cobbett, Cartwright and Brayshaw after the Napoleonic Wars. In 1820 the entire strategy depended on a simultaneous joint uprising in west central Scotland and northern England, a plan that reflected the common experience of these two regions of rapid industrialization. The rest of Scotland was quiet and virtually irrelevant to the conspiracy. The proclamation which began the Radical War also confirms this sense of shared political identity. It was addressed to the 'Inhabitants of Great Britain and Ireland' and refers in the text to the need to restore those liberties to 'Britons' which they had gained in earlier times through 'Magna Carta and the Bills of Rights' but which were now lost. The rebellion therefore showed a fusion of Scottish and English symbols of freedom but precious little evidence that Scottish independence was ever seriously on the agenda.

The overall historical significance of 1820 has also been debated by scholars. At one level, it seems yet another inglorious failure for the radical cause. Leadership and overall co-ordination of the flawed armed uprising were hopelessly inadequate. The general strategy to be followed after rebellion had broken out was vague in the extreme. The content of the *Address*, with its stress on the need for a beneficial alliance between the rich and the poor, seems more the work of romantic idealists than of hard-bitten proletarian revolutionaries. Some critics point out that the call to arms was answered by only a handful of radicals in a few localities and that overwhelmingly these tended to be villages, towns and suburbs where weaving communities predominated. This, then, for some was essentially a weavers' revolt, a pointless protest against the inevitable impact of technological and demographic change on a dying craft rather than a rebellion of the working classes of Scotland as a whole.

But most of these comments do scant justice to the real significance of 1820. Failure of any armed uprising was probably inevitable, given the continued loyalty of the army, the débâcle of the projected uprising in northern England and the unwavering support of the propertied classes for the authorities. But government was genuinely alarmed at the prospect of armed insurrection. Despite the fact that in early April it had 2,000 regular soldiers concentrated around Glasgow and Paisley at its command and the support of several armed loyalist groups in the same area, it could not guarantee control of either Ayrshire or Renfrewshire. Reports of large numbers of armed men drilling openly came from places as far apart as Bridgeton, Strathleven, Balfron and Kilmarnock. Nor were military preparations confined to the weavers. They were certainly the largest group of industrial workers in the region and their predominant role in the insurrection was therefore hardly surprising. But the lists of arrested radicals show a much wider spectrum of occupational involvement. For instance, of those tried at the High Court at Stirling in 1820, including veterans of the 'Battle of Bonnymuir', half were weavers; but there were also labourers, nailors, shoemakers and others drawn from the traditional trades of blacksmith, bookbinder and tailor. The most remarkable example of solidarity was the general strike which took place in the first few days in April and drew on the support of many occupations, including factory spinners and operatives, in Scotland's industrial heartlands. It was reckoned that only coal miners and farm servants did not take part in significant numbers. The radical challenge in 1820 was much more serious than anything government had to face in England in these troubled years after the end of the Napoleonic Wars.

The longer-term impact of the 'Radical War' is more difficult to determine. It probably had a contradictory effect on the development of Scottish political and working-class history. In the short term the abysmal failure of the rebellion once again channelled energies into trade unionism in the 1820s rather than towards discredited political action. But during the following decade, mass political movements reappeared during the crisis before the Great Reform Bill of 1832 and again in the Chartist agitation between 1838 and 1842. In both cases there was explicit opposition to the use of physical force, and Scottish Chartism in particular became identified with a 'moral force' approach.

One explanation for this might be the bitter legacy of the humiliating failure of 1820. Equally, however, Chartism also drew on the traditions established during the 'Radical War'. In 1820 the industrial labour force was recognizing for the first time common interest in a cause which transcended occupational and religious differences. That cause was the destruction of a corrupt political system and its replacement by a new democratic order which only then could deliver any social improvement. These were the essential ideas that were to inspire Chartism two decades later and were to form the backbone of working-class politics for the rest of the nineteenth century.

II

Highlandism and Scottish Identity

I

To the rest of the world in the late twentieth century Scotland seems a Highland country. The 'land of the mountain and the flood' adorns countless tourist posters and those familiar and distinctive symbols of Scottish identity, the kilt, the tartan and the bagpipes, are all of Highland origin. Yet this curious image is bizarre and puzzling at several levels. For one thing it hardly reflects the modern pattern of life in Scotland as one of the most urbanized societies in the world and the fact that, by the later nineteenth century, Scotland had become an industrial pioneer with the vast majority of its people engaged in manufacturing and commercial activities and living in the central Lowlands. Most rural areas by that time were losing population rapidly through migration to the big cities of the Forth and Clyde valleys. Yet, ironically, it was one of these regions, the Highlands, the poorest and most underdeveloped of all, that provided the main emblems of cultural identity for the rest of the country. An urban society had adopted a rural face.

This was especially surprising in the light of the attitudes towards the Highlands that prevailed among most of the Lowland political, religious and social establishment until well into the second half of the eighteenth century. The concept of the 'Highlands' does not appear in the written evidence for the period before 1400 despite the geographical division between the north and south of Scotland. When the Highlands did become part of the vocabulary in the medieval period, it was in response to a need to isolate and distinguish a part of Scotland that differed in cultural and social terms from the rest. A crucial difference was linguistic for, as Gaelic retreated from the Lowlands, the 'Highlands' became more culturally distinctive and linguistically separate from other parts of the kingdom. Very quickly, too, it became regarded by the state as a problem region. In the early modern period, Highland instability was seen as a major obstacle to the effective unification of the country. After the Reformation, the Highlands were not properly evangelized for the new faith and were regarded as irreligious, popish and pagan for generations thereafter. For the Scottish political élites and the Presbyterian Church before 1700, the Highlands were alien and hostile, in need of greater state control and both moral and religious 'improvement'. The consensus was that the society had to be assimilated to the social and cultural norms that prevailed in the rest of Scotland because it was both inferior and dangerous.

At the more popular level, attitudes towards the Highlanders were equally unfriendly. There was a long tradition of anti-Highland satire in both Lowland poetry and song which can be traced back into the Middle Ages. References in works by such poets as William Dunbar and Sir Richard Holland caricatured the Gael as stupid, violent, comic, feckless and filthy. A short poem dated from around 1560 was entitled 'How the first helandman of God was maid of Ane horse turd in Argylle as is said'. The Highlander also inhabited a physical world of desolation, barrenness and ugliness; and to the Lowland mind, before the revolution in aesthetic taste of the later eighteenth century, the north of Scotland was both inhospitable and threatening. As late as 1800, when perceptions were already changing, the author of *The General Gazetteer or Compendious Geographical Directory* (London, 1800, 11th edn) noted how: 'the North division of the country is chiefly an assembly of vast dreary mountains'.[1] Dr Johnson was also repelled and astonished by the 'wide extent of hopeless sterility' during his celebrated journey to the Western Isles in 1773.[2] When the English army officer, Edward Burt, described the mountains near Inverness in 1730, he saw them as 'a dismal gloomy Brown . . . and most of all disagreeable, when the Heath is in Bloom'. Heather-covered bens were neither romantic nor attractive (as they were later to become) but merely ugly and sinister.[3]

There can be little doubt that for Protestant Whigs in the Lowlands – and that in essence meant the political and economic ascendancy in most areas south of the Tay – the support of many Highland clans for successive Jacobite rebellions instilled an even more intense suspicion of Gaelic society. The Highlanders were no longer figures of fun and ethnic contempt but in the '45 had threatened to overthrow the Protestant succession itself, and this elicited an almost hysterical reaction. One commentator, 'Scoto-Britannicus', depicted the Highlanders as men beyond the pale of civilization. The Young Pretender had secretly landed in the remote parts of the kingdom 'amidst dens of barbarous and lawless ruffians' and a 'crew of ungrateful villains, savages and traitors'.[4] For Lowland Presbyterians, the Highland Jacobites posed a dreadful threat because of their association with popery.

The Young Pretender was identified with the Antichrist, the pope, and his followers were tainted with the same satanic origin, and therefore it is scarcely surprising that the response to the rebellion took the form not only of military and judicial repression but also in an attempt to transform Highland society and culture through legislation designed to encourage economic improvement, the expansion of Presbyterianism and the removal of cultural differences with the rest of Britain.

The strategy of assimilation, which had been pursued by southern governments since the reign of James VI and before, reached its climax with the Disarming Act of 1746. In addition to proscribing the carrying of weapons, it forbade anyone not in the army to wear Highland clothes or even to use 'plaid, philibeg, trews, shoulder-belts ... tartans or parti-coloured plaid'.[5] A government minister memorably described the bill as one for 'disarming and undressing those savages'.[6] Disobedience warranted six months in prison and transportation for seven years for a second offence and the law remained in force for 35 years. Its impact may be questioned, especially in districts far from government garrisons, and in the early 1760s enforcement seems to have been relaxed in general terms until final repeal in 1781. Yet it was precisely at this time that tartan and plaid started to become popular among the Lowland upper and middle classes of Scotland. This strange development was part of a wider process, which was all but complete by the end of the Napoleonic Wars, through which (mostly) imagined and false Highland 'traditions' were absorbed freely by Lowland élites to form the symbolic basis of a new Scottish identity. This 'Highlandism' was quite literally the invention of a tradition. What made it deeply ironic was not simply the actual historic Lowland contempt for ancient Gaelic culture that existed well into the eighteenth century but the fact that Highlandism took off precisely at the same time that commercial landlordism, market pressures and clearances were destroying the old social order in northern Scotland. Indeed, as will be seen, some of the main protagonists of this new and fashionable traditionalism were themselves Highland proprietors who had long ceased to be clan chiefs and were now becoming rapacious improving landowners.

The roots of Highlandism can be traced back to the '45 and before, but an important institutional step in its development was first taken in 1778 with the foundation of the Highland Society in London. Its avowed intention was the preservation of ancient Highland tradition and the repeal of the law forbidding the wearing of the Highland dress in Scotland, an objective achieved in 1782 when the Marquis of Graham, at the Society's behest, successfully carried the legislation through parliament. The tartan was not only quickly rehabilitated but it also swiftly became extraordinarily fashionable. In 1789, the year that Charles Edward Stuart, the Young Pretender, died an alcoholic and disappointed wreck in Rome, three of the king's sons, the Prince of Wales (later George IV) and his brothers William Henry and Frederick, were provided with complete Highland dresses. They were instructed by Colonel John Small in the wearing of 'tartan plaid, philabeg, purse and other appendages', and the future king even wore the kilt to a masquerade in London. Some years before this bizarre event, tartan seems already to have started imprinting itself on the British conscious-ness as the dress of the Scots rather than simply of the Gaels. In Allan Ramsay's poem, *Tartana*, which was written to promote native textiles, the warriors and shepherds of old Caledonia are all rigged out in plaid, and in 1773 there was the first production of *Macbeth* with the hero dressed in tartan, an innovation which quickly became established as a stage tradition.

The reputation of the Highland regiments, especially during the Napoleonic Wars, lent a new prestige and glamour to the wearing of tartan. These battalions had been specifically exempted from the ban on Highland dress in the Disarming Act of 1746 and thereafter the kilt came to be for ever associated with the heroic deeds of the Scottish soldier. During the phase of intense patriotism during the wars with France, some of the Scottish volunteer corps and fencible regiments which were mustered for a short time all over the country adopted tartan and the kilt as their uniforms. By the end of 1803, more than 52,000 Scots were serving in these forces, in addition to the even greater numbers enlisted in the regular army. The military tradition had long been an important part of the Scottish identity; now that was being decked out in Highland colours and the kilted battalions depicted as the direct descendants of the clans. Crucially, however, they now represented the martial spirit of the Scottish nation as a whole rather than a formerly despised part of it.

The apotheosis of this transformation came in 1822 with the remarkable celebration of the visit of George IV to Edinburgh in August 1822. He was the first monarch to set foot in Scotland since Charles II in 1651. The king spent two weeks in the Scottish capital and a series of extraordinary pageants, all with a Celtic and Highland flavour, were stage-managed by Sir Walter Scott for his delectation. What ensued was a 'plaided panorama' based on fake Highland regalia and the mythical customs and traditions of the clans. Scott had determined that Highlanders were what George would most like to see and he therefore urged clan chiefs to bring 'followers' to Edinburgh suitably dressed for the occasion. Seven bodies of 'clansmen', MacGregors, Glengarry MacDonnels, Sutherlands and Campbells, paraded during the visit and His Majesty's generous figure was clad in kilt, plaid, bonnet and tartan coat for the occasion. The climax came with the procession from Holyroodhouse to Edinburgh Castle when the Honours of Scotland – crown, sceptre and sword of state – were solemnly paraded before the monarch with an escort led by the once-outlawed Clan Gregor. At the banquet in Parliament Hall, the king called for a toast to the clans and chieftains of Scotland, to which Sir Ewan MacGregor solemnly replied with one to 'The Chief of Chiefs – the King'.

Scott had wished the royal visit to be 'a gathering of the Gael', but what his Celtic fantasy had in fact produced was a distortion of the Highland past and present and the projection of a national image in which the Lowlands had no part. The great ball during the royal visit in which full Highland regalia was worn has been seen as a seminal event in the acceptance of the kilt as the national dress of Scotland. After all, the head of state had now himself given it a bogus legitimacy and the Scottish ruling class was addressed as 'the chieftains and clans of Scotland' during the public events. More sceptical voices at the time were less impressed than the 'enthusiasts for the philabeg'. J. G. Lockhart, Scott's son-in-law and biographer, regarded the pageantry as a 'hallucination' in which the glorious traditions of Scotland were identified with a people which 'always constituted a small and always an unimportant part of the Scottish population'.[7] Even more appalled was Lord Macaulay. Looking back from the 1850s, he found it incredible that the monarch should show his respect for the historic Scottish nation 'by disguising himself in what, before the Union, was considered by nine Scotchmen out of ten as the dress of a thief'.[8] It was especially astonishing that this mania for tartanry coincided in time with the breaking up of the real Highland society – and, indeed, some of the leading participants in the events of 1822, such as MacDonnel of Glengarry, had themselves been to the fore in the ruthless transformation of their estates into profitable assets through forced clearances. None of this disturbed the pageantry of the royal visit. The realities of the Highland present and recent past were quite separate and distinct from the cult of Highlandism.

2

Much of the new awareness of the Highlands in the eighteenth century throughout Britain can be traced to Jacobitism in general and to the '45 in particular. The rebellion put the Highlands well and truly on the map. Polite society in Europe developed an immediate fascination with the personalities and events of the rising. Histories of the rebellion, such as *Young Juba or the History of the Young Chevalier*, were published in significant numbers, and of special interest was the story of the 'Prince in the Heather' and his months of hiding protected by loyal and heroic figures such as Flora MacDonald. The most popular account was the frequently reprinted *Ascanius or the Young Adventurer, containing a particular account of all that happened to a certain person during his wanderings in the North from his memorable defeat in April 1746 to his final escape on the 19th of September in the same year*. This bestseller was soon available in French, Spanish and Italian versions.

Even during the rebellion itself, Jacobitism had developed a seductive glamour. Jacobite songwriters portrayed Prince Charles as a gallant, charming and courageous Highlander, clad in colourful plaid; and, as William Donaldson has shown, this celebration of the Young Pretender was partly derived from the tradition of the 'Bonny Highland Laddie', a youthful figure of considerable personal beauty and sexual energy who had featured in Scottish popular song since the later seventeenth century. By borrowing from this genre, the Young Pretender was transformed from 'statesman and conqueror' to 'lover and gallant'.[9] Charles Edward Stuart became 'Bonny Prince Charlie'.

But this stereotype could not achieve wide appeal until Jacobitism itself was finally crushed and the threat of a Stuart counter-revolution permanently removed. Indeed, it was the decisive nature of the Hanoverian military victory that made possible the sentimentalization of the

Jacobite cause. Any lingering menace from the Highlands would have prevented this. The rebels were, however, effectively tamed, their martial power destroyed and the scene set for their metamorphosis from faithless traitors to national heroes. The rehabilitation of Jacobitism was enhanced when William Pitt's strategy of channelling the military prowess of the clans into the imperial service during the Seven Years War (1756–63) proved such a stunning success. The outbreak of revolution in France was also influential because 'the spectre of Republicanism rendered the traditional opposition of Hanoverian and Stuart obsolete at a stroke'.[10] The famed military song, 'The Gathering of the Clans', a reinterpretation of 'The Campbells are Coming', set out a detailed list of Highland clans ready to take the field against Napoleon. This and other similar airs of the time expressed in popular form the transfer of loyalty from the Stuarts in the '45 to the Hanoverians in the later eighteenth century. In this way Jacobitism was redefined as an ideology committed to monarchy in the abstract sense at a time when the institution in Britain was under attack from radical enemies both within and without. As such, it became politically acceptable and wide dissemination of the Jacobite myth, with its potent mixture of themes of love, loyalty, exile and loss, was now possible. Jacobitism came to be regarded as representing the heroic Scottish past, the more seductive because it was so recent, and was of course seen as synonymous with the Highlands.

Jacobitism and hence Highland 'tradition' entered the national consciousness through both music and literature and a powerful force in the process was Robert Burns, a prolific writer of Jacobite songs including such familiar tunes as 'Charlie's my darling', 'Strathallan's Lament' and 'The White Cockade'. The fact that Burns himself was a poet of Jacobite sympathy who hailed from one of the traditional strongholds of Scottish Whiggism in Ayrshire was itself a significant confirmation of the new perceptions. Burns sympathized with Jacobitism for patriotic reasons, seeing it as a movement that had fought for Scottish independence rather than for the restoration of an absolute monarchy, and his songs therefore associate the '45 with the heroic struggles of the Scottish past, from the Wars of Independence onwards. That great expression of nationalism, 'Scots wha hae', may itself have been inspired by the Jacobite rebellion. Burns's role was vital in placing Jacobitism, and so the Highlands, at the centre of the new national consciousness which was emerging in Scotland after the union. He was followed by James

Hogg, who, in his *Jacobite Relics of Scotland*, published many examples
of genuine early eighteenth-century Jacobite verse which – much to the
chagrin of the Highland Society, which had commissioned the work –
did not contain enough of the sentiment, pathos and nostalgia deemed
essential in 'authentic' Jacobite verse. Much more acceptable were the
songs of Carolina Oliphant, Lady Nairne, who composed, 'Will ye no
come back again?'. This famous lament for the exiled prince was written
by the scion of an old Jacobite family who was born only 20 years after
Charles had left Scotland for ever! Subsequently three major new
collections appeared, *Songs of Scotland* (1825), *The Scottish Minstrel*
(1828) and *The Scottish Songs* (1829). By the 1820s, melodies with a
Jacobite theme were second only to love songs in number and quality
in the popular Scottish canon.

The prose writers added to this cultural momentum. David Stewart
of Garth, Anne Grant of Laggan, Patrick Graham and, above all, Sir
Walter Scott, presented idealized images of heroic Highlanders who,
despite following an unfortunate cause, had remained true and loyal.
Scott's work, and in particular *Waverley*, more than any other single
influence made Jacobitism acceptable – and, even more, made it romantic and appealing by, skilfully embedding the Jacobite movement firmly
within a Highland context of chieftains, clans and tartans. With only
some exaggeration, one Victorian writer asserted that as a result of
Scott's novels 'the whole nation . . . went over the water to Charlie'.[11]
If the '45 put the Highlands on the map within the United Kingdom,
Scott was mainly responsible for publicizing it widely to an appreciative
reading public throughout the world.

3

The '45 was the fourth and last occasion when a Highland army under
a Jacobite leader threatened the revolutionary settlement of 1688-9. Not
surprisingly therefore, as Peter Womack rightly notes, 'the Highlanders
impressed themselves on British consciousness first of all as warriors
and their society as one where the martial virtues of courage, daring
and loyalty predominated'.[12] At first, the valour of the Highlanders in
fighting against all odds for a lost cause appealed mainly to Jacobite
sympathizers. However, as the martial energies of the Gael were successfully channelled into service in the imperial armies, the exploits of the

Highland regiments rapidly became the stuff of legend and romance and a basic factor in the development of the Highland myth.

As early as 1739, one prophetic commentator had observed:

They [the Highlanders] are a numerous and prolifick People; and, if reformed in their Principles and Manners, and usefully employ'd, might be made a considerable Accession of Power and Wealth to Great Britain. Some Clans of Highlanders, well instructed in the Arts of War, and well affected to the Government, would make as able and formidable a body for their Country's Defence, as Great Britain, or Switzerland, or any Part of Europe, are able to produce.[13]

Even before the '45 the state had started to exploit this military potential. In 1739 the Independent Companies of the Highland Watch were regimented as the 43rd and later the 42nd of foot destined for renown in many a song and story under their more familiar names: the Black Watch, the Royal Highland Regiment, 'The Gallant Forty-Twa'.[14] But it was in the years 1757–60 that the elder Pitt for the first time on a systematic basis diverted the martial spirit of the Highlanders to the service of the imperial state and in subsequent eighteenth-century conflicts over 50 battalions of Highland troops were raised, distinguishing themselves at Quebec, Seringapatam, Waterloo and several other engagements in many parts of the world. Having once been seen as lawless barbarians, the Highlanders were now perceived as vital assets when, for most of the later eighteenth century, Britain was engaged in a great struggle with France for world domination and had much need of loyal troops. Whether rightly or wrongly, the loyalty of the Highland soldier was deemed his most important virtue and this was linked with the steadfastness of the Jacobite army during the '45 and with the hierarchical structure of the clans which bound followers to chief. The fact that clanship was falling apart in this period was beside the point because the composition of the Highland regiments seemed to suggest that clan values and structures lived on within the army. Fraser's Highlanders (the 71st Regiment) had six chiefs of clans among its officers: Simon Fraser, Cluny MacPherson, Macleod, Cameron of Lochiel, Lamont and Colquhoun, as well as several clan gentry. The Highland battalions were not therefore simply daring in war but were also seen to be politically reliable because of their loyalty to their hereditary leaders. As one government paper put it in 1797, the Highlanders are 'strangers to the levelling and dangerous principles of the present age' and, unlike the rest of the population, at a time of radical unrest and republican sentiment could be trusted to bear weapons.[15] This rosy perception apparently did not take into account the series of mutinies that affected several Highland battalions in the later eighteenth century.

The Highland regiments were now a major factor in the alteration of perceptions of Highland society after the '45. The speed of the transformation from Jacobite traitors to imperial heroes is astonishing. It can be seen in the famous contemporary song, 'The Garb of Old Gaul', which celebrates the gallantry of the Highland soldier and in which, in the version published in the 1760s, several of the main ingredients of later mythology are present. There is first repeated the traditional claim that even the Romans had failed to conquer Scotland because of the valour of the Highlanders. The Highland regiments are then depicted as defending Britain from France and Spain, a remarkable reversal 20 years after Culloden, and finally Highland deeds of courage are incorporated into a Scottish tradition of heroism. Before, the Gael was alien and racially inferior; now, the exploits of the Highland soldier made him a standard-bearer for long-held beliefs about the martial virtues of the Scottish nation.

The Highland regiments were therefore crucial to the development of Highlandism. They added to the glamour of the Highlands, perpetuating the association with Jacobitism and clanship, which were also being idealized at the same time, and they also enhanced the contemporary image of a 'noble peasantry' uncontaminated by urban vice and displaying all the virtues of loyalty, courage and endurance to heroic effect. Above all, the kilted battalions, more than any other single factor, popularized Highland dress and made it the national symbol of Scotland. At the end of the Napoleonic Wars, when their prestige had never been higher, the Highland regiments took pride of place in the allied march of triumph into Paris and returned home as heroes. The Black Watch entered Edinburgh to a tumultuous reception. As the regiment's quarter-master sergeant later recalled, '. . . we entered the city amidst the loud cheering and congratulations of friends; while over our heads, from a thousand windows, waved as many banners, plaided scarfs or other symbols of courtly greetings'. Finally, they marched into the castle, 'proud of the most distinguished reception that ever a regiment had met with from a grateful country'.[16]

Soon the entire Scottish military establishment began to assume a dominant Highland image. By 1881, indeed, the connection between militarism and Highlandism was so strong that the War Office ordered all Lowland regiments to wear tartan trews and Highland-style doublets, a directive that applied equally to those who had won battle honours fighting against Highlanders. The victory of Highlandism was complete.

4

At the same time as the Highlands were winning international fame as the home of kilted heroes, European intellectual and aesthetic developments were drastically altering older attitudes to both the society and the physical configuration of the north of Scotland. Enlightenment thinkers became interested in the scientific study of man and human social evolution. John Miller argued that there was a natural progression from 'rude' to 'civilized' manners, while Adam Smith elaborated a schematic structure of evolution by which man moved from the age of hunters, through the age of shepherds to the ages of agriculture and commerce. These ideas impinged on perceptions of the Highlander at two levels. First, in a practical sense they served to give intellectual legitimacy to the varied programmes of 'improvement', ranging from the Annexed Forfeited Estates Commission to the British Fisheries Society, which endeavoured to move the Highlands from backwardness to progress; and second, they placed new emphasis on the need to explore and understand 'primitive' societies. As Charles Withers has argued: 'Highlanders fitted this notion ... rude savages in an uncultivated landscape. To the urbane *philosopher* of the late eighteenth century the Highlander was a contemporary ancestor, the Highlands the Scottish past on the doorstep.'[17] In this way, therefore, the Highlands were effectively incorporated as part of Scotland; they were no longer an alien world beyond the pale but a living illustration of the social mores of the Scottish past. At the same time, the 'primitive' and antique aspects of Highland society attracted special interest:

The Scottish Gael fulfilled this role of the primitive albeit one quickly and savagely tamed, at a time when every thinking man was turning towards such subjects. The Highlands of Scotland provided a location for this role that was distant enough to be exotic but close to be noticed; that was near enough to visit, but had not been drawn so far into the calm waters of civilisation to lose all its interests.[18]

It was these intellectual changes that were tapped and exploited so successfully by James MacPherson in his alleged 'epic', *Fingal*, of 1761. This work and associated others were supposed to have been composed by the blind old harper, Oisein or Ossian, about the heroic figure, Finn, in the third century. The tales mainly amounted to the refashioning of poems that had long been available in Ireland and the Highlands, but when they appeared, MacPherson enjoyed international success and the poems of Ossian were eventually translated into 11 languages. Throughout Europe they had a widespread impact. Napoleon was said to have been a fervent admirer and such figures as Victor Hugo, Alfred de Musset, Lamartine, Goethe, Herder and Schiller were influenced by them. They caught an intellectual and spiritual mood at a time of massive economic, social and political change which saw 'primitive' societies possessing virtues that 'modern' societies had lost. This was a notion that could easily be transferred to the eighteenth-century Highlands because there, too, into the contemporary period, lived a 'primitive' people amid a landscape which seemed hardly to have altered since the time of Ossian.

The Ossianic impact was so great because it both influenced and coincided with parallel changes in attitudes to the Highland landscape. In the later eighteenth century the land ceased to be regarded as simply repellent and came to be viewed as beautiful, romantic and inspiring. Modern notions of 'scenery' and scenic beauty were born and resulted in a transformation of aesthetic responses to the Highlands. The Ossianic craze was deeply significant in this process because the fact that the northern landscape was rugged and untamed made it entirely suitable for the 'primitive' society depicted in MacPherson's best-selling epics. This was the view propounded by Hugh Blair, professor of rhetoric and *belles lettres* at Edinburgh University, in his *Critical dissertation on the poems of Ossian, the son of Fingal* of 1740. Blair's work built on the development of the idea of the sublime which was at that time gaining currency in intellectual circles in Europe. Its theoretical basis was laid out in Edmund Burke's *Philosophical Enquiry into the Origin of our Ideas of the Sublime and Beautiful*; but Blair separated out the 'beautiful' from the 'sublime' whereas Burke stimulated quite different emotions: 'the sublime is found to be rooted in the terrific, inspiring a fear which fills the mind with great ideas and stirs the soul ... any menacing object may produce the sublime, but especially those associated with obscurity, power, privation, vastness, infirmity or difficulty'.[19]

Equally influential was the idea of the picturesque propounded by William Gilpin in his two-volume work of 1792 entitled *Observations relative chiefly to picturesque beauty, made in the year 1776 on several parts of Great Britain, particularly the High-lands of Scotland.* Gilpin enunciated the notion that the picturesque landscape required discriminating and careful observation in order to see its diverse elements as a perfect composition and that the admirer of the picturesque required judgement. Not all nature was attractive; discernment required careful selection. It was a form of cultural élitism.

These new ideas helped to transform the perception of the Highlands from a barren wilderness to a place of compelling natural beauty. By the early nineteenth century, an upper-class tourist trade was already established, partly because European travelling was made more difficult during the French wars. As Sir Walter Scott remarked in 1810, 'Every London citizen makes Loch Lomond his washpot and throws his shoe over Ben Nevis.' Scott himself contributed enormously to the popularization of Highland travel. Hitherto, touring had been confined to the frontiers of the Highlands, with the fashionable 'Short Tour' entering the region at Dunkeld and leaving via Luss with Loch Lomond as the highlight, and few penetrated the wild country to the far north and west. At first Scott's writings (and in particular the 'Lady of the Lake' of 1810) invested the Trossachs with further romance and ensured that Loch Lomond was soon eclipsed by Loch Katrine as the mecca for fashionable tourists. But his 'Lord of the Isles' put Skye on the map and extended the tourist trail to the Hebrides, where those seeking the truly 'sublime' could come face to face with truly wild mountain scenery.

But these changes in attitudes to Highland landscape did not simply reflect alterations in aesthetic taste; they were also linked to practical economic developments in the eighteenth and early nineteenth centuries. People could reach the Highlands in greater numbers because of transport improvements and among these the invention of the sea-going paddle steamer was crucial, with its intricate shipping network established up the west coast and the Inner Hebrides from the Clyde by the 1830s. Cook's tours using steamers and railways began from 1846, the very year the potatoes failed in the Highlands and caused widespread distress. The wilderness seemed less daunting when seen from a comfortable and convenient mode of transport. The Highlands now had a potent appeal in an era of profound economic transformation. Elsewhere in Britain by the early nineteenth century, the 'natural' landscape had been permanently altered by enclosed fields, neat farm steadings and improved agriculture and only the remote areas of the north seemed untouched. Despite the reality of large-scale commercial sheep farming, as efficient as any in the country, which dominated the region, the Highlands seemed to exude 'the radiance of a disappearing authenticity' which gave it a special magic.[20] The 'archaic' nature of the landscape therefore became indissolubly linked with the romanticization of the historic Highlands that was taking place at the same time. It was an essentially imaginary world into which the harsh realities of life for the Gaels in the age of the Clearances rarely entered.

5

The adoption of Highland emblems, costumes and associations as its national image by a modernizing Scotland in the nineteenth century is curious but not entirely incomprehensible. Scottish society was in a contradictory position within the union relationship with England. On the one hand, the nation's rise to prosperity depended on the new connection with her southern neighbour but, on the other, the political and material superiority of England threatened the full-scale assimilation of Scotland. At the same time, from the later eighteenth century romantic nationalism spread throughout Europe and it was unlikely that Scotland would remain isolated from this cultural and political revolution. Any vigorous assertion of national identity would, however, threaten the English relationship on which material progress was seen to depend and so Highlandism answered the emotional need for the maintenance of a distinctive Scottish identity without in any way compromising the union. On the contrary, the indissoluble link between tartanry, the Highland soldier, patriotism and imperial service bestowed a new cultural and emotional cohesion on the union relationship.

It was Sir John Sinclair, regarded as the greatest bore in the House of Commons but also the most devoted chronicler of Scottish economic transformation after 1750, who composed the resolution passed by the Highland Society of London in 1804 to wear tartan at its meetings. He did so in order to recall 'the high character of our ancestors', and in doing so he stressed the need to assert Scottish identity before 'Scotland becomes completely confounded in England'.[21] As Womack notes, 'As Lowland Scotland becomes more and more like England, it turns to the

Highlands for symbols and beliefs to maximise its difference.'[22] Among these was the notion that the kilt had been the national dress of Scotland since time immemorial. Writers such as MacPherson, Scott, Stewart of Garth and others gave emotional depth to these attitudes because they portrayed eighteenth-century Highland culture as the *Scottish* past surviving into the present. What had once been the customs and dress of *all* the nation had been lost in most parts but had been preserved in the 'archaic' world of the contemporary Highlands. It was an alluring myth for a society searching for an identity amid unprecedented economic and social change and under the threat of cultural conquest by a much more powerful neighbour.

PART THREE
1830–1939

12

The World's Workshop

I

In 1888 the Glasgow City Chambers were formally opened by Queen Victoria. The lavish internal decoration, imposing façade and marble staircases symbolized Glasgow's extraordinary progress in the previous decades and its eventual claim to the status of 'the second City of the Empire'. Earlier, in 1883, at the foundation ceremony, overwhelming civic confidence was also visible. About 100,000 spectators in George Square watched a ceremonial trades march by the skilled workers drawn from the heavy industries which by the later nineteenth century had made Glasgow one of the great cities of the world. In 1901 the second International Exhibition staged in Kelvingrove Park conveyed similar images. It was the largest event of its kind ever held in Britain and attracted an attendance of 11½ million, including the Tsar of Russia himself. The focus was on the city's economic and industrial achievements which had brought it world-wide fame. The Machinery Hall and the Industrial Hall were particularly dedicated to Glaswegian prowess in the arts of engineering and science.

The opening of the City Chambers and the second International Exhibition were striking confirmation not only of Glasgow's economic success but of the remarkable material progress of Scotland as a whole since 1830. Then the jewel in the nation's economic crown had been the textile industries, with cotton manufacture in particular having a pre-eminent role. The later nineteenth century, however, was the era of triumphant advance in the heavy industries in which Scotland developed a position of global dominance in several key sectors. By 1913, Glasgow and its satellite towns in the surrounding region of intensive industrialization produced one-half of British marine-engine horsepower, one-third of the railway locomotives and rolling stock, one-third of the shipping tonnage and about a fifth of the steel. On the eve of the First World War the Clyde not only built one-third of British output but almost a fifth of the world's tonnage, a record that was greater at the time by a considerable margin than all the German yards combined. At the heart of the heavy industrial complex with its world-wide markets was the huge range of engineering specialisms in engines, pumps, hydraulic equipment, railway rolling stock and a host of other products. Three of the four greatest firms building locomotives were in Glasgow; in 1903 they came together to form the North British Locomotive Works, 'the Titan of its trade' with a capacity to produce no fewer than 800 locomotives every year. This made the city the biggest locomotive-manufacturing centre in Europe, with engines being produced in large numbers for the Empire, South America and continental countries. In civil engineering, too, the west of Scotland was a famous centre of excellence symbolized by the career of Sir William Arrol (1839–1913), the builder of the Forth Bridge, the Tay Bridge, Tower Bridge in London and numerous other projects in many parts of the world.

It is easy to lapse into superlatives when describing the global impact of Glasgow's heavy industries at this time. But two cautionary notes are necessary. First, Scottish industrial achievement was not confined to Glasgow and the west. Second, the heavy industries were not unique in achieving massive penetration of world markets in the decades after c. 1850. It is true that cotton-spinning, 'the leading sector' of the first Industrial Revolution, was in difficulty from the 1850s when the embroidered muslin trade dramatically collapsed. Although there were still 131 cotton mills operating in Scotland in 1868, the industry came under intense pressure from foreign competition, assisted by tariffs and the impact of Lancashire producers at the finer end of the trade. By 1910, cotton-spinning had virtually collapsed, with only nine firms surviving, its demise accelerated by a failure to maintain earlier patterns of innovations, by low levels of investment and a labour force which, owners asserted, was unwilling to accept the measures necessary to achieve higher productivity. However, failure in cotton-spinning was more than compensated for by virtuoso performances in other textile sectors. When Coats of Paisley amalgamated with Patons in 1896, the world's biggest thread-making producer was created. Archibald Coats (1840–1912) became known as the Napoleon of the thread trade and his business was so profitable that 11 members of the family became millionaires. When faced with American tariffs, Coats invaded the USA and soon dominated the market in thread there. The firm eventually controlled no less than 80 per cent of the global thread-making capacity.

Just as remarkable was the development of jute manufacture in the coarse linen areas of Dundee and the surrounding districts. Jute was a fibre used in bagging and carpeting and was imported from Bengal in India. Dundee soon became 'Juteopolis', with the Cox Brothers' Camperdown Works in Lochee in the 1880s employing 14,000 (mainly women) workers, making it the biggest single jute complex in the world. Again, the product was sold throughout the globe, with booming markets in the United States and the British colonies. Other Scottish towns and cities had their own textile specializations: Kirkcaldy in floor coverings and linoleum; Galashiels, Hawick and Selkirk in the Borders, tartans, tweeds and high-quality knitted goods; Kilmarnock and Glasgow, carpets (in Glasgow, Templetons was the largest carpet manufacturer in Britain by 1914); Darval and Galston in Ayrshire, fine lace curtain manufacture, which employed around 8,000 people just before the First World War. This range of activity ensured that textiles remained an integral part of the Scottish economy despite the malaise in cotton-spinning. Indeed, the numbers employed in thread and lace-making in the 1910s in the west of Scotland fell little short of the labour force in both cotton-spinning and weaving in the 1870s.

Diversity was not confined to the textile sector. James 'Paraffin' Young (1811–83) pioneered the exploitation of the shale oil deposits of West Lothian through a series of inventions which led to the growth of a substantial industry producing 2 million tons of shale by the 1900s. Whisky distillation was, of course, a Scottish specialization, with over 20 million gallons charged for duty in 1884. At Clydebank, the American Singer Company had developed the world's largest complex for the manufacture of sewing machines with a labour force that numbered over 10,000. Further evidence that heavy industry did not have a complete monopoly was the Barr and Stroud optical factory, the Acme wringer factory and the experiments in new ventures such as automobile and aircraft making on the vast 45-acre site of the engineering giant, William Beardmore and Co. During the First World War Beardmore's alone supplied no fewer than 650 planes.

The decades before 1830 had seen radical changes in Scottish economy and society. However, major industrial development was mainly – though not exclusively – confined to cotton and linen, with only sluggish growth in coal and metals. What happened after 1830, and more especially in the second half of the nineteenth century, was a truly massive increase in the scale of development. Cotton-spinning may not have been quite as dynamic, but there was energetic diversification across a whole range of other textile trades. Even more fundamentally, coal, iron, steel, shipbuilding and engineering took off and transformed Scotland into a manufacturer for the world. All these sectors and others were emphatically committed to the export market. A small country of fewer than 5 million people in the 1900s emerged as a key player in the global economy, linking the primary producing regions of America, Africa, Australasia and Asia to the industrializing regions of Europe. Such an epochal development was bound to have deeply significant effects on the nature and structure of Scottish society. A number of these will be considered in subsequent chapters of this book but here at least four important consequences merit special mention.

First, the employment released by the new industrial economy permitted a substantial increase in Scottish population. Between the 1750s and 1831, this had risen by 88 per cent to 2.374 million. In the next 80 years, 1831–1911, there was doubling of population to 4.761 million. Some of this was accounted for by an upsurge in immigration from Ireland after the Great Famine and in subsequent decades, attracted by the employment opportunities in Scottish industry. Second, the national redistribution of population that was already evident before 1830 became even more marked in the second half of the nineteenth century. The concentration of people in the central Lowlands accelerated. The eastern region, centred on Edinburgh, grew from 785,814 to 1,400,675, but the increase in the heartland of heavy industry in and around Glasgow was much more spectacular. The western zone expanded from 628,528 to nearly 2 million people by 1901. At that date the western counties had increased their share of national population to an astonishing 44 per cent. At the same time the overall share of the eastern Lowlands remained virtually static. Elsewhere the pattern was one of general haemorrhage. The population of the Highlands peaked in 1841 and then went into absolute decline. The far north reached its maximum population level in 1861, the Borders in 1881 and the north-east in 1911. The clear gainers were the counties where manufacturing and mining dominated. For instance, the population size of Fife, Angus, Renfrew and Stirling more than doubled; West Lothian trebled and Dumbarton increased fourfold. Remarkably, numbers in Lanarkshire rose by a huge

356 per cent. Rural depopulation is often associated with the Highlands, but it is clear that hardly any area of Scotland escaped the full impact of demographic transformation in this period. Special study of one decade, the 1860s, has revealed that the overwhelming majority of parishes in all parts of the country were losing people, especially in the south-west and in the east from Moray to Berwick. It was only the textile towns of the Borders and parts of the central Lowlands which experienced significant levels of inward migration.

Third, and almost an inevitable corollary of the point already made, agriculture as an employer was in rapid retreat as mining, building and manufacturing established a hegemony in the labour market. As late as the census of 1851, there were more men and women engaged in farming than in mining and textile work combined. Thereafter the pattern altered radically. The proportion of the population working in agriculture fell from 25 per cent in 1851 to 11 per cent in the early twentieth century. Fourth, the drain of the people from the land was the essential precondition for a continued expansion in urbanization. As shown in a previous chapter, Scotland had already experienced a rapid rate of urban growth in the early nineteenth century. By 1851 it was second only to England and Wales and significantly ahead of the Netherlands in a league table of 'urbanized societies' in Europe. Yet, as late as the 1830s, just over one-third of the Scottish population lived in towns of over 5,000 inhabitants. By 1911 this proportion had risen to nearly 60 per cent. This explosion of urban development was generated primarily by the expansion of the 'big four' cities, Glasgow, Edinburgh, Dundee and Aberdeen, where more than one in three Scots lived by the beginning of the twentieth century. Once again, Glasgow stood out in the colossal and continuous nature of its exuberant growth. An army of men and women flooded into the city from the farms and small towns of the Lowlands, the Highlands and Ireland to satisfy the enormous appetite of the great staple industries for both skilled and unskilled labour. In the 1830s there were already over a quarter of a million Glaswegians. By 1871, the total had reached half a million, and just before 1914, partly as a result of boundary extensions, the magical figure of 1 million inhabitants was attained. Elsewhere, agricultural and market centres such as Lanark, Dumfries and Haddington continued to thrive, but the urban dynamic was in the final analysis primarily generated by the power of industry. Outside the 'big four', the most significant rates of growth were experienced by the Border textile towns, the iron, steel and mining centres of Lanarkshire (such as Coatbridge, Motherwell and Airdrie) and the Fife burghs.

This new industrial and urban society depended on a number of important foundations. Most crucially of all, the economy relied overwhelmingly upon access to overseas markets. Some 38 per cent of all Scottish coal production went abroad or coastwise in the 1910s, apart from that consumed by the export-orientated iron, steel and other industries. The giant North British Locomotive Company sent nearly half its engines to the British Empire in the years before the First World War, with India as the primary destination. The rise of Dundee jute was generated from the 1840s by the demand for bagging for international commodities as varied as East India coffee and Latin-American guano, as well as the enormous requirements for sandbags during the Crimean War, the American Civil War and the Franco-Prussian War. At the end of its first major phase of precocious growth in the 1840s, two-thirds of Scottish pig-iron was exported, a significantly higher proportion than the pattern elsewhere in Britain. Even in the later 1860s, around one-half of total production was still being sent overseas. The ships that poured out from the yards of Clydeside relied for orders on the condition of international trade, even if increasingly from the 1890s the needs of the Admiralty for naval vessels were becoming ever more significant. It was the same story elsewhere, from quality Border knitwear to malt and blended whiskies. As far as Scotland was concerned, the international market was the king.

It follows, therefore, that the global trade revolution of the second half of the nineteenth century was a strategic factor in Scottish industrial success. The basis of this was a new and dynamic set of commercial relationships forged between Europe and the Americas, Asia and Australia based on the exchange of foods and raw materials for manufactured goods. Grain, meat, raw cotton, timber, wool and numerous other commodities went to Europe. In return the primary producers obtained ships, locomotives, bridges and railway lines, together with many other requirements for their developing infrastructure from the countries of the northern hemisphere. The whole system was facilitated and massively expanded by a revolution in transportation: the improvement in sailing ship design and speed; the ocean-going steamship from the later nineteenth century; the spread of transcontinental railway networks which unlocked the productive potential of territories as far apart as the plains of India and the American prairies; the building of the Suez Canal, which considerably reduced the travelling time to India and beyond.

All this had dramatic consequences for Scottish industry. The effect was twofold. On the one hand, the earnings which accrued to the primary producers enabled them to purchase more capital goods. On the other, the vast investments in the global transport system opened up a voracious demand for ships, locomotives, railways, bridges and jute bagging. Scottish investors added to this momentum by themselves putting money into American, Australian and Asian railway stock, land and cattle companies, mining ventures, tea plantations and state bonds. Scottish foreign investment rose from £60 million in 1870 to £500 million in 1914, a figure that was much higher per head of population than the average for the United Kingdom as a whole. This outflow from what for the majority of the population was a poor country had a circular impact on the development of the Scottish economy, as these investments then helped to fuel demand for Scotland's great industrial staples. As Bruce Lenman has put it: 'The wheat of the Canadian or American prairies, for example, had to be taken by rail to eastern ports, and in Canada the locomotive could well be made in Glasgow while both in Canada and in America the sacks holding the grain were quite likely to have been manufactured in Dundee. The ships which crossed the North Atlantic with the grain were often enough built and engineered on the Clyde.'[1] The world economic setting was therefore the essential precondition for economic success. What will now be considered are those crucial advantages which gave the Scots a cutting edge in this international market place.

A prime foundation was the rich economic heritage which had developed in the decades before 1830. Scotland's early industrialization had given her a head start over virtually all European rivals – with the exception of the country's nearest neighbour, England. A number of key advantages were already in place which helped to provide a platform for the great achievements of Victorian times. They included a large and experienced business class; a political and social élite committed to national economic growth; a labour force which had already developed skills in engineering, mining and textiles and, crucially, had become accustomed to the more rigorous time and work disciplines of industrial capitalism; a sophisticated infrastructure of ports, roads and canals; and an international network of trading connections not only to Europe and North America but increasingly to the countries of the Empire in the southern hemisphere. Some specific connections between this varied inheritance and the halcyon days of Victorian industrial achievement are worth mentioning. The meteoric rise of Dundee jute was partly based on these relationships. Samples of jute were first sent from Bengal by the East India Company to leading textile centres in Britain in the hope that the cheapness of the coarse fibre might prove attractive to manufacturers. Dundee was the first to solve the technical problem of the dryness and brittleness of the new fibre, not only because the city and the surrounding region specialized in coarser linens but because raw jute was softened by the process of 'batching' or the application of a mix of whale oil and water. Since the later eighteenth century Dundee had become a leading whaling centre in Scotland.

An even closer link can be established in shipbuilding, which in the second half of the nineteenth century became the strategic heart of the west of Scotland's heavy industrial economy. In the early decades there was little competitive advantage in ship construction. In fact, the Clyde had limited traditional expertise in building modern ships and as late as 1835 it launched less than 5 per cent of total British tonnage. The central early advantage was the Clyde's pre-eminence in the development of steam engines for ships, which in turn depended on the range of engineering skills that had accumulated in the region during the first epoch of industrialization. Steam engines were used in the pits to pump water and raise coals and in the cotton factories they were becoming increasingly common. The foundries and workshops of the region not only built but repaired and improved engines. As James Cleland remarked in the early 1830s: 'Glasgow . . . has already large establishments for the manufacture of Steam-Engines and Machinery, and for making the machinery employed in the process of Cotton-Spinning, Flax-Spinning and Wool-Spinning. In these works everything belonging to, or connected with, the Millwright or Engineer department of the manufacture is fabricated.'[2] It was perhaps almost inevitable that from this great congeries of skills in precision engineering would come an interest in the application of steam propulsion to ships. Henry Bell's historic launch of the steamboat Comet in 1812 and its successful voyage across the Clyde demonstrated that it could be done. By 1820, 60 per cent of all British steam tonnage was launched on the Clyde, even if all these vessels were small, had low boiler pressures and consumed huge amounts of coal. The foundation of later greatness depended upon an effective solution to these basic problems of high cost and low performance. It is acknowledged that an important catalyst here was the Napier family, headed by David and, later, by his cousin Robert, who pioneered key technical improvements at their Camlachie foundry and Lancefield yard. The Napier firm became a kind of advanced school of marine engineering and construction. David Napier was the first to combine engineering and shipbuilding in one firm, while many other foundries became active in the supply of boilers and engines for ships as well as their traditional market in the mines and mills. What is striking, however, is that virtually all these engineering ships were clustered in the cotton districts of Glasgow, such as Tradeston and Camlachie. The close connection between the textile industries of the first Industrial Revolution and later fame in shipbuilding in the west of Scotland was confirmed.

These were the foundations, but a number of basic influences then helped to accelerate the transformation of Scotland into a world economic power in the next few decades. A primary factor was a remarkable rate of strategic invention and innovation in metal-working and ship construction. In iron, the seminal advance was made by James Beaumont Neilson (1792–1865), the manager of Glasgow Gasworks who had developed considerable expertise as a chemist and engineer. He revolutionized the iron industry through his hot-blast process. It resulted in great savings in material, costs and fuel and also in increased production per furnace. Neilson's invention was the basis of the exceptional growth of pig-iron manufacture in Scotland because it allowed the Scots ironmasters to undercut their English and Welsh rivals significantly. Between 1825 and 1840, Scottish output expanded 20 times to 504,000 tons. Growth was concentrated in Ayrshire and, to a much greater extent, in Lanarkshire, where the Bairds of Gartsherrie built the core of their great iron-producing empire in the Monklands area. In just 40 years from the 1830s this family developed a reputation as the world's leading pig-iron producer with, in 1870, 42 furnaces with a capacity of 300,000 tons per annum and a profit in that year alone of £3 million. Thomas Tancred, the commissioner appointed to report on conditions in the mining districts, described the Monklands in graphic terms in 1841: '. . . the groups of blast furnaces on all sides might be imagined to be blazing volcanoes at most of which smelting is continued Sunday and weekdays, by day and night without intermission. By day a perpetual steam arises from the whole length of the canal where it receives waste water from the blast engines on both sides of it and railroads traversed by long trains of waggons drawn by locomotive engines intersect the country in all directions.'³ Here was indeed the scarred industrial landscape of Victorian Scotland in its classic form.

In shipbuilding the rate of innovation was continuous from the 1830s. The Clyde achieved worldwide renown by its capacity to make radical and ingenious modes of propulsion and at the same time pioneer new materials of construction. There was a remarkable list of Clydeside firsts which kept the Scottish yards at the leading edge of the burgeoning global market for ships. These included the development of the screw propeller in place of the paddle, which increased speed, the compound marine engine which dramatically expanded power, and the use of new materials such as iron and then steel in ship construction. In the second half of the nineteenth century the fortunes of shipbuilding, iron and steel became very closely linked, primarily because the Clyde yards were so keen to pioneer new materials. In the 1840s almost all iron tonnage was launched on the Clyde and between 1851 and 1870 accounted for over two-thirds of all British production. Steel-making was established in Scotland in the 1870s. Expansion had been constrained because Scottish iron ores were phosphoric and the main steel-making techniques, the Bessemer converter and the Siemens–Martin open-hearth process, relied on low-phosphoric ores. This problem was remedied by the Gilchrist–Thomas process of the 1880s. In the event, however, the Scottish industry developed by using the open-hearth process and imported ores. By 1885 there were already 10 firms producing almost half of all British-made Siemens steel. The link between the open-hearth process and shipbuilding is deeply significant. Essentially, steel was the child of shipbuilding and the result of determination by the major yards to use metal plates of even greater strength, lightness and durability in order to maintain their leading position in world markets.

The economic achievements of Victorian Scotland were also built on local supplies of fuels and raw materials and low costs of labour. Coal reserves were abundant throughout the central belt and had helped to power the steam-driven textile mills of the early nineteenth century. However, with the vast expansion of iron-making, coal came into its own. In 1800 there were probably around 7,000–8,000 miners in the country. By 1870 this labour force had risen to nearly 47,000 men, working in over 400 pits. The Baird ironmasters accounted for their extraordinary success in large part on the fortuitous presence of rich seams of the invaluable splint coal in close proximity with reserves of blackband ironstone in Lanarkshire. From the later eighteenth century, access to coal and iron ore supplies had been much improved with the development of a network of roads and canals. From the 1820s, however, the railway added a revolutionary new dimension to the transport of heavy raw materials and finished products. It is significant that the earliest ventures, such as the Monkland and Kirkintilloch Railway (1824) and the Garnturk and Glasgow (1826), were promoted in order to maximize the exploitation of mineral deposits. Capital raised by Scottish railway companies was a mere £150,000 in 1830. By 1850 it stood at over £20 million and at nearly £47 million in 1870. Trunk lines were promoted linking Glasgow, Edinburgh, Paisley, Greenock and Ayr as early as the 1830s, followed by the creation of coastal routes to England. The railways had far-reaching effects on almost all aspects of Scottish life but their impact on the heavy industrial economy was particularly profound. They were more reliable than canals, which were likely to freeze in winter. Like them, they could shift bulk goods at low cost but did so much more rapidly and with greater regularity. It was also technically much easier for industrial and mining plants to connect to an intricate network of railways by sidings and spur lines than to a system of canals. The mineral riches of particular localities were unlocked and industries with complementary specializations could concentrate on an unprecedented scale. It was the railway more than any other factor that helps to explain the sheer density of industrial activity in parts of Glasgow, Ayrshire, West Lothian and Lanarkshire.

In spite of the marvels of the new technology, most industries still depended on human labour. Shipbuilding was to a significant extent a huge assembly activity in which skilled workers were much more crucial than machine tools. Coal mining, despite significant Scottish advances in cutting machinery from the later nineteenth century, remained a 'pick and shovel' industry. In 1890 one estimate suggests that labour costs constituted around half the overall cost of finished steel and anything between one-third and two-thirds in shipbuilding. The engineering, tool-making, metalworking, furniture, woodworking and printing industries could function only on the basis of skilled labour. In 1911, seven out of every 10 men and women in Glasgow found employment in a range of manufacturing activities. Those sectors where skilled male workers were dominant or significant accounted for almost a quarter of the entire Glasgow workforce compared to only 10 per cent in 1841.

Furthermore, Scottish labour worked for lower wages than the average in England, the country which was Scotland's main competitor for much of the Victorian period. Scholars are agreed that this gave Scottish industrialists a strategic cost advantage, even if the Anglo-Scottish gap narrowed somewhat in the later nineteenth century. Scottish wages were low in comparison to the average for the United Kingdom in iron and steel, shipbuilding, cotton and brewing, according to data for the 1880s. In the crucial sectors of iron and steel and shipbuilding, the Scottish average was £70 per annum compared to £76 for the United Kingdom. In textiles there was an even more entrenched system of low pay, based on the widespread employment of female labour. By the 1880s two-thirds of the 100,000 workforce in textiles were women. The cottonmasters in the west had embarked on a strategy of hiring low-paid women operating self-acting mules rather than men, while in Dundee the employment of poorly paid female labour was the city's first line of defence against the growing threat of Indian competition. Any bottleneck in recruitment to the collieries was eliminated in two stages. The first was the ending of collier serfdom by legislation in 1775 and 1799. These measures were not enacted in a spirit of philanthropic benevolence but rather to recruit more labour, destroy the collier trade unions or 'brotherhoods' and keep wage claims in check. The second was through the increase in Irish immigration which helped to solve any problem of labour shortage in the long term as coal production grew rapidly after c. 1820. There is little doubt that the swelling coal and iron mining communities of Lanarkshire and Ayrshire depended heavily on the Irish as production levels escalated spectacularly. In 1861 in Coatbridge, fewer than half of the colliers and miners were Scots-born. The rest were Irish migrants.

It was not simply the cost and availability of labour that was of critical importance to these great staple industries. Also of relevance was the response of the workforce. By the early twentieth century, trade unionism was expanding and labour relations became more tense. This was symbolized by the foundation of the Scottish Trades Union Congress in 1897. But the later image of 'Red Clydeside' did not fit the west of Scotland at all in earlier decades. The Glasgow Cotton Spinners' Union had successfully resisted the introduction of self-acting spinning mules, but in the strike of 1837 and the aftermath it was effectively destroyed and never again represented a threat to innovation. There were stoppages among Clydeside engineering and shipyard workers in the 1860s and again in the 1880s, and Dundee female jute workers did strike at regular intervals. But during the 1860s William Knox has concluded that 'trade unionism was all but wiped out in the shipbuilding and mining industries'.[4] Union membership was low by the standards of England and Wales and there was a much stronger tradition of small, local unions with few members and little muscle. Demarcation disputes were common, especially in metals, shipbuilding and building, and this occupational sectionalism was aggravated by sectarian tensions between Irish Catholics and Protestant Scots workers. For these reasons Scottish labour seemed both cheap and docile. It was because of this perception that the American Singer Sewing Machine Company was primarily attracted to Clydebank in 1900, where its factory soon achieved the capability of turning out 13,000 sewing machines a week. In general, during the golden years of the Scottish economic miracle the employers held the whip hand. Some, like the Bairds and the Neilsons, were resolutely opposed to trade unions as an unmitigated evil and virtually all of them took a hard line in industrial disputes, sometimes pooling their strength in such alliances as the Shipbuilders' Employers Federation, the National Association of Master Builders and the East of Scotland Association of Engineers. Employers were in a virtually impregnable position. Edward Young reported to the United States Congress in 1872 that the Clydeside workers 'must work for a mere pittance, to enable his employer to sell his goods abroad at low rates, or there will be no work for him to do, and he will be left to starve'. He added that the worldwide success of Clyde-built ships was to be explained in the final analysis by 'the abundance of skilled workmen and the low wages paid to them'.[5]

2

Some look back on the Victorian economy with nostalgia. The nineteenth century was a time when the great Scottish industries were not only owned by Scots but sent their products to all corners of the globe. Scotland was truly a force to be reckoned with in the world economy and had achieved a position of manufacturing supremacy out of all proportion to the small size of her domestic population. All this is in sharp contrast to the pattern as we approach the millennium. Scottish ownership of much of manufacturing industry has virtually disappeared, the nation's prosperity seemingly depends on the fickle decisions of overseas investors and Scotland is often dismissed as a 'branch economy' controlled by external forces over which there is little indigenous political control. Yet the temptation to glorify the Victorian and Edwardian economy should be resisted. It was seriously flawed in two respects: its impact on the welfare and standard of life of the Scottish people and the emergence of structural economic weaknesses which had a potent effect on the nation's industrial crisis after the First World War.

A handful of families did make colossal fortunes from the profits of the export industries. Sir Charles Tenant of the chemical empire, William Baird the ironmaster, Sir James and Peter Coats of the thread-making dynasty and William Weir, colliery owner and iron manufacturer, were among the 40 individuals in Britain reckoned to be worth £2 million or more between 1809 and 1914. In addition to these fabulously wealthy but exceptional tycoons there were the solid ranks of the prosperous middle classes, which ranged in occupational status from highly paid professionals, such as lawyers and doctors, to small businessmen and senior clerks. In his analysis of national income, published in 1867, the Victorian economist, R. Dudley Baxter, reckoned that 267,300 people were in this group in Scotland, had an annual income of between £100 and £1,000 and represented nearly one-fifth of the total number of what he termed 'productive persons' in the country. The impact of the spending of this middle class could be seen in the elegant suburbs that blossomed around the major cities in the nineteenth century, Broughty Ferry near Dundee, the graceful terraces of the West End of Glasgow and the substantial villas of Newington and Corstorphine in Edinburgh. The extraordinary increases in the outflow of capital from Scotland after 1870 were also in part a reflection of the increases in savings among the Scottish middle classes. For instance, in the two decades after 1870, Scottish investment in Australia grew ninefold. Most of this came through Scottish solicitors and chartered accountants raising funds on behalf of overseas clients from professional and business families at home. It was said that Edinburgh in the 1880s was 'honeycombed' with the agents of these companies who were the main channel for this substantial mobilization of middle-class capital. Middle incomes were on average fewer and lower than in London and the metropolitan area of the south, but in the early twentieth century were on a par with the major English industrial centres of Lancashire and Yorkshire.

The picture is, however, somewhat gloomier for the rest of the population. Scotland was a grossly unequal society in the heyday of its industrial success. R. D. Baxter's calculations for 1867 suggest that around 70 per cent of 'productive persons', or almost a million people in total, belonged to his two bottom categories of 'lower skilled' and 'unskilled' which consisted of male workers who earned on average below £50 per annum. For many at this level, short-term unemployment was always a threat. Shipbuilding and the other capital goods industries were subject to intense and savage fluctuation in 1884–7, 1894, 1903–5 and 1908. In this last year, unemployment among Clydeside skilled engineers rose to nearly 20 per cent and among shipyard workers to almost a quarter. In the four cities there were large pools of seasonal and casual labour, reckoned in the early 1900s at around 25 per cent of the workforce, who were engaged in jobs such as portering, cartering and street-selling and whose earnings were both paltry and unpredictable. Previous discussion demonstrated that for most of the period between 1830 and 1914 Scottish industrial wage rates were lower than the English average. The Board of Trade estimated in 1912 that real wages (after taking into account living costs) were fully 10 per cent less in Scottish towns than in their counterparts in England. Living costs on the other hand were higher. For Glasgow, recent work by Richard Rodger has shown that the city's inhabitants paid on average over 5 per cent more for their food and rent (which accounted for four-fifths of the weekly working-class budget) than the population of Manchester, Leeds, Salford and Nottingham – and this against a background of low wages and volatile levels of employment on Clydeside.

That Victorian industry was not a source of general prosperity is confirmed by the examples of Scottish migration and housing in this period. Precisely at the time when manufacturing was achieving remarkable success in overseas markets the Scots were leaving their native land in large numbers for the USA, Canada and Australasia. Not far short of 2 million people emigrated from Scotland overseas between 1830 and 1914, a rate of outward movement that was around one and a half times that of England and Wales. This did not include another 600,000 who moved south of the border. The haemorrhage was so great that it placed Scotland near the top of the European emigration league, along with Ireland and Norway. In the years of massive outward movement, such as 1904–13, when more than 600,000 people left, Scotland achieved the unenviable position of topping this table, with the highest emigration rate of any country in Europe. Again, in the 1850s, the loss of young men through emigration was considerably greater than in the years of human carnage during the First World War. Scotland was almost alone among European countries in having experienced both large-scale industrialization and a great outward movement of population. Most other societies prone to high levels of emigration were poor rural economies. It seemed that many Scots were voting with their feet in the search for better prospects than were easily available to them at home.

The condition of working-class housing in Scotland provoked endless investigation and comment by the early twentieth century. From these surveys it is abundantly clear that there was little real progress made between 1870 and 1914. Clive Lee has recently concluded that,

by the eve of the First World War Scotland stood on the brink of a housing catastrophe. In 1911 nearly 50 per cent of the Scottish population lived in one or two roomed dwellings compared with just over 7 per cent in England. Rents were significantly higher north of the Border, 1905, 10 per cent greater than in Northumberland and Durham and almost 25 per cent higher than the other English midland and northern counties. Over two million Scots in 1914, nearly half the population, lived more than two persons to a room, the contemporary definition of 'overcrowding'.[6]

The housing problem reflected the reality of low and fluctuating incomes. For families on limited earnings it made economic sense to take small tenement flats at a rental sufficiently affordable to avoid arrears or eviction. The problem was not so much availability of reasonable housing as the ability of very many to pay for it. In 1914, for instance, in Glasgow alone there were over 20,000 unoccupied houses, or about a tenth of the city's total stock. The housing crisis was the most striking manifestation of the depth of Glasgow's acute problems of poverty in the very decade when it proclaimed itself the 'Second City of the Empire'.

The achievements of Victorian industry have to be acknowledged. It was indeed a remarkable feat for a small country to dominate key sectors of the world's economy for much of the nineteenth century. In addition, the huge expansion of manufacturing and mining provided countless new jobs for Scotland's growing population. But the limitations of the success story should also be recognized. The low incomes and widespread poverty that prevailed despite industrial growth placed Scotland at a strategic disadvantage in the twentieth century when home demand for household goods, motor cars and cycles, furniture and electrical products became critical to continued economic growth. The weakness of consumer-based industries and the concentration on ships, locomotives, bridges, rolling stock and iron work in the manufacturing areas of the west of Scotland proved with hindsight to be a fatal flaw in the Victorian economy which had tragic consequences in the inter-war period. Even before 1914, the structure seemed dangerously vulnerable. The heavy industries were all interrelated, geared to overseas demand, especially in the Empire, and clearly at risk from international competition from nations such as the United States and Germany. It was inevitable, given their population size and great resources, that they would become formidable industrial powers. When half a continent starts to develop, it can produce much more than a small country, no matter how skilled and innovative the latter might be. The threat was especially potent because Scots excelled in the manufacture of basic capital goods, many of whose production methods could be rapidly imitated by overseas competitors. In addition, the resource endowment which had helped to give Scotland a cutting edge was already weakening by 1914. In the 1870s, over 2 million tons of iron ore was being mined annually. By 1913 this had slumped to 590,000 tons per year. Coal supplies remained plentiful but in Lanarkshire the richest seams were fast becoming exhausted. Hard-splint coal for use in the furnace was also much scarcer. The result was higher costs. In the west of Scotland there was substantial investment in coal-cutting machinery but even this failed to prevent a dramatic fall in labour productivity.

Of greater concern was the position of shipbuilding because the orders for the steel mills and the engineering shops of the west of Scotland crucially depended on the prosperity of the Clyde yards. Superficially all seemed well. In the years before 1914 record tonnages were launched and the reputation for technical innovation remained intact. But those historians who have scrutinized the business records of the big firms have detected two disturbing trends. First, due to competition, not least from the north-east of England, many vessels were being constructed at a loss, and this condition of 'profitless prosperity' was becoming more common in the years before the First World War. Second, some major yards, such as John Brown's and Fairfield's, became committed to the building of battleships, cruisers and destroyers for the Admiralty. It was a profitable and apparently secure strategy in the era of the naval arms race, but it could prove much less sensible in different political circumstances. Both these difficulties could be contained over the short term. Grave problems would emerge, however, for the entire heavy industrial economy if shipbuilding suffered for a longer period. On the eve of the Great War that still seemed an unlikely prospect.

3

During the period 1914–18 Scottish industry became a vast military arsenal for the greatest conflict in human history. Unrestricted submarine warfare later in the war destroyed the equivalent of nearly a third of the pre-1914 merchant fleet and created a prodigious new source of demand for the shipbuilding yards of the Clyde. Engineering and metal production were diverted to the mass production of guns and shells. The linen and woollen districts of Scotland supplied huge amounts of canvas for tenting and clothing for troops. Trench warfare, the enduring image of the Great War, would have been impossible without sandbags made from Dundee jute. By 1918 one thousand million sandbags had been shipped to the fronts in Europe. In the same year the Clyde Valley had become the single most important concentration of munitions production in the United Kingdom with the great heavy industries of the region under government control, regulation or direction. Some areas of mining and manufacturing activity lost out. The border tweed industry was hit when its sources of yarn in Belgium were cut off. The eastern coalfield, which had been enjoying dynamic growth before 1914, suffered through the loss of the German and Baltic markets and the Admiralty's decision to requisition the Forth coal ports. Overall, however, the Great War intensified Scottish reliance on a narrow range of great industries which were often interdependent. A vulnerable economy had become even more exposed.

This was especially the case when the ephemeral distortion of war was exaggerated by the boom of 1919–20. The crucially important industry of shipbuilding expanded capacity throughout Britain by nearly 40 per cent in relation to the position in 1914 in the expectation of the release of a huge pent-up demand to replace wartime losses. The problem was, however, that every other shipbuilding nation – the United States, Japan, Scandinavia and Holland – was actively pursuing the same strategy. After 1923 the latent danger of over-capacity in what had become the key influence on the Scottish industrial economy quickly became a tragic reality. Behind the façade of wartime prosperity, new difficulties were also emerging in steel-making. The nature of the steel produced changed from acid to basic, but this transformation was not matched by any similar increase in basic iron supplied from Scottish furnaces. Indeed, while steel-making expanded, not one new blast furnace was built in Scotland, a development which exacerbated the lack of integration between iron and steel and resulted in a powerful cost handicap in international competition for the future. Ironically, however, integration did accelerate on another industrial front. Because shipbuilders confidently expected a huge construction programme after 1918 in order to replace wartime losses, there was a veritable scramble among the big companies to secure supplies of ship plate by actually absorbing the steel-making firms. By 1920 this process had gone so far that only one steel producer, Stewart & Lloyds at Mossend, remained independent. Scottish steel and Scottish shipbuilding were now tightly bound together by ownership as well as by economic interest just as the post-war boom collapsed into deep recession.

The inter-war period was not all doom and gloom for Scottish industry. For those who were in a job, standards of living rose for much of the period. As a result the relatively small part of the manufacturing economy geared to domestic consumers did well. Carpets, linoleum, hosiery and knitwear were especially successful although they were relatively modest employers of labour. But the giants of the nineteenth-century economy were either in the doldrums in most years or were in acute crisis. After a brief post-war boom, jute experienced declining demand and savage overseas competition. At the depth of the depression in the early 1930s nearly half its labour force was unemployed. From the mid-1920s demand for coal ceased to grow and employment slumped from 155,000 in 1920 to 81,000 in 1933 as the industry struggled against competition in its traditional markets from the new energy sources of oil, gas and electricity. Steel-making was sluggish throughout the inter-war period and never recovered the position it had attained during the early 1920s. This was hardly surprising, since its fortunes depended on shipbuilding, which was itself in long-term decline. On the one hand, world shipbuilding capacity had more than doubled during the Great War and its immediate aftermath; on the other hand, the trade between primary producers and industrial countries, the basic engine of international commerce and demand for new ships before

1914, languished for most of the 1920s and 1930s. There was, therefore, a chronic problem of global over-capacity in shipbuilding. One estimate suggests that the difficulties were so acute that British yards could easily have built all the new tonnage required in the world between 1921 and 1939 and still be left with some spare capacity. The crisis in demand for merchant vessels was aggravated by the termination of warship orders after the signing of the Washington Treaty for the Limitation of Naval Armaments in 1921. It was cold comfort that the Clyde, because of its expertise in passenger liners, for which the market remained a little more buoyant, was not quite as badly hit as the Tyne and Wear.

It is now fashionable to stress the complexity of the inter-war period. English scholars argue that the experience of misery varied regionally. Those who managed to keep a job did well as real incomes rose. This explains the housing boom which did much to trigger high consumer expenditure in the south of England and the Midlands. Over Britain as a whole, national income per head rose by over 23 per cent between 1913 and 1937, a significantly faster rate than in the decades before the First World War. The traditional image of the period is one of depression, unemployment and decline but across the UK it was also a time of significant economic change when a new industrial structure of motor car, bicycle, aircraft, electrical goods and light engineering manufacture was born.

There are some traces of this revolution in Scotland. Middle-class employment held up well, with rarely more than 5 per cent in this group without a job. Partly for this reason, retailing giants such as Hugh Fraser and Isaac Wolfson were able to expand their business empires, while large English-based stores such as Lewis's, Marks & Spencer, Boots and Montague Burton moved into Scotland. Clearly those who were in work were able to afford to buy more. Nevertheless, while Scotland did not suffer as much as Wales, Ulster or the north-east of England, conditions were different in two key respects from those in the Midlands, London and the south of England. First, Scotland depended heavily on a small number of exporting industries which were badly hit by the slump in international trade. As a result, throughout the inter-war period unemployment was always above the UK average. In 1932, for instance, the UK figure was 22.1 per cent and that for Scotland 27.7 per cent. In the industrial heartland of the western Lowlands, over a quarter of the entire labour force, nearly 200,000 people, were out of work in the early 1930s. But even in the more prosperous Lothians the unemployment rate remained above that for the south of England. It is also important to remember that the numbers recorded as 'out of work' would have been even greater but for the great safety valve of emigration. Scotland had always been near the top of the European emigration league, but in the 1920s this traditional exodus of people rose to unprecedented levels. An average of 147,000 had left in each decade from 1801 to 1911. This figure more than doubled between 1921 and 1931.

Second, the healthy economic indicators that characterized the Midlands and the south were less common in Scotland. Gross industrial output contracted annually by 2.89 per cent between 1924 and 1935. Even more significantly, Census of Production data plainly demonstrate that the 'old' staple industries of the Victorian era were still dominant, while the 'new' industries made little headway. This was not just a failure to establish new specialisms. Pre-1914 developments, such as motor car manufacture, did not survive for long in the 1920s. Even furniture-making, a classic consumer industry, was not based on modern mass-production techniques. In the booming electrical goods sector the Scots had only a toe-hold, contributing only 2 per cent of British output – and this mainly in heavy machinery. The industrial structure of Scotland seemed to ossify. In 1939 it was not significantly different from the manufacturing economy inherited from Victorian and Edwardian times, a failure of transition which was to cost the country dear in later decades. In the last part of this chapter, therefore, it is worth pondering briefly on the reasons why there was no basic movement away from industries which are now seen to have been in long-term decline and towards the more dynamic sectors of the future.

One answer is that the staple industries were more resilient than they might appear in hindsight. A major factor in their problems was the condition of world market, and they could easily change for the better. For a business class accustomed to intense fluctuation in the demand for capital goods before 1914, it was not unreasonable to adhere to a strategy of 'wait and see' or 'Micawberism' in the hope that something would turn up. Eventually, of course, something did turn up. Rearmament began in the 1930s as international tensions mounted. The upturn began in 1934 in the steel industry and soon spread to shipbuilding. But it was not simply faith in a return to better times that maintained the morale of the captains of Scotland's traditional industries. They were also conscious that there had been considerable technical progress which increased the Scottish ability to penetrate markets more successfully when they recovered. As a result of heavy investment in mechanical mining, productivity in Scottish pits was significantly above the British average and the highest of any area in the United Kingdom except Yorkshire. In addition, contrary to popular belief, the Clyde did not lose its leading position in marine-engine design but was very active in the development of diesel engines. Its worldwide reputation in the construction of passenger liners helps explain why it won the prestigious contracts to build the *Queen Mary*, which lay idle at Clydebank as a haunting symbol of recession from 1931 to 1934, and her sister ship, *Queen Elizabeth*, which was ordered in 1936.

In steel, there was a deeper technical malaise, caused by the high costs resulting from the failure to integrate sources of raw material, iron smelting and steel-making. In a famous report the international engineering consultants, H. A. Brassert & Company, advised that the only future for the industry lay in the construction of a fully integrated iron- and steel-making plant on the Clyde at Erskine. The visionary plan was rejected, partly because Indian iron producers were able to offer Colvilles even cheaper pig-iron than the Brassert concept promised, and also because the market for steel in the late 1920s was so depressed that a costly and ambitious investment might have been counter-productive. In the event, however, steel did make some progress. One firm, Colvilles Ltd, pursued an energetic programme of merger so that by 1936 it controlled over 80 per cent of Scottish steel production. The stage was then set for a programme of improvements under the direction of Andrew McCance. His 'brilliant improvisations', as Peter Payne describes them, went some way towards the provision of more efficient production and contributed to the industry's success during the recovery of the late 1930s. Stewart and Lloyds solved the problem of integration in more radical fashion by moving much of its labour force from Mossend near Glasgow to Corby in Northampton, where it built an entirely new steelworks over phosphoric ore beds. This was a better record than shipbuilding, where the National Shipbuilders Security Ltd, formed to purchase redundant shipyards through a 1 per cent levy on sales, managed to cut capacity by almost 20 per cent but failed signally to reform methods of production or working practices. Nevertheless, merger consortia, cartels and trade associations, all of which flourished in these years, were important mechanisms for maintaining the position of the family interest which dominated heavy industries. Where a public company might have gone to the wall in the face of a huge decline in profit, private limited companies were more likely to hold on in order to protect the interests of the family both past and present.

While these powerful economic and social forces perpetuated the dominance of the staple industries, other influences, no less important, made it difficult for a 'new' service and manufacturing sector to become firmly established before the Second World War. The main feature of the 'new' industries was their commitment to the home market. Scotland was seriously disadvantaged in this respect. Apart from the Lothians area, where incomes were above the British average, Scottish real earnings were significantly lower than the national level. In 1938, for instance, at a time when the recovery of the heavy industries was well under way, Scottish per capita income stood at 89 per cent of the British average. There was therefore little incentive for manufacturers of consumer goods to move north from England and establish plants in Scotland. In more prosperous regions of the UK a boom in housing was a vital trigger in releasing demand for the products of the 'new' industries. Between 1919 and 1939, 300,000 homes were indeed built north of the border, but the rate of building was lower than in England and there was no equivalent of the huge upsurge in construction in the 1930s. Needless to say, consumer demand was cut back further by the impact of high levels of long-term unemployment in the most densely populated areas of the country. The blight of the economic crisis in the older industries also made industrial diversification difficult. The giant Clydeside firm of William Beardmore and Co. might have forged strong links between the economic world of the nineteenth century and the new possibilities of the twentieth. As one of the most influential and powerful Scottish engineering concerns, it had already moved before 1914 into the manufacture of private cars, taxis, buses, commercial vehicles, aero engines, airships and flying boats. If this range of activity had continued successfully, the economic history of the west of Scotland would have been very different and the connection between old and new industries firmly established. However, such was the scale of the contraction in markets in the 1920s that Beardmore retreated for safety to their older specializations and pulled out completely from other promising areas of enterprise. It was a similar story elsewhere in the motor car industry, which seemed to have real potential for growth before 1914. But by 1930 all the firms that had emerged in that period had disappeared, leaving the Albion Motor Co., producing commercial vehicles, as the sole survivor of an era of real promise.

The problem was recognized by the Scottish National Development Council, set up in 1930. One of its leading figures, the influential Scottish industrialist, Sir James Lithgow, saw the vital need to reduce the size of the heavy industries and expand into new sectors capable of absorbing the surplus manpower. Government interest in such an approach was signalled by the creation in 1934 of a Special Areas scheme, which included several of the counties of the west of Scotland but excluded the city of Glasgow. This was Britain's first coherent attempt at 'regional' policy but it lacked impact because, of the £2.48 million authorized for the Scottish region, most was devoted to improving amenity rather than to direct assistance. More significant was the Special Areas (Amendment) Act of 1937 which gave the Commissioner in charge the power to build factories, rent them out and allow assistance to pay rents and rates starting with industrial estates at Hillington and Shieldhall. Other sites were developed at a further three locations in Lanarkshire. By the end of 1938, £4.9 million had been spent in Scotland and 5,000 (mainly female) jobs in light industry had been created. These were worth having but made little real impact on the structural problem of male unemployment. That deeper crisis was alleviated only by the gathering momentum of rearmament which in turn ensured that the hegemony of the great staple industries would remain undisturbed for some time to come. The tragedy was that Scotland had in effect lost out in the early stages of the second Industrial Revolution whose transforming effects were, if anything, to be even greater than the first. As a result, the nation inevitably surrendered its nineteenth-century position as a power house of the global economy.

13

Politics, Power and Identity in Victorian Scotland

I

The revolutionary changes in Scottish economy and society during the Victorian era were not paralleled by similar radical developments in the political sphere. It is true that the period began with the Reform Acts of 1832, the first serious breaches in the old constitutional system which had been under attack since the days of the Friends of the People in the 1790s. Henry Cockburn, the Solicitor-General, who had helped to shape the Scottish legislation of 1832, saw it as the dawn of a new age: 'it is impossible to exaggerate the ecstasy of Scotland, where to be sure it is like liberty given to slaves: we are to be brought out of the house of bondage, out of the land of Egypt'.[1] There were, indeed, some grounds for optimism, though perhaps not for Cockburn's euphoria. By the end of 1832 the Scottish electorate had risen sixteenfold, from a tiny 4,500 to 65,000, and some recognition was given to the political implications of rapid urbanization. The number of burgh constituencies increased from 15 to 23, with Glasgow now allocated two Members of Parliament, Edinburgh an additional representative and larger towns, such as Dundee, Perth and Aberdeen, one apiece. Scotland as a whole was awarded an additional eight seats. The most important consequence was the emancipation of the middle classes in the burghs and the extension of the franchise to many tenants and owner-occupiers in the rural areas. £10 householders in the burghs received the vote and in the counties £10 owners, £10 leaseholders with a 57-year or more lease and tenants with a 19-year lease worth more than £50 per annum. This legislation inevitably transformed the politics of the towns by breaking the grip of the old oligarchies and by replacing the old system of nomination managed through the burgh councils by one of direct voting in the new constituencies. More generally, the tight ministerial

control over Scottish representation at Westminster which had dominated the nation's politics since the union was no longer possible within
the enlarged electorate. Local influences, in the absence of coherent
national parties, now became much more crucial.

But the reform legislation of 1832 was far from radical. The principal
aim of the Whig government was to absorb the urban middle classes who
were considered safe for the privilege of the vote into the government of
the country, retain as much as possible of traditional authority based
on land and so remove the threat of democracy once and for all.
Universal male suffrage was still regarded as a certain and inevitable
road to social anarchy and economic ruin. The middle classes were to
be attached to the constitution but were not to be allowed to dominate
it; rather, the Whigs intended that the Reform Acts should preserve
and not destroy landed influence and so vital elements of continuity
underpinned the legislative process. As before, property and not
numbers remained basic to the new system. Urban representation was
strengthened but only marginally and most of the groupings based on
the old Royal Burghs not only survived but, more importantly, remained
separate from the county constituencies. Thus the urban areas were
not able to influence the political complexion of the rural districts.
Throughout Scotland the spread of constituencies remained largely
biased to the country areas and hence to the electoral benefit of the
landed interest. As one recent commentator has put it: 'The regional
distribution of Scottish MPs remained substantially as it had been
between 1707 and 1832, and seats won for the newer urban areas
represented less a victory for the new social forces than a *cordon
sanitaire* placed round them by the old.'[2]

In the counties, landlord dominance was effectively consolidated.
Some tenants were given the vote but not the secret ballot and, not
surprisingly, political subjection to their landlords endured for many
years after 1832. Moreover, the manufacture of votes, one of the most
obviously corrupt practices in the old system, survived in vigorous but
transformed form into the new. In Scots law, ownership of the feudal
superiority and the physical land of an estate was separate. Bad drafts-
manship in the Act of 1832 still allowed landowners to break down
their superiorities into £10 units of value and distribute them to nominees, who were then able to vote. Indeed, some of the increase in the
number of electors after 1832 was not due to constitutional reform but
to this registration of numerous 'faggot' voters. The Tories used the

device in the south-eastern counties to good effect to build up support and the practice was also employed in a number of other seats, including the counties of Angus, Stirling and Renfrew.

The Whigs attempted to preserve the old system through an alliance with the urban middle classes; but they also aspired to constitutional finality. Reform legislation was designed to strengthen the rule of an enlightened propertied oligarchy, remove all grievances and so ensure permanent political stability. It was seen as the end of a process, not as a stage towards further extension of the suffrage. But 1832 could not be a final solution. Scotland was rapidly becoming one of the world's first urban societies, yet the new electoral arrangements were still heavily biased in favour of rural constituencies and landed power. Moreover, both in 1829 and 1832, the parliamentary reformers had used popular pressure to ensure the passage of the legislation. In Glasgow, Edinburgh and elsewhere, the 'political unions' of artisans and factory operatives took to the streets in massive processions in protest against those who resisted reform. The Whigs were quite blatantly using the working classes for their own purposes. But it was a dangerous game. As one of their Tory opponents, Robert Peel, predicted: 'These are vulgar arts of government; others will outbid you not now but at no remote period – they will offer votes and power to 2 million of men who will quote your precedent for the confessional and will carry your principles to their legitimate and natural consequences.'[3]

It was not long, however, before the chickens came home to roost. The trade unions had given enthusiastic support to reform when the passing of the final Act was followed by a wave of celebrations throughout the country which lasted for several weeks. In Edinburgh, one huge event organized by the Trades Union Council included a procession of the crafts, with numerous banners carried to the memory of such reform martyrs as Muir, Gerrald and others. The Act was undoubtedly seen as a stepping stone to the fulfilment of the historic ideals of the reform movement in Scotland which stretched back to the 1790s. As it became abundantly clear that their erstwhile Whig allies had no intention of extending the franchise any further, a sense of betrayal and disillusionment set in among the organized working classes. This was the background to the emergence of Chartism, the most famous working-class movement of the nineteenth century.

The People's Charter was devised by radical groups in London and Birmingham in 1838. Its 'six points' (of universal suffrage, abolition of property qualifications, the secret ballot, equal electoral districts, payments of MPs and annual parliaments) were meant to introduce the far-reaching reforms ignored by the Whigs in 1832 and rejected by them ever since. The Chartists soon developed a large following in Scotland. Thomas Attwood, the leader of the Birmingham Chartists, attracted a large crowd of 100,000 to a demonstration in Glasgow Green in May 1838. By the spring of 1839 no fewer than 130 Chartist associations had been organized throughout the country. The Scottish Chartists also had their own press, with a national newspaper, the *True Scotsman*, supplemented by four regional journals. Enthusiasm was not even diminished after the comprehensive rejection by parliament of the Charter in June 1839 by the overwhelming majority of 235 to 46. A network of itinerant lecturers and visiting Chartist luminaries from the south helped to maintain loyalties. Local and regional organizations were created and delegates sent to national conventions in Birmingham and London.

In large part the movement was fuelled by bitter disappointment that the Reform Act of 1832 had not heralded a new dawn of social improvement. But other factors were also relevant. Chartism drew on the long radical tradition stretching back to the Friends of the People in the 1790s which had been given recent and fresh impetus during the reform agitations of the early 1830s. At most of the great Chartist demonstrations between 1838 and 1843, the same trade society banners were carried as had been flown with pride during the huge processions of operatives in 1831-2. In fact, to understand the development of Chartism, it is essential to see the bigger picture. During the 1820s, craft unionism in Scotland virtually collapsed as few trades were able to maintain controls on entry or restrictions on apprenticeship because semi-skilled and even some skilled occupations were flooded with labour. With considerable justification the process has been described by Christopher Whatley as 'the breaking of the working class'. There were some attempts at reorganizing and regrouping in the early 1830s, and political reform in 1832 also gave some hopes for the future. But these were quickly dashed. The famous Glasgow Cotton Spinners Strike of 1837 culminated in the arrest, trial and transportation of several of the leadership. The strongest and most feared trade union in Scotland was now effectively destroyed by a combination of employer muscle and the sympathetic support of the state. The cotton spinners' case, followed by the depression years of 1838-42, was a key factor in

Chartism. The ferocity of the law doubtless intimidated some, but it also inspired others to channel their energies into a quest for political change in order to purge the state and the legal system of the pernicious influences which were seen as the enemies of the workers.

But Chartism in Scotland was reformist rather than revolutionary. No school of thought preached violent overthrow of the government, though tensions existed between those who argued for the use of 'physical force' in certain situations and others who were committed to the 'moral force' approach. The Revd Patrick Brewster of Paisley argued against violence in all circumstances, but this fundamentalist approach attracted few adherents. The majority were prepared to use force in the last resort though this strategy remained undefined and was never put to the test. The policy remained little other than a theoretical possibility, encapsulated in the motto of the Glasgow Democratic Association, 'We are determined to carry the People's Charter, peaceably if we may, forcibly if we must.' In the event, Chartists in Scotland tried to advance their cause by peaceful protest, petitions, public meetings, education for citizenship, co-operation and lectures rather than armed rebellion. In the north of England a much more aggressive and militant approach had been prompted by the imposition of the hated Poor Law Reform legislation of 1834 which introduced the workhouse test and enforced a reduction in allowances to a bare minimum. The Scottish Poor Law was far from generous but, when finally amended in 1843, did not pose the same threat to the traditional living standards of workers as its English equivalent. There had not been a legal recognition of the rights of the able-bodied unemployed to relief since the years immediately after the Napoleonic Wars. Many also recognized that insurrection on the model of 1820 had proved disastrous in the past and should be avoided at all costs. It was argued that the ruling classes would be prepared to extend the franchise only if those who sought emancipation demonstrated reason, discipline and respectability of a type deserving of inclusion in the franchise. At the Chartist delegate conference of December 1838 several speakers asserted that the failed rebellion of 1820 had not only conclusively shown the bankruptcy of any strategy of insurrection but had actually impeded rather than advanced the progress of reform.

This analysis undoubtedly appealed to the artisans and small masters who comprised the Chartist leadership. Despite the aftermath of 1832, they had not abandoned the forging of links with the reformist-minded middle classes in order effectively to sustain with them a campaign for extension of suffrage. To commit the movement to methods outside the law would be suicidal against this background and would swiftly alienate the very allies who alone could provide the political force to ensure the success of the cause. There was nothing new in this. Alliances of this kind had been established in the 1790s, again for a brief period after 1812, and once more in the early 1830s when the Scottish Political Union was formed to promote common ties between the working and middle classes. The bedrock support for Chartism came from independent outworkers, handloom weavers and skilled artisans, all of whom had a close affinity with an earlier tradition of radicalism. The leadership was also often drawn from the petite bourgeoisie who, like the workers, also found themselves excluded from the franchise established in 1832. Not surprisingly, therefore, the class element in Scottish Chartism was weak in the extreme. Chartists and the urban middle classes, for instance, co-operated successfully in the campaign for repeal of the Corn Laws and, crucially but curiously, throughout the period the enemy still continued to be identified not as ruthless employers or oppressive factory masters but as the landed classes. It was the aristocracy of the land rather than the aristocracy of wealth who were seen as the sources of all evil. As the *Chartist Circular* put it in October 1839: 'Hereditary power corrupted the whole government, poisoned the press, demoralised society, prostituted the church, dissipated the resources of the nation, created monopolies, paralysed trade, ruined half the merchants, produced national bankruptcy.'[4] It went on to argue that progress was possible from this sea of trouble and the old enemy vanquished only if 'capitalocracy united with the people'. It was difficult to conceive of a purely working-class crusade against this political background.

But to see Chartism in Scotland simply as a transitory and ultimately unsuccessful movement dedicated to peaceful means and the futile politics of petitioning is to ignore the vital impact of Chartist culture on many working-class communities. The movement had a deeply religious ethos in Scotland which reflects the continuing importance of Christian belief among the skilled working classes of the country. The brotherhood of man to which all Chartists aspired was founded ultimately on the gospels, while for many the struggle for political rights was a continuation of the historic struggle for civil and religious liberty carried on by their forefathers since the time of the Covenanters in the seventeenth century. The *Chartist Circular* exhorted its readers to 'study the New Testament. It contains the elements of Chartism.' This religious spirit afforded Scottish Chartism a moral strength which helped the movement to survive during those difficult years in the 1840s when its fortunes collapsed in England. God was on the side of the Chartists. The spiritual commitment led to the creation of Chartist churches between 1839 and 1842 as a result of the hostility shown by the established and main dissenting churches to the organization. By early 1841 there were at least 20 Christian Chartist churches in Scotland. The *True Scotsman* declared, 'A Chartist place of worship is to be found on the Lord's Day in almost every town of note from Aberdeen to Ayr.'[5] A Chartist Synod was even envisaged, while marriage ceremonies were held and baptisms performed in the local congregations. Many Chartists were also members of dissenting churches which were themselves outside the political and religious establishment and hence were likely to adopt a more critical attitude to the governing institutions of the land. At the same time, the ethical ethos in Chartism also helps to explain the suspicion of 'physical force' tactics and the commitment instead to a reasoned and disciplined crusade for social justice.

Other elements in the Chartist culture included the stress on abstinence, co-operation and education. The *Scottish Patriot* admitted in 1840 that the impact of the movement on government had been limited but that Chartism was 'forming a character for the people which they have never before possessed' through total abstinence and instruction. The issue of universal suffrage was now moving from 'the public arena' to 'the domestic hearth of the working classes' where it was 'becoming part of the social character of the people'.[6] Attachment to temperance was part of the Chartist ethos; most of the Glasgow Chartist leaders were officials in temperance societies, while the vast majority of the 3,000 members of the Total Abstinence Society in Aberdeen were Chartists. Temperance was a way of improving the moral character of the workers, raising their material standards which had been destroyed by alcohol abuse and putting pressure on government whose revenue partly depended on excise duties on spirits. The campaign had a significant impact and political meetings soon began to be held in coffee houses rather than pubs. The temperance tradition outlived Chartism and in the later nineteenth century appealed to the leadership of the emerging Labour Party. Emphasis was also placed on education as a necessary training for the responsibilities of citizenship which would come with the granting of the vote. A search for alternatives to capitalism was also pursued. The establishment of co-operative stores was directed at the competitive forces at the heart of capitalism. The National Association of United Trades, formed in 1845 by Chartists, attempted to unite labour organizations to campaign against low wages, sweated labour and unemployment. It was specifically directed against 'the power of capital'. The Chartist Land Plan, which had little practical impact in Scotland, outlined a vision of smallholding colonies and agricultural self-sufficiency as an alternative to industrial capitalism.

Chartism ceased to be a part of the political landscape by the early 1850s, the hopes of its followers dashed yet again by the rejection by parliament of the second mass petition in 1842 and the collapse of an attempted revival in 1848. Improving living standards, especially for skilled workers in the 1850s, and huge increases in emigration in the same decade gradually helped to undermine the politics of hunger and discontent. However, though Chartism failed, it was far from being a historical irrelevance. It deepened and enlarged the Scottish radical tradition which had become established since the 1790s. The values of justice, fairness, morality, self-help and the conviction that all men should work together for the common good, which Chartism inherited and refined, profoundly influenced the Labour movement of the later nineteenth century and beyond. Despite successive failures, there was a remarkable thread of continuity in the radical tradition. Chartism, among other movements, also provided a means of political leadership and organizational experience. After the 1840s, prominent Chartists channelled their energies into a variety of reformist movements, including temperance, trade unionism, co-operation and municipal politics. Several former Chartists became burgh police commissioners while others were members of parochial boards. In national politics, the demise of Chartism was to the immediate benefit of the Liberal Party. One reason for the remarkable Liberal dominance of the electoral scene in late-nineteenth-century Scotland was the loyalty and support it received from members of the skilled working classes who had done most to advance the Chartist cause in the 1840s and 1850s.

2

Scottish Liberalism for much of the Victorian era was a party of factions. The Whigs had delivered the Reform Act of 1832 and, though sympathetic to some social amelioration, were sceptical about the need for further significant political reform. The legislation of 1832 had been envisaged as a permanent solution which required only limited refinement. But urban middle-class radicals thought differently. They were committed to continued franchise reform of the kind eventually achieved in the Act of 1868 and were enthusiastic advocates of free trade and at the same time were hostile to the maintenance of the privileges of the Church of Scotland. The skilled working classes, who did not start to receive the vote until 1868, were as enthusiastic for the extension of political rights as the middle-class radicals, but they wished for more fundamental reform than the former were prepared to countenance. In addition, there was the possibility of conflict over such social issues as factory reform and trade-union rights which working-class radicals strongly supported but which were opposed by many of their middle-class counterparts. Not surprisingly, these fissures became apparent at elections, when contests were often fought, not between Liberals and Conservatives, but between Liberals with different views on issues as varied as church disestablishment, trade-union rights and electoral reform. In the later nineteenth century the tensions developed into open conflict and the Liberal Party finally split after 1886 over Gladstone's support for Irish Home Rule.

Yet, despite the inevitable friction caused by the co-existence of such a confederation of political interests, the Liberals enjoyed unrivalled hegemony in Victorian Scotland. Indeed, it was partly because of the absence of a potent Conservative threat that they were sometimes able to indulge themselves in public displays of electoral disunity over cherished points of principle and personality. In the burghs the Liberal sway went unchallenged. The Conservatives won only seven seats in nine general elections between 1832 and 1868, and in 1857, 1859 and 1865 not one Conservative candidate was returned. So overwhelming was Liberal dominance that only half the burgh elections were actually contested between 1832 and 1865. The general election after the Second Reform Act of 1868 saw half the burgh members returned unopposed, with contests between Liberals four times more common than between

281

different parties. Glasgow only once returned a Conservative MP throughout the entire period 1832–86. Conservatism remained more resilient in the counties but even here Liberalism often enjoyed spectacular and stunning success, as in the elections of 1868 and 1880. The devotion of the Scots to the great Liberal, William Gladstone, illustrated the dominant influence of his party. He became a cult figure, with engravings of his head and features adorning many a Scottish home. Michael Fry recalls how Edinburgh gave him a hero's welcome during his celebrated Midlothian campaign in 1879: 'The progress began, continued and ended in triumph. Every meeting was attended with almost mindless adulation, every telling point cheered to the echo, every restated moral principle given jubilant affirmation.'[7]

The remarkable appeal of the Liberals in Scotland was primarily due to the fact that they were identified as the party of progress, reform and liberty. The Whigs after all had started the process of reform in 1832 in the teeth of reactionary Tory opposition. The Tories, increasingly being dubbed 'Conservatives', were dedicated to the maintenance of the institutions of church and state with minimal amendment. They held out no hope of further significant improvement. From the start, therefore, the Tories were hugely unpopular; on the one hand, they were tainted with the 'Old Corruption' of the period of 50 years before 1832, when they had maintained themselves in office by blatant political chicanery and manipulation, culminating in their last-ditch attempts to impede the progress of reform. On the other, the extended electorate after 1832 was determined to reward the Whigs for giving them the vote. As Sir George Clerk reminded Robert Peel after the 1832 elections: 'The complete change in the constituency of Scotland and the importance attached by the newly enfranchised Reformers to the privilege now conferred on them rendered the chance of any Conservative, especially one who had taken part in opposing the Reform Bill, extremely doubtful.'[8] The fear that the Conservatives might make a comeback also stiffened opposition, especially as it soon became apparent in the 1830s that they were doing well in the larger county seats. Indeed, the Conservative cause was not entirely lost in that decade or destroyed simply because of the implications of 1832. Even in the burghs the party temporarily remained a significant force and was able to make something of a recovery until the early 1840s. Thereafter, however, a number of factors combined to seal their fate.

Foremost among these was the church question. In the 1830s tensions between church and state became more acute as Evangelical ministers and brethren achieved a clear majority in the General Assembly. This gave them the opportunity to renew with vigour the age-old opposition to patronage and to assert the rights of congregations to choose their own minister, whatever the views of lay patrons. An underlying factor here was middle-class hostility to aristocratic privilege and a basic issue was whether the Church of Scotland was an 'independent spiritual community', free of secular influence and state jurisdiction. This was articulated in the Veto Act of 1834 which gave congregations an absolute right to veto any minister proposed by a lay patron. Here was an explicit challenge to secular authority which was rejected by the Court of Session in a test case, in a judgement subsequently confirmed by the House of Lords. In response the General Assembly denounced the actions of parliament and the Court of Session in the Claim of Right (a term which significantly drew its inspiration from the Protestant Revolution of 1688–9) and proclaimed that the church and not the civil courts had complete spiritual independence and retained the final judgement on the rights and privileges of the Kirk. The crisis came to a head in the General Assembly of 1843 when most of the Evangelical wing, led by their leader, Thomas Chalmers, walked out to form the new Free Church. The national church virtually broke in half, with over two-fifths of the clergy and around 40 per cent of the laity seceding. The Disruption has been described as probably the single most momentous event in nineteenth-century Scotland, and its wider implications are assessed in Chapter 16. The Conservatives under Peel and his Home Secretary, Sir James Graham, rightly or wrongly were widely blamed for their failure to concede an inch on the claims of the General Assembly and for precipitating the mass exodus from the Kirk. The Free Church then attracted a loyal following among the prosperous urban middle classes of Evangelical persuasion, who soon took a terrible revenge on the Conservatives by turning the burghs into Liberal fiefdoms which remained impregnable for several decades afterwards. The year 1843 seemed to confirm the lesson of 1832: that the Tory/Conservative Party was adamantly opposed to popular rights. Its image had also been tarnished by the refusal of several Tory landlords to release sites for the building of free churches which forced some Highland congregations to worship for a time in caves and on bare hillsides. Amid a blaze of publicity the Liberal press had a field day in fully reporting these acts of reactionary discrimination.

Liberalism was going with the grain of Scottish political opinion in another respect. It came to be regarded as the party of free trade at a time when there was widespread national support for tariff reform. The Anti-Corn Law League was exceptionally popular in the Scottish towns at a time when the nation's international trade was booming and the need for any form of protectionism seemed not only superfluous but a constraint on the free flow of goods on which the prosperity of merchants and manufacturers depended. This whole issue was given huge public prominence by the crisis that led up to the repeal of the Corn Laws by Robert Peel in 1846. It is significant that at that time protectionism even failed to achieve significant support in the Scottish rural constituencies. One of the prominent advocates of Corn Law repeal was one of Scotland's best-known and most innovative farmers, George Hope of Fenton Barns in East Lothian. Protection did not seem to stir up much enthusiasm even among the mass of ordinary tenants. There was a widespread faith in the high levels of technical efficiency in Scottish farming as an effective substitute for protection. In addition, 'pure' arable agriculture was much less common in Scotland than in England. Not only was pastoral husbandry dominant in the Highlands and Borders but mixed farming was the norm in most parts of the Lowlands.

The passage of the Second Reform Act by Disraeli's Conservative government in 1867–8 might have been a solution to the problem of continued Liberal hegemony. As in the elections after 1832, it could be expected that the party that had carried the Reform would be rewarded by a grateful electorate with seats gained and opposition vanquished. However, it was not to be. The franchise was extended in the towns to ratepaying male householders and to lodgers paying £10 a year for accommodation. In the country, ownership qualifications fell from £10 to £5, the annual rental value of tenanted property from £50 to £14, and the secret ballot was finally introduced in 1872. The urban electorate in particular increased significantly, in Glasgow for instance, from 18,000 to 47,000. The majority of the new electors were from the skilled and semi-skilled working class. Before 1868 just over a third of the Glasgow electorate was working class, drawn mainly from artisan occupations. After the Reform Act, the working-class proportion climbed to nearly two-thirds. But instead of showing deep gratitude, the new electors inflicted yet another crushing defeat on the Conservatives. The Liberals won no fewer than 52 out of 60 constituencies. The

Second Reform Act had effectively strengthened the Liberal grip on Scotland, though its hegemony was still based on a small electorate of 10 per cent of the burgh population and 4 per cent of rural dwellers. Yet the new working-class voters had shown their support for traditional Liberal values by supporting the party in overwhelming numbers. As men who believed in 'respectability', self-improvement, sobriety and education, they found Liberalism their natural political home. In the second half of the nineteenth century, Liberal values represented Scottish values.

3

Some recent writers, in particular Tom Nairn and George Davie, have seen the age of Liberal dominance in Scottish politics between 1832 and 1914 as one of profound crisis in Scottish nationhood. In Europe the Scots were out of step as, throughout the continent, small, historic nations were asserting their rights to independence, while in Scotland nationalism in this form was conspicuous by its absence. The suggestion is that the middle classes, who were to the fore of the European movements, had been seduced in Scotland by the economic benefits of union and empire, but at the heavy cost of anglicization and cultural assimilation. The Scots were steadily becoming invisible as a people, as their ancient institutions and traditions were diluted and eroded by the corrosive impact of closer association with the world's most powerful nation, a process that also had devastating cultural consequences: 'Loss of confidence led to an eventual collapse of Scottish culture: literature degenerated into mawkish "kailyard" parochialism and painting into uninspired "ben and glen".'[9]

There is, on the surface, much to commend this pessimistic interpretation. The Disruption of 1843 fractured what had been the most important national institution in Scotland after the parliament came to an end in 1707. The united Church of Scotland had played a pivotal role in Scottish society. It had watched over morality, controlled education and poor relief, and its General Assembly was a form of surrogate Scottish parliament. After 1843, when 40 per cent of the Kirk's members left to form the Free Church, there was no longer a national church to act as a force for cohesion. Indeed, when the large secessions which took place before the Disruption are taken into account, Scottish

Presbyterianism had become divided into three large ecclesiastical camps, the 'auld Kirk', the Free Church and the United Presbyterian Church which was established out of the dissenting Relief and Secession Churches in 1847. Also, in 1845, one of the important civil functions of the pre-1843 church was lost when poor relief was transferred to ratepayer-elected parochial boards. Three decades later, in 1872, elected school boards were set up in every parish under the supervision of the Scotch Education Department, based in London. Scotland's greatest national institution was not only broken but was also being increasingly stripped of most of its social authority. It seemed a huge blow to the nation's sense of identity at a time when the forces of assimilation and anglicization were becoming ever more powerful. Moreover, by the 1850s, Scotland had been transformed by rapid urbanization and industrialization and the new Scotland of booming cities, burgeoning manufactures and improved agriculture seemed to have little in common with the historic nation of the centuries before the union of 1707. As Sir Walter Scott put it, 'what makes Scotland Scotland is fast disappearing'.[10]

The Scottish aristocracy and many laird families had long been sending their sons to England for education in order to maximize their career opportunities in later life. One result was that many Scottish MPs were the products of English public schools like Eton and Rugby, and they had also often attended Oxford or Cambridge and served in élite English regiments like the Life Guards and Coldstream Guards. Even merchants and other businessmen who increasingly represented the burghs had a similar educational background in the south and often had trading or military experience in the Empire. It was common also for English-based 'carpet-baggers' to sit for the burgh districts in Scotland. All in all, the Scottish MPs of this period were undoubtedly committed members of the imperial British establishment. The business and professional leaders of the west of Scotland, the nation's economic engine, were also becoming even more eager in the 1850s for further integration with England. This was shown in their support of the movement to bring the Scottish legal system – one of the basic foundations of a distinctive national identity – closer to English law. The Glasgow Law Amendment Society argued that there were important aspects of Scots law which were not suited to the present economic condition and this view was strongly endorsed and supported by the leaders of the city's business community, the Chamber of Commerce, the Merchants House and the main newspapers.

Even attempts to advance Scottish interests lacked real political credibility and influence. The National Association for the Vindication of Scottish Rights, which was formed in 1853, does show that some Scots were deeply concerned about aspects of the union relationship. The Association voiced a number of grievances, which included the pleas that Ireland received more government support than Scotland, Scotland did not have a fair number of MPs, the Privy Council should be restored, and the United Kingdom ought always to be designated 'Great Britain'. The Association took the view that there were weaknesses in the union but wanted to improve it rather than repeal it. A public meeting in Glasgow drew a crowd of 5,000 in December 1853 and many of the Association's criticisms also carried through into the Home Rule movement in the late nineteenth century and beyond. But the National Association also demonstrated how feeble political nationalism was in the 1850s. It lasted for only three years and was wound up in 1856; it did not attract significant figures, apart from the radical Duncan MacLaren and the Revd James Begg, from the mainstream of Liberalism, the dominant political ideology of the time; and the leadership was dominated by romantic conservatives. The Association's president was the thirteenth Earl of Eglinton, whose sole claim to fame was his role as host to the bizarre neo-medieval Eglinton tournament in 1839. All this was a far cry from the militant nationalist crusades that rocked the capitals of Europe in the 1840s.

Undoubtedly a good deal of the pessimistic interpretation of Scottish nationhood in the Victorian era seems supported by the history of the period. But in the last ten years or so this perspective has been subjected to radical reinterpretation by a new generation of scholars including Richard Finlay, Graeme Morton and Lindsay Paterson. Their broad argument is that Scottish national identity did not vanish but rather adapted itself to new circumstances. In addition, while political assimilation was dominant at the level of parliamentary government finances and central government, Scottish control was still paramount where it mattered most to people in the Victorian period, that is at the level of the city, the burgh and the locality. This was also a period of the reinvention of Scotland, when new or refurbished icons continued to provide the nation with crucial symbols of identity and distinctiveness within the union.

Contrary to the assimilationist interpretation, most of the actual day-to-day business of governing Scotland remained in Scottish hands for much of the nineteenth century. Only after the passing of the Education Act of 1872, the extension of the franchise to the working class on a larger scale and the creation of the Scottish Office in 1885 was there a decisive movement towards a more centralized state. Until then the United Kingdom was probably more decentralized than any other country in Europe. As in the eighteenth century, parliament in London rarely intervened on Scottish issues unless invited to do so and the Lord Advocate in Edinburgh continued to control such key areas as law enforcement and policing. In the second half of the twentieth century the enormous influence of the state, in education, health, welfare and economic management, is taken for granted. In the nineteenth century government intervention was, however, limited in the extreme and the system gave considerable autonomy to Scotland within the union state:

There was a growing tendency for Scottish MPs to settle Scottish business outside parliament, submitting the results for largely formal ratification to the full house. Thus the Scots functioned as an informal domestic parliament within the imperial legislature. For example, the English Lord Chancellor was willing to extend proposed commercial legislation to Scotland only if the Scots could first reach a consensus that this was desirable. The Scottish sub-parliament was especially important for private bills, which were far more common and influential than they are today (and had been so since before 1832). They were the means whereby the governing councils of cities, towns, universities or various other public agencies would extend their powers; they also provided the legal framework for the development of railways, docks and other large public works. A Scottish private bill would be proposed by a Scottish MP and debated by other Scottish MPs. Usually, these Scottish votes would determine the bill's fate.[11]

Below the parliamentary level the routine of government and administration was devolved to town councils and supervisory boards which grew up from the 1840s. The Scottish Board of Supervision ran the Poor Law from 1845 and the Prisons Board was set up in 1838. These two were followed in due course by others, for public health, lunatic asylums (1857) and education (1872). Scots lawyers staffed this new bureaucracy and its inspectors were Scots doctors, surveyors and architects. The Scottish Burgh Reform Act of 1833 vested the management of the towns in the broad middle class. It was a crucial piece of legislation which, taken together with the administrative revolution mentioned above, created a new and powerful *local state* run by the Scottish bourgeoisie and reflecting their political and religious values. It was this local state, rather than a distant and usually indifferent Westminster authority, that in effect routinely governed Scotland. The middle classes had therefore no reason to seek parliamentary independence or to adopt a nationalism which was hostile to the British state. They enthusiastically supported Kossuth in Hungary and Garibaldi in Italy in their struggles for national unity, but they did not feel similarly oppressed or need a national parliament to achieve what the Liberal middle classes in Scotland already possessed, namely liberty, economic prosperity and cultural integrity, the very advantages for which European nationalists had yearned for so long.

Nevertheless, it does not follow that, because the basis for a strong *political nationalism* did not exist in the Victorian era, Scottish national identity was therefore in itself inevitably emasculated. On the contrary, the economic success which helped to remove the basis of nationalist discontent was itself a tremendous source of national pride and self-congratulation. As the *Glasgow Sentinel* put it in 1853:

There is scarcely a house of eminence in commerce or manufactures in the Kingdom which does not to some extent owe its success to Scottish prudence, perseverance and enterprise, there is not an industrial department in which there is not a large infusion of the Scottish element in management. Within a comparatively short period in the history of the nation, its population has more than trebled. It has led the way in agricultural improvements. Its real property has increased in even greater proportion.[12]

Scottish talents had also been displayed on the global stage through the contribution of the nation to the development of the greatest territorial empire on earth. The British Empire did not dilute the sense of Scottish identity but strengthened it by powerfully reinforcing the sense of national esteem and demonstrating that the Scots were equal partners with the English in the great imperial mission. It was commonly emphasized at the time that the Empire was born *after* 1707 and could only have been achieved through a joint enterprise between the two nations. Empire for the Scots was a route to self-respect as well as to enhanced prosperity. Linda Colley points out that English and foreign observers alike are and were wont to refer to the island of Great Britain as 'England' but at no time describe the Empire as anything other than 'British'. Within the imperial relationship the Scots could feel that they were the peers of the English. Not only that, but the Scots had been conspicuously successful as Empire builders: 'Scotsmen, whether as soldiers, statesmen, financiers, bankers, scientists, educators, engineers, or merchants have in all our Colonies fully held their own, nay, risen to positions of eminence.'[13]

Scottish Presbyterianism might be bitterly divided at home but, as a result of the Empire, it was now exported by dedicated missionaries throughout the world, as Scottish religious colonies blossomed in Canada, Australasia and Africa. David Livingstone, the explorer and missionary, became one of the great national heroes of Victorian times. The Scots were equally proud of their proven abilities as imperial governors and administrators. A third of the colonial governor-generals between 1850 and 1939 were Scots. The Glasgow-born Sir John A. Macdonald dominated Canadian politics for over two decades after the establishment of the federal dominion in 1867. In 1884 Robert Stout, an Orkney teacher, became Prime Minister of New Zealand, while in 1908, in Australia, Andrew Fisher, a miner from Ayrshire, became the first Labour Prime Minister in the world.

Empire-building was depicted as something peculiarly Scottish and as the fulfilment of a national destiny. Historical links were drawn with the Jacobite movement. The '45 was recognized as a heroic failure but also depicted as a glorious feat of arms which epitomized the essential Scottish martial qualities of courage, loyalty, trust and fidelity which were now so vital to the achievement of the imperial mission. The exploits of the Scottish regiments, which played such an important part in the expansion of Empire, were recounted in detail in innumerable press reports, children's comics, regimental histories and military bio-graphies, all designed to appeal to a wide audience and to personify and reinforce the notion of the Scots as a truly martial race. New national heroes were constantly created: the men of the 'Thin Red Line', the 93rd Highlanders at Balaclava, Sir Colin Campbell in the Indian Mutiny and the martyred General Gordon at Khartoum in 1886 whom the chroniclers depicted as saving the Empire from barbarian enemies through his heroic death. The military glamour of Empire was also colourfully displayed at home by the numerous companies of Volun-teers, the part-time soldiers who drilled and paraded at the weekends dressed in the full uniform of their shadow regular regiments and marching to the stirring music of the pipes and drums to the pride and delight of local audiences.

It was not only Empire, however, which ensured that Sir Walter Scott's pessimistic vision of the disappearance of 'Scotland' did not come about. Religion remained a vital factor in identity despite the shattering impact of the Disruption and the subsequent removal of the Established Church's civil responsibilities. These, after all, were essentially institutional changes. At the more fundamental level of values Presbyterianism still shaped the nation's identity. As already noted, it was the religious emphasis which gave Chartism in Scotland its own special distinctiveness, despite being an integral part of a British radical movement. The Disruption itself has recently been described by David Bebbington as something which verged on religious nationalism because it articulated the Scottish Kirk's historic spiritual independence, which was rooted in the principles of the Reformation of 1560 and defended with the blood of the Scottish nation in the religious struggles of the seventeenth century. The 'Claim of Right' presented by those who opposed patronage was designed to echo the Claim of Right of 1689, which laid down the reasons for opposition to James VII, was couched in language reminiscent of the National Covenant in 1638, and specifically condemned the broken pledges on church government from the union of 1707. It was a statement of Scottish religious principles, buttressed by both explicit and oblique references to the nation's Presbyterian heritage.

In addition, it was the Presbyterian inheritance that shaped the values of thrift, independence, sobriety, the work ethic and education, which were the very foundations of the middle- and 'respectable' working-class culture. These values were propagated in such seminal texts as *Self-Help* by the Scot, Samuel Smiles from Haddington, and given political expression in the enormous loyalty shown to the Liberal Party by the Scottish electorate for virtually the whole of the second half of the nineteenth century. One of the reasons why Gladstone became such a hero during his Midlothian campaign in 1879 was because he was both of Scottish parentage and a great leader of Liberalism, the dominant political philosophy of the nation. Presbyterianism's function as the defender of Scottish values had also been brought into sharper focus with the marked increase in Irish Catholic immigration during and after the Great Famine. By the 1851 census, there were 207,367 first-generation Irish immigrants and also large numbers of earlier arrivals who maintained loyalty to the Catholic faith. Their regional concentration in the west of Scotland gave their presence even greater visibility. The result was the foundation in the early 1850s of such anti-Catholic organizations as the Scottish Reformation Society and Scottish Protestant Association and the journals *The Scottish Protestant* and *The Bulwark*. These groups were not simply defenders of the 'true' religion but also saw themselves as protectors of the Protestant Scottish nation from invasion by an 'inferior' race who, they claimed, threatened to bring disease, crime and degradation in their wake.

This was also the time when the idea of Scotland as a national entity was being reinforced through the appeal to the nation's distinctive past which was threatened with destruction by the scale of urban and industrial transformation. Sir Walter Scott himself, who feared that Scotland might become invisible, helped to pioneer with others major collections of Scottish ballads and folk tales. P. F. Tytler's monumental multi-volume and scholarly *History of Scotland*, published over a span of 15 years from 1828, reached a wide middle-class readership and so testified to the continuing interest in the nation's past. Scottish history loomed large in the most popular working-class paper of the later nineteenth century, *The People's Journal*, which by 1875 had a circulation of 130,000 copies a week and a quarter of a million on the eve of the First World War. It contained frequent series on the Scottish past and also had a pioneering interest in folklore and social history that went far beyond the orthodox focus on kings, queens and national heroes. Presbyterian religious history attracted wide interest. Thomas McCrie's biographies of John Knox (1811) and Andrew Melville (1819) were best-sellers. The Reformation, the Covenanters and the Presbyterian heroes were commemorated in the paintings of Sir George Harvey and immortalized in numerous monuments in stone erected in several Scottish towns.

But more potent were mythical and semi-mythical stories and personalities, set in the times before industrialization. Here again Scott had led the way. Through his Waverley novels and *Tales of a Grandfather* he invested the Scottish past with a magical appeal and satisfied the powerful emotional needs for nostalgia in a society experiencing unprecedented changes. Scott was a brilliant pioneer in the invention of tradition, a process which helped to develop a new set of national symbols and icons while at the same time renewing others of venerable antiquity in the contemporary image of Victorian Scotland. The tartan and kilt of the Highlands had been appropriated even before 1830 as the national dress. But its adoption was given further impetus by the heroic and well-publicized deeds of the kilted regiments in the Empire, by the growing number of Caledonian Societies in the emigrant communities abroad with their pipe bands and tartan dress and, not least, by Queen Victoria's love affair with the Highlands. The best-loved monarch of modern times built a residence at Balmoral on Deeside and, after 1848, spent the autumn of each year there on holiday. By comparison she visited Ireland only four times in her entire reign. The fact that Victoria showed such fascination with the Highlands and was sometimes even heard to proclaim herself a Jacobite at heart was bound to have a major effect. Highlandism had now been given wholehearted royal approval and tartan recognized as the badge of Scottish identity. When a company of radical volunteers was established to fight for Garibaldi in Italy they were dressed in tartan shirts and bonnets topped with a Scottish thistle. At the same time, Scottish landscape painting developed a fascination with 'the land of the mountain and the flood' in the work of such artists as Horatio McCulloch (1805–67), with his pictures of lochs, corries and waterfalls and, above all, the archetypal and hugely popular *My Heart's in the Highlands* (1860).

The adoption of romantic Highland symbolism, paradoxically at the very time when crofting society itself was experiencing the terrible agony of clearance and dispossession, was only one element in the reinvention of Scotland. The historic building tradition of castles, keeps, towers and fortifications which had died out in the later seventeenth century was rehabilitated in the Victorian period in the architectural style which became known as Scotch Baronial. A key influence here was Robert Billings (1813–74) whose series, *Baronial and Ecclesiastical Antiquities of Scotland*, published between 1848 and 1852, was the primary source for the movement. Soon turrets, battlements and towers were appearing everywhere in rich profusion, first in country houses (Queen Victoria led the way with Balmoral Castle) and then on urban sheriff courts, municipal offices and infirmaries. It was even suggested that Edinburgh Castle should be remodelled in baronial style to convert it from a military barracks into a national monument. David Bryce (1803–76), the pivotal figure in Scotch Baronial architecture, boldly proposed a huge 165-foot-high keep as a 'Scottish National Memorial to the Prince Consort' on the site. It was never built, but the idea once again illustrated the close association between the Scottish nation and the monarchy of Victoria.

Above all, the cult of national heroes became one of the most popular ways of linking urban Scotland with its history. Pre-eminent in this respect were Robert Burns and William Wallace. In the period after *c.* 1840, Burns was venerated as never before. In one Burns Festival in 1844 an estimated 80,000 were in attendance, and of this multitude 2,000 sat down to eat lunch, accompanied by numerous toasts to the poet. The enormous influence of the National Bard was seen in the countless attempts at imitations of his verse which dominated the 'poetry corners' of local newspapers throughout Scotland. But the historic Burns and his remarkable literary achievement were also moulded to suit the political tastes of a Victorian middle-class readership. He was depicted as anti-aristocratic and as a man who had succeeded by his own individual talent rather than through inherited privilege or noble birth. Burns became the apotheosis of 'the lad o' pairts', a key element in the most influential of Victorian Scottish myths, that personal ability alone was enough to achieve success in life. But he was also praised because he linked the Scots with their rural past – it was often said that the blood of the Ayrshire Covenanters flowed in his veins – and preserved the ancient vernacular language by his genius. As Lord Rosebery put it in a speech at Dumfries at the centenary of Burns's death:

For Burns exalted our race: he hallowed Scotland and the Scottish tongue . . . The Scottish dialect as he put it, was in danger of perishing. Burns seemed at this juncture to start to his feet and reassert Scotland's claim to national existence; his Scottish notes range through the world, and he has thus preserved the Scottish language forever – for mankind will never allow to die that idiom in which his songs and poems are enshrined.[14]

The cult of William Wallace in the nineteenth century was equally complex and bears little relation to the raw nationalism of Hollywood's *Braveheart* in the 1990s. There can be little doubt that Wallace was one of the supreme Victorian icons. Magnificent statues to the hero of the Wars of Independence were erected overlooking the Tweed and in Lanark, but these paled before the grandest of all of these projects, the 220-foot-high tower of the National Wallace Monument, built near Stirling between 1859 and 1869. This colossal edifice overlooked the country where the Scots at Stirling Bridge and Bannockburn had fought their most decisive battles against the English in the fourteenth century. Wallace was not only remembered in statuary and monuments. Blind Harry's fifteenth-century epic, *The Wallace*, which was vehemently anti-English in language and tone, maintained its popularity, while tales of Bruce and Wallace were always familiar features in the local press. But the Wallace cult was not designed to threaten the union or inspire political nationalism, though the membership of the National Association for the Vindication of Scottish Rights were among the most enthusiastic supporters of the proposal for a National Monument. Rather, the cult reminded the Scots of their own history in which the union had been achieved *because* of Wallace's struggle for freedom. Wallace had ensured that the Scottish people had never been conquered. As a result of their own courageous fight for independence in medieval times a fruitful union between equal partners had become possible in 1707. In addition, Wallace could appeal to a Victorian Scotland profoundly divided across class lines. To middle-class Liberals, he had saved the nation when it had been betrayed by the aristocracy which still held power in the nineteenth century and which remained the reactionary enemy of many of the urban bourgeoisie throughout the Victorian era. For working-class Chartists, who often passionately sang *Scots wha hae* at their meetings, he represented the spirit of the common man striving for freedom against oppression. The national devotion to Wallace demonstrated that pride in Scottish nationhood and loyalty to union and empire could be reconciled.

This being so, it is difficult to argue that the 'failure' of political nationalism to develop caused a crisis in Scottish culture. It was possible for a strong and coherent sense of national identity to exist within the union and provide a solid foundation for cultural achievement. There is abundant evidence of this. Scottish science, medicine and technology maintained and enhanced a world-class reputation. There were some remarkable individual scientists. They included William Thomson (1824–1907), later Lord Kelvin, and William McQuorn Rankine (1820–72) whose combined talents made Glasgow Britain's leading centre for applied science and engineering. It is interesting to note that Kelvin was driven forward in his research by the same religious motivations as some of his great eighteenth-century predecessors. He advocated the study of physics in his 1846 inaugural lecture for intellectual and practical benefit but, above all, to obtain knowledge of the laws of nature established by God 'for maintaining the harmony and permanence of his Works'.[15] James Clerk Maxwell (1831–97), Scotland's greatest scientist of the century, was the most distinguished mathematical physicist of the age whose theory of electromagnetism was basic to the development of the radio and other applications. In medicine,

Joseph Lister (1827–1912) pioneered antiseptic surgery, and Sir James Simpson (1811–70) was the first to apply anaesthetics to childbirth. But technical virtuosity was not confined to the university laboratories or the great hospitals and infirmaries. The Clyde shipbuilding yards had undisputed world pre-eminence in marine engineering design, while Scottish civil engineers were in demand throughout the globe for the building of bridges, docks and other capital works. They achieved their apotheosis in the completion of the Forth Bridge in 1890, justly regarded as the greatest civil engineering triumph of the Victorian age.

Study and awareness of Scottish philosophy in the nineteenth century has suffered because of the inordinate attention devoted by scholars to the golden age of the eighteenth century. Entire academic journals are devoted to some of the thinkers of the Enlightenment period but not a single volume has been published on their successors of the Victorian period. This is a pity, because figures like J. F. Ferrier, acclaimed by some in his own time as the most significant philosopher in Europe, and Alexander Bain, Regius Professor of Logic at Aberdeen, also with a distinguished international reputation, are very worthy of serious academic consideration.[16] In social studies, Sir James George Frazer (1854–1941) was a pioneering anthropologist. Educated at both Glasgow and Cambridge, his background in classical studies was also influenced by Sir William Thomson (Lord Kelvin), who stimulated him to search for the absolute laws of nature. His seminal work was the monumental two-volume *The Golden Bough*, first published in 1890, which gave powerful new insights into the study of early societies. His contemporary, Patrick Geddes (1854–1932) also established a world-class reputation through his studies of the new cities which were transforming all the industrializing countries and his conviction that life for their citizens could be improved through effective planning and a serious effort to understand the environment. Geddes is recognized today as a seminal influence on sociology and planning and the father of environmentalism.

In literature and the arts, the descent of Scottish culture into the abyss of the sentimental parochialism of the Kailyard has been grossly exaggerated by modern critics. Thomas Knowles has defined the Kailyard school thus:

In its 'classic' form, the Kailyard is characterized by the sentimental and nostalgic treatment of parochial Scottish scenes, often centred on the church community, often on individual careers which move from childhood innocence to urban awakening (and contamination), and back again to the comfort and security of the native hearth. Typically thematic is the 'lad o' pairts', the poor Scottish boy making good within the 'democratic' Scottish system of education, and dying young as a graduated minister in his mother's arms with the assembled parish looking on. The parishioners themselves, their dialect sometimes translated for an English audience, sprinkle their exchanges with native wit, and slip easily from the pettiness of village gossip to the profundities of rustic philosophizing.[17]

The three writers who came to be synonymous with the Kailyard were S. R. Crockett (1860–1914), Ian Maclaren (1850–1907) – the *nom de plume* of John Watson – and J. M. Barrie (1860–1937). Maclaren chose for the motto of his first novel, *Beside the Bonnie Brier Bush* (1894), two lines from Burns which included the term 'kailyard' (cabbage or vegetable patch) and thereafter it became associated with this particular genre:

> There grows a bonnie brier bush in our kail-yard
> and white are the blossoms on't our kail-yard

For almost a century the Kailyard writers have been mercilessly attacked by countless literary critics for their bad art, cultural degeneracy and sloppy sentimentality. They also committed the unforgivable sin of being hugely successful by publishing a number of best-sellers for the home as well as for the vast Scottish expatriate market. For a society that was one of the most urbanized in the world but which had strong and recent roots in the countryside the Kailyard tales had an irresistible attraction.

But Scottish culture in the later nineteenth century was much more than the Kailyard school. The three authors who have been convicted of such high literary crimes wrote only a dozen books in the course of a single decade and they had a niche market among the upper middle classes at home and abroad. But they represented only one part of a rich diversity of Scottish culture. William Donaldson's brilliant analysis of some of the several thousand serialized novels in the popular press, the principal reading-matter of the working classes, demonstrates conclusively that many Scottish writers in Victorian times did not confine themselves to parochial rural themes but commonly dealt with cities and slums, poverty, disease, workers and capitalists in grim and realistic detail. Many of these stories were told in vernacular Scots, which was still the spoken speech of the vast majority of the Lowland people. In Gaelic, the creative experience in the later nineteenth century was one of a new cultural assertiveness. The poetry of Ulleam MacDhunleibhe (William Livingstone) and Ilan Mac a Ghobhainn (John Smith) contains robust and scathing criticism of the Clearances and the representatives of spiritual and secular authority. This is an approach that contrasts vividly with the weaker and timorous tone of Gaelic verse in the early nineteenth century, which reflected a society broken by the impact of famine, mass removals and forced emigration.

This was also the era of Robert Louis Stevenson's adventure novels, *Treasure Island* (1883) and *Kidnapped* (1886). Margaret Oliphant was the author of over 100 best-selling novels, including such important portrayals of Scottish life as *Effie Ogilvie* (1886) and *Kirsteen* (1890). George Macdonald's fantastic stories for both children and adults were much admired by his friend, Charles Dodgson (Lewis Carroll), and undoubtedly influenced the *Alice* books. At the other end of the creative spectrum are the novels of William Alexander concerning the north-east Lowlands, particularly his masterpiece, *Johnny Gibb of Gushetneuk*, which explores the huge changes from peasant to capitalist farming with remarkable historical realism and attention to contemporary detail, expressed in a literary language based on the idiom of central and southern Aberdeenshire in the early nineteenth century. Alexander's work could not be further removed from the cosy world of the Kailyard. It was a similar story of rich diversity in Scottish art: 'Bens and Glens' no more dominated painting than kailyardery did literature. The land-scapes of William McTaggart contrast with the Highlandism of Horatio McCulloch and Tom Faed. Near the end of the century the 'Glasgow Boys', E. A. Walton, John Lavery, W. N. McGregor and E. A. Hornel, drew heavily on the example of the French Impressionists and placed Scotland in the mainstream of European artistic development. All of this hardly suggests that in the late nineteenth century Scottish culture was in crisis. On the contrary, Patrick Geddes in his periodical, *Evergreen*, was able to argue that the nation was experiencing a Scottish renaissance. That verdict certainly seems more convincing than the more pessimistic interpretations of later commentators.

14

The Decline and Fall of Liberal Hegemony

I

For half a century after the Reform Act of 1832 the Liberals had enjoyed virtually unchallenged electoral success in Scotland and this was only finally threatened in the 1880s. The third Reform Act of 1884, which granted the franchise to all male householders and allocated more parliamentary seats than before to the larger towns and industrial districts, was a primary factor increasing tensions within Liberalism. The party had always been a broad church, but the electoral changes of 1884 significantly increased the conflict between Whigs and Radicals. Radicalism was strengthened by the enfranchisement of more manual workers and small farmers, while in the rural areas political friction between Liberal landlords and their tenantry became more acute. The eighth Duke of Argyll, the greatest Liberal grandee, abandoned the party because he feared that the Irish land legislation of 1881 would be imposed in the Highlands. His concerns turned out to be entirely justified when, after a period of prolonged disturbances by crofters in parts of the western Highlands and Islands and investigation by a Royal Commission under Lord Napier, Gladstone's government passed the Crofters' Holding Act in 1886. This significantly curbed landlord powers and provided the small tenants of the region with security of tenure and fair rentals. A year earlier, the impact of the new Reform Act in the Highlands had been dramatically illustrated in the general election, with the defeat by the 'Crofters' Party' of the official Liberal candidates in Argyll, Ross and Cromarty and Caithness and of both a Liberal and Conservative in Inverness. The memory of the Clearances gave a special emotional edge to electoral contests in the Highlands, but in the Lowlands as well the political influence of the great Whig/Liberal families was shrinking fast. The number of landowning Liberal MPs fell from nine in 1885 to only three by the end of 1910. Divisions within Liberalism were also coming to a head in the cities where the radical wing was mounting a powerful challenge to the entrenched position of the Whigs. In 1885 the Scottish radical Liberals established the National Liberal Federation of Scotland, a body which was both independent of the party hierarchy and created to advance a wide-ranging programme of reform of the House of Lords and disestablishment of the Church of Scotland. All this was anathema to the more conservative elements in the party.

Against this background of growing tension within Liberalism, three particular factors were likely to cause even greater difficulties. First, the emergence of socialist parties with a direct political appeal to the working men enfranchised in 1884 threatened the traditional support which Liberalism had attracted from the artisan classes. Some were already losing faith anyway in a party which could be seen as a political bastion of capitalism and committed to the defence of the free market economy. One of the earliest and most famous sceptics was James Keir Hardie who, after failing miserably as a candidate in the Mid-Lanark by-election, played a leading role in the formation of the Scottish Labour Party in 1888. It was also largely owing to Hardie's influence that the Independent Labour Party (ILP) was formed after a conference in Bradford in 1893. The ILP merged two years later with the Scottish Labour Party. A significant number of the key figures in these developments were disenchanted Liberals, for example R. G. Cunninghame Graham who had been elected in 1886 as Liberal MP for north-east Lanarkshire before coming under the influence of the London-based Social Democratic Federation. Keir Hardie, Bruce Glasier and Ramsay MacDonald, all to the fore in the leadership of the ILP, doubted the Liberal Party's commitment to increasing working-class representation in parliament. There was also likely to be conflict between the party's free market principles and trade unionism, which was increasingly criticized for restrictive practices from some quarters at a time of more intense international economic competition. Significantly, in 1897 a Scottish Trades Union Congress (STUC) was formed in order to ensure that the unions could increase their political influence. It was the STUC, together with the ILP, which helped to establish in 1900 the Scottish Workers' Parliamentary Election Committee, a potentially powerful combination of political and trade-union interests and a confirmation that the aspirations of the working classes were seen by some as best secured through an organization wholly independent of Liberalism.

Second, throughout the 1880s, the campaign for disestablishing the Church of Scotland became a running sore which encouraged the spread of warring factions within the Liberal Party. The Free Church, a traditional stronghold of Liberalism, became committed to disestablishment after 1875 under the leadership of Principal Rainy. From that point on, the Liberal Party was wracked by internecine dispute between Whigs and Radicals which culminated in 1885 with the formation of the National Liberal Federation of Scotland, which tried to make disestablishment part of the Liberal programme for the next election. Gladstone resisted this and was denounced by the National Federation, which then attempted to take its revenge by presenting its own candidates at the polls. Even Gladstone's great prestige could not prevent endemic feuding on this issue. Four years later, when he finally conceded that there was a majority in Scotland for liberating the church from the state, no consensus emerged, and turmoil once again broke out in the party. The Liberals at the same time also managed to offend many ordinary members of the Established Church in a vendetta which threatened its public status and influence in Scotland.

Third, and most crucial of all, there was the question of Irish Home Rule. Outright schism had been avoided in the case of church disestablishment and even in the Highlands the breakaway 'Crofters' Party' had only a short life as, by 1895, crofting candidates were back in the fold and standing as official Liberals. The crofters had shown their gratitude to the party which had delivered them security of tenure and fair rents. The split over Gladstone's Irish policy proved much more fundamental and enduring. In endeavouring to bring peace to Ireland through the offer of limited Home Rule the Prime Minister drove a deep wedge through his party in Scotland. Opposition came from several quarters. For some, this measure was the last straw and the final confirmation of the leftward drift of Liberalism. Leading Whig magnates such as the Earls of Stair, Fife and Minto were among the first to defect. Commercial interests saw Home Rule as a threat to the Empire and to free trade. In the west of Scotland, where links with Ulster were always strong, the fear that Home Rule meant Rome Rule had a potent impact on Orange working-class communities. For many Liberal lairds, Home Rule was associated with land reform and that completed their disillusion with a party which now seemed totally under the influence of radical elements.

The most disaffected finally split to form the Liberal Unionist Party, and in the general election of 1885 they had a triumphant success, winning 17 seats, or nearly a third of the Liberal total in Scotland. 'Unionist' in this case referred to the union with Ireland. This victory was no flash in the pan. Many of the Protestant working classes of the west of Scotland swung behind the Unionists in 1885 and in subsequent elections. The formerly impregnable Liberal fortresses in the cities and towns were finally breached and in some cases overwhelmed. Indeed Unionism primarily became an urban movement at this time. Even the leading newspapers of the cities, the *Glasgow Herald*, *Scotsman* and *Daily Free Press* (Aberdeen) deserted Gladstone. The Chambers of Commerce of Greenock and Glasgow ended their traditional political neutrality and publicly condemned the Home Rule policy. Though the Liberal Unionists did not merge with the Conservatives to form the Scottish Unionist Party until 1912, they maintained close contacts with each other and entered into an alliance from 1895 to mount a more powerful challenge to Liberal hegemony from the political right than at any time since 1832. Again, their best opportunities were in the west where, in 1886, the Conservatives took 10 and the Unionists eight seats from the Liberals and established a new popular political grouping, which, also for the first time, embraced a distinctive working-class constituency.

After 1886 Scotland therefore was no longer a one-party state and Liberalism seemed in long-term difficulty. The party's share of voting support in Scotland fell from 70 per cent to 51 per cent between 1874 and 1900, and in the elections of 1895 and 1900 the Liberals again did badly. In 1895 their lead was cut back to a mere eight seats, and five years later in the Khaki Election the Conservatives achieved their first ever majority since 1832. A party official lamented: 'We have been hopelessly smashed in Scotland.'[1] The open divisions over the Boer War between Lord Rosebery and his Liberal Imperialists who supported it, and the radical wing under Sir Henry Campbell-Bannerman, who equally strongly opposed the conflict, had done much to damage the party's credibility among the electorate.

But it would be wrong to dismiss Liberalism as a political movement in inevitable decline before 1914. Certainly the overwhelming dominance of the decades before 1880 had gone but the party had much more resilience and popularity in Scotland than the setbacks of 1895 and 1900 would suggest. In the years before the Great War, the Liberals still remained the party of government north of the border. John Buchan writing in 1911 had little doubt that this was the case:

Its dogmas were so completely taken for granted that their presentation partook less of argument than of tribal incantations. Mr Gladstone had given it an aura of earnest morality so that its platforms were also pulpits and its harangues had the weight of sermons. Its members seemed to assume that their opponents must be lacking either in morals or in mind. The Tories were the 'stupid' party. Liberals alone understood and sympathised with the poor; a working man who was not a Liberal was inaccessible to reason, or morally corrupt, or intimidated by laird or employer.[2]

Buchan was commenting against a background of triumphant Liberal recovery from the reverses of 1900. In 1906 the party won a landslide victory in Scotland by trouncing its Conservative and Liberal Unionist opponents by 58 seats to 12, with Labour picking up its first two Scottish victories. This position was consolidated and marginally improved in the elections of January and December of 1910 in contrast to the pattern in England, where the Conservatives managed to recover their earlier position. All this suggests that the 1900 defeat was a freak result, brought on by fatal party divisions over the South African War, which temporarily left the Liberals in disarray, and the capacity of the Conservatives and Liberal Unionists to exploit the national mood of patriotism and imperialism aroused by the conflict with the Boers. In other contests, however, the Liberal Unionists failed to attract sustained mass support and, though the Conservatives had emerged from the moribund condition of the long period before 1886, they still made only a limited impression outside the west of Scotland. Nor was Labour yet any rival to the Liberals. In 1914, Labour had decided to field a maximum of 17 candidates but in the event decided on a total of only seven or eight. One delegate at Labour's conference in that year admitted that the party still faced an uphill struggle: 'Unfortunately Scotland was so imbued with Liberal principles that it was a harder fight there than in any other part of the country.'[3] This was conclusively demonstrated by the significantly larger number of candidates that the party intended to put up south of the border.

The resilience and continued popularity of Liberalism rested on a number of foundations. In the long run the damaging splits of the 1880s which removed Unionists and Whigs had a positive effect. Not only did the party gradually become more coherent by the early twentieth century, but it was also able to move in more radical directions and hence maintain its support among industrial workers, crofters and farm servants. In 1891 the Scottish Liberal Association decided in favour of substantial land reform in the Highlands, universal adult suffrage, the abolition of the House of Lords and the eight-hour day. The Liberal administration after 1906 became one of the great reforming governments of the twentieth century with the introduction of old age pensions, unemployment benefit and the beginning of organized medical care. It is clear that these issues of social policy were basic to political debate in Scotland in 1906 – unlike the pattern in England, where discussion on these matters was relatively muted. The leading newspapers all gave extended coverage to social questions, while several party spokesmen advocated the 'new' Liberalism as the surest way of ensuring the continuing loyalty of working-class supporters and minimizing any haemorrhage to Labour. For one element within the working classes, the Irish Catholic immigrants, the Liberal Party was regarded as the only effective vehicle for securing Home Rule for their native land. Most Catholics did not obtain the vote until 1918, but it was reckoned in 1910 that there was already an Irish Nationalist vote in 46 Scottish constituencies, ranging from as little as 1 per cent in Argyll to 24 per cent in west Fife, with most of its influence concentrated in the industrial districts in and around Glasgow. Here the Irish National League, founded in 1882, and its successor, the United Irish League, formed in 1900, exercised an effective discipline over immigrant voters and normally directed them to support Liberal candidates. The Irish National League's main organizer was the remarkable John Ferguson, a stationer and publisher of Ulster Protestant stock. He was an active figure on the executive of the Scottish Liberal Association, which invited Irish Nationalist speakers to tour Scotland during the 1890 election. Close links had also been developed between leading radical Liberals and Irish land reformers such as Michael Davitt during the campaign for crofters' rights in the 1880s. Certainly there is evidence of some erosion of the Nationalist vote to Labour in a few constituencies by 1914. John Wheatley, for instance, born in County Waterford and former president of the Shettleston Daniel O'Connell branch of the Irish National League, founded the Catholic Socialist Society in 1906 and worked hard to promote support for Labour. But by and large Irish Catholic immigrant support for the Liberals before 1914 remained solid, as shown by the threats of violence that Wheatley received from those of his co-religionists who regarded his high-profile role in socialist organizations as a betrayal of the Home Rule cause and an act of treachery against the Liberals who alone were believed to be able to advance it in parliament.

The threat of socialism to the Liberal working-class vote was reduced by other factors in the short term. The vast majority of Scottish workers remained outside the trade-union movement which weakened its ability to advance the interest of the working classes through the sponsoring of an independent working-class party. The need for this approach was starting to become evident only after 1890 due to the legal setbacks suffered by the trade unions, such as the notorious Taff Vale judgement of 1901/2 which made unions liable in actions for damages by employers for civil wrongs payable from union funds. Radical Liberalism and early Scottish socialism also shared a number of common principles such as temperance, pacifism, a belief in evangelical religion, land reform and Home Rule for Scotland. Labour leaders were to the fore in organizations like the Highland Land League and the Scottish Home Rule Association which were dominated by Liberals. The crusade against rapacious landlordism in the Highlands was an old Liberal cause and the ILP drew on this tradition to develop its own campaign against urban landlords who were charging exorbitant rents. Liberals and Labour were united in their hatred of landowners and the most famous and influential critique of the landed classes, *Our Noble Families* (1909), came from the pen of Tom Johnston, the editor of *Forward*, the ILP newspaper, which was founded in 1906. It was therefore sometimes difficult to mark out a distinction between advanced Liberalism on the one hand and the policies of the ILP on the other. Scottish craftsmen were still unwilling to sever their traditional links with a party that was able to promise real improvements in their lives through its new commitment to social reform.

Labour did make more progress in the early years of the twentieth century when it had two MPs elected in Scotland in 1906, though both had strong Liberal sympathies. The artisans of the engineering shops and shipyards of Clydeside were becoming increasingly restless as periods of unemployment became more frequent and employers reacted to foreign competition by investing more in labour-saving machinery, which threatened dilution of skills. The unemployment crisis of 1907–8 was something of a watershed in this respect. It put thousands out of work, including many skilled men, and, by the end of 1907, 7,000 people in and around Glasgow were dependent on a special relief fund. This was a bitter experience for many of the proud, independent craftsmen of the Clyde. At the same time, socialist ideas were being promoted more vigorously through lectures, the newspaper *Forward*, socialist Sunday schools and the evening classes of the Workers' Educational Association. The revolutionary left was now increasingly active through the Social Democratic Federation (SDF) and the Socialist Labour Party (SLP) which had broken away from the SDF in Scotland in 1903 through the efforts of James Connolly. The SDF and the ILP were chalk and cheese. While the ILP sought reform through parliament, the SLP envisaged workers' control of industry and the use of strike action to bring about the collapse of the capitalist system. It was a sign of the times that the charismatic Govan schoolteacher, John Maclean, a member of the SDF, was able to attract audiences of several hundreds after 1911 to his Sunday evening lectures on Marxist philosophy and economics. Nevertheless, while there was a growing ferment of socialist ideas on Clydeside before 1914 – and these were to have significant effects during and after the Great War – the electoral impact in the short run was much less obvious. There is no evidence of any kind of Labour breakthrough in these years. With only three MPs, Labour had still not managed to undermine the loyalty of the majority of working-class voters to Liberalism because the Liberals, after their election defeat in 1900, moved to marginalize their rivals on the socialist left and the Unionist right by successfully occupying the centre ground of Scottish politics.

In large part this manoeuvre was achieved through the dynamic support of organized groups of young men and women in the party. The Scottish Women's Liberal Federation had a membership of 25,000 in 174 branches in 1914, and in the elections of 1910 it had played a key role in canvassing and carrying out local registration work. It formed one part of a new and more formidable Liberal electoral machine. The other and even more influential element was the Young Scots Society. This was formed in the wake of the 1900 election defeat 'for the purpose of educating young men in the fundamental principles of Liberalism and of encouraging them in the study of social science and economics'.[4] Again, like the women's organization, the membership of the Young Scots climbed rapidly. By 1910 numbers had reached 2,500, which was not much less than the total membership of the ILP in Scotland in that year. On the eve of the Great War, the Young Scots were reckoned to have over 10,000 members in 50 branches.

They made a major contribution to the 'new' Liberalism and its electoral successes. First, they were renowned for their pioneering and aggressive campaigning techniques, involving the mass distribution of propaganda leaflets, organization of speaking tours of leading Liberal personalities such as Winston Churchill, the targeting of marginal seats and the holding of numerous open-air demonstrations. Even their Unionist and Conservative opponents admitted that this vigorous and determined approach was a key factor in the Liberal victory in 1910 and they then quickly tried to copy these successful campaigning tactics. Second, local constituencies were reinvigorated and, whenever possible, the Young Scots tried to put one of their own members up for selection as a parliamentary candidate. Their success can be seen in the fact that, between 1905 and 1914, 30 members of the Young Scots were elected to Westminster. Third, they recognized that the crucial political battle-ground was for the hearts and minds of the skilled working classes and so concentrated their fire on such social issues as poverty, housing and education. Their greatest achievement in this respect was in leading the Liberal campaign in favour of free trade against the proposals of Joseph Chamberlain for tariff protection on imports. The Young Scots relentlessly hammered home the message in open-air rallies and through mass distribution of leaflets that Chamberlain's programme was a direct threat to working-class living standards as it would inevitably lead to an increase in the price of food.

As Richard Finlay has argued it was also mainly because of the Young Scots' commitment to social reform that the issue of Scottish Home Rule became a central feature of national politics in the years immediately before the First World War. Scottish interest in Home Rule was nothing new; it had emerged in the 1880s, partly because of fears that the Irish were receiving preferential constitutional treatment ahead of the Scots and also because of concerns for administrative reforms that would make the union with England function more effectively. In 1885 the office of Secretary of Scotland was revived, the Scottish Office established in London and a Scottish Standing Committee was set up in 1894 to consider all Scottish legislation. In addition, a Scottish Home Rule Association was founded to campaign for a parliament in Edinburgh. Between 1886 and 1900, seven Scottish Home Rule motions were presented to parliament. Those submitted in 1894 and 1895 gained majorities but failed because of lack of parliamentary time. Nevertheless, the depth of the commitment to Home Rule can be questioned. The Liberal leadership were unenthusiastic, significant numbers of the Scottish party did not support it and it is sometimes difficult to determine whether genuine self-government was desired or only a further instalment of cosmetic administrative reform.

It was a different story after 1910. Home Rule was now regarded by the Young Scots as the *sine qua non* of social reform, which was being needlessly impeded in Scotland because of lack of parliamentary time in Westminster and was being delayed by the reactionary forces of English conservatism. It was claimed that 'there is not one single item in the whole programme of Radicalism or social reform today, which, if Scotland had powers to pass laws, would not have been carried out a quarter of a century ago'.[5] Practical steps were therefore taken to ensure that Home Rule became a party priority, including seeking public pledges from candidates in support of a Scottish parliament. The new impetus for constitutional change came within an ace of success when a Home Rule Bill passed its second reading in the House of Commons in May 1914. Unfortunately, the chances of its reaching the statute book were killed off when war broke out. Nevertheless, the new centrality of the constitutional issue had important repercussions for Scottish politics. The Conservatives and Liberal Unionists closed ranks in defence of the union and empire and in 1912 finally merged as the Unionist Party. The Young Scots also opened up fresh divisions within the Liberal Party as some thought their radicalism too extreme and their methods too intimidating. In the early years of their existence they had been a crucial force shaping the 'new' Liberalism. Now on the eve of war they were seen to be a powerful divisive element by the more conservative influences in Liberalism and they were also condemned for forging links with Labour. The patterns were already emerging that would contribute to the radical realignment of Scottish politics after 1918 and with it the final disintegration of the old Liberal hegemony in Scotland.

2

At first this seemed an unlikely scenario. The Liberals, as the party of government, gained from the national mood of patriotic fervour which swept the country in 1914. A few socialists did vociferously condemn the capitalist war but the trade unions and most workers were all united with the government in the great crusade against the German enemy. Thousands of young Scotsmen flocked to join the colours as the nation provided more voluntary recruits in proportion to population than any other part of the United Kingdom. Of the 157 battalions which comprised the British Expeditionary Force, 22 were Scottish regiments. However, the euphoria was short-lived. The terrible carnage on the Western Front and the endless list of casualties soon changed the collective mood to one of national grief. The human losses were enormous and unprecedented. Of the 557,000 Scots who enlisted in all services, 26.4 per cent lost their lives. This compares with an average death rate of 11.8 per cent for the rest of the British army between 1914 and 1918. Of all the combatant nations, only the Serbs and the Turks had higher per capita mortality rates, but this was primarily because of disease in the trenches rather than a direct result of losses in battle. The main reason for the higher-than-average casualties among the Scottish soldiers was that they were regarded as excellent, aggressive shock troops who could be depended upon to lead the line in the first hours of battle. The impact of the ensuing slaughter was made more devastating by the method of recruitment which often concentrated soldiers from the same village, district and occupation in the same unit. During major engagements, such as the Battle of the Somme, the death columns of local newspapers were crammed with the names of the killed and wounded. Not surprisingly, as the carnage continued inexorably, so the Liberal government drew growing criticism for its inept handling of the conflict and its failure to bring it to a conclusion.

Problems were also emerging closer to home. During the war, Clydeside had become a vast national arsenal for the mass production of ships, shells, guns and other munitions. However, in 1915 it became the focus of some of the most famous industrial disputes in Scottish labour history, involving the engineers in the great workshops of Weirs, Albion Motors, Beardmores and Barr and Stroud. Before 1914, tensions had been increasing in the engineering industry as employers turned

309

away from one-off jobs which depended on the precision skills of the skilled men to the use of mass-production methods based on turret lathes and universal milling and grinding machines. In the first two years of war the government's demand for a massive increase in production accelerated this process of innovation while at the same time encouraging employers to take on unskilled male and female labour to meet output targets. The threat to the status of the engineers was reinforced by the appointment by Lloyd George in 1915 of William Weir, who had the reputation of being one of Clydeside's most anti-union employers, as the controller of munitions for Scotland. In the 'Treasury Agreement' of March 1915 the engineering unions had agreed to ban all strikes for the duration of the war but only on condition that the government would legislate to restore pre-war working practices at the end of hostilities. The promise that this would be done was regarded at grass-roots level with open distrust which culminated in a series of strikes and disputes in the engineering firms of the Clyde in 1915. They were all unofficial actions and were associated with a group of shop stewards, the Clyde Workers' Committee, among whom were several members connected with the Socialist Labour Party such as William Gallacher, Arthur McManus and John Muir. The aim of the engineers was to protect their own craft position and standard of living and the rank and file had no wider revolutionary intentions. However, the government detected seditious influences and, after a meeting held by Lloyd George to convince the Clyde Workers' Committee of the advantages of dilution was disrupted, the leading shop stewards were deported from the west of Scotland in February 1916 and the Labour newspaper, *Forward*, was suppressed. It looked as if the Liberal government was now firmly on the side of the bosses and against the rights of workers. Their first and apparently their only priority was the successful prosecution of the war against Germany as total war demanded that individual liberties be subordinated to the essential needs of the state. This was a fundamental rejection of the essential Liberal ideals which had helped to ensure electoral dominance in Scotland for many decades and it was a lesson not lost on those who were already becoming critical of the government for its incompetent prosecution of the war. Lloyd George added fuel to the fire when he alleged that munitions production on the Clyde was being hampered by the excessive drunkenness of the region's labour force.

Even more significant, however, in the long run than the industrial troubles of Clydeside was the Rent Strike in Glasgow of 1915. The disputes of the engineering workers involved one important group bent on the protection of craft and sectional interests. The rent strikes affected whole communities and attracted the support of the entire Labour movement in the city. Glasgow's housing had long been notorious as the worst in urban Britain. Nearly half the population in 1911 lived in houses of two rooms, and more than an eighth in single rooms. This was one major area of working-class life where the Liberal welfare reforms had had no impact. The war made a bad situation infinitely worse. An influx of 20,000 munitions workers and the stoppage of building intensified overcrowding and led to a steep increase in rents in some districts. In areas such as Govan and Partick, rents rose by an average of 12–23 per cent between the spring of 1914 and October 1915. This soon produced a furious response. There was a deep sense of injustice as landlords were seen to be profiteering at the expense of families whose sons and husbands were serving their country at the front. Very quickly a massive rent strike built up and, by the end of 1915, over 20,000 tenants were refusing to pay the increases. The sense of moral outrage was graphically illustrated on some of the placards carried in demonstrations: 'Our husbands are fighting Prussianism in France and we are fighting the Prussians of Partick.'[6] Whole communities were united in the struggle, with wives and mothers playing the key role within the tenements to ensure solidarity and resist eviction. Crucially, too, the tenants won the strong support of political activists, including left-wing leaders of the suffragettes, ILP councillors, the Glasgow Trades Council and the Glasgow Central Labour Party. When some defaulting tenants were taken to court in November 1915 for arrestment of wages, munitions and shipyard workers downed tools and threatened an indefinite strike if the summoned men were either fined or evicted. The government was already considering rent control legislation and, fearful of an interruption of vital supplies for the war effort, finally acted to peg rents for the duration of hostilities.

It is doubtful, however, if this decision gained it much credit with the working classes of Scotland's biggest city because for a time it had been seen to give tacit support to rack-renting landlords. The Rent Strike, on the other hand, had demonstrated the power of workers' solidarity and also enormously increased the prestige and influence of the ILP. While the Liberal government denounced strikes and disputes as unpatriotic and came across as repressive, the ILP supported the workers' grievances over prices, rents and the evils of profiteering. The party's Scottish membership tripled between 1914 and 1918, and it gained a particularly important influence among the Glasgow working classes through forging effective networks in trade unions and many workplaces of the city. While relationships between the governors and the governed in Scotland deteriorated, the Liberal administration itself was in trouble. Asquith had formed an all-party coalition in 1915 but, at the end of 1916, Lloyd George split the party by forcing him out of office. Most Scottish Liberal MPs remained loyal to Asquith, partly because Lloyd George created a ministry dominated by Tories. Liberalism now seemed in disarray.

Among the working classes, Labour was the party likely to benefit most from Liberal misfortunes. It gained a huge potential advantage from the franchise reform of 1918. At a stroke the electorate tripled, from 779,000 in 1910 to 2,205,000 in 1918, and the vast majority of these new voters were drawn from the working classes. Labour achieved immediate success in the elections of 1918 by gaining a third of Scottish votes, more than 10 times better than any of its performances in the past. The vagaries of the electoral system, however, meant that it returned only eight MPs. It is very likely also that the result was significantly affected by a defective register and the fact that many ex-servicemen were unable to vote. In the next few years, however, a number of factors helped to advance the Labour cause further. A key development was the transfer to it of much of the Irish Catholic vote, which had for so many years been loyal to the Liberal Party which was seen as the best hope for the achievement of Irish Home Rule. This support lost its rationale with the partition of Ireland in 1920 and the formation of the Irish Free State. The Irish Catholic community in Scotland was soon converted to Labour. *The Times* argued that in the general election of 1922 the Catholic vote was 'a primary factor' in Labour support, since it made up around 20 per cent of the electorate. A few years earlier, the editor of Scotland's leading Catholic newspaper had explained Labour's likely attractions for his co-religionaries:

The formation of a powerful democratic Labour Party gives us an opportunity. Formerly the weakness of Labour impelled us to give our support where we thought it would do most for Ireland ... Toryism was an impossible thing. Liberalism, unhappily, embodied a great deal of anti-Catholic narrowness and bigotry ... The new Labour Party is indeed and in truth the people's party and as a vast majority of the Irish in Great Britain are toilers it is to that party they turn, drawn by bonds of affinity or antagonism unthinkable.[7]

At the same time, the post-war coalition government of Lloyd George patently failed to deliver reconstruction or the promised 'homes fit for heroes', while the economic boom of 1918–20 quickly turned into the slump of 1921. Labour's standing rose as, with the collapse of the Asquith Liberals in the election in 1918, it was now the only credible party not in government. It also increasingly attracted members of progressive views from the older parties, such as the prominent Liberal, R. B. Haldane, who saw Labour as the only hope for maintaining social cohesion in the new age of mass democracy. Labour also excelled in organization. A formidable election machine was built up in Glasgow under the Catholic Patrick Dollan who combined administrative flair with crusading passion. The focus was constantly on increased registration of working people on the voters' roll and on the local bread-and-butter issues of housing, rents and jobs. As John Wheatley put it, 'at our meetings we talked local politics, advocating the claims of the Far East of Glasgow rather than the Near East of Europe'.[8]

The reward came in the 1922 election, when Labour became the largest party in Scotland, returned 29 MPs to parliament, 10 of them from Glasgow, and took 32 per cent of the total votes cast. It was a notable and historic victory, even if elsewhere in Scotland the success was not quite so spectacular. In Edinburgh, for instance, Labour achieved less than 10 per cent of the overall vote. Nevertheless, the national political landscape had changed. Labour managed to push its share of the vote even higher in the elections of 1924 and 1929 and at the same time did consistently better than the party's performance in the south in all the general elections to 1935. When the Labour MPs left St Enoch's Station in Glasgow for Westminster in 1922, many thought that the dawn of a new age had broken. Several, like James Maxton, David Kirkwood, Emmanuel Shinwell and John Wheatley, were veterans of the Clydeside industrial and political struggles of the war years and they delivered emotional and eloquent speeches on the platform to an enthusiastic crowd, in which they pledged themselves 'to promote the welfare of their fellow-citizens and the well-being of mankind' and at the same time celebrated their links with the old radical tradition of Scotland by leading their supporters in the fervent singing of Covenanting psalms.

The emergence of 'Red Clydeside' and the Labour breakthrough was only one part of the realignment of Scottish politics after the Great War. The most decisive feature was the complete collapse of Liberalism as an effective electoral force. This did not happen immediately but by the election of 1924 the humiliation of the once great Liberal Party was complete and apparent for all to see. It was routed and reduced to a rump of eight seats, five of which were located in the Highlands and Islands. Such a catastrophic decline had several explanations, some of which have already been indicated in this chapter. Labour had seduced much of Liberalism's old working-class constituency, gained the lion's share of the vote of the new post-1918 electorate and converted the Irish Catholics to its cause. Ironically, Labour itself owed much to pre-war Liberal radical policies for reform of the land, education, housing and Scottish Home Rule, while a whole stream of progressive Liberals also moved over to Labour in the years after 1918; they included the Revd James Barr, J. L. Kinloch, Rosslyn Mitchell and Walter Murray. But in the class-based politics of the inter-war period Liberals, as the archetypal party of the centre, were likely also to come under pressure from the Right. The main political issue for the middle classes of Scotland in the early 1920s was the need to combine to stop the advance of socialism.

Scottish Labour was reformist rather than revolutionary, but the troubles on the Clyde during the war had raised the spectre of the 'Red Menace', despite the fact that the conflict was about pay and conditions rather than the founding of a socialist utopia by means of a workers' uprising. But middle-class fears were soon inflamed by the revolution in Russia and by a further display of workers' militancy in Glasgow in January 1919. A 40-hour strike had been called to support the demand of the Scottish Trades Union Congress that the working week should be cut to help reduce unemployment which was increasing as demobilization accelerated. The strikers were trying to prevent the removal of wartime regulation of wages and control of rents. The strike culminated in a mass demonstration of around 100,000 people in Glasgow's George Square which ended in a 'riot' as the police charged the crowds with drawn batons. The evidence suggests that there was no revolutionary conspiracy, despite the flaunting of the red flag, and that the disorder was sparked off by police over-reaction. This, however, was not how the government saw it at the time. The Scottish Secretary advised his Cabinet colleagues that the situation in Glasgow was not a strike but 'a Bolshevist rising'. That day, 12,000 troops were sent in, six tanks were stationed in the Cattle Market and machine-guns were placed at the post office and the hotels. Glasgow was an occupied city.

The strike soon petered out and the 40-hour week was not granted. However, 'Bloody Friday', as it soon came to be known, had important longer-term political effects. To many workers of the city it was yet another example of government repression that helped to deepen their disillusionment with the existing political establishment and hasten the development of support for Labour. Even more crucially, the events of January 1919, set as they were against the background of the Russian Revolution, sent shock waves through the ranks of the middle classes and crystallized their need for a political party that could halt the irresistible march of socialism. Whether this would be the Liberals or the Unionists was not at first clear. The Unionists were stronger in organizational terms and were more robustly anti-socialist, while the Liberals still had several parliamentary seats in 1919. The outcome would be decided over the following five years.

In the event, the Unionists proved the more reliable party in resisting the socialist threat. The defining moment came in 1924 when Asquith decided to throw Liberal support behind the minority Labour government, an action that was widely interpreted as one of treachery and class betrayal. United Free Church clergymen were said to have left the Liberals in large numbers at this time; the business community reacted with horror and newspapers which had previously given loyal support to the Liberal cause changed sides. The main Glasgow Liberal newspaper, the *Daily Record*, threw its weight behind Unionism which alone, it argued, could now be trusted to deliver strong and stable government. But as I. G. C. Hutchison has shown, the Liberals were also crushed by other forces. The Scottish establishment swung behind the Unionists, as the élite of the legal profession was overwhelmingly Unionist in sympathy between the wars; the leadership of the Church of Scotland moved to the right and most clergymen denounced the General Strike of 1926. While the General Assembly advocated restrictions on Irish Catholic immigration, it showed little interest in the contemporary social evils of large-scale unemployment and increasing poverty. From the mid-1920s, all the morning newspapers in the main cities became Tory in sympathy. A significant press development was the transformation of the widely read *People's Journal* from a powerful radical weekly full of social comment to an outlet for sentimental stories and knitting patterns. The Liberal press was 'effectively annihilated' in this period.[9]

In addition, however, the Unionist Party took advantage of this more favourable context to develop a more aggressive campaigning strategy, which focused specifically on the new female electorate and also revived the Junior Imperial League in order to reach younger people. By the end of the 1920s it had around 20,000 members. The inter-war period was therefore remarkably successful for the Tories in Scotland. They had more MPs than any other party in no fewer than four of the seven general elections between 1918 and 1939, a record they had managed to equal only once in the decades between the 1832 Reform Act and the Great War.

3

Between 1924 and the 1930s, Scottish politics were determined above all else by the state of the economy. The memories of the decades between the two world wars are those of material disaster and social tragedy. Industrial depression, mass unemployment, hunger marches and life on the dole are the recurrent themes most closely and popularly associated with this era in British history. But in recent years some scholars have produced new perspectives on the English experience in the 1920s and 1930s. They argue that the reality of misery in some areas and in particular periods has to be set against the evidence of steadily rising incomes, the emergence of 'new' industries and even boom conditions in some regions, especially in the Midlands and the south. Contraction in traditional manufacturing was compensated for by vibrant growth in the motor industry, electrical engineering, chemicals and building. The argument runs that England between the wars was experiencing economic transformation rather than absolute and inevitable national decline.

Some of this revisionism, as suggested in Chapter 12, can be applied to Scotland with qualifications. Around four in five of the Scottish labour force remained in employment even during the worst years of recession, and for them there were clear gains in living standards as real incomes rose and low interest rates made for easier credit facilities. Even as the dole queues lengthened, Scotland experienced a leisure revolution in these years. The new popular craze was going to the 'pictures', especially after 1929 when the talkies arrived. In the 1930s larger towns had three or four cinemas apiece and Glasgow an incredible

127. Glasgow, the metropolis of the most depressed region in the land, was also the nation's dancing capital, with young men and women flocking in their thousands to the city's 30 dance halls. Home entertainment was also revolutionized by the radio (or wireless) which, by the end of the 1930s, was to be found in over 40 per cent of Scottish homes. There were also profound differences of experience between areas and classes: in the west, whole communities faced economic ruin; Edinburgh and parts of the Lothians weathered the storm much better. The business and professional classes who were in work never had it so good. Car ownership increased significantly, while the fringes of most Scottish cities and towns came to be colonized by street after street of new bungalows, confirming that some social groups at least had money to spend. The rash of 'bungalow belts' proliferated to such an extent that the Saltire Society, founded in 1935 to promote Scottish cultural interests, denounced them as a 'form of English invasion'.

The complexity of Scottish experience in the 1930s was well captured by Edwin Muir in his *Scottish Journey*, which was published in 1935. He encountered various Scotlands in the course of his travels. The evidence of middle-class consumerism abounds in his comments. The petrol stations were spreading on the road from Glasgow to Kilmarnock, and beside Burns's cottage in Ayr the suburban street 'was crammed with parked cars'. Muir also notes the tea-rooms in Edinburgh as the exclusive preserve of the middle and upper classes, where 'the working-class, the trade union and class-conscious proletariat' rarely entered. He describes his family home on a street in the south side of Glasgow, not far distant from some of the worst slums in Europe:

Most of the people in it were better paid clerks, shopkeepers, foremen, buyers, commercial travellers: a respectable church-going lot intent on making money and rising, as the saying goes, in the world. They lived in what seemed to me comfort: that is, they had several rooms in their houses, containing safes, arm-chairs, pianos, pictures and knick-knacks of all kinds. When they went out they were well-dressed.

But Muir was also aware of the terrible human waste and suffering inflicted by the Depression and this, above all else, coloured his vision of Scotland in the 1930s. He speaks of 'a silent clearance' advancing in the manufacturing districts of the west: 'the surroundings of industrialisation remain, but industry itself is vanishing like a dream'. This was a mortal threat to the future of the nation because, even if other areas were not as badly hit, the west was 'the heart of Scotland'. His 'main impression' after his journey had ended was deeply pessimistic, even despairing: 'Scotland is gradually being emptied of its population, its spirit, its wealth, industry, art, intellect, and innate character.' And Muir was not alone. Other commentators portrayed a nation in terminal decline. George Malcolm Thomson put it succinctly: 'The first fact about the Scot is that he is a man eclipsed. The Scots are a dying race.'[10]

This collapse in confidence was rooted in the disastrous impact of an economic crisis that was deeper and lasted longer than in most parts of England outside some of its northern industrial counties. Between 1924 and 1937, the growth of Gross Domestic Product for the whole of the UK averaged 2.2 per cent; but Roy Campbell's figures for Scotland alone show a much poorer performance, with an annual average of 0.4 per cent falling to an absolute *decline* of 2.0 per cent in the depths of the Depression between 1928 and 1932. By 1931, Scottish industrial production was less than the level achieved in 1913; over 26 per cent of the insured workforce was idle, almost double the English average; and 100,000 men were reckoned to be 'permanently surplus' to working requirements. In the shipbuilding and engineering trades, the aristocracy of labour were laid off in their thousands while in the worst-hit areas of Lanarkshire and Dumbartonshire even the lower-middle classes faced personal ruin as demand for their services disappeared. It was a sign of the times that even the trickle of new university graduates struggled to find teaching posts in the 1930s. Many more Scots would have faced a grim future on the dole had it not been for the unprecedented levels of emigration in the 1920s, which meant that the total population of the nation actually fell by 40,000 between 1921 and 1931.

The devastating impact of economic collapse prompted a mood of pessimistic introspection, deepened by the fact that the nation was still coming to terms with the terrible losses sustained during the Great War. In cities, towns and villages all over the country memorials were raised to the war dead with the full panoply of civic and military ceremonial. Sir Robert Lorimer's National War Memorial was constructed at Edinburgh Castle between 1924 and 1927 and immediately became an extraordinarily popular place of pilgrimage. The numbers who visited in the 1920s were so great that the original rough stone of the floor was worn smooth after only a few years. As the authors of a *History of Scottish Architecture* (1990) point out, the Memorial could be seen not only as a commemoration of the glorious dead but as a monument to the days of imperial greatness which were now passing away. Increasingly, also, the nation was confronted with the daunting realities of its many domestic social problems. Government commissions and academic surveys brutally exposed the harsh facts. The distinguished nutritionist, John Boyd Orr, showed that in the 1930s infant mortality in Scotland was the worst in western Europe apart from Spain and Portugal. Over 300,000 houses were built between the wars and two-thirds of these were in the public sector but even this achievement failed to keep pace with the ongoing decay of old housing stock and the huge scale of the problem of endemic overcrowding inherited from the years before 1914. Yet no immediate solution was possible because of the rigorous constraints on public expenditure enforced by the economic crisis. By 1939, half of Scottish housing stock was reckoned to be inadequate and gross overcrowding was over five times worse than in England.

The majority of Scots prospered in these years because they were fortunate to escape the worst ravages of unemployment. But the hopeless plight of the very large numbers of their fellow citizens imposed acute strain for a time on the social fabric of Scotland. The razor gangs of Glasgow, captured in such graphic detail in the novel *No Mean City*, first became notorious during the recession which soon followed the post-war boom. More seriously, the baleful spectre of sectarian conflict loomed over the Depression years. The Church of Scotland and the United Free Church led a public campaign to enforce rigorous controls on Irish immigration and denounced the 'Scoto-Irish' as an inferior race who could not be assimilated despite the fact the number of migrants had actually slowed to a trickle in the 1920s. Job discrimination on the basis of religion increased in the labour market as the number of workers was ruthlessly cut back and the authority of chargehands and foremen who were often of masonic and/or Orange background was consolidated: 'For young unemployed Catholics, this was the era of "What school did you go to? Were you in the Boys Brigade? and Who was your Sunday School teacher?"'[11] In the early 1930s the anti-Catholic Scottish Protestant League won six seats on Glasgow Corporation, polling 67,000 votes against Labour's 63,000. Significantly, its main support came from the skilled working-class areas of Cathcart, Govanhill and Kinning Park, which had been very badly hit by unemployment between 1931 and 1933. In Edinburgh, John Cormack's Protestant Action advocated the disenfranchisement of Roman

Catholics and their expulsion from Scotland and in the summer of 1935 it provoked the worst sectarian incidents of the inter-war years. In the event, the potential for serious inter-communal strife was contained and Glasgow did not become a second Belfast. Labour, Unionist and Nationalist politicians distanced themselves from the extremists and the Scottish press gave them little support. Indeed, it was the *Glasgow Weekly Herald* which did much to discredit John Cormack by publishing an unedited version of one of his letters which revealed him as semi-literate. The *Glasgow Herald*, the paper of the west of Scotland middle class, undermined the Kirk's case for immigration controls by demonstrating in a series of carefully researched and authoritative articles that there was little factual foundation for most of its claims.

Nevertheless, racism and sectarianism, even if contained, were still disturbing signs of a national malaise which also seemed to affect the creative spirit of the nation. It is true that the dark years of economic depression also saw a remarkable literary revival, led by Christopher Murray Grieve, 'Hugh MacDiarmid', Scotland's greatest poetic genius since Burns, and including such major figures as Lewis Grassic Gibbon, Neil Gunn, Edwin Muir, Fionn MacColla, Naomi Mitchison and James Bridie. This 'Scottish Renaissance' was undeniably distinguished but much of it had little direct impact on the popular consciousness in the short term. MacDiarmid had a vision of a nation born again through adoption and use of the old Scots tongue. He also fought hard to restore a genuinely national culture. But he himself questioned the influence of his poetry in his 'Second Hymn to Lenin':

> Are my poems spoken in the factories and fields,
> In the streets o'town?
> Gin they're no then I'm failin' to dae
> What I ocht to ha' dune.

The truth was that his appeal was limited. As Christopher Harvie acidly comments: 'The ordinary people still read the Dundee press and went to Burns Suppers, while MacDiarmid's later poetry grew more cerebral and élitist.'[12] Indeed, much of MacDiarmid's creative genius was in response to his personal perception of the nation's sorry state. He brilliantly explored the malaise in his 2,600-line masterpiece, 'A Drunk Man Looks at the Thistle' (1926) and in his polemical journalism he scathingly denounced the mediocrity of provincial Scotland and its ruling classes with the linguistic vitriol for which he was famous, 'the whole gang of high mucky-mucks, famous fatheads . . . and all the touts and toadies and lickspittles of the English ascendancy'.

For all its literary excellence and exuberance, the 'Scottish Renaissance' failed to inspire any broader flowering of Scottish culture in the inter-war years and it was concern about the nation's cultural heritage that led to the formation of the Saltire Society in 1935. Historical research was in the doldrums, few monographs were produced, and the *Scottish Historical Review* ceased publication in 1929. It was said that sacks of valuable documents lay mouldering in the basement of Register House where they had been stored over a century before. In architecture, the era was at first one of conformity and adherence to tradition. Economic constraints and the end of the age of great patrons meant that most building carried out was of council houses and functional schools. A good deal of this was routine and unimaginative. Only later, with the development of Beaux-Arts modernity (often seen as the 'architecture of leisure' in cinemas, ice-rinks and swimming pools) and the innovative work of young architects such as Basil Spence and Giacomo (Jack) Coia for the 1938 Glasgow Empire Exhibition, was there a real renewal of creative vitality. Social and economic conditions were even less favourable to art. The 'Scottish Colourists', S. J. Peploe, Leslie Hunter, F. C. B. Cadell and J. D. Fergusson, had established their reputations and completed most of their best work before 1918. After the Great War no figure of international stature emerged and the middle-class clientele, who now dominated the art market as wealthy patronage disappeared, tended to go for the familiar and conventional rather than the adventurous in an age of insecurity.

The universities also experienced a marked decline from their former eminence. While the numbers of students elsewhere in the UK were rising, the fall in Scotland was from 10,400 in 1924 to 9,900 in 1937. The Scottish institutions were manifestly falling behind in research and, as a disturbing illustration of this, more and more of the brightest first degree students were moving south to the leading English institutions for postgraduate work, especially in science and technology. Lack of investment in research facilities was one factor, but the universities were also doubtless constrained, as were other areas of Scottish cultural life, by the slaughter of young talent on the killing fields of Flanders. Some of those who made their mark in the technologies of the twentieth century tended not to have links with the older universities. Both John

Logie Baird, the television pioneer, and John (later Lord) Reith, the first Director General of the BBC and its main formative influence, were products of Glasgow's Royal Technical College (later the University of Strathclyde). John Grierson did not attend university but became the most influential documentary film-maker of the age by encouraging the realistic treatment of social issues in such classics as *Drifters* of 1929.

4

The economic trauma of the inter-war years also shaped the politics of Scotland. For its supporters, Labour was the party of social justice best equipped to defend the working classes from the miseries of mass unemployment, poor housing and falling living standards. But Labour did not fulfil these high hopes and expectations. In May 1924 it became the party of government for the first time, albeit in a minority administration with Liberal support. Its period in office was short-lived, as in October of that year the Conservatives won a crushing victory, though the socialist vote held up better in Scotland than in England. The achievements of that first Labour government were few and far between and in the social field were confined to John Wheatley's important Housing Act, which significantly extended subsidies to local authorities and encouraged a marked increase in new building. Even this legislation, which Wheatley had guided through the Commons with consummate skill, was curtailed in 1926.

As economic problems became ever more pressing, Labour again became the largest single party in Scotland in 1929, winning 38 of the 74 constituencies and confirming that it now had electoral appeal well outside its traditional heartlands in Clydeside. But this victory was but the prelude to disaster. Economic difficulties slid rapidly into financial crisis with the onset of the Great Depression. In response, the Prime Minister, Ramsay MacDonald, formed a 'government of national emergency' with Conservatives, a few Liberals and only a rump of the parliamentary Labour Party. The left wing, including the ILP and the trade unions, stood apart since they were wholly opposed to any planned reduction in welfare benefits. When a general election was called in 1931, the National Government won an overwhelming victory, the greatest ever in British electoral history, and Labour in Scotland was reduced to a mere seven MPs. In reality, despite being led by a Labour

Prime Minister, the new administration was solidly founded on Conservative support, and this secured a Unionist hegemony in Scotland that would last from 1931 until the end of the Second World War. Labour north of the border was far from being annihilated. The concern to protect welfare benefits gave it a continuing loyalty among the industrial working classes which was clearly shown in the party's steady progress in local elections. By 1935 it controlled 19 burghs, including Glasgow. But this was poor compensation for the many years spent languishing in the parliamentary wilderness where countless numbers of Labour supporters were being exposed to the ravages of structural unemployment.

The failure of Labour between the wars was to some extent due to factors outside its own control. It did achieve power in two elections but on both occasions this depended on Liberal support and that required compromises to be made. Socialist policies were of necessity diluted and the party became committed to a gradualist and reformist approach which alienated and demoralized many of its staunchest radical supporters, including most of the ILP. Despite this, Labour's opponents were still able to brand it as the party of 'bolshevism' and a revolutionary menace to British civilization. Thus the 'red letter', supposed to be from Zinoviev, head of the Russian Comintern, and believed to contain instructions to the Communist Party to subvert Britain through infiltration of the Labour Party, was exploited for maximum propaganda benefit in the general election of 1924. In 1931 a central theme was the portrayal of Labour as a wild revolutionary movement, threatening property by schemes of widespread nationalization and placing the entire economy at risk by its financial adventures.

But Labour also had itself to blame. Like the Liberals and the Conservatives the party had no intellectual answer to the problems of the inter-war economy. A Labour Chancellor of the Exchequer like Phillip Snowden stuck rigidly to the economic orthodoxies of the time. Only latterly were Keynesian ideas of full-scale public intervention espoused by Scottish Labour figures like Tom Johnston. It is doubtful anyway if much could have been achieved through intervention because of the sheer scale of unemployment and structural crisis, but in any event a Labour government bent on wholesale job-creation would have encountered resolute opposition from the Treasury which was absolutely opposed to the funding of private industry and confined support mainly to public works in roads and housing. Throughout the period after 1926 Labour also seemed more intent on developing organizational structures and maintaining central control within the party than on engaging in the search for innovative policies. In 1926, John Wheatley published an ILP document, *Socialism in Our Time*, which encapsulated his ideas on nationalization and public spending, among key issues. He had a track record of effective and practical implementation of socialist ideals through his housing legislation of 1924 but he failed to achieve ministerial office in 1929 and died the following year. The second Labour government of 1929 crystallized the tensions and differences between left and right which also weakened the party's capacity to achieve a long-term electoral impact. Open hostilities between the ILP and the Labour Party began with the failure of the General Strike of 1926. As ILP chairman, the charismatic James Maxton vigorously supported the strike and roundly condemned the Labour leadership and the trade unions for their timidity which had led to its failure. The wounds became deeper during the Labour government of 1929 when a bitter struggle ensued between the Cabinet and the ILP which demanded nationalization and massive government intervention to cure Scotland's economic ills. The decision by Ramsay MacDonald to form a national government was seen as the final betrayal of socialist principles and in 1932 the ILP finally broke with Labour.

Earlier, the party had abandoned its historic commitment to Home Rule. Before he boarded the train for Westminster in 1922, Wheatley had proclaimed that 'there was no subject in Scotland that arouses as much enthusiasm as home rule'.[13] By the mid-1920s, however, attitudes were changing. Labour was becoming more centralist and the party hierarchy in London was developing greater authority in Scotland. The Scottish Trades Union Congress abandoned its support for Home Rule in 1931, as the harsh economic climate meant that it saw the future in the formation of larger British unions with industrial muscle which would help repair the serious damage done to the movement by the catastrophic failure of the General Strike in 1926. The Scots on their own would be vulnerable, not least because Scotland was suffering more than most regions of the UK from the effects of the recession. Even John Wheatley, Scottish Labour's leading thinker of the period, changed his mind in the new circumstances. He argued that only the power of the British state as a whole could protect the working classes from the predatory nature of international capitalism. Scotland's particular problems were so acute that they could be alleviated only through deploying the economic resources of Britain as a whole. As his colleague Tom Johnston put it, 'What purpose would there be in our getting a Scottish Parliament in Edinburgh if it has to administer an emigration system, a glorified poor law and a desert?'[14]

It was the growing indifference and, in some cases, the outright hostility of the Labour movement to Home Rule that helped trigger the formation of the National Party of Scotland in 1928. At first its main aim was to demonstrate that Home Rule was popular with the electorate and by so doing convince Labour that it neglected the national cause at its peril. Yet the aggressive intervention of nationalists in by-elections against Labour candidates had exactly the opposite effect and the gulf between the two parties soon widened. Undeniably, however, there seemed good reason to anticipate an increase in nationalist support as the crisis in the Scottish economy deepened. According to the Secretary of State in the national government, the Depression had caused some to seek a solution by the setting up of a parliament in Edinburgh. That concerns were not confined to the Left in Scottish politics was shown in 1932 when, after a secession from the Cathcart Unionist Association, which blamed Westminster for indifference to the serious difficulties north of the border, the moderate right-wing Scottish Party was established. This eventually joined with the National Party of Scotland to form the Scottish National Party in 1934.

However, the nationalists failed to capitalize on the anxieties of the electorates. In the general election of 1935 the SNP failed to win any of the seven seats it contested and in the five in which nationalists had stood before the vote for the party went down significantly. They may have been able to argue that the blight of the Great Depression proved the bankruptcy of the union so far as Scotland was concerned but the SNP had no coherent alternative strategy of economic reconstruction to put forward in its place. For its part, the government insisted that it would be suicidal for Scotland to go it alone at a time of serious recession and increasing international tension in Europe. In addition, it sought to appease national sentiment by moving the Scottish Office to Edinburgh in 1937, a development that has rightly been seen as having '. . . immense symbolic value, making Edinburgh once again a seat of government, truly a capital, rather than just the headquarters of the Kirk and Judiciary'.[15] The SNP soon started to disintegrate into competing factions of Left and Right. Party discipline collapsed and on the eve of the Second World War nationalism had ceased to be a coherent political force in Scotland for the time being.

The clear winners in these troubled years were the Unionists, who enjoyed undisputed supremacy in Scottish politics until 1945 in part because of the fracturing of their Labour and nationalist opponents. Moreover, despite the depth of the crisis that had overwhelmed Scotland, public protest against the government was surprisingly muted and confined to the National Unemployed Workers' Movement, demonstrations against cuts in the employment benefit and the hated 'means test' in 1931, followed by the hunger marches of 1933 and 1934. But the Unionists also worked hard to consolidate their hegemony. Labour was portrayed as a party of revolutionaries who would threaten savings, pensions and investments with programmes of nationalization. Unionists also feared the electoral threat posed by Liberals who, despite their much-weakened position, in many seats were the main political alternative. This was especially true in the rural areas where the farmers had in recent years become one of the main bastions of a rejuvenated unionism. The party policy was therefore to conciliate the Liberals by reaching deals on individual elections, moving further towards the centre and opposing any connection with fascism or with the Protestant extremists in Glasgow and Edinburgh and on four occasions promoting Liberals to the post of Scottish Secretary in Unionist or Unionist-dominated governments.

Efforts were made under the Scottish Secretary, Walter Elliot, a 'One Nation' Tory, to address the threat of nationalism and the economic crisis that was devastating parts of Scotland. Elliot was committed to progressive social policies, he was willing to use state intervention to tackle them and was frustrated at the seeming indifference of Whitehall to the acute problems in Scotland. His anger boiled over in 1932 when a decision was made to scrap the Cunard cruiser:

The question is not so simple from the point of view of workers on the Clyde. Government can scrap cruisers and claim the money for something else. But the people of Scotland know that officials are too apt to spend money saved on bridges in London and carrying out other work in England, while there is more than enough unemployment in Scotland.[16]

During Elliot's tenure of office, the national government developed agencies such as the Scottish Economic Committee, the Scottish

Development Council and the Special Areas Reconstruction Association to create jobs and promote economic diversification. The results only scraped the surface of a vast and intractable problem which was at last beginning to become more manageable as once again rearmament expanded employment in the heavy industries. But the agencies were nevertheless an important step forward and helped to prepare the way for the much greater state involvement in the economic system during the war and after 1945. Elliot's greatest achievement was the transfer to Edinburgh of the Scottish Office in 1937. Until that date, the administration of Scottish affairs was fragmented, with the Scottish Office in London and various boards operating from Edinburgh. With the location of the Scottish Office in a permanent home at St Andrews House in Edinburgh, the old boards were streamlined into a coherent structure of four departments in the areas of agriculture, education, health and home. Elliot was motivated by a desire to bring a more efficient form of administrative devolution to Scotland while also firmly maintaining political control at the centre of power in London. But it was indeed ironic that it was a Unionist minister who helped to boost the nation's sense of identity at a time when the cause of Home Rule was in the doldrums and the nationalists were marginalized by electoral humiliation.

15

The Scottish City

In the decades before 1830, urban growth had been fast and extensive in Scotland. However, the majority of Scots still lived on the farm, the croft and in the rural village. In the 1840s, for instance, under a third of the population was to be found in settlements of 5,000 or above. Thereafter, the growth of cities and towns was continuous and relentless so that by the early twentieth century Scotland, after England, had become the most urbanized country in the world. In 1911, 60 per cent of Scots lived in centres of more than 5,000 in population and 50 per cent in towns of more than 20,000 inhabitants. In effect the urban share of national population had doubled between 1831 and 1911. It was inevitable that growth on this scale would eventually slow down and this was indeed the case, especially in the 1920s and 1930s, when difficult economic conditions in the industrial heartlands of the central Lowlands helped to decelerate the process of urban expansion. Nevertheless, the urban population continued to increase, albeit at a slower rate. In 1981 there were 57 per cent more town and city dwellers than there had been in 1891.

The main feature of this explosion in urbanism was the increasing dominance of the 'big four' cities of Edinburgh, Glasgow, Dundee and Aberdeen. Around one in five Scots lived in them in 1851 and by 1911 this proportion had risen to one in three. City growth continued until the 1950s. In that decade, no less than 37.6 per cent of the population were city dwellers. No single Scottish city had the dominant metropolitan position of London in England or Paris in France, though Glasgow came closest, with an extraordinary rate of expansion which saw numbers rise from 274,000 in 1831 to 761,000 in 1901. Glasgow was also the urban heart of the great west central Scotland region of heavy industrialization and one of the pre-eminent centres of manufacturing in the world. By 1901, nearly 2 million of Scotland's total of 4.5 million lived and worked in the city and the surrounding port, mining and industrial towns such as Paisley, Kilmarnock, Motherwell, Airdrie and Coatbridge. Each of these was also a boom town in the Victorian era, experiencing very fast growth as new coalfields and iron ore beds were opened up as a result of the inexorable advance of industrial capitalism. In addition, below the cities there were many smaller urban centres, several of which had some industry but which also served the needs of agriculture. These included Ayr, Dumfries and Perth. The border woollen towns like Galashiels and Selkirk and the Angus linen centres of Forfar and Dundee had a more specialist manufacturing function. There were other specialist groupings, such as the fishing burghs, spa towns, seaside resorts and the many middle-class settlements that grew up around the cities in the nineteenth century such as Broughty Ferry near Dundee, Portobello close to Edinburgh and Helensburgh, north of Glasgow.

The cities did not simply grow prodigiously in population in the nineteenth century, they were also physically transformed in equally dramatic fashion. To this day the city centres of Scotland bear the indelible mark of the great era of Victorian construction and architectural innovation. Edinburgh was the first to be remade on the grand scale. The city was 'Grecianized' by architects such as W. H. Playfair in the 1820s and 1830s with work on the National Monument on Calton Hill (to be designed as an exact replica of the Pantheon), Edinburgh University and the Royal Institution, among many other prestige buildings. The New Town, which had been laid out in the 1780s, was further developed for the city's professional and business classes; by 1830 it had more than 5,000 houses and 40,000 residents, almost a quarter of Edinburgh's population. The New Town had a visual unity of housing, squares and streets and this was reflected elsewhere in the central city where the explicit aim was to create a single, integrated architectural monument that was founded on the images and styles of Greek antiquity. Edinburgh had become a classical city of renowned physical beauty, set in an equally remarkable natural landscape of exceptional vistas. It was in the 1820s that it was hailed for the first time as 'the Athens of the North' by the poet Hugh William Williams, a title which stuck. The last major project of this seminal era was Playfair's remodelling of the Mound in the 1840s and 1850s. After the Disruption of the

Established Church in 1843, he was commissioned to design the Free Church College to dominate the new skyline as physical confirmation of the centrality of the new church in the religious life of the nation. The other major project on the same site was the striking building designed to house the National Gallery and the Royal Scottish Academy.

Even as these prestigious developments were being planned, however, Edinburgh's reputation for building on the grand scale was in decline. In 1833 the city corporation was formally declared bankrupt after lavish overspending on an extension to the Leith Docks and for nearly two decades afterwards building activity all but ceased and population growth visibly slowed down. But a new Edinburgh had emerged that reflected the city's aspirations and identity. The imposing physical presence of the buildings and their dignified lineage back to the classical world were meant to impress. They legitimized the city's position as the nation's capital and the centre of Scottish law and religion while at the same time proclaiming the power and bold confidence of the urban middle classes and their ability to plan and shape their environment. The capital's development had echoes in the other cities. The core of Dundee's New Town was Reform Street, laid out in the 1830s, which later became the focus for distinguished buildings such as the Albert Institute, the Royal Exchange, the Caird Hall and the Post Office. Edinburgh also had a considerable influence on the transformation of Aberdeen. With the building of Union Street it too acquired its New Town, with flanking residential areas for the business and professional classes and a succession of Grecian public and ecclesiastical monuments designed by John Smith, the city architect, in the 1830s and 1840s. Previously granite, the local material, was considered too hard for decorative work, but by the 1830s steam-powered technology had revolutionized the cutting process and soon granite added a new dimension to the construction of classical buildings. Aberdeen now became the Granite City. Many other burghs, notably Perth, also developed improvement schemes on the Edinburgh model.

The pattern in Glasgow was on an altogether greater scale. Already by the 1830s it was attracting attention for the grandeur of its public buildings like the Justiciary Court House (1809) and the Post Office (1810). The great European architect, Karl Friedrich Schinkel, on his visit to Scotland in 1826 described the 'purity' and 'splendour' of the city's new architecture and acclaimed the advances made by both Glasgow and Edinburgh: 'there is a wondrous contrast . . . between the stone huts covered with straw in the old parts and the splendid streets full of palaces, twenty-foot wide pavements of the finest stone, iron railings and gaslight lamp-posts'. He particularly commented on 'the magnificent stone' apparent in all the great buildings, in contrast to the plaster façades in his native Prussia and the 'mean' domestic architecture of England.[1] This phase, however, was only the first step in the transformation of central Glasgow which accompanied the explosive development of the city in the Victorian era, a process that reflected the growth in middle-class incomes, power and status. It was the propertied classes above all who benefited from the vast wealth now generated by imperial and industrial expansion. Taxation had little effect on their standards of life. After 1842, taxes on personal income were low and there were none on profits:

This bourgeois revolution resulted in a speed-up in the relocation and segregation of traditional urban functions – including a new residential townscape of terraced houses and villas, interspersed with gardens, imposing churches, and parks, and a city-centre townscape with its proliferation of new building types, such as purpose-built clubs, charity institutions, bath houses, theatres, railway stations, hotels and shopping arcades and retail 'warehouses'.[2]

High status housing, designed by some of the foremost architects of the age, was built on an increasingly lavish and sumptuous scale as the middle classes steadily moved westward from the old burghal core. The principal developments included remarkable boulevards, crescents and terraces in and around Woodlands Hill and Great Western Road created by J. T. Rochead and Alexander 'Greek' Thomson. The institutions of capitalism were reflected in other majestic buildings. Grandiose headquarters were constructed for banks, insurance companies, lawyers' offices and shipping firms. The individualism and status-seeking nature of bourgeois society demanded more and more ornamentation and decoration. This even applied in death, as can be seen from the 'competitive tomb-building' in the city's burial ground for the élite, the Necropolis, which was opened in 1833 beside the medieval cathedral and modelled on Père Lachaise in Paris. The spread of numerous retail shops and 'warehouses' (the forerunners of the modern department store) along Argyle, Buchanan and Sauchiehall Streets also testified to a new mass consumerism among the middle and artisan classes. Some of the city's business élite also contributed handsomely to the cost of the neo-gothic buildings for Glasgow University by Gilbert Scott on

Gilmorehill in the 1860s. The climax to this extravagant form of public architectural display came with the construction in the 1880s of the massive and lavishly appointed Municipal Buildings, which symbolized in stone the city's commercial success, civic pride and confidence in the future.

Few cities elsewhere in Britain could equal Glasgow's remarkable architectural achievements in the nineteenth century. But similar forces were at work to a greater or lesser extent in all the other cities and several of the towns in Scotland. The planning of middle-class suburbs became common as social segregation intensified and railways and tramways allowed the travel times between home and work to be cut dramatically. For the really wealthy there were huge detached villas and mansions, like the 'jute palaces' built for the Dundee mill owners after the boom in jute production from the 1850s. Everywhere, banks, insurance offices, libraries, academies, museums, courthouses, schools and colleges, which were previously housed in 'utility structures', were now accommodated in prestigious public buildings constructed for the purpose and modelled on Greek, Italian and French tradition. They were overtly designed to impress by their formal grandeur. Even more remarkable was the mania for church-building which became almost frenzied in the years immediately after the Disruption of 1843. It reflected the passionate evangelicalism of many of the urban middle classes, competition between the three main Presbyterian churches and a renewed urge to bring the gospel to the alienated masses of city slums. Anyone who doubts the central significance of religion in the Victorian era need only reflect on the hundreds of churches completed in cities and towns in Scotland in this period. They included the three great masterpieces of Alexander 'Greek' Thomson, himself a committed member of the United Presbyterians, at Caledonia Road, St Vincent Street and Queen's Park. The railways also added a new physical dimension, particularly the Caledonian and North British with their huge shed-like stations like Edinburgh Waverley and Glasgow Central, which were also linked to equally vast and ornate hotel complexes.

The new shape and structure of the cities articulated in imposing physical form a changing sense of national identity. The very richness of the new urban setting was the most telling symbol of Scotland's status as one of the richest societies on earth, a position that was ultimately seen to rest on the union and the empire. It was therefore common on city public buildings for external friezes and sculptural schemes to proclaim loyalty to the union with England, to freemasonry and to Liberalism, the nation's dominant political philosophy. Significantly, for instance, the entrance façade to Glasgow's new and magnificent Municipal Buildings featured Queen Victoria receiving homage from the empire. But the city monuments also celebrated a strong sense of Scottishness, of a nation within a nation. Architecture was seen as a means of enshrining the events of Scottish history for a Victorian middle class very much under the spell of Sir Walter Scott's novels. The Scots vernacular style went out of fashion for over a century after 1707, but it returned from the 1820s as 'Scots Baronial' with corbelled turrets, chimneys and gables. Sheriff courts, town halls, public halls, banks, police stations, suburban villas and the remodelling of Edinburgh Castle were all presented in the Baronial style. That giant of Glasgow architecture, Charles Rennie Mackintosh, was himself deeply influenced by Scottish Renaissance, Baronial and Celtic traditions, which contributed significantly to several of his most famous achievements, including the Glasgow School of Art, Scotland Street School and the Hill House. Statues of national heroes like Knox, Burns, Wallace, Livingstone and Scott were placed in prominent positions in town squares, parks and major thoroughfares. To the ruling classes of the Victorian era unswerving devotion to the union and empire could be easily reconciled with attachment to the symbolism of the historic Scottish nation.

2

The Scottish cities of the 1840s and 1850s drew admiring comment from foreign visitors for their majestic buildings, great wealth and economic dynamism. Other reactions, however, were less complimentary. Some observers viewed these huge concentrations of population, which seemed to go on, growing ever greater in size, with a mixture of alarm, fear and horror. The cities did indeed contain beautiful buildings and elegant streets but they also suffered from appalling social problems of disease, filth, poverty and crime. Some argued that these negative forces were so powerful that they threatened to engulf and destroy urbanism. The grossly unequal distribution of wealth in Scotland was nowhere more apparent than in the cities. In Glasgow, for instance, the splendid town mansions of the city's grandees and the impressive squares being laid out to the west of the centre of the old burgh confirmed the buoyant prosperity of the urban economy. The 'wynds and closes' of the High Street, Gallowgate and Saltmarket areas, the core of the burgeoning slum district, told another story. Around 1830 it had a population of over 20,000, with numbers rising every year as migrants continued to pour into the city. This 'Augean pandemonium' was an area where, it was said, 'sanitary evils existed to perfection' and where the worst excesses of the new urban society were most in evidence:

In the very centre of the city there was an accumulated mass of squalid wretchedness which was probably unequalled in any other town in the British dominions – that in the interior part of the square bounded by Saltmarket, Trongate and Stockwell streets, and by the river Clyde, as well as in certain parts of the east side of High Street, including the Vennels, Havannah and Burnside, there was concentrated everything wretched, dissolute, loathsome and pestilential. Dunghills lie in the vicinity of the dwellings, and from the extremely defective sewerage filth of every kind constantly accumulates . . .

The people who dwell in those quarters of the city are sunk to the lowest possible state of personal degradation in whom no elevated idea can be expected to arise, and who regard themselves, from the hopelessness of their condition, as doomed to a life of wretchedness and crime . . . they nightly issue to disseminate disease and to pour upon the town every species of abomination and crime.[3]

No other city in Scotland could match Glasgow for human squalor on this scale. As the reporter of the West of Scotland Handloom Weavers Commission famously observed: 'I have seen degradation in some of its worst phases, both in England and abroad, but I can advisedly say that I do not believe until I visited the wynds of Glasgow that so large an amount of filth, crime, misery and disease existed in one spot in any civilised country.'[4]

Nevertheless, acute problems also existed elsewhere. The urban areas were steadily becoming more lethal. There were serious typhus epidemics in 1837 and 1847 and, for the first time, the dreaded cholera visited Scotland in 1832, leaving 10,000 dead, with other outbreaks in 1848, 1853 and 1866. Cholera killed swiftly and randomly and instilled widespread terror among all social classes and these epidemics in particular drew attention to the dangers of the new urban environment. But more insidious and less publicized was the inexorable increase of death rates from the more 'mundane' diseases of consumption (tuberculosis), diarrhoea and whooping cough. Between the 1830s and the late

1850s, death rates in the cities rose to peaks not seen since the seventeenth century. Even in the 1860s, when preventative measures were being put in place to address the public health problem, the mortality rate for the four cities was one-fifth above the rate for the towns and nearly 60 per cent higher than that for rural areas. The stench of the city, more than any number of learned treatises on mortality, brought home to rich and poor alike the scale of the sanitary crisis: 'To stand close to a defective sewer today is to recapture the essence of early and mid Victorian towns . . . a compound of broken or inadequate sewers, overflowing cesspools, poorly-drained cowsheds, abattoirs, domestic pigsties, exposed dung-heaps and industrial waste.'[5] One medical authority stated that the 'influence of stink as stink' was so nauseating that it could of itself have a lethal effect on 'health, loss of appetite, nausea, sometimes actual vomiting, sometimes diarrhoea, headache, giddiness, faintness, and a general sense of depression or malaise'.[6]

Systematic investigation, such as Edwin Chadwick's *Report on the Sanitary Condition of Great Britain* in 1842, and pioneers in social medicine like W. P. Alison and Drs Baird, Cowan and Watt, demonstrated the relationship between disease, water supply and cleansing. But recognition of the problem was one thing; discovering effective solutions was quite another. There were a number of obstacles. In the words of M. W. Flinn, the cities were still expanding 'at rates that would bring cold sweat to the brows of twentieth century housing committees'.[7] But the Victorians had little of the scientific and administrative expertise of later generations. There was profound conflict in the medical profession, for instance, over the origins of some of the major killer diseases and limited understanding of how best to tackle them. The debate between those who supported the 'miasma' and 'contagion' theories to explain the incidence of cholera continued for many years. But middle-class society did not entirely abandon the poor. Major efforts were made in all the 'fever' outbreaks to establish infirmaries – though in all cases these lasted only as long as the crisis itself. The main middle-class initiative until the 1850s came through the churches and the philanthropic societies. The urban crisis was seen as a moral problem: it was believed that the horrors of the slums came about in large part because of the irreligion of the masses and the destructive effect that this had had on the character of the poor who were regarded as the victims of their own failings. Despite the views of those like W. P. Alison, who stressed the environmental and economic causes of poverty, the moral argument remained dominant for many years. It was buttressed by the remarkable personal influence of the Revd Thomas Chalmers, who believed that through bringing the Christian gospel to the poor they would develop a new personal responsibility and free themselves from drink and degeneracy. The urge to cleanse the moral world was therefore at least as powerful as any concern to address directly the physical problems of the city in the 1830s and 1840s. Evangelical energy and a great deal of money were poured into church building programmes in the urban areas. A vast missionary initiative was promoted, especially in the 1850s by the Free Church and the United Presbyterian Church, to visit non-churchgoers in their homes and bring them Christian salvation. Men and women of remarkable zeal and commitment formed a host of charitable societies to aid orphans, vagrants, prostitutes, alcoholics and other unfortunates. There can be no denying that some good came from much of this activity. Equally, however, philanthropy often diverted middle-class enthusiasm to psychologically satisfying ends while postponing a fundamental attack on the basic causes of the urban crisis itself.

Radical reform demanded heavy investment of resources to improve the water supply and the sanitary system of the cities. But by the 1840s there was still no consensus that the ratepayers should be taxed so that all the inhabitants of the city should benefit. The Glasgow Police Board observed in 1840 that the slum areas were not the responsibility of 'the general community' but only of the property owners in these districts. It opposed the creation of a Board of Health 'for defraying the expense of creating buildings as hospitals, dispensaries, etc. and for appointing medical officers, district surgeons, apothecaries and inspectors'. Regulation to this extent amounted to gross interference with the sanctity of private property which was the very foundation of the Victorian social system. Moreover, 'the preservation of public health' by compulsory assessment would have disastrous consequences, so the Police Board argued, by removing the sources of charity and promoting an exodus of the wealthy from the city.[8]

It followed from this that the most effective way of advancing the cause of sanitary reform was to convince ratepayers that it would actually save money in the long run. As the *British and Foreign Medico-Chirurgical Review* put it in the 1840s, 'one broad principle may be safely enunciated in respect of sanitary economics – that it costs more money to create disease than to prevent; and there is not a single

336

structural arrangement chargeable with the production of disease which is not in itself an extravagance'.[9] But demonstrating the principle in practice to sceptical ratepayers was more difficult and promoters of the 'Sanitary Idea' experienced protracted local arguments before they managed to win general acceptance. Those aspects of civic reform that could be justified in terms of the principle of efficiency did make progress; those which could not, such as public support for working-class housing, were neglected for many decades.

By the 1850s, the advocates of clean water in the cities and improved sanitary control were making an impact. A key development was the compulsory registration of births and deaths in 1855 in Scotland, 19 years before similar legislation was passed in England. The data derived from the census made possible influential studies by W. T. Gardiner, Glasgow's first Medical Officer of Health, and his great successor, J. B. Russell. They revealed the appallingly high death rates among infants and the stark evidence of huge class variations in mortality levels within the cities. The third cholera epidemic of 1853-4, coming so soon after the very bad outbreaks of 1848-9, also concentrated the minds of the wealthier classes, who were terrified that the dreaded disease would escape from the poorer districts and cause widespread carnage in the more affluent areas. In this crisis cholera was seen not so much as an act of God as compelling proof that the slums had to be cleansed. As one doctor put it in the *Glasgow Herald*, 'the cholera has been permitted by our Creator for no other object than that of enforcing upon the rich and intelligent the amendment of the habitations of the poor'.[10] Sanitary reform now took on a moral fervour and for many became part of the evangelical crusade to establish a more godly society. Cleansing the physical environment and the moral world were no longer seen as distinct but as integral and related parts of the same mission. As Anthony Wohl suggests:

To most Victorians, epidemics were not scourges sent by God to punish man for his sins but were the consequence of man's sinful neglect of God's earth and of His injunction to care for the sick and the weak. Sanitary reform, health care, visiting the poor, slum clearance, education of the poor in matters of health and hygiene were all vital causes for a people inspired by both the evangelical concept of duty and, increasingly, a new secular concern for the well-ordering of society. Whether the inspiration was religious or secular, whether it stemmed from a sense of shame or altruistic duty, from self-interest or fear of the ravages of epidemics, the most widely held of Victorian social doctrines was that physical well-being and a pure environment were the essential foundations for all areas of social progress. There could be no moral, religious or intellectual improvement without physical improvement.[11]

Thus was born a more environmentalist concept of the urban crisis, a religious diagnosis given further support by the more secular analysis of Charles Darwin in his massively influential *Origin of Species*, with its emphasis on adaptation, survival and the external forces which fashion the human condition.

A momentum for intervention was developed. Scotland was not covered by the 1848 Public Health Act and so all initiatives had to come from the local authorities, although these were aided by the Burgh Police Act of 1861 and the Public Health (Scotland) Act of 1867. Long before this, however, many burghs had police commissions with the power to raise and spend rates for a range of purposes including paving, lighting, watching and scavenging. Under local 'police' acts, a considerable amount of cleaning and scavenging could be undertaken. The 1862 Act further strengthened these powers and led to a significant growth in the number of permanent officials, such as sanitary inspectors and medical officers of health. The MOHs of this era were a formidable group and included J. B. Russell in Glasgow, Matthew Hay in Aberdeen and Henry Littlejohn in Edinburgh: 'They led the battle for cleanliness, drainage, public parks, civic fever hospitals, better housing and collections of statistics to the continual embarrassment of City Fathers.'[12]

The greatest advance in health could be made through the capital works for bringing clean water to the cities and the disposal of sewage. Here Glasgow led the way and set an example to the whole of Britain through its spectacular scheme for drawing water from Loch Katrine, some 50 miles away in the Trossachs area of the southern Highlands. The project, opened by Queen Victoria in 1859, was hailed as a triumph of civic endeavour and unequivocal confirmation that the huge sanitary problems of the city could be addressed by an investment which benefited all the community when the connections were finally completed to standpipes in the closes and courts of the slums. The Loch Katrine scheme proved an incentive to other municipalities. Aberdeen had its water works in 1866 and Dundee in 1869. In the Glasgow case, it also formed the basis for other enterprises, as the city expanded into slum clearance, gas supply, public lighting, tramways, libraries, museums, public baths, parks and art galleries. Glasgow had more municipal services than any other city of its size by the 1890s. It served as an inspiration to the three other Scottish cities and attracted a stream of admiring visitors from abroad, especially from the United States where civic initiative on the grand scale was widely regarded as a model for the future. Nevertheless, the environmental achievements before 1900 need to be kept in perspective. The Clyde was still the main sewer until 1894 and J. B. Russell thought Glasgow remained a 'semi-asphyxiated city' from its countless coal fires and industrial chimneys. Above all, as will be discussed in more detail later, the problems of slum housing and chronic overcrowding had hardly even been touched by the end of the nineteenth century.

The contribution of medicine to the containment of the urban crisis is problematic. The period under discussion was indeed a golden age of Scottish medicine. Joseph Lister developed a system of antiseptic surgery and his ideas were taken further in the 1890s by his distinguished pupil, William MacEwen, who pioneered antiseptic surgery. Earlier, in the 1840s James (later Sir James) Simpson developed the use of anaesthetics in childbirth: 'Simpson had to fight the view that God had ordained that childbirth should be painful: this he countered with a reference to the Lord putting Adam to sleep before extracting the rib that was to become Eve.'[13] The antiseptic precautions did increase the chances of surviving a hospital operation but this good fortune affected only a tiny minority of the urban population. Existing infirmaries were extended and additional hospitals built in all the cities. From the period 1870 to 1914 can be dated the opening of such famous names as the Western and Victorian Infirmaries and Stobhill Hospital. In addition, by the end of the century those on Poor Relief could expect free treatment which was supported by local parishes and the Board of Supervision. But this still left the majority of the poor, and for them provision remained inadequate. Dr Charles Cameron, MP, described 'the multitudes of sick poor of Glasgow who cannot obtain admission to the Infirmaries, who will not go into the Poor houses, and who have no money for medical attendance at their houses'.[14] The class most vulnerable to the diseases of the urban environment was plainly the least likely to receive proper medical care. In any case, medical science had as yet no answer to tuberculosis, the greatest endemic scourge of the Victorian city, or to whooping cough and measles, which contributed to the persistence of appalling mortality rates among infants.

However, overall, the urban crisis was coming under control by the early twentieth century. The age of epidemics was over. Only in two years in the later period, 1897 and 1915, did mortality rise significantly above the average, and in both cases this was triggered by a number of infectious diseases rather than by a single major killer like typhus or cholera. Moreover, from the 1860s the cities seemed to be winning the battle on a wider front. The gap between urban and rural death rates, which had been a yawning chasm in the middle decades of the nineteenth century, now narrowed dramatically and, by 1910–12, city rates were only 17 per cent worse than the country areas. (In the early 1860s the difference had been a huge 57 per cent.) Indeed, the most recent commentators on the topic, Michael Anderson and Donald Morse, show that by 1900 the big cities no longer had the worst figures. The leaders in that unenviable league table at the turn of the century were now smaller places like Stirling, Montrose, Ayr, Coatbridge and Dumfries, where sanitary controls were not quite as well developed as elsewhere. Nevertheless, averages conceal a lot. There were still enormous differences in life-chances between the poor of the slums and the affluent in suburban areas. The 'Massacre of the Innocents' showed no signs of abating. The Scottish infant mortality rate (the annual average number of deaths under the age of one per 1,000 live births) was 120 in the 1850s but actually rose to 129 in the later 1890s. Even when long-term decline did set in during the early 1900s, the rate did not fall as quickly or to the same extent as in England. This in itself tellingly illustrates the perilously low standard of living for many of the urban masses. It also suggests that the fall in the price of basic foods in the 1870s and 1890s (leading to a better-nourished generation of mothers a couple of decades later), municipal attempts to improve milk supplies, free school meals in the early twentieth century and the widening influence of nurses, midwives and health visitors were at least as important in radically cutting back urban death rates as cleaner water and more efficient sewerage systems.

3

The problem of working-class housing in the cities was as daunting as the sanitary crisis but much more intractable. In 1871 almost a third of the houses in Scotland had only one room, and 37 per cent had only two. The position improved somewhat so that by 1911 the proportion living in one room had fallen to around 13 per cent. But overcrowding remained acute in the poorer areas of the cities, particularly in Glasgow where the density per acre in 1911 was about twice that of Edinburgh and Dundee. The full extent of the Scottish problem became apparent only when compared to England. If the standard of 'overcrowding' adopted by the Registrar-General for England and Wales, of more than two persons to a room, had been applied to Scotland in 1918, 45 per cent of the population, or a remarkable total of just over 2 million people, were living in overcrowded conditions.

Some blamed the Scottish urban tradition of tenement living for this state of affairs. The tenement was a block of flats or 'houses' of three to four storeys served by a common stairway. The houses in these blocks varied in size from one to five apartments, but the 'single end' or one-roomed flats, of which in 1913 there were 7,106 in Edinburgh and 44,354 in Glasgow, attracted criticism as a major reason for over-crowding. But the tenements as a building type had a number of attractive features. Built in stone and substantially constructed, they gave protection against adverse weather. In addition, the flats were easy to heat, an important consideration when many lived in deep poverty and in a climate of short summers and long winters. Tenants above ground were also less likely to suffer from damp conditions than their counterparts in croft houses and farm cottages in the countryside. The tenement has come to be associated with the slums, but middle-class housing in the nineteenth century was dominated by tenement flats, usually with five rooms, including dining-room, parlour, water-closet and lavishly fitted interiors. In addition, high-status tenement housing was usually differentiated by external decoration and bay windows. However, in poorer areas, intensive subdivision of space, or 'making down' within the shells of tenements and cramming additional buildings into the land behind them with warren-like passages and closes, created the dense overcrowding that was the despair of sanitary reformers. These tenements were dark and gloomy – since buildings were so closely packed that light was limited – and foul-smelling, with one privy or dry closet often serving many families. These living conditions help to explain why so much time was spent by families in the streets. Children played outdoors, women chatted at the entrance to the closes and many men sought the refuge of the local public house. Beds might be used night and day by workers on different shifts. There were also 'hole-in-the-wall' beds and 'hurley beds' on wheels that could be stored and then 'hurled out' (pushed out) at night. But such ingenuity could only go so far. Ralph Glasser gave a vivid insight into the absence of privacy in a Gorbals tenement:

In most of the houses we knew every foot of space was taken up by beds, mattresses on the floor, a few bare wooden chairs, a battered kitchen table. One or even two of the younger children commonly shared the parental bed, usually a mattress on planks resting on trestles in a curtained alcove in the kitchen.

To enable a coupling to take place in a semblance of privacy behind the curtain, the woman would step out of her shift, snatch a blanket off the bed and wrap the child in it and lay him on the floor boards near enough to the cooking range for him to get some radiated warmth from its banked-up fire. Afterwards she parted the curtains and came out naked to lift the unsleeping, finely aware child back into bed, to lie between her and the man lying open mouthed in post-coital sleep. And then mother and child might lie awake for a while, locked in unique perplexities. She, her body prompting her still, with no finality in her, turned her world over and over again in her mind's restless fingers. The child, possessed by wonder and nameless hauntings, tried to join together the heavings and creakings and groans and gasps and little cries he had heard as he lay on the floor, his mother's disturbed concentration now, his father's stillness as if felled, and the sticky warmth in which he lay between them, something more than the sweat that was there before, a substance he divined as elemental, mysterious, newly decanted, that touched his flesh and his senses with profound unattainable meaning.

If there had been two children in the bed, the other, a toddler, also put on the floor might well have slept through it all. His turn for nocturnal wonderment would come.[15]

Some argued that overcrowding was tolerated because the poor had low expectations. Living in congested tenements was no worse – and often better – than eking out an existence in the damp cabins of Donegal, the black houses of the western Highlands or the cottar dwellings and bothies on Lowland farms from which many of the cities' populations had come. But there were also more fundamental reasons for over-crowding related to the family economy of the working classes in the Victorian period. Primary poverty, the absolute minimum necessary to sustain life, was endemic. It was reckoned in the 1890s that nearly 27 per cent of the adult male workforce in Glasgow earned no more than the basic minimum of £1 per week. In addition to this number, there were the vagrants, the old, the sick and those who were employed in seasonal jobs. Large families could also have devastating economic consequences for the low paid. An investigation by J. Bruce Glasier showed that many migrants were particularly at risk because 'the bulk of them are not craftsmen' and 'they get very uncertain work'.[16] But even skilled artisans were not insulated from the threat of poverty. The economies of both Dundee and Glasgow were geared to the global economy and fluctuations in markets and hence in employment were a fact of life. In shipbuilding, for instance, volatility of demand seemed to become even more intense from the 1880s. Even in good times it was not uncommon for one or two days to be lost because of problems in maintaining work flows. Even the labour aristocracy was vulnerable to sickness, accidents and the onset of old age and, when unemployed, they could not fall back on the earnings of their wives because not many wives of skilled men had a job. Significantly, of those applying to the Charity Organisation Society for assistance with rent arrears in the 1880s, nearly a quarter were reckoned to be from the skilled trades. The Scottish Poor Law had been reformed in 1845 by establishing a Board of Supervision to oversee work in the locality, allowing for compulsory rating to support the poor transferring legal responsibility for the kirk sessions and appointing Inspectors of the Poor to manage applications for relief. But the 'able-bodied' unemployed in Scotland still had no legal right to relief, even if some support was often given in practice, and the Poor Law in Scotland remained much more parsimonious than the equivalent in England. Between 1900 and 1905, for instance, the annual cost of relieving paupers per head of population in Scotland was a full 50 per cent lower than in England. North of the border, the Poor Law hardly provided even a basic safety net for the urban working classes.

Against this background of uncertainty and poverty it was only sensible to go for accommodation, however modest, that people could afford. This was a rational strategy for other reasons. First, Richard Rodger has shown that the cost of rent and food (which represented four-fifths of working-class expenditure) in the Scottish cities was high by British standards. In 1912 the cost of living in Aberdeen was 7.4 per cent above that of Manchester, Leeds and Sheffield, 10.6 per cent greater in Dundee and 9.6 per cent more in Edinburgh than in the English cities. Second, the nature of Scottish rental leases compelled a cautious approach. Commonly, a rental of one year from Whitsunday was agreed four months before the start of the lease. This convention was in explicit conflict with employment patterns. Fixed payments had to be made for 16 months while incomes were often very volatile because of the fluctuating labour market. As Rodger comments: 'In this uncertain climate of household accounting many tenants understandably chose a level of accommodation at such minimal levels that they felt reasonably confident that whatever the nature of seasonal and casual employment in the ensuing twelve month period they should be able to maintain rental payments. It was a delicate balancing act.'[17] Third, there were draconian penalties enforced on defaulters. Non-payment of rent could and did lead to compulsory eviction. Annual evictions in Glasgow in the early years of the twentieth century were running at around 3,000 households – and, significantly, over a third of these were described as 'respectable'. In one year of very bad trade there were 20,000 petitions of eviction lodged in the city's Sheriff Courts and the majority were granted.

The only sure way to break the vicious circle of poverty and over-crowding was to subsidize working-class housing from the rates or the public purse. Eventually this did happen, but for most of the nineteenth century it was not a serious option. As late as 1911, for example, only 0.47 per cent of Glasgow's population and 0.61 per cent of Edinburgh's lived in municipal houses and the majority of these tenants were not in great need. For much of the Victorian period, the dominant belief was that the inhabitants of the slums were slothful, drunken and feckless and that they endured terrible squalor because of their own personal failure and defects of character. To house them at public expense would therefore have been intolerable. So regulation and control were the preferred options. The Corporation of Glasgow assumed powers in 1866 to 'ticket' houses that did not exceed 2,000 cubic feet in capacity. The metal 'ticket' was fixed to a door or lintel and laid down the number of occupants allowed by law and the police and sanitary inspectors were given authority to inspect these houses at any time of the day or night. The practice extended to other Scottish cities over the next 15 years and was generally confirmed by the 1903 Burgh Police Act. These extraordinary powers of interference and regulation were unequalled anywhere else in the British Isles. They illustrated an authoritarian streak in Scottish local government which derived from the old interventionist traditions of the royal burghs. Some 28,288 houses were ticketed in Glasgow alone, and the night inspections averaged 40,000 annually in the 1880s and 50,000 a year by the early 1900s. Significantly,

70 per cent of the households ticketed were let to unskilled workers, the very class that found the greatest difficulty in making ends meet. Ticketing amounted to harassment of the poor but there is little evidence that it deterred them or prevented overcrowding in any significant way.

In the 1860s the city corporations tried another approach through Improvement Acts designed to promote the large-scale demolition of some of the worst slums. Legislation was passed for Glasgow in 1866, Edinburgh in 1867 and Dundee in 1871. The impact of the Glasgow legislation has been studied most closely, where the attempt at urban renewal was partly influenced by Haussmann's ambitious scheme for transforming central Paris. Between 1870 and 1874, the Improvement Trust created by the Act cleared nearly 15,500 houses in the most crowded closes and wynds around Glasgow Cross, Calton, Trongate and Saltmarket, thus removing some of the worst slums in the city. However, the unfortunate inhabitants were displaced rather than rehoused. Overcrowding remained endemic and was aggravated further by the impact of the railway. The construction of St Enoch's station alone led to the demolition of 433 tenements. The other Scottish cities were spared this because the railway did not pass through dense working-class communities to anything like the same extent.

Yet by the early twentieth century some of the old attitudes that had constrained public intervention in housing were crumbling fast. The seminal research of Charles Booth and Seebohm Rowntree on London and York respectively had demonstrated that primary poverty was due to low income, old age, family size and illness rather than to the lack of will to work. These findings were widely debated in Scotland. The legislation of the Liberal government in the early twentieth century on old age pensions, unemployment insurance and other welfare provision was also a tacit admission that inadequate incomes rather than character deficiency were the root cause of poverty. Housing could not remain insulated from these wider developments. The labour movement was in favour of subsidized municipal housing at rentals which would meet the cost of building and maintenance and, interestingly, the ILP drew attention to Glasgow's pioneering role in gas, water and trams to demonstrate that public intervention could provide services more efficiently than private enterprise. Rent strikes during the Great War showed that housing was now a matter of urgent political and social concern. Some churchmen were increasingly throwing their weight behind the cause of social reform. Where before there had been a broad acceptance of the existing social order and an emphasis on charitable work to address its most serious problems, there was now a new spirit of social criticism. In 1891 the Report on the Housing of the Poor by Glasgow Presbytery urged action on the corporation to remedy the crisis in the slums. Ironically, the statistics suggest that the worst overcrowding, though still on a vast scale, was easing nationally in this period. In 1871, 32.5 per cent of Scottish houses had only one room, but by 1911 this had fallen to 12.8 per cent, a trend which might reflect the modest increases in real incomes in the later nineteenth century. However, problems remained acute in Glasgow where density of persons per acre was twice that of Dundee and Edinburgh in 1911, and standards were still poor across all the Scottish cities when compared with conditions in England.

The pressure for reform led the Secretary of State to establish a Royal Commission on Housing, which reported in 1917. Its conclusions were a scathing indictment of landlords and government: 'gross overcrowding and huddling of the sexes together in the congested villages and towns, occupation of one-room houses by large families, groups of lightless and unventilated houses in the old burghs, clotted classes of slums in the great cities'. The commissioners for the first time identified the sheer immensity of the problem more convincingly than in any previous survey. The majority of them believed that private enterprise had manifestly failed and that a new and radical approach was necessary: 'the State must at once take steps to make good the housing shortage and to improve housing conditions, and that this can only be done by or through the machinery of the public authorities'.[18] In addition, though not completely condemning it as a building style, they argued that the tenement was at the heart of the problem. They therefore recommended that no more single apartments should be built, tenements should not exceed three storeys and houses ought to be constructed in terraces in order to admit light and air to the back and front of the building.

These ideas were to alter the townscape of Scotland radically in future years and would place local authorities and the state at the centre of national housing development. Government action followed quickly. Lloyd George had fought his post-war election campaign on a programme of 'homes fit for heroes'. He was also mindful of the greater political muscle of the working classes after the Reform Act of 1918, as well as the rent strikes by women in Glasgow in 1915 which had shown that the housing issue could provoke civil unrest. Lloyd George's coalition government passed the Housing and Town Planning (Scotland) Act in 1919. No single piece of legislation has contributed so much to the shape and development of urban Scotland in the twentieth century. State subsidies for housing were introduced and local councils given more authority, so ending the dominance of the free market and the private landlords. A further six Acts were passed between 1912 and 1938 which refined and extended these provisions. The Act of 1924 gave an annual subsidy of £9 per house per year to the local authority. When passed on to the tenant, this amounted to an effective cut of between a third and a quarter in the weekly rental. Further legislation in 1930 and 1935 shifted the emphasis to the aiding of slum clearance and the rehousing of the inhabitants on new estates.

From this point on, the physical appearance and housing structure of the Scottish city would never be the same again. The age of the council house was born. No less than 70 per cent of the 344,209 new houses built in Scotland between 1919 and 1941 were owned by local authorities. The private landlords survived but their numbers fell over time, a process that was encouraged by legislation like the Rent Restriction Act of 1920, which limited their freedom of action and made the owning of rented property less lucrative. Moreover, the large numbers of new local authority houses marked a break with the Scottish urban tradition which changed almost beyond recognition in these years. The old type of tenement was now hardly built at all. Stone was abandoned in favour of brick. Two-storey, semi-detached and terraced cottage styles became the norm. High-density tenements were replaced by low-density houses with some garden ground. In Glasgow this was the strategy in the new estates of Knightswood, Hamiltonhill, Mosspark and Possilpark, which were built in the 1920s. The following decade, however, three-storey flatted tenement blocks were put up on cleared sites at Blackhill, Balornock and Haghill. In both Edinburgh and Glasgow there was also a general movement to build on cheaper land on the outskirts, thus creating the familiar modern urban form of the Scottish city ringed by single-class council housing estates.

This tendency towards greater segregation of the social classes had of course been developing in the nineteenth-century city but the tenement tradition had contained it to some extent. The process accelerated in the inter-war period. The theory behind much of the housing legislation in the early 1920s was that council houses would in the first instance be allocated to the better-off, who would vacate their own reasonable accommodation for the use of the poorer classes. Over time then, this 'stepladder' would ensure the elimination of the slums. Eighty per cent of the first 700 post-war Edinburgh council houses, for instance, were occupied by non-manual workers, and Glasgow's model estates at Mosspark and Knightswood were built to house the families of 'respectable' skilled artisans. By the 1930s, however, subsidies had been cut back because of the economic crisis and building costs had risen steeply as the best land in the cities had mainly been swallowed up by the low-density council estates of the early 1920s. Therefore the council houses built in the 1930s after slum clearance were much cheaper and had fewer amenities but were intended to rehouse some of the poorest people of the inner city. Manifestly the areas where they were built soon came to be seen as second class. This process imposed another form of territorial social segregation. Places like Craigmillar in Edinburgh and Blackhill in Glasgow came to be regarded as ghettos for undesirables. As one observer noted:

Built during the early 1930s the scheme had gained a city-wide reputation by the 1950s as a haven for thieves and criminals. Blackhill residents were defined by their local authority landlords and other sections of the working class as 'rabble', to be contained, controlled and policed at every opportunity. In common with many working-class housing estates, Blackhill, in the Springburn area of Glasgow, was stigmatised. Residents were (and still are) systematically blacklisted for credit by chain stores and by employment agencies, local authority services and taxi-drivers. The scheme has its 'own' police station (steel shuttered) and a complete tenement of social workers. Enclosed on three sides by motorways, physically distinct and socially segregated, it represents the failure of Scottish inter-war housing policy.[19]

During the inter-war period too, the Scottish middle classes were distancing themselves from the city. While the vast majority of Scots continued to rent rather than buy, the 1920s and 1930s saw an expansion in bungalow building in all the major cities and in many smaller towns as well. For those in steady employment during these years, real income was rising by about 15–16 per cent and the salaried and self-employed middle classes were among the chief beneficiaries. The extension of tram and bus routes and rising car ownership also allowed the reasonably affluent to live in a more desirable environment further from their place of employment in a way that the very rich in the city had been able to do for some time. The proliferation of 'bungalow belts' in cities and towns also reflected hostility to tenement living. The Saltire Society, founded to promote Scottish culture, bitterly criticized the rapid advance of the bungalow from the late 1920s, seeing it as a form of anglicization of the Scottish townscape, since as a building type it had been virtually unknown north of the border before then. But the bungalow had strong appeal over the traditional tenement. As a Department of Health report noted in 1943, 'The preference for the single storey self-contained home (bungalow) is related to the housewives' experience of the tenement or flatted house and life in a congested neighbourhood.'[20] Like the allocation policies of the council officials in public housing, the colonization of numerous streets, crescents and squares of bungalows intensified the process of spatial and social segregation within the Scottish city by creating solidly middle-class enclaves on a much larger scale.

The overall public policy of attempting to reduce overcrowding had both successes and failures. By 1951 only one-quarter of the population lived in two rooms or less compared to one-half in 1921. Much of this progress was made between the wars. Even on the bleakest estates, council tenants had a toilet and more rooms, which was a conspicuous advance on the old tenements. The lucky few who managed to obtain a house in the first developments of the 1920s were especially favoured. They had their own front door and small garden, together with combined bathroom and toilet and hot water. This was a radical improvement in family life. One Edinburgh lady recalled the thrill of the experience, 'It was paradise! For my sister and myself to share a bedroom just for our two selves, we thought this was heaven. There was a bathroom and electric light!'[21] Another remembered without a trace of nostalgia what had gone before:

I would never live in those days again, never. The houses were all crammed together and built close together and maybe one lavatory for maybe a whole stair. It was terrible living long ago. Talk about the good old days. They say, 'would you like to live them again'. I say 'no, never again'. Never, nothing would make me live in the old days gone. I've seen too much of the poverty, you know.[22]

But success was far from universal. The public building policy in the 1930s also produced dreary and monotonous rows of uniform two- and three-storey blocks with no diversity or individuality. The Treasury in London had to give its agreement before financial subsidies were made available after 1919 for local authority housing, and councils were limited to a small number of Treasury-approved designs. As the economic depression deepened, so the emphasis on the costs of design and building increased. Moreover, the Act of 1930, passed to clear some of the worst slums, often merely succeeded in creating new ones. Basic facilities had improved for the new council tenants, but people often missed the tightly knit sense of community, the support of neighbours and the close connections with family that were part of the way of life of the tenements. Those crucial supports of working-class existence, the pub, the small shop and the pawnshop, were usually missing. Some of those who had taken council houses soon moved back into the city. In fact, despite the scale of the house-building programme, the housing crisis remained unresolved on the eve of the Second World War. Scotland still remained the worst-housed area in the United Kingdom. According to the overcrowding standards defined by the Housing Act of 1935, the differences between England and Wales and Scotland were very wide. More than one-quarter of all houses were overcrowded in Scotland compared to just over 4 per cent south of the border.

It was ironic that it was a Scot, Patrick Geddes, who did most in the early twentieth century to pioneer modern town planning by stressing the value of urban life and how it could be enhanced by careful rebuilding and conservation, avoidance of social segregation and the integration of housing and recreational space. Geddes died in 1932 and there was no evidence that any of his ideas had significantly influenced the planning of cities in his native Scotland. On the contrary, municipal policy in the 1930s was in direct conflict with his prescriptions for urban improvement in almost every particular. But some of that may have been inevitable: the scale of the problems inherited from the nineteenth century was so huge and the monies available from central government so limited in the 1920s and 1930s that the response was always likely to be inadequate.

4

In 1850 a leader in *The Scotsman* proclaimed:

That Scotland is, pretty near at least, the most drunken nation on the face of the earth is a fact never quite capable of denial. It may seem strange that Edinburgh, the headquarters of the various sections of a clergy more powerful than any other save that of Ireland, should, in respect of drunkenness, exhibit scenes and habits unparalleled in any other metropolis, and that Glasgow, where the clergy swarm, should be notoriously the most guilty and offensive city in Christendom.[23]

While this comment might seem like hyperbole or even an early illustration of east–west rivalry, there was no denying the sheer scale of alcoholic consumption in the Victorian city. By the 1840s Edinburgh had around 5 licensed houses for every 30 families; Dundee's ratio was one pub to 24 families, while Glasgow's 2,300 licensed premises represented one pub for every 150 inhabitants in the city. But the licensed trade in drink was only one part of the story. In the poorer districts of the cities there was also a vast underground network of shebeens and illicit drinking dens. One survey by the *North British Daily Mail* in the early 1870s counted over 150 dram shops in the Saltmarket–Gallowgate area of Glasgow that functioned outside the law. They varied from 'respectable shebeens', which were simply illicit, to 'wee shebeens' 'on the stair head, where a drunken old hag in a greasy mutch with trembling hands pours out from her black bottle a compound of whisky and methylated spirits, a glass of which being swigged off in the dark and money paid, the recipient staggers down the stairs and out again to the streets'.[24]

The drink culture in Scotland had two distinctive features in addition to the huge quantities of alcohol that were actually consumed. First, whisky was becoming more popular than ale and stout from the later eighteenth century. The alcohol content of beer was around one-eighth that of whisky, some of which was distilled illegally as poteen in the cities by migrants who had learnt their skills in Highland glens and in the depths of the Irish countryside. Whisky did not necessarily replace beer but was often consumed in combination with it. A favourite tipple, for instance, was 'a schooner and a stick', a cocktail consisting of a pint of beer with a glass of whisky added for additional impact. The significant increase in the drinking of hard spirits helps to explain the wave of intoxication that swept across several Lowland towns in this period because, as several commentators pointed out, the level of whisky consumption always rose in years of good trade when people had more money in their pockets. A second characteristic of the drink culture in Scotland was the widespread availability of alcohol. In England, the Beer Act of 1830 made it illegal for beer-houses to sell spirits. But this did not apply to Scotland where public houses (at this time often little more than rooms in private houses) sold both, as did grocers, drapers and eating houses. In 1828 the Home Drummond Act introduced licensing of Scottish public houses for the first time. Publicans were now required to obtain a certificate from the local authority in order to carry on business, although this seemed to have little effect on the flourishing and expanding illegal sector of shebeens and cheap dram shops. There was little legal restriction on who could buy drink. Indeed, until 1903 alcohol could be sold to customers aged 14 and above at a time when the minimum age in England was 16. It was the cheapness of spirits and the ease with which they could be bought that helped to encourage the universal use and abuse of whisky. In the 1830s, for example, the official record (obviously an underestimate) stated that the consumption of spirits in Scotland worked out at over 2½ gallons a year per head of population. This per capita figure was more than seven times the consumption that would be recorded a century later.

Yet cost and availability were only part of the story. Heavy drinking also had cultural and social roots. Drinking was an integral part of all social intercourse. Weddings, christenings and funerals often occasioned feats of heroic drinking, as did the annual celebration of New Year. Hiring fairs for servants were also notorious for scenes of intoxication on the grand scale. There were numerous 'social usages', such as completion of a job, end of an apprenticeship, or the sealing of a bargain when the consumption of copious amounts of alcohol was regarded as both socially necessary and desirable. The pub itself had a much wider social role in Victorian times than today. It was a meeting place for early trade unions, political organizations and friendly societies. Until the truck legislation of the 1870s, the paying of wages in pubs was common and they long remained places for the hiring of casual labourers. All Scottish cities teemed with migrants and, for single men in particular away from home in lodgings or 'flitting' from one temporary house to another, the pub was not simply a drinking place but an ideal social centre and a source of companionship. The slum pub must also be seen in the context of Victorian street life. The emphasis was not necessarily on the family home, which was small, bereft of anything other than the simplest furnishings and overcrowded, but on the informal life of the streets, with the pubs offering drink, fellowship and entertainment: 'Imagine the dram shop's impact on a tired and bored working man, fleeing from his drab home, nagging wife or landlady and crying children.'[25] Some pubs also had entertainment. The 'free-and-easy', the forerunner of the music hall, was a room in a public house with a platform and a piano where the company would be entertained to a programme of sentimental, comic and bawdy songs. Some of these singing saloons were 'beautifully fitted up, finely painted and brilliantly illuminated', and inevitably the performances were appreciated all the more when the audience had had a good drink.[26]

The scale of alcoholic consumption in Scotland in the 1830s and 1840s was bound to provoke a reaction when evangelicalism became a dominant force in the Church of Scotland. Drinking started to be regarded as a social problem, as statistical surveys revealed seemingly unending and dramatic increases in consumption. In 1823 the duty on spirits was reduced from 9s. 4½d. a gallon to 2s. 4¾d. and, as a result, legal consumption more than trebled from 2,303,000 gallons in 1823 to 7,171,000 in 1852. A report to parliament on the numbers arrested for drunkenness between 1831 and 1851 described Glasgow as the worst city in the kingdom, 'the Presbyterian Rome and the modern Gomorrah' with 'every twenty-second person in Glasgow once a year taken drunk to the police office'. This meant that 'Glasgow is three times more drunken than Edinburgh and five times more drunken than London'.[27] Vigorous reaction came in the form of the temperance movement, whose supporters saw drink as a fundamental cause of crime and degradation. The misery of the poor was blamed not on economic and social causes but on gross abuse of alcohol. But working-class reformers, including many Chartists, were also passionately committed to the campaign against the demon drink because they believed that only a sober radicalism could be effective. This was an important strand which ran through radical politics in the nineteenth century and which also embraced the co-operative movement and members of the Independent Labour Party, although they regarded brutalizing working and living conditions as the principal causes of heavy drinking rather than the other way round.

The anti-spirits movement was launched in the late 1820s by leading evangelical laymen such as John Dunlop, a Greenock magistrate who had written a major study of Scottish drinking customs, and William Collins, the noted Glasgow publisher. But the campaign did not meet with immediate success as it was split between those who advocated teetotalism and those who supported drinking in moderation. There was greater progress by the 1840s, as demonstrated by the famous visit to Scotland of the charismatic Irish champion of temperance, Father Theobald Mathew in 1842. Not only did he address an enthusiastic crowd of around 50,000 on Glasgow Green, he was also fêted by the leaders of Scottish temperance and managed to receive the pledge of abstinence from an estimated 40,000 of his fellow Irishmen who had settled in Scotland. In the same decade, both the Church of Scotland and the Free Church of Scotland adopted the temperance cause. In 1849 the Free Church petitioned parliament, and out of this came the movement's first notable success, the Forbes Mackenzie Act of 1853, so-called from its promoter, the Peebleshire laird of the same name. The Act, unique to Scotland, closed public houses on Sundays and from 11 p.m. to 8 a.m. on all other days. Strengthened by later legislation such as the Public House Amendment Act of 1862, it remained in force for over a century. On the Sabbath, only so-called 'bona fide' travellers could now go to hotels to drink. It was a loophole in the law which many later exploited. As temperance became more respectable among the urban middle classes, town councils enhanced the powers of the police to crack down on shebeens and illicit distillers. Even more significantly, spirit duty, whose earlier fall had accelerated the trend to heavy drinking, was more than doubled between 1853 and 1860.

The crusade for sobriety was intensified in the later nineteenth century. The young were directly targeted with the formation of the Band of Hope for children, while the Salvation Army and friendly societies such as the Rechabites became resolute supporters of the anti-drink campaign. The movement embraced all denominations, with the Catholic Church establishing its own temperance association, the League of the Cross. The aim increasingly was to offer a series of counter-attractions to the seductive allure of the drinking places. Temperance songs, such as 'Whisky's Awa'', were written – and some, like 'The Wild Rover', became so popular that they re-emerged in later generations as drinking songs! Teetotal concerts were also organized as an alternative to the 'free-and-easies'. The Glasgow Abstainers Union ran highly successful concerts in the City Hall on Saturday evenings between 1854 and 1914 without a break. Competitions were held to attract new talent and Harry Lauder, later the first Scottish popular entertainer to achieve an international reputation as the purveyor of his unique brand of Scots kitsch, made his name in one of these events. The temperance reformers even had a teetotal paddle-steamer, *The Ivanhoe*, which provided excursions on the Clyde from 1880 to compete with the steamboats that were notorious as floating public houses where binge-drinking was common (thus 'steaming' as the popular Scots term for 'drunken') and were not covered by the 1853 prohibition on the selling of alcohol on the Sabbath. The movement was far from being a middle-class crusade. Many labour leaders, including Keir Hardie and the Clydesiders David Kirkwood and Willie Gallacher, received their first political education in temperance lodges. Trades Councils consistently advocated abstinence and 'the early socialist movement was steeped in temperance attitudes'.[28]

What was the impact of all this effort? The first effect was seen among the middle classes, where temperance attitudes were common by the 1850s and were founded firmly on the evangelicalism of so many of the urban bourgeoisie at that time. This coincided with a boom in middle-class recreational activity as a rational and moral way to use leisure time. Gardening, bowling and choral singing all enjoyed considerable popularity in these years. Physical activity came to be seen as a means of promoting good fellowship and strengthening the virtues of will-power, perseverance and courage. Thus curling, rambling, cricket and, above all, golf enjoyed increasing middle-class patronage. There is also some evidence that by the 1860s the respectable working classes were drinking more at home or were not drinking at all: 'In Scotland the middle class, the skilled working class and women moved out and the pub world was left to the less "respectable" male working classes.'[29] Women were increasingly excluded, both as drinkers and as barmaids, and the Scottish pub now became the male domain which it long remained down to the 1960s. Yet the temperance movement failed to make much initial impact on the consumption of drink. By the later 1840s the consumption of duty-paid spirits was actually a little higher than it had been in the 1820s, and this despite the best efforts of the anti-drink campaigns over those decades. In time, however, the increases in spirit duty of the 1850s and the stricter licensing controls after 1853 had their effect. By 1900, per capita whisky consumption had fallen by one-half in relation to the levels prevailing in the 1830s, while beer consumption rose but not in proportion to the fall in the drinking of hard liquor.

But the victory of temperance was far from complete. Spirit consumption had indeed fallen dramatically by the 1860s, but then it stabilized and was still much the same by the early years of the twentieth century. Crucially, the level of duty did not significantly alter over this period. In addition, the licensed trade proved to be resilient and adept at retaining custom. A revolution occurred in pub structure and design, mainly in England but also to some extent in Scotland:

a new phenomenon, the 'gin palace' with plate-glass windows, richly ornamented façade, gilded lettering and brilliant lamps began to arouse comment. Its style became almost universal in urban pubs, and still influences their design today. Its splendour accentuated the contrast between the pub and the squalor of its surroundings. In towns very much darker at night than they now are, the huge and elaborate wrought-iron gas lamps which hung over the pub entrance extended the brilliance of the interior into the street . . .[30]

Faced with this beguiling competition, several more draconian rounds of tax increases were necessary to reduce spirit consumption further and so transform whisky from a cheap to an expensive drink. In 1860, spirits duty stood at 10s. per proof gallon; it rose to 30s. in 1918, and more than doubled again to 72s. 6d. in 1920. It was hardly surprising that there was soon evidence of a spectacular decline in whisky-drinking. By the 1930s consumption of spirits per head of population was less than a quarter of the levels recorded in the last decade of the nineteenth century. As T. C. Smout points out, this was a victory not so much for the temperance campaign as for the Chancellor of the Exchequer and the Treasury. It also reflected deeper changes in Scottish popular culture. The hegemony of drink among the working classes was already being eroded in the later nineteenth century with the emergence of a range of alternative recreations and entertainments on which surplus incomes could now be spent.

It was inevitable that, for most Scottish people before 1914, opportunities for recreation and sport were severely limited by poor earnings and the long, exhausting hours of manual labour. But even in the 1840s and 1850s, strong drink and the public house were not by any means the only leisure alternatives for the urban masses. Robert Duncan's recent study of the mining town of Wishaw in Lanarkshire describes a surprisingly long list of activities pursued by the local population. These included throwing quoits (a sport that produced fierce rivalry between teams drawn from different pits, works and communities), pigeon racing and fancying, whippet racing, music-making (which then led to the eventual formation of brass, silver and pipe bands), and betting and gambling. If towns such as Wishaw are typical, historians need to revise their view that the workers of the new industrial towns were for the most part starved of recreation. Nevertheless, a number of factors soon came together to extend the range of opportunity significantly and eventually to create a revolution in mass leisure.

From the 1870s, if not before, real wages for many Scots in employment started to rise, in some cases – like that of skilled artisans – quite sharply. Low pay and broken time were still a feature of several jobs such as casual and general labouring but the average upward trend was undeniable. Scholars still dispute the precise timing and extent of the trend but for Britain as a whole real wages improved by around 80 per cent over the period 1850–1900 and the pattern in Scotland was not likely to be significantly different. Many workers therefore had a little more spare cash – but also the opportunity to spend it, with the spread of holidays and shorter hours. Not all benefited but, by the end of the First World War, in a number of trades average weekly hours had fallen to 48 hours (where 50–60 hours had been the norm in the later nineteenth century). The Saturday half-holiday, which was crucial to the rise of football as a mass spectator sport, was already common in many urban employments by 1900. Also from the 1880s the week-long unpaid summer holiday was appearing and in iron and steel making and some other trades many works shut down for a full fortnight of unpaid leave by 1914.

Against this background the revolution in urban transport enabled the commercialization of leisure. The development of a steamboat network on both the Forth and Clyde, followed by the expansion of the railway system from the 1840s, allowed the industrial masses in the west of Scotland to go 'doon the watter' to the Clyde seaside resorts and explore the scenic beauties of the southern Highlands by day excursion. Day trips to Loch Lomond were also common as early as 1820, and by 1844 the competition between steamboats had reduced the sail from Balloch to the head of the loch and back to 6d steerage. Temperance and friendly societies and mission halls eagerly sponsored these excursions as a way of providing a healthier moral alternative to the perceived debauchery of the traditional fair holidays. Ironically, however, heavy drinking soon became one of the attractions of a steamboat trip. By 1870 going for a sail 'doon the watter' was so popular that only the very poorest in Glasgow and the industrial towns of the western Lowlands would spend the entire summer at home. Irish immigrants could also spend a few days in the old country by taking advantage of the shipping companies' price war, which had cut the steerage fare from the Clyde to Belfast in the 1860s from 1s. to 4d.

The transport revolution was also crucial to the rapid increase in the popularity of the new spectator sports such as football. By the 1880s the railway companies were running 'specials' to take fans to the new grounds and also allowing more choice on which team to follow. The trams were even more important. By the early 1900s, Glasgow had three of the biggest sports stadiums in the world – Hampden, Ibrox and Parkhead – each capable of accommodating many thousands of spectators. The trams, which were at first horse-drawn and then powered by electric traction from 1898, provided a cheap and regular system of transport which enabled the gathering of these huge spectator concentrations.

Leisure opportunities also expanded because of the initiative of town councils, churches, temperance organizations and political groups. The city fathers built libraries, art galleries and public halls to bring 'rational' recreation to the masses while the building of parks and municipal baths was designed to improve the health of the town population. All these initiatives were designed to contribute to civic pride and distinction. Aberdeen's Art Gallery opened in 1885, the Museum of Science and Art in Edinburgh (from 1904 the Royal Scottish Museum) was housed in a handsome new building in Chambers Street constructed over three phases from 1861 and a museum and art gallery was established in Dundee in 1872. A spirit of civic competition and emulation was at work. The Glasgow museum was founded in 1870, before moving to a more opulent and impressive building at Kelvingrove in 1901. There was some concern in Glasgow that formal galleries and museums would not have an immediate appeal for the working classes. This led to the establishment of the People's Palace on Glasgow Green, a combination of museum, gallery, gardens and music hall, built specifically to meet the needs of the poorer classes in the east end of the city. In its first year it attracted more than 770,000 visitors. Glasgow was also to the fore in developing parks. By 1914 the city owned 1,561 acres of parkland – much more than any other municipality in Scotland. But most towns, large and small, laid down parks in this period. They were designed to provide space for a range of sports from putting to football, for walking past well-ordered and attractive flower beds and for summer concerts held in elegant bandstands. In addition, some towns had a policy of siting their museums in or near the new municipal park. An important feature of these council initiatives was the contribution made by wealthy benefactors, who funded halls, museums, galleries and libraries and also gifted or bequeathed fine art collections. The Coats family of thread millionaires built the museum at Paisley which opened in 1871. The Caird Hall in Dundee, the Usher Hall and McEwan Hall in Edinburgh and the Cowdray Hall in Aberdeen stand to this day as impressive monuments to this age of Victorian benefaction. A large part of Glasgow's fine art collection at Kelvingrove was also gifted by wealthy local families and their heirs. In numerous Scottish towns public libraries were supported by the Carnegie Trust, established by the hugely successful American steel magnate, Andrew Carnegie, who had been born in Dunfermline.

The churches competed vigorously with this explosion in secular leisure opportunities. Both Protestant and Catholic churches built temperance halls where, as the local parish priest at Hamilton put it in 1892, '. . . men could go after work for rational and harmless amusement. Under present conditions the only place available was the public house, and the evils arising therefrom were well known.'[31] The churches also ran excursions, picnic outings, dances and sports days. At first some churchmen fulminated against the craze for football with apocalyptic warnings that there would be no football in heaven. The Young Men's Christian Association (YMCA) annual conference in 1890 launched a vigorous attack against the 'perfectly sickening' obsession with football. But there was soon a recognition that the game was here to stay as the sport of the people and as a healthy pastime it also suited the vogue for 'muscular Christianity'. In the event the leagues eventually organized by the churches and the Boys' Brigade made a vital contribution to the development of the amateur game. Queen's Park grew out of the YMCA, and Celtic was founded by the Catholic Marist Brother, Walfrid, to provide clothing, free dinners and cash support for the poor of the Catholic parishes of the east end of Glasgow. The socialist movement approached the development of recreation with a similar enthusiasm. Much leisure activity strengthened the bonds of community and solidarity, provided an alternative to the corrosive attractions of alcohol and promoted self-improvement. All of this fitted well with the socialist ethic. Thus there were socialist swimming clubs, annual co-operative galas and picnics and socialist choirs. From one of these emerged the Glasgow Orpheus Choir in 1906, later to achieve worldwide fame under its legendary conductor, Hugh Roberton. Clarion Scouts and Clarion Campers held regular summer camps and Clarion Cycling Clubs were so numerous that a competitive league was established. The 'safety' bicycle, fitted with Dunlop pneumatic tyres after 1888, became the basis of a relatively cheap outdoor pastime which had wide appeal well beyond the socialist movement.

The late nineteenth century saw the birth of a mass entertainments industry in which the music hall and theatre, football, the cinema and dancing were the central elements. The music halls and theatres took popular entertainment in Scotland into a new phase. From the 1870s they started to replace the old 'free-and-easies' by catering for family audiences and all social classes in larger halls of increasing splendour. In the years before the First World War, even more magnificent theatrical palaces such as the King's (1904) and the Alhambra (1910) in Glasgow were opened. It was indicative of their popularity that the most successful theatrical entrepreneur in Britain of this era, H. E. Moss, first made his fortune in Scotland before establishing the renowned Moss Empires Ltd which dominated the business throughout Britain in the Edwardian era. From the new music halls first emerged the sentimentalized and tartanized caricature of the Scot as the 'Bonnie Hieland Laddie', resplendent in kilt and plaid and mouthing comic songs, couthy sayings and jokes. What was to become a familiar stereotype was first developed by W. F. Frame, who demonstrated its potential among the North American emigrants from Scotland when he took Carnegie Hall in New York by storm in 1898. When copied and further refined by Harry Lauder, the image proved irresistible to audiences throughout the world.

But the theatres were soon to feel the competition from the cinema, even if at first there was little sign that the 'pictures' would become the new working-class entertainment. The films were shown as curiosities by travelling showmen, though they were actually less popular than the lantern slides that usually accompanied them. But specialist cinemas soon developed; the first built for the purpose was the Electra Theatre, in Sauchiehall Street, Glasgow, opened in 1910. Expansion was rapid. A town like Motherwell had four cinemas by 1914, and Glasgow may have had as many as 66 before the outbreak of the Great War and 104 in 1938. The 'pictures' had a magical and universal appeal. Admission charges at 1d. to 6d. were very low compared to the theatre and it was therefore scarcely surprising that working-class women with children, who had been all but driven out of public houses by temperance legislation, made up a significant part of the audiences. In 1937 a survey of 8,000 West Lothian schoolchildren found that 36 per cent attended the cinema once a week and a quarter more than once. Only 6 per cent never went. The cinema's popularity started to affect the variety theatres, which went into relative decline in the 1920s and 1930s. They were also facing stiff competition from dancing as the great night out of the inter-war period for the adult young of both sexes. 'Dancin' daft' Glasgow had an incredible 159 registered dance halls in 1934. But Saturday night dancing was also found all over urban Scotland in civic, church and drill halls, as well as in registered dance halls. For most young adults it was a social experience, but for some, 'ballroom dancing also became a refined art form of the common people'.[32]

By the 1930s going to the cinema and the dancing were second only to watching and playing football as the most common leisure pursuits of young working-class men. Football had developed a mass following from the 1870s and 1880s. The first Scottish club was Queen's Park, founded in 1867, the Scottish Football Association was established in 1873 and by the 1890s its membership varied between 130 and 190 clubs. Football became the working man's game *par excellence*, sweeping all before it. Cricket, rugby football, rowing and bowling had all gained some popularity among the skilled working classes in the 1860s but none could eventually compete with the appeal of soccer. It was a game born out of the industrial communities of central Scotland. Football teams were often first formed as work's teams and then extended to neighbourhoods and communities. Football did not require any expensive equipment and could be played on almost any surface, an important consideration in towns where massive physical expansion often reduced space for recreation. There was also more to it than this: 'to the worker with magic in his feet, football offered a way out of the industrial system; to him for whom the magic was only in the mind it offered a few hours of escapist release'.[33] The workers became football mad. One estimate suggests that, at its peak, one in four of all males aged 15–29 in central Scotland belonged to a soccer club. But watching the game and supporting the team quickly became just as important as playing. Football became big business, with large, purpose-built stadiums charging for entry, players on professional contracts and limited liability companies governing the finances. Gates of 70,000 and above when the bigger teams met were not unknown before the First World War. The first Scotland and England International was watched by 3,500 people in 1872. In 1906 the same fixture attracted more than 121,000 spectators, and in 1937 created a world record of 149,515.

Football was not simply a sport. It also became a powerful focus of national identity. From the start there was a separate Scottish league and national team. Before 1900 Scotland beat England with gleeful regularity, but even when this was no longer the case the annual match between the two nations was invested with emotional patriotic fervour. In the late 1930s it was not uncommon for as many as 60,000 Scots to make the trip south to Wembley for the confrontation with the 'auld enemy'. Football also became an emphatically working-class game as middle-class interest fell away. The teams that emerged by their very nature reflected religious, community and ethnic differences within the population and the rivalries built on these divisions and tensions helped increase interest and attendances even further. Football promoted local identities as well as national ones. Thus Dundee Harp, Edinburgh Hibernians and Glasgow Celtic were the champions of the immigrant Catholic Irish. At first Celtic (founded 1888) enjoyed a good relationship with Glasgow Rangers, the team destined to become their deadly rivals in future years. In 1892 the *Scottish Sport* noted 'the light blues are favourites with the Parkhead' and a year later described how both teams 'are getting very pally'.[34] However, a run of Celtic victories soon put paid to this harmony. The Scottish press demanded a Scottish champion to take on 'the Irishmen', and Rangers emerged as that team. From the 1896 season it was noted that there was 'bad blood' between the two and that sectarian bitterness was already present. It culminated in a major riot at the Cup Final of 1909 which led to the uprooting and burning of goalposts and nets, followed by bloody running battles that lasted well into the evening. Nearly 100 fans were injured. Celtic and Rangers had become the standard-bearers of their two communities and their confrontations on the football field a noisy outlet for the bitter sectarian tensions of the west of Scotland.

16

Religion and Society

The issue of religious belief, practice and influence in the new urban and industrial Scotland of the nineteenth century is a contentious one. Until quite recently there was a broad consensus among historians and sociologists across Europe that the economic revolutions of the period had massively weakened the old religious loyalties and attachments. Society became more secular, so it was argued, because of the corrosive effects of scientific and technical thinking on traditional beliefs, the speed and scope of urbanization which overwhelmed the existing structure of church and chapel, and the fact that the working classes became rapidly alienated from organized religion which became dominated by the values of the urban middle classes. In effect this thesis suggested that industrialization and urbanization started the decline of religion, a process which culminated in the second half of the twentieth century when secular values became dominant in many European countries.

This was the conventional wisdom among most scholars until the last couple of decades. But these ideas have now attracted a robust critique from a new generation of historians and social scientists in Britain and elsewhere who have cast doubt on some key features of the theory of secularization. They have argued that church membership did not collapse and religious values continue to influence politics, education and welfare and to shape powerfully national identities. If secular forces did begin to influence religiosity, they started to have a major effect only in the very late nineteenth century rather than in the earlier decades of rapid urban growth.

Callum Brown, the scholar who has done most to develop the revisionist approach to religious decline in Scotland, suggests rightly that the Scottish experience offers an excellent opportunity to test the validity of these competing views. As has already been seen, over a period of less than 150 years Scotland was transformed from being a predominantly agricultural society to the position of the world's second industrial nation. Moreover, as earlier chapters of this book have shown, the Scottish rate of urban growth after *c.* 1760 was significantly faster than England's and the process of economic change more intense and convulsive than that of her southern neighbour. Here indeed was a society *par excellence* in which traditional religious structures must have been powerfully challenged by the enormous force of rapid industrialization. What, then, does the Scottish experience reveal about the validity or otherwise of the secularization theory?

I

Even a superficial examination shows that religious values continued to remain central to the ethos of Victorian Scotland. The most visible sign of Christian influence was the maintenance of the Sabbath when shops and businesses closed and even most tram services were cancelled. As late as the 1950s, Scottish pubs remained shut on a Sunday and no games or sport took place. Crucially, the keeping of the Sabbath did not always depend on law. Sunday shopping, for instance, had never been made illegal. It did not happen simply because it was regarded as socially unacceptable until the 1970s to open a shop on a Sunday. Also the Protestant Churches continued to exert a huge influence in public life. Church leaders, such as Thomas Chalmers, possibly the most influential Scot of the nineteenth century, and the first Moderator of the Free Church after it broke with the Established Church in 1843, dominated national debates on the Poor Law, education and a host of other matters of social policy. Figures of lesser eminence, like James Begg, Norman Macleod and Thomas Guthrie, were all at the centre of public discourse throughout the Victorian period and made major contributions on issues such as housing for the working classes, temperance and sanitary reform. The clergy were among the social and intellectual leaders of Scotland and from their families came a constant stream of young men and women reared in a domestic atmosphere of religious duty and educational endeavour who went on to make their mark in the Scottish professions both at home and in the empire.

The religious analysis had an impact on most areas of public policy, which was framed for much of the period in emphatic moral terms. This could have both positive and negative effects. Evangelical

Presbyterianism, for instance, was the moral dynamic behind the initiative taken by the Scots in the Edinburgh and Glasgow Emancipation Societies during the British agitation against slavery between 1833 and the outbreak of the American Civil War. On the other hand, there was also a tendency to reduce complex economic, social and political problems to a simple matter of personal religion and morality, thus over-emphasizing individual responsibility to the virtual exclusion of environmental factors outside individual control. As the Free Church newspaper, *The Witness*, put it in 1841: 'irreligion is the cause of this miserable estate of things, and . . . religion is the only cure'.[1] The result was a somewhat myopic commitment to voluntary effort for much of the nineteenth century and a passionate religious mission which often went hand in hand with a profound hostility to state intervention in industry and commerce.

From one angle it might appear that the influence of the Churches on social issues was gradually crumbling in the nineteenth century. The Poor Law Amendment Act of 1845 took exclusive responsibility for the care of the poor out of Church hands, thus ending a system that had endured from the time of the Reformation and before. In 1872 came universal state elementary education, which also transferred local power over schools to lay boards outside ecclesiastical control. But to suggest that this effectively terminated the influence of religious values in civic life would be mistaken. The membership of these new secular authorities was appointed on the basis of election and local democracy allowed elected churchmen and committed laymen to maintain the relevance of religious ideals in Scottish public life. In fact, far from religious erosion, the Victorian Age saw a quite remarkable and hitherto unprecedented fusion between Christian ethos and civic policy. Many of the great urban issues of the day, such as poor housing, sanitation, crime and the provision of public utilities, were dealt with from an overtly religious perspective. Town councillors were also often kirk elders and were not slow to bring their religious principles to bear on the many problems that confronted them in the urban environment. The influence of evangelical ministers and leading laity has been detected in areas as varied as the free access to public parks in Edinburgh and Glasgow, sanitary legislation in the 1850s, the licensing of public houses and work schemes for the unemployed and hungry in the cities and in the famine-ravaged western Highlands of the 1840s. Much Victorian social policy after 1850 was driven by a religious vision which equated social improvement with moral improvement and placed particular emphasis on the values of hard work, self-help, thrift and temperance.

Recreation was not immune from the impact of this dynamic evangelical culture. By the 1880s more workers than ever before were enjoying increasing leisure time, particularly on a Saturday. The majority also had more money in their pockets as real wages crept upwards in the later nineteenth century. The result was a boom in the leisure economy, with new attractions like the music hall, football and, by the 1900s, the picture house. But the churches were not slow to respond to this competition. Even in the field of popular culture, religious organizations and values remained important. Church-affiliated organizations, such as the hugely popular Boys' Brigade, which was founded in Glasgow in 1863, required attendance at prayer meetings but also ran swimming and football leagues for teenage boys. The Bands of Hope were founded to promote teetotalism among children but they too organized their own football competitions with over 70 teams playing in the Band of Hope Union Cup by the 1910s in the west of Scotland. The Band of Hope also provided magic lantern shows and experimented with the 'cinematograph' in order to convey its message of moral improvement. Protestant and Catholic churches held lectures, socials, dances, concerts and organized excursions to the seaside and other places of interest for their congregations. In late-nineteenth-century Scotland there was still a strong and persistent religious flavour to much popular culture.

Religion also had a significant impact on Scotland's sense of national and imperial identity. The role of the Scots in the British Empire was given a powerful moral legitimacy by the missionary movement. Empire could be seen as a territorial precondition for the expansion of God's kingdom in order to liberate countless millions from the dreadful grip of paganism. In India, Africa, the Caribbean and China, Scots missionaries were to the fore. The greatest British medical mission centre of all was in Edinburgh. Famous missionaries such as David Livingstone, the national icon who became almost a Scottish saint, Mungo Park, Mary Slessor and Christina Forsythe were celebrated at home in the press, in magic lantern shows, speaking tours, pamphlet literature and best-selling books. A key theme was how the unspeakable barbarity and terrible savagery of native peoples in far-off lands could eventually be overcome when they heard the Christian message. This not only gave a moral imperative to imperial expansion but also added a fresh glamour to Victorian religion. Mary Slessor, who had worked as a mill girl in Dundee, spent 28 years as a United Presbyterian missionary in Nigeria. When she arrived in 1876, she encountered a society based on slavery where a dead chief was accompanied to his grave by hundreds of slaves who were then killed or buried alive with him. To end such abomination was a Christian duty. It is not surprising that local communities in Scotland were keen to form their own links with missionary endeavours by raising funds and praying in church for their courageous fellow countrymen and women doing God's holy work in foreign lands. In one sense, this was an extension of the Christian mission at home which had tried to bring the gospel to the 'pagan' masses who were said to concentrate in the inner slum areas of the great cities, alienated alike from church connection and religious observance.

By underwriting the empire as a moral undertaking, religion helped to strengthen the union with England but also assumed great significance as an important factor reinforcing Scottish identity. The father of the Kirk, John Knox, was a national hero in Victoria's reign, 'a sort of theocratic Jefferson'.[2] The General Assembly of the Church of Scotland, before the Disruption of 1843 and in the absence of a Scottish parliament, provided a national forum for debate on the state of the nation. Some argue that the emergence of the Free Church in 1843 with the exodus of around a third of the ministers and even more of the laity from the 'auld Kirk' did have nationalist overtones. The dispute over patronage that led to the great schism was in opposition to a landlord class that had become significantly anglicized and it was the Westminster parliament which not only passed the hated patronage legislation in the first place in the eighteenth century, in violation of the Treaty of Union, but had then studiously ignored repeated invitations to intervene to defuse the developing crisis between church and state.

There is clear evidence, therefore, that in the era of industrialization and urbanization religion remained a powerful force in the lives of the Scottish people, influencing values, providing a guide to personal conduct and helping to fashion contemporary social, welfare and educational policies, as well as moulding both imperial and national identities. It now remains to establish the trends in church membership, because a key element in the secularization theory is that church affiliation, especially among the working classes, went into rapid decline in western Europe as urbanization advanced. The trend of churchgoing is difficult to determine, simply because censuses of church attendance took place only infrequently and differing methods of enumeration were often employed, making it difficult to compare like with like over time. Brown's work on these data, however, suggests no significant decline in *churchgoing* in the Scottish cities between the 1830s and 1890s, although afterwards there was evidence of a clearer downward trend. *Church adherence* levels, which included all those connected with a church either as adult members or as Sunday school scholars, are easier to quantify. They reveal that church membership in Scotland probably more than doubled between 1830 and 1914, at a faster rate of increase than national population growth, and peaked in 1905. Equally significant is the evidence from the Registrar-General's returns on where couples married (though, of course, a church wedding may have simply denoted a desire for respectability rather than sincere belief). In 1861–70, only 0.2 per cent of weddings in Scotland were by 'non-religious forms'. By 1881–90 the figure still remained very low, at 2.5 per cent. Only in 1901–10 is there an increase, when the proportion of weddings conducted under 'non-religious forms' rose to 6.4 per cent.

These figures are national averages which inevitably conceal as much as they reveal. They also tell us little about active churchgoing or about the inner beliefs of people. The Church of Scotland's Life and Work Committee reported gloomily in 1874 that only 174,371 of its 679,488 official adherents had been present at communion in that year and that many members were merely nominal adherents. The problem was particularly acute in the cities, where large numbers had no contact with the Church at all. This complaint echoed that of such influential figures as Thomas Chalmers, who had asserted in 1847 that the great towns contained 'a profligate, profane and heathen population' who were both a disgrace to Christian civilization and a potent menace to social order.[3] It was this alarming diagnosis of 'masses of practical heathenism' in the slums of the cities of Scotland that inspired the extraordinary wave of church building, evangelical mission and philanthropic endeavour in the urban areas which is considered in more detail below.[4] The 1890 Commission on the Religious Condition of the People concluded that the 'unchurched' were most likely to come from the ranks of the poor, the unskilled, casual and general labourers, though it also conceded that the Catholic Church had managed to attract the loyalty of many Irish immigrants who belonged to this class. But at the same time there was no general or uniform alienation of the urban working classes from the churches: 'If the vast majority of the working classes did not go to church, it remained the case that the vast majority of churchgoers were working class.[5] In fact, the backbone of most Presbyterian urban congregations was the upper working class or 'labour aristocracy' of artisans, tradesmen and clerks, who developed a strong culture of religious respectability in the Victorian era and who were to be found in especially larger numbers within the Free Church.

Outside the large towns there was still plenty of evidence of religious adherence by the mass of the population. The western Highlands and Islands had been converted to evangelical Protestantism earlier in the nineteenth century and had remained a strong citadel of Christian belief and piety ever since. In the agricultural parishes of the central and southern Lowlands, most families had a church connection though there was not the same level of religious commitment as in Gaeldom. The mining districts of Lanarkshire and the Lothians contained deeper pools of indifference. But even here the total impact of religion, whether direct or indirect, was still considerable. An illustration can be given from Motherwell in Lanarkshire, which in 1891 was a booming industrial town of nearly 19,000 inhabitants who were employed mainly in mining and iron-making. Its only substantial public building was the Town Hall, built in 1887. The local library was not opened until 1904. Yet it possessed no fewer than 11 churches, providing accommodation for about 60 per cent of the population of churchgoing age, in addition to a whole series of choirs, men's clubs, Boys' Brigades, women's guilds, temperance associations and an impressive Young Men's Christian Association Institute founded in 1899. The Motherwell case suggests a general point about the force of religion in urban Scotland. The churches were able to spread their power and influence far beyond the ranks of their *formal* membership through an active programme of social and religious action and an unremitting campaign against the urban vices of intemperance, improvidence and irreligion, conducted through a myriad of clubs, schools, classes and societies and the army of committed laity who unceasingly carried the message of the gospel into the community. This prodigious energy came from the spiritual force of evangelicalism.

2

Evangelicals took the view that faith was a matter of the heart rather than the mind and was a gift from God through revelation and conversion. Assurance of salvation rested only on the election by God of the repentant sinner. Christ alone could accomplish this but visible symbols of election could also be found in observance of the Sabbath, good works and spiritual exercises in atonement for sin. But the Evangelicals were less interested in theological debate than in action, first to transform individuals and help each human being to make his or her own personal journey to God, and second to reform society so as to make that journey easier and less hazardous. This call to action in God's name produced a huge release of missionary energy, the development of what has been termed 'aggressive Christianity'. It was the spiritual source of the endless stream of Sunday schools, mission societies, benevolent societies, Bible classes and prayer groups that enveloped urban Scotland in the nineteenth century.

By the 1830s a coherent focus had been given to these evangelical ideals of mission and conversion by Thomas Chalmers. He himself had experienced an intense evangelical conversion in 1811 and tried to put his ideas into practice as minister of the rural parish of Kilmany in Fife. His principles were based on those of the sixteenth- and seventeenth-century ideal of the 'godly commonwealth' in which there was no separation of church and state but with both bound in sacred partnership to create a society that conformed to the word of God. Kilmany almost became a laboratory for the evangelical method, with preaching, schooling, systematic visitation and effective organization of poor relief all combined to mould the community in God's image. An even greater opportunity came when Chalmers was appointed to the Tron parish in Glasgow. In 1819 a new parish of St John's was created out of this larger area and here Chalmers began his famous experiment to transform the religious beliefs, morals and social values of a poor inner-city community. Four schools were established, poor relief was radically altered and came to be based on voluntary giving rather than compulsory assessment, and an active ministry was created with dedicated lay visitors and Sunday school teachers. Despite its superficial short-term success, however, the experiment failed miserably in its primary objective of transforming the community of St John's into a 'godly' society. In fact, the whole exercise might have been counter-productive. Chalmers took the view that poverty was basically a result of personal moral failure. His rigorous experiment of imposing character tests on the distribution of meagre doles to the poor at the bottom of trade depressions could have done little to enhance his appeal among the city's working classes.

Nevertheless, the St John's scheme was of fundamental importance in the later development of 'aggressive Christianity'. Chalmers and others believed it to be a success and that the method employed would have had a deep impact on urban irreligion if only Glasgow Town Council had given more support. A true partnership between civil and religious authorities would ensure that Christianity could rise to the challenge of an industrial society and the 'godly commonwealth' would indeed be brought about. These views struck a chord with many of the urban middle classes. In part this was because Chalmers was by far the most outstanding preacher and the most charismatic church leader of the age. His pre-eminence was graphically demonstrated when he died in 1847 and an estimated 100,000 mourners attended his funeral in Edinburgh. But Chalmers had also produced an apparently effective blueprint for evangelical action which might resolve one of the most daunting and insoluble social problems of the age. In addition, his social ideas were also those of the propertied classes because, like them, he accepted the existing economic order to be divinely ordained, opposed 'democracy' as a sure route to anarchy, condemned trade unions and believed that the pursuit of self-interest would through the 'invisible hand' also promote the general welfare of all citizens. But Chalmers also argued that with the possession of wealth came the heavy responsibility of philanthropic action. This also generated a deep response among his middle-class audience:

Through responding to the call to action, evangelicalism was for the Victorian middle classes a source of identity offering separateness from the older landed élites and from the working classes: the dressing in 'Sunday best' clothes, the sense of belonging conferred by the family name inscribed at the end of the rented pew, the visible 'givings' to church missionary funds of one kind or another, or for the more wealthy the sponsoring of an evangelist or even an entire mission church in 'the "slums"'. The work of volunteers, and more especially of the growing army of 'home missionaries' from the 1840s onwards was publicised for middle class sponsors, affirming bourgeois values and separateness through the power of mission work to improve society.[6]

However, the spiritual and social power of evangelicalism was not confined to urban Scotland. One of its most remarkable manifestations was to be seen in parts of the western Highlands and Islands in the first half of the nineteenth century. Not only was there a new spiritual awakening there but religious revivals started to occur with increasing frequency in such areas as Breadalbane, Perthshire, in 1816, on a series of occasions on the Island of Lewis between 1824 and 1833 and throughout Skye and parts of the Outer Hebrides in the early 1840s. Accounts of these episodes describe communities seized with religious frenzy, convulsions, wailing and fits. But these were simply the dramatic peaks of a general increase in popular spiritual enthusiasm in many parishes in the region. In part this may have been due to the devastating impact of clearance and famine in the Highlands in this period. The evangelical message gave hope, consolation and spiritual comfort to a people racked by great psychological pressures as their familiar world disintegrated with alarming speed in the first few decades of the nineteenth century. Christian conversion was possible only through complete submission to the Divine Will. A refusal to accept suffering was tantamount to questioning the Will of God, while resignation to suffering was Christian obedience to God's plan. In the early years of the potato famine, one missionary society in the Highlands stated '. . . for He hath said I will never leave thee nor forsake thee. It is this word that your teachers are, day and night, occupied in dispensing to the starving families of the Highlands and Islands.'[7] Evangelicalism also gave a spiritual certainty amid the social trauma of the transition from clanship to clearance by concentrating the minds and emotions of the people in an intensely personal struggle for grace and election. The miseries of this life were not therefore simply to be endured but were a necessary agony for those who wished to attain eternal salvation in the next.

The religious revolution in parts – though not in all areas – of Gaeldom was also carried through by the spread of Lowland evangelicalism into the Highlands and by the development of religious forces indigenous to the region. Evangelical preaching and mission had started as long ago as the 1790s with the Society for Propagating the Gospel at Home

founded by the brothers James and Robert Haldane, who saw evangelization of the Highlands as part of their work to bring Christianity to
the heathen populations of far-off lands. Indeed their work and that of
those who came later had much in common with the foreign missions.
Preachers were itinerant, the Christian message was conveyed in Gaelic,
a direct appeal was made to the emotions and tracts were widely
distributed to maintain spiritual interest when the missionaries moved
on. Similar techniques were employed by such agencies as the three
Gaelic Schools Societies and the Highland Missionary Society which
followed in the footsteps of the Haldanes in subsequent decades.

A significant indigenous force were the 'Men' or *Na Daoine*, who
were lay preachers (so called to distinguish them from the ordained
ministers of the church). They were a spiritual élite, successors to the
tacksmen of the clan society in terms of their eventual social influence,
and a major factor in converting entire communities to evangelical
Protestantism in the first half of the nineteenth century. It must be
remembered, however, that their impact was relatively limited in many
areas, such as the Inner Hebrides below Skye and most of the central
and southern Highlands. Elsewhere, however, their dominance by the
1840s was undeniable. The power of the Men first became obvious in
Easter Ross in the 1740s and it spread to the west and north in the
following 50 years. They were as much a social as a religious élite,
providing the communal leadership that was vanishing in the traditional
society as a result of the emergence of commercial landlordism and the
growing pressures on the tacksman class. For the most part, they were
drawn from the better-off crofters and tradesmen rather than from the
underclass of cottars and squatters; but their standing and influence
depended above all on their personal qualities of intense spiritual
commitment, deep knowledge of scripture and capacity to blend and
adapt traditional Gaelic culture and speech with the Christian message
to maximum effect. Some were reputed to have the gift of prophecy,
the second sight, which indicated their close relationship with the deity,
and many employed folk tales and popular symbolism adapted to
Christian purposes. Though they did not necessarily have a formal
education, the Men were clearly individuals of great natural ability
with the personal charisma to project the Word of God in a way that
helped to stimulate the series of revivals which became an important
facet of Highland religious life in the first half of the nineteenth century.

Their early prominence can be traced to the role they played in the huge public communions which became common in many parts of Gaeldom. Because of the long distances involved, public communions were held only intermittently, but they normally attracted large crowds. In the days before the actual ceremonies, fellowship meetings were held to prepare the godly, and at these the Men emerged as lay catechists, interpreting scripture and addressing matters of spiritual concern; and in this function they could be seen, especially by parish ministers of Moderate inclination, to be a divisive influence, implicitly at least the leaders of a church within a church. They were indeed a threat to the Moderates because they branded ministers of that persuasion as ungodly and eulogized those of evangelical tendency. When the Disruption came in 1843, the Men were a crucial influence in winning most of the western Highlands and Islands for the Free Church.

Evangelicalism was at the root of this great schism in the Church of Scotland. In the 1830s the Evangelicals had gone from strength to strength. Thomas Chalmers, their leader, became Moderator of the national Church in 1832. The great religious conversions in the Highlands had established a veritable evangelical stronghold throughout the north-west and much of the Hebrides, while in the larger towns evangelical fervour and financial resources had been mobilized to great effect so that, astonishingly, over 200 churches had been built in the short period of seven years. Against this background it was not surprising that a confident Evangelical party in 1834 finally broke the historic dominance of the General Assembly by the Moderates who had maintained political control of the Church of Scotland for over two generations. The Moderate party preferred to avoid religious enthusiasm, were tolerant of intellectual deviation, more relaxed about church discipline and preferred to accept the civil power rather than confront it. The Evangelicals, however, were more uncompromising, committed to the independence of the Kirk under the sole leadership of Christ, and not prepared to surrender the sovereignty of the Church in spiritual matters to the state.

The catalyst for the so-called 'Ten Years Conflict' which racked the Church from 1833 to the final rupture in 1843 was patronage or who should have the final authority in the appointment of parish ministers. The Patronage Act of 1712 had been ambiguous; it granted individual patrons (mainly landowners) the right to present their candidate to vacant church offices within their gift. However, the presentation was to be accompanied by a 'call' signed by the male heads of family in the

374

parish, indicating their approval of the nominee. From the 1750s, however, and especially during the era of Moderate ascendancy, the popular 'call' came to be viewed as a mere formality and the Church courts increasingly upheld the rights of patrons. As Stewart J. Brown suggests: 'Patronage became a symbol of the subordination of the Church to the upper social orders, especially the landed interest.'[8] This arrogant extension of secular authority into the Kingdom of Christ provoked outrage among many of those of evangelical principles from the 1730s onwards and led to a growing exodus of tens of thousands of Presbyterians from the Church of Scotland into the secessionist Churches. But large numbers of Evangelicals still remained within the Established Church. When they achieved power in the 1830s, the Evangelicals were determined to deal with this historic grievance.

Their first initiative was the Veto Act of 1834. It fell short of an outright abolition of patronage, but it was still radical enough because it gave local congregations the absolute right to veto a minister presented by a patron. At first new appointments were settled peacefully but difficulties soon arose when some candidates appealed against the parish veto. In 1838 the Court of Session decreed, in a famous test case involving the nominee of the Earl of Kinnoul and the parish of Auchterarder, that the Veto Act had no existence in law, a judgement upheld a year later by the House of Lords. To add insult to injury, the Lords also denied the Church's claim to spiritual independence. This was certain to inflame most of the Evangelical party led by Thomas Chalmers. The 'non-intrusionists', as they were called, because of their opposition to the 'intrusions' of patrons' candidates into the ministry, held firmly to the fundamental principle of the 'Two Kingdoms' in which the state had no authority over the Church. Yet this had now been explicitly denied in a judgement handed down by the highest court in the land. In 1842 the General Assembly replied robustly with a remarkable document, the 'Claim of Right', which reiterated that only Christ had headship over the Church and that to recognize the supremacy of the state would be to deny that Divine authority.

Thereafter the crisis intensified. The Court of Session struck a second blow when it awarded damages of £15,000 to the patron and the rejected candidate in the Kinnoul case. With a further 39 patronage cases pending in the courts, it was clear that the Church faced escalating costs to maintain its principles. The alternative was for the 'non-intrusionists' to leave the Church altogether. This was thought increasingly likely, since neither parliament or the government was prepared to intervene to negotiate a compromise. Indeed, in early 1843 the government of Sir Robert Peel summarily dismissed the Claim of Right as 'unreasonable'. To accede to it might open the door to clerical tyranny. By that stage Disruption was probably inevitable and Chalmers in 1842 had already prepared a plan for the maintenance of a national Presbyterian Church through voluntary contributions alone. The climax came at St Andrews Church in Edinburgh on 18 May 1843, the first day of the annual General Assembly. After opening prayers, the retiring Moderator, the Revd Dr David Welsh, read out a long statement protesting that the British state had infringed the spiritual independence of the national Church in Scotland. When he had finished, he laid the protest on the table and walked into the street, to be followed *en masse* by the Evangelical leaders of the Church and their followers, leaving the left – or Evangelical – side of the church nearly empty. They walked in procession down Hanover Street 'through an unbroken mass of cheering people and beneath innumerable handkerchiefs waving from the windows'.[9] At Tanfield Hall the procession was joined by hundreds of other ministers, equally determined to leave the Established Church. The assembly then formally constituted itself as the 'Free Protesting Church of Scotland' and signed the Deed of Demission by which over 450 ministers resigned from the existing establishment and surrendered their churches, houses and incomes. It was a remarkable demonstration of the power of religious principle and commitment.

Secession from the Church of Scotland was not new. It had flourished and increased from the middle decades of the eighteenth century as organized dissent became more significant. But nothing on the scale of the Disruption had ever occurred before. This was a great and fundamental schism, not another secession. Nearly 40 per cent of the ministry and a third of the congregations, with some of the most dynamic and charismatic leaders, left the Established Church. The religious census of 1851 indicated that Protestantism was ruptured and that numbers attending the Free and Established Churches were now almost the same. The Free Church had a special appeal among the upwardly mobile middle class, skilled artisans and west Highland crofters and cottars who had been evangelized over the previous few decades. But despite the vast haemorrhage, the Established Church was not marginalized. It continued to attract the loyalty of the majority of the population in the Borders and maintained a considerable presence throughout the rural Lowlands as a whole. In the cities, the Established Church had most adherents among established professional and commercial groups and the urban poor.

Scottish Presbyterianism was hopelessly fractured by the 1840s, and in 1847 there emerged a third large grouping, the United Presbyterians, formed out of the two main groups of eighteenth-century seceders. Some have argued that these often bitter and competitive divisions fatally weakened the foundations of Protestantism and made it more difficult for the churches to combat secularism and apostasy in later decades. Certainly the Disruption accelerated the movement of the state into areas thought previously to be the province of the Church. In 1845 authority over poor relief was transferred from parish churches to elected boards. Religious tests for all university professorial appointments other than divinity chairs were abolished in 1852. Even in rural parishes the power of the kirk sessions to enforce moral discipline, an authority already disintegrating before the 1840s, finally collapsed in the 1850s and 1860s. From another perspective, however, the dramatic events of 1843 gave a fresh impetus to Scottish Presbyterianism. The Free Church had achieved huge credibility by vindicating the principle of spiritual independence from the state at great material sacrifice and establishing a new national institution from scratch through voluntary contributions. By 1849 it had erected 730 places of worship, built 400 manses, supported 513 teachers instructing 44,000 children and founded a college to educate its ministers, set in impressive buildings on the Mound in Edinburgh. A 'home mission' campaign to evangelize the urban poor was launched and overseas missions established. It was an exceptional achievement, based on the evangelical spirit and the contributions of the affluent urban middle and artisan classes who were the backbone of the Church's membership. In one sense, therefore, the success of the Free Church reflected the economic prosperity and dynamism of Scotland in the middle decades of Victoria's reign. There was always a danger, however, that the rich would come to see their chances of salvation measured by the value of their contributions, and the Church's mission might easily be distorted by these financial considerations.

Yet the Free Church was by no means the only expression of religious vitality in the middle decades of the nineteenth century. The Established Church had been satirized in the familiar rhyme as

The auld Kirk, the cauld Kirk
The Kirk wi'out the people

However, it still retained considerable support in Edinburgh, Glasgow and throughout the Lowlands, and it soon experienced something of a renewal under the leadership of men such as Norman Macleod of the Barony Church in Glasgow and James Robertson, Professor of Ecclesiastical History at Edinburgh. Their concern was to demonstrate that only an Established Church could be truly national and care for all the people. Numbers in the Established Church did start to rise from the 1860s. Moreover, the period was also punctuated by a series of emotional religious revivals in several working-class communities. In the 1840s there were 'awakenings' in Kilsyth and Aberdeen and, even more significantly, in the south-west and parts of the north-east in 1859–62. American evangelists such as Charles Finney and E. P. Hammond pioneered the distinctive revival service in Scotland of short, highly charged sermons, followed by the 'call' to come forward to those anxious whether or not they were among the 'saved'. The emphasis was moving away from sin and the terrible threat of eternal damnation to the joyous experience of conversion and salvation. The new formula made a considerable impact, especially when it was refined further in 1873–4 by two other American evangelists, Dwight L. Moody and Ira David Sankey. Their nationwide tour was a remarkable success. Services were orchestrated for maximum emotional appeal and special emphasis was given to the use of music. Ira Sankey made the harmonium so popular that it led to pleas in the 1870s by working-class mission congregations for the introduction of instrumental music. The reaction to Moody and Sankey demonstrated that puritanism was indeed faltering and that there was not the same appetite for hell-fire preaching.

The dynamism of Victorian religion was not confined to the Presbyterian churches. The Scottish Episcopal Church had seemed in irreversible decline in the eighteenth and early nineteenth centuries. But from the 1850s it recovered rapidly, recruiting from the anglicized upper classes who were concerned about contemporary developments in Presbyterianism and also through evangelization among the urban working classes in the later nineteenth century. Some popular support came from Irish Protestant immigrants who were originally adherents of the Church of Ireland. As they were also staunch Orangemen, they added an interesting element to the social mix of episcopalianism. Between 1877 and a peak of 1914, the Episcopal Church managed to triple its membership. Since such smaller denominations as the Congregationalists and the Baptists were also flourishing, a greater diversity was developing in Scottish religious life in the later nineteenth century. One of the most significant manifestations of this was the resurgence of Catholicism, due to the great influx of Catholic Irish and, to a lesser extent from the 1880s, the settlement of immigrants from Italy and Russian-ruled Lithuania. When the Roman Catholic hierarchy was restored in 1878 there were already perhaps some 300,000 Catholics in Scotland. The traditional areas of strength since Reformation times were parts of Aberdeenshire and Banffshire and some island and mainland districts of Inverness-shire. By the 1870s, however, the vast majority of Scottish Catholics were of Irish birth or descent and lived in the industrial towns of the west of Scotland and, to a lesser extent, Dundee and Edinburgh.

As David Hempton has noted: 'Those historians of nineteenth-century Britain who suggest too easily that urbanisation was the nemesis of organised religion would do well to ponder the Irish experience.'[10] Certainly in the first wave of immigration to Scotland down to the 1850s there was considerable haemorrhage from the faith. The Church did not have enough priests or chapels to cope in the early decades of the nineteenth century. But the pattern changed dramatically later. In Glasgow alone, where the Catholic population rose by over 100,000 in the last 30 years of the nineteenth century, the number of priests serving the archdiocese increased from 74 to 234, many of them born and educated in Ireland. In a manner reminiscent of the achievements of the Free Church after 1843 but with much fewer resources, the Catholic hierarchy and the community created a great network of new parishes, chapels, schools and halls to serve spiritual and social needs. The result was a substantial rise in religious observance. The record shows that by the 1880s a strikingly high proportion of the Irish went to Sunday Mass on a regular basis. Here was one church that enjoyed unambiguous success among some of the poorest people in the urban working classes. Their faith provided these 'strangers in a strange land' with identity, spiritual solace and a sense of community. Far from causing alienation from religion, the experience of many Catholic immigrants in Scotland fortified their connection with the Church and made it even stronger for some than it had been in rural Ireland itself.

3

For much of the nineteenth century the Scottish Churches voiced little public criticism of the existing social order. Their position is succinctly stated by the ecclesiastical historian, A. C. Cheyne:

> Churchmen, it is clear, still accepted the existing order with almost unquestioning complacency, still taught submission as the prime virtue of the disadvantaged. The greater part of Scotland's poverty and misery was still ascribed, and the role of the environment minimised or ignored. The assumptions and assertions of the classical economists were still endorsed, eagerly or with resignation.[11]

Ministers, such as James Begg, who led a campaign for better housing for the working classes, and Thomas Guthrie, who made great efforts to improve the lot of vagrant children in the cities, were very much the exceptions before the 1870s and 1880s. Thomas Chalmers gave a powerful legitimacy to the prevailing views by his unfailing trust in voluntary effort, rejection of state intervention and fierce hostility to attempts by organized labour to raise wages by industrial action. Chalmers had embraced the ideals of the classical economists so enthusiastically that 'he gave something like a divine sanction to the consequences of uninhibited free enterprise'.[12] All over Scotland in the 1840s the majority of ministers shared his views, as can be seen by their parish contributions to the *New Statistical Account of Scotland*, published during that decade.

Little change occurred in these attitudes before the 1870s. The existing order was still accepted as ordained by God and social problems were seen primarily as the result of character weakness, irreligion and immorality. The United Presbyterians were more liberal in approach, but most churchmen still regarded extension of the franchise with deep suspicion, as seen in their opposition to the Reform Act of 1867. However, in the last quarter of the nineteenth century ideas started to change in a quite radical way. Partly this revolution in thinking was due to the impact of intellectual and social forces in the secular world. Social investigations pioneered by men like Charles Booth and Seebohm Rowntree, together with a stream of Royal Commissions on housing, the Poor Law, working conditions and wages, drew more attention to the force of environmental factors in social problems and played down the significance of individual responsibility and character. In the Churches, too, there was a flood of inquiries and surveys into social issues, which culminated in the Established Church with the creation of the Glasgow Presbytery Commission on the Housing of the Poor in Relation to their Social Condition of 1888–91 and the Commission on the Religious Condition of the People of 1889–96. These investigations drew the Church's attention to some uncomfortable social facts. They also helped to forge connections between trade unionists and activists in the early Labour movement which later helped to promote the development of a Christian socialist movement. At the same time the sacred tenets of the classical economists were being rejected by Alfred Marshall and other thinkers, while British society was becoming much more sympathetic to the idea of state intervention and help for the poor, sick, old and disadvantaged. The growing appeal of socialism, evidenced by the formation of the Scottish Labour Party in 1888 and Keir Hardie's entry into parliament in 1892, suggested a greater popular awareness of the influence of the environment on the individual.

Churchmen, however, were not simply reacting to the political and social ideas of the age, though they could hardly remain entirely insulated from them. Parallel developments were also taking place in the religious sphere. Here the most potent influence on the Protestant Churches was the liberal theology of the 1880s and 1890s and its focus on Christ's teaching about the Kingdom of God. The basic principle of this new approach was that the Kingdom of God should be able to be achieved on earth as well as in heaven. The United Presbyterian Church minister, Scott Matheson, drew out the implications of this in his *The Church and Social Problems* of 1893: 'The Church is to see God's will done on earth as it is in heaven, part of that will is to grapple with social wrongs, abolish poverty, and join in all lawful efforts to obtain for labour its due reward, and for the toilers a large degree of amenity in their lot.'[13] We are a long way here from the religious principles of earlier decades and the uncritical acceptance of the existing social order. What added force and legitimacy to the views of clerics like Matheson was that their analysis was not grounded on secular theory but rather on the authority of Holy Scripture.

The public impact of this 'social theology' was soon made apparent in the actions of some of the new generation of clergy. Hostility to trade unionism started to ebb away and there was considerable support from some clergy for the workers at the time of the prolonged railway

strike of 1890–91. During the Crofters' War of the 1880s in the western
Highlands, the Free Church General Assembly did not support violent
action but did assert that the intervention of the state was necessary to
correct the manifest social injustices in the Highlands. Between 1890
and 1914, interactions between the churches and the labour movement
became stronger with the formation of a group of around 100 individuals
based in Glasgow, Edinburgh and Dundee, drawn from trade unions,
academics and MPs, together with clergy from the Established, Free,
United Presbyterian, Episcopal and Catholic Churches. As the papal
encyclical, *Rerum Novarum*, had shown, the new emphasis on social
mission was not confined to the Protestant Churches. Through this
network, churchmen were able to share ideas with social reformers and
labour activists on such important issues of the day as old age pensions
and national insurance. These connections symbolized the more sympathetic response to organized labour and ensured that the Scottish
churches avoided alienating the organized working classes in the way
that occurred in this period in some continental countries, such as France
and Germany. Indeed, some leading figures in the labour movement, like
the Protestant, Keir Hardie, and the Catholic, John Wheatley, were
committed Christians, as were several prominent members of the Independent Labour Party. In the years before the First World War, several
of the churches also sponsored social action. The Established Church
and the United Free Church gave payments to unemployed adherents
in the trade depression of 1908–9, ran baby clinics and provided homes
for slum children. By 1910, both Churches had specialist committees
devoted to the preparation of policy on social issues.

Nevertheless, Christian socialism, though influential, was never more
than a minority movement among church members. Most of the laity
in the Protestant churches were indifferent or hostile and some elders
in the Church of Scotland openly critical as they saw the strategy of
social mission as nothing other than a surrender to atheistic socialism.
Christian socialism was emphatically a clerical movement and the fact
that its roots were not very deep in the Church of Scotland was
convincingly shown in the years after the Great War. During the actual
years of conflict, however, the Churches' quest for social justice actually
intensified. After 1916, both the Established Church of Scotland and
the United Free Church committed themselves to a joint programme of
social reconstruction and reform in Scotland. They hoped that the terrible
sacrifices of the war would best be remembered by the development of a

new Scotland which rejected the economic individualism of the past and was instead committed to equality and brotherhood. To this end plans for full union between the two Churches were resurrected in order to restore Presbyterian influence in the nation and ensure that the post-war world was founded on Christian principles. When the war ended, a joint National Mission of Rededication was established to bring this about.

Yet this was the high-water mark of socialist idealism before 1939. The strategy of religious and social regeneration crumbled during the dark years of economic recession and political tension in the late 1920s and 1930s. The Russian Revolution had had a shattering impact because it showed how, in the new revolutionary utopia of the workers' state, Christianity itself could face destruction. There was always the fear that this ideological cancer would spread to Scotland where serious labour unrest had already occurred on Clydeside and the working classes had become better organized through increased trade-union membership and the growing strength of the Labour Party. Social reconstruction slipped rapidly off the political agenda with the massive victory of the Conservatives in the 1918 election and the collapse of the brief post-war economic boom in 1921.

Against this background, conservative churchmen such as John White, Alexander Martin and James Harvey reasserted their position both in the Established and United Free Churches. Supported by middle-class laymen who dominated the church courts, they revived the nineteenth-century evangelical emphasis which had been attacked before the war by the Christian socialists. Social criticism was abandoned and instead the nation's ills were blamed once again on individual failings which could be cured only by controlling laziness, intemperance, gambling and sexual licence. Puritanism was reborn. At a more sinister level, between 1922 and 1938 the Presbyterian Churches mounted a systematic campaign against Irish immigrants and Roman Catholics of Irish descent, whom they saw as driving down wages, taking employment from native Scots and also a major cause of criminality and intemperance. The 'Scoto-Irish' had also contributed significantly to the historic breakthrough success of the Labour Party in Clydeside at the general election of 1922. The Revd John Maclaglan of Glasgow declared in the General Assembly that both the trade unions and Labour organizations in the west of Scotland were dominated by 'aliens' from Ireland while the Revd Duncan Cameron alleged that nearly all the leaders of the 1926 General Strike were Irish-born. Cameron reached even greater heights of fantasy in a speech in Paisley in that year when he claimed that the Scoto-Irish Catholics were an even more dangerous enemy of the Scots than had been the German Empire in the Great War! However, the attempt to make scapegoats of the Catholic Irish failed. Neither the Conservative nor Labour Party was prepared to introduce the legislation for which the General Assemblies of the Church of Scotland and the United Free Church pressed so enthusiastically year after year. The campaign was a false trail: it did little to support the revived evangelicalism of the Churches, alienated many Scots who regarded it as unworthy of Christians and only served to give a spurious respectability to resurgent sectarianism in the 1930s. It was a low point in twentieth-century Scottish ecclesiastical history. As Stewart J. Brown notes: 'At a time when large numbers in Scotland were in real need, both materially and spiritually, the national Church of Scotland seemed more intent upon reviving its ecclesiastical authority and proclaiming an exclusive racial nationalism, than in its mission to bring the gospel to all people.'[14] Equally importantly, the Churches had once again parted company with organized Labour when they roundly condemned the General Strike of 1926.

Other signs of difficulty had started to emerge in earlier decades. In 1930 the eminent church leader, John White, spoke of the change he had seen in his lifetime from an unquestioning acceptance of Christian orthodoxy to 'a secular rationalism, atheism and the New Psychology'. In the later nineteenth century, biblical scholarship had undermined the fundamental belief that Sacred Scripture was a single inspired text to be accepted literally by all Christians. In 1881 William Robertson Smith, a professor in the Free Church College at Aberdeen, dared to suggest that the Pentateuch was written by more than one hand. He lost his chair as a result of this admission, but the new scholarship soon became widely accepted. Doubts were also spread as the evolutionary ideas of Charles Darwin were debated in the press and popular literature. Biological evolution seemed incompatible with a literal interpretation of the Bible, especially when geologists like Sir Charles Lyell found difficulty in explaining how their understanding of the earth's creation could possibly be explained in terms of the seven days described in Genesis. Natural science, and the newer disciplines of psychology, anthropology and comparative religion, were all gradually increasing uncertainty about supernatural explanation. Some churchmen argued that even more powerful enemies were the new working-class attractions of football and dancing which now had an appeal that organized religion could not match. Football, in T. C. Smout's words 'the new opiate of the people', generated an emotional enthusiasm which for many bordered almost on a quasi-religious intensity.[15]

It is very likely that the Great War accelerated unbelief. Both the Protestant and Catholic Churches had given their solemn and enthusiastic support to the national struggle against the German Empire. By 1915 it was reckoned that around 90 per cent of the 'sons of the manse' had volunteered, and many ministers joined up as both chaplains and combatants. There was no truck with pacifism. The mood was both jingoistic and self-righteous. Dr Wallace Williamson declared at the 1915 General Assembly of the Church of Scotland that: 'We have entered into the War fully conscious as a nation that if we did not enter into it we would stand as criminals before God.'[16] Attitudes changed quickly as the full horror of the terrible losses at the front became apparent, but the Churches had blessed the conflict as a holy war and the sheer scale of the catastrophe had a devastating impact on Christian morale. Investigations carried out on the religious beliefs of soldiers in the trenches in the final stages of the Great War produced worrying results. These showed that, while nearly all combatants believed in God and immortality, they were in a state of confusion and ignorance about much of Christian doctrine and only 20 per cent of the troops in Scottish regiments had a 'vital relationship' with a church, though this figure was significantly greater than for English regiments. The lowest figures of church adherence were always among working-class battalions from the cities. Equally worrying, from the perspective of the Protestant Churches, was the considerably higher level of church attachment recorded among Catholic soldiers. One of the immediate consequences of this sapping of confidence in the wake of the Great War was an acceleration of the movement towards Presbyterian unity. Through legislation in 1921, the Church of Scotland's relationships with the state were clarified in the Declamatory Articles, which stated the Church's spiritual independence and freedom from state control. This then became an important foundation for the historic union in 1929 with the United Free Church elements that had separated from the Auld Kirk on this very issue of state control in the Great Disruption of 1843.

It was unlikely, however, that organizational change could itself halt the relentless progress of secular forces between the wars. A. C. Cheyne's verdict is pessimistic:

Long-established traditions (church-going and Sabbath observance among them) continued to give ground before the onward march of technological progress and social change. Improvement in communications – faster trains, more frequent and more comfortable; the revolution brought about by the electric tram, the motor bus, and above all the private car; the coming of air transport – hastened the decline of rural society, where ancient pieties tended to be most strongly entrenched. It also undermined the hold of custom by introducing people to a new and vastly different way of life and enabling them to escape more easily from that which they no longer desired to follow. And it diminished the authority of the older generation, whose experience seemed increasingly limited and whose ideals of reverence, thrift, temperance and self-denial began to look more like superstition than wisdom. At a very practical level, the spread of new forms of lighting by gas and electricity lengthened the working day and encouraged men and women to indulge more varied interests when their work was done. Cinema, radio and the popular press had clearly taken over from the pulpit as the principal educator and entertainer of the masses, while organised sport displaced religion (and politics) as the dominant preoccupation of their leisure hours.[17]

There is no denying the force of Cheyne's insights for the whole of the century, but perhaps for the years before 1939 his analysis is too gloomy. Levels of Church membership as late as 1956 were only marginally lower than in 1905 when adherence had reached an all-time high. The real collapse did not set in until the late 1950s, and especially in the 1960s. In that decade, by the measures of church attendance, baptisms and religious marriages, the massive drift away from most of the churches was unmistakable. In the 1920s and 1930s, however, membership of the Church of Scotland was reasonably stable and fell only slightly in certain years despite high levels of emigration. After the Second World War there was again a brief resurgence in Protestant church adherence. For the Catholic Church the 1920s and 1930s were years of dynamic growth and spiritual renewal. Not only did numbers double, from 343,000 in 1892 to 614,469 in 1939, but, relieved of the crippling burden of supporting a huge school establishment by the 1918 Education Act, the Church was able to devote more resources to building churches and the promotion of religious mission. For many

Catholics the inter-war period was one of heightened spirituality symbolized by the building of the Grotto at Carfin in Lanarkshire by unemployed miners in the depression years of the 1920s and memorably described by Edwin Muir in his *Scottish Journey* (1935) as 'the only palpable assertion of humanity . . . in the midst of that blasted region'.[19]

The influence of the Presbyterian Churches on civil affairs was indeed further curtailed in 1929 when the parish councils and the elected education authorities, which had long been dominated by church representatives, were abolished, while temperance and the 'new' puritanism of the Church of Scotland were comprehensively rejected in the inter-war years when, to the dismay of the zealots, most of the local plebiscites voted in favour of public houses rather than their prohibition. But religion and religious values still played a considerable role in the lives of the Scottish people in the inter-war period including those who rarely darkened the door of a church. A clutch of oral history studies have shown how important Sunday Schools, Bands of Hope, Girls' Guildry, the Boys' Brigade and Girl Guides were for the youth of Scotland in the 1920s and 1930s. Numbers in the Boys' Brigade rose from 12,796 in 1900 to 35,922 in 1939, and most of the recruits came from the working-class districts of the west of Scotland. Despite the seductions of the cinema and the dance hall, the churches still remained major providers of leisure until the 1960s. Children were sent to youth clubs and often to Sunday Schools even when their parents were not church attenders. Protestant identities survived the horrors of the Great War and the economic trauma of much of the peace. In his novel, *The Magic Flute*, set in Govan, Alan Spence vividly recaptures the range of Protestant influences on working-class boys in the west of Scotland: Sunday School, the Boys' Brigade, Orange marches and Rangers matches at Ibrox to cheer on the 'Protestant' team.

David Hempton's summary of the current state of knowledge on the centrality of religious influence in Britain in the inter-war period also has much relevance to the particular case of Scotland:

. . . even non-churchgoers sent their children to Sunday school, dressed up on Sundays, used religious affiliations to obtain jobs and welfare relief, sang hymns as a means of cementing community solidarity, respected 'practical Christian' virtues, relied heavily on Christian sexual ethics (not least as a point of departure), derived comfort from religion in times of suffering or disaster, accepted that church and chapel or Protestant or Catholic were fundamental social divisions, and used the churches' social facilities without any need to attend more overtly 'religious' activities.[20]

17

Educating the People

For the Scots in the nineteenth century, education was much more than a matter of learning, instruction and scholarship. It had become a badge of identity, a potent symbol of Scottishness and one of the ways in which a sense of nationhood was preserved without in any way threatening the basic structure of the union with England. But education in Scotland did not play this role by promoting the study of the native literature and the national history. On the contrary, the schools were often criticized for their neglect of these aspects of the Scottish heritage, and it was only in 1901 and 1911 that chairs of Scottish history were founded at Edinburgh and Glasgow universities respectively. Schooling promoted identity through the structures of education rather than through the subject matter taught in the curriculum. The educational system was a source of great national pride. It was assumed to be excellent not only intrinsically but also compared to that of other European countries. This uncritical veneration of Scottish schooling has continued as a popular belief down to the present day despite increasing evidence that, at the very least, some of the proudest claims merit considerable qualification.

But in the past the claim of excellence did seem to rest on solid foundations. After all, the Scots could boast five universities when England had but two. A 'national' system of education had developed in the century following the Reformation and offered schooling to all, no matter their station in life, on payment of a modest fee. The Scottish system was believed to be both meritocratic and democratic, resting on a ladder of opportunity which ascended from the parish and burgh schools through to the universities, allowing able boys from the most humble background to rise to eminence simply on the basis of their own talent. In Scotland it was believed that social barriers did not obstruct the path to success of the 'lad o' pairts'. As one schools inspector put it in his report in 1872: 'The Scotch poor have enjoyed and have not abused, the boon of higher education for all who could profit by it. In England nothing short of genius will lift a boy from the National School to the University. In Scotland useful ability, prudence and hard work are the only requisites.'[1] Lyon Playfair, a leading advocate of scientific and technical education, stressed in the same year that the vital issue in Scotland was not the number who actually achieved academic success but rather the *possibility* of advancement which existed for very able lads among the working classes.

These beliefs were probably at their most potent in the Victorian period and early decades of the twentieth century, though modern scholars like Andrew McPherson have demonstrated that they continued to influence the thinking of the leaders of Scottish education down to the 1970s and beyond. However, much of the myth was constructed in the later nineteenth century. The coming of state education after the Act of 1872 lent a glow of nostalgia to the old parish schools, now seen as the basic foundations of Scotland's record of educational excellence. Around this time, for instance, references abounded in educational literature to the 'lads of pregnant parts' until, in 1894, came the first use of the term in Scots, 'lad o' pairts' in the Kailyard story, 'Domsie' by Ian MacLaren. This celebrated the sentimental story of a star pupil from a humble rural background who achieved the glittering prize of a double first degree at university. 'Domsie' was the village schoolmaster or 'dominie' whose other former pupils included seven ministers, four schoolteachers, four doctors, one professor and three civil servants. These popular tales of a fictitious and idealized rural world proved immensely popular between 1870 and 1914 with middle-class readers and exiled Scots who looked back fondly and nostalgically to the good old days of their forefathers on the farm or the croft. 'Getting on' in the colonies was a variant of the 'lad o' pairts' myth and the great success which some emigrants achieved across the seas was easily explained and legitimized in terms of the famous educational traditions of their homeland.

These assumptions were closely linked to Protestantism, another defining characteristic of Scottish identity in the Victorian period. The educational ethos and the religious faith of Presbyterian Scotland were interconnected because the schooling system of which the nation was so proud had been effectively established by John Knox and his fellow reformers in the *Book of Discipline* in the sixteenth century. No one reading the documentation on Scottish education in the later nineteenth century can be in any doubt that Knox remained the revered father figure of the system and his name was constantly invoked to provide authority for an argument, legitimize an innovation or defend the Scottish tradition from the threat of anglicization. Even when rival models of educational change were put forward, as in the debates on secondary schools in the 1890s, the parties would appeal to the Knoxian ideal to lend weight to their points despite the fact that by then the parish school as an institution had already been consigned to history. But it is not at all surprising that the *Book of Discipline* of the sixteenth century should still be relevant to the educational thinking of the nineteenth century. It was not simply that the politicians and officials who administered the system were committed Christians and hence had a natural tendency to seek justification through their Protestant heritage. It was also because the reinvented Knoxian principles of scholastic achievement on the basis of merit, hard work, ambition and seriousness of purpose had powerful appeal to the middle classes in an era of competitive individualism. Even inequality could be justified because, in theory at least and sometimes in practice, there was a ladder of opportunity up which the meritorious could climb, whatever their class background. As the President of the Educational Institute of Scotland put it in 1903:

The ideal of free opportunity for all ... whether properly called a democratic or a national ideal, is one still vitally active in the Scottish people. However checked, diverted, or modified that ideal may have been by the current of events during the last generation, and notably by Scotland's ever increasing industrial prosperity, with its consequent social cleavage ... it is still to be calculated on by those who seek to fashion our educational system, as a whole, in accordance with our traditional spirit.[2]

Here, in the very language used, traditionalism is blended with phrases such as 'our educational system', a term that covers the more structured and managed approach which had become established in Scotland since the Act of 1872. In this way the past and the present could be fruitfully blended, with the former helping to justify change in the latter.

I

Precisely because education played such a central part in the nation's sense of itself it is often difficult to penetrate below the myths, claims and assumptions about schooling to the mundane reality. Chapter 5 showed that the problem was compounded by important gaps in source materials which make it possible to provide only tentative estimates for literacy in the eighteenth and early nineteenth centuries. However, these difficulties are less acute for the 1850s and 1860s, and hence more solid conclusions can be drawn about Scottish educational standards on the eve of the landmark Education Act of 1872. In 1855 the compulsory registration of marriages for the first time produced reliable statistics for 'literacy', in this case defined as the ability of brides and bridegrooms to sign one's name. Moreover, the census of 1861 included systematic returns about school attendance which augmented the data from church and private sources. In the 1860s a major Royal Commission on Scottish education was established under the chairmanship of the Duke of Argyll; it sat from 1864 until 1868 and produced a formidable range of statistical surveys and detailed comment which can contribute to an anatomy of schooling and literacy in Scotland. All these materials have been the subject of thorough examination by the educational historian, Robert Anderson, and some of his conclusions are considered below.

The most striking initial impression is of the sheer range, complexity and diversity of schooling in Scotland in the years before compulsory elementary education was established in 1872. According to the 1851 religious census, only a minority of 25 per cent of scholars were now educated in the much-praised parochial schools and the Church of Scotland no longer had anything like a monopoly of elementary education. Other churches were very active, which once again confirmed the centrality of religion in Victorian society. The Disruption of 1843 resulted in a massive educational investment by the new Free Church; by the early 1850s it was reckoned to be supporting some 600 to 700 schools, particularly in the Church's areas of strength in the cities and in the western Highlands, although around half of these were existing foundations transferred to its control. In addition, from a limited base, the Roman Catholic Church was also making visible progress by the 1860s. According to the Argyll Commission, the Catholics had 61 schools with 5,736 pupils, though these totals still concealed continuing low levels of educational attainment among the majority of the Irish Catholic immigrant community. The most significant finding was that 44 per cent of all schools were private and subscription foundations, outside church control altogether, and educated more than one-third of all pupils in Scotland. These included 'ragged schools', originally established for street children but gradually evolving into 'reformatory' schools for delinquents and truants; charitable schools offering free education; private schools charging higher fees for the middle classes; girls' schools, which expanded rapidly in the 1850s and 1860s as public opinion moved in favour of full literacy for girls; and schools located in mining and industrial villages established by employers because they offered an obvious means of inculcating proper morality, good discipline and loyalty to the company among the labour force. This remarkable variety in schooling was itself a manifestation of the massive social and economic changes taking place in Scotland during the previous few decades as a result of heavy levels of internal migration, urban expansion and the transformation of class and occupational structures. As Donald Withrington has written:

In fact, the complex and often highly differentiated provision of schools had itself been shaped by customer demand; it reflected, whether publicly or privately supported, the changing numbers, the geographical spread, the career intentions, and the fee-paying potential of would-be pupils. In many towns, and in populous and close-knit parishes, it was not unusual for pupils to attend not one school for the whole day but two or even three schools for parts of the day, for different subjects of instruction. The teaching day was not heavily regulated: for some masters and mistresses it might stretch from 6.30 in the morning until 9.30 in the evening, in order to accommodate different groups. The curricula offered the sizes of available schools, their scales of fees, the character and professional capabilities of their teachers, the social environment of the schools and the clientele they attracted, all these gave grounds for choice.[3]

Moreover, even if the Argyll Commission thought the system 'confused' to the point of anarchy, it nevertheless produced results. Judged by the ability to sign the marriage register, 'literacy' seems to have improved considerably even before the dawning of compulsory education in 1872. In 1855, 89 per cent of bridegrooms were literate; by 1885, reflecting the state of education 15 years before, this figure had risen to 94 per cent. The rate of improvement for women was even steeper than for men, increasing from 77 per cent to 89 per cent over the same period. The suggestion is that writing was now more generally taught than in earlier decades when reading absorbed much of the learning time in the early years of education. The number of children attending schools was on an upward curve, growth was especially fast in the 1850s and 1860s and much of the increase was due to rising attendance by girls. By 1871, girls were staying at school for as long as boys, and in some areas longer. This was something of a revolution in Scotland's educational history and, indeed, in the expectations of girls and their parents. One other measure, the ratio of scholars to total population, confirms this optimistic interpretation. This reveals that Scotland was also doing well in an international context and that at least some of the claims made by the apologists for the Scottish system were indeed justified. In 1850 the figures of school attendance in a European context suggested that Scotland was behind Switzerland and Germany but somewhat ahead of France. But by the later 1860s a clear improvement had occurred so that the proportion of Scottish children on the school roll was close to the levels achieved in Prussia, where education was already compulsory. This would suggest that when compulsion took place in Scotland after the 1872 Act it was likely to result in consolidation and some improvement in an ongoing process rather than a radical reform leading to dramatic changes in educational performance.

These patterns beg two obvious questions. First, what factors contributed to this marked progress in basic literacy and school attendance? Second, if the existing educational network was working effectively, as even the Argyll Commission admitted there was no shortage of provision, why was a greater level of state intervention thought necessary in 1872? The history of the 1850s and 1860s may help to provide at least part of an answer to the first point. It was a time when wages and employment levels were rising in most years during the 'Great Mid-Victorian boom', which perhaps enabled the working classes to spend a little more on schooling their children. At the same time, population growth was slower, partly because of very heavy emigration in the early 1850s, thus allowing the churches and the private schools to catch up with provision. This was also the time when the evangelical mission in the cities was at its height. Religious conversion and schooling for the young were closely linked. Mission schools in poor neighbourhoods were established and Sabbath (or Sunday) schools were attached to many churches in working-class areas.

State support for education was also expanding even before 1872. From 1833, capital grants were available for new schools which at first were modest but, from 1846, schools were eligible for annual awards if they accepted state inspection, followed an approved curriculum and recruited state-certified teachers. The system was supervised by an inspectorate based in Scotland and a Committee of the Privy Council on Education in London. Despite the complaints which often surfaced about the threat of creeping anglicization (notably the Revised Code of the early 1860s), the majority of working-class children were being educated in schools, supported through this 'Privy Council' system by the 1860s. The contributing role of the state, even before 1872, in the improvement of literacy should therefore not be underestimated.

The state also had a part to play in ensuring the supply of teachers. David Stow had pioneered teacher-training in Scotland, principally through his 'Normal Seminary' in Glasgow, which was opened in 1837. Another normal school was established in Edinburgh, which was followed after 1843 with similar institutions founded by the Free Church. The state subsidized these foundations and after 1846 linked grants for schools to the 'pupil-teacher' system. The pupil-teachers were boys and girls aged 13 and over who taught while studying and who, at the end of their apprenticeship, could compete for a scholarship allowing them to attend one of the normal schools in order to become fully qualified. Certificated teachers who took on pupil-teachers were entitled to an additional grant and this provided a cheap supply of teaching assistants in the short term while at the same time holding out the promise of a better-qualified teaching force in the longer run.

One explanation, therefore, for the 1872 Act is that since the state was already subsidizing education in Scotland it naturally wished to impose greater control and regulation through a centrally directed structure. Withrington, for instance, has pointed out that the deliberations of the Argyll Commission in the later 1860s were driven mainly by a concern to achieve a more rigorous administration of public expenditure in an inefficient system where resources did not necessarily go where they were most needed. There were also wider educational issues. Behind the comforting averages of good performance there were undoubted black spots. Problems existed in the Western Isles and parts of the north-western mainland. Highland schools found it difficult to qualify for state grants, and fee income was often in short supply. Literacy and attendance levels were also low in some inner-city areas and industrial districts in the Lowlands. The issue was not simply an urban one because, perhaps surprisingly, the 1871 census revealed that most towns had higher attendance figures than surrounding country parishes, while cities such as Edinburgh and Aberdeen were better than virtually any rural county. But there were serious problems in Glasgow, where an estimated 15 per cent of children were reckoned not to be receiving effective schooling, and in some of the industrial towns of the western Lowlands. The mass of casual and general labourers caught in the poverty trap had to put their children into the labour market at the earliest possible opportunity and their schooling was inevitably bound to suffer as a result. There was also a correlation between below-average literacy rates and areas of Irish Catholic settlement such as Glasgow, parts of Dundee, West Lothian and some of the Lanarkshire industrial towns. The Irish were concentrated in unskilled and casual employment and were most likely to suffer from the consequences of the impact of adverse economic conditions on regular school attendance.

There was a growing recognition, therefore, that the existing resources provided by the state were not solving the problem of these less literate groups and that compulsion alone could only iron out the differences which had emerged in the surveys. In addition, the Presbyterian Churches were beginning to find their own schools an increasing financial burden. This was likely to become even more pressing in the future since pupil-teachers and adult assistants allowed the division of schools into separate classes which required bigger buildings. The idea of a new national system in which the young had to attend and be instructed in Christian values was positively appealing for some churchmen. One Free Church minister saw it as the best way of dealing with youthful alienation from religion:

The young are so easily put to labour, and become so soon independent of their parents, and are so constantly encompassed by endless temptations and means of indulgence, and at the same time parents themselves are generally so unable to discipline their children, that the only likelihood of having them reared in Christian knowledge is to provide it in the daily schools of instruction.[4]

Other broader social and political forces were also at work. The argument that an effective system of education could ensure political order and social stability by giving proper training to the next generation of citizens was even more compelling when the Paris Commune erupted in 1871 and crystallized the dangerous revolutionary potential of the urban masses. There was also concern about the growth of international economic and military competition. The military victories of the Prussian state in 1866 and 1871 and Germany's growing economic success were seen in large part as the result of a national system of compulsory education. The influential Lyon Playfair in 1870 was one of several commentators to observe that, 'In the competition of nations, both in war and in peace, their position for the future will depend upon the education of their peoples.'[5] It was against this background that the Education (Scotland) Act was finally passed in 1872.

The legislation did not establish 'state education' as such because, as has been seen, state subsidy and school inspection were already in place from the 1840s. Nevertheless, the Act was still a landmark development and was more radical than the English legislation of 1870. It imposed compulsion on all children aged between five and 13, and the existing burgh and parish schools were transferred to local boards consisting entirely of ratepayers, which could also levy rates and borrow to build their own schools. The non-parochial and private schools might maintain their independence but would have to survive without rate aid. In the event, the vast majority elected to join the state system and most of those that remained outside were Roman Catholic and Episcopalian schools. By 1878 only 28 per cent of Scotland's 3,011 schools were outside the control of the new boards. In 1914 this figure had fallen further to 10 per cent, and finally, in 1918, Catholic and other church schools were also incorporated. This overwhelming dominance of the state in Scottish elementary education contrasted with England where schooling was not at first compulsory and a large voluntary sector survived that had higher status than the public schools, which were virtually confined to the poorer classes. In Scotland, since the vast majority of pupils attended the board schools, the public system possessed no such social stigma.

Linked to this were elements of continuity. Fees were maintained at first until they were finally abandoned, 27 years after the Act. The focus was also almost exclusively on elementary education. Secondary schools were not seen at the time as a stage to follow elementary education. The 1872 Act did transfer the burgh schools to the new boards and the major ones were designated as 'higher class' schools, but the state did not contribute any finance to secondary education and boards were not permitted to spend ratepayers' money on them. It was assumed that, since such schools catered mainly for the affluent classes, they could provide finance from their own resources and from existing endowments attached to some of the leading burgh schools. The later history of secondary schooling will be considered in the next section.

Another feature of the new system was a much greater level of state intervention from the centre. The role of the churches in Scottish education was maintained through the major contribution made to the management of school boards by the local clergy and pious laity, but overall power had now effectively shifted to the government and civil servants. It was an important public symbol of the relative decline of religious authority and of the expanding empire of the secular state. A new committee of the Privy Council, called the Scotch Education Department (SED), was established to supervise the post-1872 system. It was located in London – which raised fears of anglicizing influences on Scottish education – and in 1885 came under the control of the new Secretaryship of State for Scotland. Under powerful and domineering figures like Sir Henry Craik and A. Craig Sellar, the SED soon became a force to be reckoned with. In the final analysis it held the purse strings, and the SED inspectors ensured that central policies were implemented rigorously in every board school in the land. This structure gave Scotland one of the most centrally organized educational systems in the world by 1918.

The legislation of 1872 and its subsequent implementation and development have attracted both plaudits and criticisms. Mass elementary education providing basic literacy did not start in 1872; that had already been achieved in many areas. The new system extended these standards to the urban poor, some industrial communities and the Western Isles, where levels of literacy had been significantly below the national average before 1870. Parents were not permitted to plead poverty when they kept their children away from school. Those who could not afford to send their children to school were made entitled to assistance from the Poor Law, while the School Attendance Committees and their inspectors enthusiastically went about the task of enforcing the law. Attendance became longer and more regular. In the cities and some towns an extensive building programme of large schools was launched, each split into separate classrooms for individual groups of the same age. These 'board schools' soon became a familiar part of the townscape and many stand to this day as physical memorials to enthusiastic Victorian educational endeavour. The huge expansion in state education was made possible only by a dramatic increase in the number of women teachers which radically altered the gender balance in Scottish education. Women were cheaper to employ, being paid half the rate for male teachers, and there was a contemporary belief that they were more suited to dealing with young children. By 1881, women made up 8,000 of the 13,000 workforce and 70 per cent of the elementary school teachers. Teaching provided women with a significant professional career and a new independence but, in terms of pay, promotion and status, their position in Scotland long remained much inferior to that of their sisters in England.

The growth of state intervention in education after 1872 also had an impact in the field of social welfare. The Boer War of 1899–1902 had shocked government by revealing the very poor physical condition of recruits from the urban working classes. Concern was deepened because this was the era of 'national efficiency', when the nation's military and economic strength was seen to depend on the physical health of the younger generation. Compulsory schooling under state authority since 1872 offered a means for tackling these problems. In effect, the schools were now to become agents of state welfare and social policy and through the school the next generation of citizens could be 'improved'. From 1908, therefore, school boards provided medical inspection of pupils and feeding for needy children. Action could be taken against parents whose child was thought to be 'verminous'. The education of girls in cookery and household management was also developed, as it was expected that good motherhood would become the foundation of a stronger nation. A new bureaucracy of medical officers and school health visitors came into being, while teachers were now required to check heads routinely for lice and report on children walking barefoot to school. Inspection, however, could not solve the many and deep-seated problems that came from chronic poverty. The future Labour MP, James Maxton, who taught at St James's School in Bridgeton in Glasgow, remembered that 'in a class of sixty boys and girls of about eleven years old . . . thirty-six out of the sixty could not bring both knees and heels together because of rickety malformations'.[6]

However, the 1872 Act did not escape criticism both from contemporaries and later from scholars. The initial denial of funding for secondary schooling was attacked for inhibiting opportunities for able working-class children to proceed to higher levels. Withrington scathingly denounces the mighty SED which, through its inspectorate, circulars and codes, imposed 'a dull and humourless rigidity to the classroom', where children were controlled by 'a military-style discipline'.[7] Others at the time, always conscious of the need to protect Scotland's historic educational identity, feared that one consequence of 1872 was likely to be the assimilation of practice in schools to a 'British' norm since the system was now financed from London. As Robert Anderson points out, much of the debate on anglicization, following the publication of George Davie's influential *The Democratic Intellect* (1961), has focused on the universities, with the implication that the schools remained authentically Scottish. In fact he argues rightly that, '. . . as far as its curriculum and organisation went, a Scottish elementary school in the 1900s was much more like its English counterpart than a Scottish university was like an English one'.[8]

The SED was also accused of conducting a campaign against Gaelic, and specifically of failing to implement the recommendation of the Napier Commission in 1884 that the language should be part of the curriculum in Highland schools. This sin of omission allegedly contributed to Gaelic's decline at a time when the activists of An Comunn Gaidhealach and prominent figures like John Stuart Blackie of Edinburgh University and the MP for Inverness, C. Fraser Mackintosh, were pressing to make the language a compulsory school subject. But the reality seems more complex than this. The SED inspectors, including the Gaelic speakers among them, viewed the campaign to revive the language with deep suspicion. In their view, it was the work of outside interests and sentimentalists and did not reflect the real feelings of the Highland people themselves. Despite this cynicism, however, the SED was not unresponsive and in 1878 allowed teachers of Gaelic to be paid from the grants. But it was not prepared to countenance compulsion, citing as reasons the difficulty of funding teachers and the opposition of some school boards. A basic difficulty was that the tide was running strongly in favour of English among the Highland people. Gaelic was the language of everyday life, religion, poetry and song and, as the mother tongue, was not easily abandoned. But English was seen by the Highlanders in the late nineteenth century as the language of the future, of economic opportunity and social progress. Even one sympathetic observer concluded in the 1860s: '. . . the most ardent lover of Gaelic cannot fail to admit that the possession of a knowledge of English is indispensable to any poor islander who wishes to learn a trade or to earn his bread beyond the limits of his native Isle'.[9] In the event, despite some further cosmetic concessions in 1886, 1904 and 1906, the SED did little in a major way to aid the Gaelic cause before 1918.

2

The story of Scottish secondary education after 1872 is more convoluted than the development of elementary schooling. In part, this was because the state did not initially give secondary schools the same political priority as it showed for elementary schools and only slowly did the overall structure become visible. The old burgh schools were transferred to the management of the new boards in 1872 and 13 of those located in the largest towns, including such well-known names as Ayr Academy and Glasgow High School, were designated 'Higher Class Public Schools'. This élite group was to be free from government inspection and the requirement to abide by SED codes. On the other hand, they had to support themselves from fees alone and did not receive any rate aid from local boards. By 1892, however, when a direct subsidy for secondary schools was first introduced, the government, educational experts and the SED were becoming much more committed to the development of post-compulsory education. The 1872 Act itself was a powerful symbol of the acceptance by the state of its responsibility for the education of its citizens. Once the principle was established, it could easily be extended to secondary schooling, especially because of the new concerns about international economic competition. If the British Empire was to continue to prosper in a more competitive age, the nation's best talent had to be recruited to serve the purpose of the state, and that in turn could be achieved only by establishing a solid bridge between elementary and secondary education over which the most able from all social classes could pass into the élite. G. G. Ramsay, Professor of Latin in Glasgow University and a leading figure in the educational debates of the time, argued in 1876 that *the* main factor in the future prosperity of nations was 'the disciplined intelligence of the great bulk of the community':

We cannot trust only to the intellect of our well-to-do classes; we cannot afford to allow humbly-born ability to take its chance of being able, by rare good fortune, to struggle out into usefulness and recognition; we must go to meet it wherever it is to be found, and, by a carefully organised system of graded education, placed within the reach of all such as are able to profit by it, do everything that is possible to swell the bulk and improve the quality of the national intelligence.[10]

This idea of a meritocracy based on 'equality of opportunity' could be achieved only through more state support for secondary education. It struck a particular chord in Scotland, where it had long been assumed that the old parish school system had successfully recruited intellectual talent from all social backgrounds. The extension of secondary schooling and the creation of a more structured ladder of opportunity could be seen as the adaptation of Knoxian ideals to the modern age and hence easily legitimized through the connection with a glorious national tradition. Yet behind the rhetoric of broadening opportunity for the mass of the population, the numbers expected to benefit from secondary education were very small. The SED and parliament put the figure as little more than 4–5 per cent of the age group in the 1890s. This was therefore not a project inspired by the ideals of the 'democratic intellect' but a strategy designed to ensure that the best minds were rigorously selected in order to serve the needs of the state.

Developments in the universities were encouraging a similar trend towards secondary schooling. They were now having to respond to new middle-class demands as patronage and hereditary privilege were replaced by formal qualifications and examinations for entry to professional careers. In 1858, for instance, medicine became a state-regulated profession with graduate entry and competitive examinations were established for the civil service. University reformers reacted to these trends by seeking to raise academic standards, a strategy which included the introduction of entrance examinations demanding graduation as a matter of course and moving the average age of entry from 14 or 15 to 17 or 18. This revolution in academic structure could not easily be achieved without an expansion in advanced schooling, especially after the introduction of the Leaving Certificate examinations in 1888 and the decision in 1892 to limit entry to universities to only those who possessed this formal qualification.

There were several strands in secondary expansion between 1870 and 1918. At first in the 1870s and 1880s it was led by a dynamic growth in middle-class provision where schooling was exclusive and high fees restricted education to a small élite. This phase saw the creation of four large fee-paying day schools in the capital from the endowments of the Merchants Company and the Heriot Trust for the children of the Edinburgh professional classes, and the foundation of Kelvinside Academy and the Hutchesons' endowed grammar schools for boys and girls in Glasgow. Indeed, a feature of this period was enhanced provision for middle-class girls. St Leonard's opened in St Andrews in 1877 as a boarding school on the model of English public schools and was followed by such 'proprietary schools' as Westbourne (1877), the Park School (1880), Craigholme (1894) in Glasgow and St George's (1888) in Edinburgh. When the universities were finally opened to female students in 1892, the middle classes already had a good choice of socially exclusive schools for their daughters. In addition, the growing lower-middle class of clerks, shopkeepers and elementary schoolteachers was aspiring to something more than a basic education for their children. This could be satisfied in schools partly funded by the state and charging lower fees than the established high schools. The SED Code for elementary schools included grants for specific subjects taught at a higher level. This led to the extension of so-called 'Higher Grade Schools', particularly in Glasgow, where there were fewer endowed schools on the Edinburgh model. They offered the full range of secondary subjects, with the majority of pupils leaving at 15 for commercial careers but allowing at least the possibility of going on to university for some.

In theory at least, the opportunities for secondary education widened further in 1892 when a direct state subsidy was introduced for the first time. Despite the opposition of the SED, which argued for the concentration of advanced schooling, the grant was in fact widely distributed to support a national structure of secondary education in most Scottish towns. It was a political victory for those who believed in the old parish school ideal that education should be generally available, a principle that was enthusiastically supported by the schoolteachers' organization, the Educational Institute of Scotland. An additional feature was that many of these schools were free; and scholarships also became more widely available, so opening up at least the possibility of more working-class participation in secondary education. State support for the system was enhanced further at the end of the Great War in the historic Education Act of 1918 which, *inter alia*, transferred the control of Catholic and Episcopalian schools to local education authorities which replaced the old school boards, with provisos for religious observance and church rights on teacher appointments. Catholic provision, despite valiant efforts by the Irish immigrant community, lagged far behind the non-denominational sector. In bringing Catholic schools under state control, the SED was influenced by the same concerns for maximizing 'national efficiency' which had shaped its other policies. It was feared that Catholics would become a 'pariah class' whose 'inefficiency' would threaten the strategy of improving the human resources of the state through an effective school system.

How effective the secondary system was has recently engendered considerable debate. Both H. M. Paterson and T. C. Smout conclude that it failed the Scottish people because it was geared essentially to the needs of the middle classes and had little to offer the mass of the population as a route to social mobility. Paterson is particularly scathing. In his view, the attempt to create a meritocracy was a 'particularly Scottish solution of the problems involved in sieving a nation, by the device of mass schooling so as to recruit talent to the leader class whilst, at the same time, placating and controlling the many who would never reach such heights'.[11] In Smout's view, education was 'a matter of low social priority once the perceived needs of the middle classes had been attended to' and 'a channel had been opened for a limited number of working class children to use secondary school and university as a means of upward social mobility'.[12]

These contentions can be tested against the careful research of Andrew McPherson, the most thorough examination of the subject to date. He shows that secondary education became even more available over time. In 1923 the SED extended full secondary school status to around 200 schools previously designated as 'Higher Grade'. Numbers of pupils then more than doubled, from 40,000 in 1913 to 90,000 by 1939. Leaving Certificates gained increased from 1,700 to over 4,000 over the same period. More places were available in both secondary and higher education than in England and Wales and, hence, marginally more opportunities for upward social mobility. An important difference in Scotland was that there was no dominant public school or fee-paying system that might otherwise have relegated the state secondaries to second-rate status. In 1914, one in six or seven Scottish children started a secondary course; in England it was more like one in 21. In addition, working-class students at the universities were more numerous in the years before the First World War than they had been in the 1860s. Nevertheless, the vast majority of working-class girls and boys left school as soon as they could to enter the factory, pit, farm, office or domestic service. But this was caused fundamentally by the economic pressures on ordinary families and their social expectations rather than the nature of the educational system itself. In fact, one section of the 1918 Act enshrined the principle of equality of opportunity by stating 'that no child ... who is qualified for attendance at an intermediate or secondary School, and ... shows promise of profiting thereby shall be debarred therefrom by reason of the expense involved'.[13] It was a statement of the ideal that material circumstances should not be allowed to restrict access to advanced schooling.

Important voices in Scottish education wished to make the system even more open. The Educational Institute of Scotland in the early 1920s argued for 'secondary education for all', a view shared by members of political parties and educational commentators. However, the SED had a different attitude and the decisive voice which was conditioned by its unyielding belief that only a small number of children had the intellectual ability to benefit from a full academic secondary course. As George Macdonald, Secretary of the SED, put it: '... the school population falls into two parts – the majority of distinctly limited intelligence, and an extremely important minority drawn from all ranks and classes who are capable of responding to a much more severe call'.[14]

It was the combination of this official mindset and the rigorous control of the Treasury over public finances in the troubled economic climate of the early 1920s which produced the notorious Circular 44 from the SED in 1923. This laid down the structure of secondary schooling in Scotland until the coming of comprehensive education in 1965; and this, more than any other policy directive, explains the harsh criticisms of Paterson and Smout. The Circular ended common schooling after the age of 12 years. Only schools offering full five-year certificate courses would now be designated 'secondary' and they would teach pupils who were deemed to be academically qualified at 12. The vast majority, who were not, were to complete their education in a new 'Advanced Division' sector with lower standards of staffing and resources. These schools eventually emerged as the 'junior secondaries' of the late 1930s, while the 'senior secondary' sector consisted of those granted secondary status in Circular 44. In addition, in 1924 the SED abolished the Intermediate Certificate that might have provided a bridge between the early years after primary education and the later courses leading to university entry. Ironically, when an examination at 16 years of age was finally restored in the 1960s, it led immediately to a dramatic increase in presentations for Highers in subsequent years.

The critics are correct to point out that these policies branded the majority of pupils as 'failures', intensified social divisions and produced a secondary educational system of glaring inequality. The SED strategy was imposed against the virtually unanimous opposition of Scottish educationists, including the government's own Advisory Council on Education. The opponents even produced an alternative blueprint, with common schooling in the first three years of secondary and an intermediate examination at 15 years which would provide a certificate for those who wished to leave and a qualifying examination for others who intended to continue to more advanced work. So great was the hostility to the SED's attack on the nation's 'democratic' traditions that many educational authorities disregarded its directive in the 1920s and 1930s. But Circular 44 still left a deep mark on Scottish society. In 1944 the Scottish Council for Research in Education estimated that at least a third of all pupils had the ability to be admitted to a full senior secondary course. But as late as 1951 only 5 per cent of school leavers had stayed on to complete the five-year course between the ages of 17 and 19, with nearly 90 per cent leaving at or before their fifteenth birthday. It was recognition of this 'wastage' that prompted the decision in 1955 to introduce the 'O' grade examination at fourth-year level. This was finally implemented in 1962. With the parallel development of comprehensive schooling in 1965 eventually ending the apartheid of senior and junior secondaries, staying-on rates climbed dramatically and were boosted further by the substantial rise in working-class incomes which reduced real educational costs for many families. By 1974, a remarkable 66 per cent of school leavers were gaining certification compared with 27 per cent 10 years earlier. This indeed was confirmation that the policies of the 1920s, which had moulded the development of Scottish secondary education for over 40 years, were neither fair, efficient nor founded on valid intellectual premisses.

3

Significant changes in university education in the second half of the nineteenth century reflected a number of pressures for reform. Some critics regarded them as closed corporations, governed by a self-perpetuating professorial élite. Academic standards also increasingly came under scrutiny in an age of rapid progress in medical and natural sciences which encouraged much greater intellectual specialization in these disciplines. Questions were asked in inquiries like the influential Royal Commission on Scientific Instruction and the Advancement of Science (1872–5) whether the academic resources of the universities could be more effectively devoted to the improvement of the national economy. The professionalization of several middle-class careers, such as medicine and accountancy, also created greater demand for formal training and qualifications. In 1858, for instance, medicine became a graduate-only profession, and competitive examinations became the norm in the civil service. Nor could the universities ignore the developments in school education after 1872 and, in particular, the reforms in secondary schooling culminating in 1888 with the establishment of leaving certificate examinations taken at 17. Now much of the work traditionally carried out in the junior classes of the university would become part of the curriculum in the senior levels of the schools.

Above all, there was widespread concern that the Scottish universities, which had led the world in the eighteenth century, had now degenerated into mediocrity. Complaints abounded that Scottish graduates had to go to England for advanced training, that the universities grossly neglected research studies and that the teaching curricula had hardly changed in 300 years. Some of the most wounding criticisms came from James Donaldson, rector of Edinburgh High School and editor of the *Educational News*, the journal founded by the Educational Institute of Scotland. Donaldson complained in 1882 that 'The Scottish universities are schools with curricula fixed nearly on the old Reformation programme', and he argued that 'an educational revolution' had taken place in the nineteenth century and with it had come much greater 'competition for distinction in science, scholarship, theology and all the higher intellectual pursuits'. In this context, however, the 'Scotsman has to fight with bow and arrow against men armed with rifles and cannon. He is the handloom weaver of the intellectual world.'[15]

Perhaps because of the depth of concern a whole series of reform proposals came thick and fast in the later nineteenth century. An Act of parliament in 1889 established an executive commission under the Court of Session judge, Lord Kinnear, which passed no fewer than 169 ordinances. These included a compulsory entrance examination, changes in arts, law and medical degrees including Honours courses, the setting up of separate Faculties of Science to develop the B.Sc. degree outside the Arts framework and provisions to introduce regulations for research degrees. The entrance examination was in place by 1892 and meant that the common age at entry moved upwards from 14–15 to 17, which was facilitated by the introduction of the leaving certificate for secondary schools. As late as the 1870s, only a small number of Arts students took degrees but, by 1914, there had been a transformation with most university students in Scotland now aiming to graduate. New chairs were founded, especially in medicine, a discipline which attracted no less than 40–50 per cent of the students at Edinburgh between 1860 and 1914 and substantial numbers at other universities. But the Kinnear commission also created chairs in English, History and Political Economy at Aberdeen, Edinburgh and Glasgow. Women were finally permitted to matriculate at Scottish universities in 1892, much later than in England, though their numbers grew rapidly after 1900 and by 1914 they made up 23 per cent of the student body. Nevertheless the progress of women in the academic community was slow. No Scottish woman professor was appointed before the Second World War, although some women did become lecturers or assistants.

This impressive sequence of reforms made university education in Scotland more professional, raised academic standards, increased research activity, integrated higher education with secondary schooling and prepared Scottish graduates to compete more effectively in Britain and the empire. This last function was vital. One estimate suggests that more than half the graduates of Aberdeen in the later nineteenth century left Scotland for employment in England or overseas. By 1914 Scotland's universities had an academic structure that was to remain broadly unchanged for most of the twentieth century. This achievement raises at least three issues: the intellectual and cultural consequences of reform, the impact on popular access to the universities and the relationship between higher education and the Scottish economy.

George Davie's *The Democratic Intellect* (1961) is a comprehensive indictment of the university reform movement which he criticizes as the source of a pernicious anglicization of the academic curriculum which was to have profoundly damaging effects on Scottish culture and society. He suggests that the reformers destroyed the traditional broad Scottish curriculum in favour of an alien narrow specialization leading to the single-subject Honours degree. Entrance examinations restricted entry and philosophy was removed from its former place at the heart of university education. The inevitable result, in Davie's view, was to make the universities more socially exclusive and less democratic. Since Davie wrote in the 1960s educational historians have examined the evidence for his claims in detail. There is broad agreement that his critique is most persuasive in his description of the decline of Scottish philosophy. The great tradition of the eighteenth century did not survive with Victorian times. Instead, university philosophy in most institutions in Scotland became dominated by neo-Hegelianism and chairs in the subject were usually filled by proponents of this school who had been trained at Oxford. Elsewhere, however, Davie's analysis is less convincing. For one thing, he exaggerates the degree of specialization which was imposed. Only a minority took honours degrees until after 1945, the Arts curriculum in particular remained broad-based and the 1889 commission had maintained compulsory classics and philosophy for all students. Nor is it helpful to divide the reformers into 'patriots' and 'anglicizers'. Both camps were attempting to modernize the curriculum because of the belief that the universities were failing and so the main external models were not England but Germany and France, whose economic achievements were said to be based on their national achievements in education.

Davie's critique also raises the important issue of entry to the universities and how far the reform process may have narrowed access by establishing entrance examinations and developing a more formal structure than had existed hitherto. The Argyll Commission showed from a sample of students in the 1860s that around a third came from the professional classes (especially from ministers' families) and perhaps a half from the middle classes as a whole. Nevertheless, there was a considerable 'working-class' group, though it consisted overwhelmingly of the sons of skilled workers and artisans such as carpenters, shoemakers and masons. There was only a handful of labourers, farm servants and miners. It was reckoned that a minister's son was about a hundred times as likely to go to the university as a miner's and 'most working class students were drawn from the very top stratum of their class, while neither the rural poor nor the majority of factory workers, nor the unskilled workers in the towns, had more than a token representation'.[16] The lads o' pairts clearly existed, but they were few and far between. Above all, most students of working-class origin came to university as adults, often on a part-time basis, rather than directly from the celebrated parish schools. The incentive for them was the low fees, the absence of entrance examinations and the junior classes which provided a form of 'remedial' teaching. This structure was obviously threatened by the reforms of the later nineteenth century.

In the event, however, the proportion of working-class students remained broadly the same when judged from the university matriculation records of 1910. Indeed, at Glasgow more were now coming from the shipyards and engineering shops than ever before. The growth of secondary education, the greater availability of bursaries and, crucially, grants from the Carnegie Trust, founded by Andrew Carnegie, the millionaire Scottish philanthropist, helped to preserve what limited access there was. The Carnegie scheme, established in 1900, was especially important and was covering part of the fees of about half of all university students in Scotland by 1910. Students of working-class origin also combined teacher-training and elementary teaching with attendance at university in order to gain their degree. One of the most famous examples of this was John Maclean, the revolutionary socialist, who came from a humble background and entered teaching from a higher-grade school before successfully graduating M.A. at Glasgow. But entry to the universities remained beyond the mass of the population even if, for much of the nineteenth century, a higher proportion attended university classes in Scotland than elsewhere in Europe. But in the twentieth century other countries caught up; while numbers in Scotland did rise, from 6,000 students in 1900 to 10,000 in 1938 (partly because of the admission of women students), between the wars expansion virtually came to a halt and there was little overall change in the social composition of the student body. The middle classes remained overwhelmingly dominant in the professional faculties of law and medicine and the proportion of working-class students in the general undergraduate population, who invariably took the M.A. ordinary degree and entered the teaching profession, altered little between the First World War and the 1950s.

The third and final issue for consideration is the relationship between higher education and the economy. The connection was far from close in this period. Formal qualifications were not required for most industrial or commercial careers, and university degrees were primarily required for the 'learned' professions of law, medicine, teaching and the ministry. Only in the last few decades of the twentieth century has this historic pattern altered. One study of 'business leaders' in Scotland from 1860 to 1960 confirms that a mere 15 per cent possessed a university degree while 53 per cent had received little formal education beyond elementary school. These were the men who valued practical experience and training on the job above all else. W. J. Macquorn Rankine, the renowned Professor of Civil Engineering and Mechanics in the University of Glasgow in the 1870s, pointed out how his former students had gained posts in India, Brazil, England and elsewhere but that few had made their mark in Scotland. A number of his academic colleagues denounced the industrialists of the west of Scotland in evidence to the Royal Commission on Scientific Instruction for their indifference to scientific training. However, it is perhaps not surprising that the Clydeside captains of industry were unenthusiastic about academic studies when their dominance of world markets remained for the most part unchallenged. Moreover, the faults, if they did exist, were not all on the industrial or commercial side. Even figures of the stature of Macquorn Rankine and the great Lord Kelvin were uneasy about the direct application of science to practical purposes. The former took the view that practical training should not take place in a university: '. . . there is a limit to the functions of a University, which is to impart and to certify the scientific knowledge, but not to certify the practical skill, of the candidates'.[17]

The real impact was therefore not made in the universities but through technical education in the colleges which attracted increasing government attention because technical high schools and trade schools were seen as primary factors in the economic resurgence of European countries like Germany. In Edinburgh the Watt Institution, which became Heriot-Watt College, was founded in 1885. The Glasgow and West of Scotland Technical College emerged in 1887 from three institutions, one of which, Anderson's College, had a history dating back to 1796. A Technical Institute was also opened in Dundee in 1888. By the early twentieth century these and eight other colleges specializing in art, domestic science, commercial training and hygiene, had become 'Central Institutions' under the control of the SED. In 1912 they had over 15,000 students in all, two-thirds of them attending in the evening and coming from skilled or white-collar occupations. The Glasgow and West of Scotland College, renamed the Royal Technical College in 1912, and Heriot-Watt developed higher work and established research laboratories in an attempt to meet the needs of the industrial economy. At the same time, there was evidence from the SED in 1913 that around a third of the 1,740 students who gained the leaving certificate opted to enter one of the 11 central institutions. Their emphasis on a practical education did something to fill the gap created by the more academic emphasis of the universities.

18

The Highlands and Crofting Society

I

The Irish Famine of the 1840s was the greatest human disaster in western Europe in the nineteenth century. Over 1 million people died of famine-related diseases in those terrible years when the potatoes failed and a further 2 million were forced to emigrate by the threat of starvation and acute destitution. The Irish catastrophe was unique in its horrific scale, but subsistence crises triggered by potato blight were in fact common in several countries in that decade; the fungal disease, *phytophthora infestans*, also decimated crops in mainland Britain, the Netherlands, several German states and France. There was no clear scientific understanding of the nature and origins of the blight or how to prevent it. It was plain, however, that the disease could wreak havoc not simply for one or two seasons but for several years, and it flourished particularly in regions with moderate winters and rainy summers which allowed the germination, survival and spread of the fungus spores from affected plants. In Scotland, the Highlands were most vulnerable to potato famine, partly because the climatic conditions of the maritime and insular districts were an appropriate environment for the transmission of the blight, but also because of the central importance of the potato in the diet of the people of the region.

Not until the autumn of 1846, a full year after the blight had destroyed potato crops all over Ireland, was the Highlands affected. But when the disease did strike in August and September of that year, the impact was deadly. Press reports described how the stench of rotting potatoes pervaded numerous crofting townships up and down the west coast and throughout the Hebrides. Early estimates suggested that in over three-quarters of the crofting parishes the crop had failed entirely. The Free Church newspaper, the *Witness*, concluded that 'The hand of the

Lord has indeed touched us' and proclaimed the calamity 'unprecedented in the memory of this generation and of many generations gone by, even in any modern periods of our country's history'.[1] Unambiguous signs of famine emerged. While burial registers for most Highland areas in the 1840s are few and far between, in those that have survived, deaths among the old and the very young rose significantly in late 1846 and the first few months of 1847. *The Scotsman* in December 1846 described how deaths from dysentery were 'increasing with fearful rapidity among the cottar class'.[2] In the Ross of Mull government relief officers reported that the death rate during the winter months was three times the normal. Elsewhere in Harris, South Uist, Barra, Skye, Moidart and Kintail, influenza, typhus and dysentery were spreading, unchecked, among the poor. The awful possibility of the Highlands being engulfed in a human tragedy of Irish proportions seemed to become ever more likely.

But that potential disaster was averted, despite the fact that the potato blight continued to ravage the Highlands for several years after 1846–7. By the summer of 1847, death rates had returned to normal levels and the threat of starvation receded. The mortality crisis had been contained. The different experiences of Ireland and the Highlands in this respect can be explained by a number of influences. An important factor was that of scale. In Ireland, the blight brought over 3 million people to the edge of starvation. In the Highlands, on the other hand, around 200,000 were seriously at risk, and this number diminished over time as the crisis increasingly centred on parts of the north-western coastlands, the northern isles of Orkney and Shetland and the Hebrides. By 1848, only around a quarter (or fewer than 70,000) of the total population of the Highland region were still in need of famine relief. The map of distress was in fact a complex one. The southern, central and eastern Highlands did not escape unscathed, but after 1847 relief operations were wound down there. This reflected the more resilient economies of these areas. There was less potato dependency and more reliance on grain and fish, a better ratio of land to population and stronger alternative occupations, such as commercial fishing and linen manufacture, in southern Argyll, Perthshire and eastern Inverness-shire. The concentrated and relatively small-scale nature of the Scottish famine meant that the emergency could be managed more easily by the relief agencies of the day than the crisis across the Irish Sea. The Scottish authorities were dealing with many thousands of potential victims, the Irish with several millions. The vastly different magnitude of the two famines is best illustrated by the role of government. In Ireland the state, both local and national, was the principal source of relief over several years, whereas in the Highlands direct government intervention began in late 1846 and ended in the summer of 1847. Two vessels were stationed as meal depots at Tobermory in Mull and Portree in Skye to sell grain at controlled prices. Landowners in the stricken region were able to make application for loans under the Drainage and Public Works Act to provide relief work for the distressed populations of their estates.

These initiatives apart, the main burden of the relief effort was borne by three great charities, the Free Church of Scotland and the Edinburgh and Glasgow Relief Committees, which came together in early 1847 to form the Central Board of Management for Highland Relief. The Central Board had the responsibility for relieving destitution until its operations came to an end in 1850. The relief effort went through several phases. First in the field was the Free Church, eager to come to the aid of its numerous loyal congregations in the north-west and the islands. The schooner, *Breadalbane*, built to carry ministers around the Hebrides, was pressed into service to take emergency supplies to the most needy communities. The Free Church was the only active agency during the most critical months of late 1846 and early 1847. Through its superb intelligence network of local ministers it was able to direct aid to those areas where the risk of starvation was greatest. The Free Church's relief operation was also free of any sectarian bias. Grateful thanks for supplies of grain were received from such Catholic areas as Arisaig and Mordant. Not the least of the Free Church's contribution was the imaginative plan to transport over 3,000 able-bodied men from the Highlands for work on the Lowland railways.

The Central Board assumed control of relief operations in February 1847 and by the end of that year had established a huge fund for the aid of distress of nearly £210,000. This was probably the greatest sum ever raised in support of a single charitable cause in nineteenth-century Scotland. With this resource it proceeded to divide responsibility into two sections, with Edinburgh entrusted with Skye, Wester Ross, Orkney, Shetland and the eastern Highlands, while Glasgow took charge of Argyll, western Inverness, the Outer Hebrides and the Inner Hebrides, apart from Skye. The distribution of meal was managed initially under the sections' Local Committees, appointed from each parish or district from lists supplied by local clergymen. The aim was to do enough to prevent starvation, with allowances limited to 1½lb. of meal per adult male per day and ¾lb. per female. Children under 12 received ½lb. each. In order to ensure that the people were not to be corrupted into a state of indolent dependence, work was supposed to be given in return for food. In the spring and summer of 1847, gangs of men, women and children could be seen labouring all over the western Highlands, the northern isles and the Hebrides at 'public' works, laying roads, building walls, digging ditches and constructing piers. Several 'destitution roads' survive to this day in many parts of the Highlands as physical memorials to the greatest crisis in the modern history of the region.

The relief effort did avert the threat of starvation. In spring 1847, for instance, the Glasgow Section dispatched 15,680 bolls of wheatmeal, oatmeal, peasemeal and Indian corn to the distressed districts. But critics in the hierarchy of the Central Board were soon complaining that the Highlanders were being encouraged to rely on 'pauperizing' assistance, the 'labour test' was often ignored and the distribution of meal too lavish. A campaign to establish a more rigorous system of relief started to gain momentum, partly inspired by the belief that destitution was likely to endure for much longer than one season and so some effort had to be made to ensure that the Gaels could support themselves in the future. Latent racism also came to the surface. Vitriolic attacks against the 'lazy' Highlander who was supported by the 'industrious' Lowlander appeared in the pages of *The Scotsman*. Sir Charles Trevelyan, Assistant Secretary to the Treasury, the key figure in the famine relief strategies in Ireland, was also a powerful influence on the men who ran the Central Board. Trevelyan's position was unequivocal. He regarded both Irish and Highland Celts as racially inferior to Anglo-Saxons. The potato famine represented the judgement of God on an indolent people who now had to be taught a moral lesson to change their values and attitudes so that they might support themselves. Gratuitous relief was a curse; as Trevelyan put it, 'Next to allowing the people to die of hunger, the greatest evil that could happen would be their being habituated to depend upon public charity.'[3]

The outcome was the imposition of the hated 'destitution test' throughout the distressed region. By this system of extreme stringency a whole day's work was required in return for a pound of meal, the theory being that only those facing starvation would accept help on such terms. Trevelyan stressed that 'pauperism' or dependency on relief could be avoided but insisted that 'the pound of meal and the task of at least eight hours hard work is the best regime for this moral disease'.[4]

An elaborate bureaucracy was set up to enforce the new approach, consisting of an Inspector-General, resident inspectors, relief officers and work overseers. Most were retired or semi-retired naval officers ('heroes of the quarter-deck', as one observer put it) who were accustomed to maintaining strict discipline. Meal allowances were issued only once a fortnight in order to impose habits of prudence by teaching the poor to spread their means over an extended period rather than rely on being fed on a daily basis. Labour books were kept by the overseers in which the hours of work of each recipient were faithfully recorded, the fortnight's allowance for each family calculated with care and tickets issued for presentation to the meal dealers. The destitution test was resolutely enforced by relief officers who saw it as their duty to teach the people a moral lesson. Not surprisingly, however, it provoked deep hostility. One critic commented acidly that the scheme was 'starving the poor Highlanders according to the most approved doctrines of political economy . . . the Highlanders upon grounds of Catholic affinity, were to be starved after the Irish fashion'.[5] Free Church ministers protested loudly at the programme of 'systematized starvation', which provoked angry opposition among the people of Skye and Wester Ross. Nevertheless, the test was enforced through 1848 and into 1849. In essence a great philanthropic endeavour had been transformed into an ideological crusade to reform a population represented as inadequate and in need of improvement. It was an extraordinary outcome.

However, the reasons why the Highlands did not starve were wider and deeper than the relief effort itself. Many landowners were active in supporting the inhabitants of their estates in the early years of the crisis. For instance, only 14 per cent of all west Highland proprietors were censured by government officials for negligence, though, in several other cases, pressure had to be brought to bear to ensure that landowners met their obligations, while in later years estate policy in general became much less benevolent and more coercive. Civil servants even contrasted the positive role of Scottish landowners with the indifference of many of their counterparts across the Irish Sea. A prime factor in the Scottish case was that many proprietors had the financial resources to provide support to their small tenants. Since the early nineteenth century there had been a great transfer of estates from the indebted hereditary landlord class to new owners who were often rich tycoons from outside the Highlands. Over three-quarters of all estates in the famine zone had been acquired by merchants, bankers, lawyers, financiers and industrialists by the 1840s. These men were attracted to the Highlands for sport, recreation, the romantic allure of the region and, not least, the basic desire for territorial acquisition. Typical of the breed was the new owner of Barra and South Uist, Colonel John Gordon, dubbed 'the richest commoner in Scotland', and Sir James Matheson, proprietor of Lewis and partner in the giant East India house of Jardine, Matheson and Co. The economic muscle of this élite complemented the relief programmes of government and the charities, at least in the first years of the disaster.

The different stages of economic development of Ireland and Scotland were also a crucial factor. The Scottish famine took place in an industrialized society with urbanization occurring at a faster rate than in virtually all European countries. By the 1840s Scotland had much greater per capita wealth than Ireland and an industrial economy that offered a range of jobs in general and casual labouring to temporary and permanent migrants from the Highlands. Agricultural work, especially at the harvest, the fisheries, domestic service, building, dock labouring and railway navvying were just some of the outlets available in the booming southern economy. By the 1840s, temporary migration had become a very well-developed feature of Highland life. Not only did it provide a stream of income from the Lowlands but the peak months for seasonal movement, May to September, were also the times of maximum pressure on food resources when the old grain and potato harvests were running out and the new had still to be gathered. These migration networks were of critical importance during the potato famine. The years 1846 and 1847 were by happy coincidence a phase of vigorous development in the Lowland economy, stimulated in large part by the greatest railway construction boom in Scotland of the nineteenth century. Inevitably there was an unprecedented demand for navvies, but fishing and agriculture, both traditional outlets for Highland seasonal migrants, were also very buoyant. The combination of a very active labour market in the south and the unremitting pressure of destitution in the north prompted a huge exodus from the stricken region.

Mass starvation was therefore avoided by a variety of means. But this is not to say that the Highlands escaped unscathed. The potato famine was a decisive factor in the history of crofting society because it precipitated emigration on a hitherto unknown scale. It is reckoned that perhaps a third of the entire population migrated permanently from the western mainland and the Hebrides between the early 1840s and the later 1850s. The physical remains of countless communities are still to be seen in the ruined townships and abandoned cultivation beds ('lazybeds') which litter the crofting region to this day as silent memorials to the greatest and most concentrated diaspora in Highland history. The greatest losses were experienced in Skye, Mull, Tiree, the Outer Hebrides and the mainland parishes of the Inner Sound (between Skye and the mainland). Some of the insular parishes lost up to one-half of their pre-famine levels of population.

This great emigration also stands out because of the scale of landlord-assisted emigration of the very poor, the social class which had neither the means nor the motivation to move in previous years. During the famine years, nearly 17,000 were 'assisted' to emigrate to Canada and Australia by landowners intent on ridding their properties of destitute small tenants and cottars and determined to employ the most draconian means of clearance in order to achieve their ends. The pressures making for increasing migration soon began to build up as the potato crop failed to recover and the biological disaster was soon followed by economic collapse. Between 1848 and 1852, prices slumped for black cattle, commercial fishing was in difficulty and the industrial recession of the later 1840s reduced opportunities for Highland temporary migrants in the Lowland economy. The net effect of the intensity and long duration of the crisis was to weaken the grip of the people on the land. In many parishes there developed a desperate urge to flee the stricken region, even on the part of the cottars and poorer crofters who were traditionally the most reluctant to contemplate emigration.

The incentives to promote assisted emigration became stronger. The policy of landlord relief provision was short-lived and from 1849 the strategy switched from charitable support to one designed to export the poor and the destitute for fear that the entire burden of maintaining the stricken population would fall on the proprietors. Partly, this was because the main organization for famine relief, the Central Board, intimated its intention to terminate its activities in 1850; but it was also due to the rumours, widely circulating in the region, that the government was contemplating the introduction of 'an able-bodied Poor Law' as the best means of averting the persistent threat of starvation in the Highlands. This would give the destitute, who formed the majority on most Highland properties, the legal right to claim relief, and it would also establish the principle of compulsory rating and so threaten many proprietors with financial ruin. The mere suggestion of such legislation was enough to send tremors of alarm through the ranks of the landed classes. Some suspected that Sir John McNeill, chairman of the Board of Supervision of the Scottish Poor Law, who was conducting an inquiry into Highland destitution in 1851, was likely to report in favour of such a measure; in the event, however, he advised a programme of assisted emigration as the solution to the problems of the region. Yet before government came to a decision on his report, several landlords had concluded that they were likely to be left with the final responsibility for maintaining the poor on their properties, whether through direct famine relief or through the indirect cost of contribution to a massive extension of the Poor Law. Their eagerness to support emigration derived ultimately from the fact that the costs of assisted passages were in the long run very much lower than either of these alternatives.

There was also an obvious economic attraction in thinning the population. During the later 1840s the fall in cattle prices led to an increase in arrears among the small tenants, who were also selling stock to buy meal, but in the same period sheep prices were buoyant and there was a sustained recovery from the more difficult market conditions of the 1820s and 1830s. Sheep-farming attracted, not only because it yielded higher rentals than traditional cattle-rearing, but also because returns from a few flockmasters were also more secure and more easily collected than from most impoverished crofters. The expansion of sheep-ranching, clearance of small tenants and cottars and assisted emigration schemes all became integrated into coherent programmes of action on several Hebridean estates in this period.

Compulsion became a core element in landlord policy. After 1848 the volume of summonses of removal granted to landlords in west Highland sheriff courts dramatically increased. Between 1846 and 1848, 187 writs of removal were issued to the Matheson estate in Lewis alone, and in the following three years this multiplied sixfold to 1,180. Yet it is important to note that clearance, or the threat of it, was only one of several weapons employed with great vigour to induce movement. These included the threat of confiscation of cattle stocks for those in rent arrears, prohibition of the right to cut peat supplies during the summer months for winter use, and refusal to grant famine relief to those in distress. These techniques were applied with clinical care, and only the most destitute were normally offered support. As the Duke of Argyll noted in May 1851: 'I wish to send out those whom we would be obliged to feed if they stayed at home; to get rid of that class is *the object* [underlined in letter]'.[6] On his Tiree and Ross of Mull estates, great discrimination was employed in order to remove 'all the poorest and those most likely to be a burden on the property'. Much of the strategy was designed to rid estates of that 'redundant' population which now languished in destitution as a result of the decline in kelp manufacture and it explains why, on arrival in Canada, many were compared to the Irish because of their poor and ragged appearance. On the Island of Lewis the administration tried to clear crofting townships in the west which had relied on kelp production while, at the same time, maintaining and consolidating fishing communities on the east coast which had a better record of regular rent payment. Such selective use of emigration assistance ultimately depended on the application of threats, pressure and coercion, and it was a policy that must have spread alarm and anxiety throughout the crofting region, even on estates where 'compulsory emigration' was not practised. The overall effect must have been to increase the fear of eviction and hence the attractions of leaving the Highlands for ever.

2

It was in early 1856, after a full decade of misery, that the first optimistic reports of recovery concerning Highland conditions began to appear in the Scottish press. In that year the *Inverness Advertiser* described how more people were at work in the south and east and, more significantly, that the potato crop was more productive. But the potato never again recovered the dominance in the Highland diet that it had attained in the decades before 1846 and there is abundant literary evidence by the 1870s of altered dietary habits in the region. Consumption of imported meal increased markedly – and so significant was this that it became common practice to feed the indigenous grain crop and part of the potato crop to the cattle to sustain them during the winter months, while reserving imported meal for human consumption. There was an equally important expansion in the purchase of tea, sugar, jam and tobacco. Until the 1850s these articles were rare and expensive luxuries, but by the 1880s tea drinking had become universal in the crofting districts and a familiar part of the way of life.

These alterations in diet were the most obvious manifestations of more fundamental changes in the nature of crofting society in the aftermath of the famine. To some extent, the declining significance of the potato may have reflected the relaxation of population pressure in some districts as emigration persisted and the ranks of the cottar class were thinned in most localities outside the Long Island. But the new dietary patterns were also to be found in the Outer Hebrides, where the old problems of population congestion and land hunger remained; and the more varied diet, in fact, was simply one part of a wider and deeper social transition that affected *all* areas. In the 1870s and 1880s the majority of the population of the western Highlands became less dependent on the land for survival and even more reliant on the two sources of income and employment, which had proved most resilient during the famine itself: fishing and temporary migration. They entered more fully into the cash economy, selling their labour for cash wages and buying more of the necessities of life with their earnings rather than producing these themselves.

Manufactured clothes and shoes, 'shop produce' as they were known in the region, steadily replaced the home-made varieties in the two generations after the famine. A new mechanism of credit facilitated these developments. Shopkeepers, merchants and fish curers supplied credit on which meal and clothes were bought until seasonal earnings from fishing and temporary migration became available. The running accounts were then partly paid off on the basis of these returns, but more often than not the debts persisted from year to year. In Lewis, for instance, the fishing crews purchased on credit in the curers' shops the meal, clothing and other necessities required for their families. Settlements took place at the end of the season; fishermen were credited with the price of fish delivered by them to the curers and were debited with the price of their purchases.

The entire structure depended ultimately on five factors: the recovery of the prices gained for Highland black cattle; a steep fall in world grain prices in the 1870s and 1880s; a continued expansion in steam navigation in the western Highlands; the growth of the indigenous fishing industry; and a further increase in the scale of temporary migration and casual employment. These particular influences need also to be viewed against the longer perspective of the decisive change in the economic circumstances of the west Highland population which took place from the later 1850s and continued into the 1860s and 1870s. The period from the end of the Napoleonic Wars to the potato famine had been one of contracting income and falling employment opportunities. The three decades after the crisis saw a significant recovery in both earnings and jobs but this was not wholly offset by either rising costs or new demographic pressures. Even given the important qualifications that will be entered below when living standards are considered, there had been a relative improvement in circumstances.

Price trends, between the 1850s and 1870s, were to the advantage of the people in the crofting region, and this was a dramatic reversal of the pattern before 1846. Cattle prices continued the recovery that had begun in 1852 and crofters' strikes in Lewis selling at 30s. to £2 in 1854 fetched £4–5 in 1883. Those small tenants who possessed sheep stocks gained from the upward swing in prices which lasted until the late 1860s, and the fact that they were much better fed on grain and potatoes during the winter months added to the marketability of cattle. The principal aim was now one of maximizing the potential of stock, not simply in the traditional manner in order to pay rent but as a source of the funds employed to purchase meal and other commodities.

A further expansion in sea transport facilitated both cattle and sheep exports and grain imports. In the early 1850s a single small steamer plied the route between the Clyde and Portree once a fortnight, whereas three decades later two larger vessels sailed to Skye and Lewis every week and a further three visited Barra and North and South Uist. These developments in communications were both cause and effect of the changing way of life in the region and the basis of the close involvement of the people in the money economy. Above all, they allowed the population of more areas to take full advantage of the sustained fall in world grain prices that took place after the opening up of the interior areas of North America by railroad and the new steamship connections were established with purchasing countries in Europe. In the early 1840s meal imported from the Clyde sold at an average of £2 2s. per boll in the Outer Hebrides; by the 1880s average prices were close to 16s. per boll. It was the enormous decline in costs which encouraged the practice of feeding cattle on grain produced at home and allowed earnings from cattle sales and other activities to be devoted to the purchase of cheap meal from outside.

Pivotal to the whole system of increased trade, credit and money transactions was a vast expansion in seasonal employment opportunities, and the indigenous white and herring fisheries of the Outer Hebrides achieved a new level of activity and prosperity. Fishing stations were set up at Castlebay, Lochboisdale and Lochmaddy and the number of fish curers increased from seven in 1853 to 50 in 1880. In the early 1850s, about 300 small boats were active; three decades later, around 600. The organization and capitalization of the industry were dominated by men from the east coast, but the Hebrideans gained from the new opportunities for seasonal employment, and the developing steamer services and the injection of capital from the east had given the winter white fishery in particular a fresh and vigorous stimulus. Casual jobs as stalkers and ghillies were also available on the sporting estates and in the labour squads needed to build the infrastructure of roads and lodges required by the booming recreation economy.

Finally, the expansion in temporary migration which had begun during the famine was sustained after it. Virtually all sectors – agricultural work in the Lowlands, domestic service in the cities, the merchant marine, and general labouring (such as in the gasworks of the larger towns) – produced more opportunities for Highland temporary migrants than before. Because of this, 'seasonal' migration more often became 'temporary' movement, with absences extending not simply for a few weeks or months but for the greater part of a year or even longer. The seasonality of different work peaks made it possible to dovetail different tasks outside the Highlands and at the same time alternate labour in the crofting region with work opportunities elsewhere. The classical example of this cycle was the interrelationship between the winter white fishery in the Minch, the spring herring fishery in the same waters and the east coast herring fishery during the summer months.

Nevertheless, the extent of material amelioration should be kept in perspective as the majority of the inhabitants of the region continued to endure an existence of poverty and insecurity after 1860. Despite relative improvement, life was still precarious and could easily degenerate into destitution again if any of the fragile supports of the population temporarily crumbled. Between 1856 and 1890, there was a series of bad seasons which recalled some of the worst years of the potato blight, and conditions in 1864 were briefly reminiscent of the tragic days of the 1840s. On the Duke of Argyll's estate in Mull in that year there was a rapid increase in arrears among the small tenants and cottars, and food, seed and labour had to be provided for the people who had suffered great hardship since 1862. Four years later, distress was again experienced by the population of an island that had sustained a decline in the number of its inhabitants from 10,054 to 7,240 between 1841 and 1861. Once again, meal was made available and public works started. It was successive bad seasons in 1881–2, affecting the whole of the western Highlands, that not only produced much social suffering but also provided the initial economic impetus for the great crofters' revolt of that decade. Over 24,000 people received relief in these years. Conditions deteriorated once more in 1888 when, in the Outer Hebrides, 'actual starvation' was predicted, and the inhabitants once more were supported by charitable organizations from the Lowland cities. The chamberlain of the Lewis estate himself estimated that there had been at least nine seasons between 1853 and 1883 when the proprietor had had to advance varying amounts of seed and meal to distressed crofters.

At best, then, 'recovery' was modest, insecure and interrupted by years of considerable difficulty. Typhus remained common in some localities because of hard living conditions and poor sanitation, and cattle continued to share living accommodation with human beings. Domestic squalor persisted and continued to disconcert observers from outside the Highlands. Mass clearances were a thing of the past but insecurity of tenure remained a fact of life: 'Others, not a few, continue quietly evicting by legal process and clearing by so-called voluntary emigration. The lawyer's pen supersedes the soldier's steel.'[7] At the same time the movement of the young to the New World and the Lowland cities continued unabated. Above all, the social calamities of previous decades had not been forgotten and a bitter folk memory of dispossession lingered on and fuelled the simmering discontent that finally erupted in the 1880s into open agitation.

3

The traditional stereotype of the docile Highlander as passive and apathetic during the Clearances has been much qualified by recent research. Between 1780 and 1855 more than 50 acts of defiance against landlord authority occurred, and further intensive investigation will doubtless reveal even more instances of collective protest. Sometimes resistance took place on a considerable scale, as in 1792 in Easter Ross, when the people of several districts came together and tried to drive the hated sheep flocks that threatened their way of life out of the region. More often, opposition was highly localized, sporadic and uncoordinated, a spontaneous and desperate response to imminent eviction.

Women – and men dressed as women – were often to the fore. Sticks and stones were the usual weapons. Estate factors, police and sheriff officers were assaulted and humiliated but protest usually crumbled when the army became involved. That the people were not broken by the ravages of clearance is also shown by the incidence of sheep-stealing and occasional intimidation of the flockmasters. The greatest single collective act of defiance of landlordism was probably the emergence of the Free Church in 1843, which drew many communities in the western Highlands and Islands from the established Church of Scotland. This was the climax to a long series of patronage disputes as congregations in the crofting region opposed the induction of unpopular ministers appointed by lay patrons (invariably landowners) who did not share the evangelical commitments of the ordinary people. The Disruption of 1843 was not an overtly political movement in the Highlands; it was about Christian belief rather than an explicit attack on landlordism. Nevertheless, the sheer size of the exodus from the Established Church in the teeth of landlord opposition was deeply significant.

A few years later, however, the morale of the Gaels was dealt a devastating blow by the famine and the consequent increase of eviction to unparalleled levels. The senior government relief officer during the crisis, the aptly named Sir Edward Pine Coffin, was a career civil servant not normally given to alarmist claims. Yet he was so concerned about the sheer magnitude of the removals that he wrote to his superiors, bitterly condemning landowners for seeking to bring about 'the extermination of the population'. Eviction was so rampant in 1848–9 that in his view it would lead to 'the unsettling of the very foundations of the social system'.[8] Coercion was maintained after the famine not through mass eviction, which petered out in the late 1850s, but by the rigorous control of sub-letting of land to avoid the creation of additional households within an individual tenancy. So insistent did this strategy become that the keeping of lodgers was expressly forbidden and anyone who married had to leave the croft. As the young emigrated, cottages were pulled down when the parents died. The whole process was enforced by the threat of the dreaded summons of removal. The factors on several estates came to resemble petty tyrants who ruled the people with an iron hand. One of the most notorious was John Campbell, the Factor Mòr (Big Factor), Chamberlain of the Duke of Argyll's lands in Mull and Tiree. When he died in 1872, emigrant communities across the Atlantic celebrated in uninhibited style, as reported in the satirical poem, 'Lament for the Factor Mòr':

When they heard in Canada that that beast had expired
bonfires were lit and banners attached to branches;
the people were cock-a-hoop with joy
as they met one another
and they all got down on their knees and praised God that you had died.[9]

The estate factors had awesome powers of eviction, since the small tenants held their crofts only on annual tenure. John Murdoch, the energetic champion of the crofters' cause, found the people of the Gordon estate of South Uist in such 'a state of slavish fear' in the 1870s that they dared not complain about their grievances to the factor, Ranald MacDonald, lest he force them from their homes. Similarly, in South Harris, Murdoch also found the small tenants 'paralysed by terror'.[10] As one crofter, Donald MacAskill, admitted at a land reform meeting in Skye a few years later: 'I am ashamed to confess it now that I trembled more before the factor than I did before the Lord of Lords.'[11]

It is therefore surprising, against this background of chronic fear and anxiety, that the people did eventually mount a successful challenge to landlordism in the 1880s. The protest began in the townships of Gedintailor, Balmeanach and Peinchorran, which constituted the district known as the Braes on Lord MacDonald's estate on the east coast of Skye. The crofters petitioned their landlord to have traditional grazing rights returned to them. The factor rejected this request and the crofters responded by stating that they would no longer pay rent to Lord MacDonald until their rights were restored. The landlord then attempted to serve summonses of removal on a number of tenants on the grounds that they were in rent arrears. On 7 April 1882, however, the sheriff officer serving the summonses was accosted by a crowd of around 500 people and the notices were taken from him and burned. Ten days later, the law returned in force, strongly supported by no fewer than 50 Glasgow policemen. They managed to arrest those who had assaulted the sheriff officer, but not before about a dozen constables received injuries at the hands of a large crowd of men and women throwing stones and wielding large sticks. The 'Battle of the Braes' was followed by similar forms of action at Glendale in Skye at the end of 1882.

These disturbances had several features that recalled the ineffectual protests against clearance in the decades before the 1860s, including the use of rudimentary weapons; the central role of women; the deforcement of the officers of the law; the intervention of the police and the localized nature of resistance. However, the Battle of the Braes has come to be regarded as a historic event because it also signalled a decisive change of direction from past episodes of protest. For one thing, the people took the initiative to try to regain grazing rights which they had lost 17 years before. This protest was proactive rather than reactive. For another, the rent strike, which had been employed with deadly effect on numerous Irish estates in earlier years, was a tactic that was extremely difficult for proprietors to combat without contemplating mass eviction, and this was a policy which was becoming politically unacceptable by the 1880s. The Battle of the Braes and other disturbances suggested that landlordism was now encountering a different type of opposition, but it was still small in scale, confined to only a few estates in Skye, and at this stage the authorities were still dealing with only a minor land dispute. Previous episodes of resistance like this had usually petered out in failure and imprisonment for the participants, but the Braes skirmish was the prelude to more widespread acts of insubordination, sustained on many Highland estates for several years, which involved the consolidation of rent strikes, the occupation of sheep farms, the destruction of farm fences, deforcement of sheriff officers and mutilation and killing of stock. *The Scotsman* reported in some alarm in October 1884 that: 'men are taking what does not belong to them, are setting all law at defiance, and are instituting a terrorism which the poor people are unable to resist . . . Rents are unpaid, not because the tenants cannot pay them, but because in some cases they will not, and in some cases they dare not.' It asserted that, if the law was not enforced quickly, 'the condition of the islands will soon be as bad as that of Ireland three years ago'.[12]

The Scotsman was likely to exaggerate, since the paper was a close ally of the landlord interest. There was little 'Irish'-style agrarian terrorism in the Highlands at this time and most disturbances were confined to particular districts. The western mainland was peaceful for the most part, and even in the Hebrides, where there was most overt discontent, illegal activity was concentrated mainly in Skye and, to a lesser extent, Lewis. Direct action did occur in South Uist, Tiree and Harris, but it tended to be much more intermittent than elsewhere. In part, the notion that the entire region was aflame and lawlessness everywhere rampant was the result of the remarkable success of the publicity given the disturbances by the Scottish and English press. The incidents in Skye were deemed so serious that the government sent an expeditionary force to the island, the first since the time of the last Jacobite rebellion in the eighteenth century, a decision which produced an almost hysterical reaction from certain sections of the press. A violent armed confrontation between troops and people was eagerly anticipated, the *North British Daily Mail* carrying such sensational headlines as, 'Threatened General Rising of Crofters' and 'Dunvegan Men on the March to Uig'. The 16 newspaper correspondents who were sent from the south and the two artists from the *Graphic* and the *Illustrated London News* were disappointed, however, when the expected violent conflict did not take place. Marine detachments did stay on in Skye until 1885, and on their departure from Uig in June of that year they received a friendly farewell message from the local people. The troops stationed at Staffin seem to have developed a particularly close association with the local inhabitants and, according to one observer, they had shown a considerable interest in the women of the district: 'They gave more of their time to the god of love than to the god of war.'[13]

In fact, the distinguishing feature of the events of the 1880s, or the 'Crofters' War' as they have come to be described, was not so much the spread of violence, intimidation and lawlessness throughout the Highlands as the fusion of an effective political campaign for crofters' rights with a high-profile series of acts of resistance, of which the refusal to pay rents and the 'raiding' of old lands were the most significant. By the early 1880s a crofting lobby had already grown up in the southern cities, consisting of land-reformers, Gaelic revivalists, second- and third-generation Highland immigrants, and radical liberals. From these groups and existing committees there was formed the Highland Land Law Reform Association (HLLRA) with a strategy loosely based on that of the Irish Land League. It sought fair rents, security of tenure, compensation for improvements and, significantly, redistribution of land. This was a decisive development because not only did the HLLRA link the crofters' cause with external political interests, it also, through its proliferating branches and district committees, helped to end the localism that had impeded collective action in the past.

The most remarkable example of this came with the appointment of a Royal Commission into the condition of the crofters and cottars in the Highlands and Islands under the chairmanship of Lord Napier and Ettrick. The government had responded to the perceived scale of civil disobedience and growing public sympathy for the Highlanders, so that the Commission took evidence throughout the region from the spring to the winter of 1883, with its Report finally published in 1884. When it appeared, it was much criticized, not surprisingly, by landlords because it recommended controls over their powers of ownership, but also by the majority of the people because its proposals fell far short of their aspirations. The proposals ignored the problem of the cottars and were confined to those who possessed holdings of more than £6 and less than £30 per annum. Nevertheless, the Napier Commission's Report was also a symbolic victory for the crofting agitation as, for the first time, a public body had admitted the validity of the land rights of the people, even though these were not recognized in law. The Royal Commission also proposed that the state should provide a degree of protection for their interests. The Report was reluctant to offer perpetual security of tenure but advocated that government should instead assist crofters to purchase their holdings. It was a radical change from the kind of assumptions that had governed external intervention in the Highlands during the famine years of the 1840s and 1850s.

The subsequent legislation, enshrined in the Crofters Holdings (Scotland) Act, differed in some key respects from the Commission's recommendations but it too represented a decisive break with the past and began a new era in landlord–crofter relations in the Highlands. Security of tenure for crofters was guaranteed as long as rent was paid; fair rents would be fixed by a land court; compensation for improvements was allowed to a crofter who gave up his croft or was removed from it; crofts could not be sold but might be bequeathed to a relative and, with certain restrictions, the compulsory enlargement of holdings could be considered by the land court.

This legislation did not immediately find favour with the land reformers, especially since it gave only very minor concessions to crofters' demands for more land. But its historic significance should not be underestimated. The Crofters' Act made clearances in the old style impossible, breached the sacred rights of private property, controlled landlord–crofter relations through a government body and afforded the crofting population secure possession of their holdings. The balance of power between landlords and small tenants had been irrevocably altered by 1886, a fact that was already becoming apparent earlier. In December 1884, Cameron of Lochiel had noted that the current of political and public opinion was flowing fast against the landed interest, and the following month about 50 Highland proprietors and their representatives met at Inverness to discuss the crofting agitation and agreed to provide crofters with leases, consider revision of rents and guarantee compensation for improvements. It was a tardy attempt at developing a more benevolent form of landlordism and was induced by the weakening position of the élites. The proposals were rejected as a sure sign that the landowners were finally on the run. As the *Oban Times* gleefully declared, 'the Highland lairds are on their knees'.[14] Final victory seemed only a matter of time.

In historical perspective, the events of the 1880s are quite remarkable. The crofters had not secured the return of lands from which they had been removed during the Clearances; that would have amounted to wholesale expropriation of private property and remained politically unthinkable. Yet, by imposing legislation which made the tenancy of a croft heritable, the state had in effect deprived the landlord of most of his former rights of ownership. No other class or group in late-nineteenth-century mainland Britain was given such protection as were the Highland crofters in this way. How and why they managed to achieve such privileges is the question that now will be considered.

The agitation in Skye was triggered in part by economic crisis. The winter of 1882–3 was reckoned to have been one of the worst since the disasters of the 1840s. The potato crop was partially destroyed and earnings of migrant labourers from the east coast fisheries, a key source of income in Skye and the Long Island, had fallen dramatically. Problems became more acute after a great storm in October 1882 which damaged or destroyed many boats (one estimate suggested over 1,200), nets and fishing gear. The resulting economic stresses may help to explain why 'no rent' campaigns became so popular within the crofting community. Even when there was some recovery from the difficulties of 1882–3, cattle prices collapsed throughout most of the remainder of the decade, and by the late 1880s young beasts which might have fetched £7 or £8 in 1883 were worth less than £2. The period was also one of difficulty in sheep-farming as the British market for wool and mutton was swamped by imports from the Antipodes. The big flockmasters suffered most, with many surrendering their leases, and there was wholesale conversion of sheep farms to deer forests. But small tenant income was also affected as by this time it was also usual for crofters to keep a few sheep.

These continuing economic difficulties in the western Highlands fuelled social tensions. But there had been bad times before and little unrest. The people had accepted suffering as God's judgement or as part of the natural law, not as a consequence of the injustice of man. One new factor was a changing attitude among the people. Some scholars have noted that they had more iron in their souls by the 1880s. The Gaelic poetry of the land war period, as analysed by Sorley McLean, transmits a more powerful mood of confidence and optimism and even before the Battle of the Braes there was evidence on some Highland estates of a new level of tenant truculence. By 1880, for example, on the Sutherland estate the agents were apparently willing to allow rent arrears and breach of regulations, rather than provoke the people into acts of defiance. It is also interesting to note that virtually all the famous incidents of the Crofters' War were the results of the initiative of the local populace rather than desperate responses to landlord action, as had been the pattern in the past. Young adult men and women formed the backbone of protest. They had been brought up in the better times of the 1860s and 1870s and had not known at first hand the anguish of the famine decades which had demoralized many of their parents and grandparents. The press often drew attention to the fact that many of the older people in the crofting townships were often timorous and meek while the young were more bold and defiant.

A decisive factor prompting them to action was the Irish example. Rural agitation in Ireland had led in 1881 to a famous victory, when Gladstone's government passed the Irish Land Act. This granted to tenants the rights known as the '3 F's', fair rents fixed by a land court, fixed tenure as long as the rent was paid, and free sale of the tenant's interest in the farm which allowed for compensation for improvements. The Irish triumph had obvious implications for Highland crofters. In part, information on the Irish agitation was conveyed through the regional Highland press, especially in the columns of the *Highlander*, edited by John Murdoch, who had lived in Ireland. Indeed, it was suggested by some that he devoted most of the last few issues of his journal more to Irish than to Highland matters. Even more important, however, was the personal connection between Skye and Ireland. From about 1875, many Skye men became labourers in Campbeltown and

Carradale fishing boats for the summer season in Irish waters, and these annual sojourns gave them experience of such Irish tactics as rent strikes. Indeed, the Irish connection goes a long way to explaining why in its early years the agitation concentrated mainly on Skye. In a remarkable letter to Lord MacDonald's Edinburgh agent, his factor on the island noted:

Shortly before the term of Martinmas a body of young men, the sons of tenants, most of whom had been fishing at Kinsale in Ireland and had imbibed Irish notions, came to my office and presented a petition which they had almost the whole tenants to sign, to the effect that they demanded Ben Lee in addition to their present holdings without paying any additional rent.[15]

But despite the new boldness of the men of Skye, the dispute would probably not have lasted for long if it had not been for significant changes in external attitudes to the land issue. As late as the 1850s protests against clearances had been effectively crushed, the law enforced and the rights of landed property upheld, but such brutal assertions of proprietorial privilege were politically unacceptable 30 years later. At first, the due process of law in Skye was followed against deforcement and land raiding and both the police and the military were employed; but the government recognized that it could not contemplate the full use of force because public and political opinion would not permit it. The only alternative, therefore, was to concede some of the crofters' demands eventually in order to restore law and order.

The climate of opinion was already changing in the 1870s. In 1879 the estate of Leckmelm on Lochbroom was purchased by A. C. Pirie, an Aberdeen paper manufacturer. He tried to organize 'improvements' on his property which resulted in some evictions, but the removals produced a huge outcry in the Highlands and resounding condemnation from all sections of the national press, with the predictable exception of *The Scotsman*. Four years later, J. B. Balfour referred to 'a considerable body of vague and floating sentiment in favour of ameliorating the crofters' condition' which had influenced several members of the Liberal Party.[16] These feelings were apparent at the very highest levels of government and were shared by Gladstone, the Prime Minister, and the Home Secretary in 1882, Sir William Harcourt. Harcourt had a key role to play in the unfolding of events in the Hebrides, as he had spent many years on yachting holidays there and had developed a sympathy for the condition of the people of the area. In November 1882 he refused permission for a military expedition to be sent to Skye, and in the same month he suggested to Gladstone that a Royal Commission be established instead. Significantly, he observed that among 'decent people' there was now a view that the crofters had real grievances and in an age of widening political franchise such opinions could not easily be ignored.

These latent sympathies for the crofters were exploited to the full by pro-crofter propagandists, one of the most effective of whom was Alexander McKenzie, editor of the *Celtic Magazine*. McKenzie had been using this publication to draw attention to the social problems of the western Highlands since 1877. In 1883, however, he published his best-seller, *A History of the Highland Clearances*, which conveyed in emotive prose the harrowing details of some of the most notorious mass removals. It was not a work of historical detachment but a compendium of landlord misdeeds. Works like McKenzie's portrayed Highland proprietors as heartless tyrants who had ruthlessly betrayed their responsibilities and their people.

The contemporary press played an even more central role in publicizing the crofters' cause and influencing public opinion further in their favour. This was a publicity machine which even the wealthiest landowner could never hope to equal. As one reporter who covered the events of the 1880s noted later: 'Printed paper in the shape of newspapers proved the most deadly tool against the Highland landowners.'[17] The fact the coverage was so extensive, not only on the part of the Scottish papers but also in the English press, reflected the deep interest in the Highland problem that existed throughout the country and which was facilitated by the revolution in communications in the Western Isles. By the 1880s, a network of steamer connections had spread throughout the Inner and Outer Hebrides. In addition, the telegraph now allowed eyewitness reports of disturbances to be published soon after they took place and this made the Crofters' War one of the first popular agitations in Britain in which the media of the day played a significant part not only by reporting but also by actually influencing developments.

External political and cultural forces were also important. Crofter political awareness was raised by the methods and campaigns of Charles Stewart Parnell's Irish Nationalist Party and the Irish Land League. Though the disturbances in the north were not, as some suggested, a 'fenian conspiracy', there can be little doubt about the general Irish impact, especially through the writings and speeches of the charismatic

John Murdoch, who had been politically active in Ireland for several years and was acquainted with some of the leading personalities of the Irish agitation. There was also powerful support from the Highland societies which were not active in the Lowland towns. Until the 1870s they had been devoted almost exclusively to conviviality and cultural pursuits; by the end of that decade, however, the Federation of Celtic Societies was being criticized in some quarters as being too political. Activists, such as the eloquent and energetic Professor John Stuart Blackie of the University of Edinburgh, projected a potent message of literary romanticism and political radicalism. The regional Highland press was increasingly sympathetic, notably the *Oban Times* from 1882 when Duncan Cameron became editor, and provided a faithful record of speeches at meetings of the HLLRA at local level, which lent both cohesion and momentum to the agitation. Land reformers in mainland Britain and Ireland took up the crofters' cause, and it received particularly important support from reformist sections of the Liberal Party in Scotland. Second-generation Highlanders in the southern cities were also deeply influential in certain areas.

This motley alliance became in time an effective crofters' lobby. The people of the disturbed districts did help themselves but they gained a great deal from the unparalleled levels of external support which provided experienced leadership, political muscle and organizing expertise. The most remarkable demonstration of this contribution came in the months after the setting up of the Napier Commission. Government may have seen this as a way of defusing tension and deflecting opposition, but instead it became a catalyst for further agitation and the creation of a more effective organization, especially when it became apparent that the witnesses to the Royal Commission would be guaranteed immunity from intimidation. This was a crucial development, since bitter memories of the reign of terror of the clearance period endured among the older men whose evidence of past events was vital to the crofters' case. Until the Napier Commission sat for the first time in May 1883 at the Braes in Skye, every effort was made to prepare evidence. Alexander McKenzie and John Murdoch toured the region and provided advice, and at the end of 1883 the HLLRA of London published three pamphlets, in Gaelic and English, addressed to the crofting community, highlighting past wrongs and encouraging agitation in favour of security of tenure, fair rents and reallocation of land, as well as other aims. They were urged to form district branches and use peaceful and constitutional methods in pursuit of their demands. When branches were established the rules were drawn up by central headquarters in London.

But the crofters' movement did not simply become the creature of external sympathizers in these years, although they did do much to raise expectations. One of the most significant events in the organizational process was the decision taken at a mass meeting in Fraserburgh in August 1883 of west coast fishermen engaged in the herring fishery to form land reform associations on their return home. Furthermore, subversive and illegal activity on some estates persisted despite the official opposition of the HLLRA. The successes achieved represented a joint victory for the crofters and their new allies who were able effectively to exploit the new and more sympathetic climate of opinion that had emerged in the last quarter of the nineteenth century. It was this which granted the power that previous generations had lacked.

4

The great drama of the Clearances had been played out between the landowners and the people with occasional interventions from external forces of law and order. With the passage of the Crofters' Act in 1886, however, social and economic conditions and relations in the western Highlands and Islands could never be the same again. The state had become a major factor in influencing the future development of the region, both through statute law (which in 1886 established new controls on the relationship between landlord and tenant), the formation of new agencies (such as the Crofters Commission) and, from 1897, the Congested Districts Board (which provided financial support for distressed areas, emigration and communications development). The problem of civil disorder had originally drawn government into the Highlands, but by the eve of the First World War the original aim of bringing a measure of stability to a troubled area had been replaced by a vague and ill-defined commitment to a policy of economic and social improvement for the inhabitants of the region. The notion of the Highlands as a special case deserving special treatment was already established in the thinking of British policy-makers by 1914.

The Crofters' Act was the government's main response to the problems in the Highlands in the early 1880s and its structure reflected a complex series of influences. There was a desire to stop the agitation and restore law and order through concessions to the crofters; but to interfere with the rights of private property could have serious repercussions for the maintenance of social hierarchy elsewhere in Britain. Key ministers responded to this threat by accepting that the Highlanders were a special case and that what gave them this status was not their poverty but their history. Gladstone argued that the people had a historic right to the land which had been expropriated from them by commercial proprietors in the eighteenth and nineteenth centuries. The crofters had suffered a profound injustice, which should be redressed by parliament. In terms of land law, the historical basis of this contention was false, but these 'historicist' beliefs were fundamental to the passage of the 1886 legislation. As Gladstone stated in early 1885:

For it is, after all, this historical fact that constitutes the crofters' title to demand the interference of Parliament. It is not because they are poor, or because there are too many of them, or because they want more land to support their families, but because those whom they represent had rights which they have been surreptitiously deprived to the injury of the community.[18]

He also indicated that legislation would be confined to any parish with a history of common pasturage over the previous century and in this way the crofters were isolated from other social groups suffering material disadvantage. They were, by definition, an exceptional case and action for them could proceed without necessarily being regarded as a dangerous and politically unacceptable precedent.

At first the legislation did not take the heat out of the situation. The passing of the Crofters' Act produced a good deal of bitterness and disillusion and a subsequent return to violence and confrontation in some parts of the Hebrides. The crofter MPs had opposed the legislation with their allies, the Irish nationalists, but to no avail. Their principal bone of contention was the absence of any clause which might allow the restoration of land to the people and this shortcoming drew angry condemnation from such militant districts as Kilmuir and Glendale in Skye. Even more disappointed were the cottars, the landless or semi-landless people, for whom the 1886 Act had made no provision, and this excluded group demonstrated their discontent and frustration through persistent land raids on several estates over the next four decades. Concern about the limitations and weaknesses of the Act became apparent at the HLLRA's annual conference in September

1886, when it reconstituted itself as the Highland Land League and committed its members to 'restore to the Highland people their inherent rights in their native soil'. The scene was set for further confrontation when Gladstone's government fell on the issue of Irish Home Rule and was replaced by a Conservative administration from the autumn of 1886. This government determined on a more resolute policy of coercion in the Highlands and the new Scottish Secretary, Arthur Balfour, saw no need for further concessions to the crofters. The 1886 Act had gone far enough to meet their grievances; continued disorder should therefore be punished and malcontents brought to justice, since there was no longer any justification for lawlessness.

The immediate aftermath of the passage of the Crofters' Act therefore saw several episodes of significant unrest in 1886 and 1887 and the return of military and naval forces to the Highlands in support of the civil power. Following a land raid in Tiree, troops intervened on the island to assist the police, who were losing control of the situation. Similarly, there was another military expedition to Skye in late 1886 when civil administration on the island was in danger of collapse because of the accumulation of arrears of rates. The following year the military was also used in Lewis and in Assynt in Sutherland after land raids in these areas. The disorder had taken a change of direction and instead of rent strikes the emphasis was now on the occupation of land. Increasingly, too, the cottar class assumed a higher profile in several of the incidents. The courts also took a more stringent attitude to lawlessness and handed down much heavier prison sentences; there seemed to be a new climate of opinion emerging that the major grievances of the crofters had been answered in the 1886 Act and that now there was little legitimate reason for further disorder.

Over time, the Crofters' Act itself became much more acceptable. In January 1887 the Crofters Commission published its first set of judgements on crofting rentals, and the results were a revelation. The *Oban Times*, a few days afterwards, admitted that the 1886 Act had been misjudged and, on the basis of the Commission's decision, was likely to inaugurate a new era for the Highlanders. The Commission examined 1,767 holdings in 1886–7 and recommended an average rent reduction of almost 31 per cent; and in subsequent years, down to 1892–3, the reductions ranged on average from 30 per cent to 21 per cent. Equally significant was the action taken on rent arrears, which had risen dramatically as a result of the economic crises of the early

1880s and the series of rent strikes over many estates in the western Highlands and Islands. In Wester Ross and Lewis the cancellation of arrears between 1886 and 1895 was 72 per cent, in the Inverness-shire islands it was just over 71 per cent and in Argyll around 63 per cent.

Among the crofters, however, the legislation soon came to be regarded as the Magna Carta of the Highlands. The Act of 1886 placed the crofter in a unique position, in the words of Adam Collier, 'by conferring on him most of the advantages of ownership – security and power of request – without its drawbacks'.[19] In the two decades after its passage there was substantial material improvement in the crofting counties, with an estimated 40 per cent of crofters in Barra, the Uists, Skye and Harris building new homes. The Crofters Commission in 1912 noted how cottages were replacing 'black houses' in many districts. A Royal Commission of 1895 also took the view that the legislation had given a fresh impetus to crofting society and generated a greater sense of confidence and security. The knowledge that improvements to the holding would not necessarily result in increased rent had produced a new context for development. As the Commission concluded:

we found that more attention is being paid to cultivation, to rotation of crops, to reclamation of outruns, to fencing and to the formation or repair of township roads; but most conspicuous of all the effects perceptible, is that upon buildings, including both dwelling-houses and steadings. In a considerable number of localities we found new and improved houses and steadings erected by the crofters themselves since the passing of the Act.[20]

But the improvements should not simply or even mainly be regarded as the result of legislation. The last quarter of the nineteenth century was a period of modest amelioration for many groups in addition to the crofters but the fall in world grain prices was especially significant for the Highland population because there was an increasing tendency to buy in food for human consumption and use crops produced on the croft for animals. On the west coast of Sutherland, grain prices fell by about 50 per cent between 1880 and 1914. In addition, money income in many households rose as a result of remittances from migrants.

In the longer term, critics have argued that the 1886 Act became a powerful force for conservatism, condemned crofting society to a future of inertia and stagnation by freezing an existing structure of smallholdings and ensured by its constraints and limitations that any evolution of holding size as circumstances changed was virtually impossible. What compounded the problem was the loyalty the legislation inspired, which made any attempt at amendment politically unpopular and unattractive. The Act had provided the Crofters Commission with powers to grant enlargement of crofts but these were inadequate and resulted in only marginal changes. In addition, there was no provision at all for the creation of entirely new crofts. The assumption behind the Gladstonian policy of 1886, that in some way the government was preserving an ancient way of life threatened in the past and the present by the forces of commercial landlordism, was fallacious. The crofting system had itself been created in the later eighteenth century as a response to the economic imperatives of the Age of Improvement and was not an inheritance from the distant past of clanship. Nor did the benevolent legislation of 1886 provide any long-term remedy for the fundamental economic problems of the region and for much of the twentieth century depopulation proceeded apace. The assumption behind Lord Napier's proposals was that crofting had lost much of its rationale in the first half of the nineteenth century, when several of the by-employments linked to each holding, such as kelp manufacture and distilling, went into decline. The croft was not designed to produce a full subsistence which could be secured only by combining other activities with the working of the land. It was this essential imbalance between population and land resources which the more radical proposals of the Napier Commission attempted to address. Given the political impossibility of wholesale landlord expropriation, Napier concluded that there was not enough land available to provide an adequate living for all and therefore some consolidation and reorganization were necessary which should be linked to a programme of emigration. This approach was rejected by the Liberal government, which was not in the business of producing economic panaceas. The favoured policy was based on more pragmatic and short-term criteria. The 1886 Act came about for political reasons, it was a political response to a problem of public order and it is therefore hardly surprising that its long-term economic consequences have generated considerable controversy. It was not designed to be a blueprint for economic recovery.

Nor did the Crofters' Act do anything to help the problem of the landless cottars. This class was distributed unevenly throughout the Highlands. Clearance and draconian controls over subletting on many estates after the potato famine had resulted in a decline in their numbers along much of the western mainland and some of the Inner Hebrides.

But cottar families were still very numerous in parts of Skye, Mull and, even more significantly, in the Outer Hebrides, particularly in Lewis, Harris and the Uists. Popular agitation in the years after the passage of the Crofters' Act began to grow more common in these districts as the centre of discontent switched to Lewis from Skye. The political agitation had probably raised expectations among cottars who were frustrated by the 1886 legislation that had ignored their interests. This Act, however, was proof that direct action could bring political rewards. In addition, the cottar economy in the Hebrides was hit by crisis from 1884. The income of most families depended on the earnings of seasonal workers on the east coast fishery. Herring prices fell between 1884 and 1886 as a result of record catches and higher European import duties; and wages also went into decline and became more insecure as curers moved from fixed-price arrangements with the boats to one whereby the returns depended on the fluctuating market prices for fish. The average earnings of Hebridean seasonal workers collapsed from £20–30 in the early 1880s to a mere £1 or £2 later in that decade.

This was the economic background to a series of land raids by the cottars, designed in large part to draw attention to their plight. The most celebrated was the occupation of the Park deer forest in Lewis, when several hundred young men raided part of the Matheson estate and slaughtered many animals in the process. This was a well-organized and effectively publicized incident, with lurid and exaggerated details of the mass killing of hundreds of deer reported in the press; once again the government had to draft in the military to restore order, this time in the form of the Royal Scots. The *Oban Times* concluded in December 1887 that the crofters' agitation had come to an end. It was now the turn of the cottars, the class descended from those who had lost their lands during the Clearances. For this reason, the agitation concentrated on the recovery of land. It was a movement of the dispossessed.

The Park raiders were acquitted on a technicality, which probably served to encourage more disturbances. Further raids took place in Aignish in Lewis in early 1888, which led to a bloody confrontation with troops, and in Assynt in Sutherland. Throughout the Outer Hebrides, more covert cottar protest became endemic with nocturnal dike-breaking now commonplace and almost impossible to control. In the interim, the government responded to the lawlessness not simply by sending in the army but also by establishing an inquiry into the social and economic conditions of Lewis. The subsequent report demonstrated that the breakdown in law and order was not the work of hot-headed agitators but derived ultimately from the conditions of destitution, poor housing and congestion in which the landless population lived. The scale of the human crisis, reminiscent in some ways of the terrible years of the potato famine of the 1840s, and a desire to restore stability and order, prompted government intervention. The problem demanded other responses in addition to those of repression and coercion and, in formulating these, the state became directly involved in the Highlands on a much greater scale and in the process attempted to evolve a strategy of development for the region to remove once and for all the causes of instability and economic crisis.

There were several elements in the emerging policy. First, a short-term need existed to assist with the immediate problems, and a subsidy of £30,000 in relief of rates was made available by the Conservative government in 1888. In subsequent years the Highlands received £48,000 in relief of local taxation under the Local Government (Scotland) Act of 1889 and these monies helped to relieve the acute difficulties of the late 1880s and early 1890s. Second, an ambitious scheme of assisted emigration was planned to reduce congestion in the Hebrides, in which one of the authors of the report on Lewis had envisaged the removal of 30,000 families. Lord Lothian, the Secretary for Scotland, produced a plan in 1887 by which the British government would provide a loan of £120 for each emigrant family while the Canadian authorities made available 160 acres of free land. In the event, only £12,000 was forthcoming from government, the organization of the venture was less than efficient and the two settlements in Manitoba and the North-West Territories met with only limited success. Third, there was a commitment between 1888 and 1892 to develop the infrastructure of the region and promote the fishing industry. This, however, would be done in parallel with planned emigration. By December 1890 the Treasury had agreed to an expenditure of nearly £10,000 for harbours, roads, steamboat subsidies and the extension of the telegraphic system.

All this represented a dramatic extension of government activity in the Highlands but it is probably too simple to say that the fear of recurrent agitation forced the hand of the state. Certainly the problem of law and order was a real one and it was hoped that prosperity would bring eventual stability. Yet the ruling Conservative administration did not concede the crofters' and cottars' demands for more land and matters relating to land tenure were explicitly excluded from all policy initiatives. Indeed, by helping to support fishing it was hoped that land hunger would diminish as more non-agricultural employment became available. The government's emphasis on emigration as central to the strategy was also in direct conflict with the view taken by the crofters' lobby that there was sufficient land to be redistributed.

State action could in fact be justified because there was a growing view that the Highland problem was a chronic one that would be alleviated only by external intervention. Without this, the crofting districts would lurch from crisis to crisis, with recurrent destitution and disorder compelling emergency government action which would itself be a drain on national resources. It was better by far to stabilize the situation and move the region towards a more secure economic system with a linked programme of assisted emigration, fishing expansion and development of the infrastructure. Significantly, as they pointed out in a Memorial to Lord Lothian in 1888, most of the major Highland proprietors favoured such a strategy and their initiative did much to convince the Conservative government of its value. However, despite progress in road and harbour building and in the development of the telegraph system, the policy was not brought to any successful conclusion. Investment was limited, few initiatives were completed and the government therefore failed to make any significant impact on the long-term social and economic problems of the western Highlands, despite alleviating the crisis of the later 1880s. It was not, however, by any means the last Highland development plan which would founder, as later policy-makers discovered to their cost.

Public policy in the western Highlands and the west of Ireland had often run in parallel in the last quarter of the nineteenth century as both areas suffered from chronic problems of economic difficulty which often stimulated phases of popular unrest, and Irish land legislation was also used as the model for changes in Highland land tenure. Irish developments had yet another effect in the 1890s. In 1891 the Conservative government set up the Congested Districts Board in the west of Ireland to promote economic improvement by providing new holdings on land acquired for the purpose, to support industry and to give instruction in farming. The Board had a major impact and was deemed to have achieved many of its objectives even in the poorest areas.

Such was its success that the government established a Congested

Districts Board in 1897 to improve those parts of the Highlands perceived to be suffering from the same problems of over-population as Ireland. Fifty-six parishes in the crofting counties were judged to be 'congested' and the Board's remit extended to all the islands from Barra and Tiree northwards, together with most of the maritime districts of the western mainland from Ardnamurchan. Its objectives were to promote agriculture, provide land for settlement among crofters and cottars, extend road communications and develop the fishing industry. Most of these aims had been familiar parts of government policy since the later 1880s, but what was new was the commitment to the redistribution and resettlement of land and the recognition that 'congestion' could not be reduced by encouraging emigration alone. This acceptance of the principle of land settlement was of great political significance. Even if its practical effects were limited before the First World War, it became a basic factor in public policy towards the Highlands thereafter and drew the state even further into the life of the region than could have been imagined during the land wars of the 1880s.

However, the Congested Districts Board had raised expectations among the land-hungry cottars which it could not fulfil, although some aspects of its activities during the 15 years of the Board's existence were deemed to have been a success. It assisted through providing improved seed and stock; roads, bridges and piers were constructed and vegetable growing was encouraged throughout the congested districts. But the Board would be judged mainly by its creation of new holdings and policies of land settlement. Between 1897 and 1912 it did successfully establish 640 new holdings and complete enlargements totalling 133,000 acres but this was very far from the land transformation that the population of the western Highlands had expected; frustrated expectations came to the surface in a fresh series of land raids that punctuated the years of the Board's existence. Barra, South Uist and Lewis were all affected and the threat of land occupation was often made in numerous other localities.

The evidence suggests that the cottar population expected the wholesale restoration of the lands they believed their forefathers had lost during the Clearances. But this the Board could in no way deliver as it did not possess powers of compulsory purchase and therefore could not take the initiative in the land market but had to wait until a proprietor was willing to sell. It acquired no large estates up to 1904, and after 1906 its activities were considerably restricted because of changes in government policy. Action was also hampered by inadequate funding, with a budget of £35,000 compared to the Irish Board's final income of £231,000. It was therefore hardly surprising that the impact of the two bodies was very different. The Congested Districts Board in Ireland is credited with transforming the poorer districts of that country but in the Highlands the effects were much more problematic. The Irish Board had greater powers to cajole and finally compel landlords to sell land than its Scottish counterpart and, in addition, Highland crofters were much less willing to purchase holdings than Irish tenants; this reduced the Scottish Board's potential income. There was a much greater desire to obtain tenancies under the protection of the Crofters' Act of 1886 than to assume the burdens of ownership which could lead to higher outlay on rates. More generally, the policy of land resettlement was doomed in the western Highlands because of the deep reluctance of the people in most districts to migrate to other areas. Some argued that this was because planned resettlement, no matter how potentially beneficial, was still associated with clearance. The deep scars left by the great social trauma of the nineteenth century were still there and would affect the implementation of public policy for some time to come.

The Congested Districts Board was wound up in 1912 and its function taken over by the Board of Agriculture; its demise brought to an end a period of increasing state involvement. Governments of different political colours had recognized the Highlands as a special case, requiring the development of policies, the creation of agencies and the supply of subsidy not thought appropriate in the rest of the country. A striking example of this was the establishment of the Highlands and Islands Medical Services Board in 1913, by which a grant of £42,000 was made available to allow doctors in the region to charge fixed low fees. This was a recognition of the exceptionally high costs of delivering a medical service in sparsely populated and remote districts and also of the very poor health record of the western Highlands. On the eve of the First World War the state was assuming responsibilities for the welfare of the Highland population which would have been unthinkable a few decades previously. This was not simply a result of the general increase in social expenditure which occurred in the Edwardian era, it was also because of the peculiar history and circumstances of the Highlands. Ironically, this was also one reason why public policy failed to regenerate the economy of the region. Governments could not afford to concentrate exclusively or even mainly on economic rationalization of land use and so policy had to be based in part on what was acceptable to the people. More profit and greater output might have been realized if land had been concentrated in bigger holdings, but such an approach, whatever its potential merits, was politically and socially unacceptable. As the Committee on Land Settlement in Scotland stated in 1929, 'their [the crofters'] conditions were a reproach to the nation of which they formed a part and the only way to remove that reproach was to give them the only available land'.[21] It was an unambiguous declaration that social priorities were of paramount importance in the approach to the Highland problem.

This was demonstrated conclusively with the passage of the Land Settlement (Scotland) Act of 1919, which not only provided more funds for settlement purposes but also gave the Board of Agriculture the authority to purchase land compulsorily. This accelerated the process of land settlement dramatically. From 1912 to 1925, 1,571 new holdings were created and an additional 894 were extended. In the Hebrides alone, 932 new holdings were carved out of the large farms created during the nineteenth-century clearances. In the Outer Isles, Tiree and Skye – though not in Mull, the Small Isles or most of the mainland – the removals of Victorian times were effectively reversed. Since 1886 the crofting population had also gained security of tenure and achieved virtually nominal rentals for their holdings, privileges denied any other section of the agricultural community in Scotland. State intervention successfully solved the political problem of the crofting counties; and land raiding, which reached epidemic proportions in some parts of the Western Isles among returning ex-servicemen in the early 1920s, disappeared a few years later. However, satisfying the demand for land was one thing, ensuring economic security quite another. Depopulation still continued at an alarming rate. From 1861 to 1931, the Highlands lost 230,000 persons by net outward movement. During the 1920s and 1930s, the haemorrhage was especially severe, although arguably the loss of people might have been worse but for land settlement. In the Outer Isles, where the population had actually grown until 1911, emigration accelerated on a huge scale because of the post-war collapse of stock prices and the continued decline of fishing. Crop failure in the atrocious weather conditions of 1923 produced such a grave social crisis that government had to intervene with emergency food supplies in Lewis and elsewhere. The land settlement programme was not therefore any more of an economic panacea than what had gone before, nor had it done much to relieve congestion. In the Hebrides, for instance, 83 per cent of all holdings in 1925 were smaller than 15 acres. These small crofts inevitably forced families into supplementary employments to make ends meet, but even these outlets were increasingly hard to come by in the depression years between the wars. There was, however, little further scope for further settlement as, by the mid-1920s, most of the land available had been absorbed in earlier programmes. Increasingly, government and policy-makers came to the conclusion that croft holdings were too small and enlargement was necessary for the long-term economic security of the population. On the eve of the Second World War the 'crofting problem', which had engaged the intervention of the state since the 1880s, still remained intractable.

19

Land, Elites and People

The rural Lowlands have tended to become the Cinderella of modern Scottish history, ignored or marginalized in general studies and attracting few specialist works in recent years. The reasons are perhaps obvious. The region did not experience the tragedy and drama which mark the history of the Highlands while the dominance of towns, cities and industries in nineteenth- and twentieth-century Scotland also means that rural society can too easily be dismissed as irrelevant to an informed understanding of the nation's present condition. This chapter, however, argues that an analysis of the rural Lowlands after 1830 is an essential part of the wider interpretation of the development of modern Scotland. It concentrates on two central issues which combined to influence the nature and shape of Scottish society in the twentieth century: the structure and power of landownership and the origins of mass migration from the countryside to the towns and overseas.

I

For centuries the landed classes had been the unchallenged leaders of Scottish society. However, by the 1830s this historic hegemony seemed finally to be starting to crumble. The Great Reform Act of 1832 for the first time extended the franchise well beyond landed property, the new fortunes made from trade and industry undermined the virtual monopoly of the landowners over the wealth of the country and, in 1846, the Repeal of the Corn Laws suggested that the interests of an urban society were now of much greater political importance than those of agriculture and the land. All of these were serious potential threats to landed power, but throughout the middle decades they had little direct or decisive impact on the material position of the landed classes.

Indeed, down to the 1880s most landowners in Lowland Scotland experienced several decades of prosperity and rising rent rolls. Only in the western Highlands and Islands was there a real crisis of traditional landownership as many hereditary estates disappeared in the economic collapse in that region following the end of the Napoleonic Wars. Huge losses of land were suffered by the Mackenzies of Seaforth, Campbells of Islay, McNeils of Barra and MacDonalds of Clanranald among others. By the last quarter of the nineteenth century, around 70 per cent of the mainland and insular parishes of western Argyll, Inverness and Ross were under new ownership as a result of the greatest transfer of land recorded in modern Highland history. Ironically, however, this unprecedented sale of hereditary estates merely underscored the continuing appeal of landownership since the majority of the buyers were wealthy merchants, industrial tycoons and rich lawyers from outside the Highland region. In the Lowlands, on the other hand, the stability of landed property and its enduring economic importance were demonstrated by the continuity of ownership of great estates and the overall consolidation of the landed structure inherited from the period before 1870.

The first official survey of landownership, conducted by the government in 1872–3, confirmed that the historic Scottish structure remained intact. Some 659 individuals owned 80 per cent of Scotland, while 118 held 50 per cent of the land. Among the most extraordinary agglomerations were those of the Duke of Sutherland, who possessed over 1 million acres, the Duke of Buccleuch with 433,000 acres, the Duke of Richmond and Gordon, 280,000 and the Duke of Fife, 249,000. As in the Highlands, the wealthy of the towns were acquiring Lowland estates throughout this period. Yet this process had not reversed the eighteenth-century pattern whereby the properties of greater landowners grew while those of the small lairds declined further. Studies of the land market in Aberdeenshire suggest that only a relatively small proportion of territory (less than 15 per cent of the total acreage) was bought by new families in the nineteenth century and most of these sales were of property belonging to previous incomers rather than traditional owners. Throughout most of the Lowlands, therefore, the territorial ascendancy of the most powerful families, who possessed huge estates running into many thousands of acres, remained inviolate. Buccleuch, Seafield, Atholl, Roxburgh, Hamilton and Dalhousie, to name but a few of the greatest aristocratic dynasties, still controlled massive empires. The country had the most concentrated pattern of private landownership in Europe, even more so than in England, where the territorial power of the landed aristocracy was also unusually great by comparison with other nations. A full century after the Industrial Revolution no economic or social group had yet emerged to challenge this mighty élite. Great industrial dynasties such as the Coats, Tennant and Baird families did buy into land, but their total possessions were minuscule compared to those of the hereditary landowners, while their deep interest in acquiring landed property was itself confirmation of its continuing attraction and significance.

Landed estates were not simply durable, they were also exceedingly prosperous and secure from the 1830s to the 1870s. Partly this was because of the Scots law of property and related financial arrangements which helped to give guaranteed protection to most landed families. As Sir John Sinclair famously asserted in 1814, 'In no country in Europe are the rights of proprietors so well defined and so carefully protected.'[1] From 1685, entailment laws safeguarded landed estates against the claims of creditors in the event of bankruptcy. A second strategy was the formation of trusts to supervise entailed estates if an owner became insolvent or was under age or for other reasons could not continue in direct possession of the lands. By the nineteenth century the administration of estates through trusts was common at some stage of family ownership and the associated legal arrangements became ever more secure, sophisticated and intricate. Underpinning this legal structure was the prosperity of Scottish agriculture in the middle decades of the nineteenth century. The basic context of this was the burgeoning demand for food, drink and other products of the land from the vast expansion of towns, cities and industrial communities which could not yet be satisfied on any significant scale from overseas suppliers. But both landlord and tenant farmers made a major contribution to this period of success by further investment and innovation which reduced costs of production and allowed more land than ever before to be used intensively for cropping and stock fattening. By 1830 the basic organizational structure of Lowland farming was in place. The consolidation of farms was complete, sub-tenancies had been removed in most areas and improved rotations were the norm everywhere. But the Agricultural Revolution now entered a new phase. The eighteenth-century Improvers had never solved the problem of drainage and, as a result, the rigs of the old system still remained common. This changed with the invention of the cylindrical clay pipe to act as an underground drainage channel and the provision of government loans at low rates of interest from 1846. Slowly but surely the stiff, cold acres that predominated throughout many parts of the Lowlands were transformed and the frontier of turnip and potato cultivation significantly extended as a result.

The combined transportation revolution of steamship and railways was equally decisive. The great potential of Scotland as a great cattle-fattening and breeding country was finally realized. Cattle intended for the English market had in earlier times to be sold lean to the drovers who took them south on the hoof. Then, in the 1820s, came the steamships, followed in the 1850s by the railways, which opened up the huge London market to Scottish fat cattle. The most spectacular gains were achieved in the north-east which rapidly became a specialist centre of excellence for the production of quality meat. By 1870 beef from the region carried the highest premium in London markets. The Aberdeen Angus, developed by William McCombie of Tillyfour farm, evolved into a breed of worldwide reputation. The railways also enabled the perishable products of milk and buttermilk to be brought into the expanding cities from further afield while affording farmers the enhanced opportunity to import feeding-stuffs and fertilizers like guano and industrial phosphates in huge quantity. The result was even higher yields. Steam power was now used more for threshing, and by the 1870s the greater part of the grain and hay crop was being harvested mechanically in most areas of the Lowlands. The physical face of agriculture also changed as larger, more elaborate and better-designed farm steadings spread across the countryside. Many of these impressive buildings remain to this day as lasting memorials to the prosperous days of 'High Farming' in Victorian Scotland.

Landowners in this period did not simply gain from swelling rent rolls as grain and cattle prices rose steadily and investment in the land bore profitable fruit. Industrialization also contributed handsomely to the fortunes of several magnates by affording them the opportunity to exploit mineral royalties. Among the most fortunate Scottish grandees in this respect was the Duke of Hamilton, whose lands included some of the richest coal measures in Lanarkshire, the Duke of Fife, the Earl of Eglinton and the Duke of Portland. That great symbol of the new industrial age, the railway, was warmly welcomed by the landed classes as a whole. This was hardly surprising, since one inquiry by J. Bailey Denton in 1868 had concluded that the letting value of farm land could increase by 5–20 per cent according to its proximity to a railway station. Landowners were heavily involved in railway financing and, indeed, before 1860 were second only to urban merchants as investors in the new projects. Some patrician families also benefited from considerable injections of capital from the empire to which the landed classes often had privileged access through their background and the associated network of personal relationships and connections. In the north-east, for instance, one conspicuous example of the lucrative marriage between imperial profits and traditional landownership was the Forbes family of Newe. They had owned the estate since the sixteenth century but its economic position was mightily strengthened and its territory increased from the middle decades of the eighteenth century when the kindred of the family began merchanting in India. By the early nineteenth century the House of Forbes in Bombay was producing a flow of funds for a new country seat, enormous land improvements and the purchase of neighbouring properties in Aberdeenshire. Examples of the connection between imperial profit and landownership of the kind illustrated by the Forbes family could be found in every county of Scotland.

Historians have also argued that for much of the nineteenth century it was the country house rather than the counting house that had most political influence. The House of Commons remained predominantly a landowners' club, the House of Lords was virtually a monopoly of the hereditary landed class, while in Scotland the owners of great estates continued to wield great influence at the local level as Lord-Lieutenants, Justices of the Peace and through a range of more informal mechanisms. Perhaps, however, the position of Scottish lairds was not quite as overwhelmingly dominant as that of the magnates of rural England. Even before the late nineteenth century, the land question attracted more passionate controversy north of the border. The Disruption of 1843 had unleashed great hostility to several major landowners who, like the Duke of Buccleuch, refused to make land available for Free Church buildings, and the campaign for disestablishment of the Church of Scotland from the mid-1870s kept these animosities alive. This crusade attracted the support of well over half of all Presbyterians in Scotland, while ranged against them were several prominent members of the peerage such as the Lord Balfour of Burleigh, a robust and energetic defender of the cause of the Established Church of Scotland. There were also emerging tensions in the countryside. Conflict over the game laws intensified as lairds sought to maximize the sporting potential of their estates. By the 1870s, game was being developed systematically and sporting rents were booming. But this new enterprise meant that the crops of tenant farmers increasingly suffered from the depredations of both ground game (rabbits and hares) and game birds. Farmers who killed game in retaliation could be prosecuted. The other and more serious source of tension was the law of hypothec, which gave a landlord the position of a preferred creditor for the payment of his rent by giving him a general security over a tenant's movable property. Some argued that this legal privilege allowed landowners to impose high rentals, secure in the knowledge that arrears could be recovered from a tenant's assets. Tensions on these and other issues led to the creation of the Scottish Farmers' Alliance to press for land reform and resulted in a succession of defeats at the polls for landlord candidates in the general elections of 1865 and 1868. In the event, concessions were made both on the game laws and on hypothec which helped to defuse discontent and the conflict did not develop into a full-scale revolt of the tenantry. The 1883 Agricultural Holdings Act (Scotland) also gave tenants the right to compensation for agricultural improvements. What the experience of the 1860s and 1870s did show, however, was that even at the height of their awesome power the landed classes in rural Scotland were far from omnipotent.

2

From the following decade, however, it seemed that the economic base of landlordism was finally starting to weaken. The immediate cause was a series of poor harvests in the later 1870s, though there had been harvest difficulties before and no crisis. What was new was that the reduced quantity of grain brought to market was not compensated for by higher prices due to a huge increase in cheap imports from the American prairies where a vast food-growing potential had finally been unlocked by the railroads and the steamships. Then, a few years later, the livestock sector, which had escaped relatively unscathed, was hit by the arrival of chilled and frozen beef and mutton from Australasia. Free trade had finally come home to roost for British farmers and landowners and prices for their products tumbled through the 1880s and into the 1890s. It is true that Scottish agriculture suffered less than in other areas of the United Kingdom as the greatest decline in prices was in wheat, which was a major crop only in the south-east Lowlands. The tradition of mixed farming in Scotland gave the agrarian system considerable flexibility and the capacity to adjust to changes in the market. Even in the Highlands, where hill sheep-farming was badly affected, there was often rapid diversification into deer forests. The Scottish livestock farmers operated at the quality end of the trade which gave a degree of protection against cheap overseas imports. Nevertheless, while Scottish agriculture was spared the worst effects of the Great Depression, the prosperity and confidence of the mid-Victorian era was still undermined. The average price of oats in the 1890s was a quarter less than the 1870s. Even returns from the sale of quality fat cattle from the north-eastern counties show a big slide from the mid-1880s. The net result was a parallel decline in landlord rents. Even livestock areas were not spared as the countryside adjusted to the new reality that the halcyon days of high prices and low imports were over for good. In Morayshire, a prime stock-rearing county, rents of larger farms fell by a quarter between 1878 and 1894 and the pattern was even worse in less favoured grain-producing areas, where rents of between one-half and one-third were recorded. The misery was not spread equally, however, among estate owners. The smaller proprietors often found themselves in acute difficulty, having to meet fixed obligations such as interest charges and family annuities from a reduced income stream. The larger estates fared better as their owners tended to have outside sources of income.

The economic gloom for landlords was paralleled by adverse political developments in the 1880s. The crofting agitation had been confined to parts of the Highlands and the provisions of the Crofters Holding Act of 1886 were limited to the seven 'crofting counties'. But Lowland landowners could not escape the political fallout as the 'evils of landlordism', which had led to the social problems of the Highlands, were repeatedly denounced in the press. Groups such as urban Liberals, working-class socialists and Irish nationalists could and did all unite on the single issue of the excesses of landlordism. It is significant that Lloyd George's People's Budget of 1909 with its series of land reforms was warmly welcomed by a wide spectrum of opinion in Scotland.

Indeed, the later nineteenth century seems to stand as a watershed in the fortunes of the landed classes in Scotland as one misfortune piled on top of another. Death duties were imposed for the first time in 1894. Though not significant at first, tax rates were eventually increased to more punitive levels in the new century. New taxes on land were also passed. In 1907, for instance, an unearned income surcharge payable on rents was levied. Confidence in the historic stability of land as a secure asset was further eroded by the continuing collapse of land-derived income, which fell in the UK by around 25 per cent between the mid-1870s and 1910. Not surprisingly, estate sales started to increase even among the great landlords. Lord Kinnoul realized £127,000 from the sale of his lands, while magnates such as the Duke of Fife and the Marquess of Queensberry were also selling up parts of their great properties. The pressures became even more acute during and after the First World War. Aristocratic families suffered huge personal loss in the bloody carnage of 1914–18. Altogether, 42 of the 225 relatives of Scottish peers who served in the war were killed in action. C. F. G. Masterman concluded that 'In the retreat from Mons and the first battle of Ypres, perished the flower of the British aristocracy.' During the war, he reflected, 'the Feudal System vanished' in blood and fire and the landed classes were consumed.[2] While the majority of the sons of landowners survived the conflict, the relentlessly contracting vice of higher taxes did tighten further during the Great War and its immediate aftermath. Death duties were now higher and were likely to compel sales, especially if an owner's death was followed by that of his heir killed in action. Income tax and local rates also rose steeply. The Marquess of Aberdeen, for instance, paid £800 in annual estate taxes in 1870. By 1920 his bill had swollen to £19,000. The income from agriculture, which had increased artificially during the Great War, fell back once again in 1921. The scene was set for an unprecedented escalation in land sales and the break-up of several estates. The Duke of Marlborough pronounced, 'The old order is doomed' as a direct result of the 'conspiracy' taxation of the 1919 budget, which had raised death duties to the punitive level of 40 per cent on estates of £2 million and over.

The Duke's prognosis seemed well founded in Scotland. The cream of the Scottish aristocracy, including the Dukes of Sutherland and Portland, the Earl of Airlie, the Earl of Strathmore and the Duke of Hamilton, were all selling off many thousands of acres in the early 1920s. It was claimed that one-fifth of Scotland changed hands between 1918 and 1921. A veritable social revolution was under way as former tenant farmers bought up land from the great proprietors on a remark-able scale. In 1914 only 11 per cent of Scottish farmland was owner-occupied but by 1930 the figure had climbed to over 30 per cent. The very basis of landlord power seemed to be crumbling. That the crisis was biting deeply is shown by the selling of town houses, artistic treasures and country seats. The London homes of Lord Balfour and Lord Rosebery were sold in 1929 and 1939 respectively. Lord Lothian divested himself of three of his four grand houses in the 1930s. The Duke of Hamilton closed Scotland's most impressive private home, Hamilton Palace, in 1922 and sold off more than £240,000 worth of paintings, furniture and carpets. These had hitherto been one of the public symbols of aristocratic status. Their disposal suggested a class in decline.

It seemed that the process was indeed inevitable. The passage of the Parliament Act in 1911 abolished the veto powers of the House of Lords and effectively ended its real authority. The political influence of the landlords in the country had also been massively reduced by the Third Reform Act of 1884–5 which doubled the voting population in Great Britain. By the time of the Great War the age of mass democracy had truly begun. Aristocratic candidates were rejected in Scotland in the first general election held after the war, with only the two brothers of Lord Elibank achieving electoral success. Anti-landlord sentiment was stoked by such polemical works as *Our Scots Noble Families* (1909), written by the future Labour minister and Secretary of State for Scotland, Tom Johnston. He maintained that the territorial empires of the great landed families had been created through deeds of grand larceny in the past:

Show the people that our Old Nobility is not noble, that its lands are stolen lands – stolen either by force or fraud; show people that the title deeds are rapine, murder massacre, cheating, or Court harlotry; dissolve the halo of divinity that surrounds the hereditary title; let the people clearly understand that our present House of Lords is composed largely of descendants of successful pirates and rogues; do these things and you shatter the Romance that keeps the nation numb and spellbound while privilege picks its pocket.[3]

The aristocracy had also to cope with more mundane direct threats to their material position. Mineral royalties declined in the 1920s due to the depression in coal mining and they were finally nationalized with compensation in 1938 and 1942. The government, through the Corn Production (Repeal) Act of 1921, had also abandoned its financial support for oat and wheat prices in the post-war era. The cycle of misery seemed complete.

However, any notion that these powerful forces would eventually destroy the traditional landed classes or the old estate structure as a whole is profoundly mistaken. Obviously it is the case that landowners in the twentieth century have shed their historic role as the governing class of the nation in an age of mass democracy. But landownership itself has proved to be remarkably resilient in Scotland and England, compared to other European countries and to Ireland, where large estates have virtually disappeared altogether. In Ireland there has indeed been a complete revolution in landed structure over the last 100 years. In the 1880s, half the country was owned by the aristocracy and larger gentry with estates of 3,000 acres and above. By the 1980s, virtually none. Those who have examined the Scottish case in close detail, such as Robin Callander and Roger Millman, have painted a radically different picture. Four conclusions emerge from the research of these scholars and others.

First, from the later 1930s, the selling of land on a significant scale by the great estates declined, a pattern that continued after the Second World War and lasted through to the 1970s. The tide of owner-occupation which had threatened to engulf the traditional estate structure had ebbed considerably. Second, there has been a remarkable continuity in Scottish landownership which the malaise of the decades from the 1880s to the 1930s has obscured. The nation still has the most concentrated pattern of landownership in Europe with 75 per cent of all privately owned land in the 1970s held in estates of 1,000 acres or more and over one-third in estates of 20,000 acres or more. By the 1990s this remarkable level of concentration had, if anything, increased further. The extent of land possessed by these mammoth estates has fallen since the 1870s, but the traditional structure of concentration has survived and has done so to a greater extent than in any other European country. Third, the continuities are deeply significant, as a core of fewer than 1,500 private estates have owned most of the land in Scotland during the last nine centuries. Among the owners of great estates are several families who have been in hereditary occupation for more than 30 generations. Several landed families may have lost their estates in whole or in part, but the great houses of Buccleuch, Seafield, Roxburghe, Stair, Airlie, Lothian, Home, Montrose and Hamilton and others still

457

own extensive acreages. Fourth, the historic infiltration of newcomers into Scottish landownership has persisted in the twentieth century. Merchant bankers, stockbrokers, captains of industry, pop stars, oil-rich Arabs and wealthy purchasers from Holland and Denmark are among the groups that have acquired Scottish estates in the past few decades. Nevertheless, this has not generally resulted in the break-up of the larger traditional properties, as most buying and selling has been of land that has usually had a higher turnover of ownership in the past.

It is patently clear, then, that the Scottish system of landownership and large estates in the event was not pulverized and destroyed as the alarmists and pessimists of the 1920s had predicted. Instead, the old structure has survived into the late twentieth century with remarkably few alterations. Why was this? One factor was that many of the land sales of the inter-war period were not designed to liquidate landownership but to preserve it through maintaining the core of estates and diversifying into other and more profitable assets. Thus, by the 1920s, the Earl of Elgin derived half his income from land and the remainder from directorates in banking and building societies. There was nothing new in this. In the 1880s such grandees as Portland and Sutherland were investing in British and overseas stocks and bonds. It is likely, nevertheless, that more landowners than ever before after *c.* 1920 were making the rational choice of divesting themselves of surplus territory and putting money into stocks and shares. It was crucial, too, that the land reform movement which had been at the heart of radical politics for the best part of a century virtually vanished off the British political agenda after the Great War. The vital importance of the political factor in the disintegration of private landownership was conclusively demonstrated in Ireland, where what F. M. L. Thompson describes as 'the mincing machine of land reform' effectively destroyed the system of great estates in the space of a few years.[4] In Scotland, however, the depopulation of the countryside, the dominance of urban issues in a highly urbanized society and the crisis in Scottish industry marginalized the land issue for over a generation. It may well also be that the publicity given to the avalanche of land sales in the inter-war period convinced reformers that the job was already done. Certainly there is a striking contrast between the centrality of the land question in radical politics in the 1880s and 1890s and its virtual disappearance from the public discussion soon after the Great War until more recent times. Partly because of this, the larger landowners in the United Kingdom have been spared a draconian system of land value taxation which might well have hastened their demise.

Instead, in the post-1945 period and until the 1970s, the overall tax burden on landowners continued to decline, while state subsidies to agriculture and forestry increased significantly. At the same time, average land prices in the UK rose dramatically from £60 an acre in 1945 to £2,000 an acre in the early 1980s. Despite high taxation of income, there remained considerable tax advantages in owning land, particularly if it was both owned and farmed. This has been further enhanced in some areas by the application of the Common Agricultural Policy within the European Community, with its range of farming subsidies. Ironically, the Scottish landowners in the late twentieth century now benefit more from public financial assistance than their ancestors ever did, even in the days of the Corn Laws. In addition, a free market in land persists in Scotland, although regulation and control have become the norm in virtually all other European countries. One expert from the Agricultural University at Wageningen recently commented of Scotland: 'It is very curious how people treat land [in Scotland]. Land is simply a commodity. This is wild-west capitalism. One of the most valuable assets for the future, the land, can be bought and sold at will. Elsewhere in Europe this is not the case.'[5] In this as in so many other ways, there was a significant continuity of the inherited system of landownership from earlier centuries to the modern age. This connection has in recent times become even more secure, as the opening of the great country houses to the public, mass tourism and the popular addiction to nostalgia have enabled several aristocratic families to act as guardians of the nation's heritage and personified symbols of an enduring link with the glories of the Scottish past. As will be seen in the next section, however, such levels of continuity were far from the experience of the population who lived in and worked the farms of the landed estates of Lowland Scotland in the nineteenth century.

3

'The Scots', G. T. Bisset stated in 1909, are notoriously 'migratory'.[6] Of few areas in the country was this assertion more true than the rural Lowlands. The social and labour structure that emerged in this region from the Age of Improvement made human mobility on a large scale inevitable. In Scottish tradition, migration is usually associated with the Highlands and the Clearances, and certainly during and after the Great Famine there was a huge exodus of people from the crofting society of the north-west mainland and the Hebrides. Before the 1840s, the breaking-up of joint tenancies into crofts and the permissive attitude to rampant subdivision had, when combined with potato cultivation and temporary migration, tended more often than not to anchor the people to the land. However, in the Lowlands and the southern and eastern Highlands the nature of the new social formations had exactly the opposite effect, by squeezing out those who were not essential to the effective working of the farming regime.

Between c. 1760 and 1840, the consolidation of holdings accelerated. When coherent data first became available in the 1880s, extensive holdings of over 400 acres were common in the Borders, the Lothians and Berwick, but in many other areas consolidation had much more modest effects. In 16 out of the 18 Lowland counties, at least half of all holdings were at or below 100 acres in extent, with 'family farms' significant in the central and western counties of Ayr, Lanark, Renfrew and Stirling. But despite diversity, common patterns ran throughout the region. Only a small part of the population had access to land as main tenants. Subtenancies, formerly very important in the old order, had been crushed in almost all districts by c. 1830; strict and rigorous controls were imposed in order to prevent subdivision. Only in the north-eastern counties of Aberdeen, Banff and Kincardine did the number of landholders actually increase with the development of smallholdings or crofts alongside the larger farms. But this was planned as an integral and necessary part of the new agrarian order. This region had a considerable amount of moor and wasteland and carving it up into small crofts was seen as an efficient and economical way of bringing it into regular cultivation. In most other areas, however, movement of people was inevitable as numbers rose. Labour requirements in improved farming did increase, at least until the 1850s, but not at the rate of the overall rise in population, which almost doubled between 1831 and 1911. It followed that only some of the rising population in the rural districts could be absorbed in the long run by the new agriculture. Many must have had little choice, either to find work in country trades and industries or to leave the land altogether for the towns or overseas.

This was the basic mechanism for channelling 'surplus labour' from the Lowland countryside before 1830. It meant that the region did not suffer the social problems of structural unemployment that affected many southern and eastern areas of rural England and which were the direct cause of the series of violent disturbances known as the 'Captain Swing' riots in the early 1830s. The Lowlands, by contrast, were quiet. The imbalance between those seeking work and the number of jobs available was a critical issue in the larger towns in the 1820s, but not in the countryside. This rural system continued to operate effectively as a demographic safety valve throughout the nineteenth century. Those surplus to the needs of the agrarian structure were relentlessly squeezed out, particularly since both single and married servants were accommodated on the farm, and so to be without work was also to be without a place to stay. The system ensured that people had to move. In that sense it was unambiguously coercive, even if the means of removal were not as directly oppressive as clearances in the Highlands. But by regulating the supply of labour in this way, the kind of social crisis that overwhelmed Gaeldom in the 1840s was prevented while, at the same time, wage levels for those who did manage to secure employment on the land were maintained.

However, even the impressive efficiency of the system cannot explain the sheer scale of the exodus from country districts which occurred in the late nineteenth and early twentieth centuries. In this period, for the first time, the rate of out-migration from the rural Lowlands exceeded the natural increase in population which was still occurring at more than 10 per cent per decade before 1914. It was not simply the 'surplus population' that was now being lost. In effect, the numbers who worked in agriculture and rural industry were beginning to go into rapid decline. In the 40 years between 1871 and 1911, the number of skilled ploughmen and shepherds fell by a third. The haemorrhage was even greater among women workers, who were vital on dairy and family farms and the big arable holdings of the south-east. 'Female wage earners in Agriculture' (a measure which does not take account of all women employed) fell from 40,653 in 1861 to 15,037 in 1911. The decline continued well into the inter-war period. An entirely new situation had developed. The Royal Commission on Labour in 1893 concluded that the emerging problem was now not so much lack of demand for workers on the land but rather the growing scarcity of those willing to accept employment on Lowland farms. Numerous witnesses to the Commission pointed out that wages were rising sharply as farmers tried to stem the tide of migration. Indeed, in the period 1850–1914, Scottish agricultural wages rose faster than in most other areas of Britain and only fell back temporarily in the 1880s. But still the exodus gathered pace, especially among the young. One estimate suggested that in the 1920s one-half of all male workers had left agriculture by the time they were 25. What had started as a trickle in the middle decades of the nineteenth century had now become a flood.

Migration on this scale puzzled many contemporary observers and some later commentators. Even in the difficult years of the 1920s there was little unemployment and a gradual rise in wages from 1922 to 1927. Nor was it necessarily the case that rural wages were necessarily always lower than in the towns in real terms. Urban workers had to pay for food and housing which Scottish farm servants obtained as part of their contract of employment. It was the case that the housing conditions of farm workers were often very poor, with damp cottages and inadequate sanitation attracting much critical comment well into the twentieth century. But though often perceived as a cause of depopulation, there was no obvious link between the exodus and the areas where the housing problem was most acute. In any case, the great cities and towns to which many country dwellers were being drawn in increasingly large numbers were hardly models of cleanliness and efficiency. Disease, atrocious housing and periodic unemployment were commonplace and, given the short-distance nature of most rural–urban migration, much of this must have been known to the country population. The paradox is, however, that the towns still had enormous attractive power.

Nor can the paradox be unravelled by arguing for the impact of technical change, of the influence of man and woman power being increasingly replaced by machinery. There was indeed a technological revolution in the later nineteenth century associated with the development of reapers and binders. But these innovations primarily affected harvest and casual labour and came about as a consequence rather than a cause of the scarcity of hands. From then until 1939 technical change was limited in most areas. The real transformation came with the advent of the Standard Ferguson tractor after 1945 – the *Wee Fergie* – and the combine harvester. The days of horsework were then numbered and as a result there was a great movement from the countryside by horsemen and the tradesmen associated with the traditional farming regime. Gavin Sprott recalls how a small 15-acre field near Kirriemuir in the north-east was cleared in a morning by a single combine in the 1970s, whereas in 1922 it had taken more than 40 people to cut, bind and stack the crop in the same time. The post-1945 changes revolutionized the countryside. By the end of the 1950s, horses were becoming unusual and with their demise went the whole labour-intensive system developed from the later eighteenth century. Remarkably, as a consequence those directly or indirectly associated with farming are, in the 1990s, a minority within the rural Lowland population. Technical change, therefore, hit hard in the second half of the twentieth century but it was not a central influence on 'the flight from the land' before the Second World War. The same point applies to the effect of 'agricultural depression'. As noted earlier in this chapter, the Lowland rural economy possessed considerable resilience between 1870 and 1900, as a series of bad seasons and cheap grain and meat imports from abroad combined to cause a crisis in some parts of British agriculture. The grain-producing districts of the south-east Lowlands and some Border areas were most vulnerable, but overall the fall in employment was marginal and certainly not on the scale necessary to explain the remarkably high levels of movement away from the land. By 1900, only about 10 per cent of the best land had gone out of production in Scotland, compared to 20 per cent in England.

Any convincing attempt to explain the rural exodus must begin by acknowledging that the problem was wider and deeper than the issue of the agricultural population itself, or those directly engaged in the preparation and cultivation of the land. It should be remembered that much industrial activity was still rural-based in 1830. In the central Lowlands and in some other districts, handloom weaving remained an important rural activity until the 1850s. Moreover, a multitude of skilled trades had grown up as essential supports of improved agriculture. Country blacksmiths were necessary for the making and repairing of the new iron-framed ploughs. Horses replaced oxen in the later eighteenth century and had to be shod regularly, on average every six to eight weeks. The building and rebuilding of farm steadings, with houses, byres, milkhouses, barns and stables, took place in two main phases during the 'High Farming' of the 1840s and again, to a lesser extent, in the 1870s. This created demand on a large scale not only for the building trade but also for skills in quarrying, stone-breaking, brick-making and sawmilling. In addition, the new style farming could not have been carried on without millers, joiners, masons, ditchers and dikers. Tailors, shoemakers (or 'soutars') and country weavers served the needs of the farm labouring population. The signal importance of this range of trades is often forgotten when the textbooks focus on ploughmen, women workers and bothymen.

It is clear that many of these crafts were being undermined by urban competition in the second half of the nineteenth century. Already by the 1850s, the technology of power looms was destroying the textile economy in numerous villages in Perth, Fife and Angus and promoting large-scale migration as a result. The development of a myriad branch railway lines enabled cheap factory goods to penetrate far into the rural areas and so threatened the traditional markets for tailors, shoemakers and other tradesmen. The displacement of craftsmen and their families from the smaller country towns and villages became a familiar feature of the rural exodus by the end of the nineteenth century and before. While some trades, such as the country shoemaker, vanished into oblivion, others, such as the blacksmiths, continued to thrive as long as the horse economy survived and in some cases even diversified into agricultural engineering.

However, in large part, migration from the land before the 1940s has to be explained in terms of the changing attitudes of the farm labour force itself. Here it should first be recognized that Scottish farm servants had a developed culture of mobility long before the rural exodus accelerated.

The structure of service in Lowland Scotland resulted in high levels of internal mobility in rural areas. 'Flitting' (or moving) to another farm, usually in the same parish or county, at the end of the six-month or annual term was part of the way of life. The contract of employment meant that in law servants had only one or two opportunities to move in the year. This concentrated minds at these crucial periods and there was always the temptation to seek a place elsewhere for better wages, more experience or a change of surroundings. But the reasons for movement were legion. When asked, one Lothians farm worker between the wars explained: 'Possibly the neighbours, possibly the gaffer [foreman], possibly the farmer, possibly the horses. Maybe the horses came first if they didnae have a good pair of horse, or the harness wasn't up to scratch.'[7] For married men the costs of moving were low. A house came with the job and the new employer provided transport to move the family and the household belongings. Servants could carry their own locks with them when they flitted. An East Lothian writer noted in 1861 how one married ploughman's door 'was literally covered with key-holes, made to suit the size of the lock of each successive occupant'.[8] Almost all this habitual movement was localized and over short distances but it accustomed farm servant families to levels of mobility that could in certain circumstances encourage them to leave the land altogether.

The relationship between the system of employment and migration was even more clear-cut in the case of single servants, who formed the majority of regular farm workers in the Lowlands. At marriage they faced a stark choice, because in many areas there was a distinct lack of family cottages. Some could continue in agricultural employment as day labourers and in the north-east they might seek to return to the crofts from where many had originally come as young servants. But the number of smallholdings was too few to absorb those who left full-time employment on the farms in their mid-twenties, and anyway the possibility of such a move back to the land was confined to only one area of the Lowlands. Young ploughmen had also been accustomed to a nomadic life, regularly moving from one master to another. At marriage many left the land altogether to go to the towns and other occupations. In Perthshire, for instance, which had a particularly heavy dependence on unmarried farm servants, a quarter to a third of them in the middle decades of the nineteenth century were likely to leave for another occupation by the time they were 30. In essence, migration from the land was built into the life-cycle of single servants.

This traditional exodus became a great haemorrhage from the later nineteenth century onwards. The towns and emigration overseas now exerted a magical appeal over the rural young. This was partly due to rising expectations as a result of better agricultural wage levels, the impact of compulsory education after 1872 and the penetration into the countryside of urban values, following the construction of railway branch lines throughout the Lowlands. Life on the land had always been hard, but now many came to see it as intolerable when compared to the working conditions and social attractions of the towns. Before 1914 a ploughman would rise at 5 a.m. to feed and groom his horses, yoke them at 6 a.m. and work until 6 in the evening, with a break between 11 and 1. After the Great War this was reduced to 10 hours a day and a Saturday half-day was conceded for the first time. Before this, the only holidays were Sundays, New Year's Day and the hiring days. The burden of work on family farms which were common in the south-west and the north fell particularly heavily on women. One observer in 1920 called it 'the slavery of family work'. Dairying near the cities involved very early rising at about 2 or 3 a.m. because of a popular prejudice in favour of warm milk. Similarly, dairy women in upland farms needed to milk early to ensure that milk could be dispatched to town by early morning trains. Where milk was made into cheese there was, in the words of one commentator in the years after the Great War,

an enormous amount of continuous labouring, seven days a week during six to seven months in the year . . . I have seen the women folk on such farms at 3 o'clock in the afternoon in the same garb they had hurriedly donned between 3 and 4 o'clock in the morning, having been constantly toiling, one duty succeeding another . . . it is usual for women on dairy farms to work sixteen hours per day, time for meals only being allowed for.[9]

Even the leisure activities of farm workers were dominated by work. The bothy songs were about work, and the *Kirns* that marked the end of the harvest celebrated work. Compared to the life of hard toil on the land, the town occupations of domestic servant, railway porter, policeman and carter seemed infinitely less demanding. Not only did they pay better than agricultural labouring in some instances, but they also had shorter hours, more leisure time and freedom in the evenings and weekends from employers.

In contrast, rural life had few social attractions. Scottish farm workers were dispersed in groups of cottages, bothies and chaumers attached to isolated individual farms. Long hours and the habitual turnover of labour at the end of each term confined most social life to the occasional fair or agricultural show. The hunger for a more interesting life was demonstrated after 1917 when the Board of Agriculture helped to establish the Scottish Women's Rural Institutes. They were an immediate success, despite initial male opposition, and five years later had 242 branches and a total membership of 14,000. But for many, and especially the young, this hunger could be fully satisfied only by moving from the land altogether. As the Royal Commission on Labour concluded in 1893:

there is much drudgery and very little excitement about the farm servant's daily duties, and I believe the young men dislike the former and long for the latter. By the labourers themselves slight importance is attached to the healthy character of country life in comparison with various branches of town labour.

That phase of the question sinks into insignificance in their estimation, and only the shorter hours, numerous holidays and ever present busy bustle and excitement of town life or the neat uniform and genteel work of the police constable or railway porter, are present to the mind of our young farm servant.[10]

20

Emigrants

I

Between 1821 and 1915 it is estimated that over 44 million emigrants left Europe for North America, Australasia and other destinations. The scale and volume of this great exodus of people was unprecedented in human history and was a basic factor in altering the balance of economic power between the Old and the New World. Without such a revolutionary increase in intercontinental migration, the rise of the USA to the status of global superpower would not have been possible. The specific Scottish contribution to the general European diaspora was very significant. In absolute numerical terms, the Scottish emigration of over 2 million between the 1820s and the First World War was considerably less than the 8 million who left from Italy, the 5 million from Germany and its constituent states or the 4.5 million recorded for Spain and Portugal. But a much greater number of Scots emigrated as a proportion of the national population than for any of these nations. Throughout the nineteenth and early twentieth centuries, three countries, Ireland, Norway and Scotland, topped the league table of central and western European countries with the highest rates of emigration per head of population. Ireland led the list in most decades. Norway and Scotland fluctuated in their relative positions over time because the exodus of people ebbed and flowed dramatically, depending on economic circumstances at home and overseas. However, during four great surges of emigration (in the 1850s, 1870s, the early 1900s and again in the inter-war period) Scotland either headed this unenviable championship or came a close second to Ireland. If movement to England is included in the statistics, Scotland then emerges clearly as the emigration capital of Europe for much of the period. In the quarter-century from 1825, recorded figures of emigrants were well below 10,000 in most years, and in the following quarter not far short of 20,000. Between 1875 and 1900, numbers fluctuated between 20,000 and 30,000. By the Great War they were up to 60,000 and they rose further in the 1920s and early 1930s. Edwin Muir in the preface to his *Scottish Journey* (1935) spoke for many when he sounded a note of alarm about this enormous haemorrhage of people from a small country: '. . . my main impression . . . is that Scotland is gradually being emptied of its population, its spirit, its wealth, industry, art, intellect and innate character. If a country exports its most enterprising spirits and best minds year after year, for fifty or a hundred or two hundred years, some result will inevitably follow.'[1]

All areas of Scotland were affected. The historic connection between the western Highlands and emigration is a familiar one and the crofting region did dominate in the aftermath of the subsistence crises in the 1830s and 1840s. Especially during the potato famines there was a mass exodus of crofter and cottar families, with the western Highlands losing up to a third of its population between 1841 and 1861. But during the rest of the nineteenth century, though emigration from the north-west continued, the overwhelming majority of those who left Scotland now came from the towns and cities and the rural Lowlands. Therein lies the essential paradox of Scottish emigration: it was one of the world's most highly successful industrial and agricultural economies after *c*. 1860 but was losing people in very large numbers rather than those countries traditionally associated with poverty, clearance, hunger and destitution. The evidence contained in the Poor Law Commission Report of 1844 shows that emigration was already extraordinarily common throughout the country with over two-thirds of parishes indicating that some overseas departures had occurred in the previous few years. It is also striking how widespread the pattern was in occupational terms, with farm servants, weavers, masons, carpenters, blacksmiths and many other artisans listed among the emigrant groups. But the trend overall was increasingly towards the towns and industry as the main source of emigrants by the later nineteenth century. In one sense this is not surprising since Scotland was rapidly becoming an urbanized society by this period. Yet it does underscore the point that emigration was clearly associated with areas of economic growth as well as regions of economic decline. A sampling of Scottish emigrants to the USA in the later nineteenth century reveals that over three-quarters came from the towns rather than rural areas. In the 1880s, for instance, around 80 per cent of male emigrants were from 'industrial' counties, while Canada, Australia and New Zealand still remained very attractive to tenant farmers and farm servants because of the availability of land, and well into the twentieth century these were the most popular destinations for emigrants from the agricultural counties of the north-east. Joe Duncan, the able and perceptive secretary of the Scottish Farm Servants' Union, commented on the rising tide of emigration in the years before the First World War:

There has been a fairly steady stream of emigration from the rural districts of Scotland, rising at times into something of a torrent, such as we have just had within the last three or four years. It is interesting to note the counties from which emigration has been the greatest. By far the greatest emigration has taken place from the counties of Elgin, Nairn, Banff and Aberdeen. This is probably accounted for by the fact that there are fewer industries in these districts and less chance for farm workers changing occupation within their own districts. It is in these counties too that the largest number of single men employed on the farms are to be found, while the fact that it is the custom there for the bulk of wages to be paid at the end of the six months, produces a system of involuntary saving which provides the young men with the necessary cash to pay for passage abroad . . .

The emigration has been less in the counties south of this where the wages are higher and where the opportunities of entering other employment are greater. Emigration has generally been to Canada, Australia coming next, and increasingly, and then, much behind these, New Zealand and the United States. Emigration has helped to increase wages and has also contributed to the independence of the workers remaining. It is the case today all over Scotland that there is a scarcity of suitable men for the farms, and although there seems now to be slackening in emigration it is not likely that any large increase in the number of competent men will take place.[2]

The popularity of destinations varied over time. Up to the early 1840s, British North America (which was to become the Dominion of Canada in 1867) attracted most Scots, and distinctive Scottish communities were well established in the maritime provinces and Upper Canada (later Ontario) by that time. Canada also was the most favoured choice in the years before the First World War, especially for emigrants from rural districts, as public land in the Dominion was still being offered on very easy terms. Australia and New Zealand attracted significant numbers in the gold rush of the early 1850s when around 90,000 Scots left for Australia alone. Again, in the low emigration years of the early 1860s and in the later 1870s Australasia was a popular destination. Around the turn of the century there was a flurry of emigration to South Africa. But the United States maintained the greatest lure throughout. More than half of all emigrating Scots went there between 1853 and 1914 and a still higher number made it their final destination, having first sailed to Canada before moving south. No country could match the USA and Canada for ease of access, familiarity, economic opportunity, family links and availability of cheap land.

The Scots migrants generally made a deep mark on the development of their adopted homelands. This in itself is not surprising. While some emigrants were destitute Highlanders, redundant handloom weavers, convicts exiled to Australia and orphan children under assisted passage, many others came with considerable advantages which allowed them to exploit the opportunities of the New World and influence its development out of all proportion to their numbers. Of course, it would be nonsense to assume that all succeeded. Some at least of the many thousands who returned home across the Atlantic in the later nineteenth and early twentieth centuries may be regarded as failures, though by no means all, or even the majority, necessarily were. Studies of Scots in nineteenth-century urban Ontario also reveal some evidence of downward social mobility. But even when all the qualifications have been made, the record of the emigrant Scots in the making of North America and Australasia is a formidable one. They had several advantages which gave them an edge over other ethnic groups. The overwhelming majority were Protestant and Lowland Scots, with English as their native tongue. They therefore avoided the religious discrimination that was visited upon the Catholic Irish, while maintaining a clear linguistic advantage over Germans, Scandinavians, French, Italians and others. They also came from one of the world's most advanced economies. Scottish agriculture had a global reputation for excellence and efficiency, while the nation had a leading position in areas as diverse as banking, insurance, engineering, applied science, shipbuilding, coal mining and iron and steel manufacture. The Scots who emigrated had experience of working within this system of advanced capitalism and had acquired a range of skills that few other emigrants from Europe could match. Between 1815 and 1914, as many as half of the Scotsmen who moved to the USA were skilled or semi-skilled. Also in the early 1920s, 55 per cent of adult men leaving Scotland had skilled trades, while in the two years before the First World War over one-fifth could be described as belonging to the group 'commerce, finance, insurance, professional and students'. This was the reason why Edwin Muir lamented that emigration was drawing away the life-blood of the nation. It was not simply the tradesmen of the big cities and the renowned industries of Scotland who were at an advantage. The tenant farmers, ploughmen and shepherds who had been reared on the disciplined toil and progressive techniques of improved agriculture were equally at a premium in societies that had land and raw materials in abundance but which suffered from a profound shortage of skilled labour. In a sense, it was a form of technology transfer from a sophisticated economic system to one that was more primitive and less developed. An added bonus was that the Scot often arrived with some capital. Unlike the Irish Catholic emigration to the Americas, the Scottish diaspora was not mainly the flight of the poor.

The famous traditions of Scottish elementary and higher education were also relevant to success. In the later eighteenth century almost all the colonial medical profession in North America were Scots or Scots-trained. In religion, Scots and Scottish-educated ministers dominated both the Presbyterian and Episcopal churches of America, while Scottish educators had a leading role in Princeton, the College of Philadelphia and countless Presbyterian academies in the middle and southern states. In the nineteenth century the Scottish contribution to the professions remained fundamental. The pages of the *Canadian Dictionary of National Biography* demonstrate a massive Scottish influence in religion, education, literature, medicine and journalism. Even Scottish convicts sentenced to transportation to Australia had higher levels of literacy than their English or Irish counterparts. Formal education was also only one part of the story as essential skills were acquired on the job under the apprenticeship system. The real universities of industry were the great Clyde engineering workshops where craft techniques were learnt, improved, refined and passed on to the next generation. Similarly, on the land, the young *haflin* (apprentice) passed through the various stages of horsemanship until being initiated as a true ploughman through the secret ceremony of the Horseman's Word. This faith in the traditional craftsman's training is now recognized by Canadian business historians as the key factor in Scottish dominance of much of Canadian industry in the later nineteenth century. Younger sons of Scots emigrant farmers in Ontario who were unlikely to inherit the family holding were sent in large numbers to foundries, mills and workshops where they gained the technical skills that gave them an advantage over other ethnic groups. To this was added a loyalty to other Scots which endured at least for the first and possibly second generations. In all the countries of settlement, ethnic identity among the immigrant élite was consolidated by the masons, Presbyterian churches, St Andrew's Societies and Burns Clubs which all flourished in the nineteenth century and were as much networks for the promotion of mutual business success as key religious and social institutions.

The combination of these factors helps to explain the undoubted pre-eminence of the Scots in many areas of the North American and Australian economies. The exceptional figures have often been noted. These were men like Andrew Carnegie from Dunfermline, whose mammoth corporation, Carnegie Steel, became the world's largest producer of iron and steel; or George Stephen who died Lord Mount Stephen in 1921, born the son of a Banffshire carpenter and the driving force behind the giant Canadian Pacific Railway which transformed Canada in the later nineteenth century by linking the country from east to west. But less famous Scots also dominated entire industries. In the 1880s, Scots or the sons of Scots migrants were dominant in Canadian textiles, paper, sugar, oil, iron and steel, furniture-making, the fur trade and bakery products. The level of success achieved was out of all proportion to their numbers in the Canadian population. In the later nineteenth century it has been estimated that about one-third of the Dominion's business élite was of Scottish origin, although first-generation Scots formed only around 16 per cent of the population. In the USA there was also much evidence of Scottish business success. Men like Henry Eckford, Donald Mackay and George Dickie contributed significantly to the development of shipbuilding at New York and Boston. James Forgan, the son of a golf club manufacturer in St Andrews, arrived in the United States in 1885 and eventually became president of the First National Bank. Scottish builders and operators were to the fore in the creation of the American rail network. Major-General Craig McCallum, born in Renfrewshire, during the Civil War was largely responsible for the efficiency of the federal rail system which was acknowledged as a decisive factor in the final defeat of the South.

While the deeds of these celebrated 'great men' are well recorded in the history books, of even greater significance were the countless numbers of unknown Scots who helped to transform North America –

the generations of Scots sheep farmers who left their mark on the thinly populated states of Montana, Idaho and Wyoming; the bankers, merchants and small storekeepers of Scottish origin who were found in large numbers across the expanding frontier; the warehousemen who had learnt the drapery trade in Edinburgh and Glasgow and became pioneers of the department store business in American cities. It was a similar story in the Antipodes. One of the recent evaluations of the Scottish role in New Zealand by Tom Brooking concludes that '. . . the endeavour of Scottish farmers, manufacturers and businessmen outweighed their numbers. The entrepreneurial contribution of the Scots was certainly proportionately greater than that of the more numerous English.'[3] Australian historians have a more measured view of the Scottish impact and rightly stress that the failures among the immigrants tend to be ignored while the successful receive all the attention. In the sustained depression of the 1890s, for instance, several Scottish enterprises went to the wall. In addition, the historiography in general is only now coming to grips with the 'invisible' Scots: the women, the labourers, the criminals, the diggers and the outcasts whose experience was just as important a part of Australia's heritage as that of the rich and famous. Nevertheless, the very substantial contribution of the Scots to the making of Australia is still acknowledged. It was not always a pretty story. Scots pioneers in Victoria were often land-grabbers and squatters who were notorious for their ruthlessness, and the Scots, like the English, Welsh and Irish, played a full part in the harsh treatment of the Aboriginal peoples. It was ironic that some of those most notoriously involved were Highlanders who themselves had suffered clearance and privation in the old country before receiving emigration assistance under the auspices of the Highland and Island Emigration Society in the 1850s. The great mass of the quarter of a million Scots who did reach Australia before 1900 was absorbed into the urban labour force or the up-country sheep-runs. But they also figured very prominently, as in North America, in Australian business, education, religious and cultural life. A distinctive factor in the Scottish impact on land pastoralism and mining (shared with New Zealand) was the link between Scottish capital at home and enterprise in Australia. Expatriate Scots who were active in land, cattle and sheep companies were able to draw on middle-class savings in Scotland through a network of solicitors and chartered accountants who mobilized the capital of the affluent. By the 1880s no less than 40 per cent of all Australian borrowing could be directly attributed to this source. Here was further confirmation of the close connection between Scotland's economic success in the nineteenth century and the impact of Scottish emigration overseas.

2

European migration to the New World had been under way from the period of the Discoveries in early modern times. In the second half of the nineteenth century, however, what had been a relative trickle became an enormous flood of individuals and families crossing the Atlantic. The age of mass emigration had truly begun. This was not simply because of the voracious demand for labour in North America as both the US and Canadian economies experienced unprecedented expansion. It was also made possible by the crumbling of two of the great constraints that had restricted emigration in the past, namely the distance and costs of travel, which normally meant that leaving Europe for the Americas was likely to be a permanent exile, and the traditional perception of the New World as an alien and densely forested wilderness where risks and dangers far outweighed opportunities.

Emigration, like all other aspects of human existence, was transformed by the transportation revolution of the nineteenth century. Although the cost of steamship travel was actually about a third dearer than crossing by sailing ships, the new vessels radically increased speed, comfort and safety. In the 1850s it took six weeks to cross the Atlantic. By 1914 the average voyage time had fallen to around a week. In the early 1860s, 45 per cent of transatlantic emigrants left in sailing ships, but the number fell rapidly in the next few years so that, by 1870, all but a tiny minority travelled in steamships. By drastically cutting voyage times the steamship also removed one of the major costs of emigration: the time between embarkation and settlement during which there was no possibility of earning. This was especially crucial for the skilled and semi-skilled urban tradesmen who comprised an increasing proportion of Scottish emigrants in the later nineteenth century. They were now able to move on a temporary basis in order to exploit high wages or labour scarcities at particular times in North America. This factor also explains the increasing scale of return emigration. By 1900 it is estimated that around one-third of those Scots who left came back sooner or later. It was not only transatlantic emigrants who behaved in this way.

Over the whole period 1853–1920, 1.4 million persons, virtually all of them British, went to New Zealand and it is estimated that nearly a million (not all, of course, necessarily emigrants) returned. Returners became more common over time, rising from only 36 per cent of outward sailings between 1853 and 1880 to 82 per cent of the 1 million outward sailings between 1881 and 1920. The increases correspond exactly to transport changes on the New Zealand route.

The steamship was the most dramatic and decisive advance but it was paralleled by the railway, which made it possible for emigrants to be quickly and easily transported from all areas through the national network to the port of embarkation. Agreements were commonly made between shipping and railway companies, allowing emigrants to be transported free to their port of departure. The expansion of the railroad in North America brought similar benefits. By the 1850s the completion of the Canadian canal network and the associated railway development facilitated access to the western USA by allowing emigrants to book their passage to Quebec and Hamilton and then by rail to Chicago. The links between steamships and railways led to the provision of the highly popular through-booking system by which emigrants could obtain a complete package, with a ticket purchased in Europe allowing travel to the final destination in America. The *Chambers' Journal* in 1857 described it as a 'prodigious convenience' which would 'rob emigration of its terrors and must set hundreds of families wandering'.[4]

Scots emigrants had a particular advantage because the railway system existed alongside a number of major shipping lines operating from the Clyde which by the 1850s had developed a worldwide network of services. The significant passenger companies were the Allan, Anchor and Donaldson lines, sailing mainly on a number of routes across the Atlantic; the City Line to India; the Allan Line to South Africa and, from the 1860s, the Albion Line to New Zealand. In addition, some of the major railway companies in Canada played a vigorous proactive role in the emigrant business. They recognized that the railway was not simply an easy and rapid mode of transport for new arrivals from Europe but was also the most effective way of opening the wilderness and prairie territory to permanent settlement. The mighty Canadian Pacific Railway Company (CPR) became very active in the promotion of emigration because of this. In 1880 it had been allocated 25 million acres of land between Winnipeg and the Rocky Mountains by the Dominion government. In order to generate profit, the company had to increase traffic through expanding areas of settlement and to achieve this goal embarked on an aggressive marketing campaign in Britain designed to stimulate emigration to the prairies. Scotland was specifically targeted and agents of the CPR toured country areas, giving lectures and providing information. The CPR even sought to reduce the hardships of pioneering by providing ready-made farms in southern Alberta, with housing, barns and fences included as part of the sale.

These initiatives by a large organization in attracting settlement to the prairie provinces were but one manifestation of a wider revolution in communicating the attractions of emigration to the peoples of Europe. The letters of emigrants to their families at home had always been the most influential medium for spreading information about overseas conditions. With the steamship, railway and telegraph, this traditional form of communication became even more effective as postal services became even more frequent, increasingly reliable and speedier. Emigrant letters, coming as they did from trusted family members, retained a great significance as the most credible source of information on overseas employment, prices and wages. Letters were often supplemented by remittances sent home to relatives. Alexander Buchanan, the principal immigration agent at Quebec, commented in his annual reports on the large numbers of emigrants from Scotland and elsewhere in the UK who came to join friends and relatives and who were often assisted by cash sums sent back to help cover their passage.

Returning migrants were also a key source of information. It is wrong, for instance, to assume that those who came back did so because they necessarily experienced failure and disillusion in the New World, although some were indeed in this category. The Scottish press printed articles from time to time about emigrants who had returned with 'blighted hopes and empty purses'. The steamship revolution was bound to mean that the number of emigrants returning could increase markedly when conditions in the receiving countries temporarily deteriorated. However, many 'returned migrants' had originally left Scotland with no intention of settling permanently in America. This was especially the case with tradesmen and semi-skilled workers. In the north-east, for instance, several hundred granite workers migrated annually to American yards each spring, before returning to Aberdeen for the winter. Coal miners from Lanarkshire also developed a tradition of temporary movement for work in the USA. Masons and other skilled building workers were in great demand on a seasonal basis. By the

1880s there seems to have been a willingness to go overseas at relatively short notice. In the latter part of that decade, for example, scores of Scottish building tradesmen who had responded to press adverts descended on Austin, Texas, when work on the state capital was halted by a strike of American workers. Evidence from Scandinavia, Italy, Greece and England suggests that the 'failed' returning migrants were usually in a minority. There seems no reason to suppose that the Scottish pattern was any different. 'Successful' returnees must indeed have been a potent source for spreading knowledge of overseas conditions in local communities, and even a positive influence in encouraging further emigration.

To these personal and family networks was added in the later nineteenth century a veritable explosion in the quality and quantity of information available to potential emigrants. The Emigrants' Information Office opened in 1886 as a source of impartial advice and information on land grants, wages, living costs and passage rates. Circulars, handbooks and pamphlets were made available in greater volume and were valued because of their avowed objectivity. Even more important were local newspapers. Marjory Harper has shown how significant newspapers such as the *Aberdeen Journal* were in raising interest about emigration in the rural communities of the north-east. Advertisements for ships' sailings, information on assisted passages, numerous letters from emigrants and articles on North American life were very regular features as the country population was relentlessly bombarded with all the facts of the emigration experience. Overseas governments and land companies also became more aggressive, professional and sophisticated in promoting emigration. In 1892, for instance, the Canadian government appointed two full-time agents in Scotland who undertook a tour of markets, hiring fairs, agricultural shows and village halls. The illustrated lecture, using the magic lantern, was a favourite device. W. G. Stuart, the agent for the north, was even able to deliver his presentation in Gaelic if the audience required it.

From the 1870s to the Great War, the Canadian government's aim was to settle the Prairie West with immigrants who would establish an agricultural foundation for the Dominion. The key influence on the strategy was Clifford Sifton, the Minister of the Interior from 1896 to 1905. He pioneered the first emigration communications strategy by flooding selected countries with appealing literature, advertisements in the press, tours for key journalists who then filed flattering copy on their return home, paying agents' fees on a commission basis for every immigrant who actually settled in Canada and giving bonuses to steamship agents for promoting the country in the United Kingdom. The rural districts of Scotland were particularly targeted because of their historic links with Canada and their population of experienced farmers and skilled agricultural workers.

3

The revolution in communications and marketing of emigration affected all western European countries to a greater or lesser extent. This context in itself cannot explain why Scottish levels of emigration were so high, relative to every other area of the continent. Most other societies with heavy rates of outward movement, such as Ireland and the Scandinavian countries, were relatively backward agricultural economies, whereas Scotland was one of the most successful industrial countries in the world, with rising standards of living in the second half of the nineteenth century and a global reputation for excellence in shipbuilding, engineering, iron and steel and agriculture. The Scottish haemorrhage also lasted longer than any other part of the UK. When British emigration in general fell back between the two world wars, the Scottish exodus continued at high levels. Indeed, in the 1920s Scotland topped the league table of emigrant nations with an emigration rate that was greater than in previous decades. Even in the years before the Great War, Scottish emigration was running at nearly twice the rate of the English figure. Ironically, movement *into* Scotland, particularly from Ireland, had been a significant feature from the early nineteenth century and it increased further after the Great Famine, until reaching a peak in 1891 when 218,745 first-generation Irish-born immigrants were recorded in the census. By the later nineteenth century, immigration – albeit on a much lesser scale – was also on the increase from areas of Italy and parts of northern Europe. Scotland therefore stands out in a European context as a country with high levels of *both* emigration and immigration.

Why Scotland should have such a history of heavy emigration despite its well-documented economic achievements in the nineteenth century is an intriguing question. One answer might be that the Scots had always been a mobile people who had traditionally looked overseas and to England for advancement, opportunities and employment. The

Scottish diaspora did not begin with the opening of North America and Australasia. In the sixteenth and seventeenth centuries the Scots migrated in their thousands to Poland, Scandinavia, Ireland and England as mercenary soldiers, pedlars, small merchants and (in Ulster) tenant farmers and labourers. Between 1600 and 1650, an estimated 30,000–40,000 Scots moved to Poland and a few thousand more than this settled in Ulster in the last quarter of the seventeenth century, especially during the 'Ill Years' of the 1690s. In fact, T. C. Smout suggests that the proportion of young Scotsmen (aged between 15 and 30) migrating in the middle of the seventeenth century was probably proportionately about the same as from the larger population of the mid-nineteenth century. Similarly, the Scots were among the earliest settlers in North America 100 years later. The Treaty of Paris of 1763 opened up the American back country to the settlement of an estimated 40,000 Scots by the time of the American War of Independence. They came in large numbers, especially to the frontier lands of colonial society, Georgia, the Carolinas, Canada and upper New York. International migration had therefore been a social habit for the Scots for centuries; the custom of going abroad was nothing new. It is particularly important to emphasize that the migratory culture in early modern times affected all parts of the country from the Orkneys to the Borders. The majority of those who went to Europe in the sixteenth century were natives of the eastern counties and the Northern Isles, while Ulster mainly attracted the population of the south-west and Argyll. In the later eighteenth century, there was the first major Highland exodus to North America. Mass emigration was therefore a continuum, with the great diaspora from Victorian and Edwardian Scotland a further stage in a process that was already centuries old.

But the exodus of the nineteenth and twentieth centuries also had particular causes specific to that period. These can best be considered by examining the influences at work in the three regions, the Highlands, the agricultural Lowlands and the urban-industrial areas. The place of the western Highlands and Islands in Scottish emigration history is well known. The link drawn between the Clearances and emigration is a familiar one in song, story and historical discourse. But the issues are more complex than popular accounts sometimes suggest. Emigration tended to focus mainly on the crofting region of the far west and the Hebrides. The majority who left the southern, central and eastern parishes of the Highlands moved in the first instance to the cities of Glasgow, Edinburgh and Dundee. From the later eighteenth century to the 1850s, it is clear that the Highland exodus was proportionately greater than that from other regions. For example, in the early 1840s an estimated two-fifths of all Scottish emigrants were from Highland parishes. Thereafter, however, and especially from the 1860s, as noted earlier, the Highland migration was notably less significant than elsewhere. By the later nineteenth century, most Scottish emigrants came from the towns, cities and industrial occupations. From that period it is certainly inaccurate to portray the large-scale exodus of Scots as a simple result of the social and economic problems of the Highlands.

In earlier decades, nevertheless, there were good reasons why the western Highlands should lose such a high proportion of its population through transatlantic emigration. The Gaels were more aware of opportunities outside the region than one might think. The huge scale of military recruitment in the later eighteenth century established a tradition of mobility and spread knowledge of overseas destinations. By the end of the Napoleonic Wars, around 30,000 Highlanders had already settled in North America, and the emigrant communities often maintained strong links with districts at home which helped to foster 'chain migration' later in the nineteenth century. In fact mass emigration can be dated from the 1820s because in most west Highland areas population continued to rise until that period. With the failure of kelp and the malaise in fishing, landlords came to see the region as 'over-populated', a view easily legitimized in intellectual terms from the fashionable doctrines of Thomas Malthus. The new conventional wisdom was that the Highland population was 'redundant'. It had to be removed in order to release land for the flockmasters who could pay higher and more reliable rents than a destitute tenantry just eking out an existence on the margins of subsistence. Already in the 1820s, some proprietors, such as McLean of Coll and Lord MacDonald in Skye, were supporting the passage of the 'surplus population' of their estates across the Atlantic. After the subsistence crisis of 1836–7, an ambitious scheme of assisted emigration was established with Colonial Office support. As a result, around 4,000 Highlanders were resettled in New South Wales. This was the prelude to the large-scale assisted emigration during the potato famine in the following decade when at least 16,500 people were supported to move to Canada and Australia from the Hebrides by individual landowners and charities like the Highland and Island Emigration Society. Coercion was widely deployed in this process to enforce emigration. This was the time, as seen in Chapter 18, of the most draconian clearances of the nineteenth century, when the flight of the poor was driven on by a combination of economic privation and the inexorable pressures of landlord compulsion.

It is not surprising that the Highlands loom large in the popular story of Scottish emigration. Only in that tragic region was landlord authority used directly to impose expulsion. Elsewhere in Scotland, heavy levels of emigration were also recorded, but the influences were more subtle and impersonal and did not produce the same impassioned response. Even in the Highlands, however, the subtlety of the process should be acknowledged. After the passage of the Crofters Holding Act in 1886, when mass clearance was finally outlawed, the drift from the land continued and in some areas accelerated. Even before the 1880s, the proprietors in most parts, except Lewis and South Uist, had effectively controlled the subdivision of crofts. Non-inheriting sons and daughters had to move, and in most cases this meant leaving the Highlands altogether because of the lack of alternatives to landholding in the region. Recurrent economic and subsistence crises, as in the early 1860s, the 1880s and again in the early 1920s, continued to generate periodic waves of heavy emigration. This was likely anyway because the Highlands remained the poorest part of Scotland yet the one area with a strong cultural tradition of land-holding. These features of the region often made young Gaels easy prey for the agents of Canadian land companies who could promise a way of life closer to their own experience than that of the Lowland towns or cities.

Some of the same influences were at work in the rural Lowlands. This was traditionally a society with very high levels of internal mobility. In the 1860s, for instance, the vast majority of all parishes experienced net outward movement of people. The reasons for this were varied and complex and have already been discussed in Chapter 19. But this unusually heavy incidence of internal mobility is crucial to an explanation of the roots of emigration. The rural Scots were very mobile abroad, in large part because they were also very mobile at home. There is now some evidence that from the later nineteenth century the volume of emigration varied inversely with that of internal migration. People in country farms and villages searching for opportunities elsewhere seem to have been able to weigh the attractions of the Scottish towns against those of overseas destinations and come to a decision on the basis of these comparisons. In the decades 1881–90 and 1901–10, for instance, there was heavy emigration, with 43 and 47 per cent respectively of the natural increase leaving the country. In the same twenty-year period, movement to Glasgow and the surrounding suburbs fell to low levels, while there was actual net movement out of the western Lowlands. On the other hand, during the 1870s and 1890s emigration declined but larger numbers moved to the cities and towns of the west. This pattern suggests a sophisticated and mobile population which had access to sources of information such as newspapers, letters from relatives and intelligence from returned migrants that enabled informed judgements about emigration to be made. It also highlights once again the key importance of the transportation revolution which enabled the historic and habitual internal mobility of the rural Scots to be translated fully into international movement.

Lowland rural emigration was not induced so much by destitution or deprivation – as in the Highlands for long periods – as by the lure of opportunity. Throughout the nineteenth and early twentieth centuries, Canada was the great magnet for those who wished to work the land, while rural tradesmen and industrial workers tended to opt more for the USA. From emigrant letters and newspaper articles one can piece together the attractions of emigration for both small tenants and farm servants. A primary incentive was the possibility of owning land that was cheap to acquire and increasingly made available for purchase in developed form by land companies and by the Dominion and provincial governments. In Canada and Australia land was plentiful whereas in Scotland even wealthy farmers were dependent on their landlords, with tenure regulated by a detailed lease enforceable at law and other sanctions. The tenants' agitation of the 1870s shows the tensions that these relationships could sometimes generate. In the colonies, on the other hand, owner-occupation, independence and the right to bequeath the hard-worked land to the family were all on offer and at reasonable rates. The strains imposed by the Agricultural Depression added to discontent in some areas and further increased the attractions of emigration. The Board of Agriculture in 1906 reviewed the reasons for the decline in the rural population and concluded with respect to Scotland that:

Many correspondents refer to the absence of an incentive to remain on the land and of any reasonable prospect of advancement in life, and it is mentioned in some districts, particularly in Scotland, many of the best men have been attracted to the colonies, where their energies may find wider scope and where the road to independence and a competency is broader and more easy to access.[5]

For farm servants the prospects were equally alluring. In the north-eastern counties, ploughmen placed part of their wages in local savings banks in preparation for emigration and some also took hired periods of labour in Canada before saving enough to invest in a farm.

The issue of wages was also at the heart of emigration from the urban and industrial areas. Relatively low wages might have given Scottish manufacturing a cutting edge in world markets, but they were also eventually bound to influence emigration to areas where the rewards of industry were more attractive. Of course, there was no inevitable correlation between low earnings and emigration. What matters is the relative differential between opportunities at home and overseas. Undoubtedly the economic growth of Scotland did result in some increases in real wage levels in the Victorian period, especially towards the end of the nineteenth century. However, wages were rising even more rapidly overseas in the American and Australasian economies, which were rich in land and resources but underpopulated. Those with trades and skills were especially in demand. The differences in income were often so enormous and the skills shortages so acute that many thousands could not resist the prospects. It is therefore hardly surprising that the Scottish level of emigration was significantly higher than the English. Scotland remained a poorer society than England, as shown by the migration of around 600,000 Scots to the south between 1841 and 1911 and the absence of any similar movement in the opposite direction over the same period. It followed that the Scottish people had more to gain from emigration since for them the differences between opportunities at home and those abroad were simply so much greater.

However, it was not only a question of wage levels. Scotland's manufacturing structure was founded on a small number of giant industries dependent on international markets. It was an economic system very vulnerable to the rise and fall of the trade cycle. After c. 1840 the UK became more subject to fluctuations of this type which were particularly violent in Scotland because of the tight interrelationships between shipbuilding, iron, steel, engineering and coal and the fickle nature of overseas markets which they served. Therefore, even in the heyday of the great Victorian and Edwardian industries, there was chronic economic insecurity with employment falling steeply in such periods as the later 1840s, the mid-1880s and 1906–10. Emigration tended to peak at the bottom of these cycles not simply because of the 'push' of deteriorating conditions at home but as a result of the 'pull' of high wages and employment in the USA and Canada. As Brinley Thomas showed some years ago when Britain was in depression that in the later nineteenth century America tended to experience boom conditions. In these circumstances, emigration was likely to reach unprecedented levels as the factors of 'push' and 'pull' were now both acting in unison. Before 1914, Scotland's highest recorded level of emigration was between 1901 and 1911, when the industrial economy was stagnant for several years but at a time when Canada was going through a protracted boom as prairie agriculture expanded and railroad building, mining, manufacturing and lumbering all developed vigorously. Similarly, the continuation of heavy out-migration in the 1920s and 1930s, when it was falling off elsewhere in the UK, can be explained by Scotland's characteristic mix of heavy, export-orientated industries which were peculiarly vulnerable for much of the inter-war period. At the bottom of the slump in 1931–3 more than a quarter of the Scottish labour force was out of work, compared to a little over a fifth in the UK as a whole. The Scots suffered more and, not surprisingly, tended to emigrate in greater numbers. *Plus ça change, plus c'est la même chose.*

21

New Scots

The Catholic Irish

In medieval times the nation that became Scotland had evolved from a mix of ethnic groups of Gaels, Picts, Scandinavians, Britons and Angles. To a much greater extent than either Wales or Ireland, Scotland in these earlier centuries was a heterogeneous society. When large-scale immigration once again began after 1800, however, a much more coherent sense of Scottish national identity had developed, which could have meant that newcomers who were different in religion, language and culture might be treated with suspicion, if not outright hostility. During the nineteenth and twentieth centuries, waves of Irish, Italians, Lithuanians, Jews, Poles, Asians and English people settled in Scotland. It was the most concentrated phase of immigration since the Irish, Scandinavian and Britannic tribes had established themselves hundreds of years before and was to have a powerful and complex impact on the development of modern Scottish society. This chapter explores the experience of the five groups who made up the majority of the immigrants to Scotland before the Second World War and considers the reaction of the host community to the new arrivals.

Although the nineteenth century was an age of mass migrations throughout Europe, no other country could match the sheer scale of the Irish exodus: 'Emigration became part of the expected cycle of life; growing up in Ireland meant preparing to leave it.'[1] While the Irish settled in virtually every English-speaking country in the world, Scotland attracted only a small minority of around 8 per cent of all Irish emigrants in the 80 years to 1921. But their impact on Scottish society was nevertheless significant. The Catholic Irish have been Scotland's main immigrant group of modern times, vastly outnumbering the Italians, Jews, Lithuanians (who numbered more than 40,000 together by the

1930s) and the Asians who settled in the second half of this century. Already by the 1850s there were around a quarter of a million Irish-born in Scotland and the immigration continued on a significant scale until the 1920s, when it started to decline. Indeed, even in narrow numerical terms, the Irish migration to Scotland was more important proportionately than the Irish movement to England. Only 2.9 per cent of the population of England and Wales were Irish in 1851, compared to 7.2 per cent in Scotland. While Irish migration to England was dropping steadily in the years immediately before the First World War, in Scotland the tide of new migrants showed little sign of ebbing. In 1901 there were still 205,000 Irish-born, little different from the 207,000 who had settled in the years immediately after the Famine.

The visibility of the Irish in Scottish society was significantly increased by their tendency to concentrate in particular areas, notably Glasgow, the industrial counties around the city, Dundee and the mining districts of the Lothians. Above all else, it was the jobs generated by industrialization which drew them and ensured that substantial communities of people of Irish descent grew up in boom towns like Airdrie, Coatbridge, Motherwell and several other places in the western Lowlands. The Irish who settled in Scotland in this period came overwhelmingly from the historic province of Ulster, with relatively few from other parts of the island. It followed, therefore, that though most were Catholic, a substantial minority (about a quarter to a fifth) of all immigrants in the middle decades of the nineteenth century were Protestant, the direct descendants of those Presbyterian Scots who had settled in Ulster in the seventeenth century. For obvious cultural, racial and religious reasons, they were much more easily assimilated in Scotland than the Catholic Irish. Their story is told in the next section of this chapter. But the regional origin of the migrant streams was deeply significant because it meant that the tribal hatreds of Ulster were transferred to the industrial districts of Scotland and faction fighting between Orange and Green sympathizers became a routine feature of life in several communities in Lanarkshire and Ayrshire in the nineteenth century.

The Irish made a substantial contribution to the development of the Scottish economy. Friedrich Engels claimed in 1843 that the progress of the British industrial revolution would have been impeded but for the labour power of the immigrants from across the Irish Sea. Engels was talking particularly of Lancashire, but his comment was perhaps even more valid for Scotland, where the Irish made up a higher proportion of the population and where an abundant supply of unskilled and semi-skilled labour was crucial to Scottish industrial success. In the mining districts of Lanarkshire and Ayrshire the Irish gained an unsavoury reputation as strike-breakers, hired by unscrupulous Scottish employers to break the unions in the first few decades of the nineteenth century. In the long run, however, they were complementary to the native labour force, willing and able to take on the menial and un-skilled jobs vital to the development of industrial and urban society that were not always attractive to many Scots. Young Irishmen, some of whom were working in Scotland only to earn enough to cover their passage to the land of real opportunity across the Atlantic, formed a great mobile army of navvies, moving across the length and breadth of the country, completing the harbours, railways, canals, bridges and reservoirs which became the physical sinews of the new economic order.

At the time, however, the Irish did not receive much credit for helping to sustain the Scottish economic miracle. They were 'strangers in a strange land', alien in religion, speech and culture, massed at the bottom end of the labour market, often attracting vociferous criticism for burdening ratepayers and the Poor Law with hordes of shiftless paupers, and the scapegoats for every conceivable social ill from drunkenness to the epidemic diseases of the larger towns. In response, so some commentators have argued, the immigrant Irish retreated into them-selves, became introverted, pursued a separate identity in Scotland and warmly embraced the Catholic faith which alone provided them with spiritual consolation and a sense of social worth in a hostile land. They could not relate to a Scotland which, as a stateless nation, derived its collective identity from Presbyterianism, a creed whose adherents regarded Catholicism as at best superstitious error and at worst as a satanic force led by the Man of Sin himself, the Pope of Rome. However, the enclave mentality among Irish Catholics developed only slowly, was never wholly dominant and was already showing signs of gradually crumbling in the early twentieth century. Presbyterianism itself, as shown earlier in this book, was far from monolithic and was rent for much of the nineteenth century by fratricidal disputes which made some aspects of the division between Catholics and Protestants seem tame by comparison.

The striking feature of the first wave of immigrants was the speed of their assimilation. Many of the descendants of the eighteenth-century migrants to Galloway and Ayrshire lost their Catholic faith as a result of intermarriage with the native stock and because of the absence of priests and chapels in Scotland. Part of this process was the loss of the Irish form of surname. Thus McDade became Davidson; O'Neil, McNeil; Dwyer, Dyer and so on. Many of the first and even of the second generation of immigrants quickly became invisible. Until the middle decades of the nineteenth century the Catholic Church was unable to cope with the seemingly endless flood of migrants from across the Irish Sea. In 1836 there was only one priest in Glasgow for every 9,000–11,000 Catholics. The great cathedral church of St Andrew had opened in 1816 in Clyde Street as a powerful physical symbol of the new Catholic presence in the west of Scotland. However, the building costs drained the resources of an impoverished community for years to come and slowed down the foundation of other churches in areas of burgeoning migration. One of the features of this period was the custom of priests leaving their missions to go on begging trips to England and Ireland in an attempt to raise funds. Catholic schooling, later one of the key influences maintaining the religious identity of the Catholic immigrants, was also profoundly weak. Until 1816 there was no Catholic school in the west of Scotland and, when a Catholic Schools Society was founded in Glasgow in 1817 by wealthy Protestant benefactors, most financial support came at a price. Teachers were not allowed to give instruction on the Catholic faith and the Protestant version of the Bible alone was used for religious lessons.

In the difficult years after the end of the Napoleonic Wars the Irish were sometimes seen as a scapegoat for the depressed conditions in the labour market and falling wage rates. But there was little open and violent opposition to them in the decades before the Famine. Most sectarian incidents were between Irish Catholics and Irish Protestants at the Orange marches where the tribal battles of the old country were fought out once again in a new land. The Presbytery of Glasgow and the University did oppose the passage of the Catholic Emancipation Act of 1829. But the legal and academic establishment of Edinburgh supported the legislation, and this included influential figures like Sir Walter Scott and Thomas Chalmers. Significantly the trial in Edinburgh of two of the most notorious Irishmen in Scotland of the age, William Burke and William Hare, did not incite any anti-Irish riots in the capital. Burke and Hare were two former navvies in the Union Canal who had turned their talents to the more lucrative business of selling corpses to

Edinburgh lecturers in anatomy. They tried to undercut the resurrectionists by murdering and selling no fewer than 16 unfortunates to Dr Robert Knox in 1828, their victims including several of their fellow countrymen and co-religionists. Hare and his wife turned King's evidence, on which Burke was convicted, hanged and his body dissected. Crowds of over 20,000 witnessed the execution and many subsequently viewed the corpse on the dissecting table before its public dismemberment. These gory events, however, did not spark off any violent backlash against the Irish.

Henry Cockburn was convinced that there was little conflict between the immigrants and the native Scots. He commented in his *Journal* in 1835:

The whole country was overrun by Irish labourers, so that the presbyterian population learned experimentally that a man might be a Catholic without having the passions or the visible horns of the devil. New chapels have arisen peaceably everywhere; and except their stronger taste for a fight now and then, the Irish have in many places behaved fully as well as our own people. The recent extinction of civil disability on account of the religion removed the legal encouragement of intolerance, and left common-sense some chance; and the mere habit of hating, and of thinking it a duty to act on this feeling, being superseded, Catholics and rational Protestants are more friendly than the different sects of Protestants are.[2]

In the light of these remarks, it is not surprising to find much evidence of Irish and Scottish workers combining for common purposes. The view that the Catholic Irish formed an isolated community in this period, divorced from the Scottish radical and trade-union tradition and exclusively concerned only with 'Irish' issues such as Catholic emancipation and Repeal of the Act of Union, no longer fits the facts. Certainly the immigrants were sometimes used as strike-breakers against native workers. But most of the evidence for this comes from the coal and iron industries of Lanarkshire and Ayrshire from the 1830s. Elsewhere, however, the Irish were often to the fore in much trade-union and radical activity. They dominated the membership and leadership of the Glasgow Cotton Spinners' Association and formed a large part of the handloom weavers' union in the west of Scotland by the later 1830s, at a time when the weavers were the largest group of Scottish industrial workers. The Catholic Irish in Scotland campaigned vigorously for a restoration of an Irish parliament, but members of the immigrant community, as Martin Mitchell has shown, were also deeply involved in Scottish radical movements like the United Scotsmen of the 1790s (itself powerfully influenced by the United Irishmen), the secret societies in and around Glasgow after 1816, the Chartist movement of the 1830s and the Suffrage Association of the following decade. The common experience of migration, urbanization and industrialization helped to fuse the aspirations of many Irish and Scots workers before the 1840s towards those common political goals which were seen as the real keys to social and economic improvement. Moreover, the cause of Irish parliamentary freedom was one that drew sympathy from many Scottish radicals. Daniel O'Connell was received rapturously when he visited Scotland in 1835 and he addressed crowds estimated at nearly 200,000 when he spoke in Glasgow Green.

The period from the Great Famine to the early twentieth century forms a second distinctive phase in the immigrant experience. In the aftermath of the crisis Scottish attitudes to the Catholic Irish undoubtedly hardened. Latent anti-popery sentiments were stimulated by the decisions of Pius IX in 1850 to restore the English Catholic hierarchy. For a year and more, meetings were held throughout Scotland and numerous petitions submitted to parliament in an attempt to combat the menace of 'papal aggression'. Anti-Catholic hostility was also generated by the unprecedented increase in the movement of impoverished Irish to Scotland during and immediately after the Famine. Never before in modern Scottish history had there been immigration on such a scale over such a short period of time. In 1851 the numbers of Irish-born in Scotland had risen to over 207,000, and they still stood at 204,000 10 years later. They were the destitute refugees from the most appalling human disaster in nineteenth-century Europe. Between 1845 and 1854 the authorities in Scotland shipped back some 47,000 Irish paupers, but many more were able to stay on and attracted native hostility and a Protestant backlash against the new wave of immigrants. The Scottish Reformation Society was founded to 'resist the aggressions of Popery, and to watch over the designs and movements of its promoters and abettors'. It soon had 38 branches spread up and down the country. Anti-Catholic demagogues attracted large audiences for a few years. Notable among them was John Sayers Orr, the self-proclaimed 'Angel Gabriel', whose meetings incited ugly riots in Greenock and Gourock in 1851 and 1852, and Alessandro Gavazzi, a former Catholic monk, whose lectures on the iniquities of popery had, according to the *Glasgow*

Herald, a drawing power in the Scottish cities equalled only by Jenny Lind, the popular singer of the time known as the 'Swedish Nightingale'. Anti-Catholic periodicals, such as the *Bulwark* and *The Scottish Protestant*, were also founded in the 1850s. The latter drew a causal link between the flood of Famine immigrants and the menace of popery on the march: 'If the hopes of Popery to regain her dominion of darkness in this kingdom of Bible light are beginning to revive, it is because she is colonising our soil, from another land, with the hordes of her barbarised and enslaved victims, whom she proudly styles her "subjects".[3] But this phase of overt hostility did not last for long and had virtually ended by the late 1850s. Sectarian disturbances after that decade were confined mainly to the west of Scotland, where the settlement of Protestant Irish fuelled tensions with their ancient enemies, the immigrant Catholics. Dundee, which had a large immigrant population, and Edinburgh were usually quiet. The Scottish economy of the 1850s was growing vigorously as a result of the rapid expansion of coal mining and iron manufacture and was able to absorb even the large number of the new arrivals relatively easily in unskilled and semi-skilled employment. Moreover, the north of Ireland, from where most of the migrants to Scotland had come, suffered less than many other parts of the island from the catastrophic effects of the potato blight. The scale of the movement to Glasgow and the western Lowlands, though greater than before, was much less than the huge destitute influx to Liverpool which originated from districts in Ireland that suffered more acutely than the counties of Ulster. It was also fortuitous that Scotland's own potato famine in the Highlands in the 1840s was effectively contained by charity and government effort, thus preventing a mass flight of the poor to the south and reducing the danger of an ethnic clash between Scottish Gaels and the Irish in the cities of the Lowlands.

It may be, however, that the tensions of the early 1850s were one factor in the shaping of a more introspective Irish Catholic community than had existed earlier in the nineteenth century. Certainly, Catholic identity was strengthened as never before in the half-century after the arrival of the Famine immigrants. Even when they were virtually overwhelmed by the numbers under their care, the priests, who were also often from Ireland, continued to identify with the plight of the poor. The clergy considered it an obligation to visit the sick and provide the last rites to all who wished them. Some buckled under the strain of the task but a loyalty existed among the majority of Irish Catholics (around an estimated two-thirds in Glasgow in the 1840s) who did not attend mass on a regular basis. In the 1830s, Bishop Murdoch took advantage of this support and quickly removed a church debt of over £9,000 when he appointed collectors to gather weekly contributions from both the practising and the nominal Catholic population in the tenements of the city centre. From the pennies of the poor and eventually, by way of loans, from the tiny immigrant middle class of pawnbrokers, publicans, shopkeepers and ham-and-egg merchants a formidable parish network slowly came to be established. By 1878 the number of priests in Glasgow had risen to 134 and further increased to 234 in 1902. The parishes expanded over this same period from 60 to 84, and a total of 44 new chapels were also built. While some of the Protestant churches were arguably losing touch with the urban poor at this time, the Catholic clergy were forging ever closer contacts with them. A new social Catholicism was emerging which created almost an alternative community in Scotland for the Irish immigrants and their descendants.

Intermarriage with Protestant Scots, the quickest way to assimilation, became less common and was made more difficult still by the Vatican's rigorous *Ne Temere* decree of 1908. Catholic social agencies, such as the St Vincent de Paul Society, created to help the poor, and the League of the Cross, established to combat the evils of drink, grew up in most parishes. It became common to open halls adjacent to chapels so that Catholic young men and women could find acceptable recreation in the evenings and mix only with those of their own faith. Celtic Football Club was first mooted by the Marist brother Walfrid to help feed and clothe the poor of the parishes in the east end of Glasgow. But he was also worried about the dangers of young Catholics meeting Protestants after work and by the fear that Protestant soup kitchens might tempt them into apostasy. The new football club would not only help the poor but also keep young Catholics together in their leisure time. A major effort was invested in the provision of Catholic schooling. The 1872 Education Act made education compulsory for all children; but the Catholic schools continued to rely mainly on voluntary contributions, which in turn led to an enormous and continuing fund-raising campaign drawing on weekly offerings, collections, bazaars, fairs, concerts and soirées. All of this also enhanced community pride and identity powerfully. By 1876 there were 171 certificated teachers and 357 pupil-teachers in 192 institutions serving over 20,600 day and 3,300 night scholars. It was a remarkable achievement by an overwhelmingly poor community.

Yet even these sacrifices were not enough to prevent the Catholic schools lagging behind the public system in quality of buildings, resources and numbers of teaching staff. This handicap, together with the constraints of poverty and discrimination in the job market, helps to explain why upward social mobility among the 'Scoto-Irish' was still very limited before 1914.

At the same time as the Catholic ethos was becoming more pronounced, the 'Irishness' of the community was also becoming more firmly established. At first sight this seems strange, because the proportion of new immigrants was steadily falling and many of the Scoto-Irish, the second, third and fourth generations, had never set foot in Ireland. But they, like the rest of the global Irish diaspora, were affected by the upsurge in Irish nationalism, culminating in the foundation of the Home Rule Movement in 1870 which campaigned for the repeal of the 1800 Act of the Union with Ireland and Great Britain and the creation of a parliament in Dublin. Branches of the organization were soon established throughout the urban and industrial districts. Coatbridge, where a sense of ethnic Irishness was fortified by its endemic Orange and Green disputes, boasted the largest branch in Britain in the 1890s and one of the most generous contributors in the whole of the kingdom to Home Rule funds. Many of the Catholic clergy were also sympathetic to Home Rule and often spoke at Home Rule meetings. Until the 1850s the mainly Highland and north-east leadership of the Church was reluctant to accept too many Irish priests for fear of establishing an Irish clerical imperial ascendancy in Scotland. But the desperate shortage of priests after the Famine immigrations caused a change of heart and, by 1867, 20 of the 167 clergy in the western district of Scotland were Irish, many of them with strong nationalist sympathies. The influence of the Home Rule Movement was also intensified by the *Glasgow Free Press*, the weekly paper of the Irish in the west of Scotland from 1851 to 1868. (It eventually folded after being condemned by Rome but until then maintained an aggressively nationalist stance on all Irish issues.) At the local branch level, the main function of the movement from the 1880s was to mobilize the Irish communities at general elections behind pro-Home Rule candidates. Usually the vote was placed at the disposal of the Liberal Party, which introduced Home Rule bills in 1886, 1892 and 1912, but on occasion those candidates regarded as at all lukewarm on this single issue did not receive endorsement.

By 1900, then, the Irish immigrants and their descendants seem to have developed almost as a distinct and introverted ethnic community in Scotland with its own chapels, schools, social and welfare organizations and political agenda. Bonds were further reinforced and links fostered with the old country by bodies such as the Gaelic Athletic Association, the Gaelic League and the Ancient Order of Hibernians. Irish musical festivals, language classes and lectures on Irish history drew large attendances. The immigrants also had their own football teams. The first, Edinburgh Hibernian, was founded in 1875 and was quickly followed by several 'Harps', 'Shamrocks' and 'Emeralds', each attached to a local area. The proudest sporting symbol of the community became Glasgow Celtic which, after a string of early successes after its foundation in 1888, went on to win an unprecedented six successive Scottish championships, from 1905 to 1910. The origins of Celtic were unambiguously Irish-Catholic. The first patron was the Archbishop of Glasgow, Archbishop Eyre, and Michael Davitt, the great Irish nationalist leader, laid the first sod of 'real Irish shamrocks' at the new Celtic Park in 1892. Several of the team's officials were also well-known supporters of the nationalist cause.

But the notion of an ethnic enclave, insulated and divorced from the rest of Scottish society, can be pressed too far. The Irish and the Scots shared a common experience in the workplace and, as in the early nineteenth century, the Irish also became involved in trade-union organization, including the National Labourers Union and the Dock Labourers Union in Glasgow. Irish workers in the Dundee jute industry were already unionized before 1914. The focus on Irish Home Rule also had implications for Scottish domestic politics. It instilled in unskilled workers a political awareness they might not otherwise have obtained and allowed men of ability from the ranks of the immigrant community to develop organizational skills which could be used in other spheres. This was the background of John Wheatley (1869–1930), founder of the Catholic Socialist Society and a future Government Minister, who became a major influence encouraging the descendants of the immigrants to move towards the new Labour Party. From the Edinburgh immigrant community emerged James Connolly (1868–1916), who also received his earliest political education through the Irish question but went on to become a leader of unskilled workers and a famous revolutionary socialist before being executed for his part in the 1916 Easter Rising in Dublin. Even before 1914, loyalty to the Liberal Party was beginning to become more uncertain because of its failure to achieve Home Rule. Influential leaders of the Irish interest, like John Ferguson, were beginning to show a desire to make common cause with Labour interests on issues such as a just wage and shorter working hours. Common interests also united Irish Home Rulers, Liberal Scots politicians and radical activists over the issue of land reform in the Highlands and Ireland. Michael Davitt vigorously supported the cause of the crofters and was even offered a Highland parliamentary seat, Charles Stewart Parnell addressed Highland societies on the land issue in Glasgow in 1881, while John Murdoch, the well-known campaigner for crofting rights, sought to revive the ancient cultural links between Ireland and Scotland.

The Scoto-Irish did not therefore entirely inhabit a closed world. Indeed, the social aspirations of the clerical and lay leaders of the community differed little from those of the wider Scottish establishment in their enthusiasm for education, self-help, improvement and temperance. During and after the First World War the connections with Scotland became even stronger as it seemed that the ties with Ireland were finally starting to weaken. The immigrant community shared fully in the bloody sacrifices of the Great War. The Roman Catholic Archbishops of Glasgow and Edinburgh blessed the conflict as a just war, large numbers of Scots Irish enlisted even before conscription in 1916, and six members of the community were decorated with the Victoria Cross. Any doubts about the loyalty of the Irish in Scotland to the British state were conclusively removed. Throughout the conflict, the immigrants' newspaper, the *Glasgow Observer*, never faltered in its support and continuously publicized the heroic deeds of Catholic soldiers at the front. The year the war ended saw the passing of the 1918 Education (Scotland) Act. Section 18 of that legislation has been described as the Magna Carta of Scottish Catholicism in the twentieth century. It brought the Catholic schools, which until then had been supported by voluntary effort, into the state system. At a stroke one of the poorest sections of Scottish society was relieved of an increasingly intolerable burden because, in addition to financing their own schools, they had also to pay the general educational rate. However, this was educational integration with a difference, not found in any other mainly Protestant country. In exchange for agreeing to the transfer of their schools, the Catholic authorities won three crucial concessions: full rights of access to the schools by priests, religious instruction to be maintained at existing levels and, most importantly of all, only teachers acceptable to the Church 'in regard to religious faith and character' were to be appointed. The distinctive ethos of the schools was preserved while the cost of running them became the responsibility of the state. Not surprisingly, at the time this remarkable settlement provoked furious protest from some members of the Church of Scotland who complained bitterly of 'Rome on the Rates', and it has been condemned by others ever since as a prime factor in the perpetuation of sectarian differences in Scottish society. From another perspective, however, the 1918 Act had a more positive effect, becoming in the long run a key factor in the promotion of Catholic assimilation. Without it, the Scoto-Irish may have been unable to grasp the educational opportunities of the twentieth century and as a result be condemned to the enduring status of an underprivileged and alienated minority. Instead, 1918, and the later changes promoting access to higher education after 1945, enabled the eventual growth of a large Catholic professional class, fully integrated into the mainstream of Scottish society.

But all this was still far in the future. In the short run, during and immediately after the Great War, Irish issues continued to dominate the political interests of the immigrant community. The Easter Rising of 1916 at first attracted condemnation as a crazy exploit that threatened the final peaceful resolution of the Home Rule question. However, when the rebels were executed by the British, they instantly became martyrs. Increasingly, sympathy among those of Irish birth and descent in Scotland was transferred to Sinn Fein, the separatist Irish party, especially when news began to filter through of the atrocities committed by British irregular forces, the Black and Tans, in whose ranks were many battle-hardened Scottish soldiers who were veterans of trench warfare in France and Belgium. By 1920 there were 80 Sinn Fein clubs in Scotland, all strongly committed to the military struggle against British rule. In the same year, Glasgow had an estimated 4,000 IRA volunteers and on at least two occasions high-ranking officers came from Dublin and secretly reviewed the troops in the west of Scotland. Throughout the years of struggle, Scottish sympathizers were the main source of powder and gelignite obtained from the quarries, coal pits and shale mines where Irish labour was widely employed throughout the central Lowlands. The money and materials which came from Scotland far exceeded those from anywhere else, including Ireland itself. Eamon de Valera, in thanking the Irish Scots for their efforts, proclaimed that it had been the main factor in the success of the Sinn Fein campaigns. This, however, was the high point of interest in Irish politics. The outbreak of the bloody Irish Civil War in 1921 disenchanted many, while the establishment of the Free State and self-government in 1922 effectively brought to an end the need for vigorous Irish political activity in Scotland. Thereafter, the immigrant vote went to Labour as it promised the best hope of social justice and improvement for an under-privileged community and because influential figures in the community, such as John Wheatley, were already building the foundations of support long before 1920. Loyalty to Labour brought the Catholics into the mainstream of British politics for the first time. As Tom Gallagher puts it:

For all its shortcomings Labour was crucially important, not for the material gains it brought ordinary Catholics, which were pitiably few till the 1940s, but because such an involvement set a lot of them on the road to integration. In time identification with Labour helped reconcile them to their place in the British state and the horizons of many would widen to the extent that loyalty to their class, union or occupation would become more important than loyalty to their parish or ancestral homelands.[4]

But the pattern outlined by Gallagher would still take several decades to mature and did not become fully established until the second half of the twentieth century. Only then did the erosion of discrimination in the labour market, better career opportunities in the public services, wider openings in higher education and the support provided by the Welfare State promote rapid assimilation of the Scoto-Irish. If anything, indeed, the fortress mentality and suspicion of the host society were strengthened in the inter-war period by a renewed outbreak of anti-Catholicism which has been described as the most intense phase of sectarian bitterness in Scotland since the seventeenth century. The terrible human carnage of the Great War, followed by economic depression, mass unemployment and a huge increase in Scottish emi-gration, created a grave crisis of national insecurity. The Scoto-Irish, widely regarded by many as alien in race and religion, became for some the obvious scapegoats for Scotland's calamities.

From 1922 the General Assembly of the Church of Scotland cam-paigned vigorously against the supposedly malign effects of Irish immi-gration. Its Church and Nation Committee in 1923 approved the notorious report, *The Menace of the Irish Race to Our Scottish*

Nationality, which accused the Irish Roman Catholic population of taking employment from native Scots, of being part of a papist conspiracy to subvert Presbyterian values, and the main source of intemperance, improvidence, criminality and much else besides. The only remedies were control of immigration from the Irish Free State, deportation of natives of that country who were in Scottish prisons or receiving poor relief and absolute preference given to native Scots in public works because Scotland 'was over-gorged with Irishmen'. The demographic assumptions of the report were seriously flawed. Irish migration had virtually collapsed because of the slump in Scottish industry, Irish workers were among the many thousands emigrating from a distressed Scotland in the 1920s, and the vast majority of the 'Scoto-Irish' community had in fact been born in Scotland. But the main conclusions of the report still formed the context for annual debates in the General Assembly until the eve of the Second World War.

By the later 1920s a politicized anti-Catholic movement had also emerged at grass-roots level, represented by Alexander Ratcliffe's Scottish Protestant League in Glasgow and Protestant Action led by John Cormack in Edinburgh. At their peak, a third of the votes and several seats in council elections in these cities were taken by those parties. In 1935, Cormack's Protestant Action assembled a hostile mob of nearly 10,000 in the capital which disrupted a civic reception for the Catholic Young Men's Society. Two months later they also interfered with a reception for the Roman Catholic Prime Minister of Australia, Joseph Lyons. The most serious violence occurred in June when Protestant Action launched a systematic series of attacks on the Catholic Eucharistic Congress, including the stoning of coaches carrying Catholic children. Throughout the summer of 1935 sectarian violence was endemic and Catholics organized 'all night vigils' to protect chapels from vandalism. As Stewart J. Brown has argued, while no Presbyterian clergy took part in these outrages, 'the national Church's campaign against the Scoto-Irish community since 1922 had clearly contributed to the mood of violence, giving an aura of respectability to racism and sectarianism'.[5]

This period of sectarian tension was short-lived. It ended with economic recovery and the outbreak of war in 1939. Moreover, both the Church of Scotland and its allies, the United Free Church, failed to gain the support of any of the main political parties for its campaign to restrict immigration or to deport 'undesirable' Roman Catholics. Labour gave strong support to the 1918 Act and the Conservatives actively distanced themselves from the extremists in the kirk. The Scottish press – and notably the *Glasgow Herald*, which published a convincing refutation of the Church of Scotland's case – was broadly unsympathetic to the sectarian position. Nevertheless, Protestant demonstrations of the 1920s and 1930s had attracted many thousands and the Protestant parties had achieved some electoral success at local level. Oral evidence suggests also that existing discrimination in the labour market was strengthened by the serious economic recession of the time which hit hardest in those parts of Scotland where Catholics were most concentrated. It would take some time for these scars to heal before the process of Irish Catholic integration could be completed later in the twentieth century.

The Protestant Irish

For Irish Presbyterians, Scotland in the early nineteenth century was not a strange land. Their ancestors had left Ayrshire, Wigtownshire and Argyll in the seventeenth century to colonize the Ulster plantation, and the links with the mother country had been strengthened in subsequent decades through trade, education and family connections. The distance separating the Antrim coast from Scotland is barely 20 miles and by the later eighteenth century daily passenger sailings were established between Donaghadee (located in the strongly Scots Presbyterian Ards peninsula) and Portpatrick in Wigtownshire. Two of the most notable examples of the regular intercourse that took place between Ulster and Scotland before 1800 were the movement of Irish Protestant bleachers and weavers to provide instruction in the Scottish linen industry in the 1780s and 1790s and the attendance of Presbyterian Irish students at Glasgow and, to a lesser extent, Edinburgh universities. At Glasgow, the 'Scotch' Irish never made up less than 10 per cent of the student body in any one decade in the eighteenth century. They were attracted by the university's Presbyterian traditions and low course fees. When they returned home to become teachers and ministers they were important channels for the dissemination in Ulster Protestant society of the Enlightenment ideas of their Scottish professors, such as the charismatic Francis Hutcheson.

Political developments in the 1790s forged even stronger links between Ulster and Scotland. The failure of the United Irishmen's rebellion in 1798 was significant in boosting Protestant Irish emigration. Ulster Presbyterians had been heavily involved in the abortive revolution.

They opposed the legal penalties imposed on them by the Established Church of Ireland ruling class and the tithe payments required in support of the clergy of the Established Church. Areas of United Irishmen strength, such as north County Down, were often also areas where the Presbyterian radicalism of small tenant farmers and linen weavers flourished. The brutal crushing of the rebellion compelled many to flee to Scotland, where some at least took part in the agitations that eventually culminated in the 'Radical War' of 1820. Sectarian passions were also intensifying in Ireland in the 1790s. The passage of the Catholic Relief Acts in 1792 and 1793 created widespread alarm among the Protestant community that a Catholic armed uprising was imminent. Anxieties were further heightened by the growth of 'Defenderism', a movement of Catholic secret societies determined to evict Protestants from the land, and by the fact that the '98 Rebellion itself had ended in a sectarian bloodbath which left around 30,000 dead. These political and religious forces of themselves led to an increase in migration to Scotland, but they were enhanced by powerful economic attractions. Some Ulster Protestants were small farmers, but many others were weavers, bleachers, skilled tradesmen and labourers. During the Napoleonic Wars, economic opportunities and wage rates were increasing much faster in Scotland than in Ireland as the former entered its first phase of rapid industrialization. Not surprisingly, many Irish Protestants determined to emigrate to a land which was more secure, shared a common religious identity, was familiar in cultural terms and offered more material promise than Ireland.

By the 1830s the Irish Protestants probably made up about a quarter of the overall Irish migration to Scotland, though in some areas and occupations their numbers were much greater than the general average suggests. This was the case, for instance, in such weaving centres in the south-west as Wigtown, Glenluce, Newton Stewart, Maybole, Girvan and Calton in Glasgow. The Irish Protestant presence in some of the cotton mill communities, such as Blantyre in Lanarkshire, was also significantly greater than that of Irish Catholics. Moreover, the immigration of Irish Protestants was not only confined to the first phase of textile-based industrialization in Scotland before 1830, when most entered weaving, bleaching, finishing and cotton-spinning. A statistical snapshot from the later nineteenth century shows that between 1876 and 1881 83 per cent of Irish immigrants into Scotland came from Ulster. Of these, over 58 per cent were natives of the four counties

– Antrim, Down, Londonderry and Armagh – all with substantial
Protestant majorities. By this time Irish Protestants were well established
in the mining and iron-making districts of Lanarkshire (with important
settlements in Larkhall and Airdrie), in the collieries of West Lothian
and in the shipbuilding centres of Glasgow at Govan, Whiteinch and
Partick. Only in the later nineteenth and early twentieth centuries
did the inflow from the Protestant areas of Ulster begin to decline
significantly as the Catholic counties of the north of Ireland, particularly
Donegal and Cavan, became Scotland's major source of Irish immigrants
from then until recent times.

The Irish Protestant migrants in nineteenth-century Scotland are
usually differentiated by historians from the Catholic majority in two
ways – they were normally to be found in higher-skilled occupations
and, because they encountered no racial or religious animosity, they
had no inducement to develop a sense of separate group identity.
Assimilation into the mainstream of Scottish society was easy and
predictable for them. There is much substance in the first argument.
Often Protestants arrived in Scotland as a result of being directly
recruited by employers for skilled or semi-skilled employment because
many skilled Scots craftsmen in the second half of the nineteenth century
were opting for emigration. Advertisements were placed in the Belfast
newspapers offering specific jobs in the mines and iron and steel works
in Lanarkshire and Ayrshire. Those who applied travelled to Scotland
with warrants provided by their firms, with houses allocated to them
and company school places provided for their children. Higher-status
transport workers in Glasgow, such as goods guards and train drivers,
were recruited in a similar way. The greatest Scottish iron-making firm
of the Victorian era, Bairds of Gartsherrie, ensured that the skilled jobs
at its massive Coatbridge works were always monopolized by Scots
and Irish Protestants, while Irish Catholics were employed as unskilled
labourers and furnacemen. It was said that there was not one Catholic
member of the local branch of the Amalgamated Society of Engineers
until 1931.

It was a similar story in the Clyde shipyards. Irish Protestants were
well represented among the skilled occupations, particularly the boiler-
makers, and they tended to live in better-quality working-class housing
in such shipbuilding districts as Partick and Govan. Their position as
a labour élite could easily be perpetuated because apprenticeships in
the yards were arranged by the craft unions in consultation with the

foremen. The combination of craft exclusiveness, the desire to maintain standards, restricted entry and the overall influence of religious loyalties usually ensured that boys from unskilled Catholic families would be permanently excluded from the best jobs. But to stereotype the Protestant Irish immigrant simply as a labour aristocrat is going too far. There was in fact considerable diversity over time and among different places and occupations. Until the 1830s and 1840s, the majority of Ulster Protestants who settled in Scotland worked as linen and cotton weavers. This was a trade often subject to falling earnings, dilution and a gross oversupply of labour from the end of the Napoleonic Wars. Many of the Irish weavers were trying to escape from an industry that was itself in terminal decline in Ulster, only to find the Scottish manufacture itself in chronic difficulty in several years of the 1840s and 1850s. Graham Walker's survey of Glasgow Poor Law records for the later 1860s shows significant numbers of Irish Protestant weavers, labourers, domestic servants and millworkers seeking support, although most of the destitute in the areas considered were Irish Catholics. Away from Glasgow and Lanarkshire, occupational patterns seem also to have been more complex. The majority of Irish Protestants in the 1880s in Greenock were general labourers employed at the port. In the steel-making areas of the Garnock Valley in Ayrshire during the same decade, the Protestant Irish were to be found in unskilled and semi-skilled grades as well as in the better-paid occupations. Our knowledge of their profile in other areas where they also settled, such as Dumbarton, Stirling and West Lothian, is less clear but there is no reason to believe that it was significantly different in these localities.

The Irish Protestant identity in Ulster was forged by the influence of political, religious and social forces in the north of Ireland in the seventeenth and eighteenth centuries. It was significant that the first important wave of migration in the 1790s coincided with a period when the sense of Protestant Ulster collective consciousness was being fortified as never before. The Protestant role in the 1798 Rebellion was as much a powerful assertion of the community identity of Ulster-Scots as a struggle for political emancipation and radical republicanism. Furthermore, as suggested earlier, sectarian passions also reached unprecedented levels as the rebellion ultimately degenerated into a bitter and bloody tribal conflict between Catholics and Protestants. The group identity of Irish Protestants had long been conditioned by chronic fear of the ever-present Catholic menace. Now there was even more reason for mutual defence against the common enemy. Not surprisingly, these deep loyalties came with the Ulster migrants when they crossed the sea to Scotland. Collective identity was, if anything, strengthened further by the even greater contemporaneous emigration of their ancestral Catholic enemies to the very same industrializing areas of the western Lowlands.

The main agency for the transmission and consolidation of this identity was the Loyal Orange Order, founded in Armagh in 1795 to defend Protestants against the Catholic secret societies which were becoming aggressively active in the region. The Order was named after King William III, the Prince of Orange, who had secured the future of the Reformed Faith in Ireland by his famous victory at the Battle of the Boyne in 1690. The organization was based on a hierarchical system of lodges, ranging from local, district and counties to the National Grand Lodge of all Ireland at the pinnacle of the structure. The cohesion of the organization was further enhanced by an elaborate system of grips, degrees, sign and passwords which ensured security, developed a sense of collective brotherhood and was based on the ritual of earlier Protestant secret societies and Freemasonry. The Order proved hugely popular and spread very quickly across Ulster, with 315 lodges founded only a year after the first was established. Equally importantly, they were able to prove their militant anti-Catholicism by helping to crush the 1798 Rebellion in the north through joining the Yeomanry as well as special bodies like the Orange Volunteers.

The Order's expansion in early nineteenth-century Scotland was at first somewhat less spectacular, but by 1830 lodges were well established in Galloway, Ayrshire and Glasgow. Of course not all Orangemen were Irish Protestants and not all Irish Protestants became members of the Orange Order. Nevertheless, they seem to have been the backbone of the movement until at least the 1850s and beyond and their children and grandchildren played a significant role thereafter in maintaining the tradition. The correlation between areas of Orange strength and Irish Protestant settlement is very striking. For instance, all six Glasgow lodges in the 1830s were located in the weaving district of Calton, where significant numbers of Ulster Protestants had settled. The identification with the 'old country' was made apparent later in the century through lodge names. Among many examples were 'Antrim True Blues' LOL 78, Glasgow, Enniskillen 'True Blues' LOL 155, Paisley, and 'Sons of Ulster' LOL 348, Port Glasgow. By the later nineteenth century membership of an Orange lodge had become a family tradition in many working-class communities, with a son joining his father's lodge when reaching adulthood. The bonds were enhanced as many lodges took on a welfare function and as Orangeism influenced the basic rituals of life. Weddings were celebrated in the local Orange Hall, and Orange funerals, with the brethren acting as pallbearers in full regalia, became a recognized part of the culture.

But the public face of Orangeism in Scotland remained confrontational with Irish Catholics either through the celebration of the Boyne anniversary by means of a procession or 'walk' on the 12th of July, intended to demonstrate Protestant ascendancy, or by violent affrays and faction fights with their hereditary enemies. Sectarian violence was not common in nineteenth-century Scotland, partly because the authorities were often quick to ban Orange parades if they disturbed the public peace, and the Scottish judiciary (unlike its Ulster counterpart) was quite prepared to hand down exemplary sentences to troublemakers, no matter what their religious allegiances. When 300 Orangemen returning from a march were attacked at Airdrie and routed by a large body of Catholics in 1857, the 12th of July parades were banned for a decade in Lanarkshire. Earlier, in 1834 in the same town, Sir Archibald Alison, Sheriff of Lanarkshire, unmoved by the Orangemen's protestations of loyalty to the constitution, intervened at the head of a troop of dragoons to prevent an Irish Protestant march, dispersed the crowd and led 28 prisoners back to Glasgow. The ringleaders were later sentenced to transportation. Where incidents did occur, however, they tended to be endemic, for the most part, in areas of the Lanarkshire coalfield (such as Coatbridge and the surrounding district) and Ayrshire in the middle decades of the nineteenth century where Irish Protestants and Catholics lived cheek by jowl and where immigration was running at high levels because of the impact of the Great Famine in the 1840s and the rapid expansion in Scotland in mining and metal manufacture.

The communal identity of Irish Protestants and the association of many with the Orange Order was further strengthened with the influx of skilled men from Belfast to the Clyde shipyards from the 1860s. Much of this was a form of temporary migration, as workers moved back and forth depending on employment opportunities. This in itself helped to maintain close ties between Ulster and Glasgow. But there was also considerable permanent movement which generated a marked increase in the number of Orange lodges in the shipbuilding districts of Partick, Govan and Whiteinch. Further expansion took place downriver, with new foundations in the 1880s and 1890s at Clydebank, Port Glasgow and Greenock. It was no accident that the local Orange Hall in Clydebank was built outside the main gates of John Brown's, the town's world-famous shipbuilding firm. By 1914, the three largest Orange jurisdictions in the country were located in the shipbuilding centres of Greenock, Partick and Govan. Their connections with Irish Protestantism were strong. The 'Scottish Orange Notes', regularly published in the *Belfast Weekly News* in the 1920s, record the many prominent Orangemen of Irish birth who had migrated to Scotland in the last four decades of the nineteenth century. The lodges could provide a range of personal contacts and initial support for migrants, which goes a long way to explaining their appeal. Significantly, Orangeism was weak in east coast cities such as Dundee because there the immigrant community was overwhelmingly Roman Catholic and the Protestant Irish were thin on the ground.

That the Ulster heritage had not been forgotten was powerfully demonstrated during the Irish Home Rule crisis in the years before the Great War. Grass-roots alliances between the Orange Order and the Conservative Party to vigorously oppose Home Rule were established. Many rallies were held, of which the most impressive was that addressed in a packed St Andrew's Hall in Glasgow in October 1913 by Sir Edward Carson. The Ulster Covenant was signed by 'the Ulstermen of Glasgow', pledging resistance to Home Rule. An extremist preacher, the Revd James Brisby, himself an Ulsterman, of the 'Christian Union Church' located in the Irish Protestant stronghold of Calton, organized a contingent of volunteers drawn from Glasgow, Rutherglen and Clydebank, who paraded in public and were committed to the protection of Protestant rights in the north of Ireland. The movement had earlier attracted more numerical support with the establishment of the Harland & Wolff shipyard in Govan in 1912, which brought numerous workers from Belfast to the Clyde when it opened. With hindsight, however, these events were the high-water mark of militant Irish Protestant activity in Scotland. After the Great War, Ulster Protestant migration to Scotland slowed to a trickle and as a result the links to the old country inevitably became more tenuous. The fact that the recent Troubles in Northern Ireland have not engulfed the west of Scotland or stirred the same depth of emotions as the issue of Irish Home Rule earlier in the century is testimony to that fact. Yet not all the traditional loyalties have disappeared. As Graham Walker points out, 'the tribal folk memory still counts for something and Orange songs and banners and slogans spell out the claim to an indivisible bond between Scotland and Ulster for those who desire, or think it important to hear it'.[6]

Lithuanians

The mecca for the vast majority of European migrants in the nineteenth century was the United States, the land of economic opportunity and cheap land. Passage to America was now less costly, speedier and more reliable because of the intercontinental transport revolution associated with the steamship and the railway. Not all emigrants, however, from central and eastern Europe travelled directly to the USA. Some used the United Kingdom as a staging post and found it cheaper to land at Hull or Leith, travel by train to Liverpool or Glasgow, and then take ship again for the Atlantic crossing. A minority of these 'transmigrants' stayed on and established new migrant communities. The two most important groups in Scotland were the Lithuanians and the Jews. Lithuanians originated from the area bordered by the Baltic Sea on the west and German Prussia to the south. Lithuania was an ancient independent nation, but by the later eighteenth century it had been swallowed up in the Russian Empire. Nevertheless, the people maintained their national identity and, despite relentless persecution, were still loyal to the Catholic religion which the migrants took with them to Scotland.

The movement to Scotland was a small part of a much greater exodus from Lithuania between the 1860s and 1914 which resulted in a total emigration of between one-quarter and one-third of the national population. The emancipation of serfs in the Russian Empire in 1861 indirectly worsened conditions for the Lithuanian peasantry by driving up both rents and taxation levels. These economic pressures were accompanied by a ruthless programme of Russification which attacked all facets of Lithuanian culture, imposed the Orthodox faith as the state religion and enforced compulsory military service in the Tsarist army on the population. These pressures were enough to generate huge increases in emigration which were also fuelled by the immensely greater economic opportunities that were available in western Europe and North America. The major Scottish coal- and ironmasters, such as the Bairds and Merry and Cunninghame, were already recruiting young men from Lithuania for unskilled work in the pits and at the blast furnaces in the 1870s and 1880s. Company housing was often provided and, when the labourers had saved enough after a few years, wives, families and sweethearts were brought over to Scotland to join them. So too were male friends and relatives who were attracted by the glowing accounts in emigrant letters of the rewards to be had working in Scottish industry. Witnesses to the Royal Commission on Alien Immigration described how 'the letters tell them what an Eldorado this country is' and that 'this was the place for good wages'. Even in 1886, when the Census of Wages confirmed that Scotland in general was still a low-wage area in coal mining and pig-iron manufacture, the sectors where most Lithuanians worked offered good earnings above the average for the UK. Against this background, immigration from the Baltic accelerated so that by 1914 there were nearly 8,000 Lithuanians settled in towns in Lanarkshire, Ayrshire, Fife and West Lothian. It was common for the first arrivals who worked in the pits to club together to bring over more young men from other communities in Lithuania. In addition, some established immigrants assisted the migration of men of working age in order to profit from their labour in Scotland.

The first reaction of the native Scots workers to this swelling tide of alien immigration was one of bitter hostility. Keir Hardie himself claimed that 'foreigners' had been brought into the Ayrshire coalfield to drive down wages, break strikes, reduce working conditions and dilute the power of the unions. Friction intensified after 1900 as depression in the coal trade caused successive reductions in miners' wages while Lithuanian immigration in an over-supplied labour market continued. There was indeed clear evidence of Lithuanian labour being used to undercut wages and break strikes in Lanarkshire in the 1890s. But this phase of industrial friction was short-lived. Pressure emerged from the Lithuanian community itself to defuse the emerging tensions. A minority had already become committed to socialism in their native land and in 1903 a branch of the Marxist Lithuanian Social Democratic Party was founded in Bellshill in Lanarkshire, one of the main areas of Lithuanian settlement in Scotland. The arrival of political refugees from the 1905 Revolution in Russia may also have encouraged a more class-based approach to community relations. Gradually the Lithuanian presence in the mining unions increased, even at a time when fellow countrymen were still being used by the coal companies to break strikes.

An important sign of their involvement was the decision by the Miners' Federation of Great Britain to print its rules in Lithuanian and soon afterwards to extend full union benefits to all immigrants. Over just two decades the unskilled Lithuanian labourers had learnt to identify with the interest of the Scots workers for their own economic advantage, and they gave a convincing display of their loyalty to the union cause when they took part in the national miners' strike of 1912. This commitment to the solidarity of all workers undoubtedly reduced any inter-communal tensions which might have built up in the years before the Great War.

However, assimilation was initially confined to the realms of politics and industrial relations; in all other spheres the Lithuanian communities were mainly separate and distinct. While they did not live in ghettos, the tendency to cluster in particular streets of a few towns in central Scotland made them easily visible. The women and children stood out because of their colourful dress. Virtually all marriages in the first generation also took place within the community. Lithuanians attended the local Catholic churches, but they also developed the St Casimir Society, an organization unique to their community. Within the home, the language, food, dress, furnishing arrangements and even the celebration of Christmas were all Lithuanian. Mothers were crucial to the maintenance of the Lithuanian identity by teaching language, songs and folklore to their children. Women also played a key role in the social functions of the community and eventually in 1929 founded the Lithuanian Catholic Women's Society to promote the national culture. Two weekly newspapers had appeared in Lithuanian by 1914 and they did much to foster identity by featuring news and comment about the homeland and publicizing information on topics as varied as religious events, cultural societies, dances and musical evenings. Lithuanian clergy held services in the national language. The community also developed a number of insurance and friendly societies. There was a vibrant social life. Orchestral concerts (the immigrants had their own orchestra), choral evenings and dramatic presentations were held on a regular basis. This culminated in 1905 in a Lithuanian Festival in the City Hall, Glasgow, which included displays of folk dancing and choirs singing traditional Lithuanian songs. The immigrants had their own shops, providing such favourite foods as rye bread and sausages. It seemed a confident, self-contained community with a strong sense of national cohesion and cultural identity.

In the space of the next two generations much of this disappeared. An early indicator of faltering confidence was that a growing number of Lithuanians abandoned their names, sometimes for anglicized versions, but more often for new names which bore no relation at all to the old. For instance, 'Lesaukas' became 'Smith' and 'Ramkevicius' was transformed into 'Black'. In the early days of immigration some Lithuanians had had anglicized names imposed on them by Scots foremen and bosses for easier recognition. But now, and especially in the 1930s, Lithuanians themselves were choosing to remove one of the key hallmarks of their own identity. This was in contrast to the Italians in Scotland, who tended to retain their names, except in the years of strong anti-Italian feeling during and after the Second World War when some changing did take place. The first-generation Lithuanian young men had avoided intermarriage with the Scots and brought their partners from their native land. But intermarriage soon became much more common between the wars. For the new generation the school was also an important agency of assimilation because it taught not only a new language but also a new culture. Second-generation Lithuanians recall that, when returning home from school, they stepped back into 'a foreign country' where Lithuanian alone was spoken. Unlike the large Jewish community in the Gorbals in Glasgow, where education was provided in three Jewish schools with Jewish teachers, the dispersed Lithuanian population had no option but to attend local schools where the language, values, history and literature of the host community alone were taught. Inevitably, the immigrant identity came under pressure, not least from the peer pressure of school friends as the new generation grew into young adulthood.

Dress, food and leisure pursuits were all affected. Assimilation also accelerated as some Lithuanians gained entry into higher education. In Lanarkshire alone, almost 20 became teachers before 1939 and, significantly, nearly half of these were women. Some of the old established communities in the 'Lithuanian streets' of the industrial towns were disrupted by the inter-war local authority house-building programmes and the dispersal of families which took place as a result. But the process of assimilation was far from complete by the 1940s. Lithuanian cultural events, concerts and religious services still flourished. The highlight of the year was the national pilgrimage to the Catholic grotto at Carfin, where many appeared in Lithuanian dress and the ceremonials were punctuated by the powerful and emotive singing of national hymns from a congregation which had come in large numbers from all over central Scotland. However, Ellen O'Donnell, the most recent historian of the community, is in little doubt that much of that spirit had started to disappear by the 1990s. Numbers at the celebrations have dwindled to a few and those who do come belong in the main to an older generation. What was a vibrant and distinctive community in the first half of the century may well be on the verge of extinction in modern Scotland.

The almost total submergence of an ethnic group within the main-stream host culture is not inevitable. Both the Jews and the Catholic Irish have demonstrated that it is possible to achieve integration without complete assimilation. Why were the Lithuanians unable to do so? The small size of the community (at less than 8,000 in 1914) was one factor. A sharp drop in these numbers occurred in 1917 when over 1,000 men were compulsorily repatriated under the Anglo-Russian Military Agreement to fight as 'Russian subjects' on the eastern front. In the 1920s there was a further haemorrhage as a result of emigration to the USA and return migration to the now independent Lithuania. Only after the Second World War were there some new arrivals in Scotland, when Lithuania was annexed by the Russians. Here was an obvious contrast with the Irish, whose sense of identity was constantly refreshed and renewed by a continuing flow of fresh migrants over several gener-ations from the early 1800s through until the 1950s. The Scottish Lithuanians, on the other hand, were effectively isolated after 1920 because of the restrictions on alien immigration which followed the Great War and the deteriorating economic circumstances of Scotland in the inter-war period which made it a much less attractive destination for their fellow countrymen.

The community was also weakened by both internal and external pressures. Behind the façade of community cohesion there were deep tensions between the minority of immigrants who had socialist sympa-thies and who became associated with the Lithuanian Socialist Feder-ation of Great Britain (itself linked to the broader British movement) and the 'conservative' majority who looked to the Catholic Church for leadership and guidance. These stresses did not result in an absolute split, but they did diminish ethnic solidarity. This was put to the test most severely during the economic crisis of the 1930s. In the worst years of the Depression, areas of Lithuanian settlement suffered terribly from unemployment. It was reckoned, for instance, that Bellshill in

Lanarkshire, where many lived, had a male unemployment rate of 70 per cent in 1932. Unlike the Italian community, who could find work for their fellow countrymen in their own shops and cafés, most Lithuanians were confronted by the bleak prospect of the dole and long-term unemployment. They were likely also to suffer discrimination in some areas of the labour market because of their Catholicism and their distinctive identity. Many families still had memories of being described by officialdom as 'alien' and experience of friends and relatives being repatriated during the Great War. The realistic strategy in such circumstances seemed to be to submerge their identity, keep a low profile and become part of the Scottish community. By changing their name, their original nationality could be concealed and the chances of securing a job improved. It is significant that name changes became much more common in the Catholic marriage records of the 1930s. Many Lithuanians were adapting to life in Scotland by becoming invisible.

Italians

Before the later nineteenth century, Italians were to be found in Scotland, but until the 1880s they were few in number and consisted mainly of a few highly skilled craftsmen, itinerant musicians and street pedlars. As late as 1881 there were only 328 people of Italian birth recorded in the Scottish census. Yet, on the eve of the Great War, not only had numbers swollen to around 4,500 but an identifiable Italian community had emerged. Indeed, to this day a large number of Scots Italian families can trace their roots to this phase of immigration between 1880 and 1914. In 1908 a newspaper, suitably titled *La Scozia*, was published to serve the new arrivals, though it survived for only a year. Earlier, in 1891, the *Societa de Mutuo Soccorso* was founded to provide welfare assistance and financial aid. Italian 'colonies' grew up in the Gorbals and Garnethill in Glasgow, in the Edinburgh Grassmarket and Aberdeen's Castlegate. The biggest Italian community in Scotland, of around 3,000 people (and the third largest in the UK), was located in Glasgow. But one of the major features of the Italian migration was dispersal rather than concentration and this pattern differentiated them from the other immigrant groups considered in this chapter.

The Italians in Scotland quickly became committed to the catering trade, with families owning and running ice-cream parlours and fish and chip shops. Built into this distinctive structure was a need for the businesses to disperse geographically into other localities and new towns in order to survive and to accommodate the opening of new shops by members of the next generation or by more recent migrants belonging to the extended kindred living in Italy. The Italians brought new consumer delights to the working-class areas of Scotland. The 'pokey hats' (ice-cream cones) were universally popular and the fish supper became the original 'fast food' of the common man. The cafés flourished against a social background of steadily rising real incomes for those in employment between the 1880s and 1920s. There were now many more people with a little extra to spend on reasonably priced luxuries. The cafés were able to fulfil that demand because not only did they stock confectionery and cigarettes as well as ice-cream but they and the fish and chip shops stayed open late into the evening, long after their Scottish competitors had closed for the night. They also had an enormous attraction for young people who wanted somewhere to meet away from the family home.

This did not escape criticism from some quarters. In evidence to a Parliamentary Committee on Sunday Trading in 1906 it was suggested that ice-cream parlours might be 'morally contaminating', since 'young people of both sexes congregate there after legitimate hours and sometimes misbehave themselves . . . that is the one great attraction of the ice-cream shops and not the ingredient itself'.[7] The police also insisted to the same committee that the standard of behaviour in these shops was 'acceptable only to their alien owners and to people of loose moral habits'.[8] On the other hand, the Italians attracted important allies from the powerful and influential temperance lobbies, who considered that their cafés offered a real and attractive alternative to the destructive alcoholic temptations of the public house. The fish and chip shops and the pubs were actually more complementary than this. By the 1920s it was common to buy fish suppers when closing time came at 10 p.m. and then to eat them in the streets, a tradition which has been maintained by successive generations of thirsty and hungry Scots to the present day. The food was not always consumed peacefully, especially on Saturday nights. Bruno Sereni, who arrived in Glasgow in 1919, recalled in his book, *They Took the Low Road*, that fighting in the shop was not unusual. The first words of English he ever learnt to say were 'big fight in shop' when he was sent to the local police station as a boy to ask for help after yet another affray in his father's café.

Modern Italian migration to Scotland can be traced back to the *figurinai* who settled in London from the 1850s. The *figurinai* were itinerant makers of statuettes and figurines who travelled across the country in small groups of five to seven men, selling their wares to the local people. Some worked their way north to Scotland in the search for new business, and a few settled there. This established an important migrant stream directly from Italy. It was in this period that the first links were started with villages such as Barga in Lucca province and the communities in the Abruzzi in the south from which numerous Scots Italian families migrated during the next 100 years. The connection was enhanced by the *padroni* (employers or patrons) system. The *padroni* brought over new migrants, paid their fares and then gave them employment. For instance, Leopold Guliani, by 1900 the wealthiest Italian in Scotland, paid the passage of many young boys from his native village of Barga, who then worked in his great ice-cream empire. These young men in turn aspired to their own businesses when they grew to adulthood and their success stimulated further waves of chain migration through their family and local networks in Italy. At first ice-cream was sold from barrows and hand-carts, and only gradually did cafés become more common. But investing in a barrow, sometimes with the help of a benefactor (normally a relative or employer) who would later be repaid from the earnings of the business, was much less costly than leasing a shop and it ensured that many more were able to establish an independent operation in these early years of settlement. But this could be achieved only through hard and continuous toil. Federico Pontiero of Cambuslang recalled:

Aye, it was heavy, heavy work and it was quite a wee bit hard life tae build up the business. When I did come here the day start seven in the mornin, didna finish till one o'clock, maybe two o'clock in the mornin' and that was for eight solid year. There were one night we went to the pictures, the three o' us and when we went back home, they told us, 'No more pictures!' We hadna a night off nor nothing. I mind o' Mr Rinaldi, I think he was the first Italian settled in Cambuslang, he used to go down the Clyde there and cut the ice. They cut the ice in the Clyde at that time so it must have been an aufu' number of year ago because I never seen a Clyde frozen since! (laughs) It was breakin' ice off for the ice-cream. Aye it was a struggle, you know, it wasna money made easy I assure you.[9]

Later, when shops became more common than itinerant selling, the more affluent Italians would open cafés, stock them and then sell them on as going concerns, allowing the value to be paid back by weekly or monthly instalments.

The business life of the community was based on trust, family loyalty and personal knowledge, which were the essential factors for economic success in a strange land. This in turn conditioned the nature of migration in the future. To a much greater extent than any of the other ethnic groups considered in this chapter, the Italians who settled in Scotland from 1870 came from a very limited number of locations in their native land. The migrant streams consisted of members of the same extended families, neighbourhoods and villages associated with the pioneering settlers of the later nineteenth century. Two distinct areas around 250 miles apart were most important: the province of Lucca in northern Italy and Frosinone in Lazio, south of Rome. A long tradition of temporary migration in these areas facilitated permanent movement which became more necessary in the last quarter of the nineteenth century as rapid population increase brought an archaic agrarian system to the verge of crisis. One Italian lady who moved to Scotland as a child in the early twentieth century recalled the countryside of her native land, 'full of grapevines, lots of trees and animals and chickens'. But the poverty was 'terrible', and in her view all the migrants were 'glad to escape the hard life they had over in Italy'.[10] However, migration from Italy fell to a trickle as a result of the Aliens Act of 1919 and the opposition to emigration by the fascist government in Italy during the inter-war years. The Scottish community therefore stabilized at around 5,500 people. It attracted much less hostility from the native Scots than did the Catholic Irish and Lithuanians. The Italians offered a popular service. They were few in number and virtually all worked in businesses owned by Italians. They therefore posed little threat either to native workers or to wage levels. The community was not concentrated by the 1930s in any single large Italian colony which might have attracted hostile attention, but was to be found the length and breadth of the land. It was an introspective community which, outside working hours, had few social contacts with the rest of Scottish society, though by the 1930s a few Italians were finding their way to university. Oral evidence from the time suggests that Italian was spoken at home, food was in the Italian style, children were expected to marry Italians and strong parental control ensured that they did so throughout the 1920s, 1930s and beyond. The social life of the girls of the family was especially restricted. Most time was spent in the shops because of the long working hours, and the back shops became the meeting points for friends and relatives, where the men would gather for card games and to hear the latest gossip from the village back home. Increasing prosperity meant that visits to the old country could become more common. For many the hope, and for some the reality, was eventually to return to Italy, and therefore any attempt at assimilation into Scottish society seemed pointless.

This sense of Italian identity was strengthened even further by the impact of the policies of the fascist government in the 1920s. Mussolini wished to embrace all the emigrants from the motherland as full members of a reborn Italian state. *Fasci*, fascist clubs, were established in the emigrant communities, led by prominent local figures and army veterans who had served in Italian regiments during the Great War. The *fascio* in Glasgow was founded in 1922 and over time developed a remarkable number of social and cultural activities, including Italian evening classes for children and a Union of Italian Traders which had a membership of 1,000 by 1939 and brought the small shopkeepers and retailers together for the first time as an occupational association. A telling illustration of the new vibrancy of the community was the opening in 1935 of the *Casa d'Italia* in the prestigious area of Park Circus in Glasgow as a centre for the large number of cultural, literary, social and professional activities that were now taking place under the sponsorship of the fascist clubs. There were other clubs in Edinburgh, Aberdeen and Dundee, with a network of representatives also strung out across the country. They were hugely popular. A 1933 Italian government census indicated that almost 50 per cent of those who responded in Scotland were registered Fascist Party members. The annual reunion of the 'Italian fascisti' was held on 15 August, the Feast of the Day of Assumption, when Italians from all over the country met to celebrate their nationhood. Undoubtedly the fascist government's public concern for the exiled communities had a deep emotional impact on those emigrants who had felt abandoned by their motherland in the past but who had not yet become assimilated into Scottish society. Much of the attraction of fascism was therefore clearly patriotic rather than ideological in nature.

Nevertheless, the community's open support for the fascist movement meant that it paid a terrible price when Mussolini declared war on Britain on 10 June 1940. A few hours after his announcement, crowds went on the rampage, in Glasgow, Edinburgh, Falkirk, Greenock, Port

Glasgow, Irvine, Hamilton, Stonehaven and many other places. The windows of Italian cafés were smashed, stock ransacked and furnishings destroyed. The rioting occurred throughout the UK but was especially widespread and vicious in Scotland, which may partly be explained by the anti-Catholicism which flourished in some areas in the 1930s. In one of the most serious disturbances in Edinburgh, police had to baton-charge a crowd of around 1,000 twice before they dispersed. The Italians were shocked and bewildered at the intensity of the hatred. They had lived at peace with their neighbours for generations and many had been born in Scotland. As one witness, Dominic Crolla, recalled, 'It seemed as if the work of fifty or sixty years had vanished into thin air.'[11] The orgy of destruction was followed by the internment of Italian men between the ages of 17 and 60, many of whom were transported overseas, some as far away as Australia. The most tragic incident in the entire history of the Italians in Scotland came about because of this policy. On 2 July 1940 the *Arandora Star* carrying 712 Italian 'enemy aliens' to Canada was torpedoed in the Atlantic by a U-boat. Altogether, 450 internees drowned. The dead from Scotland were mainly harmless café owners, small shopkeepers and young shop workers.

A disaster on this scale for a time destroyed the self-confidence of the community which had flourished in the 1930s. Business which had been severely damaged had to be rebuilt from scratch after 1945. Terri Colpi notes that 'Many Italians were reluctantly forced to accept that it was not a good thing to be Italian and sought to mask their ethnicity.'[12] Naturalization figures were at their highest in the 1950s. The change is evident in the career of the distinguished and influential Scots Italian architect, Giacomo (Jack) Coia. Before 1939 Coia designed several Catholic churches in the west of Scotland in which Italianate detail was prominent both internally and externally, a demonstration of pride and confidence in his origins. Those buildings he worked on in the 1950s were devoid of Italian influence and reflected the changing environment of the post-war period.

In the last few decades, assimilation has intensified. Most of the younger generation now marry Scots. Moreover, unlike the pattern in London and elsewhere in England, there has been no significant post-war 'new' Italian migration to Scotland. The expansion of higher education also encouraged a large-scale movement of the able young into the professions of law, medicine and teaching. As a result, integration has occurred but has not eliminated a sense of Italian identity. Throughout the 1950s, 1960s and 1970s, Italian priests ministered to the Glasgow Italian community, and during the same period the Dante Alighieri Society had a number of thriving branches and did much to maintain an interest in Italian culture. Business networks still exist among restaurant, hotel, shop and café owners of Italian descent. Most importantly of all, family links with Italy have been maintained and even strengthened through modern air transport which allows regular travel from Scotland to those same small communities in the north and south of Italy from which the first immigrants had come, over a century ago.

The Jews in Glasgow

It was only after the 1870s that Jewish migration to Scotland reached significant levels. The Jewish Scottish community in that decade numbered less than 1,000, was concentrated in the cities of Glasgow, Edinburgh and Dundee, and consisted of families who had achieved considerable economic success in merchanting, tailoring, the jewellery trade, the manufacture of fancy goods and a range of other business activities. This pattern changed abruptly in the later nineteenth century, the period of mass Jewish migration from central and eastern Europe. This was stimulated in large part by a wave of anti-Semitic pogroms in the Russian Empire, encouraged also by the hope of economic improvement in the West and facilitated by the faster and cheaper mass travel made possible by the railway and steamship. In all, several million Jews were on the move from the 'Pale', the Jewish settlement area in eastern Europe. The vast majority were intent on migrating to the United States, *die goldene medine*, the 'Golden Land', and only a relatively small number settled in Britain. But the UK was used as a staging post on the journey from the Baltic ports to America and the Hull–Liverpool and Leith–Glasgow railway links became important in carrying immigrants overland. There were Jews crossing Scotland on their way to the USA as early as the 1860s, and numbers increased significantly in the next few decades. Some decided to stay on and not continue across the Atlantic and, by the end of the 1880s, the main centre of Jewish settlement in Glasgow had shifted from the prosperous area of Garnethill in the West End to the Gorbals, south of the Clyde. In 1914 there were around 10,000 Jews in the city, with most of them living in the Gorbals area. This represented more than 90 per cent of the Jewish community in Scotland, with smaller pockets in Edinburgh,

Dundee, Falkirk, Greenock and Ayr. The passage of the 1905 Aliens Act rigorously limited further large-scale immigration from eastern Europe and curtailed the expansion of the Scottish Jewish population. There was a further trickle of refugees from Nazi persecution in the 1930s but this was probably counterbalanced by a steady emigration of families who were already settled in Scotland to the United States and the English cities.

The new arrivals were quite different from the established Jewish communities. In the main they were poor, Yiddish-speaking Jews of Russian and Polish extraction who could speak little or no English. The Gorbals district attracted them because it was close to the railways and shipping of the Clyde and because housing was relatively cheap. Above all, as the Jewish colony developed there, it became an enclave which could provide welcome, support and employment for the tired and disorientated immigrants who had just arrived from the East. As Ralph Glasser recalled:

The new arrival was quickly spotted. A man with a week's growth of beard, eyes bleary from wakefulness in his long journey, would shuffle wearily through Gorbals Street with his *peckel*, his belongings, strapped in a misshapen suitcase, listening for the familiar tones of this lingua-Judaica from the East European Marches, and approach such a group with the sureness of a questing bloodhound. He would fumble in the pocket of a shapeless coat and show them a much-thumbed envelope.

'*Lansmann! Sogmer, wo treffich dos?*' ('Fellow countryman. Tell me. Where can I find this address/person?')[13]

The Gorbals soon had two synagogues, a *Talmud Torah* school for religious education and a Zionist Reading Room. There were more than 60 Jewish stores and workshops in the area. Chaim Bermant's description of the district before the Second World War illustrated its Jewish ethos:

There were Yiddish posters on the hoardings, Hebrew lettering on the shops, Jewish faces, Jewish butchers, Jewish bakers with Jewish bread, and Jewish grocers with barrels of herring in the doorway . . . One heard Yiddish in the streets, more so in fact than English, and one encountered figures who would not have been out of place in Barovke.[14]

The growth of such a large and well-defined Jewish colony in the heart of Scotland's biggest city did not, however, unleash a wave of anti-Semitism, though there was certainly some harassment, prejudice and discrimination. Ralph Glasser was brought up in the old Gorbals and experienced 'relentless' persecution at school. His father also advised him to keep his head down so as not to attract attention which could lead to intimidation: 'He handed down to me the lesson of the Pale.'[15] Few tenements were occupied solely by Jews, since a mixed building 'was less likely to attract the impulsive anti-semitic attack'.[16] There were public criticisms of the Jews for violating the Christian Sabbath and attempts were made by some Presbyterian churches to carry out missionary work among the Jewish young in the hope of converting them. Jewish employers of immigrant 'sweatshop' labour which worked excessively long hours for pitifully low wages attracted both hostility and condemnation from trade unions. In addition, before the Great War, it was said to be common knowledge in Glasgow that some house factors were unwilling to let accommodation to Jewish families. But all of this, of course, pales into insignificance when compared to the ingrained and vicious anti-Semitism of eastern Europe from where the migrants had escaped. Glasser emphasized that until the advent of Mosley's Blackshirts there was 'little organized molestation' of Jews, which he attributed in large part to 'the quiet influence of the Christian clergy'. He even suggested that the Irish Catholics, who made up the other large ethnic group in the Gorbals, had easier relationships with the 'Sheenys' (as they called the Jews) than with the Scots Protestants.'[17]

The absence of widespread native hostility was due to a number of factors. The tensions over the threat of 'sweated labour', apart, most Jews did not compete directly with Scots in the labour market. The Jewish immigrant economy also was remarkably self-contained. The majority ran or worked in Jewish-owned businesses as tailors, cigarette makers, hawkers, pedlars and travellers. Films such as *Fiddler on the Roof* portray the Jews from the East as poor peasant farmers. In fact, large numbers of those who came to Scotland were from towns and cities. They possessed skills developed in the urban economy in Europe which they were able to utilize when they settled in Glasgow. There was no real wish, therefore, despite their poverty, to compete alongside the Irish and the Lithuanians for menial work in the docks, mines and steel mills. In addition, there developed a remarkable network of Jewish welfare schemes to support new immigrants so that they were not seen to be a drain on the Poor Law and other public welfare agencies. In part this was due to the initiative of the more affluent and longer-established community and their concern for their own people. But there was also some tension between the two groups. It was feared that the new arrivals might stimulate anti-Semitism and increase the financial burden on those already settled. Despite this, through their efforts and the self-help of the immigrants themselves, a number of relief organizations were set up in the 1890s and 1900s, including the Boot and Clothing Guild, the Sick Visiting Association and the *Hacknosas Orchin* or Society for Welcoming Strangers. Another vital influence was the assistance given by the Glasgow Hebrew Benevolent Loan Society to enable Jewish pedlars and travellers to expand their businesses by making interest-free loans available to them.

Like the Catholic Irish, however, the Jewish community was far from being insulated from the rest of Scottish society. Zionism, still in its infancy in the early 1900s, attracted a great deal of support and had close links with the Labour Party. Other Glasgow Jews were active in the ILP and the Socialist Labour Party. The Bolshevik Revolution in Russia, with its promise of an end to despotism and class exploitation, inspired many in these groups. One of the most celebrated political figures to emerge from this background was Emmanuel (Manny) Shinwell, later one of the Clydesiders, a government minister and eventually a life peer. By the 1920s and 1930s there were also signs of social and cultural assimilation. Yiddish, once spoken in most houses, was dying. Yiddish newspapers folded, one after another, until finally, in 1928, only the *Jewish Echo* published in English remained. There was more evidence of upward mobility than in any other Scottish immigrant community of the time. By the 1914–18 war, the great Jewish tradition in medicine in Scotland was already being established. In the early 1920s there were nearly three dozen Jewish medical students at Glasgow University alone and others at Edinburgh. As they moved up the social ladder the Jews did not experience the same kind of systematic discrimination that was the lot of many Scots of Irish Catholic descent in the inter-war period. Nevertheless, social prejudice still flourished. Some bowling clubs refused to accept Jewish members, and it was because of entrenched discrimination that Jewish golfers founded their own club at Bonnyton in 1928. But all this reflected the growing economic success of the community. By this period, some of the best-known businesses in Glasgow were Jewish-owned, with Frutins in the theatre and entertainments industry, Morrisons in dress-making and Goldbergs in retail trading among the most prominent. The steady movement of Jews into the lower-middle classes was illustrated in the drift from the Gorbals to the richer suburbs to the south of the city, a process that reached its climax in the 1960s with the massive redevelopment of the Gorbals. The Glasgow Jewish community of the late twentieth century still maintains a wide range of religious welfare and cultural associations, but it is now centred on Giffnock, one of the most affluent areas of the city, and its membership is drawn mainly from the business and professional classes.

22

Scottish Women:
Family, Work and Politics

I

The place of women in Victorian society was based on the assumption
that they would marry and take responsibility for home and family.
The middle-class ideal of 'the angel in the house' was complemented by
the working-class expectation that women would acquire the necessary
domestic skills to be a good wife, mother and home-maker. Whatever
the realities, these social assumptions affected all aspects of a woman's
life by conditioning the jobs they did, the wages they earned, and the
education they received. In the 1860s around four-fifths of Scotswomen
in their early fifties were married, a figure that had altered little by the
1930s. But, though common, marriage was far from being universal.
Men tended to die earlier than women and so widows were numerous.
The 1911 census recorded that 12 per cent of the female population
over 25 were widows. Many of them had been left with families
to support after the premature death of a young husband who had
succumbed to one of the many endemic diseases of the time. Single
parenthood is therefore by no means unique to the later twentieth
century. However, normally it was death of a partner rather than
divorce that ended a marriage. Only 142 individuals sued for divorce
in 1900, and as late as the 1960s there were only 2,000 divorces a year
in Scotland.

Much more significant in increasing the pool of the unmarried was
celibacy, which varied considerably between regions and classes. The
key factor in this was the balance between men and women of marriageable age in the population (the sex ratio). Where the ratio was out of
balance, the availability of partners might reduce the frequency of
marriage. In Scotland women have outnumbered men throughout the
period considered in this chapter. This was not simply because of higher

levels of male mortality but as a result of the very heavy levels of internal migration and emigration in Scotland. Until the early decades of the twentieth century, young men in their twenties were more likely to migrate than their sisters and in some areas this haemorrhage was so serious that it produced a marked distortion in sex ratios. Most rural regions were affected, but the imbalance was particularly acute in Orkney, Shetland, Caithness and the Highland counties. In many rural parishes there were simply not enough partners for women and spinster-hood was therefore often inevitable. Thus, at the census of 1931, nearly 30 per cent of women aged 50–54 had never been married in the far north and Highland counties, a factor which, as much as large-scale emigration, condemned these regions to an inexorable process of popu-lation decline. In the cities, and especially in the western Lowlands, a better balance between the sexes encouraged a much higher rate of marriage. Even in the urban areas, however, with their large populations of young migrants, celibacy was not uncommon, especially among the middle classes. The long training required of professional men for the church and medicine led to a late age of marriage and households of bachelor brothers and spinster sisters, with the sister taking the place of the wife as manager of the home, were not uncommon. One recent study of the families of Glasgow ministers between 1830 and 1900 reveals that as many as half of the daughters who lived to adulthood never married. Since marriage was regarded by contemporary bourgeois society as an almost compulsory norm, it is easy to imagine the pain, anxiety and even humiliation experienced by many of these women. But the prevalence of spinsterhood and widowhood in all strata of society meant that the conventional image of Victorian households comprising parents and children does need to be qualified to some extent.

Most women, however, did marry and their lives were then dominated by the producing and rearing of children. With an average life-expectancy of 47 years among the working classes in the 1900s, few women would have known life without dependent children in the household. The census data confirm that Scotland in the early twentieth century was a society of large families. In 1911 in the country as a whole when a woman was married at the age of 22 to 26, the average number of children born to her was 5.8. In addition, no less than a fifth of this group had 10 or more children. Significantly, however, there were marked differences between regions, occupations and classes. High average family sizes were common in much of the north-west, parts of

Ayrshire, the central belt and the western parishes of East Lothian, confirming that crofters and miners tended to have large families of seven or more. Workers in heavy industry and shipbuilding averaged over six children, while the family size was slightly lower among textile workers, especially those occupied in woollens in the Borders. By and large, however, the distribution in the number of children across working-class groups was not significantly different, with the great majority of these families averaging out at between five and seven children in the early twentieth century. It goes without saying that this must not only have intensified overcrowding in the single and double rooms in which most working-class Scots lived, but it also placed great pressure on the meagre family budgets with which wives and mothers had to struggle endlessly in order to make ends meet.

Where the distinctions, however, were truly remarkable was between working-class and middle-class family size. In 1900 doctors, lawyers, teachers and ministers all tended to have average families under five. So too did booksellers, fruiterers, clerks, innkeepers and grocers. There were many fewer children in middle-class homes in the suburbs of Glasgow, Dundee and Edinburgh and in small market and country towns than in the mining villages and industrial centres of the central Lowlands. Moreover, the class divide in this most important aspect of life was becoming wider over time. Already by the 1870s, it was more common for wives of professional men to cease child-bearing entirely by their early thirties. For several upper-middle-class groups having children was being concentrated more and more in the early years of marriage and as a result the number of offspring was being steadily reduced. It would be no exaggeration to say that even before the First World War the trend towards the two-child family characteristic of the second half of the twentieth century was already becoming established among such groups as physicians, surgeons and clergymen in advance of the trend becoming common among the population at large. Indeed, by the inter-war period, working-class family size was falling faster than that of the middle classes. Births fell from an annual average of around 131,000 in the 1910s to approximately 90,000 in the 1930s, despite the fact that the number of women in the child-bearing age groups actually increased over the same period. This was a revolutionary development with huge implications for the future development of Scottish society. It was also happening elsewhere in western Europe, though Scotland was among those countries in the vanguard. Demographic historians have traced the origins of this silent revolution to the 1860s, but for the mass of the population it really took effect only from the 1920s. The data published in 1911 showed that women, married between the ages of 22 and 26, had an average of six children. By contrast, women marrying in the 1920s aged between 20 and 24 had on average under three children by the early 1950s. That was the scale of the transformation.

The origins of this so-called 'demographic transition' have long puzzled scholars. The cause cannot have been a sustained increase or decrease in the procreation of children outside marriage. Illegitimacy was certainly common in nineteenth-century Scotland which belied the image of a society firmly shackled by Calvinist orthodoxy and institutions. *The Scotsman* started a national controversy when it reported that illegitimacy levels in Scotland came second in Europe only to those of Austria. This was an exaggerated conclusion, but it was certainly the case that the ratio of illegitimate births was higher than in England and most of Europe and that bastardy was particularly common in parts of the north-east (in the years 1855–60 the percentage of illegitimate births in Banff per 1,000 live births, for example, was no less than 15.4) and in the south-western counties of Ayr and Wigtown. In some rural areas there was an 'illegitimacy subculture' in which bearing children outside marriage did not attract the same social stigma as elsewhere. As the population became urbanized, illegitimacy in Scotland declined in national terms though still surviving in some of the country areas where it had been traditional practice. But illegitimate births were never more than 10 per cent of all births in this period and were also falling in the same way as the overall national trend. Two other possible influences, a rise in the age of marriage and a declining frequency of marriage, also had little impact. Both these measures showed little significant variation. The average age at marriage for women in the 1830s was 25. By 1911 this had risen only slightly to 26, which was not sufficient to affect a woman's child-bearing cycle markedly. If these factors are of minor consequence, the main reason for the dramatic decline in birth rates in many social classes by the 1920s must have been some form of birth control within marriage. Quite simply, birth rates were halved between the late 1870s and the early 1930s because more and more couples decided to have fewer children. This was indeed a historic change within the family. Large families remained common, especially among the Scottish working classes before 1939, but the trend in favour of fewer children was unmistakable and accelerated after the Second World War.

Definitive explanation of this silent revolution in sexual behaviour is still not possible. Artificial contraception may have made some contribution for, by the 1870s, birth control 'appliances' were being marketed in the larger towns. But they probably had little significant effect on the population at large because of cost and availability. The much-publicized trial of Charles Bradlaugh and Annie Besant on a charge of obscenity in 1877 for distributing birth control propaganda also made the use of the rubber sheath better known. The trial itself and the resulting controversy led to the formation of the Malthusian League which sought to give even wider publicity to contraception. On the other hand, there was widespread opposition to artificial contraception from the churches and from some political parties. In 1918 the Church of Scotland demanded that the sale of anti-conception devices be 'rigorously repressed'. The Roman Catholic Church was even more uncompromising and in the 1920s managed to obtain promises from ILP candidates to oppose birth control. Indeed the Scottish Labour movement as a whole was far from supportive of the dissemination of birth control information. In 1927 a majority of Labour councillors in Glasgow voted against allowing the magazine, *Birth Control News*, into the city's public libraries. Leading members of the ILP, including James Maxton, John Wheatley and Stephen Campbell, were among those who campaigned against the provision of medical advice on contraception. As Minister for Health in 1924, for example, the Catholic John Wheatley refused to change existing policy which prohibited doctors or health visitors giving contraceptive advice.

In fact, such evidence as there is on this elusive subject tends to suggest that *artificial* methods of birth control were not widely practised among the mass of the Scottish population before 1939. The best data came from the Royal Commission on Population in 1948. Rosalind Mitchison reckons that the evidence contained in it shows that four-fifths of couples marrying in the later 1930s in the UK who were capable of having large families (that is, excluding those of low fertility) were probably practising contraception. Unskilled workers were least likely to limit births, and contraceptive 'appliances' were more common among the middle and upper classes than among the mass of the population. The Royal Commission had little doubt that throughout the 1920s and 1930s *coitus interruptus* and, to some extent, abstinence were responsible for the steep fall in conceptions.

These conclusions came from a Britain-wide study but with one significant qualification they are also likely to apply to Scotland. Scottish families remained significantly larger than those in England for much of the twentieth century because the middle class was smaller than in England and the decline in fertility was most pronounced initially among the business and professional classes. The Royal Commission evidence confirms that the trend towards smaller families depended on the desire of couples to limit the number of children rather than the ready availability of new contraceptive devices. No costs were attached to 'natural' methods, only the will to use them. In the later nineteenth century, middle-class groups were motivated by rapidly rising material standards and expectations and the increasing outlay necessary to prepare children for careers. From the 1870s, the range of consumer goods and leisure opportunities for the reasonably comfortable among the working classes also expanded as never before. For those in work there was a considerable rise in real incomes, not only in the 1870s and 1880s, but extending into the decades between the world wars: 'this was the era when mangles and gas cookers, bicycles and pianos entered some working-class and many lower-middle-class houses and when those who had a little surplus cash and not too many family responsibilities could begin to enjoy occasional trips by train or to the music-hall and even a week at the seaside'.[1] Also of possible significance in the long term was a decline in mortality among babies. Many pregnancies may have been a strategy to compensate for the large numbers of babies who died in infancy and early childhood for much of this period. High birth rates can be seen as the corollary of high infant death rates. As these were cut back and more children survived into adulthood, parents may have decided to limit births – the 'insurance' of numerous pregnancies was no longer quite so necessary.

The fall in the number of children dying in infancy started to take place only slowly and sporadically at the end of the nineteenth century, and, for some decades later, most families had to suffer the inevitable loss of young brothers and sisters. Only after the Second World War could most mothers reasonably expect that all their children would survive to adulthood. The grim details of the high mortality before that period are evident to this day in the many names recorded on the gravestones of Scottish cemeteries with the brief description 'died in infancy'. For every 1,000 babies born in Scotland in the early 1850s, 150 would die under the age of one. The death rate remained stubbornly high for the rest of the nineteenth century even though mortality in general was in decline. Indeed, in the 1890s it moved to an even higher plateau of 129 per 1,000 in the later part of that decade. Inevitably, there were striking class differences in the incidence of infantile mortality. J. B. Russell, Glasgow's Medical Officer for Health, was able to demonstrate this conclusively from the available statistics: 'In Port Dundas, Brownfield, Gorbals and Cowcaddens, one infant death occurred in every five born compared with one in eleven born in Langside, Mount Florida and Kelvinside, and one in thirteen born in Hillhead, Pollockshields and Strathbungo.'[2] Russell also noted that nearly a third of the children in the city who died before reaching the age of five in the 1890s had lived in houses of one room. At the other end of the social scale, only 2 per cent of deaths under five years of age were in families with homes of five apartments or more. The premature deaths of young children was yet another burden that was borne disproportionately by the poor. As Russell commented in memorable terms: 'There they die, and their little bodies are laid on a table or on the dresser, so as to be somewhat out of the way of their brothers and sisters, who play and sleep, and eat in their ghastly company.'[3]

By the early twentieth century, however, this latter-day 'slaughter of the innocents' was beginning to decline and then it disappeared entirely in subsequent decades. From the peak of 130 children in every 1,000 dying before reaching the age of one, the rate fell to 109 on the eve of the Great War and to 77 by the end of the 1930s. After the Second World War, the number of infant deaths fell steeply once again, reaching 40 per 1,000 in the 1950s, or less than half the rate of the early twentieth century, as antibiotics were introduced for the first time on a wide scale. But by that time the mortality revolution among young children was well under way and its roots must therefore be sought in previous decades.

A crucial factor was the health of mothers. The fall in the infant death rate in the 1900s, for instance, may reflect the fact that many women were becoming better nourished from the 1870s and 1880s, years of cheaper food prices, with more imports from the New World, and hence average increases in real wages. For those families where the breadwinner remained in work, these gains continued into the inter-war period. But improvements were not universal. In the 1950s there was an unexpected rise in certain types of stillbirth and recent medical research has related this to the malnourished condition of mothers born between 1926 and 1937 and whose fathers suffered long-term unemployment during those years of industrial depression. The direct causes of mortality decline also included the control and then the steady reduction of the lethal diseases of childhood, measles, diarrhoea, whooping cough, scarlatina and diphtheria. This was achieved by the provision of free milk and medical inspection in schools and the series of strategies introduced from the later nineteenth century to improve the urban environment through the provision of cleaner water and better sewerage. By the inter-war period, the efforts of doctors, nurses, midwives and health visitors were also beginning to be felt more directly in working-class communities. Even rickets, the classic children's disease of urban malnutrition and deprivation, became less common. By 1950–54 it was affecting less than 1 per cent of school-children in Glasgow.

The trend towards smaller families and the fall in death rates among young children made for a better life in the long term for working-class wives and mothers. But the improvements must also be kept in perspective. Larger families were still common outside the middle classes into the 1930s. Moreover, housing conditions did not change quickly or radically. Until the Second World War and beyond, most Scottish families were reared in very cramped space. In 1911 almost half the population lived in houses with one or two rooms. By 1951 there had been some improvement, but still a little less than a third of all Scottish dwellings had no more than two rooms. As late as 1951, 43 per cent of all Scottish households did not have access to a fixed bath. It was a common family tradition for the men and boys to go out on a Friday night so that the women and girls could bathe in a tub placed in the living-room. Sharing toilet facilities was also commonplace. A third of Scottish households shared a WC in 1951. This was a national average and the figures were much higher in some places, with between 40 and 50 per cent of families sharing in such towns as Dundee, Falkirk, Motherwell, Wishaw and Paisley. This was the stark material environment which shaped the lives of working-class married women until the second half of the twentieth century. Michael Anderson eloquently summarizes their experience:

Under these circumstances . . . working class married women's lives remained a constant grind. Keeping homes and husbands and children clean, carrying and heating water, preparing meals with few convenience foods and almost no domestic appliances, systematically starving themselves to allow their husbands and young children an adequate diet, last to bed and first to rise: it is hardly surprising that photographs of working class women right into the 1950s so often show them worn out and old before their time, easy to see why so many succumbed to the strains of pregnancy and disease.[4]

From an early age girls were prepared for these tasks by helping with child-minding and household chores. There was a clear sexual division of labour: domestic work was women's work with men confined to tasks such as bringing in coal and chopping wood. One Stirlingshire woman with experience of the 1920s and 1930s, on being asked, 'Did your father help your mother with any jobs in the house?' replied: 'No. No. No, my father was very well looked after in the house even to the fact that his tea was poured out for him, and everything was just there for him to sit down. He was the worker o' the house.'[5] The constant round of domestic toil was not alleviated by labour-saving appliances. Gas cookers, vacuum cleaners and washing machines were all available by the 1930s but they found their way only into affluent households. In 1939 a small élite of 4 per cent of families in the UK owned a washing machine. For the overwhelming majority of married women with no domestic help, the weekly washday was a huge task involving soaking, boiling, scrubbing, rinsing, starching, hanging up and ironing. For poorer women these continuous household tasks often had to be combined with paid work to eke out the family income, a pattern which shattered the stereotype of the working husband with a wife confined at home to family and domestic responsibilities. In fact, many of these part-time jobs, such as child-minding, sewing, taking in lodgers and laundering, took place within the home and so escaped the notice of the census enumerators.

The working-class wives of this period were engaged in a hard and relentless struggle to make ends meet and provide for their families. Unemployment, illness and broken time all frequently played havoc with delicately balanced and meagre family budgets. Oral and other evidence suggests also that married men typically kept some of their wages for themselves as pocket money to spend on drink, cigarettes and football. In addition to their own strength of character and personal courage, these women were able to develop strategies to help them survive. One of the best pieces of evidence of this comes from a study of Blackhill in Glasgow, the local authority rehousing scheme built in the 1930s, but there is no reason to believe that the findings would have been significantly different for other working-class communities in the period before the Second World War. The inhabitants of Blackhill were desperately poor. Most of the men were unskilled labourers and incomes were low and irregular. The majority that had moved to Blackhill came from the Garngad area of Glasgow, known as 'Little Ireland' because of the large numbers of Irish immigrants crammed into its teeming tenements. One of the most striking features of the women of Blackhill was the mutual support they gave one another in the daily struggle for survival. They shared food, 'making soup for the close', helped each other to pay the rent, made nappies for new babies, baked for weddings, funerals, birthdays and christenings, and looked after neighbours' children during illness and childbirth. Collective self-help was employed as a means of defence against poverty and the insidious threat of eviction if the rent payments were not maintained. But the close camaraderie among these women also helped to sustain their morale in daunting circumstances. It was a world of robust and good-humoured female solidarity, so memorably re-created in the play, *The Steamie*, Tony Roper's hugely popular evocation of the old public wash-houses of working-class communities.

2

In pre-industrial times it was common for married women to combine the roles of wives and mothers with paid industrial or agricultural employment. By the second half of the nineteenth century, some evidence suggests that this traditional integration of home and work had broken down. Among the middle classes the notion of 'separate spheres', with the woman's role concerned exclusively with domestic duties, had become accepted as an ideal to which all affluent households should aspire. Increasingly also among the working classes, the new attitudes became widely influential. Trade-union discussions in the later nineteenth century often assumed that the 'proper place' of a woman was in the home while the husband through his wages maintained his non-working wife and dependent children. After 1900, state welfare policy was constructed on the same premisses with the convention of a 'family wage' for the male earner and the 'supplementary wage' for women.

The evidence of the occupational census does seem to confirm that only a minority of women in Scotland worked for wages after marriage. According to the 1911 census, only one in 20 employed women in Scotland were married, a significantly lower proportion than in England. There was, however, a hidden labour economy that was not recorded in the census categories. This included homework, such as sewing and laundering, seasonal tasks on farms and casual employment as charwomen or as baby-minders. The wives of labourers with poor wages and fluctuating incomes were almost inevitably driven to seek part-time or temporary work. Similarly, though not enumerated in the census because it was unpaid work, wives were vital to the running of Scotland's numerous crofts and smaller farms. Even among the middle classes, where the ideal of the 'angel in the home' was most pervasive, married women sometimes worked long hours in the business firms owned by their husbands. In Dundee the jute mills entirely depended on the work of married women. A survey carried out by the Dundee Social Union in 1904 found that around half the wives in their sample of nearly 6,000 households were either working or were temporarily unemployed. Dundee had a reputation as a 'women's town', where women not in paid employment were regarded as lazy and the men who remained at home were referred to as 'kettle boilers' who prepared the meals. But the city's employment profile was unusual and elsewhere in Scotland marriage was normally a major watershed for women workers. For the 'respectable' working classes a stigma was attached to married women who worked. In teaching, a bar on married women remained in place during the inter-war period, while other occupations operated an informal embargo. As one Edinburgh shop assistant remembered: 'If you were allowed back to work after marriage they would have said "what a shame she's got to go and work". So even if you were hard up, the last thing was to go back to work. It was not the done thing – Oh no! In those days the man was supposed to be the provider.'[6]

The pattern of employment of women who did work had several distinctive features. In the 1840s women were overwhelmingly concentrated in four areas: domestic service (the biggest employer of females until the Second World War), agriculture, clothing and textiles. Nine out of 10 women worked in these sectors in the middle decades of the nineteenth century. The concentration in a narrow range of occupations can be partly explained by the nature of the Scottish economy between 1830 and 1914. The growth areas were virtually all in heavy industry which was very much a male preserve. This enhanced a division of labour based on gender. As men moved in increasing numbers into heavy industry and mining, agriculture in Scotland came to depend more on women's labour than in England. In 1871 more than a quarter of 'regular' Scottish farm workers were women, a figure which does not include the great army of female seasonal workers who were essential to bring in the annual grain, potato and soft fruit harvest. Work on the farms remained popular with women until after the Great War, but even in the later nineteenth century they were streaming off the land in increasing numbers to find new jobs in the towns and cities. Not all of these were in traditional areas. By 1900, more women than ever before were employed as clerks within the booming commercial sector, and there were also many more female teachers, nurses and midwives than ever before.

But even where women found work in formerly male preserves, a sexual division of labour remained. In tailoring, men monopolized the first-class shops catering for the most skilled work, while women were dominant in the ready-made trade where sewing machines were used extensively. Similarly in printing, female compositors were confined to typesetting, with the other processes controlled by men. Female entry to teaching was positively encouraged. David Stow, the influential educational pioneer, believed that schools should resemble a family and that 'no infant school can be perfect ... without a female hand'. Following the establishment of the state-financed pupil-teacher system in 1846, girls were recruited from the skilled working and lower-middle classes in large numbers, comprising 35 per cent of the profession in 1851 and 70 per cent in 1911. Nevertheless, the promotion prospects of women remained limited. They could go no further than the post of infant mistress in the elementary schools after the First World War, and the higher reaches of the profession continued to be dominated by men. The entry of women into medicine was much more difficult. In 1901 there were still only 60 women doctors in Scotland and in hospitals they were invariably confined to the low-status specializations of obstetrics and children's diseases, as even in the care of the sick the sexual division of labour exerted a powerful influence. The concept of 'women's work' was not fixed but it still maintained a continuing validity despite the changing complexity of the economy.

Of equal significance was the notion of a 'woman's wage'. An enduring feature of the century from 1830 to 1939 was that most women's work remained low both in status and in earning power. In the 1900s women in Scotland earned around 45 per cent of average male wages with some modest variation around this in different jobs. In textiles, one of the largest employers of female labour, the annual average wage of a woman was 53 per cent of a man's. The fact that these huge differentials persisted for so long and were only slowly in decline even in the two decades after the Second World War reflected deep-seated social beliefs about women and work. The male wage was that of the family 'provider'. Women's earnings were at best supplementary. Women were destined for marriage and to play the role of home-makers. Their time in the labour market was assumed to be of short duration and as a result they were not expected to have the commitment to acquire skills or develop responsibilities. Other assumptions included the notion that it took more to keep a man than a woman and that female workers were physically weaker and less healthy, as demonstrated by their higher rates of absenteeism.

These stereotypes were often used simply to justify lower wages for women rather than to reflect any objective evaluation of their real role in the world of work. Even where men and women performed the same jobs requiring the same skills, significant differentials in earnings remained. This was the case in teaching between the wars, where women could earn only up to 80 per cent of the male rate, a difference justified by the fact that men were likely to be family breadwinners. But the assumption that women were economic dependants did not always stand up to serious scrutiny. Eleanor Gordon reckons that in 1911 there were over 560,000 women in Scotland who did not rely on the earnings of a husband and, in the same year, 12 per cent of the female population were widows, many of them with families to support. The convention of the 'woman's wage' as less than half that of an average man's undoubtedly condemned large numbers to penury and a ceaseless struggle against destitution. Nevertheless, Scottish trade unions were committed to maintaining the traditional differentials. Women were feared as sources of cheap labour who could be used by unscrupulous employers to undercut men's wages and dilute masculine craft skills.

Some unions went so far as to try to exclude women from skilled jobs. Thus, in 1910, the Scottish Typographical Association and the printing employers' association agreed that no new female apprentices would be taken on. As a result, women compositors had virtually disappeared in Scotland by the 1940s, though they had been fairly common in Aberdeen and Edinburgh before the Great War. But the concerns of male trade unionists went much deeper than this. No less fervently than middle-class moralists, they strongly supported the ideal of 'separate spheres', in which the woman's place was very much in the home. For them it was the natural order of things and the only way properly to safeguard the integrity of the family. Greedy employers who threatened to violate this by attracting married women into the labour market had to be strongly resisted.

These beliefs were threatened by the First World War. Women now had to take the place of men who had been absorbed into the armed forces in unprecedented numbers. Women flooded into the munitions factories, engineering workshops, railways and numerous other areas of the economy formerly dominated by men. There seems little doubt that the experience of learning new skills and the female camaraderie of the huge industrial complexes of the time had a very liberating effect. It is no coincidence, for instance, that this was a period of heightened industrial militancy on Clydeside in which women and women's issues were very much to the fore. Female numbers in the trade unions rose significantly and strikes involving women became more common, including the famous Clyde rent strikes of 1915 and the clothing industry strikes of 1917. But the forces of social continuity were still very powerful. It is no longer possible to speak about the Great War as a turning point in the emancipation of women. Women over 30 did gain the vote in 1918 and achieved completely equal voting rights with men 10 years later. But in the workplace women were soon rapidly displaced by demobbed soldiers. Once again domestic service, textiles and clothing became the dominant female occupations, with some expansion in such areas as shop and clerical work where the 'feminization' of formerly male preserves was already under way before 1914. The debates at the Scottish Trade Union annual conference in 1918 revealed that the time-honoured conventions of 'separate spheres' and the sexual division of labour remained more powerful than the ephemeral impact of war. Charles Robertson of the Motherwell Trades Council asserted that the role of women in industry during the Great War had had 'a depressing effect upon public morality' and that women's 'natural sphere' was in the home to which they should now return.

Against this background it is tempting to paint the experience of women in the inter-war period in dark colours. By the standards of the later twentieth century they did face discrimination and inequality based on gender differences. But women at the time did not see their lives in such negative terms. For young girls in work, this was a period of rising incomes and more opportunity to spend on such pastimes as the cinema and dancing. Some might see women 'ghetto-ized' in the home and in poorly paid jobs, but oral evidence suggests that groups as varied as domestic servants, shop assistants, seamstresses, teachers and nurses derived considerable satisfaction and pride from their work. Most crucially, the same sources, and notably the Stirling women's history project, reveal the pivotal status and importance of wives and mothers in the family who may not have carried out paid employment but who had a demanding and fulfilling responsibility in bringing up several children, keeping their homes clean and tidy and managing tight household budgets.

3

The campaign for votes for women before the Great War is dominated by a series of dramatic images: suffragettes being fed in prison when on hunger strike, the burning of private and public buildings and high-profile assaults on politicians. Orchestrated by the Women's Social and Political Union (WSPU), the militant wing of the suffragettes, a number of sensational incidents kept the issue of votes for women in the news in Scotland virtually on a daily basis on the eve of the First World War. In July 1914, for instance, the 27-year-old Rhoda Fleming jumped on the bonnet of the King's motor car and tried to smash its windows. Dr Elizabeth Smith, a medical doctor, mother of six and wife of the minister of Calton Parish Church, Glasgow, was caught red-handed when trying to burn down a house in the west end of the city. Attacks on pillar boxes and the cutting of telephone lines had begun in 1912 and they were followed by a series of arson attacks in subsequent years on unoccupied mansion houses. The hope was that insurance companies that had to pay for the damage would bring pressure on government to grant the vote. Public buildings, such as the

Gatty Marine Laboratory in St Andrews and the Western Meeting Club in Ayr, were set on fire. In one extraordinary incident in August 1913, two women hid on the golf course at Lossiemouth and assaulted the Prime Minister himself. Episodes such as these ensured that the cause of women's suffrage was bound to feature repeatedly on the front pages in the months before the outbreak of the Great War. But the women's movement at this period was much more than a succession of colourful and spectacular incidents, nor was it exclusively concerned with the right to vote. The physical courage shown by the suffragettes when they endured prison, hunger strikes and force-feeding demonstrated increasing frustration as government adamantly refused to budge on the issue of the vote. But the strategy of arson and bombing was not put in place in Scotland until 1913, and the WSPU, which was mainly responsible for developing these militant tactics, was founded in the UK only in 1903 and the Scottish branch not established until 1906. For all the drama associated with the campaign of 1913–14, it was the short and final phase in a long struggle for votes for women.

The trigger for the suffrage movement was the passage of the Reform Acts in 1867 and 1868 which significantly extended the franchise for male voters. John Stuart Mill's amendment to this legislation to incorporate some women was defeated and led to the formation of women's suffrage societies in London, Manchester and Edinburgh. The collection of 2 million signatures from Scotland in petitions to parliament seemed to demonstrate the popularity of the cause. However, from the start the movement was overwhelmingly dominated by middle- and upper-class women. Some had honed their organizational skills in promoting the vast range of good causes covering every conceivable philanthropic endeavour in the Victorian city. For most women from the propertied classes, paid work was neither necessary nor acceptable and charitable work was an important surrogate for the display of their talents and interests. For a few, the experience gained became a foundation for involvement in local politics, especially when the 1868 Reform Act gave women ratepayers the local vote in elections for school boards, Poor Law boards, town councils and county councils. More generally, the impetus given to the extension of the franchise was an integral part of a wider and more vigorous assertion of their rights throughout society by some middle-class women. It was no coincidence that the issue of votes for women came alive at the same time as demands for access to higher education and the professions. Ladies' Educational Associations, founded in the Scottish cities from the 1860s, were concerned to promote entry to the universities, an objective that was enthusiastically supported by many male lecturers, professors, teachers and church ministers and that was finally achieved in 1892. In 1893 the first women graduated from Edinburgh, though the struggle was more protracted in the field of medical education. Electoral reform, therefore, was seen as part of a general campaign to emancipate women. As Lady Frances Balfour, a prominent suffrage activist of the 1870s, put it, the issues for women were 'education, medicine and suffrage' in that order.

Even during the more high-profile campaigns of the WSPU in the years before the Great War, the organized movement in Scotland for votes for women remained dominated by ladies from a genteel background. This is not to say, however, that working-class women had no role at all. One of the most notable activists was Jessie Stephen, organizer of the Domestic Workers' Union in Glasgow, who took part in the co-ordinated attack on Glasgow pillar boxes in February 1913, when envelopes containing bottles of acid were posted to destroy the mail. She saw her working background as a positive advantage: 'I was able to drop acid into the postal pillar boxes without being suspected, because I walked down from where I was employed in my cap, muslin apron and black frock . . . nobody would ever suspect me of dropping acid through the box.'[7] Support sometimes also came from women trade unionists. The Dundee Union of Jute and Flax Workers, for instance, which was overwhelmingly female, was very sympathetic and indeed in 1907 petitioned against the imprisonment of suffragettes. The Scottish Co-operative Women's Guild (SCWG), founded in 1892 and with 157 branches by 1913, also lent formal and public support by consistently passing resolutions in favour of votes for women at its annual conferences. But these connections were few and far between and working-class activists like Jessie Stephen were rather thin on the ground. No suffrage society branches were set up in working-class communities while both the WSPU and the Women's Freedom League were dominated by bourgeois women. As Helen Crawford, one of the most famous Scottish suffragettes of the time, put it, 'The women who became most prominent in the WSPU were middle-class women to whom the best paid professions were closed because of their sex.'[8]

The class composition of much of the suffrage movement produced a complex response from organized labour. At one level the relationships were close as Sylvia and Emmeline Pankhurst, who had founded the

WSPU in 1903, were active members of the Independent Labour Party. In Glasgow and the west of Scotland this connection was maintained, notably by Tom Johnston, the editor of *Forward*, who regularly covered the activities of the WSPU, gave it a regular column to publicize its views and afforded other forms of practical support. When Mrs Pankhurst spoke in Glasgow, Johnston ensured that she had a bodyguard of brawny dockers and navvies who promptly ejected a group of university students when they tried to disrupt her meeting. But there were also deep tensions. The suffragettes did not favour universal suffrage, just votes for women on the basis of the existing property franchise. But that franchise was still relatively narrow; only around 54 per cent of men in Glasgow had the vote as late as 1911. In poorer working-class areas of Scottish cities the proportion of enfranchised men was even less than this. It was feared that to give the vote to women from the propertied classes would both strengthen the electoral advantage of the Conservative Party and, if the property qualification was maintained, do nothing for the majority of women in the country who belonged to the working classes. Compounding this concern was the conviction among socialists that middle-class female voters in local elections were essentially a reactionary force and this did not bode well for their role in national elections if admitted to the parliamentary franchise. In 1882 only single women or widows who were householders had been given the local vote. The conventional wisdom among Labour activists who failed at the polls was that they had been defeated by the 'old women' (who made up over a third of the electorate in some middle-class areas) in alliance with 'the Churches'.

The movement for women's suffrage was then spearheaded by the upper and middle classes but it does not follow from this that working-class women were apathetic or indifferent. Working-class women were not in the vanguard of the franchise movement partly because the property qualification meant they were unlikely to achieve the vote even if gender restrictions were abolished. But they were often active in other spheres of direct importance to their own lives and those of their families. The stereotype of the passive female has little relevance to Scottish history. In the eighteenth and early nineteenth centuries, women were active in meal mobs, patronage riots, anti-clearance protests (where they usually played a key role), the Owenite socialist movement and Chartism. There was a line of continuity between these protest movements and those of the later nineteenth century. Some employers may have regarded women as cheap, malleable and docile labour, but between 1850 and 1890 there were at least 100 strikes involving them, particularly concentrated in the textile industry where the vast majority of women worked in this period. In Dundee, women strikers in the jute industry would commonly carry effigies of the employers they most hated and would subject the millowners to ridicule by catcalling and heckling them in the streets of the city. The famous dispute in 1911 at the massive Singer Works at Clydebank which employed over 12,000 workers, a quarter of them female, was instigated by women in the cabinet-polishing department. While most remained outside formal trade unionism, there was a significant increase after 1890 in the establishment of unions specially conceived to represent women's interests. These included the Women's Protection and Provident League (1888), the National Federal Council for Women's Trades (1893) and the Women's Trades Union League (1891). Equally, the ILP attracted a significant number of women, not least because the leadership regarded them as effective allies in their long-term political strategy. Keir Hardie argued in 1894 that the Scottish Labour Party should select women as candidates in school board elections. By attracting wives and mothers to the movement he contended that the next generation would also be won over to the cause of socialism.

But by far the most important working-class women's organization of the pre-1914 period was the Scottish and Co-operative Women's Guild, founded in 1892, which attained a membership of 12,420 by 1913. The main work of the Guilds was concerned with fund-raising for convalescent homes and meetings were devoted to such 'domestic' issues as cookery and dress-making. Unlike the suffrage societies of the middle classes which implicitly challenged the notion of 'separate spheres', the Guilds could be seen as confirming the domestic role of women as wives and mothers whose place was very much in the home. But crucially they also provided a bridge to wider political involvement through developing the abilities of individual women, giving them experience of organizing and promoting the development of skills in public speaking. The Guilds took a keen interest in schooling, Poor Law legislation, women's suffrage and other political issues which they regularly debated at length in their meetings. This helps to explain why members of the Women's Guilds played leading roles in the renowned Glasgow Rent Strike of 1915. The escalating rent increases and eviction threats of the spring of that year elicited an angry and vigorous response from several working-class communities in Glasgow. It was at its root a women's campaign with the organization managed by housewives through tenement and kitchen committees and co-ordinated by the Glasgow Women's Association. Sharp increases in rents were an attack on the home and its defence was often a woman's responsibility, especially when so many husbands and sons were fighting with the armies in France. The climax to several months of agitation and protest came on 17 November 1915 when 18 tenants were due to appear in court for refusal to pay rent increases. Strikes in support of the dependants were combined with a huge demonstration in George Square of women, children and men determined to oppose the right of landlords and factors to set any level of rent they wished. Not only was the case against the defaulters dismissed but before the end of the year government had introduced a Rent Restrictions Act which went a long way to meet the demands of the strikers. It was a famous victory.

PART FOUR
1939–2007

23

War and Peace

I

Like the rest of the United Kingdom, Scotland expected Hitler's bombers to inflict massive urban devastation in the first few months of the war in 1939. Mass evacuation of children and mothers from the cities took place as a necessary precaution as the nation awaited with dread the inevitable destruction and huge loss of life. In the event neither transpired. Even in the worst months of the Blitz in 1940 and 1941, Scotland escaped relatively unscathed. The exception was the night of 13–14 March 1941, when Clydebank and Glasgow suffered a ferocious night blitz which damaged all but seven of Clydebank's houses and left 35,000 of its 47,000 inhabitants homeless. The population took to the moors around the town to escape the intensity of the onslaught. Greenock, Aberdeen and the coastal burghs of the north-east were also all bombed during the war. But, Clydebank apart, none of this was on the horrific scale of relentless aerial bombardment suffered by London and several other English cities. Yet, while the military damage directly inflicted on Scotland was negligible, the impact of total war was just as great as in other parts of the country. Greenock and the Clyde were the main staging posts for the crucial Atlantic convoys. Scapa Flow in the Orkney Islands once again became the fortified anchorage of the Home Fleet. Orkney was a floating fortress and its peacetime population of *c.* 20,000 soon more than quadrupled as the sailors and garrison troops steamed north. It was not a posting that appealed to everyone:

> All bloody clouds, all bloody rains
> No bloody kerbs, no bloody drains
> The Council's got no bloody brains
> In bloody Orkney

Everything's so bloody dear
A bloody bob for bloody beer;
And is it good? – no bloody fear
In bloody Orkney

The bloody flicks are bloody old
The bloody seats are always cold
You can't get in for bloody gold
In bloody Orkney

Best bloody place is bloody bed
With bloody ice on bloody head,
You might as well be bloody dead,
In bloody Orkney.

Captain Hamish Blair, *c.* 1940[1]

The wide spaces of the Highlands were exploited for military training (most famously for commandos and other special forces in Lochaber and elsewhere) and the construction of airfields and port facilities. In consequence, new roads were built in the Outer Hebrides as well as in the Northern Isles and a hospital at Raigmore in Inverness. Much of the east coast of Scotland from Burntisland in the south was regarded as a potential target for German invasion. Blockhouses, minefields and barbed-wire barriers were hurriedly put in place and the coastline defended by Polish troops who had fled to Britain. General Sikorski, commander of the Polish Army in exile, had a headquarters in Perthshire as well as in London. The Poles turned the heads of many Scottish girls. As one lady from Aberfeldy recalled: 'Well, let's face it. Our Scotsmen are not all that courtly, nice as they are. With the Poles there was an excessive clicking of heels, kissing of hands and just general adoration of womanfolk – which we're not accustomed to here!'[2] When Poland came under Russian control after the Yalta conference in 1945, many Polish ex-servicemen in fear of their lives decided to remain in Scotland, and the Polish presence is still marked today in the number of entries under 'Z' in telephone directories for parts of the Highlands and eastern Lowlands.

War had a massive effect on the rural counties as the government mounted a systematic campaign to increase home-produced food supplies by hook or by crook. Incentives and benefits were lavished on the farming community. By the autumn of 1940, farmers had guaranteed prices for all staple products and assured markets for most of them, a position of security which was in dramatic contrast to the bitter experience of agricultural depression in the 1930s. Moreover, farmers were given a subsidy of £2 per acre of grassland which they brought under the plough. Over the course of the war, wheat and barley acreage doubled. Farmers experienced a new prosperity, with even Highland hill farmers and crofters benefiting not only from subsidy but from grants awarded under the marginal agricultural production scheme. For the UK as a whole it is reckoned that agricultural incomes rose faster between 1938 and 1942 than wages, salaries, professional earnings and profits. Average net incomes for farmers during this period increased by a remarkable 107 per cent. At a stroke the previously sceptical agricultural community was converted to state intervention and regulation. This problem of supplying labour to serve the huge expansion in grain production had already been taken into account in pre-war forward planning: '. . . if the Nazis fielded a much more professional army, the British had a more professional war economy, and farming was part of that'.[3] By the Restriction in Engagements Order of 1940, farm workers were prevented from leaving the industry. Further legislation in 1941 stopped workers at the end of their engagements moving to another master without good reason. The difficulty in procuring labour led to an unprecedented improvement in rural housing because unless decent accommodation was offered farmers had difficulty in attracting men. But more workers than before were needed and one answer was the Women's Land Army which numbered around 80,000 in the UK as a whole by 1944. Both Italian and German prisoners-of-war also worked in the fields, many of them living in the farm steading, and soldiers stationed at home. An impetus was also given to mechanization, particularly to the adoption of the tractor, a process that reached a climax in the immediate post-war years with radical consequences for the traditional horse economy of the Scottish farm.

Once again the Scottish industrial economy came into its own as a producer of ships, shells, fuses, guns and a host of other war materials. Already by the end of 1938 the demand for sandbags had become so enormous that it absorbed the entire output of the Dundee jute manufacturers. The Clyde was rejuvenated after the dark years of depression and unemployment in the early 1930s. In 1943 the shipyards were turning out an average of five vessels a week to replace the terrible British losses being sustained in the Battle of the Atlantic. By 1945, the ascendancy of the heavy industries in the Scottish economy had been consolidated and extended. At the end of the war, coal, steel, iron and engineering employed around a quarter of the insured labour force compared to 16 per cent in 1939. The full order books for the traditional industries and the imposition of conscription from the beginning of the war meant that unemployment rapidly declined and virtually ceased to exist by 1943. For most of the war years it was around 1.6 per cent of the employed labour force. This was effectively a condition of full employment.

Nevertheless, there were some worrying trends. One or two of the staple industries were still in difficulty despite the voracious demand for everything they could produce. Coal in particular, the foundation of Scotland's first Industrial Revolution, could not respond effectively because many pits were reaching the end of their lives. Astonishingly, output slumped by over 30 per cent between 1939 and 1945 and levels of productivity collapsed. This was not a happy portent for the future. In addition, though the renewed growth of the great staples was essential in order to prosecute the war effort successfully it did mean that, as in the Great War, the Scottish economy became even more dependent on a small number of heavy industries with all the potential future risks that that development implied. Dispersal of new manufactures from England might have helped to promote healthy diversification and some of this did in fact occur. The giant Rolls-Royce factory at Hillington near Glasgow built Merlin engines for Spitfires and Lancaster bombers and employed nearly 10,000 women at peak production. After 1942, factory construction proceeded apace and by 1945 the Ministry of Aircraft Production alone employed 100,000 workers in Scotland. But, in general, dispersal did not go very far and the basic policy was most often to bring workers to existing factory complexes rather than vice versa. This strategy led to one of the most controversial incidents of the war. In 1943 the Ministry of Labour transferred convoys of unmarried Scottish girls in their twenties for work in the Midlands munitions factories. Around 13,000 young women were sent south in specially reserved railway compartments under the charge of female guides. Feelings in Scotland ran high and the most dramatic demonstration of resentment occurred in the winter of 1943 when six members of a nationalist youth organization bombed and slightly damaged the ICI headquarters in Blythswood Square, Glasgow, in protest.

This furore was triggered by one part of the colossal structure of regulation and control developed by government to mobilize the total human and material resources of the nation. In 1941 not only was the war going badly both in North Africa and the Atlantic, but manpower at home was reckoned to be 1 million under the necessary strength. In December of that year, Britain became the only nation on either side to conscript women aged between 20 and 30. Women had served in the forces, munitions work and essential industries between 1914 and 1918 but not on the same scale as in the Second World War. At the Hillington aero-engine factory, for instance, fully skilled men accounted for less than 5 per cent of the labour force. Most of the rest were women. Agnes McLean recalled: 'I liked engineering. I loved the idea of these big enormous machines where you could move handles and something valuable came out. The only difference was that you'd applied your skill and intelligence and this valuable thing went into an aero-engine which helped to win the Battle of Britain.'[4] Bella Keyzer from Dundee moved from the jute mills to learning welding in the shipyards: 'This was heaven – what a difference from the monotonous clickety-clack of the weaving shed. Here was this ship being built, a thing of beauty. There was a pride in the job they didn't have in the jute trade. I dearly loved that job.'[5] Women moved *en masse* into engineering work, where they were engaged on precision tasks. One firm, Bertrams Ltd of Edinburgh, specialized before the war in paper-making machinery. Soon it was supplying gun barrels, bomb cases, howitzer parts, anti-submarine devices and ball-bearing turntables for Bofors anti-aircraft guns. All this munitions production ultimately relied on training women who then worked on three shifts around the clock for seven days a week.

In 1940 a dilution agreement allowed engineering employers to allow women to do jobs formerly done by skilled men and, in a historic decision, give women the same rate as men after they had worked for 32 weeks. Even the Amalgamated Engineering Union and the Electrical Trades Union, citadels of the male labour aristocracy, swallowed its pride and admitted women as members. But equal pay was not always easily obtained. A court of inquiry in 1943 found that Rolls-Royce at Hillington had systematically evaded the 1940 agreement. But the women refused to accept the tribunal's settlement and only after several thousand workers went on strike was the dispute finally settled. There was another major confrontation at Barr and Strouds, and in contrast to the coercive strategy of the state in the Great War these disputes were settled peacefully through conciliation and arbitration. There is much evidence that after 1943 British women were more likely than men to take strike action. This did not always meet with the approval of their sisters, as one veteran of the Hillington strike recalled: 'They were bawling at us, that their men were out fighting for the war and there we were going on strike, and I got a big tomato on the side of my face. I always remember that they just didn't know the circumstances and maybe they just didn't want to know.'[6] In many ways indeed, the Second World War was more of a watershed in women's employment history than the First World War, not least because more women managed to hold on to their wartime jobs than had been the case after 1918. Partly this was because of the continued vigour of the economy after 1945 and the parallel political commitment to full employment. The permanent disappearance of the marriage bar during wartime also helped. However, full equality for women in wages and opportunities across the economy as a whole still remained only a distant possibility.

As well as controlling the movement of labour, the state regulated the purchase and distribution through the 'bureaucratic Leviathan', the Ministry of Supply, which employed 50,000 civil servants by 1943.[7] As far as the ordinary man and woman in the street were concerned, its primary impact was felt in the rationing of essential foods such as tea, butter, jam, sugar and meat. Rationing of major foodstuffs lasted until 1954 before being finally abandoned and some unrationed foods like fish were in very short supply. Astonishingly, however, the nation was healthier and fitter than ever before and the lot of the poor and the slum dwellers in particular improved. The number of Scottish children dying in their first year fell by 27 per cent between 1939 and 1945, the biggest fall in western Europe, while the average height of Glasgow children aged 13 rose by just under two inches. This was a victory for better distribution of food to the many Scottish families who had been inadequately nourished before the war. It also reflected the new nutritionist concerns of government. Lord Woolton, who presided over the monster Ministry of Supply, had been influenced by the work of the gifted Scottish scientist, Sir John Boyd Orr, who concluded in his *Food, Health and Income* (1936) that 'a diet completely adequate for health according to modern standards is reached only at an income level above that of fifty per cent of the population'. Boyd Orr also argued that there had always been rationing of food, but in a more draconian form, imposed on the poor by the ruthless mechanism of prices. A new, idealistic concern for the most vulnerable in society was shown in the National Milk Scheme to provide free milk for the poorest mothers and children. The government also had an intrinsically practical reason for ensuring fair distribution and price controls: 'To defeat Germany citizens must be sufficiently well nourished to work harder and longer than in peacetime; food was a factor in the production of heavy bombers.'[8] This was not all. The tragedies, destruction, scarcities and multiple inconveniences of war concealed one salient fact on the home front. Full employment generated a remarkable rise in average personal incomes. Money income per head in Scotland doubled, from £86 in 1938 to £170 in 1944. When adjusted for prices, this meant an overall increase in real terms of around 25 per cent. To a significant extent, then, people were eating better because they were paid more. All of this, of course, could not compensate for the anguish of wartime or the deaths of husbands, sons and brothers in battle, even if the horrendous human carnage of 1914–18 was not repeated on anything like the same scale on the Western Front or in North Africa and south-east Asia between 1939 and 1945.

Scotland's wartime supremo was the former Red Clydesider and Labour MP for West Stirlingshire, Tom Johnston, who had been appointed regional commissioner charged with responsibility for civil defence north of the border at the outbreak of hostilities. His success in that post and Churchill's determination to avoid the industrial troubles on the Clyde during the Great War led the Prime Minister to appoint a man with a long and distinguished left-wing pedigree to the office of Secretary of State for Scotland in February 1941. Churchill had chosen wisely. Johnston was a giant figure in Scottish politics and is revered to this day as the greatest Scottish Secretary of the century. His experience of planning for a better society went back to his time on Kirkintilloch Town Council between 1914 and 1918:

To a modern observer the range of successful municipal enterprises engaged in by Johnston and his cronies in that ancient but semi-industrial town outside Glasgow seems incredible. They boosted higher education by holding popular boxing and dancing classes for those who also agreed to study English or mathematics; they formed a big, long-lived municipal bank to invest local money in building waterworks, gas and roads; they set up a municipal cinema, built municipal showers and houses, and bought bulk orders of English suits and baby food and sold them on at cost price; and they pasteurised milk and improved the food supply for the poorest children, halving the infant mortality rate in three years.[9]

Running Scotland during a total war gave Johnston the opportunity to apply these earlier lessons of municipal socialism on a national scale. He was no political theorist but a man of action who was committed to achieving practical results for Scotland. Several factors helped him. First, the war gave Johnston an opportunity to implement his passion for planning and state reform. His Scottish empire was simply one part of a great government apparatus of control and intervention which all parties agreed was essential if the nation was to mobilize effectively in order to defeat Hitler. Whether Johnston would have been equally successful in peacetime is an interesting question. Perhaps wisely, he withdrew from politics in 1945 to run the Hydro Board. Second, if his *Memories* are to be all believed, Johnston presented Churchill with a slate of demands before he accepted the Scottish Office: 'I would be given a chance to inaugurate some large-scale reforms under the umbrella of a Council of State, and which reforms, if we emerged intact at the end of the war, might mean Scotia resurgent.'[10] In essence, Johnston was promised the powers of a benign dictator. His daughter recalled her father being greeted by Churchill at a Downing Street reception later in the war with the words: 'Ah, here comes the King of Scotland!'

Third, Johnston's interventionist approach was not a complete break with the past. Even some Unionist MPs and leading Scottish business figures had experienced a sense of impotence in the 1930s Depression that the free market alone could no longer deliver prosperity and government agencies such as the Scottish Development Council and the Scottish Economic Committee were already in being in 1939. Johnston was able to exploit this more sympathetic climate of opinion towards state intervention and so expand the role of government on an unprecedented scale. Fourth, he was able to use the 'nationalist threat' in Cabinet as a cudgel to extract more concessions in Scotland. The reality of this 'threat' has often been debated. Certainly, SNP candidates during the war did better than their fellows who had lost disastrously in the 1930s. In 1945 the Nationalist, Robert MacIntyre, gained Motherwell and Sir John Boyd Orr, an Independent standing on a Home Rule ticket, won the Scottish Universities seat. Perhaps more seriously from the point of view of the Churchill government, there seems to have been an undercurrent of discontent about the conduct of the war north of the border. Indeed, Johnston himself confided to Sir John Reith in July 1943 that he feared the rise of nationalism. Certainly, as Herbert Morrison remembered in his *Autobiography* (1960), Johnston used these concerns to Scotland's advantage: 'He would impress on the Committee that there was a strong nationalist movement in Scotland and it could be a potential danger if it grew through lack of attention to Scottish interests.'[11]

In the event, Johnston was given a virtually free hand in Scotland and was advised by a 'Council of State' which consisted of all living former Secretaries of State. They met infrequently and their impact was not as significant as the grandiose title suggests. But the Council did help to legitimize Johnston's reforms by conferring on them the bi-partisan stamp of approval. The initiatives were numerous. He fought fiercely against the concentration of industrial production in the Midlands and the south of England and managed to attract 700 enterprises and 90,000 new jobs north through the establishment of a Scottish Council of Industry. By so doing, he helped strengthen the union by demonstrating that it could be exploited to Scotland's advantage. Post-war reconstruction was also high on his agenda, with no fewer than 32 sub-committees set up to tackle a host of problems, ranging from juvenile delinquency to hill sheep farming. Scotland also became the first part of the United Kingdom to operate tribunals to regulate the level of wartime rents. Even more spectacularly, Johnston created a kind of prototype National Health Service on Clydeside. On the expectation that enemy bombing would cause enormous civilian casualties, several hospitals had been built in the late 1930s to take the many hundreds of thousands certain to be killed and maimed by the Luftwaffe. But the slaughter never came and the hospitals, though well staffed, were lying virtually empty. Johnston now used them to treat workers in the munitions factories. As he recalled in his *Memories* (1952): 'The success of the experiment by April 1945 was such we had wiped out the waiting lists of 34,000 patients on the books of the voluntary hospitals – was such that our scheme had been extended from the Clyde Valley to all of Scotland and blazed a trail for the National Health Scheme of post-war years.' Perhaps, however, Johnston's most enduring achievement was his creation of a comprehensive scheme for the provision of hydro-electricity in the Highlands. The idea had been around for a long time but its implementation had been obstructed by vested interests. Johnston managed to obtain parliamentary support in 1943 for the scheme and a guarantee of £30 million to bring a domestic electrical supply to the northern glens. The Act went through the House of Commons without a division. Apart from its many benefits to the people of the Highlands over the next couple of decades, this legislation was the necessary precondition for the development of a mass tourist industry and the ubiquitous bed-and-breakfast establishment of modern times.

Johnston's administration was a powerful vindication that the state could be an effective instrument for improving the life of all its citizens. It raised expectations that the post-war world would bring with it better times and the misery of the 1930s could finally be consigned to history. The British state as a whole had shown its muscle as it pervaded every aspect of human existence in the struggle for victory. If state intervention could help defeat the might of Hitler's armies, then surely it was also capable of tackling the evils of poverty, unemployment and social deprivation. Moreover, those who had argued in the dark days of the Depression that governments were powerless to combat a crisis in economic activity were now proved wrong. The class system and class tensions did not disappear during the war but the government had worked hard to instil a sense of common purpose in which everyone made a contribution in the fight against the common foe. Those who had made a common sacrifice, however, were not prepared to return to the bad old days before 1939. In essence, a new contract had been established between the state and the people. 'Never again' became the watchwords.

The new mood was crystallized by the publication of the famous Beveridge Report in December 1942. Immediately, the Report and the Summary became best-sellers; large queues formed outside the shops of His Majesty's Stationery Office to buy them and a Gallup Poll discovered that 19 out of 20 people had heard of the proposals a mere fortnight after publication. Copies soon found their way to the troops at the fronts and in POW camps. Stuart Hood recalled: 'I was in a prisoner-of-war camp when the Beveridge Report came out. Somebody had a copy sent to them and the excitement that this caused was quite marked and there were big discussions and debates about why we had been fighting. It always seemed clear to me that the army, by and large, was going to vote left.'[12]

Beveridge provided a blueprint for the post-war society that would commit government to conquest of the historic enemies, of Want, Disease, Ignorance, Squalor and Idleness. Family allowances should be given for all children, mass unemployment could be avoided by state planning and intervention in the economy, and a National Health Service must be established. Contributors would be covered for all their needs from cradle to grave through a single weekly contribution. At the heart of the proposals was the idea of the 'national minimum', a basic level of income below which no one should be allowed to fall. All this had a magical appeal for the mass of the population and the few criticisms were mainly reserved for the proposals on old age pensions and rates for sickness and unemployment benefit which were judged too low. The government was less enthusiastic. The War Minister banned discussion of the Report in the army's compulsory current affairs classes, while the Cabinet equivocated before agreeing to accept any of the recommendations in principle, and also insisting that only a new government elected after the war could implement the necessary legislation. The Tories, however, were regarded as lukewarm on Beveridge's plans and concerned about their potential cost. Perhaps this and Johnston's successes in implementing collectivism helped to seal their fate in Scotland in the election of 1945. To the 'stupefied surprise' of the *Glasgow Herald*, Labour swept to power in the UK, notched up 37 Scottish seats and attracted nearly 48 per cent of the votes cast north of the border.[13] It was a substantial electoral foundation for a reforming government committed to the Welfare State and management of the economy for the public good.

2

But at first the omens were not good. Britain had helped to win the war, but there was real uncertainty whether she would win the peace. The nation was financially exhausted. The cost of the Second World War had been twice as great as for the First World War. No less than 28 per cent of the country's wealth had been wiped out and a huge balance-of-payments debt of £3 billion to the sterling area had been accumulated. Crucially, within days of Japan's surrender, the Americans had cut the vital financial lifeline of Lend-Lease. Britain was now in desperate straits and yet because of her status as a great power was committed to the costly maintenance of an army of occupation in Germany. Keynes's astute warning to the Cabinet in the closing months of the war, 'We are a great nation, but if we continue to behave like a

Great Power we shall soon cease to be a great nation', had gone unheeded in the euphoria of victory.[14] It was a sign of the times that bread was rationed for the first time in 1946. Then in 1947 came a natural calamity to add to the economic woes. The winter of that year was the coldest of the century and for several weeks during the worst of the weather the country came to a virtual standstill because of an acute shortage of coal. In Scotland unemployment had risen to 5 per cent by the end of 1946 and between 1945 and 1948, suffered a fall in average real income by 9 per cent, which was around double that for the country as a whole. Ominously, in 1945 and 1946, a number of English companies closed down their Scottish branches. The brave new world promised by the politicians still seemed as far away as ever.

But quite suddenly things changed. From 1947 Marshall Aid from the USA to war-devastated Europe opened up huge new export markets for British industry. At the same time, the government maintained a fiscal squeeze on home consumption in order to allow resources to flow into a drive for the exports now regarded as vital to national survival. This was all to the benefit of Scottish heavy industry which had traditionally been strongly committed to overseas markets. In addition, the war had eliminated (for at least several years) the impact of competition from Germany and Japan, two of Scotland's most formidable rivals in the shipbuilding and heavy engineering industries. Scotland also continuously gained from high replacement demand for capital goods and manufactures, which was given additional impetus by the Korean War. Shipbuilding is a case in point. In 1951 it was still very much the biggest industry in the land and now forged ahead to a position of rejuvenated pre-eminence. Between 1948 and 1951, Scottish shipbuilders launched no less than 15 per cent of the world's and one-third of British tonnage. Their success was mirrored in the resounding export achievements of the other great staples of steel and engineering. In effect, the post-war boom had consolidated the hegemony of Scotland's traditional industries. By 1958 the country had become even more dependent on them than it had been in the 1930s.

The other remarkable trend of the first decade of peace was a revolutionary extension in the power and influence of the state. Between 1945 and 1950, Labour delivered on its election manifesto, *Let Us Face the Future*. The Beveridge Plan of national compulsory insurance for all 'from the cradle to the grave' was put into effect, with child allowances, universal state retirement pensions, unemployment benefit and finally, in 1948, what was for many the jewel in the crown, the National Health Service. Scotland's problems of poverty, low incomes and poor health had always been more serious than the average for the UK as a whole and these historic reforms were likely to have a disproportionate effect for good on the welfare of her people.

State intervention in key areas of the economy became all-embracing. Coal was nationalized in 1947, railways and electricity in 1948, and iron and steel in 1949. Regional policy had its foundations in the 1934 Special Areas Act but was significantly strengthened by the Distribution of Industry Act of 1945. Through it the Board of Trade could acquire land, build factories and provide some financial assistance for capital equipment in designated 'development areas'. In addition, the Board was able to use wartime licence controls (which remained in force until 1954) and planning permission after 1947 to influence the location of new factories. Powers were further increased by another Act of 1950 which significantly extended the Scottish Development Area to include some Highland districts. By 1950, Scotland had attracted 13 per cent of all new industrial building constructed in Britain. Ten years later, the west of Scotland alone had 18 industrial estates and 29 other factory sites, providing jobs for around 65,000 people. Among the new companies were several American multinationals that were seeking to exploit the large European market and at the same time circumvent high European tariffs. US investment in Scotland was not unknown before 1939, notable examples being Singers of Clydebank and the North British Rubber Company, but the scale of inward movement in the 1940s and 1950s was unprecedented and set a trend that was to become even more firmly established in the 1960s and beyond. The first arrivals included Honeywell, IBM, Euclid, Goodyear and Caterpillar. Several of them introduced industries entirely new to Scotland, such as electronic data processing and earth moving equipment. Their effect, therefore, cannot simply be evaluated on the narrow basis of the number of jobs they created, which still remained a relatively small proportion of all those employed in Scotland.

The role of the state also extended widely into agriculture and rural society in general. There was a marked degree of continuity between the wartime regime of guaranteed farm prices and financial subsidies simply because absolute shortages and problems of food importation persisted after 1945. The farmer had to be supported and given security for the greater good of the population at a time when strict rationing was still enforced. The Agriculture Acts of 1947 and 1948 did this by maintaining guaranteed prices. In 1950 Scotland secured about £3 million out a total of £20 million for the UK as a whole, with much of this sum going on hill sheep and cattle subsidies, which attracted higher levels of support and brought great benefit in particular to the marginal hill farming districts of the Highlands. Even before the war the state's presence in agriculture was assuming more importance with the work of the Forestry Commission and the Scottish Milk Marketing Board, which had been set up in 1933. In forestry, new legislation was necessary to repair the destruction of timber reserves which had taken place during the war. As part of this strategy the Forestry Commission, founded in 1919, was made responsible on Scottish matters to the Secretary of State for Scotland. By the 1950s, the Commission had become the largest landowner in Scotland and its policies led to the greatest single physical transformation in the Scottish countryside in this century.

Indeed, the post-war period was one of dynamic growth for agriculture as a whole and success was not simply based on the cosseting of government subsidies. Productivity rose by 300 per cent between 1939 and 1960, as this was the era of the second Agricultural Revolution when mechanization based on the tractor changed the nature of rural society in a more fundamental way than at any time since the eighteenth century:

The change-over to the new regime came with great rapidity. By 1952 horses were dwindling rapidly. By the end of the decade they were becoming unusual. By the end of the 1960s they were a rarity. With the horses went the whole labour-intensive system – the ploughmen and their families, the tradesmen, and in many cases the old steadings themselves which had been designed around horse-working. The depopulation and all the attendant factors are not hard to imagine.[15]

In the Highlands no other government initiative could match the impact of the North of Scotland Hydro Electric Board (Hydro). From 1951 the Scottish Office gained control of Scottish electricity production, which had itself been nationalized since 1948. The Hydro then became not simply a source of electrical power but an instrument for economic and social regeneration in the Highlands. By 1960 a quarter of the Board's 400 roads had been handed over to local authorities free of charge, and by the early 1970s 90 per cent of crofting households were connected to the grid, despite the fact that over 25 per cent of the Board's customers were being supplied on an uneconomic basis. None of this regenerated the Highlands or stopped the constant drift of the younger generation to the cities and overseas. But the social consequences were nevertheless profound in terms of the quality of life of the people of the Highlands. The provision of domestic electricity '. . . can be regarded as one of the outstanding achievements of any public-service body in post-war Britain and was certainly the most fundamental contribution from any agency in twentieth century Highland history'.[16]

Elsewhere in Scotland, by far the most pressing social problem was housing. The sheer enormity of overcrowding and squalor in parts of the nation's cities and towns had been starkly revealed in several pre-war surveys. The restriction in housebuilding during the war and bomb damage in Clydeside had simply made the problem more acute. By 1945 planning for the future was well under way. As early as 1940, the Barlow Report advocated the dispersal of people from the cities to relieve congestion through the planning and control of public agencies. The need for such a strategy was underscored by a report prepared by Glasgow's Town Clerk revealing that 700,000 people were living in a space of 1,800 acres in the centre of the city. This meant that an incredible one-third of the entire population of west central Scotland was squeezed into a space of three square miles in the heart of the region's biggest city. The Clyde Valley Plan, prepared by Sir Patrick Abercrombie and a team of planners, sought to repair some of the social damage inflicted by nearly two centuries of rampant industrial capitalism by arguing that Glasgow's population should be rehoused outside the city boundaries through overspill policies and the creation of new towns.

What transpired over the next two decades was nothing less than a housing revolution. Houses were built at a staggering pace, over 564,000 in the 20 years after 1945, an increase of around two-thirds on those constructed between the wars. The striking feature in Scotland was the overwhelming predominance of council houses. Some 86 per cent of those built between 1945 and 1965 were in the public sector. In cities such as Glasgow and in towns like Airdrie, Coatbridge and Motherwell, the proportion was even higher. This was much greater than anywhere else in the UK, so much so that Scotland by the 1970s had probably the largest share of public housing of any advanced economy outside the communist bloc. The state underpinned this through a system of subsidies and rental controls, while private building was limited in the immediate post-war years because of materials shortage and elaborate licensing procedures. In the final analysis, therefore, the numerous Scottish tenants who benefited from the vast building programmes of the 1940s and 1950s were shielded from the economic realities and costs of housing: '. . . even allowing for a central government grant towards building them and a statutory local subsidy, it was reckoned that in March, 1952 the average Scottish council house tenant would have to pay 3.5 times his current gross rent before he was paying the real cost of his accommodation'.[17] This, in turn, had considerable implications for the patterns of political behaviour of large sections of the Scottish population.

Housebuilding on this massive scale changed the face of many Scottish towns. The provision of decent homes was seen by councillors and planners alike as a crusade against the slums and all they represented in terms of poverty, squalor, disease and social injustice. In removing the slums, local authorities believed they were also ushering in a new and better life for the people. Demolition became an unquestioned orthodoxy. Pat Rogan, the Edinburgh chairman of housing from 1962, recalled: 'It was a magnificent thing to watch, as I did many times, whole streets of slum tenements being demolished, just vanishing into dust and rubble.'[18] The County Architect for Lanarkshire, which by 1966 had built the eighth-largest stock of post-war local authority housing in the UK, was equally ecstatic about the achievement when he looked back in 1975: 'You'd find it hard now to discover a "slum" in rural Lanarkshire. We'd almost completely cleared the old miners' rows, and most pre-World War I property that wasn't owner-occupied.'[19] As the slums and old tenements fell to the bulldozers, those who had lived in them were 'decanted' to the new peripheral 'schemes' (of which Glasgow's huge developments at Pollok, Castlemilk, Drumchapel and Easterhouse were the biggest and best known) and to the new towns of East Kilbride, Cumbernauld and Glenrothes. The next stage, from the early 1960s, was the construction of colossal tower blocks of 30 storeys or more on cleared sites in inner cities as land for building started to run out and local authorities looked for even faster methods of creating new accommodation. Glasgow in this process was the European pioneer in high multi-storey living but the enthusiasm soon spread to Motherwell, Edinburgh and Dundee. The multi-storeys symbolized modernity and the sharpest possible break with the old and rejected world of the slums. Though some council leaders were aware that they were in conflict with all the best principles of planning, they were unrepentant. As David Gibson, Glasgow's Housing Convener after 1961 and the driving force behind the city's multi-storey revolution, proclaimed in evangelical and optimistic style:

In the next three years the skyline of Glasgow will become a more attractive one to me because of the likely vision of multi-storey houses rising by the thousand . . . The prospect will be thrilling, I am certain, to the many thousands who are still yearning for a home. It may appear on occasion that I would offend against all good planning principles, against open space and Green Belt principles – if I offend against these it is only in seeking to avoid the continuing and unpardonable offence that bad housing commits against human dignity. A decent home is the cradle of the infant, the seminar of the young and the refuge of the aged.[20]

It has become fashionable to criticize the massive post-war expansion in Scottish public housing for monotonous buildings, poor construction, the absence of amenity, pubs and entertainment in the large schemes around the cities, inadequate transport and the break-up of old communities. Evidence can certainly be found in abundance to support these claims. Billy Connolly's description of the big estates as 'deserts wae windaes' rings true for many observers. But two points also need to be borne in mind. First, the truly appalling scale of the housing crisis which had to be confronted, especially in Glasgow and some of the western industrial towns, made local authorities go for rapid construction of dwellings almost to the exclusion of all else. One housing official in Glasgow recalled, 'I can remember an endless stream of older women coming to me in 1957–9, all with the same question: "When's ma hoose comin' down?" They just couldn't get out of the old condemned houses fast enough.'[21] As late as 1958, Glasgow still had a housing waiting list of 100,000 families. Figures like these concentrated the minds of the politicians. Second, and not to be forgotten, for the first time large numbers of Scots had a decent home equipped to modern standards. Rising expectations and a continuing increase in standards since the 1950s cannot alter that judgement.

3

In 1957 Harold Macmillan famously remarked: 'Let's be frank about it, most of our people have never had it so good.' His comment had particular relevance to Scotland which had endured a good deal of pain for much of the inter-war period. Unemployment, the curse of the 1930s, fell to historically low levels. Between 1947 and 1957, Scottish unemployment was remarkably stable and only varied between 2.4 per cent and 3 per cent of an insured labour force which had actually increased significantly by over 690,000 between 1945 and 1960. There were now jobs for virtually everyone who wanted to work. Full employment also brought rising incomes. The income of the average working-class household in 1953 was reckoned to be 2.5–3 times greater than in 1938. For a time, even the gap in average wage levels between England and Scotland narrowed. The nation's health improved, not simply because of the new prosperity but also as a result of legislative changes and scientific advances. The National Health Service from 1948 extended free treatment to all, while by the Education (Scotland) Acts of 1945 and 1947 local authorities could insist on the medical inspection of pupils and provide free treatment. Antibiotics were introduced for the first time on a large scale in the mid-1940s and soon wiped out tuberculosis, the killer disease of young adults in the past. By 1960, Scotland's infant mortality rate was the same as that of the USA and close to the figures for England and Wales.

Rising living standards in the 1950s were shown by the steady increase in the range of new appliances, such as washing machines, vacuum cleaners and electric cookers, which made homes easier to run. Leisure patterns were transformed by the television and, for a long time after its introduction, cinema audience figures tumbled. The number of TV sets grew from 41,000 in 1952 to well over 1 million 10 years later, an explosion that was fuelled partly by the huge demand for televisions at the time of the Coronation in 1953. The BBC soon had local competition when STV emerged in 1955, headed by the Scots-Canadian tycoon, Roy Thomson, who memorably described his new company as 'a licence to print money'. However, as Christopher Harvie points out, 'it was certainly not a cultural monument', at least in its early years.[22] But some such monuments were indeed built at this time. In 1947 the Edinburgh Festival was founded, followed 13 years later by the launch of Scottish

Opera by the charismatic conductor of the Scottish National Orchestra, Alexander Gibson. A development of much wider popular appeal – and one which was to have an enduring impact on modern Scottish culture – came in the 1950s with the revival of folksong. From 1951 Hamish Henderson organized the People's Festival Ceilidhs which brought the best of the country's native musical traditions to an urban audience. It was also the time when Ewan MacColl, Jimmy McBeath and Jeannie Robertson made their marks on what soon became known as 'the folk scene'. The new prosperity also fostered a spirit of independence among young people. The 1950s was the decade of the 'Teddy Boys', who cut a figure with their individually coiffed hairstyles, tight trousers, winkle-picker shoes and velvet-collared jackets. The transatlantic influence was an even more potent force for most of Scotland's youth than the native folk revival. Bill Haley introduced a new and more powerful music cocktail to packed cinema audiences with *Rock Around the Clock*, while American stars like Elvis Presley and Buddy Holly became cult figures for a new generation of Scottish teenagers.

Full employment also had important effects on the impact of women in society. The 1951 census showed a marked increase in the proportion of married women in the labour force in relation to 1931 and by the 1960s the majority of female workers were married, indeed a revolutionary transformation of the patterns of the nineteenth and early twentieth centuries. The trend towards smaller families, earlier marriage and the concentration of child-bearing in the first years of wedlock created new opportunities for many women to go out to work. As the new domestic technology became more widely available it was also easier for married women to combine domestic responsibilities with part-time work. There were more light engineering jobs, especially in the industrial estates and the expansion of the state bureaucracies, both at local and national level, after 1945 established many new openings for female clerks and secretarial staff. Women were still paid less than men, though in teaching something of a breakthrough was achieved in the 1950s with the award of equal salaries for both sexes.

The better times helped to attract a new stream of immigrants. Full employment made it difficult to fill menial or unpleasant jobs and Irish immigration (Scotland's main earlier source of casual, low-paid labour) had dried up. Instead, Asian workers started to move into occupations such as driving and conducting in the transport departments of the cities and unskilled and semi-skilled work in bakeries, the building industry and the jute mills. Many of them were recruited from the industrial areas of the Midlands and Yorkshire and by 1960 there were already 4,000 Asians in Scotland. In the same period, Indian and Pakistani bus drivers and conductors made up more than half the labour force in the Glasgow Corporation Transport Department. One intriguing consequence was that when India and Pakistan went to war in 1965 the city fell into chaos. The public transport system came to a virtual standstill when all the Asian workers took time off to follow the momentous events on television and radio. By 1970 the Asian community had grown to 16,000 and now included Chinese migrants from Hong Kong. The reaction of the Scots was not always friendly. When Asian grocery shops started to appear, they were sometimes subjected to undisguised prejudice. Their route to survival and prosperity lay in staying open late, often until midnight, and cutting prices. In time, however, the Pakistani corner shop became as much a part of the Scottish retail scene as the Italian ice-cream parlour established many decades before. Racial tensions north of the border never reached the acute levels of some English cities, though this may have been mainly due to the relatively small number of coloured immigrants to Scotland in these years.

Ironically, at the same time as the Asian community was experiencing suspicion and some hostility, the barriers were coming down for the descendants of the Irish Catholic migrants. The crucial changes came in the labour market. Until the 1950s and 1960s, Catholics were markedly under-represented in skilled trades and professional occupations. In some of the shipyards and engineering shops, the power of foremen with Orange and Masonic loyalties to hire and fire made it difficult for Catholics to start an apprenticeship. Alex Ferry, later President of the AEU, confirmed that in the 1940s few Catholics in the engineering trade were taken on as apprentices. From the 1950s, however, institutionalized discrimination started to disintegrate. Now there was an acute shortage of skilled labour and religious affiliation seemed less important than the ability to do the job. Furthermore, foreign-owned firms were totally dismissive of old Scottish prejudices, while nationalization and the mushrooming growth of the public sector created many new avenues for upward social mobility for university-educated Catholics outside the historic citadels of discrimination in the heavy industries. This tended further to strengthen the loyalty of both working- and middle-class Catholics to Labour, which was seen as the main progenitor after the war of the vast expansion in state employment and public services and the political engine of increased social justice.

4

The 1940s and 1950s have often been described as the high point of modern British unionism. However, in 1945 it seemed that Scottish politics might go in a different direction. In that year the SNP leader, Dr Robert McIntyre, won the party's first ever parliamentary seat in a by-election at Motherwell. But it was a false dawn. In the general election a few weeks later, the seat was lost and over the next 15 years or so the SNP made little impact on Scottish politics, which were first dominated by Labour and then, in the 1950s, by the Unionists. At the SNP conference in Glasgow in 1942 the party had broken in two. The pretext for conflict was the election to the chairmanship, won by Douglas Young, a lecturer in Greek at Aberdeen University, who was then on bail after being sentenced to 12 months' imprisonment for resisting conscription as contrary to the Treaty of Union. The defeated candidate was the elderly journalist, William Power, who was supported by the powerful figure of John MacCormick, the party secretary and its single most influential voice. MacCormick believed it was more important to develop a broad consensus among the Scottish people in favour of Home Rule than to pursue the goal of Scottish independence, which he regarded as having only limited electoral appeal. He immediately announced his resignation from the SNP when Young was elected and, with a number of allies, established a body eventually named the Scottish Convention which would stand outside party politics but would seek to demonstrate to government the national desire for Home Rule by mobilizing all sections of Scottish opinion in pursuit of that primary objective. Meanwhile, the SNP became a narrow and exclusive nationalist organization, dominated by the pro-independence hardliners and appearing to those outside more like a sect than a political party. Its membership was tiny, numbering no more than 1,000 in the mid-1950s. Even this rump was vulnerable to further schism. In 1955 opposition to the leadership of Dr McIntyre, which was regarded as increasingly feeble, led to the exodus of about a third of the membership. The party was now virtually irrelevant to the electoral process and hardly took part at all in the general elections of 1950 and 1951. Even in 1959, when opinion in Scotland swung against the incumbent Conservative government, the nationalists failed to make an impact. Scottish discontent was expressed through support for Labour and the SNP polled a mere 0.8 per cent of the national vote.

On the face of it, MacCormick's Scottish Convention was much more successful. Indeed, its high public profile helped to draw support away from the SNP which undoubtedly suffered from the contemporary public perception of nationalism as an ideology that had spawned Nazism and devastated Europe in a terrible war. The spirit of the times favoured international co-operation rather than the development of new national divisions which had come to be associated with conflict and intolerance. The Scottish Convention was in tune with these ideals. It was non-partisan, consensual and did not fight elections, it had a gradualist agenda and a moderate approach to constitutional reform, preferring Scottish self-government within the UK to full-blown separatism. Even during the war it made an impact, with branches established across Scotland, and in March 1947 held a Scottish National Assembly in Glasgow with 600 delegates from a number of bodies, including the Church of Scotland, trade unions and Chambers of Commerce. It produced proposals which became known as 'the Blue Print for Scotland' advocating a Scottish parliament which would have authority over most areas of government, apart from defence, foreign affairs and the currency. The campaign was then taken further through MacCormick's idea of establishing a new 'national covenant' of the kind that had expressed Scottish religious ideals in the seventeenth century.

The Covenant was launched in the autumn of 1949 and eventually collected about 2 million signatures in favour of Home Rule. When it was presented to the third National Assembly on 29 October 1949, MacCormick waxed eloquent in his description of the occasion:

Unknown district councillors rubbed shoulders and joined in pledges with the men whose titles had sounded through all the history of Scotland. Working men from the docks of Glasgow or the pits of Fife spoke with the same voice as portly business-men in pin-striped trousers. It was such a demonstration of national unity as the Scots might never have hoped to see and when, finally, the scroll upon which the Covenant was inscribed was unrolled for signature every person in the hall joined, patiently in the queue to sign it.[23]

Even if it did contain some forgeries and the names of a few dead celebrities, the Covenant had undoubtedly attracted mass support.

However, as a vehicle for delivering Home Rule it proved a failure. Self-government could be achieved only through the ballot box, by voters backing candidates prepared to advocate self-government. The Covenant movement was avowedly non-partisan and apolitical. Moreover, the Labour government had good reason to suspect MacCormick and some of his allies. The Secretary of State for Scotland, Arthur Woodburn, regarded the movement as a front organization composed of Labour's enemies and aimed at the overthrow of the Attlee government, judgement which was not entirely based on ministerial paranoia. Mac-Cormick had joined the Liberal Party in 1945 and stood as a Liberal candidate in the election of that year. In December 1947, with Liberal, Unionist and Covenant support, he contested a by-election at Paisley against Labour, with the other parties agreeing not to put up candidates in order to maximize his chances. A joint declaration of this peculiar coalition was published which stated that 'central control' (for this read 'nationalization') imposed from Westminster was in danger of threatening Scotland's very existence if it continued for much longer. The idea that the Unionists were converted to Home Rule was, of course, ludicrous. Instead, they were skilfully playing the Scottish card against Labour for party electoral advantage rather than for any broader purpose. The tactic failed and MacCormick lost. This, however, was most certainly not the way to convince the Labour Government of the need for constitutional change.

The Covenant was ignored and the movement soon fell apart into political irrelevance and made little impact on the general elections of 1950 and 1951. Yet Nationalist sentiment survived. Partly, it was diverted into romantic exploits, as when four young student supporters of MacCormick seized the Stone of Destiny from Westminster Abbey on Christmas Day 1950. The Coronation Stone of the Kings of Scotland was a powerful symbol of national sovereignty and had been removed to London by Edward I during the Wars of Independence to demonstrate his suzerainty over the Scots. In one sense the episode was a stunt but it still provoked an excited public response. Eventually the Stone turned up again in Arbroath Cathedral, enveloped in the Scottish Saltire. Moreover, the Tory argument that nationalization north of the border would simply transfer control of Scottish industry to a Whitehall bureaucracy hit home in some quarters, as Hector McNeil, the Scottish Secretary, acknowledged in a memorandum to the Cabinet in 1950. Certainly the Unionists thought there was considerable electoral mileage in exploiting national sentiment, since they played the Scottish card to the full in their years in opposition. Winston Churchill told an Edinburgh meeting that Labour centralization threatened to absorb the Scottish nation in a 'serfdom of socialism' run from London which was in conflict with the Treaty of Union of 1707 itself. Scottish pride was also aroused by the decision, ironically taken by Churchill, to call the new monarch Elizabeth II, although she was first by that title in the history of Scotland. The journalist, Arnold Kemp, recalled the reaction in his own Edinburgh middle-class household: 'This caused widespread and genuine outrage. I remember my parents' fulminations very well. They went on about it for years.'[24] Legal challenges against the decision were mounted and a few postboxes with the QEII symbol blown up. The Scottish factor also entered the realm of religious dispute in the 1950s with the 'Bishops in the Kirk' controversy. The Anglican and Presbyterian churches had been having joint discussions on closer relations for some years and these culminated in the publication of a report in 1957 which recommended that the Church of Scotland should adopt a form of episcopacy in the interests of unity and that each presbytery would have a bishop selected from its membership. The idea might have been good for ecumenism, but it provoked fierce opposition in Scotland when made public, including widespread and vitriolic condemnation in the press. The criticisms were as much inspired by a rejection of anglicizing forces as by the need to maintain the ecclesiastical purity of the Scottish Kirk.

The Scottish dimension, therefore, never disappeared from political life after 1945, despite the irrelevance of the SNP and the collapse of the Covenant movement. Nevertheless, the cause of parliamentary devolution was certainly in the doldrums. Unionists had never supported it and now Labour too began to falter in its historic commitment. The Home Rule pledge was still in the party's manifesto in 1945, but in 1950 the Scottish Trades Union Congress overwhelmingly rejected a motion from the miners to support a Scottish parliament. In the 1950 election Labour dropped its manifesto commitment to self-government altogether. Six years later, Hugh Gaitskell confirmed that Labour was against Home Rule and in 1959 the Scottish conference itself withdrew support. For the first time in a long time, devolution was off the political agenda. The reasons are not far to seek. The two Unionist parties, Labour and the Tories, presided over an unprecedented increase in personal incomes, living standards and health care in these decades.

Westminster had delivered to the Scots where it mattered most, in jobs, wages and welfare. Indeed, full employment meant more north of the border because of the ravages of the Depression in the 1930s. Tom Johnston's effective stewardship of the Scottish Office during wartime had also shown how an able Scottish politician could work the existing system so as to obtain concessions from central government without the need for full-scale constitutional change. During the war too, despite very real national pride in the famous exploits of Scottish units, like those of the 51st Highland Division in the North African and European campaigns as key elements in Montgomery's armies, a keener sense of Britishness was also instilled in the common struggle for survival against the Nazi foe. Moreover, in the 1940s and 1950s the strategic planning for economic improvement through the Redistribution of Industries Act of 1945 and the Town and Country Planning Act of 1947 could be implemented only on a British basis because it was based on the attraction of industry from the prosperous areas of the south to the depressed regions of the north.

During the 13-year period of Tory rule from 1951 to 1964, little concession to devolutionary sentiment might have been expected but, in addition, successive Conservative administrations did much for most of this period to defuse further any potential nationalist discontent. In the general elections between 1950 and 1964, the Unionists averaged 46 per cent of the vote in Scotland, compared to 47 per cent for Labour. This was a remarkable result, given the relatively small size of the Scottish middle class, the party's natural constituency. In 1955 the Unionists also managed to attract 50.1 per cent of the vote, a unique achievement in Scottish electoral history. To some extent they were fortunate because they inherited the benefits of a booming economy after the austerity years under Labour and they still had loyal support from many Protestant working-class voters in the west of Scotland, where sectarian divisions between Catholic and Protestant were often mirrored in the political divisions between Labour and Unionist. The 1959 Coatbridge and Airdrie contest was a classic example of religious voting. Labour's candidate was a well-known local councillor, James Dempsey, who was also a Catholic. The Unionists nominated Miss C. S. Morton, a relative of the footballer, Alan Morton, who had played for Rangers between the wars. Against the trend in Scotland, Dempsey's majority in a safe Labour seat was cut to a mere 795. This also demonstrated, however, that the Tories had a distinct identity north of the border and that they appealed to a particular Scottish constituency. But, at the same time, the Tory government faithfully followed the collectivist and interventionist route mapped out by their Labour predecessors. James Stuart, the Secretary of State after the 1955 election, even managed to exceed Labour's council house building programme by a third, started the Forth Road Bridge and embarked on the electrification of the railway system in and around Glasgow. It was easy to see why many Scots now associated growing affluence with Tory rule.

But all was not as well as it appeared and by the late 1950s the good times seemed to be coming to an end. There were a number of worrying signs. Deflation in 1957, primarily the result of greater defence expenditure during the Suez Crisis of 1956, combined with the phasing out of National Service, doubled unemployment from 58,010 in 1958 to 116,000 a year later. The figure would have been higher but for persistently high levels of emigration even during the prosperous early 1950s. Between 1950 and 1960, over half a million people left Scotland, roughly divided between those who moved overseas and those who settled in England. The continuation of the exodus to the south was a confirmation that wages were still higher and unemployment lower there than in Scotland. In other ways Scotland was also lagging behind. Scottish Gross Domestic Product (GDP) rose by 59 per cent, but British GDP outstripped that to increase by 70 per cent. It was now recognized by the early 1960s that the UK was growing at a significantly slower rate than some other European countries, but plainly Scotland was doing even less well.

Gradually it became apparent to the politicians and the planners that the nation was living, in William Ferguson's words, in 'a fool's paradise'.[25] The economic boom was now seen to depend on the temporary conditions of replacement demand after 1945 and the virtual absence of international competition while the ravaged economies of Europe and the Far East recovered from the devastation of war. There had still been precious little industrial diversification. Indeed, the heavy industries were more dormant by 1958 than they had been in the later 1930s. In the west of Scotland, core of the traditional industries, the rate of entry of new companies in the 1950s was about half that of the 1940s. Ominously, indigenous enterprise was also much less in evidence. Before the Second World War, most companies in the region were Scottish-controlled. By 1960, over 60 per cent of all manufacturing firms employing more than 250 people were owned by non-Scottish interests.

However, the most serious concerns were voiced about the condition of the industrial staples. Coal in particular faced a bleak future. The once rich Lanarkshire field was virtually worked out, while many consumers were moving to electricity, oil and gas. The conversion of locomotives from coal-burning to diesel engines and steel furnaces to oil-burning cut deeply into much of the traditional market for coal. Steel was better placed. In 1957 Scotland's first integrated iron and steel works, built at a cost of £22.5 million, was brought into production at Ravenscraig near Motherwell. But by the later 1950s Europe had recovered from the war, much more steel was being produced and, with a world surplus building up, price-cutting became a common strategy. Despite the Ravenscraig investment, the Scottish steel industry remained vulnerable because of its inland location and consequent high costs for ore and delivery of finished products. Even before the late 1950s, shipbuilding was losing much of its world ascendancy as although global demand for ships was still very buoyant the Clyde's share of output was already in steady decline. In 1947, Clyde yards launched 18 per cent of world tonnage but this slumped to 4.5 per cent in 1958. Scottish shipbuilding, once a world-class industry, was in a sorry state and its many grievous problems had simply been concealed by the post-war replacement boom. Certainly German, Dutch, Swedish and Japanese yards had the benefit of more lavish state support, but it was still the case that many of the wounds of Scottish shipbuilders were self-inflicted. While their rivals adopted streamlined assembly-line techniques, invested extensively in mechanization and designed well-planned yards, the Scots stood still, apart from the replacement of riveting by welding and improvements in prefabrication. They were losing their competitive edge. In the later 1950s German yards could frequently deliver ships in half the time quoted by Clyde builders. Indecisive management and workers caught up in numerous demarcation disputes bore a collective responsibility for this state of affairs which was by no means inevitable but which before too long would bring a once mighty industry to the brink of total collapse.

The difficulties of the Scottish economy had immediate political repercussions. In the 1959 general election, Scotland voted against the UK trend and Labour emerged as the biggest single party in the country, with 38 seats to the Unionists' 32. There was also more activity in the smaller parties. Liberalism had been little more relevant than Nationalism throughout the 1950s; but after 1957, under Jo Grimond's energetic leadership, the party started to have much more public impact. On the face of it the SNP remained moribund, contesting only five seats in the 1959 general election, but the organizational foundations were now being laid for the party's achievements in the 1960s. Arthur Donaldson admitted at the time that all the party's activists could have been carried in a small passenger plane which, if it crashed without survivors, would have destroyed the cause of Scottish independence for a generation. By the early 1960s, however, under the organizational direction of Ian Macdonald, local SNP branches were being set up across the land. Before 1962 there were fewer than 20, but by 1965 the number had risen to 140. The party first showed its electoral teeth at the West Lothian by-election in 1962. It was won by Tam Dalyell, the Labour candidate, but William Wolfe, later leader of the SNP, pushed the Unionists into third place, in the process attracting nearly 10,000 votes in a rock-solid Labour constituency. What was interesting was the changing compos-ition of the activist group which supported Wolfe's campaign. They were now mainly drawn from the skilled working class and lower-middle class and differed radically from the SNP old guard of professionals, writers, academics and upper-class lawyers: 'these were more sober types, less interested in poetry than in digging out figures on the Scottish economy'.[26]

The economy was once again at the centre of the political battleground and as fears mounted that Scotland might slip back to the dark days of the 1930s the Conservative government, under two successive Scottish Secretaries, John S. Maclay and Michael Noble, embarked on an ambitious programme of economic planning and intervention. The inspiration came partly from the 1961 Toothill Report, called after its chairman, Sir John Toothill of Ferranti Ltd. He identified the major structural weakness of the Scottish economy as the over-reliance on traditional industry, the inability to adapt to new world markets, and the failure of the new science-based manufactures to become established on any significant scale. In some ways the emphasis was unfortunate, since the Report tended to equate good with new and bad with old. Some diversification was clearly imperative but the 'old' industries, apart from coal, still had considerable potential if they had attracted government investment to the same extent as their overseas competitors and had more imaginative and dynamic management strategies. In the event, the Tories did try to preserve traditional industry while at the same time generating new growth areas through the Scottish Development

Department (established in 1962) and a Central Scotland Plan. Their strategy was designed as much to shore up their weakening political position as to halt Scottish economic decline.

Prodigious sums were poured into prestige projects. A loan of £50 million was virtually forced upon Colvilles Ltd in 1958 to encourage the firm to construct a state-of-the-art strip mill at Ravenscraig despite the commercial judgement of the directors – and Sir Andrew McCance in particular – that the market in Scotland was not great enough to warrant such a vast investment. From the start the whole viability of Colvilles as a steel-making enterprise was threatened by the burdens imposed by this major development. Then, in May 1963, the Duke of Edinburgh opened the Rootes car plant in Linwood, the first built in Scotland for 30 years, amid a blaze of publicity. It cost another £23.5 million and was designed to reach a staggering output of 150,000 cars a year when in full production. Finally, in December 1964 the British Motor Corporation set up a great truck plant at Bathgate. Whatever the economic future of these projects, they manifestly failed to repair Tory fortunes. In the same year as Bathgate started production, Labour won a narrow victory in the general election on Harold Wilson's campaign slogan of '13 wasted years' of Conservative rule. Scotland made a decisive contribution to this triumph by returning no fewer than 43 Labour MPs. Labour scraped home nationally with a majority of six. Wilson's narrow victory depended in large part on the Scottish electorate who had turned against the Tories despite their extraordinary spending spree on great factories and industrial investment.

24

The Scottish Question

The most sensational by-election result in Scotland since 1945 came in Hamilton in Lanarkshire in November 1967 with the victory of the young Glasgow solicitor, Winifred Ewing, over Labour. The SNP won with 46 per cent of the vote – and this in one of the safest Labour seats in the party's political heartland of the west of Scotland. Mrs Ewing travelled to London in triumph by train, accompanied by large numbers of enthusiastic SNP supporters, before being driven to Westminster in a scarlet Hillman Imp built at the Linwood car plant. The victory truly put the SNP on the British political map and attracted huge press and television interest. The success also sent shock waves through the other political parties. Hamilton was no freak result. At the local elections in May 1968, the SNP had won a remarkable 34 per cent of the votes cast, had performed strongly in the Labour fiefdom of Glasgow, which was afterwards ruled by an SNP–Conservative coalition, and made 101 net gains as against overall Labour losses of 84. The Labour Party was increasingly dependent on support from Wales and Scotland to counter the effect of the strong Conservative vote in England. But now even the loyalty of the Celtic fringe seemed threatened by the growth of rampant nationalism. In the same year that the SNP won its famous victory at Hamilton, Plaid Cymru also achieved successes in a by-election and in local contests against Labour. As the veteran nationalist, Oliver Brown, wryly observed, 'a shiver ran along the Labour backbenches looking for a spine to run up'.[1]

The Conservatives, already anxious about their declining popularity in Scotland, were the first to respond positively to the perceived national-ist menace. Richard Crossman noted in his diaries the comment of the Tory leader, Ted Heath, that nationalism was the 'biggest single factor in our politics today'.[2] As the party in opposition, the Conservatives may have exploited the constitutional issue to put further pressure on the

Labour government. This was the background to Heath's remarkable Declaration of Perth in 1968 when, to the horror of many in the audience at the Scottish party conference, he committed the Conservatives to a devolved Scottish Assembly, thus reversing at a stroke an entire century of consistent Tory opposition to Home Rule.

After 1967 and 1968 Scottish politics would never be the same again. However, at first the SNP achievements did seem a mere flash in the pan. In the general election of 1970, while the Nationalists doubled their vote, they lost Hamilton and gained only one seat, the Western Isles. The gains at local authority elections were quickly reversed as it soon became clear that many of the new SNP councillors were both inexperienced and ineffective. A vote for the SNP came to be regarded as an act of protest, a manifestation of Scottish discontent about government policy rather than a commitment to Scottish independence. All the opinion polls confirmed that only a small minority of those who actually supported the party in elections wished to see Scotland separated from the United Kingdom. Harold Wilson's policy of prevarication towards nationalism seemed to be amply justified by the course of events. He had appointed Lord Crowther to head a Royal Commission on the Constitution in 1969 but was in little doubt that this body would take a lot of time before producing a report and recommendations. The Prime Minister had once famously declared that Royal Commissions spent years taking minutes. The SNP performance in the 1970 general election, though its best to date, gaining 11 per cent of the vote but only one seat, confirmed the Labour government's view that delaying tactics on the Scottish constitutional issue were by far the most effective approach to an irritating problem.

However, the nationalist challenge had not run out of steam. Early indications that the SNP were once again on the move came in March 1973, when it polled 30 per cent of the vote in Dundee East, and again in November of that year, when the charismatic 'blonde bombshell and darling of the media', Margo MacDonald, won the rock-solid Labour seat of Glasgow Govan. In the first general election of 1974, the SNP broke through as a real parliamentary force in Scotland, gaining seven seats and 22 per cent of the vote. Within a week, the incoming Labour government embraced devolution as a real commitment despite having fought the election on a platform opposed to it. Even diehard opponents of Home Rule like the formidable Secretary of State for Scotland, Willie Ross, the 'Hammer of the Nats', were forced to eat their words. In the second election of 1974 in October the SNP did even better by pushing the Tories into third place in Scotland and achieving 30 per cent of the vote. The party still had only 11 seats, but more alarming from Labour's point of view was the fact that the SNP had come second in no fewer than 42 constituencies. As Michael Foot confided to Winnie Ewing: 'It is not the eleven of you that terrify me so much, Winnie, it is the 42 seconds.'[3] Within three months Labour published a White Paper, *Devolution in the UK – Some Alternatives for Discussion*, which set out five options for change. Even though many in the Labour Party in Scotland were opposed to this appeasement of the hated nationalists the Cabinet was determined to press for some form of change, not in order to improve the UK constitution, but to end the threat of separatism. Roy Jenkins, then Home Secretary, admitted:

The fundamental trouble was that the Labour Party leadership, I think this was true of Wilson, I think it was true of Callaghan, I think it was to some substantial extent true of Willie Ross, saw the need for some declaration to avoid losing by-elections to the Nationalists, and not to produce a good constitutional settlement for Scotland and the UK. Any question of separation would be very damaging for the Labour Party because, while it might give Labour a very powerful position in Scotland, if you do not have Scottish members of parliament playing their full part in Westminster then the Labour Party could pretty much say goodbye to any hope of a majority ever in the UK.[4]

The Labour leadership was therefore enraged when, in June 1974, the Scottish executive rejected all five options in the White Paper by a narrow margin at a meeting that was poorly attended, reputedly because it was held at the same time as a World Cup football match in which Scotland was playing! A special conference of the party was then ordered to be held two months later in the Co-operative Halls in Glasgow to reverse the decision. The debate was bitter and bad-tempered, with many arguing that nationalism was in direct conflict with socialism and that devolution would dilute the benefits of central planning which had brought so many economic benefits to Scotland since the end of the Second World War. In the end, the union block vote was used to push through a motion in favour of devolution, the Scottish Trade Union Congress having for some time become an enthusiastic convert to Home Rule. Constitutional change for Scotland was firmly back on the political agenda within seven years of the SNP's historic victory at Hamilton and was due in large part to the two great surges of support for the party in 1967–8 and again in 1973–4.

Hamilton stands out as a landmark in the rise of the SNP but it did not come out of the blue. There were already clear signs of a revival in the party's fortunes earlier in the 1960s. Under the dynamic leadership of Arthur Donaldson as chairman, the number of branches rose from 20 in 1960 to 470 in 1969 and the party claimed an increase in membership over that period from 1,000 to 125,000. Organization improved under the former farmer, Ian MacDonald, and was shown to good effect in by-elections at Glasgow Bridgeton in 1961 and West Lothian in 1962. One reason for Winnie Ewing's victory in 1967 was the ability of the SNP to flood the Hamilton constituency with an army of eager young canvassers and volunteers who proved more than a match for the moribund local Labour Party organization. The SNP in these years also entered into discussion with the Liberals with a view to possible co-operation against the two big parties. The Liberals had already achieved early success, having been brought back from virtual oblivion by their solitary MP and leader, Jo Grimond, and they wrested three northern seats from the Conservatives in 1964, followed by the victory of the 26-year-old David Steel in the Roxburgh, Selkirk and Peebles by-election, a year later. In 1964 and 1967 both parties met to discuss an electoral pact. Though the talks foundered, they tellingly illustrated SNP ambitions and the growing force of third-party politics in Scotland. Labour and Conservatives might stand for socialism and capitalism, but the very classlessness of the SNP gave it a distinctive appeal, especially for new voters and for those with no previous party affiliations. A series of studies have shown that the SNP had a special attraction in this period for non-manual workers who had been upwardly mobile from the working classes, those who 'were renouncing the class of their homes, while not yet entering the middle class' and first-time voters.[5] The very vagueness of SNP policy on a number of issues (apart from the core factor of the constitution) also made the party an appealing vehicle for those who wanted a focus for a range of political discontents.

In the final analysis, however, the rise of the SNP and the new centrality of the Scottish question in national politics by the early 1970s was based not so much on the party's intrinsic attractions as on the broader historical context of the times. Few Scots, even at the height of the party's electoral popularity in 1974, wished to break the union but sought to improve it to Scottish advantage. Opinion polls revealed that, while a third of Scots had voted for the SNP in that year, only 12 per cent supported independence. The SNP's success alarmed governments and was seen as an effective way of drawing attention to Scotland's problems. At the same time, however, deeper changes were under way which were to the party's advantage. 'Britishness' may have had less appeal than before. That linchpin of the union, the British Empire, was disintegrating at remarkable speed. India had gained independence in 1947 and a decade later even the African possessions, starting with Ghana, were winning freedom from British rule. Other former colonies followed in quick succession. Britain was seen to be a nation of declining influence on the world stage. Having won the war, she seemed to be losing the peace. Successive governments had great power pretensions but the façade could not disguise the real erosion of Britain's standing. The Suez Crisis in 1956 conclusively demonstrated the international dominance of the USA, with Britain tagging along as merely a junior partner in the 'special relationship'. In 1963 the British government of Harold Macmillan was humiliated when its application for membership of the Common Market was summarily rejected at the insistence of the French President, Charles de Gaulle, who dismissed the idea by claiming that the United Kingdom was unfit for full membership. Not until 1973 did the UK finally join. A year later, John Mackintosh argued in the *New Statesman* that whatever the other political parties offered to stem the SNP advance would not be enough 'so long as there is no proper pride in being British'.[6] Ironically, it was the attempt to maintain Britain's status as a world military power that helped to alienate some in the new generation of Scots. In November 1960 Prime Minister Macmillan announced that the country's main nuclear deterrent, the Polaris submarine, would be based in the Holy Loch in Scotland, a decision confirmed in 1964 by the Labour government of Harold Wilson. These decisions boosted the membership of the Campaign for Nuclear Disarmament (CND) in Scotland, while opposition north of the border had a particular force because of the realization that the Scots would be in the front line in the event of nuclear war. This galvanized hostility across the political spectrum. But the SNP was the only party to voice outright opposition to nuclear weapons in the 1960s, especially after Hugh Gaitskell succeeded in reversing the policy of unilateralism espoused by Labour in 1960. Some leading figures in the SNP of future years, such as William Wolfe, Isabel Lindsay and Margo MacDonald, had been members of CND. It was partly because of the success of the familiar CND symbol of the time that the SNP adopted what soon became its own equally recognizable image, the thistle-loop.

More fundamental – at least in the short term – than the issue of Britishness was the impact of economic change on the fortunes of the SNP. Harold Wilson's government had taken office in 1964 with the promise of bringing the 'white heat of the technological revolution' to bear on Britain's endemic problems. Planning was to be the panacea for both economic decline and regional disadvantage. Willie Ross, the Secretary of State, was the man responsible for ensuring that Scotland obtained at least its fair share of the resources to be dispensed through this strategy. Ross was in office from 1964 to 1970 and again from 1974 to 1976. He was the dominant Scottish politician of the day, an elder of the kirk, and a former army major and schoolmaster, who was a formidable champion of Scotland's cause in Cabinet. A ferocious opponent of the SNP, who was fond of referring to it as the Scottish Narks Party, he was yet utterly determined to fight Scotland's corner against all comers. The late John Smith, who served as his parliamentary private secretary in 1974, recalled:

There was a legion of people he didn't like, but he had real bearing and style. He was a proper Secretary of State. He could charm the birds off the trees. I saw him at functions at Edinburgh Castle when he would absolutely charm foreign bankers. He was passionately Scottish too. He has some wonderful achievements to his credit. He could get things through. He was extremely good in Cabinet. He achieved enormous success in what he could get for Scotland in expenditure terms. I think his technique was to secure Scotland somehow and then support the Chancellor in doing everybody else down. I said, 'Why don't you boast of your success?' He said, 'You don't understand: the day you do that you can never do it again'. He was willing to give up the taking of credit in order to secure the advance.

When I was at the Department of Energy [in 1974–5] and Willie was Secretary of State, he expected Scots in other ministries really to be ambassadors for Scotland. He would say, 'You know what your duty is here'. He felt I was on loan, from him to the Department of Energy.[7]

Under Ross, Labour in Scotland did deliver at first. Public expenditure rose spectacularly by 900 per cent to £192.3 million between 1964 and 1973 as the Secretary of State successfully extracted as large a share as possible from the public purse for Scotland. Identifiable public spending per head north of the border moved to one-fifth above the British average. The whole of Scotland except Edinburgh was designated as one large development area within which over £600 million of aid was dispensed through a new Scottish Office Department. No area of the country was left untouched. The Highlands and Islands Development Board was set up in 1965 with executive authority over transport, industry and tourism. The north also gained when the Dounreay fast breeder reactor started in 1966, followed by the Invergordon smelter in 1968. A huge new pit at Longannet was opened, bringing with it the promise of 10,000 new jobs. The Forth Road Bridge was completed in 1964 and the Tay Road Bridge in 1966. Achievements were by no means confined to infrastructure and industry. Following the publication of the Robbins Report in 1963, the number of universities doubled to eight with the foundation of Strathclyde (1964), Heriot-Watt (1966), Dundee (1967) and the only entirely new institution, Stirling (1968). There was a huge growth in the teaching profession of over 20 per cent between 1963 and 1973, which led to the opening of three colleges of education, at Ayr, Hamilton and Falkirk in 1964–5. Technical colleges also boomed at the same time. In the 1960s, comprehensive schooling was introduced into Scotland, more successfully than in England. By 1974, under half the children south of the border were in comprehensives, compared to 98 per cent in Scotland. The fact that so many of the larger Education Authorities were controlled by Labour helped facilitate the process. Local government itself was not immune from the wind of change. A Royal Commission was appointed under Lord Wheatley to recommend reforms in a system which had hardly altered since the 1920s.

The social and economic impact of all this activity can hardly be doubted. Scotland was gaining from the union as public revenues were channelled north in the form of massive regional assistance and other benefits. Ross had demonstrated that, like Tom Johnston before him, the union relationship could be maximized to Scottish advantage. Labour was rewarded with a general election victory for Wilson's government in 1966 in which the Conservatives lost three of their 24 seats in Scotland. This, however, was the lull before the storm. Planning and lavish state expenditure had created expectations which could not always be fulfilled. The vast Labour spending on the National Plan made it difficult to balance the budget. This in turn led to wage restrictions and increases in duties on foreign imports. A dockers' strike in 1966 compounded the problems and pushed sterling down further. The government was soon forced to devalue but Harold Wilson's boast that 'the pound in your pocket' was still secure did not convince a sceptical electorate. This was the political background to the SNP's advances at the by-election in Pollok and the victory at Hamilton in 1967. Planning had now degenerated into crisis management and no longer could the state guarantee the employment levels and the material standards to which the Scots had become accustomed. This triggered support for the SNP in the short term, though much of it soon melted away. Articulate opponents, such as the eloquent and energetic Jim Sillars, then a prominent unionist member of the Labour Party, were able to launch a devastating attack on the SNP's Achilles heel, namely the absence of any coherent ideological position on social and economic issues. At the same time, the inept performance of many SNP councillors, some of whom resigned soon after their election, conveyed to the public the image of a party which had come much too far too fast. In the 1970 South Ayrshire by-election, Labour, with Sillars as its candidate, overwhelmed the SNP and effectively derailed their bandwagon. At the general election later that same year, the Tories triumphed under Ted Heath. But it was unlikely that the constitutional relationship between Scotland and the rest of the UK would disappear as an issue. Heath's new Secretary of State, Gordon Campbell, was the first since 1945 to belong to a government that did not possess a majority of votes or seats in Scotland. Before long, this and other factors were to cause trouble for the new incumbents.

A basic cause of the growing prominence of the SNP in Scottish politics in the 1960s and 1970s was the decline in the Tory Party as the most effective challenge to the hegemony of Labour in Scotland. The Conservatives had stood above all for Unionism. Indeed, it was only in 1964 that the Scottish party dropped the 'Unionist' label in favour of the more anglicized 'Conservative' one. For decades it had been a powerful vehicle north of the border for the expression of British patriotism. Now the decay of the party gave Nationalism its chance. The vote against Labour, which earlier might have gone overwhelmingly to the Unionists, now sometimes went to the SNP. The Liberals, despite their successes in rural Scotland, proved to be less significant than in England where in the two 1974 elections, when the SNP was at its peak, they took over 20 per cent of the vote compared to around 8 per cent north of the border. The decline in Unionist popularity was as swift as it was sudden. As recently as 1955, the Unionists had attracted just over 50 per cent of all Scottish votes, the only party ever to have managed that electoral achievement. But in retrospect, this was to prove a watershed in their fortunes. In 1959 the number of Unionist MPs fell from 36 to 31, then to 24 in 1964, and it dropped again to 20 in the 1966 general election. It was still not a disaster on the scale of the elections of 1987 and the 1990s, but it was nevertheless still an enormous humiliation for a party that was the most successful in Scottish politics since the end of Liberal hegemony after 1918.

Increasingly the Unionists presented a remote élite and an anglicized image that seemed out of touch with current Scottish problems. In part, this was due to the combination of the difficulties of the older industries and the inexorable decline of indigenous control of manufacturing and enterprise with nationalization, numerous mergers and the penetration of American capital. The great Scottish captains of industry and leaders of the Clydeside dynasties who had formerly ruled the party were fast disappearing and their place was once again being taken by lairds and aristocrats who had received an entirely anglicized education. The huge changes in urban housing after the Second World War also affected the party's fortunes. The massive working-class peripheral housing estates around Glasgow and Edinburgh established new Labour fiefdoms in former rural areas, while the flight of the middle classes to the suburbs eroded the Conservative vote in the heart of the cities. It may seem remarkable from the perspective of the 1990s, but as late as 1951 the Conservatives held as many as seven seats in Glasgow, only one less than Labour. By 1964, however, they were left with two, one of which was already very vulnerable.

The secret of Conservative success for much of the twentieth century had been the ability to reach out well beyond the middle classes to the respectable, skilled and semi-skilled working classes in Scotland. To them the party represented Protestantism, Unionism and imperial identity. Even in 1986, 45 per cent of the members of the Church of Scotland claimed to vote Tory. In Dundee in 1968, nearly 40 per cent of Protestant manual workers voted Conservative, compared to 6 per cent of Roman Catholics of the same class. These figures were produced when the pattern of voting along religious lines – at least for Protestants – was already in decline. It is very likely that in the 1950s and early 1960s political and religious cleavages in Scotland were even deeper. Nevertheless, the bedrock Protestant working-class support for Conservatism was crumbling in the 1960s and 1970s. Britishness had less appeal and the empire was fading fast. The influence of the Kirk was also ebbing. Church membership reached a peak in the mid-1950s and then went into serious decline. In 1956, 46 per cent of Scots had a formal Church connection. By 1994, this proportion had fallen to 27 per cent. The rate of decline for the Church of Scotland was even greater because, until recent years, the overall haemorrhage from the Catholic Church was much less. A 'membership catastrophe'[8] occurred during the 'Swinging Sixties'. Many young people lost contact with religion altogether. The numbers attending Sunday School plummeted and the proportion of marriages being religiously solemnized fell, especially from 1964/5. That Scotland was becoming a more secular society was also illustrated by the decline of sectarian employment practices, encouraged by the impact of new foreign-owned industry, the nationalization and/or decay of the older staple manufactures, where discrimination against Catholics in skilled occupations had flourished, and the effect of full employment in the 1950s and early 1960s on the labour market. As a result, the Protestant monopoly of many skilled jobs was broken. Mixed marriages and the growing integration of the Catholic community into Scottish society as a result of better educational opportunities in colleges and universities after 1945 also diluted, although they did not yet end, the bitterness of historic religious divisions. It was a sign of the times when (the then) Archbishop Winning in 1975 became the first Catholic priest to address the General Assembly of the Church of Scotland, a body which just before the Second World War had campaigned vigorously against Irish Catholic immigration. Seven years later, Pope John Paul II met with the Moderator under the statue of the great reformer, John Knox, during his historic visit to Scotland. There were occasional 'No Popery' demonstrations during the visit, but it was significant that most people regarded them as unrepresentative of Scottish public opinion as a whole. The Conservatives suffered most as a result of this growing tolerance and the associated secularization of Scottish politics. As early as 1964, when they suffered the shattering loss of the Pollok constituency in Glasgow, party managers first became aware that they were losing the old working-class religious vote. On the other hand, the Catholic Labour vote remained solid for another generation, while in the 1970s support for the SNP was overwhelmingly Protestant. The Tories were therefore squeezed by two forces: the desertion of many of their working-class supporters to new allegiances and the still unquestioning loyalty to Labour of the Catholic population in numerous west of Scotland constituencies.

Nevertheless, in 1970 Scotland found itself once again under Conservative rule, although the party itself was in a minority north of the border. The new Prime Minister, Ted Heath, had been one of the first modern British politicians to acknowledge the importance of devolution for Scotland in his Declaration of Perth. However, the SNP performed poorly in the general election of 1970 by winning only the Western Isles. Some now thought it a spent force. Heath then took the opportunity to shelve the plans for a Scottish Assembly formulated by Lord Home's constitutional committee which he had appointed. From that point on, devolution had little appeal for the Tories. However, two factors during the period of Conservative administration rejuvenated the SNP and led to a spectacular performance in the two elections of 1974 which placed constitutional change once again at the centre of political debate for the rest of the decade. First, the Heath government tried to mount a radical assault on the interventionist economic policies that had sustained both Labour and Tories alike since 1945. There was to be more competition, industrial 'lame ducks' should not be propped up with taxpayers' money, overwhelming union power had to be crushed and a more discriminating approach undertaken to state welfare provision. The attempt to reform housing finance in Scotland under the Housing Financial Provisions (Scotland) Act provoked furious resistance from local authorities under Labour control, since low rents had been one of the key foundations of the vast post-war housing programmes around the Scottish cities. The Tories now proposed not only to raise them but also to end subsidized rents by demanding that local authorities balance the books on their housing accounts. This was political anathema. No fewer than 25 authorities refused to co-operate and came into line only when they were taken to court and fined for their truculence.

More serious was the plight of Upper Clyde Shipbuilders (UCS), one of two large combines established on the Clyde in 1967–8 to increase the competitive potential of a flagging industry. In 1971, UCS announced it was going into receivership with the potential loss of 8,500 jobs. Dole queues were already lengthening in Scotland during the first year of the Heath government, and the collapse of UCS was seen as a potentially mortal blow to the tottering edifice of the old industrial structure. Clydeside shipbuilding was seen as a Scottish icon, a great symbol of the country's glorious industrial past which could not be allowed to disappear and was now threatened with bankruptcy only because of the uncaring actions of a government for which the Scots had not voted. Under the charismatic and skilful leadership of two young Communist shop stewards, Jimmy Reid and Jimmy Airlie, a campaign of resistance to closure began which attracted widespread national support. In June 1972 an estimated 80,000 people marched to a rally in Glasgow in support of the workers' right to work. Nothing like it had ever been seen in this century, not even during the heyday of Red Clydeside. Reid himself argued later that the fight was initially to save the yards but it was eventually transformed into a wider struggle to protect the Scottish economy and the rights of the Scottish people to have some control over their destiny. UCS was reprieved and the government gave in. Protest was seen to work.

Second, the credibility of the government was undermined by economic crisis and industrial action. Heath's Industrial Relations Act, far from curbing union power, swiftly unleashed an unprecedented wave of unrest in the workplace which culminated in the mighty National Union of Mineworkers' refusal to accept the government's pay policy. This led to an overtime ban, a state of emergency and finally to power cuts and a three-day week in the depths of the winter of 1973. Inflation stood at 18 per cent in November of that year and the balance of payments slipped into a huge deficit as the Arabs' limits on oil production after the Yom Kippur War with the Israelis led to a quadrupling of prices. In early 1974, Heath was forced to go to the country on the issue of 'Who Governs Britain?'. The nation was in acute crisis and there seemed little hope of recovery from the British disease of unemployment, balance-of-payments problems and poor labour relations.

However, the SNP argued that there was a way out of the spiral of decline if an independent Scotland took control of the enormous oil resources now becoming available in the North Sea. In October 1970, BP struck oil 110 miles off Aberdeen in what was to become the giant Forties field. The inflation in world oil prices after the Arab–Israeli War meant that even marginal fields could have huge potential value. Recovery of the 'black gold' and expansion in the area of exploration proceeded apace. The SNP oil campaign began in 1971 and brilliantly exploited the contrast between, on the one hand, the fabulous wealth found off Scotland's coasts and, on the other, the fact that by then the Scots had the worst unemployment rate in western Europe and were yoked to a British state that stumbled from crisis to crisis. Oil also gave the nationalist argument a new credibility by demonstrating that an independent Scotland might indeed survive out of its own resources. In November 1973 Margo MacDonald's victory at Govan for the SNP, one of the safest of Labour seats, was the prelude to sweeping gains in the two general elections in 1974, including the scalp of the Tory Scottish Secretary, Gordon Campbell. Indeed the nationalists did especially well in former Conservative seats. Nine of the 11 that they won were from the Tories. The SNP was once again regarded as an effective instrument for exerting pressure on London government to respond to Scottish grievances. However, its problem was that only a small minority of its supporters agreed with the long-term strategy of full independence, while its voting strength was notoriously soft and volatile and liable to dissipate when grievances became less pressing.

Nevertheless, the electoral success of the SNP in 1974 meant that Home Rule remained at the top of the UK political agenda for the next several years. Labour had gone to the country in October 1974 as a strong supporter of devolution, and its first attempt at honouring the election pledges came in 1975 when *Our Changing Democracy* was published, proposing a Scottish Assembly of 142 members, funded by a block grant and with control over most Scottish Office functions but with no revenue-raising powers. Jim Sillars, by now a convinced and enthusiastic devolutionist, thought the blueprint lacked economic teeth. He and one other MP, John Robertson, defected to form the Scottish Labour Party in early 1976, an ephemeral grouping prone to Marxist infiltration that lasted for a mere three years. The departure of Sillars exposed the deep Labour divisions on Home Rule. Some still believed that strong centralist powers were needed to solve Scotland's economic problems and this sentiment inspired the foundation of the Scottish Development Agency in July 1975. Others thought that devolution was essential to stop the SNP bandwagon, while the opposing view was that conceding anything to the Nationalists would accelerate movement towards the break-up of the United Kingdom. Essentially, however, the party's public support for Home Rule was founded on the paramount importance of halting the progress of the SNP while, at the same time, minimalizing factionalism on the issue among its MPs. Tam Dalyell, MP for West Lothian and arch-enemy of Home Rule in all its forms, was able to mount a sustained and effective campaign against what he contemptuously dismissed as illogical proposals designed to placate nationalism which would lead inevitably to separation between England and Scotland. By 1977 the Labour government was weak in the extreme. It had only a small majority and from March of that year depended on Liberal support for its very existence. The Cabinet also faced a multitude of intractable economic problems. Throughout the UK, over 1,250,000 were unemployed, the balance-of-payments deficit approached £1 billion and annual inflation stood at 16 per cent. The Chancellor, Denis Healey, was forced to go cap in hand to the International Monetary Fund for a substantial loan during the sterling crisis of September 1976. This rescue package was to be agreed only if draconian cuts in government expenditure were implemented. The government had by now become widely unpopular and did not possess either the moral authority or the power in parliament to manage effectively the most important constitutional change in the United Kingdom since the emergence of the Irish Free State in 1922.

Difficulties soon emerged when the Scotland and Wales Bill was presented in the House of Commons. To avoid intensifying the damaging splits on devolution, the government was forced to concede a referendum. Michael Foot, who was responsible for taking the Bill through parliament, admitted that it was forced on the Cabinet by threatened backbench disaffection. At least 140 MPs signed a motion urging a referendum and stating they would not vote for the Bill unless it was granted. A government with a tiny majority had no choice but to concede. The referendum was at best a delaying tactic and at worst a wrecking device; cheered by this victory, the anti-devolutionists pressed on to other triumphs. The attempt to impose a guillotine on further parliamentary discussion of the Bill after its second and third readings failed, leaving opponents of the legislation with the opportunity to table amendments which could water down the original proposals even further. The most crucial of these was the motion proposed by the Labour MP for London Islington, the Scot George Cunningham, that if less than 40 per cent of those voting in the referendum voted 'yes' then an order should be laid before parliament for the repeal of the Scotland Act. This amendment was passed on Burns Night, 25 January 1978. For those bent on destroying devolution it proved a potent weapon. Cunningham's coup has been described by some political scientists as the most significant backbench intervention in any parliament since 1945. The Scotland Act was finally agreed by the Commons in

February 1978. Now the verdict of the Scottish people was awaited.

When they gave their answer on 1 March 1979 it was inconclusive, ambivalent and confusing. The majority of those who voted did vote 'yes', 51.6 per cent or 1.23 million Scots, as against 48.4 on the 'no' side. But on such a major constitutional issue the margin of victory was very slim indeed and, since the 'yes' vote represented just less than a third of the whole electorate, was well below the 40 per cent required by the Cunningham amendment. This was hardly a ringing endorsement of Home Rule. Moreover, just 63.8 per cent of those entitled to vote did so, which does not suggest that the Scotland Act had engendered mass popular enthusiasm. More seriously, much of the rural north and south of Scotland voted against devolution. The Borders, Dumfries and Galloway, Tayside, Grampian and the Orkney and Shetland Islands all recorded 'no' majorities, suggesting they were more in fear of domination from the Labour-controlled cities of the Lowlands than with rule from London. The SNP launched a 'Scotland Said Yes' campaign to urge the government to press on with devolution. But the cause was lost. The truth was that less than a third of the electorate had actually voted for the most important constitutional change in Scotland's history since the union of 1707 and the detailed results of the referendum demonstrated conclusively that the Scottish people were hopelessly divided on the issue. Since the Callaghan government failed to deliver devolution and had proved incapable of controlling its backbenchers during the passage of the Bill through parliament, the SNP thought it had no option but to table a motion of no confidence in an increasingly discredited administration. This succeeded by one vote and, in the general election that followed, the Conservatives under Margaret Thatcher swept to power with a radical agenda for curing Britain's ills in which constitutional change had no part. For the SNP, the election was a disaster. It lost nine of its 11 seats, thus confirming James Callaghan's famous gibe that the censure of the nationalist MPs on his government was the first recorded instance in history of turkeys voting for an early Christmas. The election failures were bad enough but, in addition, 'No institution, no region of the country, no section of society was clearly converted to their cause. They had on the contrary been shown beyond doubt that, while young Scots saw themselves as a useful tool for securing reform, few actually shared their aspirations.'[9] The campaign for Home Rule which had dominated much of Scottish politics in the 1970s collapsed in acrimony, bitterness and disillusion. Turnbull's cartoon in the *Glasgow Herald*, depicting the Scottish lion admitting, 'I'm feart', captured the mood of despondency in the pro-devolution camp.

A number of factors combined to cause the failure of 1979. The nationalist tide had been rising in 1977 and the SNP did well in the district elections of that year. But by 1978 the party was less popular and lost two important by-elections to Labour. Significantly, a *Scotsman* opinion poll, published a fortnight before Referendum Day, showed the SNP as a poor third in national popularity with half the support of the Conservatives and Labour. The electorate were mainly concerned with strikes, industrial relations and unemployment, and a mere 5 per cent of those interviewed gave any priority to devolution. Equally significantly, the Tories were doing well in these surveys and, alone among the major parties, were committed to opposing devolution. At a time when the country seemed to lurch from crisis to crisis, people appeared to be more concerned with jobs and living standards than with constitutional reform. 1978–9, saw the notorious 'Winter of Discontent', when Britain was rocked by a series of industrial disputes as the big unions smashed through the government's pay norms. Television images of uncollected rubbish piled high on the streets and hospital workers out on strike conveyed an image of public anarchy. At one point even the dead went unburied. A government which had demonstrated such incompetence was hardly in a position to convince the Scots of the merits of the Scotland Act.

The 'Yes' camp was also fundamentally split. Indeed, the divisions within it were almost as deep as between them and the opponents of devolution. The SNP and Labour 'Yes' campaign would not co-operate, in part because they had different aspirations, the former seeing the Act as but a stepping-stone on the road to full independence, the latter arguing that devolution would help to strengthen the union. Three high-profile Labour MPs, Robin Cook, Brian Wilson and Tam Dalyell, ran a 'Labour Says No' campaign and managed to attract considerable media attention. It did not help that the Assembly, its powers mangled and steadily reduced by parliament and the civil service, was 'an emaciated figure' by the time the Scotland Act reached its final stages, and not a national body likely to inspire either confidence or enthusiasm.[10] On the other hand, the 'No' campaign was much better organized and was well financed from Scottish business which denounced the proposed legislation as likely to raise taxes, endanger industry, produce yet more bureaucracy and increase the danger of conflict with London at a time of mounting economic difficulty in Britain as a whole. The 'Yes' camp had little effective answer to this heady mix of reasoned argument and scaremongering. The 'No' campaign was boosted further in the final weeks before the referendum with the late intervention of the former Tory Prime Minister, Lord Home, who had been chairman of Ted Heath's constitutional committee a decade before. He had had a reputation since then as a devolutionist, which increased the impact of his plea to the Scottish people to vote 'No'. He condemned the Scotland Act as inadequate and dangerous and argued that only through the rejection of this patently flawed legislation could a better set of proposals be put together by a future Conservative government. Whatever its impact on Scottish opinion as a whole, Home's intervention, in the words of one Glasgow Conservative activist, had 'a powerful, indeed devastating effect on Scottish Tories'.[11]

25

A Nation Reborn?

I

The débâcle of the 1979 referendum result was soon followed by the worst economic recession since the 1930s. To some extent the forces at work were global in scale, particularly the impact of the steep increase in oil prices during the 1970s on world demand for manufactures; but the depth of the crisis was intensified by factors peculiar to Scotland and the UK. North Sea oil, which doubled in price between 1977 and 1981, pushed up the value of the pound and cut back even further the market for those exports on which Scottish industry had a traditional dependence. This coincided with the election of a new Conservative government with a radical economic strategy fundamentally opposed to the consensus approach that had been an integral part of British politics since 1945. There was no sudden break with the past, as the last Labour administration had already been forced to introduce restraints on government expenditure in order to control the spiralling problem of debt in the public finances, but Mrs Thatcher and her colleagues now pursued these policies with unrelenting vigour. A new word, 'Thatcherism', coined by the journal *Marxism Today*, entered the political lexicon. Thatcherism came to mean monetary control, privatization, the liberalization of free markets, reduction in trade-union power and a concern to inspire a national revival of the virtues of self-help in a people perceived as too long wedded to state support and welfare subsidies. Thatcherism did not emerge fully formed in 1979–81 but rather evolved over the course of the 1980s. However, even in the early years, the full rigour of monetarist policy was imposed on an economy already mired in the most serious depression since the Second World War. Control of inflation would now take absolute priority over the safeguarding of full employment and the principal weapon to achieve

591

this was to be a rise in interest rates to ensure that the growth in the money supply was halted. By the end of the first year of the Conservative government, Bank of England base rate had gone as high as 17 per cent. The results of this policy were catastrophic for whole sectors of Scottish industry and this time the state would not shelter ailing and uncompetitive businesses from the harsh winds blowing through the market economy. Even if the social consequences proved damaging, there was to be no reversal of economic policy or a repetition of Ted Heath's ignominious surrender in the face of trade-union power in the early 1970s. As Mrs Thatcher famously declared at the Conservative Conference in 1981: 'You turn if you want; the lady's not for turning.'

Against this background the chairman of the Scottish Council (Development and Industry) predicted in October 1980 that Scotland would be more vulnerable than many parts of England in the new economic and political climate. He was proved right. Between 1979 and 1981, Scottish manufacturing lost 11 per cent of output and around one-fifth of all jobs. Manufacturing capacity fell all over the UK, but the decline in Scotland at 30.8 per cent between 1976 and 1987 was greatest of all. Worst hit was the traditional heavy industrial region of the west of Scotland, which experienced a fall of 36.9 per cent and the textiles area of the Borders, which lost 64.0 per cent of all manufacturing capacity. The great staples of the Victorian economy had been in difficulty for much of the period since the 1920s, though revived by war demand and post-war booms. Now they virtually all crumbled with astonishing swiftness. Scottish mining had long suffered from poor productivity levels but had been kept alive because the state-owned electricity industry was required to purchase coal from 1977. In the 1980s, however, the number of active pits fell from 15 to two. By 1997, with the failure of the miners' buyout at Monktonhall, this once mighty industry was reduced to the single Longannet complex on the Firth of Forth. The fate of shipbuilding was little better. In 1979–80 Scottish yards accounted for half of all the losses incurred by the nationalized British shipbuilders, and the rundown of the labour force was therefore inevitable. Only a handful of yards remain in the 1990s on the virtually silent River Clyde, Yarrows specializing in warships, Kvaerner at Govan (whose future is uncertain in 1999) and the small Ferguson company at Port Glasgow. In 1987, when the QE2 was re-engined with diesels, the work was not carried out where she had been built but in a German yard. It was a potent sign of the times. Textiles did not escape either. The last cargo of jute to Dundee from Bangladesh was landed in October 1998 as the industry had fallen victim to substitutes, including paper and plastic bags, bulk handling and containerization. Little remains in the 1990s of the Scottish textile industry except the high-quality production of knitwear in the Borders.

By the 1970s it was also clear that the steel industry was in acute difficulty. Demand for steel was falling generally in the UK in the later part of that decade and the Scottish plants were exposed in cost terms. Losses per ton were higher north of the border than in any of the other divisions of the British Steel Corporation because of the smaller scale of production and higher fuel and transport costs. But 'rationalization' with limited regard for political and social consequences was much harder to achieve in steel, even if the slimming down of the industry might be justified in the eyes of government by narrow economic and accountancy criteria. The Lanarkshire plants were the biggest electricity customer in the land and provided half of all the freight traffic in Scotland. They were also important suppliers to the North Sea construction yards at Clydebank, Nigg and Ardersier. The closure of the Linwood car plant in 1981, which had been a key market for strip steel, was therefore a serious blow but not a mortal one because business leaders and politicians of all parties were agreed that a Scottish steel-making presence was essential to attract other industry to Scotland. The survival of the great Ravenscraig works began to assume a totemic significance as the symbol of Scotland's historic status as a great industrial nation. Its closure was therefore unthinkable. Even the Tory Secretary of State, George Younger, indicated that the closure of 'the Craig' would be for him a resignation issue. But the plant did die, although it was death by a thousand cuts. During the 1980s, Ravenscraig was starved of investment, steadily reduced in capacity (including the closure of the Gartcosh rolling mill) and threatened with a complete shutdown on two occasions. Despite this, the workforce, under their energetic union convener, Tommy Brennan, agreed a package of productivity reforms which meant that they soon consistently outperformed the rival works at Llanwern in Wales. Nevertheless, when the privatization of the British Steel Corporation took place, Ravenscraig's days were clearly numbered. In January 1992 British Steel announced that the plant would close in the following year and when production finally ceased in June 1993 the end was accepted with resignation rather than protest.

Yet it was not simply the traditional pillars of Scottish industry that disintegrated with such frightening speed in the Thatcher years. Even many of the regional policy successes of the post-war years succumbed in significant numbers: 'A list of closures included Singers in Clydebank, Goodyear in Glasgow, Monsanto in Ayrshire, Massey Ferguson in Kilmarnock, BSR in East Kilbride, Wiggins Teape pulp mill in Fort William, Talbot's Linwood car plant, the Invergordon aluminium smelter, Caterpillar in Uddingston, Burroughs in Cumbernauld, Plessey in Bathgate, Rowntree Mackintosh in Edinburgh.'[1] Other multinationals, like Timex, Hoover and SFK, shed tens of thousands of jobs between 1976 and 1988, while commentators talked freely of the deindustrialization of Scotland as unemployment soared to levels not seen since the 1930s. The prominent SNP activist and former Labour MP, Jim Sillars, voiced the worst fears of many when he wrote in late 1985 that even Scottish Conservatives were alarmed at the serious threat to 'Scotland's place as an industrial nation'. The seemingly endless lists of closures were 'hammer blows at main pillars of Scottish economic life' and the optimism of the 1970s had now been replaced by a mood of deep pessimism: 'Today ours is a fearful anxious, nail-biting nation ruminating on Burns's salutation to human despair, "An' forward tho' I canna see, I guess and fear".'[2]

Sillars articulated the worries of many Scots at the prospect they faced of a seemingly inexorable process of national economic decline. It was these concerns which in large part fuelled popular hostility to the Thatcher governments, on whom fell the blame for the series of economic disasters. There was precious little discussion of the deep-seated weaknesses in several Scottish industries which were the major long-term causes of their collapse. The Conservatives were also accused of favouring the south-east and the Midlands where lay the foundations of their electoral supremacy and of ignoring the terrible effects of unemployment in Scotland, Wales and the north of England where they were much less popular. The Conservatives were punished in the general elections of the 1980s in Scotland and by 1992 had seen their vote collapse to historically low levels. No one can deny the political consequences of the perception of decline or of the personal suffering endured by many families caught up through unemployment in the vortex of economic change. Manufacturing as an employer is less prominent in Scotland in the 1990s than at any time since the Victorian era. In the 1980s it employed 800,000 Scots but only around half that number by the 1990s. Scotland now has a lower proportion of the population engaged in manufacturing than the average for the UK as a whole. But 'decline' is too simple a word to describe the entire process of change in the 1980s.

Sector	Number in Employment (thousands)			Change in Employment (percentage)		
	1979	1989	1994	1979	1989	1994
Agriculture, Forestry, Fishing	48	29	26	×40	×10	×46
Energy and Water Supply	72	57	49	×21	×14	×32
Manufacturing	604	402	354	×33	×12	×41
Construction	155	130	101	×16	×22	×35
Distribution, Hotels and Catering, Repairs	392	400	416	2	4	6
Transport and Communication	135	113	107	×16	×5	×21
Banking, Finance, Insurance and Business Services	123	176	204	43	16	66
Education, Health and Other Services	573	651	704	14	8	23
All Industries and Services	2102	1957	1963	×7	0.3	×6.6

Table 25:1. Employees in mployment in Scotland by major industry or service sector. Source: A. Brown, D. McCrone and L. Paterson, *Politics and Society in Scotland* (London, 1996), p. 75.

Table 25.1 shows that Scotland experienced a revolution in employment in these years. The number of workers in manufacturing, agriculture, fisheries fell by nearly a half between 1979 and 1994, while the total number of workers in financial and public services has expanded dramatically. By the 1990s, the service sector had become the most dynamic part of the economy and this is a development that Scotland shares with other advanced countries in western Europe and North America. 'Services' are complex and include hotels and catering, transport, tourism, business services, education and health. In the private sector, the jewel in the crown is finance. In terms of turnover, 10 of the 15 largest Scottish companies in 1993–4 were in finance, and Scotland by some measures is reckoned to be fourth in Europe in the provision of financial services after London, Frankfurt and Paris. In 1992 no fewer than 220,000 people were engaged in this area of employment. Tourism has also become big business, with a turnover in the early 1990s as great as agriculture, fisheries and mining combined. Ironically, one of the attractions for visitors was the plethora of heritage museums and industrial theme parks designed to recapture the glories of Scotland's industrial past which was now vanishing fast from the real manufacturing economy.

Yet though the extraction of coal and the making of ships were in irreversible decline, new growth points were emerging in the recovery of North Sea oil and gas and in electronics manufacture. Commentators are divided on the precise economic impact of each. Scottish heavy industry was neither transformed nor saved by the coming of oil. The North Sea was exploited so quickly by a government eager to provide licences to harvest its riches in order to solve the crisis in the public finances that Scottish firms did not have the opportunity to develop the expertise to compete against experienced international suppliers. Nevertheless, construction yards for drilling and production platforms were established at Ardersier, Dundee, Nigg, Stornoway and Loch Kishorn, though they all suffered massive redundancies between 1985 and 1987 when oil prices plummeted. In addition, some Scottish companies, like the Aberdeen-based Wood Group, have become key players, supplying both engineering and drilling services to the industry. While the overall impact of oil on Scottish manufacturing as a whole may be doubted, its impact on employment (and on house prices!) in the north-east and Shetland is undeniable. By the 1990s, Grampian region had emerged as one of the most prosperous areas in the UK and Aberdeen became the oil capital of Europe.

In addition, Scotland was now as famous for electronics manufacture as it had been for shipbuilding in earlier generations. Output increased fourfold in the 1980s and by 1990 the sector produced 42 per cent of the country's manufactured exports. 'Silicon Glen', stretching from Ayrshire to Dundee, now included one of the largest concentrations of high-technology industry outside the USA and by the early 1980s Scotland was the recognized leader in Europe in semiconductor manufacture. But some voiced doubts about this remarkable success story. Overwhelmingly, the new plants were the fruit of American, Japanese and then Asian inward investment, brought to Scotland by government aid, custom-built facilities, a favourable location to penetrate the European market and, perhaps not least, labour costs that were around half the going rate in California in the later 1980s. Many companies have pressed home this last advantage by recruiting mainly women and operating effective non-union policies. The fear has often been expressed that some of these companies regard their Scottish operations as 'branch factories' which are vulnerable to closure when the parent organization is in difficulty, that they are engaged in simple assembly work with limited research and development activities, and they may be tempted in the future to migrate to even lower-cost locations in eastern Europe. In 1998 these concerns were fuelled by the mothballing of the Lite-On plant in Lanarkshire and job losses at Compaq in Irvine, Viasystems in the Borders, National Semiconductor at Greenock and Motorola in East Kilbride – a clutch of firms which include both newcomers and well-established companies with solid foundations in Scotland. On the more optimistic side, however, came the important news of the development of Project Alba, which seeks to establish a unique collaboration between industry, government and academia that will attempt to position Scotland at the leading edge of semiconductor research and design. Success in that vital area and in the enhancement of software capability would do much to provide a more secure and stable future for electronics in Scotland.

In the 1980s then, Scotland went through an economic revolution which, if not as fundamental as that of the later eighteenth and early nineteenth centuries, still left a deep mark on the country's historical development. Though there were pronounced regional variations within Scotland, as between the prosperous Grampian and Edinburgh regions at one extreme and Glasgow and much of the western Lowlands at the other, overall unemployment rates in the mid-1980s in the country as a whole were worse than the average in England. The employed labour force fell by 3 per cent in the UK between 1979 and 1986 but by 8 per cent in Scotland. The publication of these figures fuelled a passionate debate about an uncaring and partisan government which was allegedly condemning Britain to a bleak future divided between a poor North and a wealthy South. By the early 1990s, however, Scotland seemed to have weathered the storm, albeit at considerable human cost. In the 1990s recession Scotland fared better than many parts of England and had lower unemployment rates than some of the older industrial regions such as the north-east and Wales. In addition, the Scottish economy was now more diversified. The old and risky dependence on one or two exporting giants had been reduced and instead the industrial structure now resembled more closely that of the UK as a whole. The judgement of one senior economic historian in 1992 was that 'industry in Scotland is more healthy than it has been for generations'.[3]

This economic transformation has had profound social effects. Accelerating technological change, deskilling and assembly-line techniques substantially increased the employment of women in a range of activities. They now form the majority of the paid labour force in Scotland, although large numbers are in part-time jobs and average wages are around 70 per cent of the male rate. With the increase in single-parent families and the huge haemorrhage of men from the older industries (male employment fell by 234,000 between 1979 and 1994) women often became the main earners in many households. Technological change also had a radical impact on rural society. The tractor revolution had substituted machines for horses and the adoption of combine harvesters and hay and straw balers completed the mechanization of agriculture. Although little noticed among the bitter public controversies following the spate of industrial closures, there was also a huge decline in employment on the land. Between 1951 and 1991 jobs in agriculture, forestry and fishing fell by over two-thirds, from 100,000 to 28,000. This highlighted the fact that though technology was achieving greater wealth for society it was also a factor in the wave of redundancies in the Scotland of the 1980s and replacement jobs for men in particular were not always to hand either in the same place or at the same time. One response was a political one: the toleration of levels of unemployment which would have been unacceptable and unimaginable in the 1950s and 1960s. By 1991, and despite 'recovery' from the nadir of the early 1980s, 220,000 people were registered as unemployed, or 8.7 per cent of those able to work, according to official statistics. These figures concealed wide regional and local disparities. In parts of Glasgow, for instance, unemployment rates were as high as 38.2 per cent in the city centre and over 30 per cent in some of the great peripheral schemes constructed with such optimism in the post-war period. Despair, drink and drugs often took over in some of these communities.

Yet, despite their public posture, the Conservative governments did not disengage entirely from either the promotion of economic regeneration or the provision of a safety net for those who were the victims of structural economic change. Identifiable public expenditure per head in Scotland still ran at 20 per cent above the average for the UK. Industrial 'lame ducks' were ruthlessly sacrificed but social security payments expanded by half in the 1980s (paid for, so it was said, by the revenues from North Sea oil) because of record increases in unemployment, the greater incidence of single-parent families and the results of part-time working for women. In industrial policy the priority changed to the vigorous encouragement of inward investment. For the first time, in the early 1980s a dedicated organization to manage inward investment strategy was created. Locate in Scotland (LIS) soon chalked up some remarkable successes and was reckoned to have attracted some 50,000 additional jobs to Scotland during the 1980s. Regional policy was not so much abandoned by the Tories as made more selective. They developed a strategy of enterprise zones in 1980 in areas of high unemployment such as Inverclyde and Tayside. Firms locating in these zones could expect exemption from development land tax and local rates. The most spectacular example of continued government intervention after 1979 came in Glasgow. There, a redevelopment programme in the city's east end, one of the most run-down areas in western Europe where deindustrialization and slum clearance had wreaked havoc on many communities, attracted over £300 million in public investment and a further £200 million from the private sector between 1976 and 1987. The Scottish Development Agency co-ordinated the Glasgow Eastern Area Renewal Project (GEAR). Housing was built, including some owner-occupied developments, the environment improved and a large shopping complex constructed on the derelict site of the old Beardmore works at Parkhead Forge, although the impact on long-term employment in the area was much less impressive. All of this demonstrated that even the most radical of governments could not easily roll back the frontiers of the state. Indeed, it was a considerable irony that structural economic change contributed to a steep increase in social security benefit payments which were being received by half a million people in Scotland in 1989. During the Thatcher years personal dependence on the state, far from declining, became a way of life in many working-class neighbourhoods.

2

At the end of 1979, the prospects for Home Rule for Scotland seemed as bleak as the future of the nation's traditional industry. Despite the fact that a narrow majority had voted in favour of devolution in the referendum, there was a sense of defeat and disillusion that a historic opportunity had not been embraced with more enthusiasm. The writer William McIlvanney caught the mood of the time in his allegorical tale, *The Cowardly Lion*, in which the king of beasts slinks back into his open cage, afraid of the freedom which is being offered. The new Conservative government was firmly against the Scotland Act and one of Mrs Thatcher's first moves was to repeal it in June 1979. In the early 1980s the Scottish Grand Committee began to meet in Edinburgh, but this was only a token gesture and elicited little public interest or response. It seemed that as a political issue devolution was well and truly off the agenda.

The two parties, SNP and Labour, which had campaigned for a 'Yes' vote in 1979 were soon mired in their own internal troubles. The SNP was demoralized and internal tensions that had been festering for some time now came to the surface. The party suffered an electoral disaster in 1979 as the number of its MPs fell to only two. The post-mortem on this débâcle and the debate on the best way forward from it led to open warfare among different factions. The '79 Group, which included Margo MacDonald, Jim Sillars and the young Alex Salmond, wished to move the party to the left in order to give it a distinctive ideological identity which would be recognized by the electorate. The newsletter of the group carried the masthead, 'For a Scottish Socialist Republic', while members gave vocal public support to workers whose factories, such as the Invergordon Aluminium Smelter and the British Leyland Bathgate truck plant, were threatened with closure. The right to civil disobedience was asserted. The most notorious example of this last campaign came in October 1981 when Sillars and some companions broke into the Royal High School building in Edinburgh, which had been refurbished in preparation for the new Assembly, in order to hold a debate on Scottish unemployment in the empty chamber. Sillars was arrested and fined £100 for vandalism. Another group to emerge at the same time was *Siol Nan Gaidheal*, the Seed of the Gael, comprising young men from the traditionalist wing of the party who liked to parade in Highland dress with bagpipes, drums and dirks. They posed as a kind of nationalist militia and were fond of the ritualistic public burning of Union Jacks. While their militaristic image pleased some supporters who were in despair at the collapse of the SNP's electoral fortunes, the '79 Group and their allies regarded *Siol*'s antics as tantamount to fascism. The party leader, Gordon Wilson, concluded that the SNP would fragment into hostile factions if drastic action were not taken. At the annual conference in Ayr in 1982 it was therefore agreed that all groups should be disbanded. Eventually, six members of the '79 Group were expelled from the party, though most returned after they accepted the conference decision. But the events of 1982 left a legacy of great bitterness and personal animosities that took time to disappear and which limited the party's political effectiveness for several years. At the 1983 general election it held on to its two seats but secured only 12 per cent of the vote. Not until Jim Sillars's victory at the Govan by-election in 1988 did the nationalists achieve another major public success. However, in the mean time, one longer-term effect of the blood-letting of the early 1980s was that the SNP did define itself more distinctively as a left-of-centre party. In due course this transformation was to bring electoral dividends.

The Labour Party in the UK was in even more serious trouble than the Scottish Nationalists after 1979. The former's response to defeat was to swing far to the left, a process accompanied by the infiltration of the Trotskyist Militant Tendency into many local constituency organizations in England. At the 1980 annual conference, the Left coasted to a sweeping victory as the party adopted withdrawal from the EEC, unilateral nuclear disarmament and removal of the power of MPs to select the leader as official policy. While ideologically pure, this programme ensured that Labour would be consigned to the electoral wilderness for some time to come. The following year, the 'Gang of Four', David Owen, Roy Jenkins, Shirley Williams and Bill Rodgers, split from Labour and founded the Social Democratic Party (SDP). The official parliamentary opposition was now reduced to division and impotence and so was unable to exploit the undeniable national unpopularity of the Thatcher government in the early 1980s. Labour's left-wing manifesto for the general election in the summer of 1983 was convincingly dubbed by Gerald Kaufmann 'the longest suicide note in history'. The combination of this programme, a divided opposition and, crucially, the impact of the successful British campaign in the Falklands War resulted in a crushing Conservative victory. Labour's performance was disastrous, its national vote falling to the lowest point since 1918. The year 1983 thus marked the start of a long period of Conservative rule which was to last without interruption for a further 14 years.

However, even at this point, clear differences were emerging between the pattern of politics in Scotland and in England. Labour still retained its dominance north of the border in 1983 by returning 41 MPs, nearly twice as many as the Tories. Because of this, the first mutterings were heard that the Thatcher government did not have a mandate in Scotland. The Scottish party also remained moderate. Significantly, in March 1982, under the new rules for the selection of MPs, not a single sitting member was deselected in Scotland. Nor was there much leakage to the alliance between the SDP and the Liberals, which had been formed in June 1981. Charles Kennedy, an SDP MP from 1982, thought that this was because Labour in Scotland was regarded as more sane and responsible than the party in parts of England. The late John Smith argued that '. . . the Labour Party owes a great debt to Scotland, because we were the ballast, we held the ground, the necessary ground, during the years in which the Labour Party faced up to its problems'.[4] It was in the 1980s that talented Scots, such as Smith himself, Gordon Brown, Robin Cook, Donald Dewar, George Robertson and others, came to the fore in the Labour Party and after the 1997 election went on to form the largest group of Scottish MPs ever to sit in a British Cabinet. Labour was still overwhelmingly the electoral focus for anti-Conservative opposition in Scotland. The Alliance had done well in 1983, winning over 25 per cent of the vote, but had gained only eight seats compared to Labour's 41. The problem was, however, that though Labour could win with ease north of the border the Conservatives were impregnable in the Midlands, London and the south-east, where British general elections were usually decided. This fact alone was sufficient to bring the constitutional issue back on to the agenda, especially as the unpopularity of the Thatcher government in Scotland was set to increase even further after 1983.

The government's economic policies were depicted as anti-Scottish when, in 1985, the British Steel Corporation was allowed to close Gartcosh cold mill in Lanarkshire which was Ravenscraig's biggest customer, despite a nationwide campaign to save the plant. Rightly or wrongly, the collapse of these symbols of Scotland's past industrial greatness was laid at the door of the Conservatives. The Scottish press, which was overwhelmingly anti-Tory, tended to focus on the story of industrial decline with much less emphasis on the growth points that were also emerging in the economy. The miners' strike in 1984 ended in complete victory for the government and the humbling of the once-all-powerful National Union of Mineworkers. But the miners' cause evoked great sympathy in Scotland, despite the uneconomic nature of much of the industry, and the government was accused of seeking to achieve efficiency while indifferent to the resulting human costs. The public services, which had attracted massive political support in Scotland since 1945, also came under a new discipline. Strict controls were imposed on the spending of local authorities and cuts in services and unemployment among council workers followed. When first Lothian Regional Council and then Stirling and Edinburgh refused to comply, the Secretary of State, George Younger, used his powers to cap spending and enforce a reduction in rates.

The vexed issue of local authority finance was also to be the focus of the most notorious and controversial Tory innovation in Scotland of the 1980s, the community charge or 'poll tax'. The regular revaluation of the rates had been postponed in 1983 in order to allow discussions on reform. When it went ahead, it became clear that some would experience a huge increase in their bills. This was politically unacceptable to the government since many of those affected were likely to be traditional Tory voters. The party's standing in Scotland was bad enough without risking an even greater political disaster and an electoral backlash of epic proportions. The horror of grass-roots Tories at the scale of the estimated rate increases was passionately articulated at the party's annual conference at Perth in 1985. But George Younger was able to tell his relieved audience that rates would be replaced by a community charge. Two years later, in May 1987, Mrs Thatcher announced to ecstatic applause at the same conference that the new tax had received royal assent. It would be a flat-rate charge, payable by all adults in a local authority for services provided. The government argued that this would ensure spendthrift local councils would therefore be held accountable to a wider section of the community. In practice, it was widely regarded as an unjust tax which took no account of the ability to pay. Moreover, it had been imposed by what many in Scotland regarded as a minority government in the teeth of opposition from MPs of other parties, local government and professional opinion. Crucially, also, the poll tax, as it soon became known, was levied in Scotland before England, and this stoked suspicions that the Scots were being used as guinea-pigs. When the poll tax was eventually killed, its demise was ensured not by a massive campaign of non-payment in Scotland (in its first year an astonishing 700,000 summary warrants for nonpayment of the tax were issued) but because of riotous protest in England and the likely impact on Conservative electoral fortunes. More than any other single policy, the poll tax drove home the message to many Scots that they were being ruled by an alien government. On the eve of its introduction, the leaders of the three largest Scottish churches condemned the tax as 'undemocratic, unjust, socially divisive and destructive of community and family life'.[5]

Not all Conservative policies roused the venomous fury unleashed by the poll tax. Allowing parents more freedom to choose their own schools for their children and giving council tenants the right to buy their own home proved very popular. Between 1979 and 1989, 150,000 council houses were sold and, for the first time in this century, the majority of Scots came to own their own homes. The government complained that they were not given the credit for these reforms in Scotland but this was partly because they were counterbalanced by others which were much less favoured. The Conservatives cut income taxes in the 1980s but only by raising indirect taxes to finance the reduction. Overall, taxes rose, but the transfer to indirect taxes had major redistributive effects: 'while the poor got relatively poorer, the rich got absolutely richer, before as well as after tax'.[6] Many middle-class Scots were appalled by the Tory attack on the welfare state, not least because large numbers of them earned their living in the very public services threatened with financial squeeze. Managers introduced into the health service in 1985 were often recruited from the private sector. The chief executive of the NHS in Scotland, for instance, was Don Cruickshank, who came with experience of Times Newspapers and Richard Branson's Virgin Group. Relationships between the new managerial élite and health care professionals were not always easy, especially in 1989 when the government introduced new plans to develop a market philosophy in the health service without consulting the profession. Universities were also subjected to a new regime of rigorous accountability, external research assessment and financial pressures. Student numbers rose from 46,597 in 1978–9 to 55,133 in 1988–9, an increase of around 25 per cent. But resources did not increase in proportion. At Dundee, for instance, staff–student ratios deteriorated from 8:1 to 14:1. Some institutions suffered grievously. The 500-year-old University of Aberdeen endured a savage round of cuts in 1986 which cost more than 200 redundancies and closed six arts faculty departments. One consequence of all this was that the Scottish principals, who had mainly been against devolution of university financial control from London to Edinburgh in 1979, became eager converts to the idea when it was mooted again in 1991.

It came as little surprise when in the general election of 1987 the government suffered a heavy defeat in Scotland. The Tories lost 11 of their 21 MPs, the party's worst result since 1910. Support had halved since 1955, while Labour enjoyed its greatest ever electoral triumph in Scotland by winning no fewer than 50 of the 72 seats in the country. Labour's euphoria, however, was short-lived. The Conservatives had won in the UK with a majority of over 100 and were determined to press on with a full programme of privatization and other radical measures which Labour in Scotland was incapable of stopping. The newly elected SNP Member for Banff and Buchan, Alex Salmond, christened the great new intake of Scottish Labour MPs 'the feeble fifty'. Mrs Thatcher, far from accepting her rejection at the Scottish polls and adjusting her policies, concluded that only a further dose of market reforms would finally wean the Scots away from bad habits which were grounded in 'a dependency culture'. This was the message driven home by her Chancellor, Nigel Lawson, on a visit to Scotland. He argued that whole areas of Scottish life were 'sheltered from market forces and exhibit a culture of dependence rather than that of enterprise'.[7] The Scottish edition of the *Sun* put over Lawson's point in its own inimitable style: 'Will you stop your snivelling, Jock'. At the same time, a number of English Conservative backbenchers started to attend Scottish debates in parliament and took the opportunity whenever it was presented to vociferously criticize the scale of public expenditure in Scotland doled out through what one MP termed the 'slush fund' of the Scottish Office. All this encouraged the view that the Thatcherite government was anti-Scottish. The SDP MP, Charles Kennedy, accurately described Mrs Thatcher as 'the greatest of all Scottish nationalists' because she successfully managed to unite most of the nation against her policies. In May 1988 the Prime Minister came to Edinburgh to address the General Assembly of the Church of Scotland. She delivered what has become known as the 'Sermon on the Mound' and outraged the majority of the ministers and elders who had gathered to listen by equating the professed Conservative values of hard work, thrift, enterprise and self-reliance with the Christian virtues. The Moderator, recognized 'leader' of the Church of Scotland, then presented the Prime Minister with two Church reports on housing and poverty which were both very critical of government policies and advised her to read them carefully. Mrs Thatcher went on to face another larger and very different audience at the Scottish Cup Final at Hampden, where she was loudly booed by the massed legions of Celtic and Dundee United fans who also showed her thousands of red cards which had been issued before the game.

3

Scottish opposition to Thatcherism went much deeper than simple hostility to an unpopular government. While the Scots remained loyal to the idea of state and community, the Conservatives made a virtue out of promoting nationalism, competition and privatization. The government's values had been rejected in the humiliating defeat of several Conservative candidates in 1987 but were nevertheless still to be imposed because of its electoral ascendancy elsewhere in the UK. Scottish protests against the poll tax, introduced to popular fury on April Fool's Day 1988, or against the privatization of public utilities were ignored. Mrs Thatcher disregarded the tradition of the union as a partnership in which Scottish interests had been taken into account and instead seemed to consider there to be no limit to the absolute sovereignty of the Westminster parliament. When Michael Forsyth became Scottish Minister for Education and Health in 1987, he vigorously pursued a strategy of appointing ideological supporters of the government to the committees and quangos of the Scottish Office which advised on a range of important matters and which had hitherto jealously guarded their professional autonomy. Forsyth saw this as essential to the success of the free market revolution and the destruction of the corporatist consensus. But his opponents saw the strategy as an intolerable undermining of independent bodies for reasons of party political advantage and a sinister confirmation of the inexorable centralization of power taking place under the Tories. Increasingly, the problem of governance in Scotland was seen not simply as being rooted in Thatcherism but instead derived from the very nature of the British constitutional system itself.

Canon Kenyon Wright, later chair of the cross-party Constitutional Convention, articulated the new perception:

There were I think two fundamental reasons why [Mrs Thatcher] was midwife at the birth of something in Scotland which will grow and flourish. First we perceived that she was imposing on Scotland not just policies broadly rejected and even detested – the Poll Tax being the single most painful and obvious example of many – but worse was the imposition of an alien ideology that rejected community and expressed itself as an attack on our distinctive systems of education and local government. This behaviour was seen in Scotland as a moral and ideological issue and not simply as a series of unpopular policies. The second reason was even deeper – the grim centralisation of power, the determined attack on all alternative sources of real corporate power in local government and elsewhere. There was also the use of Royal prerogatives to extend ministerial control through quangos and in other ways. All this made us see with a clarity that we had never had before, that we could never again rely on the British state or live comfortably with its constitutional doctrines of the absolute authority of the crown in parliament.

We came to see that if Mrs Thatcher could so insure the powers of her office, the crown prerogatives, the extent of patronage and the parliamentary system to cut down all real power elsewhere in the name of spurious individualism, then any future Prime Minister could do the same. We realised that our real enemy was not a particular government whatever its colour, but a constitutional system. We came to understand that our central need, if we were to be governed justly and democratically was not just to change the government but to change the rules.[8]

The Conservative victory in 1987 gave a new impetus to a still-moribund Home Rule movement. After 1979 the torch for devolution had been kept alight by the Campaign for a Scottish Assembly (CSA) which aimed to deliver Home Rule by bringing together Labour, Liberal Democrats, the SNP and representatives of Scottish civil society to plan a way forward. But for most of the 1980s it was virtually a voice crying in the wilderness. After 1987, however, the CSA's time had come. It appointed a steering committee chaired by the distinguished academic, town planner and public servant, Sir Robert Grieve, and composed of notables drawn from the churches, trade unions, business and the universities to consider the setting up of a Scottish Constitutional Convention which would examine the case for an assembly and outline the measures that should be taken to achieve it. Labour was increasingly sympathetic. The nightmare 'doomsday scenario' of a mammoth Labour triumph in Scotland coinciding with another Tory victory in the UK in 1987 once again inspired the party with a new enthusiasm for devolution, not least because of fear that the voters would soon lose patience with 'the feeble fifty' Labour MPs and start to move their allegiance to the SNP. In addition, the 'modernization' of the Labour Party under Neil Kinnock diluted the traditional commitment to central economic planning and nationalization, which in turn opened the way for a new approach to political devolution. The SNP had also recovered from the internal turmoil of the early 1980s. At its conference in 1988 it unveiled the new flagship policy of 'Independence in Europe' and adopted the identity of a left-of-centre party through advocating a mass campaign of non-payment against the poll tax. By arguing for Scottish independence in Europe, the SNP sought to destroy the charge of separatism usually levelled against the nationalists while, by moving to the left, it gave notice that it intended to take the fight into Labour's traditional heartlands. The party claimed an early success with this strategy in November 1988, when Jim Sillars took Govan from Labour in a by-election.

There was also a new vitality in many aspects of Scottish culture which helped to underpin the growing interest in Home Rule. Research into Scottish history, literature, politics and society expanded as never before. Novelists such as James Kelman, Alasdair Gray, William McIlvanney, Iain Banks and, later, Irvine Welsh enjoyed enormous international success with works grounded in the gritty realities of urban Scotland and often written in the working-class vernacular. Rock bands like Deacon Blue, the Proclaimers and Runrig were emphatically Scottish in style but nevertheless were able to convey their music to a much wider overseas audience. Runrig celebrated Gaelic culture in particular and Scottishness in general to a younger generation of Scots increasingly confident in their own national identity. The paintings of the 'New Glasgow Boys', Steven Campbell, Adrian Wizniewski, Ken Currie and Peter Howson, graced the walls of rich and famous collectors throughout the world, while the gifted composer, James MacMillan, established an international reputation at an early age. In television and radio the Scottish emphasis manifestly increased. Gus Macdonald, then managing director of Scottish Television, argued that 'The Scottish media used to be very un-Scottish. That's no longer the case. Our research shows that the nation wants its own agenda.'[9] Radio too often developed a serious interest in Scottish culture, as in Billy Kay's pioneering series, *Odyssey*, with its exploration of history through the perspective of oral tradition. In 1990 the government agreed to provide funds for a Museum of Scotland to house the national collections, and the magnificent new building, designed by Gordon Benson and Alan Forsyth, was eventually opened by the Queen on St Andrew's Day 1998. Political scientists have drawn attention to the 'Quiet Revolution' which occurred in Quebec in the early 1960s. They see this as an increase in cultural activity which helped to heal some of the breaches in the community that had emerged after 1945 and so enabled a more unified movement towards self-determination among the Quebecois. Something akin to this cultural awakening took place in Scotland in the 1980s and helped to infuse the crusade for Home Rule with a new impetus and confidence. However, it is important to recognize that in fields like literature at least the revival was part of a vibrant and continuing tradition that stretched back to the era of MacDiarmid and the 'Scottish Renaissance' of the 1920s. The major figures included such great names as the poets Sorley Maclean, Norman MacCaig, Iain Crichton Smith and Edwin Morgan and the novelist George Mackay Brown, much of whose work spanned the intervening decades from the 1940s to the 1980s.

It was against this background of cultural vigour that the CSA committee of 'prominent Scots' issued *A Claim of Right for Scotland*. The title of the document was intended to echo previous Scottish acts of resistance to the state when such 'claims' had been used to articulate opposition to the arbitrary monarchy of James VII in the 1680s and government interference in the Kirk in 1842 before the Disruption. The *Claim of Right*, published on 6 July 1988, was drafted by Jim Ross, a retired civil servant with long experience of the framing of devolution legislation in the 1970s. It combined historical analysis with a statement of the intellectual case for a Scottish assembly, together with the recommendation that a 210-strong constitutional convention should be established, consisting of MPs, representatives of councils, trade unions and the churches to discuss how Home Rule should be achieved. Perhaps the most striking feature of the document was its nationalism with a small 'n'. It asserted, for instance, that 'the Union has always been, and remains, a threat to the survival of a distinctive culture in Scotland'. The *Claim* went on to argue that, contrary to much received opinion at the time, the Scottish Enlightenment of the eighteenth century was not founded on the union of 1707 but on indigenous Scottish roots and relationships with Europe. Mrs Thatcher came in for scathing criticism and was accused of wielding more arbitrary power than virtually any English or Scottish monarch of the past. The document concluded with the following statement, which is worth quoting in full:

Scotland faces a crisis of identity and survival. It is now being governed without consent and subject to the declared intention of having imposed upon it a radical change of outlook and behaviour pattern which it shows no sign of wanting. All questions as to whether consent should be a part of government are brushed aside. The comments of Adam Smith are put to uses which would have astonished him, Scottish history is selectively distorted and the Scots are told that their votes are lying; that they secretly love what they constantly vote against.

Scotland is not alone in suffering from the absence of consent in government. The problem afflicts the United Kingdom as a whole. We have a government which openly boasts its contempt for consensus and a constitution which allows it to demonstrate that contempt in practice. But Scotland is unique both in its title to complain and in its awareness of what is being done to it.

None of this has anything to do with the merits or demerits of particular policies at particular times, or with the degree of conviction with which people believe in these policies. Many a conviction politician contemptuous of democracy has done some marginal good in passing. Mussolini allegedly made the Italian trains run on time. The crucial questions are power and consent; making power accountable and setting limits to what can be done without general consent.

These questions will not be adequately answered in the United Kingdom until the concentration of power that masquerades as 'the Crown-in-Parliament' has been broken up. Government can be carried on with consent only through a system of checks and balances capable of restraining those who lack a sense of restraint. Stripping away the power of politicians outside Whitehall (and incidentally increasing the powers of Ministers inside Whitehall) restores power not to the people but to the powerful. The choice we are promised in consequence will in practice be the choice the powerful choose to offer us. Through effectively answerable representative institutions we can edit the choices for ourselves.

Whether Government interferes unnecessarily or fails to interfere where it should, political institutions answerable alike to consumers and producers, rich and poor, provide the means of correcting it. If these institutions are removed, restricted or censored, Government do not get accurate messages – or can ignore any messages they do not like. If past conduct of politics has given cause for complaint, the answer is to open up and improve politics to give more accurate messages sooner, not to close politics down so that the few remaining politicians can invent the messages for themselves.

It is a sign of both the fraudulence and the fragility of the English constitution that representative bodies and their activities, the life-blood of government by consent, can be systematically closed down by a minority Westminster Government without there being any constitutional means of even giving them pause for thought. It is the ultimate condemnation of that constitution that so many people, in Scotland and beyond, have recently been searching in the House of Lords for the last remnants of British democracy.

Scotland, if it is to remain Scotland, can no longer live with such a constitution and has nothing to hope for from it. Scots have shown it more tolerance than it deserves. They must now show enterprise by starting the reform of their own government. They have the opportunity, in the process, to start the reform of the English constitution, to serve as the grit in the oyster which produces the pearl.

It is a mistake to suppose, as some who realise the defects of our present form of government do, that the route to reform must lie through simultaneous reorganisation of the government of all parts of the United Kingdom. That will lead merely to many further years of talk and an uncertain prospect of action. Tidiness of system is a minor consideration. The United Kingdom has been an anomaly from its inception and is a glaring anomaly now. It is unrealistic to argue that the improvement of government must be prevented if it cannot be fitted within some pre-conceived symmetry. New anomalies that force people to think are far more likely to be constructive than impossible ambitions to eliminate anomaly.

Even if Scots had greater hopes than they have of voting into office a Party more sympathetic to the needs of Scotland, it would be against the long-term interests of Scotland to offer credibility to the existing constitution. There is no need for Scots to feel selfish in undermining it. They can confidently challenge others to defend it.

We are under no illusions about the seriousness of what we recommend. Contesting the authority of established government is not a light matter. We could not recommend it if we did not feel that British government has so decayed that there is little hope of its being reformed within the framework of its traditional procedures. Setting up a Scottish Constitutional Convention and subsequently establishing a Scottish Assembly cannot by themselves achieve the essential reforms of British government, but they are essential if any remnant of distinctive Scottish government is to be saved, and they could create the ground-swell necessary to set the British reform process on its way.[10]

Not surprisingly, the Conservatives refused to join the proposed convention, but Labour, the Liberal Democrats, 59 of Scotland's 65 regional, island and district councils, the STUC, the Scottish churches, representatives of ethnic minorities, the Green and Communist parties and the Scottish Convention of Women did so. Clearly, nationalist sentiments were no longer the monopoly of the SNP. The SNP itself, though at first interested, did not take part. Many of fundamentalist opinion in the party feared the convention would be dominated by Labour and also took the view that devolution would impede the movement to independence rather than facilitate it, especially since the by-election victory at Govan suggested that the SNP bandwagon was rolling once again. The absence of the SNP, however, may have made Labour more willing to make concessions than might otherwise have been the case. Under the joint chairmen, Sir David Steel, the former Liberal leader, Harry Ewing, who had been a devolution minister, and Canon Kenyon Wright, the chair of the executive committee, the convention drew up a blueprint for a Scottish parliament. Malcolm Rifkind, then Secretary of State for Scotland, was reported to have said that 'if the disparate parties reached a common conclusion he would jump off the roof of the Scottish Office'. He was not held to his promise when, on St Andrew's Day 1990, the convention unveiled its report which proposed a legislature elected under proportional representation, financed through 'assigned revenues' from taxes raised in Scotland.

In some ways the recommendations were vague and inconclusive. For instance, the principle of equal representation for women in the new parliament was agreed but the method of implementing it was not. Equally, the vexed question of Scottish representation at Westminster after devolution was not considered. Above all, the proposals could not be implemented until the robustly unionist Conservative administration was removed from office. Nevertheless, the work of the convention was still important because by bringing Labour, the dominant party in Scotland, into the heart of the Home Rule movement it made it politically unacceptable for any future Labour government to deny the Scots a parliament. Equally, the vital concession of proportional representation was likely to make areas outside the Labour empire of the central Lowlands look more favourably on the concept of an Edinburgh parliament than had been the case in 1979. Finally, the political advances made in the convention gave a further impetus to the whole movement for Home Rule. The convention's ideas may have engaged the interest of no more than a minority of the Scottish population, but even some of the silent majority warmed to the defiant words of Kenyon Wright in response to the expected disapproval of the iron lady: 'What happens if that other voice we all know so well responds by saying, we say no. We say no and we are the state. Well, we say yes and we are the people.'

Ironically, in the same month in 1990 that the blueprint was produced by the convention, Mrs Thatcher was forced to resign after the Conservative Party became increasingly split over Europe and its popularity plummeted as a result of the poll tax. With the most implacable opponent of constitutional change gone from the political scene, the Home Rule movement was united as never before, the SNP was revitalized and scoring well in the polls and a Tory defeat in a future UK general election looked more likely than at any time since the 1970s. By the time the new Prime Minister, John Major, called the election in the spring of 1992, Home Rule was once again a significant factor in Scottish political debate. Media expectations became almost frenzied after a *Scotsman* opinion poll in January 1992 suggested that 50 per cent of Scots favoured independence. Distinguished journalists predicted that there would be a Tory-free Scotland after polling day and the SNP released yet another over-optimistic slogan, 'Free by 1993'. The *Sun* thought it commercially worthwhile to back the SNP in the battle for readers with the other mass circulation paper, the *Daily Record*. On 23 January it revealed its new nationalist loyalties to a bemused readership with the words 'Arise and be a Nation again' alongside a huge saltire. Even John Major made the defence of the union the central theme of the last week of the election campaign. It seemed at last that the Scots were indeed approaching a historic watershed.

However, it was not to be. Major held on with a reduced majority and, far from the Tory vote collapsing in Scotland, there was a marginal increase in its share from 24 per cent to 25.6 per cent. Yet the fact remained that parties advocating Home Rule or independence had won the support of 75 per cent of the electorate and 85 per cent of the seats in Scotland. This was not enough, however, for disenchanted nationalists like Jim Sillars who, in frustration at losing, vented his spleen on the Scots and accused them of being 'ninety-minute patriots' who had 'bottled out' at the crucial moment of decision. Sillars left politics soon afterwards. 1992 was certainly not, as the SNP had hoped, the independence election and, while Home Rule remained unfinished business, the result was a major setback for the constitutional movement which had seen such progress since the late 1980s. As Andrew Marr commented acidly, 'Those who live by the hype shall die by the hype.'[11]

In retrospect, however, there had clearly been an overwhelming vote for those parties committed to constitutional change and the Conservative performance seemed meritorious only when judged against earlier disastrous election results and the inflated expectations of nationalist politicians and some journalists. The party held its ground because John Major aroused much less hostility in Scotland than Margaret Thatcher and because the menace of nationalism might well have provoked Tory unionists to turn out in large numbers.

In the aftermath of the election, groups such as Scotland United, Common Cause and Democracy for Scotland tried to keep the spirit of Home Rule alive. The last of these was the most enduring and maintained a vigil outside the parliament building on Calton Hill until the referendum result in 1997. Common Cause brought some Scottish intellectuals together, while Scotland United, an alliance of politicians, novelists and pop stars, held two successful rallies and proposed a multi-option referendum on the constitution. These two organizations soon withered on the vine. But 'people power' was far from dead. It was demonstrated in December 1992 when 25,000 marched in Edinburgh during the summit meeting of European Community leaders, demanding democracy in Scotland, and even more emphatically when over 1 million people in Strathclyde region or 97 per cent of those who took part in the postal ballot, rejected the government's plans for water privatization in a postal ballot. This was not rioting in the streets, but it plainly articulated the strong opposition which existed in Scotland to key aspects of Tory policy.

The event above all others which was eventually to seal the fate of John Major's government and prepare the way for a landslide Labour victory had already taken place in the first year of his term of office. This was Black Wednesday, 16 September 1992, when the UK had to withdraw from the European exchange rate mechanism despite throwing many millions of pounds sterling into an abortive attempt to protect it. This was both a humiliation and an indictment of gross economic incompetence from which the Conservative government never recovered. Yet in material terms Scotland was doing relatively well in this period. In 1993 and 1994 it had a marginally lower unemployment rate than the rest of Britain. In 1996 personal disposable income per head in Scotland was £9,100, compared to England's £9,140. In the early 1990s the Scottish economy, particularly in manufacturing output, was growing faster than the UK average. But the Tories were given little credit for these achievements. When the two-tier local authority structure of regions and districts was dissolved in 1995, the Tories failed to win control of a single local council. The government's problems seemed set to increase in Scotland in 1995 when Michael Forsyth, the right-wing scourge of the health and education services in the 1980s, was appointed to succeed Ian Lang as Scottish Secretary when the latter was promoted to a senior Cabinet position. However, before the eyes of an astonished nation, Forsyth metamorphosed into a Scottish patriot. He remained resolutely opposed to constitutional change, for that would imperil the union, but all other assertions of Scottishness were to be embraced with enthusiasm. Forsyth wrapped himself in tartan – on one occasion literally, when he became perhaps the first Secretary of State to appear in full Highland dress when he attended the première of the film, *Braveheart*. The Tories introduced a new slogan, 'Fighting for Scotland', and Forsyth then pulled off a spectacular coup of 'gesture politics' when he secured the return of the Stone of Destiny from Westminster Abbey in a ceremony which must rank as an especially fine example of the invention of tradition. Plans were laid to boost the Scottish film industry and the Secretary of State even called for a Standard Grade course in Scottish history to remedy the deficiencies in the teaching of the subject in schools. But the real impact of all this flag-waving may be doubted because in the real world the government had still pressed ahead with the unpopular reform of local government and extension of the market principles in the health service. However, in one particular area Michael Forsyth did hit the target when he subjected Labour's new financial plans for a Scottish parliament to sustained attack.

The death of John Smith, the Labour leader who had succeeded Neil Kinnock in May 1994, put a question mark against Labour's commitment to Home Rule. Smith's popularity in Scotland and elsewhere was unquestioned and his grave on the Island of Iona soon became a place of pilgrimage. Since the 1970s John Smith had been a fervent advocate of devolution and in the Callaghan government he was given responsibility for the legislative process to achieve Home Rule, which had foundered after the referendum result in 1979. His devolution credentials were impeccable and when elected leader of the Labour Party he was fond of the assertion that the establishment of a parliament was now 'the settled will of the Scottish people'. It remained to be seen, however, whether Home Rule would survive the radical review of Labour policy undertaken by his successor, Tony Blair.

In the event it did, and Labour gave support to the constitutional convention's proposal that the new parliament should be able to vary the basic rate of income tax by up to 3p in the pound. Michael Forsyth relentlessly exploited this arrangement. He recognized that the Labour Party was exposed on the taxation issue and was absolutely determined to rid itself of the old 'tax and spend' reputation if it was to return to office. For Forsyth and other Tory spokespersons, the revenue-varying powers were nothing other than the 'tartan tax' imposed on the Scottish people simply for being Scottish. The attack struck home and the Labour response sent tremors through the ranks of those who had long campaigned for Home Rule. To the outrage of its partners in the constitutional convention and the fury of many of its own supporters in Scotland, the Shadow Cabinet decided in June 1996 that a general election victory was not in itself sufficient for such a momentous constitutional reform. Instead, a referendum would also be held to secure the creation and continuation of a parliament. Moreover, two separate questions would be posed, one on the principle of a parliament and another on its tax-raising powers. Critics saw this as an attempt to dilute the essential but limited financial powers without which the parliament would be stripped of economic authority. Suspicion abounded that Blair was intent on ditching the whole devolution project.

In the event, all this mistrust proved unfounded. Labour's landslide victory in 1997 was soon followed by the promise of a referendum on 11 September, a speedily produced but well-crafted White Paper on Home Rule and a new Secretary of State, Donald Dewar, with impeccable pro-devolution credentials. The omens for a successful outcome looked good, though the tragic death of the Princess of Wales in a Paris accident meant that effective campaigning had to be confined to a short and hectic period of about 100 hours. But the pro-Home Rule camp was united as never before. Under its pragmatic leader, Alex Salmond, the SNP campaigned as vigorously as did Labour and the Liberal Democrats, under Donald Dewar and Jim Wallace respectively. The opposing camp was weak by comparison. Scottish business, which had vociferously condemned devolution in 1979, was mainly silent. The one high-profile critic, Sir Bruce Patullo, Governor of the Bank of Scotland, was condemned from several quarters and some of his customers threatened to move their accounts elsewhere. On the other hand, other major Scottish companies, such as the insurance giants, Standard Life and Scottish Widows, declared they were comfortable with the proposals.

'Think Twice', the anti-devolution campaign, had few of the financial resources or personalities of the organizations which had opposed devolution in 1979. Then, when Mrs Thatcher decided to intervene and give their cause her public support, the fate of the 'no' campaigners was effectively sealed.

When the results were declared, 74.3 per cent of those who voted supported a Scottish parliament and 63.5 per cent agreed that it should have tax-varying powers. Unlike 1979, there was clear support in all regions, though Orkney and Shetland voted against the tax powers and the majorities were lowest in those regions which were hostile in the previous referendum. Nevertheless, this truly was the 'settled will' of the Scottish people. The parliament which had now been resoundingly approved would have power over all matters apart from foreign policy, defence, macro-economic policy, social security, abortion and broadcasting. It could raise or lower the basic rate of tax by 3p, or £450 million in total. Although Westminster would continue to have responsibility for relations with Europe, there would also be a Scottish representative office in Brussels and Scottish ministers could be expected to take part in the UK delegation to the EU Council of Ministers. The elections in May 1999 were by a form of proportional representation and, because the legislation only specifies the powers to be reserved to Westminster, it enables the new body to develop a potentially wider role in support of Scottish interests. Thus, when the first Scottish parliament since 1707 met in Edinburgh in July of 1999, the Scottish nation undeniably embarked on another exciting stage in its long history.

26

End of Empire

I

Most of the great territorial empires in world history have broken up slowly over generations or even centuries of decline and decay. This was not the British experience. As late as 1945 its empire was still virtually intact with British rule extending across the oceans of the globe and populations of around 700 million people. A mere two decades later, this figure had fallen to 5 million, of which 3 million were concentrated in Hong Kong. In June 1997, even that last major outpost of empire was handed back to the Chinese when the Black Watch played 'Auld Lang Syne' as the Union Jack was lowered over the territory for the very last time.

The end of empire was not only rapid, it was also remarkably peaceful. True, there were outbreaks of nationalist hostility in Cyprus, Aden and Kenya during the imperial retreat. But in mainland Britain itself, if Northern Ireland is excepted, all was calm. Indeed, as several scholars have noted, the British seem to have accepted the collapse of their empire with an equanimity bordering on indifference. Here contrasts are often drawn with the experience of France and Portugal. Both had much smaller empires than the British in Africa, Asia and Indo-China. Yet in these two countries decolonization was followed by social trauma and political convulsion at home.

In one important sense the relative silence in Britain, outside the right wing of the Conservative Party, is intriguing. As the break-up of empire loomed, some commentators predicted that imperial decline must place considerable strain on the Anglo-Scottish Union. As early as 1937, Andrew Dewar Gibb, Professor of Constitutional Law at the University of Glasgow and a prominent nationalist with deep imperial sympathies, noted in his *Scottish Empire* that 'The existence of the Empire has been the most important factor in securing the relationship of Scotland and England in the last three centuries'.[1] He implied that without empire this ancient political connection might not stand the test of time. Similarly, in his last published work, Sir Reginald Coupland – a distinguished imperial historian of the old school – considered the potential rise of Scottish and Welsh nationalism in the aftermath of decolonization and gloomily concluded that Ireland might not be the last of the nations of the British Isles to leave the United Kingdom.

This theme was taken up even more vigorously in the 1960s and 1970s as the SNP began to achieve its first spectacular successes in elections. Several commentators outlined a causal connection between the end of empire and the dissolution of the Union. H. J. Hanham's *Scottish Nationalism*, published in 1969, two years after Winnie Ewing's sensational SNP by-election victory at Hamilton, observed: 'Now that the Empire is dead many Scots feel cramped and restricted at home. They chafe at the provincialism of much of Scottish life and at the slowness of Scottish economic growth, which is related to that provincialism. To give themselves an opening to a wider world the Scots need some sort of outlet, and the choice appears at the moment to be between emigration and re-creating the Scottish nation at home'.[2] For Jan Morris, an author who had written extensively about the British empire, there was no longer much scope for a shared pride between the nations of the United Kingdom with the acceleration of decolonization. All that remained in the Union, she memorably remarked, was 'this grubby wreck of old glories' in which few could take any satisfaction.[3] Hence, the time was ripe for a new constitutional beginning. It was then left to the Marxist writer, Tom Nairn, in *The Break-Up of Britain* (1969) to provide a full-scale analysis of those issues. For him, the end of Britain was not only inevitable, but necessary as a constructive response to the crisis in the Union triggered by the end of empire.

These observers and others had, on the face of it, a plausible case. The British empire was seen traditionally as a vital economic cement of union as, for the Scots from the later eighteenth century onwards, it provided a remarkable set of opportunities in trade, the professions, military service and administration for the Scottish upper and middle classes. The entire production structure of Scottish industry from the age of cotton to the era of heavy industry was also built around imperial markets. Since the empire supplied a powerful material rationale for Union, it therefore seemed attractive to argue that with its disappearance the economic anchor which had for so long bound Scotland to England would easily be cut adrift. This point was apparently given added force by the analysis of Nairn and others of the long-run history of nationalism in Scotland. For them the nineteenth and early twentieth centuries were an epoch of profound crisis for Scottish nationhood. In Europe during these decades the Scots were out of step as, throughout the continent, small historic nations asserted their rights to self-determination and independence. In Scotland, however, nationalism in this form was conspicuous by its absence. In their view, the Scottish professional and mercantile élites were seduced by the glittering prizes of empire, selling in the process their distinctive identity and ancient autonomy for a share of the imperial spoils. With decolonization, on the other hand, nationalist aspirations could once again come to the fore. As John Mackenzie has put it in his commentary on this argument: 'With the end of Empire the Scots could at last escape from their self-interested complicity and reunite nation with state after the dramatic rupture of that particular Union. With the loss of the colonies, the imperial cataracts can be removed from the eyes of the imperial collaborators and a new democratic dispensation can be discerned emerging from which the national ophthalmologist can free the Scots as much as the subordinate peoples of the white settler territories, India and the dependent empire'.[4]

Thus far, however, more than fifty years after the independence of India, the dire predictions of the disintegration of the Union have proven to be false. Indeed, arguably it is more secure now than it has been at any time since the late 1960s and 1970s when Scottish nationalism seemed to have achieved an unstoppable momentum. In 2005 the SNP is becalmed, with around 25 per cent of the popular vote in Scotland and the pro-Union parties are in the ascendant in the Scottish Parliament. George Robertson, a former Secretary of State for Scotland and Director-General of NATO, famously observed that devolution would kill Scottish political nationalism stone dead. Whether or not this is a correct diagnosis only time will tell, but it is still tolerably clear at least that the advent of a Scottish Parliament has not precipitated a headlong rush to full independence, despite the fears of many unionists. In 2007, three centuries of the Anglo-Scottish Union will be commemorated.

In truth, of course, the Union was itself transformed by the devolving of important powers to Edinburgh in 1999. But any direct or convincing link between the end of empire and the new constitutional settlement has yet to be demonstrated. Political scientists and modern Scottish historians have tended to look elsewhere for the root causes of devolution and have found them in the disenchantment felt in Scotland in the 1960s and 1970s when neither Tory or Labour, the two 'unionist' parties, were capable of delivering long-term economic and social benefit as UK governments struggled against recurrent currency crises and the menace of rising inflation. However, these pressures were not yet enough to trigger fundamental hostility in Scotland to the terms of the constitutional relationship with England, as the failed referendum on a Scottish Assembly in 1979 made clear. Only in the 1990s did such a consensus emerge. Then it was fashioned not by any nostalgia for lost imperial glory but by the profound economic dislocation of the 1980s, the 'democratic deficit' caused by the cleavage between Scottish and English voting patterns and, perhaps above all, by growing opposition to the social policies of a succession of Conservative governments. Mrs Thatcher has an infinitely greater claim to be the midwife of Scottish devolution than the factor of imperial decline.

Indeed, historically, Scottish Home Rule and empire were not incompatible. The first search for some form of devolution for Scotland took place in the late nineteenth century at the high noon of the British empire and was partly seen by its protagonists as a means of ensuring that the governance of empire might be improved. This was not just a theoretical discussion. A series of Home Rule Acts were promulgated between the 1880s and 1914. In 1913 the policy had secured widespread agreement and was merely awaiting parliamentary time and the solution of the Irish question. The outbreak of the First World War, however, put paid to this aspiration.

There is also the problem of chronology in associating the rise of Scottish political nationalism with imperial decline in the 1940s and 1950s. The Scots mainly identified with the colonies of white settlement – Canada, South Africa, Australia and New Zealand. These were the countries which had experienced mass Scottish immigration since the eighteenth century. Ties of kindred, friendship and identity with them were close. But these dominions had enjoyed autonomy since the Statute of Westminster in 1931 while at the same time retaining a symbolic and sentimental form of attachment to the mother country through the monarchy and the British Commonwealth of Nations. The process of decolonization in Asia and Africa after 1945, which was chronologically closer to the rise of the SNP, evoked little protest or opposition in Scotland. On the contrary, the Church of Scotland vigorously supported the cause of black nationalism in Africa and, through its annual General Assembly, criticized the government for not conceding independence more quickly. The position of the church on this issue was deeply significant. To a much greater extent than today it was a national church with a membership which reached an all-time high in the late 1950s. Traditionally, in this stateless nation, the Church of Scotland was regarded as a kind of surrogate parliament which spoke for the country on matters of contemporary political and social importance as well as religious issues through its General Assembly. The proceedings of this body were then widely reported and discussed in the Scottish press.

2

We are therefore left with a conundrum. Historians claim that Scotland was heavily involved with the imperial project, yet the passing of empire seems to have had little significant consequence for the nation's politics. Certainly the anticipated causal relationship between the end of empire and the dissolution of the Union has proven thus far to be fallacious. One possible way of resolving the puzzle is to question the very premise that the British empire was of central significance to the British people. This view has a long pedigree. Some time ago, for instance, the novelist H. G. Wells famously remarked that nineteen Englishmen out of twenty knew as much about the British empire as they did about the Italian Renaissance. More recently, however, a powerful and detailed exploration of this thesis has come from the pen of Bernard Porter in *The Absent-Minded Imperialists: Empire, Society and Culture in Britain* (2004). Despite its subtitle, Porter's focus is almost entirely Anglocentric. In 108 pages of end-notes and 30 pages of 'select' bibliography, there is only one article with a Scottish emphasis. Essentially, therefore, it is for English historians to judge the overall validity of his argument. What can be said, however, is that Porter's general thesis hardly convinces in a specific Scottish context. Far from being a marginal factor in the nation's domestic history, empire was crucial to the Scottish experience during the eighteenth and nineteenth centuries. Indeed, so intense was Scottish engagement with empire that it had an impact on almost every nook and cranny of Scottish life over these two centuries: economy, identity, politics, intellectual activity, popular culture, consumerism, religion, demographic trends and much else.

In the 1700s the colonial tobacco and sugar trades were two of the key drivers of Scottish industrialization, while during the Victorian and Edwardian eras the Scottish heavy industrial economy was strongly biased towards export markets and the principal outlets for ships, locomotives and engineering products were the British colonies. Dundee became 'Juteopolis', its booming textile industry founded on the importation of raw jute from India. Gordon Stewart, later an historian who went on to write an important study of jute, recalled the imperial connections of his native city:

I grew up in Dundee and I thought that the Scottish city was the centre of the world jute trade. This impression was dinned into me by my geography lessons at school and by a host of childhood encounters with jute. When I felt depressed by the drabness of life amidst the row of identical, rain-stained buildings on the housing scheme where I lived, I would pedal my bike down to the docks and watch hundreds of bales of jute being unloaded from the holds of great cargo steamers which had sailed half-way round the world from Chittagong and Calcutta. On the way home from school I would sit on city buses crowded with women workers coming off their shifts with wisps of jute sticking to their hair and clothes and their hands roughened rad by the handling of jute in the factories . . . Because of the names on the sterns of the cargo ships and the faces of the crewmen, I understood there was an Indian dimension to jute. I also learned of this connection by listening to family stories about relatives and friends of my parents who had spent time in India.[5]

In Glasgow, the economic connections were equally deep. It arrogated to itself the description 'Second City of the Empire' (a term first used as early as 1824) while the broader west of Scotland region was later celebrated as 'The Workshop of the British Empire'. Scottish society more generally had strong ties to empire. As one author has put it, the Scots professional and middle classes claimed 'not merely a reasonable but a quite indecent share of the [imperial] spoils'.[6] Throughout the eighteenth and for much of the nineteenth centuries, Scottish educators, physicians, soldiers, administrators, missionaries, engineers, scientists and merchants relentlessly penetrated every corner of the empire and beyond so that when the statistical record for virtually any area of professional employment is examined, Scots are seen to be over-represented.

This elite emigration was but one element in a greater mass diaspora from Scotland. As seen in Chapter 20, between 1825 and 1938 over 2.3 million Scots left their homeland for overseas destinations. This placed the country with Ireland and Norway in the top three of European countries with the highest levels of net emigration throughout that period. The emigrants had three main destinations – the United States (after 1783), British North America (which became the Dominion of Canada in 1867) and Australia. After *c.* 1840 the USA was the choice of most who left, but Canada predominated in the early twentieth century. Also in the 1850s Australia, for a period, was taking more Scots than each of the two North American countries considered individually. These huge levels of emigration generated a vast network of family and individual connections with the colonies and dominions which were consolidated by return migration (in one estimate averaging more than 40 per cent of the total exodus in the 1890s), chain migration, letter correspondence and widespread coverage of the emigrant experience in the Scottish popular press and periodical literature.

The British empire also had a potent influence on Scottish national consciousness and identity. For the Scots elite in the years before 1914 nationalism was not in conflict with the Union but rather was integrated closely with it. The empire was the means by which the Scots asserted their equal partnership with England after 1707. In the Victorian era it was commonplace to assert that substantial imperial expansion only occurred *after* the Union and hence was a joint endeavour between the partners in which the Scots had played a full part. This was no empty boast. Scottish publicists, through such works as John Hill Burton's *The Scots Abroad* (2 vols., 1864) and W. J. Rattray's monumental four-volume *magnum opus*, *The Scot in British North America* (1880), were easily able to demonstrate the mark that Scottish education (especially at college and university level), presbyterianism, medicine, trading networks and philosophical enquiry had had on the colonies. Pride in the Scottish achievement was taken even further by those who saw the Scottish people as a race of natural empire-builders. Thus Andrew Dewar Gibb argued in 1930:

... the position of Scotland as a Mother nation of the Empire is at all costs to be preserved to her. England and Scotland occupy a unique position as the begetters and defenders of the Empire. They alone of all the Aryan peoples in it have never been otherwise sovereign and independent. Ireland and Wales, mere satrapes of England, can claim no comparable place. Scotsmen today are occupying places both eminent and humble throughout the Empire, and Scottish interests are bound up with every colony in it.[7]

Nonetheless, it might be objected that the argument thus far ignores the important factor of differences in the attitudes of social class to empire. Bernard Porter focuses especially on this aspect. He sees the upper and middles classes as most committed to the imperial project while the working classes were 'either apathetic towards the empire or superficial in their attitude to it'. Porter also claims a deep ignorance about the empire on the part of the majority of the British people.

Again, this interpretation hardly fits the Scottish case. While it is impossible, of course, in the current state of knowledge to determine in precise terms what the ordinary Scot thought about empire it is nevertheless unlikely that the words 'apathy' and 'ignorance' are at all appropriate terms to use of public opinion. Exposure to imperial themes started early in Scotland. In 1907 the Scottish Education Department in its memorandum on the teaching of history in schools directed that the curriculum should develop from the study of Scotland to British and then international themes but always throughout stressing the nation's role in the empire. Text books embodying this approach were soon available in schools. The most popular was *Cormack's Caledonia Readers* which placed very considerable emphasis on empire. The British empire had a key part to play in late nineteenth-century history teaching because it provided the kind of blend of British and Scottish history which reflected Scotland's position in the union state.

But this was not all. The 1900s also saw the widespread celebration of 'Empire Day' when flags were exchanged between Scottish schools and those elsewhere in the empire. The stories of such imperial heroes as General Gordon, Sir Colin Campbell (of Indian Mutiny fame), the missionary Mary Slessor and, above all, David Livingstone, would have been very well known to Scottish schoolchildren. Biographies of Livingstone, the 'Protestant Saint' and the most famous and venerated Scotsman of the nineteenth century, were widely read and also awarded as prizes in schools and Sunday schools, a practice which continued unabated through to the 1960s. Of course it was not simply children who were taught to respond to these imperial heroes. They were also celebrated by the trade-union movement, working-men's clubs and Labour politicians, such as Keir Hardie, as models of Scottish virtue and exemplars for the nation. Knowledge of and loyalty to empire was also communicated by such organizations as the Junior Empire League with around 20,000 members and the Boys' Brigade which not only promoted Christian values but also inculcated fidelity to the imperial ideal within its membership. The 'BBs' were enormously popular among ordinary young Protestant Scots boys well into the twentieth century.

Among the mass of the population, however, perhaps the main symbols of empire were the Scottish regiments. Recognized as the spearheads of imperial expansion, and widely celebrated in music, story, painting and statue as the tartan-clad icons of the Scottish nation, they enjoyed, as Stuart Allan and Allan Carswell have put it, 'unchallenged prominence in Scottish society as symbols of national self-image'.[8] Ironically, however, despite the fame of the Highland soldier, the kilted battalions were mainly recruited during the Victorian age from the working class of the Scottish cities. Their exploits were widely reported not simply in the popular press but in such famous paintings as *The Thin Red Line*. The regiments made a remarkable impact on Scottish consciousness. Seen as the heirs of a martial national tradition which went back for centuries, they also acted as important catalysts for the wide diffusion of the military ethic throughout the country. One major spin-off was the Volunteer movement, which developed into a permanent reserve force for the army and attracted many thousands of young Scotsmen. The Volunteers were a focus for local pride but they also strongly identified with the British empire. Both the Volunteers and the Boys' Brigade adopted army ranks and nomenclature, undertook military drill and were regularly inspected by army officers. The important influence of both organizations goes a long way to explaining the exceptional scale of voluntary recruitment into the army in Scotland when war broke out in 1914. More generally, the fame and significance of the Scottish military tradition lives on even to the present day as illustrated by the extraordinary and continuing success of the Edinburgh Military Tattoo and political controversies during the 2005 General Election over the proposed reorganization of the historic Scottish regiments.

3

There therefore seems to be a huge gap between the imperial enthusiasms of the nineteenth century and the apparent equanimity with which Scotland accepted decolonization in the middle decades of the twentieth century. It will be argued here that the crucial period for understanding this transformation in attitude to empire was between the 1920s and early 1950s, not during decolonization itself.

On the face of it, of course, imperial sentiment still flourished in these decades. The massive war losses suffered by Scotland, officially counted at 74,000 but unofficially reckoned to be over 110,000, were commemorated in the Scottish National War Memorial, completed in Edinburgh Castle in 1927. It was not simply a remarkable tribute in stone to the nation's fallen, but also to the sons and grandsons of Scotland from the empire. The Roll of Honour included all those who had served in Scottish regiments and in those of the dominions overseas, an eloquent affirmation of the continuing importance of the imperial bond. The link between empire and the nation church also seemed to be robust. The cult of David Livingstone reached its apotheosis in the 1920s when many small donations by ordinary Scots financed the creation of the Livingstone Memorial Centre in Blantyre, Lanarkshire, in the cotton-mill complex where the legendary explorer and missionary had worked as a boy. The Centre remained a very popular place of pilgrimage for schools and Sunday schools until the 1950s. The public face of imperial Scotland also seemed to have changed little. A great imperial exhibition was held in Glasgow in 1938, the fourth in a series which since the 1890s had attracted literally millions of visitors. As late as 1951 a colonial week was held in the same city. Empire was also still very much on the political agenda. In the inter-war years factional arguments raged in the Scottish nationalist movement over the nature of the relationship which a self-governing Scotland would have with the empire. Even the Labour Party temporarily diluted earlier hostility and some of its leading intellectuals in Scotland, including John Wheatley, argued that through the empire could come not only economic regeneration but also the hope of protecting a socialist Britain from the menace of international capitalism.

In some ways, however, all this was a mirage, a false image of continuity after the trauma of the Great War. Dewar Gibb in 1937 recognized the change. With the granting of dominion status to the colonies of white settlement, he observed '. . . the hegemony of Britain in the Empire is steadily becoming more formal and more ornamental'.[9] Popular imperialism also waned. Scholars now regard the Glasgow Empire Exhibition of 1938 not so much as a catalyst for regenerating imperial enthusiasms as an event of mere nostalgic significance. In the 1945 election both Scottish Tory and Labour candidates referred even less frequently in their manifestos to imperial themes than their English counterparts. This was a symbolic and ominous prelude to the results of that election, when the Unionists, *par excellence* the party of empire, were roundly defeated by Labour which had a quite different set of political and social priorities for the future governance of Scotland.

The traditional career route of middle-class Scots into imperial administration was also crumbling. In this respect the Indian Civil Service (ICS) had long enjoyed pre-eminence in the rank order of colonial administrations. By 1939, Scots still accounted for 13 per cent of the Europeans on the ICS books. This was marginally greater than the Scottish proportion of UK population. Nonetheless, it was a significantly lower ratio than in the eighteenth and for much of the nineteenth centuries. Indeed, demoralization was rampant in the ICS after 1918 because of a perceived decline in its career prospects as Indian self-government became an ever closer prospect. Though recruitment to the service did not dry up entirely, the ICS was confronted with a critical shortage of satisfactory recruits from Britain which became especially acute from the 1920s.

Scottish elite families were still exporting their male progeny but were no longer constrained to the same extent by opportunities within the formal empire. The great Scottish business syndicates of Jardine, Matheson and Co., the Hongkong and ShangHai Bank, Burmah Oil Company, Guthries and Company and several others had by the twentieth century become global rather than simply imperial corporations. The USA, Latin America, China and Japan, in addition to British colonies, now all provided rich pickings for ambitious and educated Scots. They no longer felt, if they ever had done, restricted by imperial frontiers. Above all, career goals were still more easily satisfied in London than in faraway places. Historians have been more interested in the exotic and have therefore tended to concentrate on Scottish transoceanic activities. In truth, the London financial and business world had always been crucial. The 'Scottish Raj' in the UK Cabinet and the high-profile Scottish presence in the British media at the start of the new millennium are simply the latest variant in a trend which goes back a very long way.

No single cause conspired to weaken the emotional attachment of the Scots to empire but the profound crisis which overwhelmed the nation between the World Wars was arguably of primary significance. Unemployment soared to unprecedented levels in the early 1930s. In the industrial heartland of the western lowlands, 'The Workshop of the British Empire', over a quarter of the entire labour force, nearly 200,000 individuals, were out of work in 1932. New industries failed to develop and poor housing and slum conditions remained as bad as ever, with overcrowding six times greater in 1935 than south of the Border. Fears were expressed in the business community of long-term economic decline and the erosion of indigenous Scottish control as several failing firms were bought up by financial interests from England. The unprecedented scale of emigration in the 1930s intensified these anxieties. So great was the exodus that the Scottish population actually fell by nearly 40,000 in that decade, the only period since records began in which absolute decline between censuses occurred.

Now, rather than being seen as evidence of the virility of an imperial race, emigration was viewed as a scourge and confirmation of a terminal national crisis. The novelist and poet Edwin Muir saw it as a 'silent clearance' in which 'the surroundings of industrialization remain, but industry itself is vanishing like a dream'. The journalist George Malcolm Thomson went further: 'The first fact about the Scot is that he is a man eclipsed. The Scots are a dying race'.[10]

The most arresting illustration of the new economic irrelevance of empire was the experience between the wars of the Dundee jute industry. Already, by the 1890s, Bengal had overtaken its Scottish parent to become the world's dominant centre for the jute sacks and hessian cloth which carried the world's foodstuffs and raw materials. Not surprisingly, in the depressed market conditions of the 1930s, Dundee jute interests pleaded on numerous occasions for tariffs to be imposed on the cheap imports from Calcutta. But their pleas were in vain. Now it was Dundee which looked more like the colony, and Bengal the metropole: '. . . jute presents an unusual example of a powerful industry emerging in a colonial setting which almost destroyed the rival industry back in Britain while the empire was still flourishing'.[11]

All this shattered faith in Scotland as the powerhouse of empire. Long before decolonization took place, the old imperial markets were no longer seen to be of vital benefit. Though the economy recovered during the Second World War and the immediate postwar period, the fully enfranchised masses now had other social priorities which could be delivered through the ballot box. It was therefore hardly surprising that the majority of the Scottish people reacted to the end of empire with equanimity, despite Scotland's historic role before 1900 in imperial expansion. After 1945, as imperial decline set in, government intervention in industry, political commitment to full employment and, above all, the Welfare State, slowly delivered unprecedented security and material improvement to the mass of Scots. These were the issues which now had widespread popular appeal, especially in the light of Scotland's history of working-class poverty over the previous century. The age of empire may have passed, but, ironically, the Union in the 1940s and 1950s was now even more important than before. As one of the poorer parts of the United Kingdom, Scotland was likely to gain more than most other regions from the introduction of an interventionist social and economic policy which was being implemented in the very decade that decolonization began with the independence of India. It was now welfare support from cradle to grave which became the real anchor of the union state.

27

After Devolution

The opening by the Queen of the first Scottish Parliament since 1707 on 1 July 1999 was a memorable occasion. Proceedings were dignified but devoid of the pomp surrounding the state opening of the Westminster legislature. The monarch and her consort listened attentively as the folk singer, Sheena Wellington, gave a powerful rendition of Burns's great hymn to democracy, 'A Man's a Man for a' That', with its eloquent condemnation of rank and privilege:

> Ye see yon birkie [i.e. fellow] ca'd a lord,
> Wha struts, and stares, and a' that;
> Though hundreds worship at his word,
> He's but a coof [i.e fool] for a' that:
> For a' that, and a' that,
> His riband, star, and a' that,
> The man of independent mind,
> He looks and laughs at a' that!

The Queen seemed to enjoy the proceedings, though her reaction to the impertinent language of the Bard was not recorded. At any rate, the symbolism of the day conveyed the impression of a parliament which intended to do things differently from its older and more venerable counterpart in London. Perhaps, however, the real highlight of the ceremony was Donald Dewar's speech as the first First Minister. Dewar had advocated devolution virtually all his political life and had then played a key role in delivering it. His eloquent address was full of passionate conviction and reflected his deep, personal understanding of Scotland's history:

This is about more than our politics and our laws. This is about who we are, how we carry ourselves. There is a new voice in the land, the voice of a democratic Parliament. A voice to shape Scotland as surely as the echoes from our past –

the shout of the welder in the din of the great Clyde shipyards;

the speak of the Mearns, with its soul in the land;

the discourse of the Enlightenment, when Edinburgh and Glasgow were a light held to the intellectual life of Europe;

the wild cry of the Great Pipes;

and back to the distant cries of the battles of Bruce and Wallace.

Dewar hoped that future generations would see 1 July 1999 as 'a turning point', a day when democracy was renewed in Scotland. With these words he further boosted the high expectations about the impact of the new Parliament, assumptions which would quickly come back to haunt the architects of the devolution settlement.

Not all commentators were so positive in their predictions. Some thought the coming of the Parliament was fraught with serious constitutional and political risk. Andrew Neil, expatriate London Scot and successful newspaperman, spoke for the pessimists. To him, devolution was 'a heady, unstable brew' which would undermine the Union by breathing new life into both Scottish and English nationalism. He thought the cardinal weakness was the provision to finance the Edinburgh Parliament almost entirely by a block grant from London. In Neil's view this would perpetuate the begging-bowl mentality (long attributed to Scotland) and, when Westminster failed to stump up, resentments would inevitably grow in Scotland:

A system more designed to exacerbate tensions between London and Edinburgh would be hard to conceive. The Nationalists must already be licking their lips. The only way to avoid a bust-up would be to make the Edinburgh parliament responsible for raising every penny it plans to spend. It would add a dose of realism to the Scottish political debate.[1]

Few were quite as forthright as Andrew Neil in predicting disaster. But also, alongside the high expectations, was an undercurrent of concern about the robustness and durability of this unprecedented constitutional reform. Thus far (as this is written in 2006) none of the more extreme fears have been realized. On the eve of the tercentenary of the Act of Union of 1707, the Union is still intact, albeit since 1999 informed by a different type of political and legal relationship to that which had existed for nearly 300 years. Nor is there any sign of a significant rise in tensions between Edinburgh and Westminster or of the unleashing of rampant nationalism on either side of the border. Support for Scottish independence has remained stable at around 25 per cent of the electorate. The next Scottish parliamentary elections are expected in spring 2007 but, thus far, the SNP has failed to make any significant breakthrough, even in such a controversial by-election as Glasgow Cathcart in September 2005, called because of the resignation of the sitting Labour MSP, Lord Watson, who had been jailed for a bizarre act of fire-raising in an Edinburgh hotel. Nor do the English appear to be too concerned about Scottish devolution. A major study at Lancaster University concluded that: 'English people like the Scots and are happy with the Scottish parliament . . . they are not annoyed about it'. One senior Scottish journalist scathingly dismissed the much-predicted English backlash as 'a figment of the febrile imaginations of Tory MPs and their press tribunes'.[2]

Thus the transition to devolved government has happened smoothly and without provoking the kind of dramatic reaction which some anticipated. Indeed, the opinion polls suggest that the Scots have become somewhat weary of constitutional politics and, like others throughout much of the western world, are increasingly less likely to vote in elections. This constitutional stability has a number of causes. The last few years and more have shown sustained economic growth and healthy levels of employment which not only generated material improvement but substantially increased the budgets of the Scottish Executive. Indeed, in 2005 it was reported that the job market in Scotland had improved consecutively for two and a half years, with Glasgow generating one in three of the new positions. The housing and employment markets have not only remained vigorous over the same period, but more buoyant than those south of the border where economic growth has slowed since 2004. Thus, the predicted financial tensions between London and Edinburgh have not materialized. Moreover, administrative devices developed since 1999 have helped to lend flexibility and pragmatism to the devolution arrangements. The best known are the so-called 'Sewel Conventions', named after Lord Sewel, the UK Government Minister who introduced them. Under these, it can be agreed that Westminster legislates in areas formally devolved to Scotland. The Conventions were enacted on 41 occasions from 1999 to 2003, leading to criticism that Holyrood was surrendering too many responsibilities to Westminster. Most crucially, however, devolution has had a good wind because Labour was the main party of government in both London and Edinburgh. Potential problems can therefore usually be dealt with through party channels and personal connections. What all this means, however, is that the settlement has yet to be fully tested. That scenario will only come about when there are two different dominant parties in Holyrood and Westminster and/or when UK financial circumstances (and hence the value of the block grant to Scotland) become more difficult.

The political challenges within Scotland itself came much more quickly for the new Executive and Members of the infant Parliament but whether Donald Dewar and his team were up to them is now debatable. Recent revelations suggest that Dewar's virtuoso perform- ance at the royal opening of Parliament belied his real state of mind and health. Dewar, despite his political standing, was prone to black moods and self-doubt. In the view of one of his closest friends, Fiona Ross, broadcaster and daughter of Willie Ross, the redoubtable Labour Secretary of State for Scotland in the 1960s, the worst time was when the future First Minister himself was Scottish Secretary in the months before the Scottish Parliament elections in 1998. At this point he seemed to run out of steam, a year before the daunting task of leading Scotland's first devolved government. According to Ross, remorseless media hostil- ity, rows over the selection of candidates for the Parliament and pressures at Westminster 'as various English colleagues suddenly woke up to the extent of the constitutional changes they had agreed to' all combined to affect him. In her view, he sank into a serious depression, complained of being very tired and started to suffer from a chest infection. The man who so many looked to for leadership in the new Scotland was clearly ailing:

At this point, hardly a year into the Labour Government, the Secretary of State who'd spent 18 years in the political wilderness, and finally had the job he'd always aspired to, was threatening to walk away. Donald was exhausted and said on several occasions, 'I can't go on like this. This constant grind. On an endless treadmill' . . . the discussion of resignation was serious. He considered not standing for the Scottish Parliament and remaining at Westminster. How- ever, the option he favoured was to resign from the Cabinet and simply retire at the next election. 'If I gave up this job', he said, 'I would miss it but not much'.[3]

Ross surmised that Dewar's acute heart problems, which were eventually to cause his premature death, probably date from that bleak period. The omens for successful leadership as devolved government began were not good.

In the event, Dewar's period in office was tragically short. He served as First Minister for less than eighteen months and for six months of that period he was battling ill health. In addition, after the high hopes and euphoria of the referendum campaign, his administration was dogged by problems and mishaps. Dewar and his ministerial team seemed in a constant state of crisis. Sections of the print media which had long opposed devolution relished in denouncing the new Parliament for some of its first decisions in 'voting itself huge salaries, allowances, a three-day week with short hours, 17 weeks holiday a year and a medal'.[4] Every little peccadillo was picked over and the tabloid newspapers in particular fuelled public scepticism by their exposures. The Executive and MSPs had to become used to such relentless and often hostile scrutiny and did not always handle it well. There was, in truth, plenty of meat to throw to the tabloid wolves. Inaccurate Higher Grade results were sent out by the Scottish Qualifications Agency in the summer of 2000, causing a national furore and a long period of uncertainty for school pupils seeking university entrance. Two of Dewar's senior advisers resigned, one of whom, John Rafferty, was his chief of staff. He had wrongly told reporters that the Health Minister, Susan Deacon, was under police protection because she had received death threats. The national fuel protests of September 2000 then threatened to bring the country to a halt. Though a UK-wide phenomenon, the bitter dispute still conveyed the impression of a devolved administration lurching from crisis to crisis. One commentator sympathetic to devolution called it a 'catalogue of calamity'.[5]

But these events were as nothing compared to the gathering storm over the escalating costs of the building of the new Parliament at Holyrood and the controversy over the legal provision, Section 28 (2A). Dewar had wished for an iconic building to house the new Parliament and the choice of site – opposite the Royal Palace of Holyroodhouse in Edinburgh – was very much his decision. Criticism started to mount that the costs of the project had been drastically underestimated and many feared the nation was to be landed with a huge bill for construction. Again, it was easy to portray the Executive as incompetent, though, in fact, the project had been started before the first sitting of Parliament.

Donald Dewar's short period in office spared him, however, from the full ferocity of the media backlash as the enormous scale of the Holyrood fiasco only really became clear at a later date.

More serious in the short-term was the furore over Section 28 (2A). The decision was taken to abolish this legal provision which prohibited local authorities (and hence local authority schools) from 'promoting' homosexuality. Dewar told the Parliament that Clause 2A had to go because it 'singles out a minority in our community for stigma, isolation and fear'. The decision to legislate was announced in autumn 2000 by Wendy Alexander, the Communities Minister. It was not long before fierce opposition began to emerge. An alliance of the *Daily Record*, Scotland's biggest-selling tabloid, the Catholic Church, led by the high-profile Cardinal Tom Winning, and the millionaire bus tycoon, Brian Souter, an evangelical Christian, orchestrated a massive protest. This included a postal vote, funded by Souter, in which 87 per cent of respondents voted to keep the Clause. Opponents voiced a clear message: abolition was in their view merely the thin end of the wedge, the essential preliminary to gay lessons being made available in schools. Amid the hysteria, the Executive stuck to its guns and the Clause was abolished. The episode showed that, whatever one's point of view, a Scottish Parliament could indeed make a difference and that Dewar himself was not always the cautious politician so often portrayed. His social liberal credentials were obvious for all to see even if many others sincerely saw this legislation as a sinister and unacceptable attack on family values. He proudly proclaimed at the Labour Party Conference later that year: 'We stood firm in the blizzard . . . section 28 is no more'.[6] But the reform was achieved at the expense of much electoral unpopu-larity. The First Minister's poll ratings fell to even lower levels. Cardinal Winning, a previously influential enthusiast for devolution, now pro-claimed the Parliament an 'utter failure' and added that he was almost ashamed of Scotland's politicians. There was a general sense among the hierarchy of the Catholic Church in Scotland that the Executive was more interested in addressing a politically correct agenda than in defending traditional moral principles. The Church of Scotland, on the surface at least, seemed less concerned. Perhaps even more significant politically, however, was Dewar's apparent inability to control his Cabinet. There was constant infighting and leaks to the press by the opposing camps. The First Minister confided to close colleagues that he ought to have had more of 'the killer instinct' and should have sacked the offenders. After his heart operation, there was, of course, near certainty that Dewar would retire before too long. The jostling for position among the main contenders for the succession, Henry McLeish, Jack McConnell and Susan Deacon, intensified.

When Donald Dewar died suddenly in October 2000 all of this was forgotten. The national mourning was real and sincere. Dewar was enormously respected as a man of integrity and the key figure in the delivery of devolution. His funeral in Glasgow Cathedral was the closest Scotland had come in recent times to a state occasion. The entire UK Cabinet, the cream of Scottish civil society as well as numerous friends, admirers and colleagues attended in large numbers. The popular press now performed an extraordinary *volte-face*. In a series of hagiographic obituaries, the previously dull, stumbling and incompetent Donald was transformed into 'The Father of the Nation'. Most space was devoted to his influence on the making of the Scottish Parliament, less was given to his two major achievements during his short period in office: his plans for radical reform of land ownership in the Highlands (which were eventually implemented two years after his death in January 2003) and the revolutionary idea to transfer Glasgow's huge council housing stock to tenant-managed housing associations. The new land reform bill, *inter alia*, gave rural communities the right to collectively purchase sections of the estates where they lived whether or not owners wanted to sell. If the majority decided they wanted to buy, the property's value was determined by an independent assessor and could then be bought by using lottery money that went into a government fund. The Scottish Landowners' Federation raged against the measure as a threat to liberty and private property while land reformers welcomed it as an attempt to right what they saw as some of the wrongs of the Highland Clearances and a small step towards correcting Scotland's historic pattern of highly concentrated estate ownership. The plans for Glasgow housing also addressed an old problem. The UK government took over the council's £900 million housing debts, which were eating up 40p of every £1 of rent collected, thus releasing an income stream for improvement and refurbishment of many thousands of decaying homes. One recent commentator has described the strategy as 'the biggest revolution in social housing since the Housing Acts of 1919 and 1924 created council housing'.[7] Behind the negative headlines and incessant criticism, then, there had been some real achievements. Moreover, despite the many problems, Dewar had been undeniably a politician of UK standing who had helped to give legitimacy to the Parliament in its early months. In the short term no similar figure of such eminence and experience was likely to emerge as his successor.

The Enterprise Minister, Henry McLeish, was selected as First Minister over the rival candidate Jack McConnell by the Labour MSPs. But his victory hardly amounted to a ringing endorsement. Despite being strongly backed by heavyweight London politicians such as Gordon Brown, McLeish was elected by a mere 44 votes to 36, a majority of only 8. However, one clear and very popular policy advance did emerge during McLeish's term of office. Free personal care for the elderly, an idea strongly opposed by the Blair government in London, became law, partly because of the enthusiastic support of Labour's coalition partners in the Scottish Parliament, the Liberal Democrats, and also that of the SNP and Conservatives. Only time will tell whether this legislation represents an historic landmark in society's support for the old or a disastrous decision with potentially enormous costs which will seriously imperil the nation's finances in the future. At the very least, however, the controversy over personal care demonstrated that the new Parliament was not always prepared to toe the London line. McLeish should be given considerable credit for resisting the pressures which came his way over this issue from the Treasury and the UK Department of Social Security, headed then by the Scottish lawyer, Alistair Darling.

This success apart, however, the McLeish administration was mainly distinguished by its mediocrity. Above all, in most areas, the new First Minister lacked personal authority or even confidence in his own ability. In his previous role as Enterprise Minister, McLeish had performed creditably in the Chamber. Now the top job seemed to overwhelm him. He was prone to verbal mishaps, which became known as 'McLeishés' which were widely and amusingly reported by an unsympathetic press. Scotland's First Minister was in danger of becoming a comic figure. Insiders interviewed by the respected journalist, Brian Taylor, bluntly told him that McLeish had been over-promoted and was simply not up to the job. In the end he did not hold it for very long. A year after his election, Henry McLeish resigned on 8 November 2001 over a failure to end speculation about office cash allowances when he had been a Westminster MP. The writing had been on the wall since his appearance on BBC TV's *Question Time* when he comprehensively failed to provide satisfactory answers to the issues which had been raised before a national television audience.

This was for many pro-devolutionists a worrying and depressing time because it was not simply McLeish's political career which lay in ruins. For those who had devoted many years to promoting the devolution cause the loss of two First Ministers in as many years, the public fiasco over the relentless cost increases in the Holyrood building project and the widespread cynicism about the quality of MSPs, all seemed to put the entire devolution project in jeopardy. The Queen herself noted as much when she addressed the Parliament in its temporary home in Aberdeen in May 2002. She also added some wise words of perspective: 'After what might be considered a Parliamentary adjournment of almost three hundred years that process [of building a new political culture] will inevitably take time. In an age which tends to instant judgements, this is something we would all do well to remember'.[8]

The monarch's supportive words were well received. There is little doubt that circumstances had indeed worked against the Parliament's early success. Expectations were certainly too high, the departure of two First Ministers in quick succession was very bad luck and, unfortunately, devolution came at a time when, throughout western Europe, politics and politicians had fallen into a degree of disrepute. But the Executive had also scored some truly spectacular own goals, of which the most damaging was the series of blunders over Holyrood. The former Tory minister, Lord Fraser of Carmylie, was appointed to find out why an unrealistic initial budget of £40 million had spiralled to a colossal £431 million. After hearings lasting for 49 days and a million words of evidence, he concluded in a damning report that there was no single villain of the piece but that the civil service in Scotland should bear most of the blame for allowing enormous cost overshoots and not keeping their Ministers and MSPs informed about the emerging disaster.

After 'Officegate', which had ended McLeish's career, only two likely successors were available: Jack McConnell, who had been narrowly defeated a year earlier in the last election, and Wendy Alexander, a protégé of Donald Dewar and a young politician widely respected for her intellectual ability and work rate. After much soul-searching, Alexander pulled out of the race, leaving McConnell as the sole candidate to claim the spoils of victory. McConnell was soon criticized for his lack of vision, commitment to 'doing less better', which sometimes tended to reduce Scottish politics to a mind-numbing condition of boredom, and for his 'Jack the Lad' image. After the immediate post-devolution traumas, however, there was perhaps some sense in 'bedding down' the new institutions, avoiding potential crises and going for stability. Certainly, to a greater extent than either Dewar or McLeish, McConnell was in command of his Cabinet, not least because he removed virtually all personal opposition to him on the Labour side soon after becoming First Minister. Only Wendy Alexander remained for a time, but, soon after being given a massively overloaded ministerial portfolio, resigned her post for the backbenches. Thus far, moreover, the McConnell years have not been devoid of significant policies though little credit is given for them by what MSPs see as a consistently malign Scottish press. The attack on Scotland's age-old sectarian culture, the attempts to grapple with anti-social behaviour, the ban on smoking in public places which became law in spring 2006 and the so-called Fresh Talent Initiative, which seeks to help address Scotland's potentially shrinking population, are all very relevant to the contemporary needs of the nation. Above all, perhaps, was the decision to seek to introduce proportional representation in local government. This legislation will be implemented in 2007. At a stroke it could end the hegemony of the Labour Party at local level, usher in coalition politics, give the main opposition a major increase in representation in every town hall and, in the view of its supporters, stimulate more vitality in some semi-moribund councils. Yet, as this is written, the real impact of all these policies has yet to be fully tested.

Eight years after the Scotland Act was passed and on the 300th anniversary of the Treaty of Union of 1707 some aspects of devolution have become clear. The new Parliament has been severely criticized, some of it deserved, and in the view of many Scots has failed to live up to expectations. But more positively, in the successful operation of coalition politics, its relative transparency, the functioning of its special committees, the enhanced scrutiny of the civil service in Scotland and the passing of some significant and distinctive legislation on local government, land, health care and student fees, the Parliament has indeed made a difference. With the royal opening of its new home at Holyrood and the international architectural accolades it has received (including, in 2005, the prestigious Stirling Prize, when the judges described the building as one of 'sparkling excellence' and, without irony, as 'money well spent'), memories of the exorbitant cost of construction started to fade. By the end of 2005 more than a million visitors, most of them Scots, had visited the new building and the vast majority left with a positive impression. Also, so far as the public was concerned, there was no going back on devolution. In 2003, only a quarter of Scots said they were opposed to devolution although nearly half of those sampled agreed with the proposition that 'the Parliament has made no positive difference to life in Scotland and has been a failure so far'. Obviously the new breed of Scottish politician has much still to prove. Intriguingly, however, not only does the nation want to maintain devolution but increasingly wishes the Parliament to develop greater powers. Every test of opinion since 1999 confirmed this aspiration. For instance, a Mori poll in autumn 2005 showed that 58 per cent of Scots wanted more powers for Edinburgh as against 24 per cent who did not. Devolution, in the form defined by the legislation of 1999, has not yet become 'the settled will' of the Scottish people.

2

In spring 2004, the then Chair of Highlands and Islands Enterprise, Dr Jim Hunter, gave a presentation to Members of the Scottish Parliament in Edinburgh. His report on job creation in the north was very positive as he outlined the development of several innovative projects and, even more importantly, the reversal in some areas of the problem of population decline which had plagued the Highland region for generations. But Hunter began his speech in a much more downbeat fashion by pointing to the pessimistic attitudes which in his view ran through much of public discourse in Scotland: 'we just don't do optimism . . . especially in an economic context . . . once in Scotland we paid preachers pittances to tell us we're no bloody good. Now we pay press columnists big fees to do the same. And to do so in defiance of the facts . . . saddling us in the process with an unremittingly pessimistic commentary'.[9] A case in point soon came in the public intervention by Stuart Cosgrove, Channel 4's Director of Nations and Regions, when he denounced his fellow Scots as a nation in love with a culture of miserabilism. He was soon followed in quick succession by the ex-Glasgow Academy Harvard historian Niall Ferguson, who likened his native land to 'the Belarus of the West' and by a commentator in the *Irish Times* in early 2006 for whom modern Scotland is bent on committing suicide as, in his view, it inexorably surrenders to subsidies, welfare dependency and a culture of worklessness!

The issue was brought into even sharper focus when Carol Craig, dubbed by some as 'a California-style happiness guru', published her much discussed *The Scots' Crisis of Confidence* in 2003. She argued that there were dark aspects of the Scottish psyche which inhibited transformational change, especially in the area of economic development and cited in support the 2000 study of the Hunter Centre for Entrepreneurship at Strathclyde University which reported that Scots, more than the inhabitants of any other developed nation, saw 'fear of failure' as the biggest constraint on starting a business and that 'a dependency culture' was holding back the progress of the nation. So taken were some with Dr Craig's analysis that the Scottish Executive and several prominent businesses helped to support the establishment of her 'Centre for Confidence and Wellbeing' which was launched in the full glare of publicity within the precincts of the Holyrood Parliament in 2004. Indeed, an intriguing aspect of the response to this pessimistic analysis was the enthusiastic reaction of some of Scotland's leading entrepreneurs. The social science academic community, on the other hand, remained not simply sceptical but scornful.

Other commentators have speculated about the origins of this so-called 'Scottish cringe'. For some it is one result of the dread effects of Calvinism on the Scottish character and value system, an interpretation, however, which has little to commend it, since in the heyday of evangelical Calvinism in the Victorian era, Scotland was a world leader in trade and industry and played an absolutely central role in the governing and operation of the British empire. Not surprisingly, this extraordinary story of successful enterprise, recorded in detail earlier in this book, fashioned not only a social confidence in the national élite but an overweening ethnic conceit bordering on triumphalism which depicted the Scots as a chosen imperial race destined by their character and values to play a world role in culture, politics, economy, intellect and much else.

More compelling is the thesis which views 'the confidence problem' as the consequence of the catastrophic decline from the nineteenth-century position of hegemony after the Great War. For much of the twentieth century the Scottish people indeed had a hard time. The terrible losses of young men on the Western Front, the collapse of Scottish heavy industry in the early 1930s and the unprecedented levels of emigration between the Wars, all induced a mood of profound uncertainty. Recovery from this trauma was inevitably slow and piecemeal despite rising levels of employment during the Second World War and thereafter. Even the improved standards of living which started to be recorded from the 1950s were no panacea as, during the 1960s and 1970s, Britain's relative economic decline continued to produce a sense of anxiety. This could not have been helped by the sheer pace of deindustrialization in the 1980s when the old manufacturing and mining economy melted away within the space of a few years. The process was not simply one which had short-term social costs in rising unemployment, poverty and insecurity. Deindustrialization also triggered a crisis of national identity because so much of Scotland's modern collective psyche was invested in the great traditional staples of shipbuilding, heavy engineering and coal mining. Since the Victorian era the Scots saw themselves as a nation *par excellence* which made things and sold them around the world. Yet for all this, over much of the twentieth century the market economy had failed most Scottish people and had not delivered a decent standard of living for the majority of the working classes. It is, therefore, scarcely surprising that after 1947 they warmly embraced the basic securities of the Welfare State, responded with angry hostility during the years of the Thatcher governments when these seemed to be threatened and still retained a left-of-centre consensus into the new millennium.

However, whether all this suggests a 'crisis of confidence' in the first decade of the twenty-first century is more open to question. For a start, the assertion rests on an unproven premise with merely hunches, impressions and anecdotal evidence in support. There is no robust comparative data to demonstrate how 'confident' or 'unconfident' the Scots are in relation to other peoples. Indeed, some social scientists even doubt that such an exercise can be carried out meaningfully given the many imponderables involved. Perhaps, above all, the rhetoric of pessimism is in direct conflict with the actual history of Scotland over the last quarter of a century. The establishment of the Scottish Parliament was at least in part the political affirmation of a stronger sense of Scottish identity than had existed in the 1970s when the first devolution referendum failed in 1979. Chapter 25 has also outlined the evidence for a flourishing national culture covering such varied areas as literature, art, music (both popular and classical), theatre, architecture, history-writing and much else besides. Literature in particular is flourishing with writers such as J. K. Rowling, Ian Rankin, Irving Welsh, Alexander McCall Smith, Alasdair Gray and Ali Smith attracting an international readership. Behind this group of well-known names are many other figures producing high-quality work in fiction, poetry and drama. It was a sign of the times when in 2004 Edinburgh was designated the world's first UNESCO City of Literature, an accolade awarded, at least in part, as a tribute to the capital's thriving literary scene. Even more fundamental were the profound and rapid changes in Scottish economy and society which had come about since the early 1980s. Quite simply, Scotland, over that period, had been transformed to an extent unknown since the epoch of the Industrial Revolution of the later eighteenth and early nineteenth centuries. The Scotland of the 1950s was closer in overall economic and social structure to the Victorian Age than to the country of 2007. As the authors of an important study of social trends since *c.* 1980 concluded: 'Scotland [in 2004] is now barely recognizable as the same place'.[10]

Heavy industry, the heart of the old economy, was still growing into the later 1950s. Yet deep coal mining has now disappeared, as has steel making (virtually), while shipbuilding is but a shadow of its former self. Today, *all* manufacturing accounts for less than a fifth of Scottish GDP and the service sector, making up almost 70 per cent of GDP, dominates the economy. Scotland has reinvented itself as a post-modern economy in less than two decades, a process which has been contrasted favourably by some US economists to the continuing travails of the 'Rust Belt' regions in their own country. The new economic pillars are financial services, oil and gas, tourism, light engineering, public services, retailing and bio-sciences. The economy is arguably more diversified and resilient in the face of challenges from the low-cost economies of India, China and Eastern Europe than at any time since Scotland's old global pre-eminence started to crumble in the early twentieth century.

Scottish growth rates in the public discourse are often treated like a political football with journalists, polemicists, opposition MSPs and Scottish ministers the main players in the game. But, despite the controversies, the main outlines of development are reasonably clear. Since the late 1980s, Scotland has been doing rather well, albeit not quite as well for most of the period as England, whose economy has itself been outpacing most of Europe in recent years. From 1981 to 2000, for instance, absolute Scottish GDP was about 1.8 per cent per annum with the UK standing at 2.0 per cent over the same period. However, as Christopher Bryant has recently shown, the superior UK average is primarily due to the performance of London and the South-East. When the figures are disaggregated (as in Table 27.1), for 1991–2002 Scotland moves ahead of Wales, Northern Ireland and six of the nine English regions. By 2005, the pattern of Scottish employment was even healthier. The Bank of Scotland reported at the end of that year that permanent posts were rising at a faster pace than at any time since 2000. Job market conditions had improved for 28 successive months. By the end of 2005 Scottish unemployment had fallen to a thirty-year low while economic growth north of the border had not slowed to the same extent as in other parts of the UK. Edinburgh, the Lothians and the Grampian region are often seen as the new motors of the economy but in this process of employment expansion Glasgow posted the strongest growth of the Scottish cities. Indeed, data from the Office for National Statistics confirmed that in 2005 Glasgow generated one in three of Scotland's new jobs.

Of course, not everything in the Scottish economic garden is rosy. Labour productivity levels are weak by international standards. New company formation is still disappointing and take-up of new technologies below the European average. But the tendency still remains to exaggerate these difficulties and play down the bright spots. Major Scottish businesses, such as the Royal Bank of Scotland and HBoS in banking, the Wood Group and Cairn Energy in oil, Scottish Power in energy and Stagecoach and Firstbus in transport have had considerable global success. The number of high-tech companies created by university academics is small but on a per head of population basis ranks ahead of the UK, USA and Canada. When some of the world's most eminent economists gave the Allander series of lectures they broadly concluded that excessive pessimism about the Scottish economy was unwarranted – the overall performance was far from being disastrous, though further scope for improvement clearly existed. That much is taking place was confirmed by evidence from the Global Entrepreneurship Monitor (GEM) at Strathclyde University for 2006. Scotland had lagged behind the UK since the study began in 2000 in new-business activity rates. Slowly, however, the gap has narrowed over the six-year period, with the most recent evidence suggesting that Scotland for the first time matched the UK average rate for early-stage entrepreneurial activity. There is still some way to go, however, to equal the levels of London and the economic dynamo of the south-east of England. Yet long-term and patient investment in entrepreneurial education and start-up schemes may finally be paying off.

	GVA per head (UK = 100)		Gross Disposable income per head (UK = 100)		Unemployment rate (%)		Unemployment claimant count rate (%)	
	1991	2001	1991	2001	1999	2003	1998	2002
United Kingdom	100.0	100.0	100.0	100.0	6.2	5.1	4.6	3.1
North-East	84.5	76.4	88.3	88.9	10.1	6.6	7.1	5.2
North-West	90.8	89.8	94.2	93.7	6.5	5.1	5.1	3.6
Yorks & Humber	90.4	86.4	93.7	91.9	6.7	5.5	5.4	3.7
East Midlands	94.9	91.9	95.0	92.8	5.3	4.3	4.0	2.9
West Midlands	92.0	90.4	88.7	94.1	6.9	5.9	4.5	3.5
East	109.4	110.1	109.7	104.9	4.4	4.2	3.3	2.1
London	130.5	133.2	117.8	120.4	7.8	7.1	5.2	3.6
South-East	110.2	120.1	109.9	109.0	3.8	3.9	2.6	1.7
South-West	92.9	89.3	101.4	99.3	5.0	3.9	3.4	2.0
England	101.8	102.5	101.3	101.4	6.0	5.1	4.3	3.0
Wales	83.3	78.9	89.8	87.5	7.4	4.6	5.5	3.6
Scotland	99.5	94.7	96.3	97.3	7.5	5.7	5.4	3.7
Northern Ireland	76.4	78.4	85.1	88.7	7.6	5.4	7.3	4.5

Table 27.1: Economic trends by nation and English region.
Source: C. G. Bryant, *The Nations of Britain* (Oxford, 2006), p.53.

More sceptical commentators unfavourably contrasted the Scottish experience of steady and relatively slow growth to the exciting drama of the Irish 'Tiger Economy' across the sea. This has been a favourite ploy of those who argue that the unprecedented economic miracle which has taken place in Ireland provides a convincing lesson for Scotland of the material benefits of national independence. It would be crass to suggest that Ireland does not provide useful models for Scotland, notably about the value of a national consensus for and commitment to an agreed economic strategy over the long run. But the two cases are in fact quite different. The Irish were trying to move from a poor to a rich economy. Scotland in the 1980s was, by contrast, a mature industrial economy which was experiencing renewal and a fresh start. The spectacular growth rates of Ireland were simply not repeatable in Scotland. The Irish starting point of a low-wage, low-cost environment with a deep pool of unemployed labour made a rapid take off possible. Scotland did not have these 'advantages' and hence could not sustain the year-on-year high growth rates of the Irish economic miracle. In this context, renewal was a greater challenge than take off.

However, the equally radical change in the Scottish economic system had indeed been accompanied by a general increase in affluence. Scotland was reckoned to be three times richer in 2003 than in the 1950s, a leap in average real incomes greater than in any such previously recorded time-frame. Between 1996 and 2004 overall median income rose by 3.3 per cent with growth even higher among low-income earners who benefited from such public policy initiatives as tax credits. Over the last four decades car ownership has risen by 200 per cent. Housing has been transformed. The old Scottish problem of overcrowding in housing, still an issue in the 1950s, was solved over the next few decades. By 2001, in addition, ninety-three per cent of the population had both their own shower or bath and central heating – conveniences which for the current generation's grandparents were the preserve of a rich minority. Owner-occupation had massively increased, with only a quarter of Scots renting from the local councils by 1999. The old industrial cities of Dundee and Glasgow have been reinvented. Glasgow is now the second biggest shopping centre after London, its central streets crowded with new restaurants, bistros and pubs. It enjoys an international reputation – as the *National Geographic* magazine's 'Capital of Cool' – while being lauded by the prestigious *Frommer's Guide* at the top of the visitors' list for American visitors to European cities in 2006. Dundee is now more famous for bio-science than jute. The city's University was rated fourth in the world's best life-science institutions by *The Scientist*, with Dundee and Glasgow being the only two UK universities to make it into the top five. The most recent survey of employment in Dundee showed that 40 per cent of male workers have white-collar jobs. All around Scotland, urban regeneration, the general habit of eating out and the huge popularity of overseas holidays are testimony to the new prosperity enjoyed by the majority.

It is clear, then, that the economic outlook is more positive than some commentators have suggested. With its well-educated workforce, excellent universities and government strategies, such as the 'Smart Successful Scotland' initiative, Scotland seems well placed to compete in a global economy where brainpower and talent are much more important than muscle power. But the prospects are not uniformly bright. For instance, at first glance the demographic picture looks to be quite positive. In the new millennium, Scotland's age-old problem of mass net emigration seems to have temporarily abated. In the 1990s, migration has been in broad balance, although, ethnically, Scotland remains more homogeneous than most other parts of the UK with Asian and Caribbean immigration still limited in the extreme. The country's biggest immigrant group are the English, with no less than 406,900 first-generation migrants from south of the border recorded in the 2001 census. Far from being the retired 'white settlers' of legend, the vast majority of these immigrants are employed in skilled and professional jobs and live in the cities and towns of the Lowlands rather than in the remote communities of the far North. Even more recent are significant new arrivals from the eastern bounds of the European Community with young Poles, Lithuanians and Slovaks featuring prominently. But alongside this the high birth-rates of previous generations have, for the time being, disappeared. Fertility has fallen, families are smaller. So concerned was the Scottish Executive that a Fresh Talent Initiative was launched in February 2004 with the aim of attracting 8,000 (net) skilled, new migrants to Scotland in an effort to ensure that the national population does not fall below the psychologically symbolic 5 million level. Obviously this 'demographic time-bomb' is bad news. A shrinking cohort of the economically active young will have to support an ever-increasing army of the elderly and the pensioned as medical advance continues to extend average life spans. There are, however, three qualifications to this very real concern. First, historically, demographic predictions are a notoriously imprecise science. Indeed, the Scottish demographic apocalypse (breaching the 5 million barrier) was originally scheduled to take place in 2009. The Registrar-General has now postponed this prediction to 2017 at the earliest as the birth rate and immigrant levels have risen more recently. Second, this trend in population is a feature of the developed world and is not unique to any one country. In fact, only Albania and the Faroe Islands currently (2006) have total fertility rates above the estimated 'replacement level' of 2.1 births per female. Scotland sits squarely in the middle of the European league of fertility rates, above the countries of the central and southern regions of the continent which are facing even more serious demographic problems. Third, the prophets of doom take little account of improvements in economic productivity which theoretically could solve the problem of producing much more value with less labour.

In fact, demography may not be the main challenge for the nation. In the autumn of 2005, *Scotland on Sunday* revealed the 'State's Grip on Scotland' by quoting the view of Sir John Ward, Chair of Scottish Enterprise, that public-sector spending was reaching 'Eastern bloc' levels across the country. In 2002–3 his agency claimed that total public spending in Scotland was around £40 billion, partly as a result of the Chancellor of the Exchequer's largesse, or 55 per cent of the nation's total economy. Some areas of west-central Scotland are indeed over-whelmingly dependent on state spending – in Argyll and Clyde the proportion generated stands at 76 per cent, in Ayrshire and Arran, 74 per cent and in Lanarkshire, around 72 per cent. Only in oil-rich Grampians (35 per cent) and the Lothians (39 per cent), with the Edinburgh financial dynamo at its heart, did Scottish levels fall below those of the UK average, where state spending (2005) accounted for approximately 40 per cent of the economy.

A spokesman for the Confederation of British Industry (Scotland) was reportedly horrified at these figures: 'To have that much of the economy generated by wealth-spending rather than wealth-creating can't be good for Scotland in the long term'.[11] Conservative critics contended that the widespread availability of 'safe' jobs with secure pensions fortified Scotland's so-called 'dependency culture' while some academic economists, although recognizing the difficulty of measuring productivity levels in the public service in precise terms, worried that reform is still required in health and education where, so it is claimed, providers of services do not always have an incentive to deliver the outcomes users want when the disciplines of the market and the profit motive are absent. Increasingly, there is a public and political demand for 'value for money' in these sectors. More seriously, Scotland has become accustomed to the budget generosity of Gordon Brown. There is no certainty that will continue for ever and a day. If the tap is turned off, Scotland will be one of the first to suffer, given its disproportionate reliance on the public finances.

Equally, however, and more positively, it has to be recognized how vital the modern public sector is to the nation's capacity to generate prosperity. Good health and excellent education are central to that strategy and neither, in present circumstances, can be provided easily or widely by private enterprise. The whole issue of public spending in Scotland is in fact more complex than the views of those commentators and others who gleefully likened Scotland to the former Soviet Union would suggest. Scottish public expenditure was perhaps the fourth highest in Europe. What, however, was given much less attention by the alarmists was that two of the continent's most successful economies, Denmark and Sweden, had an even higher share of public spending than Scotland!

Yet economic concerns do not in themselves explain the pessimistic analysis which, in the midst of plenty, often underpins much of Scottish public discourse. One clue might be found in recent academic work where some economists now realize that men (and women) do not live by bread alone and, as a result, they are trying to measure the level of 'subjective well-being', using a more varied and sophisticated range of indicators than GDP alone. There is now a world database on 'happiness' and analysts try to evaluate such questions as: 'On the whole, are you very satisfied, fairly satisfied, or not at all satisfied with the life you lead?'. Table 2.7, showing UK patterns, suggests there has been a modest improvement in Great Britain as a whole but that the position in Scotland, despite the new affluence, has not changed much since the early 1970s. Rising living standards are, on the basis of this evidence, not making most Scots any happier.

We can only speculate why this may be so. There is undoubtedly a widespread perception that modern consumerism has brought with it a decline in community and neighbourhood and a more competitive, self-seeking, narcissistic, opportunistic and individualistic society. In such a society relativities matter. People are more inclined to compare their lot with others, aided and abetted by advertising and the mass media. Some believe that the decline in influence of the Christian religion which has accelerated, especially among the young, since the 1960s has left a moral vacuum where essential values are ignored or attacked and sexual responsibilties abdicated. In 2002, for instance, just over 11 per cent of Scots went to church on a Sunday. Numbers have been in decline for over forty years and show no sign of abating. Between 1994 and 2002, Church of Scotland membership slumped by 22 per cent and Roman Catholic by 19 per cent. Conservatives in the USA have tapped into these feelings to good effect and so helped to win George W. Bush a second election victory in 2004. The sheer speed of economic and social change has resulted in a loss of security and certainty for many people. But these elements are not peculiarly Scottish. The challenges are international and face all developed societies. The comment below comes from Australia, the so-called land of sunshine and easy living:

	% not at all satisfied	% not very satisfied	% fairly satisfied	% very satisfied
a) GB				
1973–1977	4	11	54	31
1978–1982	4	10	53	33
1983–1987	4	10	55	31
1988–1992	4	10	55	31
1993–1997	3	10	57	31
1998–2002	2	9	55	35
b) Scotland				
1973–1977	3	12	57	28
1978–1992	2	10	62	26
1983–1987	5	9	61	25
1988–1992	4	11	58	27
1993–1997	4	11	58	27
1998–2002	3	11	58	28

Table 27.2: Life satisfaction, Scotland and Great Britain, 1973–2002.
Source: Eurobarometer Surveys 1973–2003 from D. Bell and D. G. Blanchflower, 'The Scots may be Brave but they are neither Healthy or Happy' in *Institute for the Study of Labour (IZA), Bonn. Discussion Paper 1909* (December 2005). I am most grateful to Professor Rod Cross of Strathclyde University for drawing my attention to this paper. For a discussion of the methodologies and problems involved in measuring 'satisfaction' and 'wellbeing' see D. G. Blanchflower and A. J. Oswald, 'Wellbeing over time in Britain and the USA', *Journal of Public Economics*, Vol 88, July 2004, pp. 1359–86.

Contemporary society seems overwhelmed by social problems. At a time of apparent economic prosperity, community anxiety about family breakdown, drug abuse, youth suicide, violence and home invasion continues to mount. Widespread ambivalence about the benefits of economic change is reflected in a rising tide of community concern about negative social consequences ... although these things are difficult to quantify, there can be little doubt that since the late 1960s our society has seen the collapse or erosion of many of the social structures around which people built relationships, personal worth and belonging.[12]

The revolution in the position of women over the last three decades may also be significant. For the first time most women are now in formal employment (55 per cent) and they account for the majority of employees in education, health and some other areas in the public services. The automation of domestic drudgery, effective contraception and the transition to a service-based economy have all helped to make this possible. Underlying these new economic roles for women have also been key demographic changes, such as later age at marriage, postponed child-bearing and smaller family size. For many women this is a liberation, but others are employed in insecure, part-time and poorly paid jobs. For working mothers, in particular, the need to combine home and work responsibilities can often lead to heightened stress levels. Hence, more income for the household may not necessarily lead to a higher quality of life. The classical 'family' of two parents and dependent children is now the exception rather than the rule as different relationships begin to dominate household formation which are much more fluid than those of the past. Personal fulfilment for some can also lead to insecurity, anxiety and uncertainty for others.

More generally, the demand for professional and skilled labour in the new economy, together with the vast expansion of higher educational provision and the greater need for formal credentials have resulted in general social mobility on an unprecedented scale. Studies by sociologists at Edinburgh University show that, in terms of census descriptors, among adults of working age in 2001, almost two-thirds have moved to a different social class from that of their parents. In fact, nearly half of men born between 1937 and 1966 have been upwardly mobile. There is some evidence that this rate of movement may be declining for those born in more recent times but this is not necessarily because of an increase in social inequalities. Rather, 'a lower proportion of the total population moves upwards simply because a lower proportion comes from manual-class backgrounds. Likewise, a higher proportion are immobile because they are already at the top of the class structure as children'.[13] Table 27.3 shows the sharp growth in managerial, professional and non-manual employment and a shrinkage of semi-skilled and unskilled jobs. Scotland is therefore a more 'middle-class' country than at any period in its history. The transformational effects of these movements on Scottish society were obviously profound and their implications have yet to be fully worked out.

One striking illustration of this is that Scottish Catholics, making up around one in six of the population and mainly the descendants of the poor immigrant Irish of the nineteenth century, are no longer disadvantaged in employment. The Scottish Household Survey of 2001 shows them not to be under-represented among the nation's managers and professionals and younger Catholics (aged 35 and below) have

% in columns		Year	
Socio-economic group	1981	1991	2000
Employers and managers, large establishments	4.4	4.2	9.3
Employers and managers, small establishments	4.4	8.5	7.1
Professionals, self-employed	0.5	0.8	1.1
Professionals, employees	2.9	3.9	5.1
Intermediate non-manual	10.2	14.5	16.2
Junior non-manual	19.3	21.0	18.9
Personal service	6.1	4.7	6.1
Foremen and supervisors	2.6	2.4	4.4
Skilled manual	19.3	14.2	10.5
Semi-skilled manual	12.4	10.8	9.6
Unskilled manual	7.7	7.0	5.1
Other self-employed	2.3	4.0	3.8
Farmers (employers, managers and self-employed)	1.2	1.1	0.7
Agricultural workers	1.4	1.1	1.1
Armed forces	0.9	0.8	0.5
Inadequately classified	4.5	0.9	0.5
Sample size	240,135	207,378	5,733

Table 27.3: Socio-economic group of economically active population aged 16 or older, 1981–2000.
Source: Table taken from L. Paterson, F. Bechhofer and D. McCrone, *Living in Scotland* (Edinburgh, 2004, p. 85).

achieved broad occupational parity with the rest of their age group. This achievement has taken some time. The Irish diaspora in the USA reached this position in the early twentieth century. The evidence seems to suggest that comprehensive education from the 1960s, increased access to higher education, opportunities in the public service, a marked decline in discrimination from the 1960s and the academic success of Catholic schools have been the main facilitators.

But despite these positive indicators all is not well. Scotland remains a deeply divided society where profound inequalities still exist. Many have not been able to become part of the new meritocracy. Fears are voiced of the emergence of a new Scottish underclass, the excluded people outside the knowledge economy whose lives are blighted by poverty, low educational attainment, poor health, petty crime and a rampant drug culture: 'the people with no knowledge'. In 1995, for instance, 60 per cent of council tenants in Glasgow were on income support while deep pools of concentrated relative deprivation also existed in Lanarkshire, Ayrshire and Dumbartonshire – where deindustrialization has hit hard the council estates around Edinburgh and parts of Dundee, Stirling and Aberdeen. The journalist Alan Taylor graphically described the story of modern Glasgow as a 'tale of two cities' with unemployment, illness and a thriving benefit economy in uneasy coexistence with a new cultural vitality and unbridled consumerism: 'it would need a Dostoevesky to do justice to such a scenario'.[14] Partly for this reason Scotland performs badly compared to the rest of the UK and much of the developed world in almost all measures of health. Male suicide rates are significantly higher than the English average, as are the rates of violent crime. One in twenty children in Scotland under 16 had a problem drug-using parent in 2003, some 41,000–59,000 children in all, though recent evidence suggests an actual decline in drug misuse from the late 1990s. Elsewhere, however, there is precious little sign of improvement. In diabetes, coronary heart disease, strokes and liver disease the so-called 'Sick Man of Europe' has an unenviable reputation.

The real depth and extent of inequality was revealed by an extensive *Scotsman* investigation in early 2006. Using NHS data, the newspaper compiled a 'deprivation index' for the country's 830 postcode areas. In one sense, the results were unsurprising, confirming once again the stark contrast between affluence and poverty. But what the survey brought out more clearly than before was the dramatic magnitude of the differences. 'Prime Scotland', the best 100 neighbourhoods, had the highest life expectancy anywhere in the world at 80 years and above, even ahead of such global leaders as Iceland, Japan, Sweden and Australia. Alongside these areas with remarkably good qualities of life were some of the poorest districts in the western hemisphere. This 'Third Scotland', with life expectancy closer to that of the third world (around 65 years) was mainly, but not exclusively, concentrated in the east end of Glasgow and parts of the other cities where life expectancy was lower than Lebanon, the Gaza Strip or Bosnia. The difference in this measure between the 'best' and 'worst' postcode areas was 22 years in Edinburgh, 17 years in Paisley, 15 years in Perthshire and 9 years in the Highlands. In the heart of 'Third Scotland', the Glasgow districts of Dalmarnock, Calton and Townhead, male life expectancy was below 60, a figure which had been passed by the UK as a whole during the Second World War.

This depressing picture helps to explain the incomprehension of many middle-class Scots when they read that their country is a drugs black-spot and one of the murder capitals of Europe: 'it is an image incompat-ible with their lives, or the lives of their elderly relatives'.[15] Their reactions reflect the deep social divisions within urban Scotland where the new affluence of the many has not substantially eased the relative living standards of the poorer minority. Nor can the problem simply be solved by increasing resources in deprived areas. As one local man from Calton in Glasgow, where worklessness is rife, commented: 'If you want a job, you can get a job. It's not that people don't want to work, it's just that it's not worth it. Why work for a tenner when you can get more on the dole'.[16] For him, many of the next generation in his area will rationally chose welfare if it pays more. As a result, an inter-generational culture of worklessness becomes embedded in some communities with children growing up in households devoid of role models, where few fathers and mothers are regularly engaged in employ-ment. This and related problems form a lugubrious list. They are probably the main social challenge confronting the Scottish Executive and Parliament as devolution matures and the transformation of Scottish society intensifies in the early decades of the new millennium.

Afterword

The fact that in 2007 a union of two historic nations has survived so long is remarkable, even if, in that year of its three hundredth anniversary, the connection had more critics in Scotland than at any time since the eighteenth century and the Anglo-Scottish political relationship had also been changed permanently by devolution. For as European history shows mere geographical proximity is not in itself sufficient to sustain a long-term union between two different states. Britain and the Republic of Ireland, Spain and Portugal, Norway and Sweden all provide examples of associations that have proved ephemeral. The possibility of a similar breach between England and Scotland remains possible and for some has become a much more realistic scenario since the rise of Scottish nationalism from the 1960s and its electoral triumphs in very recent years. Nonetheless, in the words of one scholar: 'For unions between distinct and established medieval kingdoms of some reputation, like England and Scotland, to last for four hundred years (if we date it from the 1603 Union of Crowns), is a rare thing in European history'.[1] Since the last few chapters of this book have often been concerned with some of the factors which might erode that age-old bond, it is worthwhile briefly reflecting here on the elements which have primarily influenced the survival of the union over the centuries. The discussion will then focus in on the last few years of Scottish history when the very future of the relationship is at stake.

Both nations for the most part shared the common language of English, even if usage was complicated by local dialect and accent. The successful dominance of the Protestant Reformation in both countries was also self-evidently a key ideological support. There may have been crucial differences of governance, custom and usage between Presbyterian Scotland and Anglican England but these were of less account in the eighteenth century when both nations had to remember what united rather than divided them as they were confronted with a new hundred years war with the menace of Catholic France, often in alliance with Catholic Spain. Nor should the clauses of the Treaty of Union itself, which came into force on May Day 1707, be ignored in this regard. Allowing the Scots to maintain their Presbyterian church, formally established in 1690, was with hindsight a masterstroke. Most European monarchies in the early modern period were committed to religious uniformity within their dominions. At root, that was the cardinal factor that had led to the horrific Thirty Years War of the seventeenth century. State authorities knew that religious faith was more likely to attract emotional loyalty from their populations than political dogma, although the two were inextricably linked in the contemporary mind.

Yet the decision to guarantee the position of the Kirk in perpetuity was based more on expediency than on statesmanlike vision. Indeed, it is highly likely that without such a declaration from Westminster the unionist cause might well have foundered. Even the suspicion of an Episcopalian/Anglican settlement would have unleashed a passionate Presbyterian campaign against the proposed legislation and only given comfort to the Jacobite interest. In the event, the recognition in law of the Church of Scotland was of profound importance in the maintenance of the Union. Not only did it provide a focus of Scottish identity within the new relationship but the role and influence of the Kirk were also crucial to the survival of a distinctive system of education, poor law and, for many generations, a moral ethos in the localities of Scotland. More pragmatically, Presbyterian Scots did not experience discrimination in the Empire on religious grounds, a great boon to successful careers in that global context.

In the short-run, however, none of these factors necessarily secured the long-term future of the Union. For nearly four decades after 1707 it was widely unpopular as the promised economic advantages failed to come through. Taxation levels rose to punitive levels and London interference in church governance inflamed pious Presbyterians. The history of Jacobitism and its appeal in Scotland cannot be understood without full recognition of the deep anti-union alienation that was a crucial strand in support of the Stuart cause.

Yet, by the 1760s, there was a new stability in the Anglo-Scottish relationship. The tobacco and linen trades flourished while Culloden and its savage aftermath had finally laid to rest the Jacobite threat. Scottish officers, merchants, educators and physicians were claiming an indecent share of the imperial spoils. Some frictions, however, remained. The English Whig elites had not quite forgotten the fright they had had during the traumatic months of the '45 when an attempted counter-revolution, incubated in Scotland, had posed a mortal threat to the Hanoverian state. This memory took time to fade, as was shown in 1757 when the Militia Act established a force in England and Wales for home defence, a strategy which was not, however, extended to Scotland. The suspicion north of the Border was that Westminster still regarded many Scots as crypto-Jacobites who were not to be trusted with the bearing of arms. Moreover, as late as the 1790s, London cartoonists continued to lampoon the Scots as treacherous and parasitic mendicants feasting off England's riches both at home and abroad.

The turning-point probably came during the two great conflicts of the late eighteenth century, the American War of Independence (1776–83) and, even more critically, the Revolutionary and Napoleonic Wars (1795–1815). The Scots were not only loyal to the British cause, conspicuously so in the American War when the Irish were seen to exploit imperial weakness for political advantage, but had also contributed generously in blood to the final victory over France in 1815. The heroism of the Highland regiments came to personify a sacrifice that now entitled the Scots to an equal partnership within the Union.

In reality, of course, that could never be. Scotland was 'in bed with an elephant', as the Canadian premier Pierre Trudeau once put it in his description of the imbalance in relationships between his own country and the USA. The English outnumbered the Scots by about 5:1 at the time of the Union and around 10:1 by the First World War. London was not only the centre of imperial rule but, pace the Scottish Enlightenment, the hegemonic source of culture, fashion, ideas and economy within the British Isles. Indeed, by the early nineteenth century, the concern in Scotland was that the elephant was close to absorbing the northern nation as the new entity of 'North Britain'. Some Scottish intellectuals of the time thought that 'the end of Scotland' was nigh. For Henry Cockburn, it was 'the last purely Scotch age' while Sir John Sinclair feared that his country might be 'completely confounded in England'.[2] If this danger had become a reality, a 'nationalist' backlash, founded on the traditions of a nation with antecedents dating back to the Wars of Independence, might well have been on the cards. After all, the mid-nineteenth century was the age of both romantic and political nationalism, the very decades when the ancient Habsburg Empire was torn apart by ethnic-based revolutions in Italy, Hungary and other regions. True, the Scottish upper and middle classes were doing rather well out of the union-inspired connection and it is indeed hard therefore to see them as rabid nationalists manning the political barricades. Nevertheless, if the historic identity of Scotland had been overwhelmed with 'Englishness' or the nation marginalised as a mere province of a dominant and aggressive English state, then the 1707 settlement might well have been destabilised.

The reality, as earlier chapters of this book have shown, was, however, very different. Political nationalism in nineteenth-century Scotland was virtually extinct. The Union had never been more stable. This was the age of unionist-nationalism: pride in Scotland as a nation, yes, but with it a deep loyalty to the connection with England forged in 1707. Why?

Obviously unprecedented Scottish economic success in the Victorian era was crucial. By that time contemporary Scottish historiography had adjusted to the new realities by depicting pre-Union Scotland as a land of faction and obscurantism while the post-Union nation shone as a beacon of enlightenment, civilization and economic progress, all securely founded on 1707. But the material factor was not the only relevant influence. This was the era when the dual identity of 'Scottishness' and 'Britishness' was fashioned. Allegiance to the British Empire and pride in British global hegemony and loyalty to the popular British monarchy of Victoria ran in close parallel with the invention of a new and distinctive Scottish identity founded on the cults of

Burns, Knox and a reappraisal of Wallace, historical memories burnished and mythologized by Scott and others and the notion of the Scots as a pre-eminent race of empire builders, heroic soldiers, educators, doctors and engineers. Highlandism, the process by which metamorphosed symbols of the Gael, such as the tartan, kilt and sporran, became identified with the nation as a whole rather than simply the poorest part of it, spoke of an innocuous sartorial nationalism that was perfectly compatible with the union state. That state was also far from interventionist, at least until the last quarter of the nineteenth century. For much of the earlier period Scotland mainly governed itself through burgh councils, a host of voluntary and philanthropic organisations and official boards of various kinds managing everything from welfare to prisons and lunatic asylums. Westminster was remote and indifferent most of the time. The local Scottish 'state' ran Scotland.

Even when the British state started to flex its muscles from the 1860s, Scotland's distinctive legal system ensured that there had to be a form of administrative devolution in order to facilitate the passage and implementation of specifically Scottish legislation. Thus, in 1885, not only was the office of Secretary of State for Scotland revived but the Scottish Office was set up in London and a Scottish Standing Committee established in Westminster to consider Scottish bills. Even Home Rule for Scotland from the 1880s attracted sympathetic interest from London and came within an ace of success in 1914, just failing to become law because of the outbreak of war in 1914.

It is arguable that the first five decades of the twentieth century saw the very zenith of unionism. The Conservative and Unionist party won no fewer than four of the seven general elections between the wars. During the general economic crisis of these years Scottish voters clung to the protection of Britain rather than risk any nationalist adventure. The foundation of the SNP in 1934 showed that not all Scots were in the unionist camp but its successive failures at the polls demonstrated conclusively that the vast majority were to be found there in massive numbers. Indeed the emergence of the SNP itself came about in part because of the growing indifference to Home Rule on the part of the more established Liberal and Labour parties. The outbreak of the Second World War further buttressed British identity. For a time plucky Britain and its Empire stood alone against an evil foe. Every nook and cranny of life was affected as the nation geared up for total war. The age-old distinction between combatants and non-combatants faded as the civilian population on the home front struggled against enemy bombers, food shortages and, until 1942, the fear of invasion. The legacy of Britain united in a good cause lived long in the folk memory, even of the post-1945 generation via the extraordinary popularity (and longevity) of war comics, books and films.

This was not the only vital factor buttressing Britishness. The foundation of the Welfare State, promising cradle to grave security and the commitment to full employment in the post-war world, had enormous appeal for Scots who had suffered the full impact of market failure in the 1930s as evidenced by serious unemployment levels and appalling housing conditions. Even the beginnings of the end of Empire with the independence of India and Pakistan in 1947 did not disturb the union connection. As living standards finally started to improve in the 1950s and the years of austerity faded into the past, unionism in Scotland seemed impregnable. Indeed in 1950 the Labour party dropped its long-standing commitment to Scottish self-government while the SNP remained a political irrelevance. 1955 saw the Unionist party famously attract just over half of the popular vote, a unique and remarkable achievement in Scottish electoral history.

But this political consensus did not mean that 'Scottishness' had in any sense evaporated. On the contrary, the mass interest in the Scottish Covenant of 1949, advocating a Parliament in Edinburgh within the Union and attracting nearly 2 million signatures, suggested that Scotland's sense of itself remained robust. Moreover, by the later 1950s all was not well with the Scottish economy. The long period of Britain's post-war relative decline against international competitors, which lasted from the 1960s to the 1990s, had begun. The balance between 'Scottishness' and 'Britishness' now started slowly to shift. The rise of the SNP, the new and pragmatic interest in devolution by Westminster and a fresh vitality in Scottish culture were all signs of the times. A key decade was the 1980s when the 'elephant' for the first time since the eighteenth century seemed to move to the Scottish side of the 'bed', with the imposition of highly unpopular social and economic policies by the Thatcher governments for which Scotland had not voted. The experience put more steel into the Scottish electorate and their politicians. Any ambiguity about the relevance of a Scottish Parliament to the future of the nation quickly receded.

Over half a century on from the high noon of unionism in the 1950s the key issue, as this is written at the end of 2011, is whether the time-honoured connection between Scotland and England will survive for much longer in the new millennium. Certainly, a sense of Scottish identity has apparently never been as strong since the eighteenth century. In 2004, around three-quarters of Scots felt 'exclusively' or 'mainly' Scottish, a significantly higher proportion than the equivalent 'ethnic' measures in England and Wales. These 'Scottish' loyalties are especially common among the younger generation. But that awareness need not mean that political independence is inevitable. It may be yet another manifestation of the Union's historic capacity not only for flexibility but for giving full and easy scope for the Welsh, English and Scots to express their cultural and ethnic identities within a UK framework. The most recent research by the Economic and Social Research Council suggests that the old dual identity is not yet extinct. Perhaps inevitably, however, much recent comment both in the media and among academic analysts has been about the reasons for the decline of 'Britishness' over the last half century. The check list might include the waning of Protestantism (a key ideological British resource for earlier generations); the end of Empire and Britain's subsequent fall for a time to the status of a second-rate power; the huge and increasing importance of Europe and the parallel decline in the authority of the British state and, not least, the ebbing of respect for the institution of monarchy. Moreover, since the end of World War Two and the collapse of the Soviet threat, there is the loss of a clear 'other', or of a major external enemy which could help to sustain British national solidarity against a common foe.

In the last few years the terms of the debate on Scotland's constitutional future has changed radically. The key reason for this is the surge in SNP support and the new political authority of the party in the

Scottish Parliament. In 2007 the nationalists became the largest force in Holyrood by one seat and formed a minority government. In May 2011 the SNP won a stunning electoral victory which has the potential to change British history. With a total of 69 seats they achieved what was not thought to be possible – an overall majority in the new Parliament. At a stroke, the political landscape in Scotland was transformed. No longer could opposition parties block nationalist plans for a referendum on Scottish independence, the policy that was and is the raison d'etre of the SNP. Soon such a referendum was promised by Alex Salmond within the five-year lifetime of his administration.

The SNP's vote jumped by 13 per cent while Labour's declined. The results were devastating for the party, which had ruled central Scotland in particular for decades with the SNP taking Labour seats in every city in Scotland and the political scalps of several of its leading figures. The Liberal Democrats were wiped out, paying a terrible price for their Westminster coalition with the Tories, with hundreds of thousands of erstwhile supporters switching en masse to the SNP. The Scottish Conservatives continued to languish as a tiny electoral rump. It was a sign of the comprehensive nature of the SNP victory that in the following few months all three leaders of the failed opposition parties fell on their swords and were replaced by new and relatively unknown faces.

The reasons for the SNP triumph were many. The party was seen to have performed competently in government over the previous few years. Its message to the Scottish electorate was upbeat, positive and aspirational while Labour in particular was perceived to be fighting a much more negative campaign. In Alex Salmond the nationalists had as leader one of the most accomplished politicians, not simply in Scotland, but in the whole of the UK. Scottish voters had also long mastered the habit of supporting one party in Holyrood elections – who were thought more able to run Scotland itself – and another, usually Labour, at Westminster.

The post-mortems suggested that much of the defeat of the Labour party was self-inflicted. The veteran journalist and historian Neal Ascherson described its campaign as 'hopeless'.[3] But there were also deeper, more structural problems. Scottish Labour seemed more committed to resisting the nationalists than exploiting devolution energetically in an attempt to solve Scotland's myriad social problems of poor health and deep-seated disadvantage in some parts of the country's cities. There were also those traditional Labour voters who were alienated by Blairite neo-liberalism and memories of the Iraq war. The SNP, with its left-wing programmes could easily be portrayed as the heir of Old Labour, or at least as its ideological cousin. The talent deficit in the party at Holyrood was also there for all to see. Labour's 'big hitters', Cook, Brown, Reid, Darling and Alexander preferred London to Edinburgh while some bright contenders from the new generation were driven out of politics by factionalism and personal vendettas.

At the moment (late 2011) it would seem that the SNP is monarch of all it surveys in the Scottish political landscape. The unionist parties in Holyrood are in continued disarray and will take some time to recover from the drubbing they received at the last election. Even more seriously, they have not yet managed to produce an entirely credible and convincing intellectual case for the retention of the Union. Achieving that will be crucial when the debate on independence intensifies after the date for the promised referendum is called. Equally, support for the Union seems to be weakening in other parts of the UK. One British-wide opinion poll in November 2011 indicated that of the English and Welsh voters asked about the constitutional future for Scotland, 39 per cent were in favour of the status quo, 24 per cent preferred full independence and 15 per cent backed increased powers for Holyrood within the Union.

Against this background, the SNP government is adopting a two-stage strategy. The first priority seems to be to greatly strengthen existing proposals in the Scotland Bill currently under consideration at Westminster. This contains suggestions made by the Commission on Scottish Devolution, also known as the Calman Commission after its convener, Sir Kenneth Calman, Chancellor of Glasgow University. This was established by a Scottish Labour party motion passed by Holyrood in 2007 with the support of the Conservative and Liberal Democrats but opposed by the SNP. It was widely seen as an attempt by the unionist parties to augment existing devolved authority and so undermine the nationalist campaign of full independence for Scotland. The recommendations included modest powers for the Scottish Parliament to set income tax rates but with reduction in the block grant from Westminster by a corresponding amount and the right to borrow up to £2bn to finance public works. The SNP government now seeks to extend these proposals by negotiating for control of corporation tax and a significant rise in borrowing powers to £5bn.

The second objective is to hold a referendum in the latter part of the parliament offering the Scottish people the opportunity to vote for the option of independence. With typical confidence, Alex Salmond declared on nationwide television in October 2011 that Scots would back independence when the time came: 'In my heart, in my head, I think Scotland will become an independent country within the European community, and with a friendly cooperative relationship with our partners in these islands'.[4] Nevertheless, the major challenge in delivering such an outcome was underscored in the First Minister's speech to the 2011 SNP conference around the same time when he suggested a second option, in addition to the status quo, could be offered in the referendum: 'The first question would be a straight yes/ no question [on] independence.' Alongside this would be 'a second question, in the same way as we did in 1997, in which we'd offer a fiscal autonomy option.'[5] Critics were quick to point out that Salmond was guilty of 'hedging his bets' and hence not quite as confident as he seemed about winning the vote on independence itself.

There are in fact a number of challenges for the SNP in this regard. It has long been accepted that voting for the party does not necessarily mean support for Scottish independence. Again, the recent SNP triumph may be more fragile and ephemeral than some suggest. The Scottish electorate may return in large numbers to its traditional Labour loyalties at the next UK General Election. Furthermore, all the polling evidence since 1997 suggests that with minor fluctuations support for the independence option has usually hovered around the 25–30 per cent mark. On the other hand, devolution, with increased tax and fiscal powers (the so-called 'devo-max' option) has appealed more to voters, regularly scoring over 50 per cent in polls conducted over the same period. There are other major imponderables: how will the pro-independence vote fare in the new scenario of the credit crunch, the crisis in the Eurozone, an age of austerity and reduced public expenditure stretching for several years into the future and, not least, the catastrophic failure of the Royal Bank of Scotland and the Halifax Bank of Scotland, only saved from bankruptcy by UK state intervention?

On the other hand, the SNP can rightly point to the stability of its core vote for independence, despite all these vicissitudes, which should serve as an important foundation for a referendum campaign when it begins in earnest. In December 2011, Sir Gus O'Donnell, the Cabinet Secretary and Head of the Civil Service, publicly questioned whether the UK would exist in a few years time, pointing out that one of the 'enormous challenges' facing British governments was how 'to keep our Kingdom united'.[6] His remarks illustrated how seriously the possibility of Scottish independence is taken at the highest political level. The Scottish Government has promised that the referendum campaign will be the best financed and organized in the history of the nation. Only when that grand debate starts will it be easier to see how Scots might respond to the greatest constitutional decision for the country since the passage of the Treaty of Union of 1707.

Notes

1: Scotland in Great Britain

1 Quoted in W. Ferguson, *Scotland's Relations with England: A Survey to 1707* (Edinburgh, 1977), p. 201.
2 J. M. Gray, ed., *Memoirs of the Life of Sir John Clerk of Penicuik* (Edinburgh, 1892), p. 42.
3 D. Duncan, ed., *History of the Union of Scotland and England by Sir John Clerk of Penicuik* (Edinburgh, 1993), p. 118.
4 Ibid., p. 121.
5 Rosalind Mitchison, *A History of Scotland* (London, 1970), p. 326.
6 Quoted in John S. Shaw, *The Management of Scottish Society 1707–1764* (Edinburgh, 1983), p. 86.
7 Ibid.
8 Ibid., p. 1.
9 Quoted in Janet A. Smith, 'Some Eighteenth Century Ideas of Scotland', in N. T. Phillipson and R. Mitchison, eds, *Scotland in the Age of Improvement* (Edinburgh, 1970), p. 109.
10 Ibid., p. 113.
11 Quoted in E. C. Mossner, *Life of David Hume* (London, 1954), p. 372.

2: The Jacobite Challenge

1 Murray G. H. Pittock, *Jacobitism* (London, 1998), pp. 44–5.
2 *Culloden Papers* (London, 1912), I, p. 62.
3 Quoted in W. Donaldson, *The Jacobite Song* (Aberdeen, 1988), p. 46.
4 *Glasgow Journal*, 28 April 1746.

3: The Union and the Economy

1 Quoted in G. Holmes, *British Politics in the Age of Anne* (London, 1967), p. 393.
2 D. Duncan, ed., *History of the Union of Scotland and England by Sir John Clerk of Penicuik* (Edinburgh, 1993), p. 114.
3 Linda Colley, *Britons* (London, 1995 edn), p. 135.

4: Roots of Enlightenment

1 Quoted in Andrew L. Drummond and James Bulloch, *The Scottish Church, 1688–1843* (Edinburgh, 1973), p. 2.
2 Ibid.
3 G. C. Mossner and I. S. Ross, eds, *The Correspondence of Adam Smith* (Oxford, 2nd edn, 1987), p. 309.
4 Quoted in Richard B. Sher, 'Commerce, Religion and the Enlightenment in Eighteenth Century Glasgow', in T. M. Devine and G. Jackson, eds, *Glasgow Volume I: Beginnings to 1830* (Manchester, 1995), p. 321.
5 John Hill Burton, ed., *The Autobiography of Dr Alexander Carlyle of Inveresk 1722–1805* (London, 1910), pp. 93–4.
6 Quoted in J. K. Cameron, 'Theological Controversy: A Factor in the Origins of the Scottish Enlightenment', in R. H. Campbell and A. S. Skinner, eds, *Origins and Nature of the Scottish Enlightenment* (Edinburgh, 1982), p. 121.
7 Quoted in John Butt, *John Anderson's Legacy* (East London, 1996), pp. 20–21.
8 Ibid.
9 Quoted in T. C. Smout, *A History of the Scottish People 1560–1830* (London, 1969), p. 285.
10 Quoted in Anand Chitnis, *The Scottish Enlightenment* (London, 1976), p. 99.

5: The Parish State

1 Quoted in Rosalind Mitchison and Leah Leneman, *Sexuality and Social Control* (London, 1989), pp. 35–6.
2 Sir John Sinclair, *Analysis of the Statistical Account of Scotland* (London, 1826), p. 83.
3 Quoted in R. A. Houston, *Scottish Literacy and Scottish Identity, 1600–1800* (Cambridge, 1985).

4 L. M. Cullen and T. C. Smout, eds, *Comparative Aspects of Scottish and Irish Economic and Social History 1600–1900* (Edinburgh, n.d.), p. 10.
5 Ibid.
6 Rosalind Mitchison, 'The Poor Law', in T. M. Devine and Rosalind Mitchison, eds, *People and Society in Scotland, Vol. I, 1760–1830* (Edinburgh, 1988), pp. 253–4.

6: Scotland Transformed

1 Quoted in T. M. Devine, *The Tobacco Lords* (Edinburgh, 1975), p. 46.

7: The Rural Lowlands: the Old World and the New

1 Sir John Sinclair, *Analysis of the Statistical Account of Scotland* (Edinburgh, 1825), 1831 edn, vol. I, pp. 229–33.
2 Quoted in A. J. S. Gibson and T. C. Smout, *Prices, Food and Wages in Scotland 1550–1780* (Cambridge, 1995), p. 231.
3 W. Fullarton, *General View of the Agriculture of the County of Ayr* (Edinburgh, 1793), p. 21.
4 Sir John Sinclair, ed., *The Statistical Account of Scotland, 1791–97* (Edinburgh, 1791–7, new edn, Wakefield, 1975–9), volume for Lanarkshire, p. 498.
5 Ibid., volume for Ayrshire, parish of West Kilbride.
6 J. Galt, *The Last of the Lairds* (Edinburgh, 1976 edn), p. 25.
7 Quoted in Donald J. Withrington, 'Schooling, Literacy and Society', in T. M. Devine and R. Mitchison, eds, *People and Society in Scotland, Volume I, 1760–1830* (Edinburgh, 1988), p. 172.
8 Scottish Record Office, GD150/2388, Morton Papers, Report of the Acre Land of Aberdour, 1801.
9 Scottish Record Office, BD45/18/2268, Dalhousie Muniments, Memorandum on Edzell Estate, 1767.
10 All quotations on this page from T. M. Devine, *The Transformation of Rural Scotland* (Edinburgh, 1994), p. 140.
11 Scottish Record Office, CH2/378/3, Kirk Session of Wiston, 7 June 1752.
12 Quoted in Devine, *Transformation of Rural Scotland*, p. 144.

8: Urbanization

1 I. H. Adams, *The Making of Urban Scotland* (London, 1978), pp. 90–93.
2 A. S. Wohl, *Endangered Lives: Public Health in Victorian Britain* (London, 1983), p. 80.
3 Quoted in T. M. Devine, *Exploring the Scottish Past* (East Linton, 1995), p. 129.

9: The Disintegration of Clanship

1 D. Defoe, *A Tour Through the Whole Island of Great Britain* (London, 1971 edn), p. 663.
2 Quoted in T. M. Devine, *Clanship to Crofters War* (Manchester, 1994), p. 34.
3 A. I. Macinnes, 'Scottish Gaeldom: the first phase of Clearance', in T. M. Devine and R. Mitchison, eds, *People and Society in Scotland, I, 1760–1830* (Edinburgh, 1988), p. 72.
4 Second Report by the Committee of Management to the Edinburgh Section for 1850 in *Reports of Edinburgh Section of the Central Board* (Edinburgh, 1847–50), p. 11.

10: The Old Regime and Radical Protest

1 Quoted in William Ferguson, *Scotland: 1689 to the Present* (Edinburgh, 1968), p. 245.
2 Quoted in Michael Fry, *The Dundas Despotism* (Edinburgh, 1992), p. 146.
3 *Caledonian Mercury*, 2 September 1790.
4 Quoted in John Brims, 'From Reformers to "Jacobins": the Scottish Association of the Friends of the People', in T. M. Devine, ed., *Conflict and Stability in Scottish Society, 1700–1850* (Edinburgh, 1990), p. 13.
5 Quoted in ibid., p. 35.
6 *The Edinburgh Gazetteer*, 7 December 1792.
7 Quoted in Brims, 'From Reformers to "Jacobins"', p. 38.
8 Ibid., p. 39.
9 Ibid., p. 43.
10 E. W. McFarland, *Ireland and Scotland in the Age of Revolution* (Edinburgh, 1994).
11 Quoted in Norman Murray, *The Scottish Handloom Weavers, 1790–1850: A Social History* (Edinburgh, 1978), p. 76.

12 Strathclyde Regional Archives, E1/1/10, 3 February 1820.

13 Quoted in F. K. Donnelly, 'The Scottish Rising of 1820: A Re-interpretation', *Scottish Tradition* (1976), p. 24.

11: Highlandism and Scottish Identity

1 Quoted in T. C. Smout, 'Tours in the Scottish Highlands from the eighteenth to the twentieth centuries', *Northern Scotland*, 5 (1983), p. 120.

2 S. Johnson, *A Journey to the Western Islands of Scotland in 1773* (London, 1876), p. 32.

3 Quoted in P. Womack, *Improvement and Romance* (London, 1989), p. 1.

4 Quoted in W. Donaldson, *The Jacobite Song* (Aberdeen, 1988), p. 46.

5 21 Geo II c.34.

6 Quoted in Speck, *The Butcher*, p. 174.

7 H. Trevor-Roper, 'The invention of tradition: the Highland tradition of Scotland', in E. J. Hobsbawm and T. O. Ranger, eds, *The Invention of Tradition* (Oxford, 1983), p. 10.

8 Quoted in ibid., p. 31.

9 Donaldson, *Jacobite Song*, p. 66.

10 Ibid., p. 94.

11 Quoted in ibid., p. 94.

12 Womack, *Improvement and Romance*, p. 27.

13 *Gentleman's Magazine*, IX, June 1739.

14 Donaldson, *Jacobite Song*, p. 71.

15 Quoted in Womack, *Improvement and Romance*, p. 50.

16 Quoted in Donaldson, *Jacobite Song*, p. 92.

17 C. W. J. Withers, 'The historical creation of the Scottish Highlands', in I. L. Donnachie and C. A. Whatley, eds, *The Manufacture of Scottish History* (Edinburgh, 1992), p. 147.

18 M. Chapman, *The Gaelic Vision in Scottish Culture* (London, 1978), p. 19.

19 Smout, 'Tours in the Scottish Highlands', p. 101.

20 Womack, *Improvement and Romance*, p. 80.

21 Quoted in ibid., p. 145.

22 Ibid.

12: The World's Workshop

1 Bruce Lenman, *An Economic History of Modern Scotland* (London, 1977), p. 193.

2 James Cleland, *Enumeration of the Inhabitants of the City of Glasgow* (Glasgow, 1832), p. 151.

3 Quoted in A. Slaven, *The Development of the West of Scotland 1750–1960* (London, 1975).

4 W. Knox, 'The Political and Workplace Culture of the Scottish Working Class, 1832–1914', in W. Hamish Fraser and R. J. Morris, eds, *People and Society in Scotland II 1830–1914* (Edinburgh, 1990), p. 147.

5 *Labour in Europe and America* (Washington, DC, 1876).

6 C. H. Lee, *Scotland and the United Kingdom* (Manchester, 1995), p. 46.

13: Politics, Power and Identity in Victorian Scotland

1 H. Cockburn, *Journal* (Edinburgh, 1874), p. 5.

2 Michael Dyer, *Men of Property and Intelligence* (Aberdeen, 1996), p. 45.

3 Quoted in Derek Fraser, 'The Agitation for Parliamentary Reform', in J. T. Ward, ed., *Popular Movements* (London, 1970), p. 51.

4 Quoted in W. Hamish Fraser, 'The Scottish Context of Chartism', in T. Brotherstone, ed., *Covenant, Charter and Party* (Aberdeen, 1989), p. 71.

5 Quoted in Alexander Wilson, *The Chartist Movement in Scotland* (Manchester, 1970), p. 147.

6 Quoted in ibid., p. 124.

7 Michael Fry, *Patronage and Principle. A Political History of Modern Scotland* (Aberdeen, 1987), p. 92.

8 Quoted in I. G. C. Hutchison, *A Political History of Scotland* (Edinburgh, 1986), p. 1.

9 W. Ferguson, *Scotland 1689 to the Present* (Edinburgh, 1968), p. 317.

10 Quoted in R. J. Finlay, 'The Rise and Fall of Popular Imperialism in Scotland', *Scottish Geographical Magazine*, 113 (1997), p. 14.

11 Lindsay Paterson, *The Autonomy of Modern Scotland* (Edinburgh, 1994), p. 49.

12 Quoted in Richard J. Finlay, *A Partnership for Good? Scottish Politics and the Union since 1880* (Edinburgh, 1997), p. 17.

13 Ibid., p. 26.

14 Quoted in Richard J. Finlay, 'The Burns Cult and Scottish Identity in the Nineteenth and Twentieth Centuries', in Kenneth Simpson, ed., *Love and Liberty* (Edinburgh, 1997), p. 71.

15 Quoted in Crosbie Smith and M. Norton Wise, *Energy and Empire* (Cambridge, 1989), p. 84.

16 I owe these points to Gordon Graham, Regius Professor of Moral Philosophy, University of Aberdeen.

17 Thomas D. Knowles, *Ideology, Art and Commerce: Aspects of Literary Sociology in the Late Victorian Scottish Kailyard* (Gothenburg, 1983).

14: The Decline and Fall of Liberal Hegemony

1 Quoted in I. G. C. Hutchison, *A Political History of Scotland, 1832–1924* (Edinburgh, 1986), p. 176.
2 Quoted in Michael Fry, *Patronage and Principle* (Aberdeen, 1987), pp. 129–30.
3 Quoted in Hutchison, *Political History*, p. 164.
4 Quoted in Richard J. Finlay, *A Partnership for Good? Scottish Politics and the Union since 1880* (Edinburgh, 1997), p. 52.
5 Quoted in T. M. Devine and R. J. Finlay, eds, *Scotland in the Twentieth Century* (Edinburgh, 1996), p. 70.
6 Quoted in T. C. Smout, *A Century of Scottish People, 1830–1950* (London, 1986), p. 169.
7 *Glasgow Observer*, 26 October 1918.
8 Quoted in I. Donnachie, Christopher Harvie and I. S. Wood, eds., *Forward! Labour Politics in Scotland 1888–1988* (Edinburgh, 1989), p. 31.
9 I. G. C. Hutchison, 'Scottish Unionism Between the Two World Wars', in Catriona M. M. MacDonald, ed., *Unionist Scotland 1800–1997* (Edinburgh, 1998), p. 81.
10 G. M. Thomson, *Caledonia or the Future of the Scots* (Edinburgh, 1982), pp. 18–19.
11 John Cooney, *Scotland and the Papacy* (Edinburgh, 1982), pp. 18–19.
12 Christopher Harvie, *No Gods and Precious Few Heroes* (London, 1981), p. 133.
13 Quoted in Finlay, *Partnership for Good*, p. 96.
14 Ibid., p. 100.
15 Fry, *Patronage and Principle*, pp. 184–5.
16 *Daily Record*, 12 February 1932.

15: The Scottish City

1 Quoted in M. Glendinning, Ranald MacInnes and Aonghus MacKechnie, *A History of Scottish Architecture* (Edinburgh, 1996), p. 220.
2 James Schmeichen, 'Glasgow of the Imagination', in W. H. Fraser and Irene Maver, eds, *Glasgow Volume II: 1830–1912* (Manchester, 1996), p. 488.
3 Quoted in T. M. Devine, 'The Urban Crisis', in T. M. Devine and G. Jackson, eds, *Glasgow Volume I: Beginnings to 1830* (Manchester, 1995), p. 406.

4 Quoted in Ian Adams, *The Making of Urban Scotland* (London, 1978), p. 155.

5 Anthony S. Wohl, *Endangered Lives* (London, 1983), p. 81.

6 Quoted in ibid., p. 81.

7 M. W. Flinn, ed., *Report on the Sanitary Condition of the Labouring Population of Great Britain by Edwin Chadwick* (Edinburgh, 1965), p. 4.

8 Anon., *Notes explanatory of the Heads of a new Police Bill for Glasgow* (Glasgow, 1842), pp. 14–15.

9 Quoted in Asa Briggs, *Victorian Cities* (Harmondsworth, 1968), p. 21.

10 Quoted in W. H. Fraser and Irene Maver, eds, *Glasgow Volume II: 1830–1912* (Manchester, 1996), p. 406.

11 Wohl, *Endangered Lives*, pp. 6–7.

12 M. A. Crowther, 'Poverty, Health and Welfare', in W. H. Fraser and R. J. Morris, eds, *People and Society in Scotland, Volume II, 1830–1914* (Edinburgh, 1990), p. 285.

13 Sydney and Olive Checkland, *Industry and Ethos* (London, 1984), p. 106.

14 Quoted in Fraser and Maver, eds, *Glasgow*, p. 425.

15 Ralph Glasser, *Growing up in the Gorbals* (London, 1987), pp. 77–8.

16 Quoted in Richard Rodger, 'Employment, Wages and Poverty in the Scottish Cities 1841–1914', in George Gordon, ed., *Perspectives of the Scottish City* (Aberdeen, 1985), p. 27.

17 Ibid., p. 49.

18 Quoted in 'Housing', in D. Daiches, ed., *A Companion to Scottish Culture* (London, 1981), p. 171.

19 Ann McGuckin, 'Moving Stories: Working Class Women', in E. Breitenbach and E. Gordon, eds, *Out of Bounds: Women in Scottish Society 1800–1945* (Edinburgh, 1992), p. 204.

20 Quoted in Richard Rodger, 'Urbanisation in Twentieth-Century Scotland', in T. M. Devine and R. J. Finlay, eds, *Scotland in the Twentieth Century* (Edinburgh, 1996), pp. 142–3.

21 Annette Carruthers, ed., *The Scottish Home* (Edinburgh, 1996), p. 81.

22 Ibid.

23 *The Scotsman*, 22 May 1850.

24 Quoted in Elspeth King, 'Popular Culture in Glasgow', in R. A. Cage, ed., *The Working Class in Glasgow, 1750–1914* (London, 1987), p. 161.

25 Brian Harrison, 'Pubs', in H. J. Dyos and M. Wolff, eds, *The Victorian City, Volume I* (London, 1973), p. 171.

26 Shadow, *Midnight Scenes and Social Photographs being Sketches of Life in the Streets, Wynds and Dens of the City* (Glasgow, 1858), p. 85.

27 Quoted in Andrew L. Drummond and James Bulloch, *The Church in Victorian Scotland 1843–1874* (Edinburgh, 1975), p. 25.

28 Fraser and Maver, eds, *Glasgow* p. 328.

29 W. H. Fraser, 'Developments in Leisure', in W. H. Fraser and R. J. Morris,

eds, *People and Society in Scotland, Volume II, 1830–1914* (Edinburgh, 1990), p. 243.

30 Harrison, 'Pubs', p. 170.

31 *Glasgow Observer*, 31 December 1892.

32 Callum G. Brown, 'Popular Culture and the Continuing Struggle for Rational Recreation', in T. M. Devine and R. J. Finlay, eds, *Scotland in the Twentieth Century* (Edinburgh, 1996), p. 214.

33 Bill Murray, *The Old Firm* (Edinburgh, 1984), p. 41.

34 Quoted in ibid., p. 27.

16: Religion and Society

1 Quoted in A. C. Cheyne, *The Transforming of the Kirk* (Edinburgh, 1983), p. 114.

2 Sydney and Olive Checkland, *Industry and Ethos: Scotland 1832–1914* (London, 1984), p. 5.

3 *Free Church Magazine*, August 1847, p. 250.

4 Quoted in Callum G. Brown, *Religion and Society in Scotland Since 1707* (Edinburgh, 1997).

5 Ibid., p. 120.

6 Ibid., p. 107.

7 Quoted in V. E. Durkacz, *The Decline of the Celtic Languages* (Edinburgh, 1983), p. 129.

8 Stewart J. Brown and Michael Fry, eds, *Scotland in the Age of Disruption* (Edinburgh, 1993), p. 6.

9 Henry Cockburn, *Journal* (Edinburgh, 1874), Vol. II, pp. 21–2.

10 David Hempton, *Religion and Political Culture in Britain and Ireland* (Cambridge, 1996), p. 90.

11 Cheyne, *Transforming of the Kirk*, p. 118.

12 A. L. Drummond and J. Bulloch, *The Church in Late Victorian Scotland 1874–1900* (Edinburgh, 1978), p. 128.

13 A. S. Matheson, *The Church and Social Problems* (Edinburgh, 1893), p. 14.

14 Stewart J. Brown, ' "Outside the Covenant": The Scottish Presbyterian Churches and Irish Immigration, 1922–1938', *Innes Review*, XLII, 1991, p. 43.

15 T. C. Smout, *A Century of the Scottish People, 1830–1950* (London, 1986), p. 202.

16 Quoted in Cheyne, *Transforming of the Kirk*, p. 181.

17 Ibid., p. 182.

18 E. Muir, *Scottish Journey* (London, 1935), p. 170.

19 Hempton, *Religion and Political Culture*, p. 137.

17: Educating the People

1 Quoted in R. D. Anderson, *Education and the Scottish People, 1750–1918* (Oxford, 1995), p. 154.

2 *Educational News*, 3 January 1903, pp. 9–10 quoted in ibid., p. 261.

3 Donald J. Withrington, *Going to School* (Edinburgh, 1997), p. 57.

4 Quoted in ibid., p. 58.

5 L. Playfair, *Subjects of Social Welfare* (London, 1889), p. 306.

6 W. Knox, *James Maxton* (Manchester, 1987), p. 202.

7 Withrington, *Going to School*, pp. 65–6.

8 Anderson, *Education and the Scottish People*, p. 299.

9 J. Ramsay, *A Letter to the Lord Advocate of Scotland on the State of Education in the Outer Hebrides* (Glasgow, 1863), p. 4.

10 Quoted in Anderson, *Education and the Scottish People*, p. 242.

11 W. M. Humes and H. M. Paterson, eds, *Scottish Culture and Scottish Education 1800–1900* (Edinburgh, 1983), p. 200.

12 Smout, *Century of the Scottish People*, p. 223.

13 Quoted in A. McPherson, 'Schooling', in A. Dickson and J. H. Treble, eds, *People and Society in Scotland, Volume III, 1914–1990* (Edinburgh, 1992), p. 88.

14 Quoted in Smout, *Century of the Scottish People*, p. 227.

15 *Contemporary Review*, xli (1882), p. 150, quoted in R. D. Anderson, *Education and Opportunity in Victorian Scotland* (Edinburgh, 1983), p. 269.

16 Ibid., p. 152.

17 Quoted in R. H. Campbell, *The Rise and Fall of Scottish Industry 1707–1929* (Edinburgh, 1980), p. 46.

18: The Highlands and Crofting Society

1 *Witness*, 21 November 1846.

2 *The Scotsman*, 12 December 1846

3 Scottish Record Office, Edinburgh, HD6/2, Treasury Correspondence, Trevelyan to Baird, 19 March 1847.

4 Ibid.

5 T. Mulock, *The Western Highlands and Islands of Scotland Socially Considered* (Edinburgh, 1950), pp. 81–2.

6 Inveraray Castle, Argyll Estate Papers, Bundle 1558, Duke of Argyll to Chamberlain of Mull and Tiree, 5 May 1851.

7 Quoted in T. M. Devine, *Clanship to Crofters' War* (Manchester, 1994), p. 207.

8 Ibid., p. 60.

9 Donald C. Meek, ed., *Tuath is Tighheara* (Edinburgh, 1995), p. 204.

10 Quoted in I. M. M. Macphail, *The Crofters' War* (Stornoway, 1989), p. 1.

11 Ibid.

12 *The Scotsman*, 15 and 18 October 1884.

13 Quoted in Macphail, *Crofters' War*, p. 120.

14 *Oban Times*, 24 January 1885.

15 Quoted in Macphail, *Crofters' War*, p. 120.

16 Quoted in James Hunter, *The Making of the Crofting Community* (Edinburgh, 1976), p. 143.

17 Quoted in Macphail, *Crofters' War*, p. 11.

18 Quoted in E. A. Cameron, 'Public Policy in the Scottish Highlands' (Unpublished Ph.D. thesis, University of Glasgow), p. 19.

19 A. Collier, *The Crofting Problem* (Cambridge, 1953), p. 98.

20 Quoted in Devine, *Clanship to Crofters' War*, p. 233.

21 Quoted in Collier, *Crofting Problem*, p. 104.

19: Land, Elites and People

1 Quoted in Robin T. Callander, *A Pattern of Landownership in Scotland* (Finzean, 1987), p. 73.

2 Quoted in David Cannadine, *The Decline and Fall of the British Aristocracy* (London, 1992 edn), p. 81.

3 T. Johnston, *Our Scots Noble Families* (1909).

4 F. M. L. Thompson, 'English Landed Society in the Twentieth Century: I Property: Collapse and Survival', *Transactions of the Royal Historical Society* (5th series, 40, 1990), p. 17.

5 Quoted in Andy Wightman, *Who Owns Scotland* (Edinburgh, 1996), p. 191.

6 Quoted in M. W. Flinn, ed., *Scottish Population History* (Cambridge, 1977), p. 459.

7 Quoted in R. Anthony, *Herds and Hinds* (East Linton, 1997), p. 37.

8 Ibid.

9 Quoted in T. M. Devine, ed., *Farm Servants and Labour in Lowland Scotland, 1770 to 1914* (Edinburgh, 1996 edn), p. 108.

10 Ibid., p. 253.

20: Emigrants

1 Edwin Muir, *Scottish Journey* (London, 1935), p. 3.

2 Richard Anthony, *Herds and Hinds* (Edinburgh, 1997), p. 94.

3 Tom Brooking, '"Tam McCammy and Kitty Clydeside". The Scots in New Zealand', in R. A. Cage, ed., *The Scots Abroad* (London, 1985), p. 172.
4 Quoted in M. Harper, *Emigration from North-East Scotland* (Aberdeen, 1988), II, p. 22.
5 Ibid., p. 55.

21: New Scots

1 Brenda Collins, 'The Origins of Irish Immigration to Scotland in the Nineteenth and Twentieth Centuries', in T. M. Devine, ed., *Irish Immigrants and Scottish Society in the Nineteenth and Twentieth Centuries* (Edinburgh, 1991), p. 1.
2 *Journal of Henry Cockburn, 1831–34, Volume I* (Edinburgh, 1874), 15 March 1835. I owe this reference to Dr Martin Mitchell.
3 Quoted in James E. Handley, *The Irish in Modern Scotland* (Cork, 1947), p. 100.
4 Tom Gallagher, 'The Catholic Irish in Scotland: In Search of Identity', in Devine, ed., *Irish Immigrants and Scottish Society*, p. 27.
5 Stewart J. Brown, '"Outside the Covenant"; The Scottish Presbyterian Churches and Irish Immigration, 1922–1938', *Innes Review*, vol. XLII, Spring 1991, p. 40.
6 Graham Walker, 'The Protestant Irish in Scotland', in Devine, ed., *Irish Immigrants and Scottish Society*, p. 63.
7 Billy Kay, ed., *Odyssey, The Second Collection* (Edinburgh, 1982), p. 15.
8 Ibid., p. 16.
9 Ibid., p. 14.
10 Ibid., p. 18
11 Ibid.
12 Terri Colpi, *The Italian Factor: The Italian Community in Great Britain* (Edinburgh, 1991), p. 179.
13 Ralph Glasser, *Growing up in the Gorbals* (London, 1987 edn), p. 18.
14 Chaim Bermant, *Coming Home* (London, 1976), pp. 52–3.
15 Glasser, *Growing up in the Gorbals*, p. 22.
16 Ibid., p. 21.
17 Ibid., p. 22.

22: Scottish Women: Family, Work and Politics

1 M. Anderson and D. J. Morse, 'The People', in W. H. Fraser and R. J. Morris, eds, *People and Society in Scotland, Volume II, 1830–1914* (Edinburgh, 1990), p. 42.

2 W. H. Fraser and Irene Maver, eds, *Glasgow, Volume II: 1830–1912* (Manchester, 1996), p. 360.

3 Quoted in T. Ferguson, *Scottish Social Welfare, 1864–1914* (Edinburgh, 1958), p. 104.

4 M. Anderson, 'Population and Family Life', in A. Dickson and J. H. Treble, eds, *People and Society in Scotland, Vol. III, 1914–1990* (Edinburgh, 1992), p. 41.

5 Quoted in A. McIvor, 'Gender Apartheid? Women in Scottish Society', in T. M. Devine and R. J. Finlay, eds, *Scotland in the Twentieth Century* (Edinburgh, 1996), p. 192.

6 Quoted in Elspeth King, 'The Scottish Women's Suffrage Movement', in Esther Breitenbach and Eleanor Gordon, eds, *Out of Bounds: Women in Scottish Society, 1800–1945* (Edinburgh, 1992), p. 137.

7 Ibid.

8 Ibid.

23: War and Peace

1 Quoted in Seona Robertson and Les Wilson, *Scotland's War* (Edinburgh, 1995), p. 24.

2 Ibid., p. 41.

3 Gavin Sprott, 'Lowland Country Life', in T. M. Devine and R. J. Finlay, eds, *Scotland in the Twentieth Century* (Edinburgh, 1996), p. 180.

4 Quoted in Robertson and Wilson, *Scotland's War*, p. 59.

5 Ibid., p. 61.

6 Ibid., p. 63.

7 Angus Calder, *The People's War* (London, 1969), p. 381.

8 Ibid., p. 384.

9 Andrew Marr, *The Battle for Scotland* (Harmondsworth, 1992), pp. 102–3.

10 Quoted in Christopher Harvie, 'The Recovery of Scottish Labour, 1939–51', in I. Donnachie, Christopher Harvie and I. S. Wood, *Forward! Labour Politics in Scotland 1888–1988* (Edinburgh, 1989), pp. 71–2.

11 Herbert Morrison, *An Autobiography* (London, 1960), p. 199.

12 Quoted in Robertson and Wilson, *Scotland's War*, p. 188.

13 Quoted in Harvie, 'The Recovery of Scottish Labour', p. 77.

14 Quoted in Peter Clarke, *Hope and Glory: Britain 1900–1990* (London, 1996), p. 233.

15 Gavin Sprott, 'Lowland Country Life', in T. M. Devine and R. J. Finlay, eds, *Scotland in the Twentieth Century* (Edinburgh, 1996), p. 182.

16 Ewen A. Cameron, 'The Scottish Highlands: From Congested District to Objective One', in Devine and Finlay, eds, *Scotland in the Twentieth Century*, p. 162.

17 Bruce Lenman, *An Economic History of Modern Scotland* (London, 1977), p. 243.

18 Quoted in Miles Glendinning and Stefan Muthesius, *Tower Block* (New Haven, 1994), p. 237.

19 Ibid., p. 240.

20 Ibid., p. 220.

21 Ibid.

22 Christopher Harvie, *No Gods and Precious Few Heroes* (London, 1981), p. 141.

23 Quoted in Marr, *Battle for Scotland*, p. 97.

24 Arnold Kemp, *The Hollow Drum* (Edinburgh, 1993), p. 87.

25 W. Ferguson, *Scotland: 1689 to the Present* (Edinburgh, 1968), p. 387.

26 Marr, *Battle for Scotland*, p. 117.

24: The Scottish Question

1 Quoted in Alan Clements, Kenny Farquharson and Kirsty Wark, *Restless Nation* (Edinburgh, 1996), p. 50.

2 Quoted in James Mitchell, *Conservatives and the Union* (Edinburgh, 1990), p. 55.

3 Clements, et al., *Restless Nation*, p. 66.

4 Ibid., pp. 63–4

5 F. Bealey and J. Sewel, *The Politics of Independence: A Study of a Scottish Town* (Aberdeen, 1981), p. 160.

6 Quoted in James Mitchell, 'Scotland in the Union, 1945–95', in T. M. Devine and R. J. Finlay, eds, *Scotland in the Twentieth Century* (Edinburgh, 1996), p. 97.

7 Quoted in Arnold Kemp, *The Hollow Drum* (Edinburgh, 1993), p. 108.

8 Callum G. Brown, 'Religion and Secularisation', in A. Dickson and J. H. Treble, eds, *People and Society in Scotland, Vol. III, 1914–1990* (Edinburgh, 1992), p. 53.

9 Michael Fry, *Patronage and Principle* (Aberdeen, 1987), p. 250.

10 Kemp, *Hollow Drum*, p. 152.

11 Quoted in Mitchell, *Conservatives and the Union*, p. 91.

25: A Nation Reborn?

1 James Mitchell, *Conservatives and the Union* (Edinburgh, 1990), pp. 103–4.

2 Jim Sillars, *Scotland. The Case for Optimism* (Edinburgh, 1986), p. 1.

3 Peter L. Payne, *Growth and Contraction. Scottish Industry, c. 1860–1990* (Dundee, 1992), p. 48.

4 Quoted in A. Clements, K. Farquharson and K. Wark, *Restless Nation* (Edinburgh, 1996), p. 89.

5 Quoted in Kenyon Wright, *The People Say Yes* (Glendaruel, 1997), p. 55.

6 Peter Clarke, *Hope and Glory. Britain 1900–1990* (Harmondsworth, 1996), p. 395.

7 Quoted in Mitchell, *Conservatives and the Union*, p. 113.

8 Wright, *The People Say Yes*, pp. 140–41.

9 Quoted in M. Linklater and R. Dennistoun, eds, *Anatomy of Scotland* (Edinburgh, 1992), p. 136.

10 Owen Dudley Edwards, ed., *A Claim of Right for Scotland* (Edinburgh, 1989), pp. 51–3.

11 Andrew Marr, *The Battle for Scotland* (Harmondsworth, 1992), p. 230.

26: End of Empire

1 A. D. Gibb, *Scottish Empire* (London, 1937), p. 311.

2 H. J. Hanham, *Scottish Nationalism* (London, 1969), p. 212.

3 *The Daily Telegraph*, 24 February 1979, cited in Keith Robbins, ' "This Grubby Wreck of Old Glories": the United Kingdom and the End of the British Empire', *Journal of Contemporary History*, 15 (1980), p. 84.

4 J. M. Mackenzie, 'A Scottish Empire? The Scottish Diaspora and Interactive Identities' in T. Brooking and J. Coleman, eds., *The Heather and the Fern: Scottish Migration and New Zealand Settlement* (Otago, 2003), p. 19.

5 Gordon Stewart, *Jute and Empire* (Manchester, 1998), p. ix.

6 D. Allan, *Scotland in the Eighteenth Century* (Harlow, 2002), p. 85.

7 A. D. Gibb, *Scotland in Eclipse* (1930), p. 187.

8 S. Allan and A. Carswell, *The Thin Red Line: War, Empire and Visions of Scotland* (Edinburgh, 2004), p. 40.

9 Gibb, *Scotland in Eclipse*, p. 187.

10 Edwin Muir, *Scottish Journey* (Edinburgh, 1935), p. 110; G. M. Thomson, *Caledonia or the Future of the Scots* (Edinburgh, 1932), pp. 18–19.

11 Stewart, *Jute and Empire*, pp. 2–3.

27: After Devolution

1 Andrew Neil, 'Sleep-walk to Devolution' in Alan Taylor, ed., *What a State! Is Devolution for Scotland the End of Britain?* (London, 2000), pp. 29–30.

2 *Sunday Herald*, 4 September 2005.

3 Fiona Ross, 'As a Friend' in Wendy Alexander, ed., *Donald Dewar: Scotland's first First Minister* (Edinburgh, 2005), p. 46.

4 'Holyrood must raise its game', *Scottish Daily Mail*, 6 May 2000.

5 Peter Jones, 'The Modernising Radical' in Alexander, ed., *Donald Dewar*, p. 168.

6 Ibid., p. 168.

7 D. MacLennan, 'Real Devolution: In Housing' in Ibid., pp. 180–187.

8 Quoted in Brian Taylor, *Scotland's Parliament* (Edinburgh, 2002), p. 315.

9 James Hunter, 'Creating Britain's Celtic Tiger: How Scotland's Parliament is turning round the Highlands and Islands', Scottish Parliament, 5 May 2004. I am grateful to Professor Hunter for sending me a copy of his speech.

10 L. Paterson, F. Bechhofer and D. McCrone, *Living in Scotland* (Edinburgh, 2005), p. 149.

11 *Scotland on Sunday*, 9 October 2005.

12 Lindsay Tanner, 'The Loneliness Crisis', School of Business, University of Sydney, 2000.

13 Cristina Iannelli and Lindsay Paterson, *Education and Social Mobility in Scotland in the Twentieth Century* (*www.ces.ed.ac.uk/SocMobility/mobility.htm*).

14 *Sunday Herald*, 5 February 2006.

15 *The Scotsman*, 4 January 2006.

16 Ibid.

Afterword

1 T. C. Smout, 'Introduction' in T. C. Smout, ed., *Anglo-Scottish Relations, 1603–1900* (Oxford, 2005), p. 2.

2 Quoted in T. M. Devine, *Scotland's Empire, 1600–1815* (London, 2003), p. 346

3 Neal Ascherson, 'Wolves in the Drawing Room', *London Review of Books*, vol. 33, 2 June 2011, p. 8.

4 *Guardian*, 23 October 2011.

5 Ibid.

6 *Daily Telegraph*, 22 December 2011.

Further Reading

1: Scotland in Great Britain

W. R. Brock, *Scotus Americanus* (Edinburgh, 1982).

K. M. Brown, *Kingdom or Province? Scotland and the Regal Union, 1603–1715* (London, 1992).

Linda Colley, *Britons* (Yale, 1992)

T. M. Devine and J. R. Young, eds, *Eighteenth Century Scotland: New Perspectives* (Edinburgh, 1999).

W. Ferguson, *Scotland's Relations with England: A Survey to 1707* (Edinburgh, 1977).

Alexander Murdoch, *The People Above* (Edinburgh, 1980).

N. T. Phillipson and Rosalind Mitchison, *Scotland in the Age of Improvement* (Edinburgh, 1970).

P. W. J. Riley, *The Union of England and Scotland* (Manchester, 1979).

J. Robertson, ed., *A Union for Empire: Political Thought and the Union of 1707* (Cambridge, 1995).

P. H. Scott, *1707: The Union of England and Scotland* (Edinburgh, 1979).

J. S. Shaw, *The Management of Scottish Society, 1707–1764* (Edinburgh, 1983).

T. C. Smout, 'Problems of Nationalism, Identity and Improvement in Later Eighteenth Century Scotland', in T. M. Devine, ed., *Improvement and Enlightenment* (Edinburgh, 1989).

Christopher A. Whatley, *Bought and Sold for English Gold: Explaining the Union of 1707* (Dundee, 1994).

2: The Jacobite Challenge

W. Donaldson, *The Jacobite Song* (Aberdeen, 1988).

J. A. Gibson, *Lochiel of the '45* (Edinburgh, 1994).

B. P. Lenman, *The Jacobite Risings in Britain, 1689–1746* (London, 1980).

B. P. Lenman, *The Jacobite Clans of the Great Glen, 1650–1784* (London, 1984).

M. Lynch, ed., *Jacobitism and the '45* (London, 1995).

Allan I. Macinnes, *Clanship, Commerce and the House of Stuart, 1603–1788* (Edinburgh, 1996).

F. J. McLynn, *The Jacobites* (London, 1985).

Murray G. H. Pittock, *The Myth of the Jacobite Clans* (Edinburgh, 1995).

Murray G. H. Pittock, *Jacobitism* (London, 1998).

W. A. Speck, *The Butcher* (Oxford, 1981).

Daniel Szechi, *The Jacobites* (Manchester, 1994).

3: The Union and the Economy

R. H. Campbell, *Scotland since 1707* (Oxford, 1965).

S. G. Checkland, *Scottish Banking: A History* (Glasgow and London, 1975).

T. M. Devine, *The Tobacco Lords* (Edinburgh, 1975).

T. M. Devine, 'The English Connection and Irish and Scottish Development in the Eighteenth Century', in T. M. Devine and D. Dickson, eds, *Ireland and Scotland 1600–1850* (Edinburgh, 1983).

T. M. Devine, 'The Union of 1707 and Scottish Development', *Scottish Economic and Social History*, 5 (1985).

A. J. Durie, *The Scottish Linen Industry in the Eighteenth Century* (Edinburgh, 1979).

Richard Saville, *The Bank of Scotland: A History 1695–1995* (Edinburgh, 1996).

C. A. Whatley, 'Economic Causes and Consequences of the Union of 1707: A Survey', *Scottish Historical Review* 68 (1989).

C. A. Whatley, *The Industrial Revolution in Scotland* (Cambridge, 1997).

4: Roots of Enlightenment

David Allan, *Virtue, Learning and the Scottish Enlightenment* (Edinburgh, 1993).

Christopher J. Berry, *Social Theory of the Scottish Enlightenment* (Edinburgh, 1997).

Alexander Broadie, *The Tradition of Scottish Philosophy* (Edinburgh, 1990).

Alexander Broadie, *The Scottish Enlightenment. An Anthology* (Edinburgh, 1997).

R. H. Campbell and Andrew S. Skinner, eds, *The Origins and Nature of the Scottish Enlightenment* (Edinburgh, 1982).

Anand C. Chitnis, *The Scottish Enlightenment* (London, 1976).

David Daiches, Peter Jones and Jean Jones, *A Hotbed of Genuis: The Scottish Enlightenment 1730–1790* (Edinburgh, 1986).

George E. Davie, *The Scottish Enlightenment and Other Essays* (Edinburgh, 1991).

J. Dwyer and R. B. Sher, eds, *Sociability and Society in Eighteenth Century Scotland* (Edinburgh, 1993).

Andrew Hook and Richard B. Sher, eds, *The Glasgow Enlightenment* (East Linton, 1995).

Colin Kidd, *Subverting Scotland's Past* (Cambridge, 1993).

Ian Ross, *Life of Adam Smith* (Oxford, 1995).

Richard B. Sher, *Church and University in the Scottish Enlightenment* (Edinburgh, 1985).

5: The Parish State

R. D. Anderson, *Education and the Scottish People, 1750–1918* (London, 1995).

R. D. Anderson, *Scottish Education since the Reformation* (Dundee, 1997).

Andrew Blaikie, *Illegitimacy, Sex and Society, Northeast Scotland, 1750–1900* (Oxford, 1993).

R. A. Cage, *The Scottish Poor Law* (Edinburgh, 1981).

G. Henderson, *The Scottish Ruling Elder* (London, 1935).

R. A. Houston, *Scottish Literacy and the Scottish Identity: Illiteracy and Society in Scotland and Northern England, 1600–1800* (Cambridge, 1985).

R. A. Houston, *Social Change in the Age of Enlightenment: Edinburgh, 1660–1760* (Oxford, 1994).

R. A. Houston and I. D. Whyte, eds, *Scottish Society, 1500–1800* (Cambridge, 1989).

1600–1800 (Cambridge, 1985).

Rosalind Mitchison, 'The Making of the Old Scottish Poor Law', *Past and Present*, 63 (1974).

Rosalind Mitchison, 'The Poor Law', in T. M. Devine and Rosalind Mitchison, eds, *People and Society in Scotland, Vol.1, 1760–1830* (Edinburgh, 1988).

Rosalind Mitchison and Leah Leneman, *Sexuality and Social Control: Scotland 1660–1780* (London, 1989).

D. J. Withrington, 'Schooling, Literacy and Society', in T. M. Devine and Rosalind Mitchison, eds, *People and Society in Scotland. Vol. I, 1760–1830* (Edinburgh, 1988).

6: Scotland Transformed

R. H. Campbell, *The Rise and Fall of Scottish Industry, 1707–1939* (Edinburgh, 1980).

S. G. Checkland, *Scottish Banking: A History, 1695–1973* (Glasgow and London, 1975).

T. M. Devine, *The Tobacco Lords* (Edinburgh, 1975).

T. M. Devine and G. Jackson, eds, *Glasgow Volume I: Beginnings to 1830* (Manchester, 1995).

T. M. Devine and R. Mitchison, eds, *People and Society in Scotland, Volume 1, 1760–1830* (Edinburgh, 1988).

B. T. Duckham, *A History of the Scottish Coal Industry, 1700–1815* (Newton Abbot, 1970).

A. J. Durie, *The Scottish Linen Industry in the Eighteenth Century* (Edinburgh, 1979).

A. J. S. Gibson and T. C. Smout, *Prices, Food and Wages in Scotland, 1550–1780* (Cambridge, 1995).

B. Lenman, *An Economic History of Modern Scotland* (London, 1977).

T. C. Smout, *A History of the Scottish People, 1560–1830* (London, 1969).

Christopher A. Whatley, *The Industrial Revolution in Scotland* (Cambridge, 1997).

7: The Rural Lowlands: the Old World and the New

T. M. Devine, *The Transformation of Rural Scotland* (Edinburgh, 1994).

T. M. Devine, ed., *Farm Servants and Labour in Lowland Scotland, 1770–1914* (Edinburgh, 1996 edn).

R. A. Dodgshon, *Land and Society in Early Scotland* (Oxford, 1981).

Alexander Fenton, *Scottish Country Life* (Edinburgh, 1976).

M. Gray, 'Scottish Emigration: The Social Impact of Agrarian Change on the Rural Lowlands, 1775–1875', *Perspectives in American History*, VIII (1973).

I. D. Whyte, *Agriculture and Society in Seventeenth Century Scotland* (Edinburgh, 1979).

I. D. Whyte, *Scotland before the Industrial Revolution* (London, 1995).

8: Urbanization

Ian Adams, *The Making of Urban Scotland* (London, 1978).

T. M. Devine and G. Jackson, eds, *Glasgow, Volume I: Beginnings to 1830* (Manchester, 1995).

Enid Gauldie, *Cruel Habitations* (London, 1974).

G. Gordon, ed., *Perspectives of the Scottish City* (Aberdeen, 1985).

J. H. F. Robertson, *Observations on the Early Public Health Movement in Scotland* (London, 1952).

9: The Disintegration of Clanship

E. R. Cregeen, 'The changing role of the House of Argyll in the Scottish Highlands', in N. T. Phillipson and R. Mitchison, eds, *Scotland in the Age of Improvement* (Edinburgh, 1970).

T. M. Devine, *Clanship to Crofters War* (Manchester, 1994).

Robert A. Dodgshon, *From Chiefs to Landlords* (Edinburgh, 1998).

P. Gaskell, *Morvern Transformed* (Cambridge, 1980).

M. Gray, *The Highland Economy, 1750–1850* (Edinburgh, 1951).

J. Hunter, *The Making of the Crofting Community* (Edinburgh, 1976).

A. I. Macinnes, *Clanship, Commerce and the House of Stuart, 1603–1788* (East Linton, 1996).

M. McLean, *The People of Glengarry: Highlanders in Transition, 1745–1820* (Toronto, 1991).

E. Richards, *The Leviathan of Wealth* (London, 1973).

E. Richards, *A History of the Highland Clearances* (London, 1982 and 1985), 2 vols.

A. J. Youngson, *After the Forty-Five* (Edinburgh, 1973).

10: The Old Regime and Radical Protest

Christina Bewley, *Muir of Huntershill* (Oxford, 1981).

T. M. Devine, ed., *Conflict and Stability in Scottish Society, 1700–1850* (Edinburgh, 1990).

T. M. Devine and R. Mitchison, *People and Society in Scotland, Volume I, 1760–1830* (Edinburgh, 1988), Chapters 13 and 14.

F. K. Donnelly, 'The Scottish Rising of 1820: A Re-interpretation', *The Scottish Tradition*, vi, (1976).

W. H. Fraser, *Conflict and Class: Scottish Workers 1700–1838* (Edinburgh, 1988).

M. Fry, *The Dundas Despotism* (Edinburgh, 1992).

K. J. Logue, *Popular Disturbances in Scotland* (Edinburgh, 1979).

E. W. McFarland, *Ireland and Scotland in the Age of Revolution* (Edinburgh, 1994).

H. W. Meikle, *Scotland and the French Revolution* (Glasgow, 1912).

Norman Murray, *The Scottish Handloom Weavers, 1790–1850* (Edinburgh, 1978).

C. A. Whatley, 'Labour in the Industrialising City, *c.* 1660–1830', in T. M. Devine and G. Jackson, eds, *Glasgow, Vol. I* (Manchester, 1995).

11: Highlandism and Scottish Identity

M. Chapman, *The Gaelic Vision in Scottish Culture* (London, 1978).

W. Donaldson, *The Jacobite Song* (Aberdeen, 1988).

L. Leneman, 'A New role for a Lost Cause: Lowland Romanticisation of the Jacobite Highlander', in L. Leneman, ed., *Perspectives in Scottish Social History* (Aberdeen, 1988).

M. Pittock, *The Invention of Scotland* (London, 1991).

J. Prebble, *The King's Jaunt* (London, 1988).

T. C. Smout, 'Tours in the Scottish Highlands from the Eighteenth to the Twentieth Centuries', *Northern Scotland*, 5 (1983).

H. Trevor-Roper, 'The invention of Tradition: The Highland Tradition of Scotland', in E. J. Hobsbawm and T. O. Ranger, eds, *The Invention of Tradition* (Oxford, 1983).

C. W. J. Withers, 'The Historical Creation of the Scottish Highlands', in I. L. Donnachie and C. A. Whatley, eds, *The Manufacture of Scottish History* (Edinburgh, 1992).

P. Womack, *Improvement and Romance: Constructing the Myth of the Highlands* (London, 1989).

12: The World's Workshop

R. H. Campbell, *The Rise and Fall of Scottish Industry 1707–1939* (Edinburgh, 1980).

W. Hamish Fraser and Irene Maver, eds, *Glasgow, Volume II: 1830–1912* (Manchester, 1996).

J. R. Hume and Michael S. Moss, *Workshop of the British Empire* (London, 1977).

Clive Lee, *Scotland and the United Kingdom* (Manchester, 1995).

Bruce Lenman, *An Economic History of Modern Scotland* (London, 1977).

S. G. E. Lythe and J. Butt, *An Economic History of Scotland* (London, 1975).

A. Slaven, *The Development of the West of Scotland* (London, 1975).

T. C. Smout, *A Century of Scottish People, 1830–1950* (London, 1986), Chapters 4 and 5.

13: Politics, Power and Identity in Victorian Scotland

Dauvit Broun, R. J. Finlay and Michael Lynch, eds, *Image and Identity: The Making and Re-making of Scotland through the Ages* (Edinburgh, 1998).

William Donaldson, *Popular Literature in Victorian Scotland* (Aberdeen, 1986).

Michael Dyer, *Men of Property and Intelligence* (Aberdeen, 1996).

R. J. Finlay, 'Heroes, Myths and Anniversaries in Modern Scotland', *Scottish Affairs*, 18 (1997).

R. J. Finlay, *A Partnership for Good? Scottish Politics and the Union Since 1880* (Edinburgh, 1997).

Michael Fry, *Patronage and Principle* (Aberdeen, 1987).

Douglas Gifford, ed., *The History of Scottish Literature*, Vol. 3 (Edinburgh, 1988).

Christopher Harvie, *Scotland and Nationalism* (London, 1977).

I. G. C. Hutchison, *A Political History of Scotland 1832–1924* (Edinburgh, 1986).

Colin Kidd, 'Sentiment, Race and Revival: Scottish Identities in the Aftermath of the Enlightenment', in L. Brockliss and D. Eastwood, eds, *A Union of Multiple Identities* (Manchester, 1997).

Duncan Macmillan, *Scottish Art 1460–1990* (Edinburgh, 1990).

Tom Nairn, *The Break-Up of Britain* (London, 1977).

Lindsay Paterson, *The Autonomy of Modern Scotland* (Edinburgh, 1994).

Alexander Wilson, *Chartism in Scotland* (Manchester, 1970).

14: The Decline and Fall of Liberal Hegemony

T. M. Devine and R. J. Finlay, eds, *Scotland in the Twentieth Century* (Edinburgh, 1996).

I. Donnachie, Christopher Harvie and Ian S. Wood, eds, *Forward! Labour Politics in Scotland, 1888–1988* (Edinburgh, 1989).

Richard J. Finlay, *Independent and Free* (Edinburgh, 1994).

Michael Fry, *Patronage and Principle* (Aberdeen, 1987).

I. G. C. Hutchison, A Political History of Scotland, 1832–1924 (Edinburgh, 1986).

I. G. C. Hutchison, 'Scottish Unionism Between the Two World Wars', in Catriona MacDonald, ed., *Unionist Scotland 1800–1997* (Edinburgh, 1998).
James Mitchell, *Conservatives and the Union* (Edinburgh, 1990).
Marshall Walker, *Scottish Literature Since 1707* (Harlow, 1996).

15: The Scottish City

Ian H. Adams, *The Making of Urban Scotland* (London, 1978).
Annette Carruthers, ed., *The Scottish Home* (Edinburgh, 1996).
S. B. Checkland, *The Upas Tree: Glasgow, 1875–1975* (Glasgow, 2nd edn, 1982).
W. H. Fraser and Irene Maver, eds, *Glasgow Volume II: 1839–1912* (Manchester, 1996).
W. H. Fraser and R. J. Morris, eds, *People and Society in Scotland, Volume II, 1830–1914* (Edinburgh, 1990), chapter 8.
Miles Glendinning, Ranald MacInnes and Aonghus MacKechnie, *A History of Scottish Architecture* (Edinburgh, 1996).
George Gordon, *Perspectives of the Scottish City* (Aberdeen, 1985).
G. Gordon and B. Dicks, eds, *Scottish Urban History* (Aberdeen, 1983).
R. H. Holt, *Sport and the British: Modern History* (Oxford, 1989).
Bill Murray, *The Old Firm* (Edinburgh, 1984).
R. Rodger, ed., *Scottish Housing in the Twentieth Century* (Leicester, 1988).
T. C. Smout, 'Patterns of Culture', in A. Dickson and J. H. Treble, eds, *People and Society in Scotland, Volume III, 1914–1990* (Edinburgh, 1992).
N. L. Tranter, 'The Social and Occupational Structure of Organised Sport in Central Scotland during the Nineteenth Century', *International Journal of the History of Sport*, 4 (1987).
William Walker, *Juteopolis* (Edinburgh, 1979).
Anthony S. Wohl, *Endangered Lives: Public Health in Victorian Britain* (London, 1983).
Frank Worsdall, *The Tenement* (Edinburgh, 1979).

16: Religion and Society

D. W. Bebbington, *Evangelicalism in Modern Britain* (London, 1989).
Callum G. Brown, *The People in the Pews* (Dundee, 1993).
Callum G. Brown, *Religion and Society in Scotland since 1707* (Edinburgh, 1997).
Stewart, J. Brown, *Thomas Chalmers and the Godley Commonwealth* (Oxford, 1982).

Stewart J. Brown, '"Outside the Covenant": The Scottish Presbyterian Churches and Irish Immigration', *Innes Review*, (1991).

Stewart J. Brown and Michael Fry, eds, *Scotland in the Age of the Disruption* (Edinburgh, 1993).

S. Bruce, ed., *Religion and Secularisation: Historians and Sociologists Debate Modernisation Theory* (Oxford, 1992).

A. C. Cheyne, *The Transforming of the Kirk* (Edinburgh, 1983).

T. M. Devine, ed., *Irish Immigrants and Scottish Society in the Nineteenth and Twentieth Centuries* (Edinburgh, 1991).

A. L. Drummond and J. Bulloch, *The Church in Victorian Scotland 1843–1874* (Edinburgh, 1975) and *The Church in Late Victorian Scotland, 1874–1900* (Edinburgh, 1978).

David Hempton, *Religion and Political Culture in Britain and Ireland* (Cambridge, 1996).

D. McRoberts, ed., *Modern Scottish Catholicism* (Glasgow, 1979).

Graham Walker and Tom Gallagher, eds, *Sermons and Battle Hymns* (Edinburgh, 1990).

17: Educating the People

R. D. Anderson, *Education and Opportunity in Victorian Scotland* (Edinburgh, 1983).

R. D. Anderson, *Education and the Scottish People 1750–1918* (Oxford, 1995).

R. D. Anderson, *Scottish Education since the Reformation* (Dundee, 1997).

George E. Davie, *The Democratic Intellect* (Edinburgh, 1901) and *The Crisis of the Democratic Intellect* (Edinburgh, 1980).

W. M. Humes and H. M. Paterson, eds, *Scottish Culture and Scottish Education 1800–1980* (Edinburgh, 1983).

Andrew McPherson, 'Schooling', in A. Dickson and J. H. Treble, eds, *People and Society in Scotland, Volume III, 1914–1990* (Edinburgh, 1992).

Lindsay Paterson, 'Liberation or Control? What Are the Scottish Education Traditions of the Twentieth Century?', in T. M. Devine and R. J. Finlay, eds, *Scotland in the Twentieth Century* (Edinburgh, 1996).

Donald J. Withrington, *Going to School* (Edinburgh, 1997).

18: The Highlands and Crofting Society

Ewen A. Cameron, *Land for the People? The British Government and the Scottish Highlands c. 1880–1925* (East Linton, 1996).

Adam Collier, *The Crofting Problem* (Cambridge, 1953).

T. M. Devine, *The Great Highland Famine* (Edinburgh, 1988).

T. M. Devine, *Clanship to Crofters' War: the Social Transformation of the Scottish Highlands* (Manchester, 1994).

James Hunter, *The Making of the Crofting Community* (Edinburgh, 1976).

James Hunter, *The Claim of Crofting: The Scottish Highlands and Islands, 1930–1990* (Edinburgh, 1991).

L. Leneman, *Fit for Heroes? Land Settlement in Scotland after World War I* (Aberdeen, 1989).

I. M. M. Macphail, *The Crofters' War* (Stornoway, 1989).

W. Orr, *Deer Forests, Landlords and Crofters* (Edinburgh, 1982).

19: Land, Elites and People

Landownership

Robin T. Callander, *A Pattern of Landownership in Scotland* (Finzean, 1987).

R. H. Campbell, *Owners and Occupiers* (Aberdeen, 1991).

David Cannadine, *The Decline and Fall of the British Aristocracy* (London, 1992 edn).

T. M. Devine, ed., *Scottish Elites* (Edinburgh, 1994).

David McCrone et al., *Scotland the Brand: The Making of Scottish Heritage* (Edinburgh, 1995).

F. M. L. Thomson's articles on landed society in *Transactions of the Royal Historical Society*, Fifth Series, 1990–93.

Andy Wightman, *Who Owns Scotland* (Edinburgh, 1996).

Leaving the Land

Richard Anthony, *Herds and Hinds: Farm Labour in Lowland Scotland 1900–1939* (East Linton, 1997).

Ian Carter, *Farm Life in Northeast Scotland* (Edinburgh, 1979).

T. M. Devine, ed., *Farm Servants and Labour in Lowland Scotland 1770–1914* (Edinburgh, 1996 edn).

M. Gray, *Scots on the Move* (Dundee, 1990).

20: Emigrants

Dudley Baines, *Migration in a Mature Economy* (Cambridge, 1985).

R. A. Cage, ed., *The Scots Abroad 1750–1914* (London, 1985).

T. M. Devine, ed., *Scottish Emigration and Scottish Society* (Edinburgh, 1992).

Malcolm Gray, *Scots on the Move* (Dundee, 1990).

Marjory Harper, *Emigration from North East Scotland*, 2 vols (Aberdeen, 1988).

David S. Macmillan, ed., *Canadian Business History* (Toronto, 1972).

M. D. Prentis, *The Scottish in Australia* (Melbourne, 1987).

W. Stanford Reid, *The Scottish Tradition in Canada* (Guelph, 1976).

21: New Scots

Kenneth Collins, ed., *Aspects of Scottish Jewry* (Glasgow, 1987).

Kenneth Collins, *Second City Jewry* (Glasgow, 1990).

Terri Colpi, *The Italian Factor: The Italian Community in Great Britain* (Edinburgh, 1991).

T. M. Devine, ed., *Irish Immigrants and Scottish Society in the Nineteenth and Twentieth Centuries* (Edinburgh, 1991).

Tom Gallagher, *Glasgow: The Uneasy Peace* (Manchester, 1987).

Ralph Glasser, *Growing up in the Gorbals* (London, 1986).

James E. Handley, *The Irish in Scotland* (Glasgow, 1964).

Billy Kay, ed., *Odyssey* (Edinburgh, 1980).

Billy Kay, ed., *Odyssey: The Second Collection* (Edinburgh, 1982).

Elaine McFarland, *Protestants First: Orangeism in Nineteenth Century Scotland* (Edinburgh, 1990).

Bashir Maan, *The New Scots* (Edinburgh, 1992).

Henry Maitles, 'Attitudes to Jewish Immigration in the West of Scotland to 1905', *Scottish Economic & Social History*, 15 (1995).

Bill Murray, *The Old Firm* (Edinburgh, 1984).

22: Scottish Women: Family, Work and Politics

Esther Breitenbach and Eleanor Gordon, eds, *The World is Ill Divided – Women's Works in Scotland in the Nineteenth and Early Twentieth Centuries* (Edinburgh, 1990).

Esther Breitenbach and Eleaor Gordon, eds, *Out of Bounds: Women in Scottish Society 1800–1945* (Edinburgh, 1992).

Eleanor Gordon, *Women and the Labour Movement in Scotland 1850–1914* (Oxford, 1991).

Elspeth King, *The Scottish Women's Suffrage Movement* (Glasgow, 1978).

Leah Leneman, *A Guid Cause* (Aberdeen, 1991).

J. Melling, *Rent Strikes* (Edinburgh, 1983).

23: War and Peace

Peter Clarke, *Hope and Glory, Britain 1900–1990* (London, 1996).

T. M. Devine and R. J. Finlay, eds, *Scotland in the Twentieth Century* (Edinburgh, 1996).

Miles Glendinning, ed., *Rebuilding Scotland. The Postwar Vision 1945–1975* (Edinburgh, 1997).

Andrew Marr, *The Battle for Scotland* (London, 1992).

J. Mitchell, *Conservatives and the Union* (Edinburgh, 1990).

K. O. Morgan, *The People's Peace: British History, 1945–90* (Oxford, 1992).

P. L. Payne, *Growth and Contraction, Scottish Industry c. 1860–1990* (Glasgow, 1992).

Richard Saville, ed., *The Economic Development of Modern Scotland 1950–1980* (Edinburgh, 1985).

A. Slaven, *The Development of the West of Scotland 1750–1960* (London, 1975).

24: The Scottish Question

David McCrone, *Understanding Scotland: The Sociology of a Stateless Nation* (London, 1992).

Andrew Marr, *The Battle for Scotland* (London, 1992).

James Mitchell, *Strategies for Self-Government* (Edinburgh, 1996).

25: A Nation Reborn?

Alice Brown, David McCrone and Lindsay Paterson, *Politics and Society in Scotland* (2nd edn, Edinburgh, 1998).

A. Clements, K. Farquharson and K. Wark, *Restless Nation* (Edinburgh, 1996).

Owen Dudley Edwards, ed., *A Claim of Right for Scotland* (Edinburgh, 1989).

C. H. Lee, *Scotland and the United Kingdom* (Manchester, 1995).

Magnus Linklater and Robin Dennistoun, eds, *Anatomy of Scotland* (Edinburgh, 1992).

Catriona M. M. MacDonald, *Unionist Scotland 1800–1997* (Edinburgh, 1998).

James Mitchell, *Strategies for Self-Government* (Edinburgh, 1996).

Lindsay Paterson, ed., *A Diverse Assembly. The Debate on the Scottish Parliament* (Edinburgh, 1998).

Kenyon Wright, *The People Say Yes* (Glendaruel, 1997).

26: End of Empire

John Darwin, *The End of the British Empire* (Oxford, 1991).

T. M. Devine, *Scotland's Empire, 1600–1815* (London, 2003).

T. M. Devine, D. H. Lee and G. Peden, eds., *The Transformation of Scotland: The Economy since 1700* (Edinburgh, 2005).

Michael Fry, *The Scottish Empire* (Edinburgh, 2001).

Marjory Harper, *Emigration from Scotland between the Wars* (Manchester, 1998).

Tom Nairn, *The Break-Up of Britain* (London, 1969).

Gordon Stewart, *Jute and Empire* (Manchester, 1998).

27: After Devolution

Wendy Alexander, ed., *Donald Dewar: Scotland's first First Minister* (Edinburgh, 2001).

D. Bell and D. G. Blanchflower, 'The Scots may be Brave but they are neither Healthy or Happy', *Discussion Paper, No. 1909, December 2005, Institute for the Study of Labor, University of Bonn.*

Christopher G. A. Bryant, *The Nations of Britain* (Oxford, 2006).

Diana Coyle *et al*, eds., *New Wealth for Old Nations. Scotland's Economic Prospects* (Princeton, 2005).

John Curtice *et al*, eds., *New Scotland, New Society?* (Edinburgh, 2002).

Tom Devine and Paddy Logue, eds., *Being Scottish: Personal Reflections on Scottish Identity Today* (Edinburgh, 2002).

Michael Keating, *The Government of Scotland: Public Policy Making after Devolution* (Edinburgh, 2005).

W. L. Miller, ed., *Anglo-Scottish Relations from 1900 to Devolution and Beyond* (Oxford, 2005).

Lindsay Paterson *et al*, eds., *New Scotland, New Politics?* (Edinburgh, 2001).

Lindsay Paterson, Frank Bechhofer and David McCrone, *Living in Scotland: Social and Economic Change since 1980* (Edinburgh, 2004).

Brian Taylor, *Scotland's Parliament: Triumph and Disaster* (Edinburgh, 2002).

Index

Muir, Edwin 320, 629
Scottish Journey 317–18, 387, 469, 472
Muir, John 310
Muir Thomas 207, 208
Mull 174, 184, 424–5, 427
see also Hebrides
Mulock, T:
The Western Highlands and Islands . . . 417
Munro Clan 39
Murdoch, Bishop 493
Murdoch, John 427, 432, 434–5, 495
Murray, A. L. 19
Murray, Bill:
The Old Firm 361, 362
Murray, Lord George 43, 44
Murray, Norman:
The Scottish Handloom Weavers 222
Murray, Walter 314
Museum of Scotland 608–9
music 356, 509, 562–3, 608
in church 378
see also songs and ballads
music halls *see* theatre and music halls
Muthesius, Stefan:
Tower Block 560, 561

Nairn, Tom 285
The Break-Up of Britain 619
Nairne, Lady *see* Oliphant, Carolina
Napier, David 257
Napier, Robert 257
Napier Commission, 1883–4 299, 400, 430, 435, 440
see also Scottish land reform
Napier and Ettrick, Lord 299, 430
see also Napier Commission
Napoleonic Wars 27, 155, 163, 166, 169, 184–5, 241, 658
economic effects 190–91, 194–5, 216, 224, 449, 501
National Association of Master Builders 261
National Association of United Trades 280

National Association for the Vindication of Scottish Rights 287, 295
national characteristics 27, 28, 30, 291–2, 354, 360, 578, 641
Highland Clans 170, 171, 172, 175, 181–3, 185, 192
Highland regiments 234–5, 239–41, 245, 290
national debt 13, 20
National Federal Council for Women's Trades 541
National Health Service (NHS) 553, 555, 557, 562, 604
National Labourers Union 495
National Liberal Federation of Scotland 300, 301
National Milk Scheme 551
National Mission of Rededication 383
National Party of Scotland 325
National Shipbuilders Security Ltd 270
National Unemployed Workers' Movement 326
National Union of Mineworkers 585, 602
National Wallace Monument 294
nationalism 28, 30, 574–5
see also Irish Home Rule; Scottish nationalism
nationalization programmes 324, 557, 558, 564, 567
naturalization 517
Navigation Acts, 1650–72 5, 13, 54
the navy *see* Royal Navy
Ne Temere (papal decree), 1908 493
Neil, Andrew, 632
Neilson, James Beaumont 62, 117, 257, 261
Nenadic, Stana 112
New Lanark 115, 157
New Party *see* Squadrone Volante
New Statistical Account of Scotland 380
see also Sinclair, Sir John
new towns 560
New Zealand 476
Scottish contribution to 474
Scottish emigrants to 290, 470–71, 621

INVERCLYDE LIBRARIES
748

ALLEN LANE
an imprint of
PENGUIN BOOKS

Recently Published

Dominic Sandbrook, *Seasons in the Sun: The Battle for Britain, 1974-1979*

Tariq Ramadan, *The Arab Awakening: Islam and the New Middle East*

Jonathan Haidt, *The Righteous Mind: Why Good People are Divided by Politics and Religion*

Ahmed Rashid, *Pakistan on the Brink: The Future of Pakistan, Afghanistan and the West*

Tim Weiner, *Enemies: A History of the FBI*

Mark Pagel, *Wired for Culture: The Natural History of Human Cooperation*

George Dyson, *Turing's Cathedral: The Origins of the Digital Universe*

Cullen Murphy, *God's Jury: The Inquisition and the Making of the Modern World*

Richard Sennett, *Together: The Rituals, Pleasures and Politics of Co-operation*

Faramerz Dabhoiwala, *The Origins of Sex: A History of the First Sexual Revolution*

Roy F. Baumeister and John Tierney, *Willpower: Rediscovering Our Greatest Strength*

Jesse J. Prinz, *Beyond Human Nature: How Culture and Experience Shape Our Lives*

Robert Holland, *Blue-Water Empire: The British in the Mediterranean since 1800*

Jodi Kantor, *The Obamas: A Mission, A Marriage*

Philip Coggan, *Paper Promises: Money, Debt and the New World Order*

Charles Nicholl, *Traces Remain: Essays and Explorations*

Daniel Kahneman, *Thinking, Fast and Slow*

Hunter S. Thompson, *Fear and Loathing at Rolling Stone: The Essential Writing of Hunter S. Thompson*

Duncan Campbell-Smith, *Masters of the Post: The Authorized History of the Royal Mail*

Colin McEvedy, *Cities of the Classical World: An Atlas and Gazetteer of 120 Centres of Ancient Civilization*

Heike B. Görtemaker, *Eva Braun: Life with Hitler*

Brian Cox and Jeff Forshaw, *The Quantum Universe: Everything that Can Happen Does Happen*

Nathan D. Wolfe, *The Viral Storm: The Dawn of a New Pandemic Age*

Norman Davies, *Vanished Kingdoms: The History of Half-Forgotten Europe*

Michael Lewis, *Boomerang: The Meltdown Tour*

Steven Pinker, *The Better Angels of Our Nature: The Decline of Violence in History and Its Causes*

Robert Trivers, *Deceit and Self-Deception: Fooling Yourself the Better to Fool Others*

Thomas Penn, *Winter King: The Dawn of Tudor England*

Daniel Yergin, *The Quest: Energy, Security and the Remaking of the Modern World*

Michael Moore, *Here Comes Trouble: Stories from My Life*

Ali Soufan, *The Black Banners: Inside the Hunt for Al Qaeda*

Jason Burke, *The 9/11 Wars*

Timothy D. Wilson, *Redirect: The Surprising New Science of Psychological Change*

Ian Kershaw, *The End: Hitler's Germany, 1944-45*

T M Devine, *To the Ends of the Earth: Scotland's Global Diaspora, 1750-2010*

Catherine Hakim, *Honey Money: The Power of Erotic Capital*

Douglas Edwards, *I'm Feeling Lucky: The Confessions of Google Employee Number 59*

John Bradshaw, *In Defence of Dogs*

Chris Stringer, *The Origin of Our Species*

Lila Azam Zanganeh, *The Enchanter: Nabokov and Happiness*

David Stevenson, *With Our Backs to the Wall: Victory and Defeat in 1918*

Evelyn Juers, *House of Exile: War, Love and Literature, from Berlin to Los Angeles*

Henry Kissinger, *On China*

Michio Kaku, *Physics of the Future: How Science Will Shape Human Destiny and Our Daily Lives by the Year 2100*

David Abulafia, *The Great Sea: A Human History of the Mediterranean*

John Gribbin, *The Reason Why: The Miracle of Life on Earth*

Anatol Lieven, *Pakistan: A Hard Country*

William Cohen, *Money and Power: How Goldman Sachs Came to Rule the World*

Joshua Foer, *Moonwalking with Einstein: The Art and Science of Remembering Everything*

Simon Baron-Cohen, *Zero Degrees of Empathy: A New Theory of Human Cruelty*

Manning Marable, *Malcolm X: A Life of Reinvention*

David Deutsch, *The Beginning of Infinity: Explanations that Transform the World*

David Edgerton, *Britain's War Machine: Weapons, Resources and Experts in the Second World War*

John Kasarda and Greg Lindsay, *Aerotropolis: The Way We'll Live Next*

David Gilmour, *The Pursuit of Italy: A History of a Land, Its Regions and Their Peoples*

Niall Ferguson, *Civilization: The West and the Rest*

Tim Flannery, *Here on Earth: A New Beginning*

Robert Bickers, *The Scramble for China: Foreign Devils in the Qing Empire, 1832-1914*

Mark Malloch-Brown, *The Unfinished Global Revolution: The Limits of Nations and the Pursuit of a New Politics*

King Abdullah of Jordan, *Our Last Best Chance: The Pursuit of Peace in a Time of Peril*

Eliza Griswold, *The Tenth Parallel: Dispatches from the Faultline between Christianity and Islam*

Brian Greene, *The Hidden Reality: Parallel Universes and the Deep Laws of the Cosmos*

John Gray, *The Immortalization Commission: The Strange Quest to Cheat Death*

Patrick French, *India: A Portrait*

Lizzie Collingham, *The Taste of War: World War Two and the Battle for Food*

Hooman Majd, *The Ayatollahs' Democracy: An Iranian Challenge*

Dambisa Moyo, *How The West Was Lost: Fifty Years of Economic Folly - and the Stark Choices Ahead*

Evgeny Morozov, *The Net Delusion: How Not to Liberate the World*

Ron Chernow, *Washington: A Life*

Nassim Nicholas Taleb, *The Bed of Procrustes: Philosophical and Practical Aphorisms*

Hugh Thomas, *The Golden Age: The Spanish Empire of Charles V*

Amanda Foreman, *A World on Fire: An Epic History of Two Nations Divided*

Nicholas Ostler, *The Last Lingua Franca: English until the Return of Babel*

Richard Miles, *Ancient Worlds: The Search for the Origins of Western Civilization*

Neil MacGregor, *A History of the World in 100 Objects*

Steven Johnson, *Where Good Ideas Come From: The Natural History of Innovation*

Dominic Sandbrook, *State of Emergency: The Way We Were: Britain, 1970-1974*

Jim Al-Khalili, *Pathfinders: The Golden Age of Arabic Science*

Ha-Joon Chang, *23 Things They Don't Tell You About Capitalism*

Robin Fleming, *Britain After Rome: The Fall and Rise, 400 to 1070*

Tariq Ramadan, *The Quest for Meaning: Developing a Philosophy of Pluralism*

Joyce Tyldesley, *The Penguin Book of Myths and Legends of Ancient Egypt*

Nicholas Phillipson, *Adam Smith: An Enlightened Life*

Paul Greenberg, *Four Fish: A Journey from the Ocean to Your Plate*

Clay Shirky, *Cognitive Surplus: Creativity and Generosity in a Connected Age*

Andrew Graham-Dixon, *Caravaggio: A Life Sacred and Profane*

Niall Ferguson, *High Financier: The Lives and Time of Siegmund Warburg*

Sean McMeekin, *The Berlin-Baghdad Express: The Ottoman Empire and Germany's Bid for World Power, 1898-1918*

Richard McGregor, *The Party: The Secret World of China's Communist Rulers*

Spencer Wells, *Pandora's Seed: The Unforeseen Cost of Civilization*

Francis Pryor, *The Making of the British Landscape: How We Have Transformed the Land, from Prehistory to Today*

Ruth Harris, *The Man on Devil's Island: Alfred Dreyfus and the Affair that Divided France*

Paul Collier, *The Plundered Planet: How to Reconcile Prosperity With Nature*

Norman Stone, *The Atlantic and Its Enemies: A History of the Cold War*

Simon Price and Peter Thonemann, *The Birth of Classical Europe: A History from Troy to Augustine*

Hampton Sides, *Hellhound on his Trail: The Stalking of Martin Luther King, Jr. and the International Hunt for His Assassin*

Jackie Wullschlager, *Chagall: Love and Exile*

Richard Miles, *Carthage Must Be Destroyed: The Rise and Fall of an Ancient Civilization*

Tony Judt, *Ill Fares The Land: A Treatise On Our Present Discontents*

Michael Lewis, *The Big Short: Inside the Doomsday Machine*

Oliver Bullough, *Let Our Fame Be Great: Journeys among the Defiant People of the Caucasus*

Paul Davies, *The Eerie Silence: Searching for Ourselves in the Universe*

Richard Wilkinson and Kate Pickett, *The Spirit Level: Why Equality is Better for Everyone*

Tom Bingham, *The Rule of Law*

Joseph Stiglitz, *Freefall: Free Markets and the Sinking of the Global Economy*

John Lanchester, *Whoops! Why Everyone Owes Everyone and No One Can Pay*

Chinua Achebe, *The Education of a British-Protected Child*

Jaron Lanier, *You Are Not A Gadget: A Manifesto*

John Cassidy, *How Markets Fail: The Logic of Economic Calamities*

Robert Ferguson, *The Hammer and the Cross: A New History of the Vikings*

Eugene Rogan, *The Arabs: A History*

Steven Johnson, *The Invention of Air: An experiment, a Journey, a New Country and the Amazing Force of Scientific Discovery*

Andrew Ross Sorkin, *Too Big to Fail: Inside the Battle to Save Wall Street*

Malcolm Gladwell, *What the Dog Saw and Other Adventures*

Steven D. Levitt, Stephen J. Dubner, *Superfreakonomics: Global Cooling, Patriotic Prostitutes and Why Suicide Bombers Should Buy Life Insurance*

Christopher Andrew, *The Defence of the Realm: The Authorized History of MI5*

Dominic Lieven, *Russia Against Napoleon: The Battle for Europe, 1807 to 1814*

Peter Maass, *Crude World: The Violent Twilight of Oil*

Glyn Williams, *Arctic Labyrinth: The Quest for the Northwest Passage*

Michael Sandel, *Justice: What's the Right Thing to Do?*

Diarmaid MacCulloch, *A History of Christianity: The First Three Thousand Years*

Cass R. Sunstein, *On Rumours: How Falsehoods Spread, Why We Believe Them, What Can Be Done*

Robert Skidelsky, *Keynes: The Return of the Master*

Richard Overy, *1939: Countdown to War*

David Priestland, *The Red Flag: Communism and the Making of the Modern World*

John Gribbin, *In Search of the Multiverse*

Andrew Roberts, *The Storm of War: A New History of the Second World War*

W. Brian Arthur, *The Nature of Technology: What It Is and How It Evolves*

Alistair Cooke, *Alistair Cooke at the Movies*

Amartya Sen, *The Idea of Justice*

Peter H Wilson, *Europe's Tragedy: A New History of the Thirty Years War*

Stephen Green, *Good Value: Choosing a Better Life in Business*

Martin Jacques, *When China Rules The World: The Rise of the Middle Kingdom and the End of the Western World*

Patrick Hennessey, *The Junior Officers' Reading Club: Killing Time and Fighting Wars*

Richard P Bentall, *Doctoring the Mind: Why Psychiatric Treatments Fail*

John Armstrong, *In Search of Civilization: Remaking a Tarnished Idea*

Frank Wilczek, *The Lightness of Being: Big Questions, Real Answers*

Daniel Goleman, *Ecological Intelligence: The Coming Age of Radical Transparency*

Richard Overy, *The Morbid Age: Britain and the Crisis of Civilisation, 1919 - 1939*

Parag Khanna, *The Second World: Empires and Influence in the New Global Order*

Tristram Hunt, *The Frock-Coated Communist: The Revolutionary Life of Friedrich Engels*

Christopher Caldwell, *Reflections on the Revolution in Europe: Immigration, Islam and the West*

Nandan Nilekani, *Imagining India: Ideas for the New Century*

John Micklethwait and Adrian Wooldridge, *God is Back: How the Global Rise of Faith is Changing the World*

Boris Cyrulnik, *Resilience: How Your Inner Strength Can Set You Free from the Past*

John Gray, *Gray's Anatomy: Selected Writings*

R. W. Johnson, *South Africa's Brave New World: The Beloved Country Since the End of Apartheid*